Ireland For Dummies
2nd Edition

S0-BBW-502

The Ring of Kerry

NORTHERN IRELAND

Dublin ★

REPUBLIC OF IRELAND
COUNTY KERRY

NORTH ATLANTIC OCEAN

Clare
River Shannon

Tarbert

Ballybunion
R551

R552
Limerick

Mouth of the Shannon

Kerry Head

Listowel

Ballyheige
N69

Ballyheige Bay
R551

Kerry

Tralee Bay
Fenit Spa
N21

Mt Brandon ▲
R560 Blennerville **Tralee**

Camp
SLIEVE MISH MOUNTAINS

Connor Pass

Ballyferriter
Annascaul
Castlemaine
R561
N23
Farranfore Airport ✈

Dunquin Ventry **Dingle**
Farranfore

R559
Inch
1 Killorglin

Slea Head
2 **2**
R562 R563
Killarney
N72

GREAT BLASKET ISLAND
Glenbeigh
Caragh Lough

3 Ring of Kerry
KILLARNEY NATIONAL PARK

VALENTIA ISLAND
Lough Leane
Lough Guitane
N22

4 N70
Carrauntoohil ▲

5 Cahirsiveen
MacGillycuddy's Reeks
N71
8 **8** ▲
R569

Portmagee
R567
8
Kilgarvan

R565
Lough Currane
Ring of Kerry
8
Cork

R566
Waterville
Sneem
7 Kenmare
R571

Ballinskelligs
6 **6**
Parknasilla

SKELLIG ROCK
Caherdaniel
Lauragh
N

Ballinskelligs Bay
Kenmare River
CAHA MOUNTAINS

0   10 miles
0   10 kilometers

ACCOMMODATIONS ■
Foley's Shamrock **8**
Lansdowne Arms Hotel **8**
Scarriff Inn **6**
Towers Hotel **2**
Wander Inn **8**

SHOPPING ▲
Cleo **8**
Nostalgia **8**
Pat's Craft Shop **3**
Quills Woolen Market **8**

DINING ◆
The Blue Bull **7**
d'Arcy's **8**
Purple Heather **8**
Virginia's Restaurant and Wine Bar **8**

NIGHTLIFE ☾
Bianconi **1**
Caitin Baiters **4**
The Point Bar **4**

ATTRACTIONS ●
Derrynane House National Historic Park **6**
Kenmare Heritage Centre and Heritage Trail **8**
Kerry Bog Village Museum **2**
The Skellig Experience **5**

For Dummies: Bestselling Book Series for Beginners

Ireland For Dummies, 2nd Edition

Cheat Sheet

Learning the Lingo

Refer to this helpful list of lingo while touring Ireland.

An Lar	city center	**lift**	elevator
bonnet	car hood	**mna**	women (Gaelic)
boot	car trunk	**off-license**	liquor store
Bord Fa'ilte	Irish Tourist Board (Gaelic)	**press**	cabinet
cheers	thanks	**petrol**	gas
crack, craic	good times, fun	**quay**	waterfront (pronounced *key*)
creche	day care	**quid, or bob**	pounds, or money
deadly, brilliant	great, excellent	**sla'inte**	cheers or goodbye (Gaelic — pronounced *sclan*-cha)
fa'ilte	welcome (Gaelic)		
fir	men (Gaelic)	**take-away**	fast food, to go
footpath	sidewalk	**tins**	canned goods
garda	policeman		

Ireland Mileage Guide

Use this mileage chart to help plan your itinerary.

Belfast	Cork	Derry	Donegal	Dublin	Galway	Killarney	Limerick	Sligo	Waterford	Wexford
264	**Cork**									
73	266	**Derry**								
112	250	43	**Donegal**							
104	160	147	138	**Dublin**						
190	130	169	127	136	**Galway**					
271	54	274	235	192	120	**Killarney**				
201	65	204	184	123	65	69	**Limerick**			
128	209	84	41	135	86	213	144	**Sligo**		
207	78	238	222	98	137	120	80	182	**Waterford**	
192	116	235	231	88	157	158	118	191	39	**Wexford**

Copyright © 2003 Wiley Publishing, Inc. All rights reserved.

Item 5455-7.

For more information about Wiley Publishing, call 1-800-762-2974.

For Dummies: Bestselling Book Series for Beginners

FOR DUMMIES

The fun and easy way™ to travel!

Ireland FOR DUMMIES®

2ND EDITION

by David G. Allan

WILEY

Wiley Publishing, Inc.

Ireland For Dummies,® 2nd Edition

Published by
Wiley Publishing, Inc.
909 Third Avenue
New York, NY 10022
www.wiley.com

Copyright © 2003 by Wiley Publishing, Inc., Indianapolis, Indiana

Published simultaneously in Canada

No part of this publication may be reproduced, stored in a retrieval system, or transmitted in any form or by any means, electronic, mechanical, photocopying, recording, scanning, or otherwise, except as permitted under Sections 107 or 108 of the 1976 United States Copyright Act, without either the prior written permission of the Publisher, or authorization through payment of the appropriate per-copy fee to the Copyright Clearance Center, 222 Rosewood Drive, Danvers, MA 01923, 978-750-8400, fax 978-750-4470. Requests to the Publisher for permission should be addressed to the Legal Department, Wiley Publishing, Inc., 10475 Crosspoint Blvd., Indianapolis, IN 46256, 317-572-3447, fax 317-572-4447, or e-mail permcoordinator@wiley.com

Trademarks: Wiley, the Wiley Publishing logo, For Dummies, the Dummies Man logo, A Reference for the Rest of Us!, The Dummies Way, Dummies Daily, The Fun and Easy Way, Dummies.com and related trade dress are trademarks or registered trademarks of Wiley Publishing, Inc., in the United States and other countries, and may not be used without written permission. Frommer's is a trademark or registered trademark of Arthur Frommer. Used under license. All other trademarks are the property of their respective owners. Wiley Publishing, Inc., is not associated with any product or vendor mentioned in this book.

For general information on our other products and services or to obtain technical support, please contact our Customer Care Department within the U.S. at 800-762-2974, outside the U.S. at 317-572-3993, or fax 317-572-4002.

Wiley also publishes its books in a variety of electronic formats. Some content that appears in print may not be available in electronic books.

Library of Congress Control Number: 2002114826

ISBN: 0-7645-5455-7

ISSN: 1531-152X

Manufactured in the United States of America

10 9 8 7 6 5 4 3 2 1

2B/QW/QS/QT/IN

®Wiley Publishing, Inc. is a trademark of Wiley Publishing, Inc.

About the Author

David G. Allan has taken the wanderlust plunge into a one-year trip around the world, from Mongolia to Cuba and including his favorite country, Ireland. He is also the author of *Scotland For Dummies*.

Author's Acknowledgments

I would like to thank my girlfriend, Kate Rope, who helped with this update and is the world's best travel companion; and my mother, Deborah Gilmartin. Thanks to Sinead O'Brien, coauthor of the first edition of this guide, and Clem McCloskey. The excellent editorial team at Frommer's, especially Christine Ryan, deserves my thanks for their support. Also, thank you to Paul McDonagh and Ruth Moran, with the new Tourism Ireland Board, for their assistance.

Publisher's Acknowledgments

We're proud of this book; please send us your comments through our Dummies online registration form located at www.dummies.com/register/.

Some of the people who helped bring this book to market include the following:

Editorial

Editors: Elizabeth Kuball, Christine Ryan

Cartographer: Roberta Stockwell

Editorial Supervisor: Michelle Hacker

Editorial Assistants: Stephen Bassman, Carol Strickland

Senior Photo Editor: Richard Fox

Assistant Photo Editor: Michael Ross

Cover Photos: Richard Cummins

Cartoons: Rich Tennant, www.the5thwave.com

Production

Project Coordinator: Nancee Reeves

Layout and Graphics: Amanda Carter, Carrie Foster, Joyce Haughey, Stephanie D. Jumper, Tiffany Muth

Proofreaders: John Bitter, Andy Hollandbeck, Susan Moritz, Angel Perez, Charles Spencer, TECHBOOKS Production Services

Indexer: TECHBOOKS Production Services

Publishing and Editorial for Consumer Dummies

Diane Graves Steele, Vice President and Publisher, Consumer Dummies

Joyce Pepple, Acquisitions Director, Consumer Dummies

Kristin A. Cocks, Product Development Director, Consumer Dummies

Michael Spring, Vice President and Publisher, Travel

Brice Gosnell, Publishing Director, Travel

Suzanne Jannetta, Editorial Director, Travel

Publishing for Technology Dummies

Andy Cummings, Acquisitions Director

Composition Services

Gerry Fahey, Vice President of Production Services

Debbie Stailey, Director of Composition Services

Contents at a Glance

Introduction *1*

Part I: Getting Started *7*

Chapter 1: Discovering the Best of Ireland 9
Chapter 2: Deciding When and Where to Go 33
Chapter 3: Deciding On an Itinerary 43
Chapter 4: Planning Your Budget 53
Chapter 5: Tips for Travelers with Special Needs 59
Chapter 6: Getting to Ireland 67

Part II: Ironing Out the Details *79*

Chapter 7: Getting Around Ireland 81
Chapter 8: Booking Your Accommodations 91
Chapter 9: Money Matters 97
Chapter 10: Tying Up the Loose Ends: Last-Minute Details and
Other Things to Keep in Mind 103

Part III: Dublin and the East Coast *117*

Chapter 11: Dublin 119
Chapter 12: Easy Trips North of Dublin: Counties Meath and
Louth 175
Chapter 13: Easy Trips South of Dublin: Counties Wicklow and
Kildare 185
Chapter 14: The Southeast: Counties Wexford, Waterford,
Tipperary, and Kilkenny 205

Part IV: The South *239*

Chapter 15: County Cork 241
Chapter 16: County Kerry 267

Part V: The West and Northwest *303*

Chapter 17: Counties Limerick and Clare 305
Chapter 18: County Galway and Galway City 333
Chapter 19: Counties Mayo and Sligo 353
Chapter 20: County Donegal 367

Part VI: Northern Ireland *377*

Chapter 21: Counties Derry, Fermanagh, and Tyrone 379
Chapter 22: Belfast and County Antrim 393
Chapter 23: Counties Down and Armagh 411

Part VII: The Part of Tens 421

Chapter 24: The Top Ten Highlights of Ireland and
Northern Ireland 423
Chapter 25: Ten Tips for Shopping Wisely in Ireland 427

Appendix: Quick Concierge 431

Worksheets 437

Index 441

Maps at a Glance

Ireland 10
Ireland's Regions 34
Irish Bus Routes 87
Irish Rail Routes 89
County Dublin and the East Coast..........................120
Dublin Accommodations and Dining.....................126
Temple Bar..131
Dublin Attractions 140
Attractions around County Dublin 156
Dublin Shopping..160
Dublin Nightlife...166
Counties Meath and Louth 177
Counties Wicklow and Kildare 187
The Southeast 206
Wexford Town 211
Waterford City 219
Kilkenny Town...232
County Cork..243
Cork City 245
Kinsale..259
County Kerry..269
Killarney...273
Killarney National Park 277
Tralee 292
Counties Limerick and Clare 307
Limerick City 309
County Galway 334
Galway City..336
Inishmore, Aran Islands 343
Counties Mayo and Sligo...355
Sligo Town..357
County Donegal..368
Donegal Town...371
Counties Derry, Fermanagh, and Tyrone 380
Derry City 383
County Antrim..394
Belfast...397
Counties Down and Armagh......................................412

Table of Contents

Introduction 1
 About This Book 1
 Conventions Used in This Book 2
 Foolish Assumptions 3
 How This Book Is Organized 3
  Part I: Getting Started 3
  Part II: Ironing Out the Details 4
  Part III: Dublin and the East Coast 4
  Part IV: The South 5
  Part V: The West and Northwest 5
  Part VI: Northern Ireland 5
  Part VII: The Part of Tens 5
 Icons Used in This Book 6
 Where to Go from Here 6

Part 1: Getting Started 7

Chapter 1: Discovering the Best of Ireland 9
 Don't Know Much about Ireland's History? 9
  Invaders welcome 9
  Rebel with a cause 11
 Who's Who in Irish Mythology 13
 Who's Who in Irish Literature 14
 Ireland for the Irish: Digging Up Your Roots 15
  Doing your own research in advance 15
  Tapping into research agencies in Ireland 16
  Finding sources in Ireland for doing your own research 17
 Talking to the Irish 18
  Understanding the lingo 18
  Translating Gaelic place names 19
  Guarding against miscommunication 20
 Ireland Dining and Irish Cuisine 20
  Eating out: What to expect 21
  Checking out meal prices 21
 It's Emily Post Time!: Irish Meal Times and Dining Customs 22
  Deciphering the menu 22
 Livin' the Pub Life 23
  Absorbing a little pub history 23
  Snuggling up 24
  Savoring the black stuff: Guinness 24
  Sampling other Irish brews 25
  Sipping some Irish whiskey 25
  Noshing on pub grub 26
  Examining pub hours and drink prices 27
  Tipping like a local 27

Appreciating Irish Music 27
Enjoying Sports and the Great Outdoors 28
    Golf 28
    Fishing 30
    Running, cycling, walking, and more 30
    Sailing 31
    Horseback riding 31
    Spectator sports 31

Chapter 2: Deciding When and Where to Go 33

Everywhere You Want to Be: What This Book
    Covers and Why 33
    Experiencing the beauty of Dublin 33
    Touring the southeastern counties 35
    Swinging by the southern counties 35
    Wandering the western counties 35
    Rambling through Northern Ireland 36
The Secrets of the Seasons 36
    Summer 36
    Fall 37
    Winter 37
    Spring 38
Walking on Sunshine and Singing in the Rain:
    Ireland's Climate 38
Calendar of Festivals and Events 39
    March 40
    April 40
    May 40
    June 40
    July 41
    August 41
    September 42
    October 42
    November 42
    December 42

Chapter 3: Deciding On an Itinerary 43

Planning Your Own Itinerary 43
    The base camp approach 43
    The nomadic approach 44
Dealing with the Daily Tourist Grind 45
Finding the Itinerary That's Right for You 46
    Hitting the highlights: Ireland in one week 46
    Bringing the kids: A one-week itinerary for families 48
    Hitting the links: The nine-day, all-golf Ireland tour 50

Chapter 4: Planning Your Budget 53

Getting a Handle on Your Total Trip Costs 53
    Finding out what things cost 53
    Sketching a skeleton budget 54
    Outlining a low-end, one-week tour budget 55

Saving Money: Some Tips 56
Setting Priorities: Three Corners You Should Not Cut 58

Chapter 5: Tips for Travelers with Special Needs 59
Family Planning: Tips on Traveling with Kids 59
Hints and special services for families 60
Publications for family travelers 60
A World of Possibility: Travel Advice for Savvy Seniors 61
Discovering how to get travel discounts 61
Publications for senior travelers 61
Simple Suggestions for Travelers with Disabilities 62
Tips and services for travelers with disabilities 62
Publications for travelers with disabilities 63
Making a Shoestring Budget Work: Help for Students 63
Recommendations for Gay and Lesbian Travelers 64
Tips and travel services for gay and lesbian travelers 64
Publications for gay and lesbian travelers 65
Finding gay/lesbian B&Bs 66
Hunting Down Vegetarian Meals 66

Chapter 6: Getting to Ireland 67
Travel Agent: Friend or Foe? 67
The Ins and Outs of Package Tours 68
Telling the deals from the duds 68
Picking a peck of pickled packagers 69
Buying packages through the airlines 70
Touring by Bus: Escorted Tours 70
Asking the escorts: Important questions to
keep in mind 71
Hopping on the magic bus 71
The Independent Traveler: Making Your Own Arrangements 72
Knowing who flies where 72
Picking an arrival airport 73
Getting the best airfare 73
Booking through bucket shops 74
Reserving your tickets online 74
Getting through security 75
Finding Other Ways to Get There 75
Connecting through Britain 76
Taking ferry service between England and Ireland 76

Part II: Ironing Out the Details 79

Chapter 7: Getting Around Ireland 81
Seeing Ireland by Car 81
Booking a rental car 81
Considering your rental options 82
Paying for a rental car 83
Figuring out the rules of the road 84
Getting the scoop on driver's licenses and insurance 85

Driving on the wrong side of the road 85
Understanding parking rules and regulations 86
Doing the Bus Thing 86
Getting to know the major bus companies 86
Enlisting bus packages and tours 88
Riding the Rails 88
Finding train packages and tours 90
Combining bus and rail packages 90
Getting Out to the Islands 90

Chapter 8: Booking Your Accommodations 91

Figuring Out the Costs 91
Lodging in Luxury 92
Staying in Casual Comfort: Bed-and-Breakfasts and
Guesthouses 93
Enjoying Self-Catering Cottages 94
Exploring Hostel Options 95
Considering Other Accommodation Options 96

Chapter 9: Money Matters 97

Cash in Hand: Making Sense of the Irish Currency 97
Understanding the exchange rates 97
Finding a place to exchange money 98
Accessing ATMs, Just Like at Home 99
Using Credit Cards on the Road 99
Considering Traveler's Checks: Old-Fashioned or Useful? 100
Dealing with Stolen Cash and Credit Cards 101

**Chapter 10: Tying Up the Loose Ends: Last-Minute
Details and Other Things to Keep in Mind 103**

Papers, Please!: Getting Your Passport 103
For U.S. citizens 104
For non-U.S. citizens 105
Keeping your passport safe 105
And no, you don't need a visa 106
Getting more information on passports 106
Well, I Do Declare: Understanding the Customs of Customs 107
What you can't bring in 107
Customs channels: Red, green, or blue? 107
Buying Travel and Medical Insurance 108
Trip-cancellation insurance 108
Medical insurance 109
Dealing with Getting Sick Away from Home 110
Communicating with the Folks Back Home 110
Using the phones 110
Making calls from and within Ireland 111
Using your U.S. calling card 112
Using Internet Cafes 112
Sending and Receiving Snail Mail in the Republic and
Northern Ireland 113

Packing It Up 114
   Deciding what to bring and what to leave at home 114
   Ireland unplugged: Leaving that electric nosehair
       trimmer at home 115
Making Your Plane Ride More Comfortable 116

Part III: Dublin and the East Coast 117

Chapter 11: Dublin 119
Getting to Dublin 119
   By plane 120
   By ferry 121
   By train 121
   By bus 121
Orienting Yourself in Dublin 122
Getting Around Dublin 123
Where to Stay in Dublin 124
Where to Dine in Dublin 130
   Pub grub 132
   Dublin's top restaurants 132
Exploring Dublin 139
   Saving yourself some time and money 139
   Seeing the top sights 139
   Taking in some Dublin landmarks 145
   Finding other fun stuff to do 148
Seeing Dublin by Guided Tour 155
Suggested One-, Two-, and Three-Day Sightseeing
   Itineraries 158
Shopping in Dublin 159
   Locating the best shopping areas 159
   Finding Ireland's best wares 162
Hitting the Pubs and Enjoying Dublin's Nightlife 165
   Pulling a pint: Pub life 165
   Sipping a cocktail: Hip bars 169
   Pulling an all-nighter: Late-night bars 170
   Tapping your feet: Traditional music venues 170
   Striking a pose: Club life 171
   Yes, Virginia, there is other nightlife in Dublin 172
Fast Facts: Dublin 173

Chapter 12: Easy Trips North of Dublin:
Counties Meath and Louth 175
What's Where?: Meath and Louth's Major Attractions 175
Touring Meath and Louth 176
   Where to stay in Meath and Louth 177
   Where to dine in Meath and Louth 179
   Enjoying the area's top attractions 180
   Shopping and other fun stuff to do 183
Perusing Pub Life 183
Fast Facts: Counties Meath and Louth 184

Chapter 13: Easy Trips South of Dublin: Counties Wicklow and Kildare 185

What's Where?: Wicklow and Kildare and
   Their Major Attractions 185
County Wicklow 186
   Getting to and around Wicklow 188
   Where to stay in Wicklow 188
   Where to dine in Wicklow 190
   Exploring Wicklow 191
   Shopping in Wicklow 196
   Hitting the pubs 198
Fast Facts: County Wicklow 198
County Kildare 199
   Getting to and around Kildare 199
   Where to stay in Kildare 199
   Where to dine in Kildare 200
   Exploring Kildare: The top attractions 201
   Shopping in Kildare 203
   Hitting the pubs 204
Fast Facts: County Kildare 204

Chapter 14: The Southeast: Counties Wexford, Waterford, Tipperary, and Kilkenny 205

What's Where?: The Southeast Counties and
   Their Major Attractions 205
County Wexford 209
   Getting to and around County Wexford 209
   Where to stay in County Wexford 210
   Where to dine in County Wexford 212
   Exploring County Wexford: The top attractions 213
   Shopping in County Wexford 216
   Pub life in County Wexford 217
Fast Facts: County Wexford 217
County Waterford and Waterford City 218
   Getting to and around Waterford City 218
   Where to stay in Waterford 220
   Where to dine in Waterford 221
   Exploring County Waterford: The top attractions 222
   Joining an organized tour 224
   Shopping in Waterford City 224
   Pub life in Waterford City 225
Fast Facts: County Waterford 226
County Tipperary 226
   Getting to and around County Tipperary 226
   Where to dine in County Tipperary 227
   Exploring County Tipperary: The top attractions 227
   Joining an organized tour 229
   Shopping in County Tipperary 230
   Pub life in County Tipperary 230

Fast Facts: County Tipperary 231
County Kilkenny 231
    Getting to County Kilkenny 231
    Where to stay in County Kilkenny 233
    Where to dine in County Kilkenny 233
    Exploring County Kilkenny: The top attractions 234
    Shopping in County Kilkenny 236
    Pub life in County Kilkenny 236
Fast Facts: County Kilkenny 237

Part IV: The South **239**

Chapter 15: County Cork **241**

What's Where?: County Cork's Major Attractions 241
Cork City and East County Cork 242
    Getting to Cork City 244
    Getting around Cork City 244
    Where to stay in Cork City and East County Cork 246
    Where to dine in Cork City and East County Cork 247
    Exploring East County Cork 249
    Joining an organized tour 254
    Shopping in Cork City and East County Cork 254
    Pub life in County Cork 256
Fast Facts: Cork City and East County Cork 257
Kinsale and West County Cork 257
    Getting to Kinsale and West County Cork 257
    Where to stay in Kinsale and West County Cork 258
    Where to dine in Kinsale and West County Cork 260
    Exploring Kinsale and West County Cork:
      The top sights 262
    Joining an organized tour 263
    Shopping 264
    Pub life in Kinsale and West County Cork 264
Fast Facts: Kinsale and West County Cork 265

Chapter 16: County Kerry **267**

What's Where?: County Kerry's Major Attractions 267
Killarney Town and Killarney National Park 270
    Getting to Killarney 270
    Getting around Killarney 270
    Where to stay in Killarney 271
    Where to dine in Killarney 274
Exploring Killarney and Killarney National Park:
    The Top Attractions 275
    Joining an organized tour 278
    Shopping in Killarney 280
    Pub-crawling in Killarney 281
    Going clubbing in Killarney 282
    Finding live music 282
Fast Facts: Killarney 283

Kenmare and the Ring of Kerry 283
    Getting to and around Killarney and the Ring 284
    Where to stay in Kenmare and along the Ring 284
    Where to dine in Kenmare and along the Ring 285
Exploring Kenmare and the Ring: The Top Attractions 287
    Joining an organized tour 288
    Shopping 289
    Pulling a pint: Pub life along the ring 290
Fast Facts: Kenmare and the Ring of Kerry 291
Tralee and the Dingle Peninsula 291
    Getting to and around Tralee and
        the Dingle Peninsula 292
    Where to stay in Tralee and Dingle 293
    Where to dine in Tralee and Dingle 294
Exploring Tralee and Dingle Peninsula: The Top Attractions 296
    Joining an organized tour 298
    Shopping 299
    Pulling a pint: Pub life in Tralee and Dingle 300
Fast Facts: Tralee and Dingle Peninsula 301

Part V: The West and Northwest 303

Chapter 17: Counties Limerick and Clare 305

What's Where?: Limerick and Clare's Major Attractions 305
County Limerick and Limerick City 308
    Getting to and around Limerick 308
    Where to stay in County Limerick 310
    Where to dine in County Limerick 311
Exploring County Limerick: The Top Attractions 313
    Top Limerick City landmarks 315
    Joining an organized tour 316
    Shopping 317
    Pub-crawling in Limerick 317
Fast Facts: County Limerick 319
County Clare 319
    Getting to and around County Clare 319
    Where to stay in County Clare 320
    Where to dine in County Clare 322
Exploring County Clare 323
    The top attractions 323
    The top landmarks 327
    Other fun things to do 327
    Joining an organized tour 328
    Shopping 329
    Pulling a pint: Pub life 330
Fast Facts: County Clare 331

Chapter 18: County Galway and Galway City 333

What's Where?: Galway's Major Attractions 333
Getting To and Around Galway City 335

Getting to and around the Aran Islands 337
Where to Stay in County Galway 337
Where to Dine in County Galway 340
Exploring County Galway 342
    Galway's top attractions 342
    The top Galway City landmarks 345
    Other fun stuff to do 346
Joining an Organized Tour 347
Shopping 348
Pub-Crawling in Galway City 350
Fast Facts: County Galway 351

Chapter 19: Counties Mayo and Sligo 353

What's Where?: Mayo and Sligo's Major Attractions 353
Getting to Mayo and Sligo 356
Where to Stay in Mayo and Sligo 356
Where to Dine in Mayo and Sligo 359
Exploring Mayo and Sligo 361
    The top attractions 361
    Other fun things to do 364
Shopping in Mayo and Sligo 364
Pub Life in Mayo and Sligo 365
Fast Facts: Counties Mayo and Sligo 366

Chapter 20: County Donegal 367

What's Where?: County Donegal's Major Attractions 367
Getting to and around County Donegal 369
Where to Stay in County Donegal 369
Where to Dine in County Donegal 372
Exploring County Donegal: The Top Attractions 373
Shopping in County Donegal 375
Pub Life in County Donegal 375
Fast Facts: County Donegal 376

Part VI: Northern Ireland 377

Chapter 21: Counties Derry, Fermanagh, and Tyrone 379

What's Where?: Derry, Fermanagh, and Tyrone's
    Major Attractions 379
Getting to and around Derry, Fermanagh, and Tyrone 381
Where to Stay in Derry, Fermanagh, and Tyrone 382
Where to Dine in Derry, Fermanagh, and Tyrone 385
Exploring Counties Derry, Fermanagh, and Tyrone:
    The Top Attractions 386
More Fun Things to Do: The Top Derry Landmarks 389
Joining an Organized Tour 389
Shopping 390
Pulling a Pint: Pub Life 391
Fast Facts: Counties Derry, Fermanagh, and Tyrone 392

Chapter 22: Belfast and County Antrim 393

What's Where?: Belfast and County Antrim's
  Major Attractions 393
Getting to Belfast and County Antrim 395
Getting Around Belfast and County Antrim 396
Where to Stay in Belfast and around County Antrim 396
Where to Dine in Belfast and around County Antrim 400
Exploring Belfast and County Antrim 402
  The top attractions 402
  More fun stuff to do in Belfast and around
    County Antrim 405
Joining an Organized Tour 407
Shopping in Belfast and County Antrim 407
Enjoying Nightlife in Belfast and County Antrim 408
  Pulling a pint: Pub life 408
  Striking a pose: Club life 410
Fast Facts: Belfast and County Antrim 410

Chapter 23: Counties Down and Armagh 411

What's Where?: Counties Down and Armagh and
  Their Major Attractions 411
Getting to Counties Down and Armagh 413
Where to Stay in Counties Down and Armagh 413
Where to Dine in Counties Down and Armagh 414
Exploring Counties Down and Armagh 415
  The top attractions 415
  More fun stuff to see and do 417
Pulling a Pint: Pub Life 418
Fast Facts: Counties Down and Armagh 419

Part VII: The Part of Tens *421*

**Chapter 24: The Top Ten Highlights of Ireland and
Northern Ireland** 423

Driving the Ring of Kerry 423
Standing atop the Majestic Purple Cliffs of Moher 423
Bending Over Backward to Kiss the Blarney Stone 423
Pub-Crawling in Temple Bar 424
Watching Glass Blowers at the Waterford Crystal Factory 424
Taking a Ferry out to the Stark Aran Islands 424
Driving Around Killarney's Mountains and Lakes 424
Walking Out on the Giant's Causeway 424
Strolling amid the Stately and Magnificent
  Powerscourt Gardens 425
Discovering the Ancient Secrets of Newgrange and
  the Hill of Tara 425

Chapter 25: Ten Tips for Shopping Wisely in Ireland 427

Shop Around 427
Peruse Street Markets 427

Forget Designer Clothing 428
Shop Selectively 428
Don't Let Yourself Be Led by the Nose 429
Act like an Old Shopping Hand 429
Dress Respectably, but Not Too Well 429
Count Your Change and Check Your Receipt 429
Ship Breakables Home 430
Evaluate Your Carrying Capacity 430

Appendix: Quick Concierge *431*

Fast Facts 431
Toll-Free Numbers and Web Sites 434
    Airlines 434
    Car-rental agencies 435
Where to Get More Information 435
    Contacting Irish tourist boards 435
    Surfing the Net 436

Worksheets *437*

Index *441*

Introduction

● ●

You've seen it in movies and on television: lush and green, with rolling hills and effervescent waters, and dotted with magnificent castles and cathedrals — and plenty of quaint little towns in between. That's Ireland, without question, but it's only part of the story. Although that incredible backdrop really is the stuff the country is made of, there's so much more to Ireland that doesn't make it in the travel brochures. Ireland is characterized by its lush scenery and remarkable natural phenomena, but it also has its share of cosmopolitan cities and is an archaeological gold mine, a cultural hotbed, and a land of myths, legends, beauty, history, and charm.

So which of these things are you looking to find? It could be one of these or all of them. Whatever the reason, the island is one of the fastest-growing tourist destinations in Europe — and rightly so.

Your Ireland vacation can capture all Ireland has to offer, but it takes some planning and the inside scoop on what to see and what to avoid. Take it from me, putting forth a little extra effort in the planning stage will pay off big-time in the long run.

About This Book

In this book, I've tried to anticipate every question you may have about traveling to Ireland and provide the answers. If you've never been to the country before, I show you what to expect and how to plan for it. If you're an old Ireland hand, you've probably bought this book because you don't want to waste a lot of time sorting through a billion different hotels, restaurants, and attractions, trying to find the absolute best ones. You want a quick and easy, yet comprehensive, source of information, and that's exactly what I give you here.

Of course, you don't have to read the whole book. And you don't have to start at the beginning either. This is a reference book. Check out the Table of Contents, and then read the parts that answer your specific questions.

Besides just being practical, I've also written with the idea that the whole subject of travel should be just plain fun, so don't expect any dry lectures. That's just not my style.

Please be advised that travel information is subject to change at any time — and this is especially true of prices. Write or call ahead for confirmation when making your travel plans.

Conventions Used in This Book

In this book, I include write-ups on the best sights in Ireland; reviews of the best hotels, pubs, restaurants, pubs, shops, pubs, and more; and a quick-and-easy introduction to everything you'll experience in planning your trip and visiting the Emerald Isle.

Ireland For Dummies, 2nd Edition, employs a few conventions designed to convey critical information in a simple, straightforward manner.

In the hotel section, the listed price is a *rack rate* (the official rate published by the hotel, though the actual prices you'll pay are often discounted) and is good for one night only; additionally, parking charges are for one night only, unless otherwise noted.

In the restaurant section, the listed prices are the general range for the cost of a main course on the dinner menu, unless otherwise noted.

In the attractions sections, I provide an entry called "Suggested Visit" at the end of each listing. This is my estimate of how much time you should budget to do and see most of what's available at each attraction. This length of time is just a suggestion — you may find you need more or less time depending on your interests.

The following is a list of the credit card abbreviations used in the listings in this book:

AE	American Express
DC	Diners Club
DISC	Discover
ER	enRoute
EURO	Eurocard
JCB	Japan Credit Bank
MC	MasterCard
V	Visa

Foolish Assumptions

In this book, I make some assumptions about you and what your needs may be as a traveler. I assume you are one of the following:

- ✔ An inexperienced traveler looking for guidance when determining whether to travel to Ireland and how to plan for it.

- ✔ An experienced traveler who hasn't yet visited Ireland and wants expert advice when you finally do get a chance to go.

- ✔ A traveler looking for a book that focuses on only the best and most essential Irish sights, tastes, and experiences — the places that'll give you big-time bragging rights for years to come.

If you fit any of these criteria, then *Ireland For Dummies,* 2nd Edition, gives you the information you're looking for!

How This Book Is Organized

This book is divided into seven parts. Parts I through III get you ready to go, and Parts IV through VII deal with what you'll be seeing and doing after you're there. Each regional chapter begins with important and helpful information about how to get there and how to get around and includes information like emergency contacts and addresses for Internet cafes, local genealogical resources, and tourism offices.

Part 1: Getting Started

This book starts exactly where it should: at the beginning. This part is your guide to figuring out the best time of year to plan your vacation and when and how to divide your precious time when you're there. I introduce you to each of the regions in Ireland and give you the information you need to decide which parts you want to include in your trip. I give you a season-by-season description of what you can expect by way of temperature, crowds, costs, and the legendary precipitation. Then I introduce you to all the top festivals and events around the island.

These chapters also answer all those nagging questions you've been asking yourself, such as how to get there, whether to book a package tour (with tips on finding the best deal if you do), and how much it's all going to cost (with lots of advice on how to make the most of your hard-earned dollars while you're traveling around Ireland). I also acquaint you with all the different options for getting to Ireland so you can make educated decisions about what's right for you. I help you plan your own itinerary and give advice for those with special needs and requirements. You'll also find addresses, phone numbers, and Web sites where you can get more information on trip planning. I also give a concise history of Ireland and a short list of films to get you psyched about your upcoming adventure.

Part II: Ironing Out the Details

Part II takes care of all the loose ends when you're ready to head off to the hills and valleys of ol' Ireland — such as how to get around the country, what kind of accommodation options you'll have, and what the best ways are for carrying money (and getting more, if you run out). I've created a good packing checklist (including important pointers on what not to bring, like your hair dryer), a glossary of fast facts all about the island, a rundown of various things you should know before you go (like how to protect your valuable documents and money while abroad and what to do if they're lost), and tips on how to keep in touch with your family and friends while you're on the road.

Part III: Dublin and the East Coast

Part III is dedicated to Dublin and the surrounding counties, heading north to the border of Northern Ireland and south to County Cork.

Dublin is Ireland's capital and its largest city. No other city in Ireland surpasses it in terms of what to do and see, and we give you all the top picks to choose from. I preview it all, from the best cathedrals and most interesting landmarks to the top tours and which pubs have the best Irish music. Dublin is one city where you could get overwhelmed by everything going on, but with my help you're sure to see the best highlights. Chapter 11 is full of insider advice, money-saving tips, and easy-to-use maps.

Also covered in Part III are Counties Meath and Louth, just north of Dublin. These counties are the island's treasure trove of prehistoric sights, including the remarkable burial mounds at Knowth and Newgrange and the storied Hill of Tara, ancient seat of the Irish high kings. South of Dublin, the beautiful southeastern counties of Wexford, Waterford, Kilkenny, and Tipperary greet you with gardens, historic homes, horse farms and racetracks, and of course, the famous Waterford Crystal.

Part IV: The South

Part IV only covers two counties, Cork and Kerry, but together they attract the lion's share of visitors to Ireland, who come for popular attractions like the Blarney Stone and the Ring of Kerry and great towns like Cork City and Killarney. I fill you in on all the best places to eat, stay, and see as you make your way along the coast.

Part V: The West and Northwest

This part bundles the entire western side of Ireland into one neat package, from County Limerick all the way up to Donegal. You'll visit the amazing Cliffs of Moher and the otherworldly region known as The Burren in County Clare, a reproduction of John Wayne's cottage from *The Quiet Man* in County Mayo, the amazing Aran Islands off the coast of Galway, poet W. B. Yeats's grave in County Sligo, and much more.

Part VI: Northern Ireland

Part VI covers the separate country of Northern Ireland, which may be last in this book but is not least in terms of great and picturesque places to visit. Belfast is the largest city in Northern Ireland and, along with the walled town of Derry and the Antrim Coast, provides plenty of magnetism to attract your compass needle north. I give it the full treatment and explain the differences you can expect while visiting this British region.

Part VII: The Part of Tens

The Part of Tens chapters include a synopsis of some of the most amazing elements of the Ireland experience. I also give you tips on getting bargains when shopping for Irish products like linen and fisherman's sweaters.

You'll also find two other elements near the back of this book. I've included an appendix — your "Quick Concierge" — containing lots of handy information you may need when planning your trip, and a bunch of worksheets to make your travel planning easier. Among other things, the worksheets help you determine your travel budget and keep a handy record of your flight arrangements. You can find these worksheets easily because they're printed on yellow paper.

Icons Used in This Book

Keep an eye peeled for these icons, which appear in the margins:

Find out useful advice on things to do and ways to schedule your time when you see the Tip icon.

Watch for the Heads Up icon to identify annoying or potentially dangerous situations such as tourist traps, unsafe neighborhoods, budgetary rip-offs, and other things to beware.

Look to the Kid Friendly icon for attractions, hotels, restaurants, and activities that are particularly hospitable to children or people traveling with kids.

Keep an eye out for the Bargain Alert icon as you seek out money-saving tips and/or great deals.

Check out the No Blarney icon for humorous, curious, or just plain bizarre facts about Ireland and the Irish.

Where to Go from Here

Now you're ready to go! Put a Chieftains CD on the stereo, pour yourself a glass of Guinness, and get ready to fling yourself headlong into the historic, friendly, beautiful, and ever-hip experience that is Ireland today.

Part I
Getting Started

The 5th Wave By Rich Tennant

WHILE ON VACATION IN IRELAND, BILL AND DENISE WATCH A LOCAL FAMILY WORKING ON THE TRADITIONAL THATCHED ROOF COTTAGE, THATCHED ROOF SATELLITE DISH, AND THATCHED ROOF JEEP CHEROKEE.

In this part . . .

Before you can start planning your trip to Ireland, you have to do some legwork. When should you go? What parts of the country do you want to visit? How much will it cost? This section is where you'll find the answers to all these questions and more.

In Chapter 1, I introduce you to Ireland with a brief overview of Irish history and culture. I also clue you in to some of the basics of daily life in Ireland, such as dining, words and phrases that Americans may find confusing, and pub life. If you're hoping to hunt down information on your ancestors while in Ireland, I tell you what you need to do before you go to make sure you have a successful search.

If you're not sure when to go to Ireland or what part of the country you want to visit, Chapter 2 will help you out. I describe each region of the country, discuss the impact the different seasons will have on your trip, and tell you about some great festivals and events throughout the country that you may want to see. Then I help you start planning your itinerary in Chapter 3 and give you suggested itineraries to work from.

Wondering if you can really afford this trip? Turn to Chapter 4, where I help you figure out what this adventure realistically is going to cost you. I give you lots of money-saving tips as well as my opinions about what you *shouldn't* scrimp on.

I wrap up the first part of this book with Chapter 5, where I share traveling tips and resources for those with special needs, such as seniors, families, gays and lesbians, and travelers with disabilities.

Chapter 1

Discovering the Best of Ireland

. . . .

In This Chapter

▶ Taking a short course in Irish history

▶ Talking, eating, and drinking like an Irishman

▶ Appreciating Guinness and Irish whiskey

▶ Getting the lowdown on golf, fishing, and other sports in Ireland

. . . .

*I*reland is a mighty travel destination because of its riches —
verdant beauty, ancient history, rich culture, and friendly people.
And it doesn't hurt that millions of people around the world have Irish
ancestors.

In this chapter, I introduce you to the Irish and answer all the questions
you didn't even know you had about Irish culture and history, so that
when you get there, you'll be totally clued in to who's who and what's
what. If you're more interested in your own history, I provide a section
on tracing your Irish ancestry.

Don't Know Much about Ireland's History?

Ireland has one of the most storied and complex histories of any
nation, and in this section I tell you all about it. Don't worry, though!
This is the CliffsNotes version.

Invaders welcome

From the beginning, Ireland wore a welcome sign to invaders, or so it
seems. The first wave came around 500 B.C. with the Celts, who stayed
and laid roots, splitting into tribes and even creating Ireland's four
provinces — Munster, Leinster, Ulster, and Connaught. Well-intended
Christians came in the fifth century A.D., and among them, brought as a
slave by the Celts, was the future patron saint of Ireland, St. Patrick.
Christianity took off like wildfire.

Ireland

The Viking invasions abruptly ended centuries of peace. The Vikings came to plunder, but they fell in with the Irish way of life and decided to make a home there. Vikings founded the first towns in Ireland: Dublin, Cork, Waterford, and Limerick. The Irish were none too happy about the unwelcome visitors, though, and the great Brian Boru, one of the High Kings, defeated the Viking armies and sent them sailing.

Ireland flourished until the 12th century, when the Normans (or British) attacked. They, too, loved the land, and despite Irish efforts to make them leave, the Normans set up permanent camp.

Beginning around the 1500s, Irish history turned bloody and ugly. The Irish had for years held the Normans at bay, keeping them in one spot around Dublin called "the Pale" (from which comes the phrase *beyond the Pale*), but then Henry VIII dubbed himself king of Ireland and set out claiming the whole island.

Rebel with a cause

Ireland is a land that has seen its share of invasions, but it's also a place that has launched its share of rebellions. In 1600, the first of many rebellions was set in motion in defiance of Elizabeth I's ruling that increased her armies in Ireland and forced Irish lords to hand over their land. The rebellion was quickly quelled.

For a hundred years, Britain imposed harsh *Penal Laws,* which completely crushed Catholics and the practice of their religion. Irish Catholics were so persecuted and disenfranchised that by the end of the 1600s, Protestants — only 20% of the population — owned 86% of the land. Thanks to the cruelty of Oliver Cromwell, an agent of Britain, all opposition was swiftly and murderously stopped.

In 1798, war between Britain and France gave Ireland a window of opportunity for another rebellion. Irishman Wolfe Tone conspired with the French to invade his own country, with hopes of driving the British out, but his rebellion failed pitifully, and the great patriot Tone slit his own throat before facing execution by his enemies.

Ireland secured an edge when Daniel O'Connell, known as The Liberator, pushed the Catholic Emancipation Act through Parliament in 1828, but progress was stopped in its tracks when the Great Famine struck in 1845. For five years, potato crops failed, and as a result, 2.5 million people either died or emigrated to America.

The Irish kept fighting to regain their country, despite such crushing blows. Although many groups were working for Ireland's freedom, they weren't working together, which made the struggle more difficult. Charles Stewart Parnell, Ireland's representative to the British Parliament, finally united the groups in the late 1800s, laying the groundwork that would lead to independence.

The Irish flag

Ireland's flag, three thick vertical strips of green, white, and orange, first flew publicly over Dublin's General Post Office during the Easter Rising of 1916. The green represents Ireland's Catholics, the orange represents Protestants (symbolic of William of Orange, a 17th-century king of Britain), and the white is the hoped-for peace between them.

These newly united factions staged Ireland's most famous rebellion on Easter Monday in 1916. Fifteen hundred freedom fighters, led by Patrick Pearse and James Connolly, took Dublin's General Post Office, from the steps of which Pearse read the Proclamation of the Irish Republic. This rebellion led to swift attack by the British, who sailed gunboats up the River Liffey and heavily shelled the town. After six days of battle, the rebels were overwhelmed. Connolly, Pearse, and 13 other leaders of the Rising (as the rebellion was called) were taken to Kilmainham Gaol (Jail), tried, and shot. The Irish were outraged at the savage executions, especially that of Connolly, who had been so badly injured from fighting that he couldn't stand and had to be tied to a chair to face the firing squad. The murdered patriots became martyrs in Ireland, and the Irish commitment to fight for freedom was secured.

In 1918, Sinn Fein (pronounced shin fine) won the General Election and began the first independent Parliament, essentially claiming independence from Britain. Britain retaliated, and the Irish launched what has come to be called the War of Independence. Michael Collins led the Irish forces and persuaded the British to negotiate.

The Anglo-Irish Treaty of 1921 gave autonomy to 26 of Ireland's 32 counties. The remaining six counties stayed part of the United Kingdom (U.K.) and became known as Northern Ireland. Many Irish, eager to finally reach peace, accepted the accord for the Irish Free State, even though it kept Ireland in the British Commonwealth. Others, led by Eamon de Valera, disagreed. A civil war broke out, Collins and many others were killed, and de Valera's side won control. In 1937, he forced complete independence from England.

The question of British control of the North never ceased to be a catalyst for anger, though, and another war broke out in 1969. The IRA battled pro-British forces through nearly 30 years of guerilla warfare, mostly in the North. Today, although violence does still break out among radical factions of the IRA, Northern Ireland is operating under a semi-autonomous agreement and the Sinn Fein is a pro-Catholic political arm with members holding seats in British Parliament.

Who's Who in Irish Mythology

Some of the folks I describe in this section lived more verifiably real lives than others, but all have entered the mythology to such an extent that you're almost sure to hear them mentioned at some point in your trip.

- ✔ **Cuchulainn (pronounced coo-*cul*-in):** The famous Celtic warrior of ancient myth. Many legendary stories are told of his feats, in which Cuchulainn grows to enormous size and strength (he can kill scores of men with one swing of a sword). A statue stands in Dublin's General Post Office (GPO) depicting Cuchulainn in bloody action.

- ✔ **Queen Maeve (pronounced mave):** Cuchulainn's enemy, who legend credits with stealing the prize bull of Ulster and killing Cuchulainn, among other evil exploits.

- ✔ **Finn MacCool:** An Irish hero immortalized in poems by his son Ossian and in many *Fenian ballads,* named after the Fenians (or Fianna), professional fighters whom Finn was said to have led in the third century. Finn and his men defended the country from foreign aggressors and hunted for food; these two activities are the main subjects of the stories. He is often portrayed as a giant with supernatural powers, accompanied by his pet hound, Bran.

- ✔ **Ossian (pronounced o-*sheen*):** Finn MacCool's son, a great leader and warrior, as well as one of the first poets of Ireland. The name means "fawn," and legend claims that his mother spent part of her life as a deer.

- ✔ **Turlough O'Carolan:** One of the best-known of the Irish harpers (sometimes called Carolan). After smallpox blinded him in his teens, he learned to play the harp and for the rest of his years traveled throughout Ireland as an itinerant musician. He wrote more than 200 compositions that are still played today, more than 300 years later.

- ✔ **Children of Lir:** This legendary story tells of how the wicked new wife of King Lir (pronounced leer) put a spell on his children to turn them into swans for 900 years. She later regretted her evil deed but couldn't reverse the spell, so she gave the birds the gift of song instead. (Today it is illegal in Ireland to kill swans.) A beautiful sculpture depicting the Children of Lir is the centerpiece of Dublin's Garden of Remembrance.

- ✔ **St. Patrick:** The patron saint of Ireland. Brought to the country as a teenage slave, he later escaped, only to return to Ireland later as a missionary. His legendary feat of driving the snakes out of Ireland has been proven false by scholars, who say that snakes are simply not indigenous to the island. His feast day is well known and celebrated with great enthusiasm far beyond Ireland's borders.

✔ **St. Brendan:** The "other" Irish saint. A wandering monk, he traveled all over the present-day U.K. during the sixth century before finding religious paradise in Ireland. His legend is an odyssey of difficulties. A mountain in County Kerry is named for him, and his feast day is May 16.

Who's Who in Irish Literature

The Irish are fiercely proud of their rich literary tradition, and many standouts have places of honor around the country. You can't go to County Sligo without tripping over references to W. B. Yeats, and repeated references to the novels of James Joyce fill Dublin. The hallowed walls of Dublin theaters practically resonate with the plays of O'Casey, Shaw, and Beckett.

Here are some bite-sized bios of the literary wonders you're most likely to hear about:

✔ **James Joyce (1882–1941):** A controversial writer who set his famous pseudo-trilogy *Portrait of the Artist as a Young Man, Dubliners,* and *Ulysses* in Dublin. *Ulysses* was banned in Ireland until the 1960s, and up until the euro conversion, Joyce's picture was on the £10 Irish note — talk about ironic.

✔ **Samuel Beckett (1906–1989):** A Nobel Prize–winning playwright and novelist, known for surreal writing. The best-known and most performed of his plays is *Waiting for Godot.*

✔ **W. B. Yeats (1865–1939):** A Nobel Prize–winning poet and playwright who cofounded Dublin's Abbey Theatre. Many of his poems, such as "Easter Rising, 1916," capture the horror and irony of Irish rebellion.

✔ **Sean O'Casey (1880–1964):** The famed Abbey Theatre playwright who shocked theatergoers with controversial plays based on his early, poverty-stricken days. Best known are *Juno and the Paycock* and *The Plough and the Stars.*

✔ **George Bernard Shaw (1856–1950):** Nobel Prize–winning author of *Pygmalion, Major Barbara,* and *St. Joan.* As a 15-year-old dropout, Shaw spent a lot of his time at the National Gallery in Dublin. Later, he bequeathed it a third of his royalties.

✔ **Brendan Behan (1923–1964):** Despite a youth full of run-ins with the law and a stint with the IRA in his teens, this playwright, columnist, and novelist made the most trouble with his politically charged plays *The Quare Fellow* and *The Hostage,* both dealing with the Irish rebellion.

> ✔ **John Millington Synge (1871–1909):** A noted Abbey Theatre play-
> wright, Synge is best remembered for plays that explore the rural
> life of western Ireland, among them *Riders to the Sea, Shadow of
> the Glen,* and *Playboy of the Western World.*

For more information about Ireland's rich literary history, pick up a
free copy of *Literary Ireland,* an enlightening brochure and country-
wide map on areas of literary interest. It's available at the larger tourist
offices and some bookstores.

Ireland for the Irish: Digging Up Your Roots

If there's one thing more popular these days than going to Ireland, it's
being Irish. Those lucky enough to have an *O* or a *Mc* in front of their
names usually wear it like a badge of honor. It's inherently harder for
people with names that smack of other national origins to gain Emerald
Isle respect.

So if you're sick of people saying, "You? Irish? With a name like
Fornatale?" there's only one thing to do: Prove it! You can easily trace
your Irish roots thanks to endless resources created for the sole purpose
of revealing your Irish ancestry. This kind of family-tree-tracing can
enrich your whole trip to the homeland. Imagine visiting the places
where your grandparents worked or your great-grandparents were born!

Doing your own research in advance

Your research should begin at home. The most immediate and valuable
sources are living family members, whose own family papers and even
traditions can give clues. Sometimes Irish Americans named their homes
after their old town or parish. Details like surnames, occupations, and
religion are all important clues needed for a successful search.

Start the paper trail before you consult any agency — showing up
empty-handed will get you nowhere. Birth, marriage, and death certificates (civil and parochial), census returns, and immigration papers are
all valuable. Don't carry originals overseas; bring copies.

In the United States, the **National Archives,** 700 Pennsylvania Ave. NW,
Washington, DC 20408 (☎ **866-325-7208;** E-mail: inquire@nara.gov),
has a great service for helping you trace your family back to the port of
origin. In Canada, the bulk of research is being done at the Department
of Irish Studies at **St. Mary's University** in Halifax, Nova Scotia, B3H
3C3 (☎ **902-420-5553;** E-mail: research@stmarys.ca). Australia has
kept extensive records of the many Irish immigrants who went down

under. The best sources there are the **National Library in Canberra, ACT 2600** (☎ **61-2-6262-1111;** Internet: www.nla.gov.au), and the **Mitchell Library** in Sydney (☎ **61-2-9273-1466**).

Tapping into research agencies in Ireland

After you exhaust your home resources and have insight about where to start looking, you're ready to get help from a research agency.

Costs range from small fees for copies of certificates to paying researchers by the hour. Even though these services cost you some cash, they save a lot of time and hassle. They're probably also able to get information that someone off the street could never find.

Common Irish names and where they come from

Here are just a few popular Irish surnames and the counties where they originated. Many of these families later spread throughout the island and beyond. Each name has plenty of variations; for instance, FitzGerald has derivations of Fitzpatrick, Flanagan, Flynn, Fogarty, Foley, and Gaffney.

Ahearne: Clare, Limerick

Butler: Kilkenny

Donoghue: Cork, Kerry

FitzGerald: Cork, Kerry, Kildare

MacCarthy: Munster

Maguire: Ulster

Martin: Connaught

Murphy: Sligo, Tyrone, Wexford

O'Brien: Clare, Limerick

O'Donnell: Donegal

O'Keeffe: Cork

O'Kelly: Galway

O'Neill: Ulster

O'Sullivan: Tipperary

Power: Waterford, Wicklow

Regan: Dublin, Meath

Ryan: Limerick, Tipperary

Walsh: Dublin, Kilkenny, Leitrim, Waterford, Wicklow

What's in a name? Ages ago, the prefixes of Irish last names signified a great deal. *Mc* or *Fitz* meant "son of," and *O* before a name meant "grandson of" or "from the family of." So the name O'Brien means "ancestors of the Brien family" (in this case, the ancestors of Brian Boru, the most famous of the High Kings of Ireland). You'll also occasionally see a name with an *Ní* prefix (such as Ní Dhomhnaill), but this configuration is, for the most part, archaic. Literally, it means "formerly of," as in Triona Briain Ní Dhomhnaill, the name Triona might go by if she were a proud Dhomnaill who married a Briain.

The leader of the pack is the **Hibernian Research Company,** P.O. Box 3097, Dublin 6 (☎ **01-496-6522**), the oldest and largest genealogical agency in Ireland. Its staff is trained under the Chief Herald of the Genealogical Office.

In Northern Ireland, the two best-known companies are the **Irish Heritage Association,** Queens Road, Belfast (☎ **028-9045-5325**), and the **Ulster Historical Foundation,** Balmoral Buildings, 12 College Sq. East, Belfast BT1 6DD (☎ **90-33-2288**; Fax: 90-23-9885; E-mail: enquiry@uhf.org.uk; Internet: www.ancestryireland.com).

Finding sources in Ireland for doing your own research

In addition to the following organizations, counties throughout Ireland have local genealogical sources that I list in the different chapters of this book. These sources function more as record-storage facilities or archives than as full-service research services.

- ✔ **Irish Genealogy Ltd.,** 5th Floor, 25–28 Adelaide Rd., Dublin 2 (☎ **01-6617-334**; Fax: 01-6617-332). A good starting point for narrowing your search. Cost: Initial consultations start at €45. A full family history report can cost between €150 and €300, depending on the level of detail you require.

- ✔ **Births, Deaths, and Marriages** (records office), General Registrar House, Joyce House, 8/11 Lombard St. East, Dublin 2 (☎ **01-671-1000**). Cost: Varies for type of research and certificate obtained.

- ✔ **The Genealogical Office of the National Library of Ireland,** 2 Kildare St., Dublin 2 (☎ **01-603-0200**). The Library houses pre-1880 records, newspapers, trade directories, and more. Cost: Advisory service for genealogy is free.

- ✔ **National Archives,** 8 Bishop St., Dublin 8 (☎ **01-407-2300**). The largest variety of sources, including health and school records, parish registers, land titles, wills, and grants or public and private sources. Cost: Varies for type of certificate obtained.

- ✔ **The Public Records Office of Northern Ireland,** 66 Balmoral Ave., Belfast BT9 6NY (☎ **028-9025-1318**; Fax: 028-9025-5999). The office has baptism, marriage, and burial records for the North on microfilm. Cost: Just the price of photocopying.

For more information about searching your Irish roots, pick up a free copy of *Tracing Your Ancestors in Ireland,* a good introductory guide providing more details on how to trace your ancestors. It's available at the larger tourist offices and some bookstores.

Talking to the Irish

Sure, they speak English in Ireland, but between occasional odd words and the accent (which is particularly heavy in small, remote towns), it sounds like a foreign language at times. Read these handy glossaries so that you don't have to keep one of those polite but puzzled smiles on your face while talking with locals.

Understanding the lingo

Some of the following terms are slang or just Irish usage, and some are bona fide Gaelic:

- **An Lar:** City center (Gaelic)
- **Bonnet:** Car hood
- **Boot:** Car trunk
- **Bord Fa'ilte (pronounced board *fal*-tea):** Irish Tourist Board (Gaelic)
- **Cheers:** Thanks
- **Crack, craic (pronounced crack):** Good times, fun (Gaelic)
- **Creche:** Day care
- **Deadly, brilliant:** Great, excellent
- **Fa'ilte (pronounced *fal*-tea):** Welcome (Gaelic)
- **Fir:** Men (Gaelic, sometimes used on bathroom doors)
- **Footpath:** Sidewalk
- **Garda:** Policeman
- **Lift:** Elevator
- **Mna (pronounced just like it's spelled):** Women (Gaelic, sometimes used on bathroom doors)
- **Off-license:** Liquor store
- **Petrol:** Gasoline
- **Press:** Cabinet
- **Quay (pronounced key):** Waterfront
- **Quid, sterling, or bob:** Pounds, or money
- **Sla'inte (pronounced *schlan*-cha):** Cheers or goodbye (Gaelic)
- **Take-away:** Fast food, to go
- **Till:** Cash register

✔ **Tins:** Canned goods

✔ **Windscreen:** Windshield

Translating Gaelic place names

Picture this: You're passing through a quaint town with an even quainter name. Wonder what it means? Use the following list to mix and match parts of names to get their Gaelic meaning. For example, Tullamore translates into Great Small Hill (tul + mor). Sounds better their way, huh?

✔ **Ard:** Height, hill

✔ **Aw, ow:** River

✔ **Bal, bally:** Town

✔ **Bawn:** White

✔ **Beg:** Small

✔ **Carrick, carrig:** Rock

✔ **Cloch:** Stone

✔ **Derg:** Red

✔ **Doo, du:** Black

✔ **Dun:** Fort

✔ **Drom, drum:** Ridge

✔ **Innis, ennis, inch:** Island

✔ **Glen, glas:** Valley

✔ **Kil, kill:** Church

✔ **Knock:** Hill

✔ **Lis, liss:** Fort

✔ **Lough:** Lake

✔ **Mone, mona:** Bog

✔ **Mor:** Great, large

✔ **Owen, avon:** River

✔ **Rinn, reen:** A point

✔ **Ross:** Peninsula

✔ **Shan, shane:** Old

✔ **Tra, traw:** Beach

✔ **Tul, tulagh:** Small hill

Guarding against miscommunication

When you're in Ireland, you may recognize certain words but not understand the way they're used. This can lead to some potentially embarrassing situations. For instance, when looking for someone to drive you someplace, ask for a lift, not a ride. Asking for a ride is the equivalent of asking for a roll in the hay. Along the same lines, holding two fingers up in a *V* with your palm faced inward is the same as raising your middle finger to someone. Careful when ordering two pints!

On the other hand, the Irish have some sayings that may sound quite rude to you but actually are acceptable and mean no offense. Here are some examples:

- ✔ *Piss take* or *Take the piss out of you* just means, essentially, "pulling your leg" or "messing with you."

- ✔ *Feck* and *shite* are not what you think. Both words are a bit worse than *shoot,* but fall more into the *crap* or *suck* category.

- ✔ *Slagging you* means "teasing you."

And if someone asks if you have a "fag," they just want a cigarette.

Ireland Dining and Irish Cuisine

Yes, there is such a thing as Irish cuisine, and it's good, so if you think food in Ireland is all potatoes all the time, you're just plain wrong.

For years, the boundaries of cooking in Ireland stretched to no great limits. Food consisted mainly of overcooked and oversalted meats, accompanied by butter-laden vegetables and potatoes, making Ireland the true home of meat and potatoes.

But all that has changed, drastically and for the better. The country appears well aware of its cooking renaissance, too, and takes great pride in wowing restaurant patrons with succulent sauces and masterful preparation of worldwide cuisine.

Even traditional Irish food, while still solidly established in the average diet, has had a makeover. Hearty stews and soups are still everywhere, but their quality has been jacked up a few notches, and the selection is vast. Specialty dishes like *boxty* (a potato pancake stuffed with various meats) and *colcannon* (potato, scallions, and kale) abound, but unlike their older counterparts, these meals now have flavor and variation and don't rely so heavily on salt for taste.

The Irish are particularly proud of their delicious farmhouse cheeses. Opting for a cheese course after dinner rather than a dessert isn't exactly making a sacrifice.

Homemade bread, baked daily, is everywhere, and although considered a quite humble food, it's one of the country's most delicious (and addictive) offerings. Visitors rave about the classic, hearty brown bread and slightly sweet soda bread long after they return home.

Eating out: What to expect

If you're looking for a real traditional Irish meal, you can often find it in a hotel restaurant, where tradition holds court and quality and succulence reign. Aside from the hotels, you won't find many traditional Irish restaurants that aren't geared toward tourists, like **Gallagher's Boxty House in Dublin** (see the section on dining in Chapter 11).

Loads of small cafes and lunch counters offer hearty soups and sandwiches. Even more plentiful are *chippers* and *take-aways,* fast food places where you can get, among other things, traditional fish and chips.

In larger cities, you may be surprised to notice the number of ethnic restaurants in Ireland. You can get a fine Italian meal here that rivals some in New York City. And although the Irish have always had a taste for Chinese food (from fast food to classy), Indian Tandoori and other Eastern cuisines are making a major breakthrough as well. And don't laugh, but American food is big, from gargantuan hamburgers to pizza, and usually served up at American-themed restaurants. Even vegetarian food has carved out a niche for itself.

If you have your heart set on eating at a posh restaurant in one of the larger cities during the summer, you should probably make reservations. But generally speaking, reservations aren't necessary.

Checking out meal prices

Fortunately, you probably won't have to pay for breakfast, which usually comes standard with your room. Lunch typically sets you back around €12 ($11.40) if you eat in a restaurant or as little as €5 ($4.75) if you have fast food or carry-out, like the ubiquitous fish and chips.

Dinner is more expensive, with entrees ranging from €8 ($7.60) to €12 ($11.40) on the low end to €16 ($15.20) and way up on the high end. After you factor in wine and service, the tab can get rather high. I include a few dining-related money-saving tips in Chapter 3.

Restaurants in the "Dining" sections of this book are categorized by the following scale, based on the price of a main course:

$	€8/£5.10/$7.60 or less
$$	€8–€13/£5.10–£8.30/$7.60–$12.35
$$$	€13–€19/£8.30–£12.15/$12.35–$18.05
$$$	€19/£12.15/$18.05 or more

It's Emily Post Time!: Irish Meal Times and Dining Customs

Rules of dining are similar to those in the States, with just a few exceptions. One, which you may notice right away, is that the Irish, like many Europeans, keep the knife in their right hand and lift food on the fork with the left hand. Table settings are the same, except that often a large soup spoon lays across the top of your place setting.

Meal times mirror those in the States, with breakfast beginning around 7 a.m. and finishing at 10 or 11 a.m. Lunch goes from noon to about 3 p.m. Having lunch between 1 and 2 p.m. is difficult in major towns and cities; most places will be a madhouse. Dinner is served beginning at 5 p.m. and goes as late as 11 p.m. or so, but expect to order by around 9 p.m.

Choice restaurants often have set lunch menus that are reasonably priced and offer the same good food as at dinnertime. Some restaurants also have early-bird menus, which are similar to those at lunch: three to four courses, good food, and low prices. Also, you should know that pubs serve some of the best and most traditional Irish food you'll find anywhere. They're a popular place for lunch, too. Pub grub is fully covered later in this chapter.

Deciphering the menu

Here are a few food terms you may run up against. Some are Irish, some derived from the Brits, and some just vaguely European.

- **Aubergines:** Eggplants
- **Barn brack:** A cake-like bread
- **Boxty:** Potato pancakes filled with meats and vegetables
- **Chassuers:** Mushrooms
- **Chipper:** Traditional fast food
- **Chips:** French fries

- ✔ **Courgettes:** Zucchini

- ✔ **Crisps:** Potato chips

- ✔ **Dublin coddle:** A thick stew made with sausages, bacon, onions, and potatoes

- ✔ **Mange tout:** Snap peas

- ✔ **Minerals:** Sodas

- ✔ **Rasher:** Bacon

- ✔ **Shepherd's pie:** Ground beef and vegetables topped with mashed potatoes

- ✔ **Sultanas:** Similar to raisins but with a slightly different taste

Livin' the Pub Life

Irish pubs are much more than places to have a drink. They have a culture of their own, providing people with a place to meet, laugh, eat, hear music, and relax. Great care is taken to preserve the mood of the rare auld times, with even the newest pubs filled with antiques and tons of old-looking woodwork. Music and good food enhance the magic, all combining to create what the Irish call *craic,* or good times.

If you're drinking with a group, think rounds. Everyone takes turns buying each person a drink, so don't think you're hanging out with the friendliest and most generous people in Ireland when someone buys you a pint; you're expected to reciprocate.

Absorbing a little pub history

Going back to the Middle Ages, Irish pubs began as places for merchants and travelers to replenish themselves with a drink. Later, when the strong arm of Britain was upon Ireland, these watering holes flourished even though they'd been declared illegal, serving as a wonderful escape from the colonial tyranny. In Victorian times, pubs went from being drab and dark to being beautifully decorated, and many of the older establishments still bear their original counters and elaborate windows.

The word *pub* has an interesting story. *Pub* is short for *public house,* which was the opposite of a *private house,* where only members could go. The people who frequented public houses often were the hard-working lower classes. Someone who ran a pub was called a *publican.*

Pubs also have a grand place in Ireland's history, because they're the places where many revolutionaries secretly met and planned for the country's freedom fights. Irish literary figures graced many Dublin pubs with their presence. (See the section on organized tours in Dublin in Chapter 11.)

Snuggling up

In many pubs, you'll notice small partitioned areas called *snugs*. These are great places for quiet conversation or to get away from the crowd. But that's not what they were for originally. Until the late 1960s, it was impolite for women to drink in public, so they were confined to the snugs. The barman would pass drinks (only half pints, of course!) through a small opening.

Savoring the black stuff: Guinness

You may have had one or two pints of Guinness beer in the States. But the pint of Guinness you have in Ireland will taste like nothing you've had before. Call it the home-court advantage or credit the fact that the stuff is as fresh as all get-out in Ireland, but it's a fact that the Guinness you'll have in Ireland is a high cut above the Guinness you'll have anywhere else.

When Arthur Guinness took over a small brewery in Dublin, he had fantastic foresight. He may not have known then that his brew would account for one of every two pints sold in Ireland or would be sold in 150 countries, but he definitely was going for longevity — in 1759 he signed a 9,000-year lease on the brewery's site!

I want to clear up a few misconceptions about Guinness. One misconception is that it has a huge number of calories. Actually, a pint of Guinness has about as many calories as a pint of skim milk — around 100. Another misconception is that Guinness is a particularly heavy drink, an idea that probably comes from the look of it. Really, Guinness is very easy to drink and refreshing — don't let the thick head scare you. An extra bonus is that the famous ad campaign, "Guinness is good for you," is pretty much on the mark. With only four all-natural ingredients — barley, hops, yeast, and pure Irish water — and no preservatives, Guinness is almost guaranteed not to give you a hangover. (But note: I can't be responsible if you start downing shots of whiskey with it!)

Finally, five words to live by: A good pint takes time. Barkeeps draw the pint halfway and let it sit for about two minutes. Then, by pushing the tap forward so the stout comes out even slower than the first draw, they fill the glass the rest of the way (some fill the glass in a three-step process). This slowness isn't cruel taunting; it's how a real pint is pulled. Even when you finally get the pint in your hands, don't drink just yet. Wait until it has settled completely and has turned a deep ruby, almost black. A good test is to take a coin and tap it against the glass, working upward. When the coin makes a heavy thud throughout the glass, rather than a tinny tap, your brew is ready!

Sampling other Irish brews

You may not believe it, but there are other Irish beers. Just because most people tend to forget that doesn't mean you should, too. Some of the more popular are Harp, a light lager that's good for people who aren't into dark beers; Caffreys, an ale that settles like a stout; Smithwicks, a dark ale; Kilkenny, an ale very popular across Europe; Murphy's Amber, a thick-tasting ale; Murphy's Stout, which is a bit sweeter than Guinness; and Bulmer's Cider, a sweet, entirely too drinkable hard cider.

Wondering what the difference is between Guinness and Murphy's Stout? Well, employees at St. James's Gate, where Guinness is brewed, have an idea. According to rumor, a drawing inside the brewery shows a donkey drinking from a trough labeled "Guinness." Behind the donkey is another trough, in which the animal is urinating. This trough, of course, is labeled "Murphy's." I assume Murphy's has its own ideas about its rival.

Sipping some Irish whiskey

Monks did a lot for Ireland. They painstakingly crafted the Book of Kells and protected Irish antiquities in their round towers during invasions. But ask your average man on an Irish street, and you can bet he'll say the best thing monks did for Ireland was invent whiskey.

You read that right — monks invented whiskey. In the sixth century, missionary monks brought the secret of distillation home from the Middle East, forever changing the face of Ireland. Irish whiskey is known all over the world for its smoothness and quality, and it has done more than brighten the lives of many Irish; it has brought Ireland huge revenues over the centuries. The original Gaelic term for whiskey, Uisce Beatha (pronounced *ish*-ka *ba*-ha) means "Water of Life." Even today, every European country that distills a native spirit refers to theirs as the Water of Life: *Eau de Vie* in France, *Akvavit* in Scandinavia, *Lebenswasser* in Germany, *Agua de la Vida* in Spain, and *Aqua della Vita* in Italy.

Poteen

You may have heard of a potent potable called Poteen and wondered just what it is. Well, poteen (or potcheen) is unlawfully distilled clear whiskey, banned since 1661. Basically, it's the Irish equivalent of moonshine. Not too long ago, though, the government gave a license to **Bunratty Mead and Liqueur,** Bunratty, County Clare (☎ **061-36-2222**), to make poteen, so you can now legally get a bottle of Ireland's original spirit. (But you can't bring it into the States; it's too potent.) I triple-dog dare you to try some.

Scotch versus whiskey

Irish whiskey and Scotch whisky have always been in healthy competition, but it was the Irish who taught the Scottish how to make the spirit.

Distillation of Scotch began around the 13th century, making Irish whiskey nearly twice as old. (You'll notice that Scotch whisky is spelled without the letter *e*.)

Whiskey became more than just a home brew in 1608, when the world's first distillery license was given to Old Bushmills Distillery. Next came John Jameson & Son in 1780 and John Powers & Son in 1791. These licenses blew open the whiskey export trade in Ireland, and the world's love affair with Irish whiskey began. By the end of the 19th century, more than 400 brands of it were available in America alone!

The money stopped rolling in when Prohibition was introduced in America in 1919. Bootleggers began distributing lousy liquor under the respected name of Irish whiskey, destroying its reputation. Meanwhile, Ireland and England were recoiling from Irish insurrection and engaged in an economic war. They stopped buying each other's products completely. With Irish whiskey out of the picture, Scotch jumped in to fill the void. It's only recently that Irish whiskey has regained a foothold in American markets and is rebuilding its international lead.

Irish whiskey has a distinctive smoothness, and that's no accident. Unlike any other whiskey, the Irish distill theirs three times before it's ready to drink. (By way of comparison, American whisky is distilled only once and Scotch twice.)

If you're interested in the distillation of Irish whiskey (or just love the stuff), go on the Irish Whiskey Trail. You can tour the country's three historic and popular distilleries: **The Old Bushmills Distillery,** County Antrim (☎ **080-12657-31521**), **The Old Jameson Distillery,** Dublin (☎ **01-872-5566**), and **The Old Midleton Distillery,** Cork (☎ **021-61-3594).** They're pretty spread out over Ireland from north to south, but they're worth the trek. Each hosts tours daily.

Noshing on pub grub

Pub food in Ireland is much more than a bag of peanuts or a basket of pretzels. On the whole, pub grub is hearty, wholesome food that makes for a great meal. You can find beef and lamb stews, soups, meaty sandwiches, salads, and, of course chips (which are like steak fries).

One thing to keep in mind is that many pubs serve food only during lunchtime, from noon to 3 p.m. You can't even get a crust of bread after that in some places. On the other hand, plenty of pubs do serve all day.

If you just want a little something to keep the wolf from the door, one particular nosh offered in many Irish pubs could change your attitude toward junk food forever: Hot Nuts, which are spicy cracker-coated peanuts. Look for the lighted little roasters on the bar. At around €1 (95¢) for a tiny cupful, they're no great bargain, but one taste and you won't be able to stop.

Examining pub hours and drink prices

Most pubs open at 10:30 a.m., for you go-getters. They close at midnight, with last call at about 11:30. Clubs can get special licenses to stay open as late as 3 a.m.

A pretty strict rule in Ireland says pubs can't open before noon on Sundays; this is to keep people out of the pubs before they go to Mass with their families. Another part of the rule says that late-night bars are supposed to close up at midnight on Saturdays — because at midnight it's actually Sunday — but this part of the law is rarely enforced.

One of the most fun evenings you can have in Ireland is when the doors of the pub close with you inside. This wink-and-nod arrangement usually happens only in small-town places and shouldn't be expected. But there's a chance that the publican will allow a small gathering to stay, a situation that often ends up in music, conversation, and getting to know the locals. It's then that you're liable to make lifelong friends.

Wondering what a night in a pub will run you? Ballpark figures are about €2.50 ($2.35) for a pint in a small town to as much as €3.50 ($3.35) in the city. The price for a glass of liquor (called a *short*) ranges from €2.75 ($2.60) on the low end to €3.70 ($3.50) for the more expensive areas. If you're a nondrinker, keep in mind that a small bottle of soda costs nearly the same as a pint of Guinness!

Also, if you order a mixed drink (a vodka tonic, for instance), don't be surprised when the barkeep hands you a glass with ice and liquor and a bottle of tonic. It's not out of laziness; that's just how it's done.

Tipping like a local

Thanks to the proliferation of American tourists, many barkeeps know of the Yankee tendency to tip when given a drink, so they're not surprised when some money is left after the round is paid for. It's not really customary, though. More common is buying the bartender the odd drink for his labor. After leaving some silver on the bar, I watched a bartender pick it up, look at it quizzically, and then toss it atop a shelf. Many will run after you with your change, even if it's just a few pence!

Appreciating Irish Music

This should say something about the importance of music in Ireland: It's the only nation in the world with a musical instrument as a national symbol. The Tara Harp appears on all official documents of the Irish government. You can see the oldest Tara Harp in Ireland on display in the Old Library of Trinity College in Dublin (see Chapter 11).

Thankfully, traditional Irish music enjoyed a huge revival in the folk music days of the 1960s, with credit due to such popular groups as The Dubliners and the Wolfe Tones. Today you'll hear those unique Celtic sounds from Irish bands like Solas, Clannad, and The Corrs.

The best place to hear Irish music is in a pub, where music is as vital to the whole experience as having a pint. Irish songs tell the story of Irish history and can alternate from the raunchy and hilarious to the moving poignancy of a hero's last moments.

You can find scheduled music in many pubs, especially during the high season. Another type of music, which isn't necessarily scheduled, is a *session.* This is a group of people informally playing traditional instruments — the tin whistle, uillean pipes (the Irish version of bagpipes; pronounced *ill*-un), the bodhrán (a handheld drum, pronounced *bow*-ron), and fiddle.

Enjoying Sports and the Great Outdoors

All that green Irish grass gets used for more than feeding sheep, and whether you want participatory sports like golf or fishing, spectator sports like soccer or rugby, or traditionally Irish sports like hurling or Gaelic football, you'll find it in Ireland — and in this section, so read on.

Golf

Ireland, it's said, is one large golf course with a few towns and hills scattered around it, the whole thing surrounded by a huge water hazard. More than 250 courses are spread around a country that's only about the size of Maine. That's remarkable but not surprising, given that the country likes to take credit for starting the sport.

Irish courses compare favorably with the perfectly groomed courses in the United States. Although the grass is not as chemically enhanced as it is in the States and many clubhouses are not as decked out, the lush Irish countryside makes for excellent natural courses and hazards.

Golf clubs in Ireland are used to catering to tourists, and most rent clubs. The cost is generally €10 to €15 per round, depending on the quality of the clubs.

Golf package tours

If you're a golf enthusiast, you may want to consider a golf package tour, which allows you to book your play and your stay all together.

Here are a few of the best tour companies that merge the links and the land for an unforgettable golf vacation:

- ✔ **Jerry Quinlan's Celtic Golf,** 1129 Rte. 9 South, Cape May Court House, NJ 08210 (☎ **800-535-6148;** Fax: 609-65-0670; E-mail: Celticgolf@aol.com; Internet: www.jqcelticgolf.com). This place will customize your vacation package and personally host golf tours.

- ✔ **Irish Links Tours & Travel,** 400 Main St., Suite 315, Stamford, CT 06901 (☎ **800-824-6538** or 203-363-0970). Tee times are on the best courses with this package, and you stay in choice accommo-dations, from B&Bs to luxury hotels (seven-day packages begin at $995 per person).

- ✔ **AtlanticGolf,** 237 Post Rd. West, Westport, CT 06880 (☎ **800-542-6224** or 203-454-1086). These golf tours are all-inclusive, including the top courses, airfare, accommodations, and more.

- ✔ **The Tower Hotel Group,** 44–45 Middle Abbey St., Dublin 1 (☎ **01-677-3333**). With excellent accommodations in Dublin, Waterford, Killarney, and Sligo, the Tower Group has golf and hotel packages at fantastic courses. Contact them for their brochure, *Tee Time in Ireland.*

Some hotels have deals with local golf courses in which they give greens fees discounts to guests. See individual hotel reviews throughout the book for information on nearby courses.

More golf information

For further information about good courses near the areas you plan to visit, stop by the local tourism center in the area. Many regional publi-cations for golfing are available, including the new annual *Golfing in Ireland: The Official Golfers Guide to Ireland* covering the best courses, events, and nearby accommodations to courses. It's available at the larger tourist offices.

Golfing Ireland, a booking service and good source of contact informa-tion on courses around the Republic, can be reached at 18 Parnell Sq., Dublin 1 (☎ **053-39-962;** Fax: 053-39-977; Internet: www.golfing-ireland.com). Its Northern Ireland counterpart is **Golfers Abroad,** 6 Park St., Wombwell, Barnsley, South Yorks, England (☎ **01226-75-1704**).

The **Golfing Union of Ireland,** 81 Eglinton Rd., Donnybrook, Dublin 4 (☎ **01-269-4111**), publishes a calendar of golf events. Contact them for a copy.

For a rundown of some of the best Irish courses, see the perfect Irish itinerary for golfers I've outlined in Chapter 3.

Fishing

With its many lakes (called *loughs*) and coastal villages, Ireland is an excellent country for serious anglers as well as for those who like to just cast a reel and then kick back and relax.

You can fish year-round, but the popular salmon season begins in February, and the sea trout season begins in March; both run until the end of September. Angling licenses are required and are available at most tackle dealers.

The **Irish Federation of Sea Anglers** (☎ 01-280-6873) has information on fishing areas in the Republic, and the **Kingfisher Angling Centre** (☎ 028-2582-1301) has the same for Northern Ireland. For more informal advice, **Rory's Fishing Tackle,** 17a Temple Bar, Dublin 2 (☎ 01-677-2351), is the most popular and well-stocked fishing store in Ireland.

The best resource for a fishing vacation is *The Anglers Guide to Ireland,* printed by Guinness. It's 80 pages of places to go, accommodations near fishing locales, and tips and insider advice on different types of fishing in Ireland. Pick one up at the Dublin Tourism Centre.

Running, cycling, walking, and more

You're bound to do quite a bit of trekking while you're in Ireland, but if you're more serious or more competitive, here are a few options you may want to explore:

✔ **The Golden Pages Dublin Marathon:** More than 3,000 runners participate in this popular and circuitous route through the capital on the last Monday in October. For information and entry forms, contact the Dublin Marathon Office, 2 Clare St., Dublin 2 (☎ 01-676-4647; Fax: 01-676-1383).

✔ **The Co-operation North Maracycle Event:** Thousands of cyclists race between Dublin and Belfast on this 206-mile round-trip in June. Contact Alison McCrum, organizer, 37 Upper Fitzwilliam St., Dublin 2 (☎ 01-661-0588; Fax: 01-661-8456).

✔ **The Wicklow Mountains May Walking Festival:** This festival organizes walks of between 9 and 16 miles in West County Wicklow in the first week of May. For more information contact the **Wicklow County Tourism Office** in Kilmantin Hill, Wicklow (☎ 0404-66-058).

✔ **Kenmare Walking Festival:** The town of Kenmare in County Kerry holds a walking festival in April, with guided walks during the day and entertainment venues in the evening. Contact the **tourism office in Killarney** (☎ 064-31-633) for more information.

Walking Ireland — The Waymarked Ways is a complete guide to walking trails in the country. You can pick it up at the Dublin Tourism Centre and other tourism offices for routes to the Wicklow Way, Royal Canal Way, Grand Canal Way, and 22 other trails throughout the country. In addition, the **National Sports Council** (☎ 01-873-4700) has information on long-distance walking routes in the Republic, and the **Sports Council of Northern Ireland** (☎ 028-9038-1222) puts out Ulster Way leaflets detailing walking routes in the North.

Sailing

Ireland's clear waters and Gulf Stream winds rival the Caribbean, so if you want to do some sailing, you're in luck. Contact the **Irish Sailing Association**, 3 Park Rd., Dun Laoire, County Dublin (☎ 01-280-0239), for a list of approved teaching schools that rent boats.

The charming fishing village of Kinvarra, County Galway, is host to **Cruinniu' na mBad** (literally, "Gathering of the Boats") at the end of August, featuring all kinds of sailing. Contact the **Galway Tourist Office** for information (☎ 091-56-3081).

Horseback riding

Seeing Ireland from atop a beautiful steed is a remarkable way to tour some of the island's rural areas. For more information about places that offer horseback riding, contact the **Association of Irish Riding Establishments,** 11 Moore Park, Newbridge, County Kildare (☎ 045-43-1584), in the Republic, or the **British Horse Society,** House of Sport, Upper Malone Road, Belfast (☎ 028-9038-3816), in Northern Ireland. To plan a horse-riding vacation, contact **Equestrian Holidays Ireland,** 1 Sandyford Office Park, Foxrock, Dublin 18 (☎ 01-295-8928).

Spectator sports

Spectator sports are hugely popular in Ireland. Many pubs, especially in larger cities, have the local game on — whether it's football (soccer), Gaelic football, hurling, or horse racing. You'll also have plenty of opportunities to see live sports — provided you can get tickets.

Horse racing

Steeplechases are year-round. The flat season (races without hurdles) is from mid-March to early November. The Irish Tourist Board draws up an Irish Racing Calendar every year. Here are some of the highlights:

- ✔ **The Kerrygold Dublin Horse Show:** Held during the first two weeks in August at the Royal Dublin Society (RDS) Showgrounds, Ballsbridge, Dublin 4. Contact Niamh (pronounced Neeve) Kelly at ☎ 01-668-0866 or fax 01-660-4014. One of the biggest social and sporting events in the country, this show has the best in Irish horses, fancy balls, and awards the Nation's Cup and the Aga Khan Trophy.

- ✔ **Christmas Horse Racing Festival:** Three days of thoroughbred racing at Leopardstown Racetrack, in Dublin, in late December. Call ☎ 01-289-3607 for information.

- ✔ **Irish Grand National:** Takes place at Fairyhouse in County Meath. For information, call ☎ 042-825-6167.

- ✔ **The Budweiser Irish Derby:** Held in the Curragh, County Kildare, on the last Sunday in June or the first weekend in July. For information, contact the Curragh Racecourse Office at ☎ 045-441-205.

- ✔ **The Ulster Harp National Steeplechase:** Takes place in Downpatrick, County Down, in mid-February. Call ☎ 0396-61-2054 for information.

Greyhound racing

Greyhound racing takes place around the country, usually Monday through Saturday at 8 and 10 p.m. The largest racetracks are the **Shelbourne Park Stadium** in Dublin and **Kingdom Greyhound Stadium** in Tralee. For more information, contact the **Irish Greyhound Board** (☎ 061-31-6788; Fax: 061-31-6739).

Rugby, soccer, hurling, and Gaelic football

These four sports are played throughout the country. Gaelic football is a rough-and-tumble sport that combines the best aspects of American football, soccer, and rugby. Hurling is a fast-paced and thrilling game akin to field hockey or lacrosse and is played with a stick called a hurley stick. The game is traced to the pre-Christian folk hero Cuchulainn (see "Who's Who in Irish Mythology" earlier in this chapter). Big matches are played in Croke Park in Dublin City (north of O'Connell Street). You can get schedule information from the **Gaelic Athletic Association (GAA)** at ☎ 01-836-3222. The **Football Association of Ireland** is located at 80 Merrion Sq., Dublin 2 (☎ 01-676-6864).

Chapter 2

Deciding When and Where to Go

• •

In This Chapter

▶ Discovering the Emerald Isle, region by region

▶ Visiting Ireland: Any time is a good time

▶ Experiencing Ireland's best festivals and events

▶ Planning your trip: A few quick tips

• •

*B*ad weather, too many tourists, being stuck in a small town for too long, not having enough time to see the big attractions — these are all factors that can ruin a vacation. This chapter will help you avoid these and other poor-planning pitfalls. I also help you decide which areas of the country you should visit.

Everywhere You Want to Be: What This Book Covers and Why

Should you fly into Limerick or Dublin? Do you want to see the Ring of Kerry or Donegal? Is Northern Ireland worth the time? If you've never been to Ireland, you're not yet prepared to make these big decisions. Here's your quick primer to the various regions of the island so you can make informed choices about where to spend your precious vacation time.

Experiencing the beauty of Dublin

Sometimes people fly into the Dublin airport and set off to the western, more scenic, part of the country before their plane even comes to a complete stop. Unless you know there's an honest-to-goodness pot o' gold waiting for you out west (and I'll bet there's not), there's no reason to rush away. **Dublin,** with its big-time hotels, restaurants, clubs, and museums, is a place whose imprint will last in your memory.

Ireland's Regions

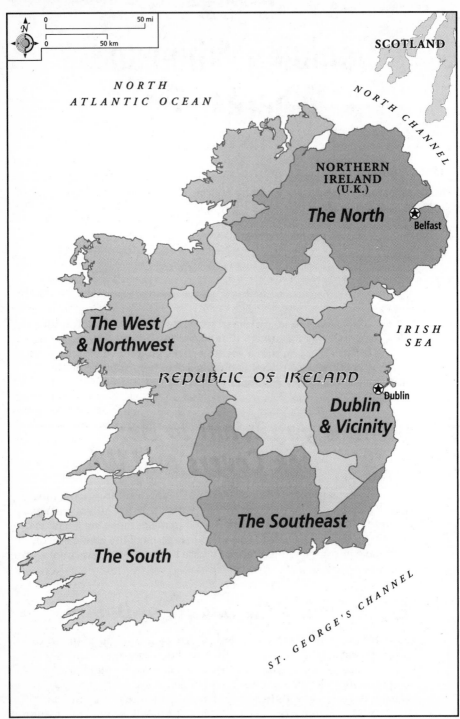

SCOTLAND

NORTH
ATLANTIC OCEAN

NORTH CHANNEL

NORTHERN
IRELAND
(U.K.)
The North
★ Belfast

**The West
& Northwest**

IRISH
SEA

REPUBLIC OF IRELAND
★ Dublin
**Dublin
& Vicinity**

The Southeast

The South

ST. GEORGE'S CHANNEL

South of the city, Wicklow and Kildare contain some of the best of the Irish outdoors. And just north of Dublin are Meath and Louth, which contain magnificent ancient ruins. Prepare to be amazed.

Touring the southeastern counties

If you pass through all the southeastern counties of **Wexford, Waterford, Kilkenny,** and **Tipperary,** you'll take in a city, a vivid harbor town, verdant farmland, and an impressive archeological site. Sound good? It is — read Chapter 14 to find out more.

One thing that brings numerous tourists to this region is the world-famous Waterford Crystal Factory. The tour's great, and if you're even the slightest fan of the pristine crystal, you'll be hard-pressed to pass up the well-stocked shop that you visit when the tour's over.

Swinging by the southern counties

Cork City and its surrounding towns aren't just pretty and bustling, they have plenty of historical importance as well. If shopping for great Irish souvenirs is your passion, you'll love the wide array of trinkets and baubles you'll find here. All of this comes second, though, to County Cork's leading attraction: the **Blarney Stone.**

If the southern counties of Ireland were a high school, County Kerry would be the prom queen. It's long been Ireland's hottest tourist spot, and it doesn't look as if that's going to change anytime soon. Beginning with the **Ring of Kerry** and **Killarney National Park,** the area is a natural wonder. And when you throw the quaint and timeless towns of Killarney, Tralee, and Kenmare into the mix, you have tourist heaven.

Wandering the western counties

Immortalized in some of the most unforgettable Irish ballads and rebel songs, the west of Ireland seems to typify the country. The visual evidence is striking: the **Cliffs of Moher,** the stark **Aran Islands,** the lush land of **Sligo** that prompted poet W. B. Yeats to adopt it as his home. It's also where you'll find many of the amazing, storied Irish sights you've been told not to miss: **the Burren, Bunratty Castle,** and **John Wayne's cottage from the movie** *The Quiet Man.*

In this region, Irish hospitality reigns. Whether you're in a bustling restaurant on one of Galway's busy streets, in a roadside tavern you found while hunting down the Cliffs of Moher, or up in Donegal, splurging on some of the county's famous seafood, you'll find a level of friendliness and welcoming that's never breached. You're sure to hear "You're very welcome" quite often — and they really *mean* it!

Rambling through Northern Ireland

When you cross that invisible border between the Republic and Northern Ireland, the first thing you may notice is that you don't notice anything. The landscape is as green, the people are as friendly, and the history is the same as the Republic. There's no immediate difference between the two areas, and if you blink, you could miss the uneventful border crossing altogether. Not much really separates the two countries, except for their governments. (Though, as on the rest of the island, the accents change from region to region.) Here you can visit **Derry City,** one of Europe's only completely walled-in cities; **St. Patrick's grave;** and bustling **Belfast,** the second-largest city in Ireland.

The Secrets of the Seasons

If you're lucky enough to have the luxury of traveling whenever you want to, here's a list of the highlights and drawbacks of the four seasons (see Table 2-1 for the average temperature of each month).

Summer

The most popular and arguably the best time to tour Ireland is the summer. For the unsure traveler, this is your time to go; you'll have lots of touristy company and plenty of leads to follow.

Summer is great because

- ✔ Ireland is just plain gorgeous during this time of year. Just think of your hotel's high-season rates as a cover charge for the great weather. Temperatures stay comfortably warm and breezy during the day and drop to that perfect light-sweater temperature at night. Don't hold me to this forecast — you'll still get caught in the rain, but it will be a bearable, if not pleasant and refreshing, experience.

- ✔ It is the busiest tourist season by far, which can be a good thing. Empty pubs don't make for lively fun. Shops, streets, and attractions that are teeming with people may only enhance your trip. Ireland is such a friendly place in general that throwing a ton of people into the mix makes for a spirited atmosphere.

But keep in mind

- ✔ Summer is the high season, so during the months between May and August, every major attraction, hotel, and restaurant is jam-packed. If you'd rather escape crowds, this is not the time to go.

- ✔ Most of the people who operate visitor services make nearly their entire year's income during the high season, so they increase their prices for the summer.

Fall

Fall is probably the most underrated time to visit Ireland, but, at the risk of making my Irish friends and family mad (because it's such a well-kept secret), I'll tell you that I'm a huge advocate of going in the fall. Days are mild with not too much rain, and daylight lasts until nearly 9 p.m., which is great for marathon sightseeing.

Fall is great because

- ✔ Beginning around October, the high season ends and prices drop. Some tours also cost less, and even restaurants offer new menus (translation: same food, lower price).

- ✔ Plenty of people still travel the country during the fall, so Ireland certainly isn't a desolate place and you'll still get that feeling of being among a group. In addition, you're more likely to have the chance to hang out with the natives: Many Irish have just done the same as many of you and gone on holiday during the summer months. So in the fall, you're likely to find pubs filled with the Irish residents rather than tourists.

But keep in mind

- ✔ Honestly, I can't think of any downside to traveling to Ireland in the fall.

Winter

Okay, if I didn't love Ireland so much I'd probably tell you to hightail it down to the warm and sunny Caribbean for your winter vacation. But I'm such an unabashed Celtophile that, although winter is not the ideal time to travel to Ireland, I'll still point out the benefits of going in this harsh season.

Winter is great because

- ✔ Prices are at their lowest all across the country, and you're likely to find the cheapest fares of the year to get there.

- ✔ From November to March, you're liable to have the run of the country! And the landscape is still beautiful — winter doesn't take as hard a toll on Ireland's plants and trees as it does in many U.S. states.

But keep in mind

- ✔ Ireland is spared snow for the most part, and the temperature doesn't dip to extreme lows, but the elements are, well, miserable: It's cold, rainy, and windy.

✔ Lots of things close for the season, including many attractions and some small hotels and B&Bs. Other places have shorter hours during this time, too. This is all because tourism slows to a crawl. You can still find plenty of things to see, but you'll get an abbreviated tour offering fewer highlights that you'd see during the other seasons.

Spring

Many argue that spring is the perfect time to travel in Ireland.

Spring is great because

✔ The warmer temperatures, lush scenery, and longer days combine to make wonderful circumstances for touring the country.

✔ The locals are fresh from their own break from tourists and are ready to start playing host. On the whole, it's quite a nice time to go.

But keep in mind

✔ Almost all the factors involved in going during the summer apply here. This is the beginning of the high season, so prices go up. Tourists start flooding in (though it's not as crowded as in the summer).

✔ The weather's pretty rainy in the spring, but often the rain showers last only part of the day, opening up the sky to sun and yes, even rainbows.

Walking on Sunshine and Singing in the Rain: Ireland's Climate

If there's one stereotype about Ireland that actually rings true, it's about the rain. Yes, no matter what time of the year you go, chances are slim that you'll make it back without having had the raindrops falling on your head. But that's all part of the ambience! You'd be cheated out of the full Ireland experience if it didn't happen.

Rain falls heavier and more often during certain times of the year — winter especially. Also, certain places on the island see more rain than others. The southwest of the country (Counties Limerick, Clare, and Kerry) tends to get more rain all year round. See Table 2-1 for the average monthly temperature in Ireland.

Table 2-1	Average Monthly Temperature in Ireland	
Month	*Temp (F)*	*Temp (C)*
January	34–46	1–8
February	35–47	2–8
March	37–51	3–10
April	39–55	4–13
May	43–60	6–15
June	48–65	9–18
July	52–67	11–20
August	51–67	11–19
September	48–63	9–17
October	43–57	6–14
November	39–51	4–10
December	37–47	3–8

Most visitors are surprised to see palm trees when traveling through certain parts of Ireland. The country has a fairly high latitude but is spared very cold weather thanks to the curved path of the Gulf Stream, which roars out of the Gulf of Mexico, through the straits of Florida, across the Atlantic, and along Ireland's west coast. But don't be fooled: Despite the palm trees, you can bet it won't feel tropical!

Weather and temperatures aren't the only factors involved in deciding when to go. The amount of daylight varies greatly from season to season. Ireland is situated at such a high latitude that summer days are blissfully long (sunset as late as 10:30 p.m.), but winter days are tragically short (sunset as early as 4:30 p.m.). The more daylight there is, the more sights you'll get to see.

The best site on the Web for Ireland's weather forecasts is http://cnn. com/WEATHER/cities/world.html. It gives the four-day forecasts for seven Irish cities as well as the sunset and sunrise times.

Calendar of Festivals and Events

No matter when you visit Ireland, some sort of event or festival is sure to be going on. About a zillion events are held each year, of all sorts and kinds, but I've sorted through and picked only the best.

Some of these dates can fluctuate each year by a day or two, depending on when weekends fall and so on. Call ahead to confirm dates.

Attention sports fans: Check out Chapter 1 for the sections on golf, horse racing, hiking, and fishing for events of particular interest to you.

March

St. Patrick's Day (March 17): The feast day of the patron saint of Ireland. It's a religious day for most of the country but there are parades and festivities and lots of drinking everywhere, especially in Dublin, Cork, Limerick, Armagh, and Downpatrick (where the ol' saint is buried). The biggest parade is in Dublin, down O'Connell Street. Call for information. ☎ 01-676-3205 or 1550-22-4324; E-mail: info@paddyfest.ie.

April

International Pan-Celtic Festival (April 17–22): A festival of Celtic music and dancing that includes street entertainment, poetry readings, and a Celtic Pub Trail in Tralee, County Kerry. ☎ 066-80-050; Internet: www.panceltic.com.

Dublin Film Festival (April 6–16): The best of Irish and world cinema, as well as seminars and lectures on filmmaking, all centered around the Irish Film Centre of Temple Bar and other theaters. It's one of the best-attended film festivals in Europe. UCG Cinemas, Parnell Street, Dublin 1; ☎ 01-679-2937; Fax: 01-679-2939; Internet: www.iol.ie/dff.

May

Belfast City Summer Fest (May 22–June 6): Festivals, parades and floats, exhibitions, bands, concerts, and tours for two weeks throughout the city. Contact the **City Events Office** at ☎ 028-9027-0345.

June

The Music Festival in Great Irish Houses (June 10–19): Classical music by internationally renowned musicians combined with some of Ireland's best architecture. Homes are in Dublin and neighboring counties Wicklow and Kildare. Contact **Crawford Tipping** of the Blackrock Post Office at ☎ 01-278-1528 or fax 01-278-1528.

Bloomsday (June 12–16): This festival commemorates Leopold Bloom, the main character in James Joyce's 900-plus page novel *Ulysses,* which takes place in Dublin on June 16, 1904. Restaurants and pubs do everything to look the part, pretending to be part of the book or just celebrating its homage to Dublin. You can take guided tours and attend ceremonies in areas associated with the story. Contact the **James Joyce Cultural Centre** at 35 North Great George's St., Dublin 1 (☎ **01-878-8547;** Internet: www.jamesjoyce.ie).

Dublin Writers Festival (June 13–16): Overlapping with the famous Bloomsday celebration, this new addition to the festival scene honors writers from all over the world with readings by Irish and visiting writers, a poetry slam, a jazz and poetry night, and events planned specifically for children, including workshops with children's poets and writers. Most of the events are free to the public. For more information call ☎ **01-874-1415.** Internet: www.dublinwritersfestival.com.

The Budweiser Irish Derby (last Sunday in June or first Sunday in July): Held in the Curragh, County Kildare, this is Ireland's version of the Kentucky Derby. For information, contact the **Curragh Racecourse Office** at ☎ **045-441-205.**

July

Irish Open (first week of July): This golf championship attracts the best of the best, and each year one of the country's top courses plays host. Because the venue changes from year to year, contact the organizers for more information so you can stand rough-side to the world's most famous masters. ☎ **01-662-2433;** Internet: www.murphysirish open.ie.

Galway Arts Festival (second half of July): Two weeks of concerts, street theater, and children's shows that ceremoniously end with the famous Galway horse races at the end of the month. Contact the **Galway Arts Festival Office** at ☎ **091-509-700;** Fax: 091-562-655; Internet: www.galwayartsfestival.ie.

Lughnasa Fair (last Saturday of July): Medieval harvesttime fair with crafts, entertainment, and costumes, all set inside and on the grounds of the 12th-century **Carrickfergus Castle,** in County Antrim. Call the castle for more information at ☎ **028-9335-1273.**

Galway Arts Fest (last two weeks of July): Located in the old part of town, the medieval city shines with varying entertainment these two weeks. Concerts, parades, street theater, and more showcase the town and serve as an exciting kickoff to five days of Galway horse racing at the town racecourse. Call for more information at ☎ **091-56-1516.**

August

Rose of Tralee Festival (August 20–25): Five days of concerts, entertainment, horse races, and a beauty pageant in this County Kerry town to pick the new "Rose of Tralee." Contact ☎ **066-712-1322.**

September

All-Ireland Hurling and Football Finals (first two weeks of September): Tickets to the live matches (held at Croke Park in Drumcondra, outside Dublin) are impossible to get, games are televised, and the excitement shouldn't be missed. Contact the **Gaelic Athletic Association** for more information by calling ☎ 01- 836-3222.

Galway Oyster Festival (end of the month): Besides eating, other events at Galway's major mollusk fest (or should I say feast?) include dancing, an oyster-shucking competition, a golf tournament, and a yacht race. Call ☎ 091-52-7282 for information.

October

Wexford Opera Festival (October 15–November 1): The biggest event in Southeast Ireland, attracting the best and most prestigious in the business. The featured artists change annually. Contact **Theatre Royal,** Wexford, at ☎ 051-87-4402.

Halloween (Shamhana) (October 31): Celebrated a bit differently from in the United States, with fireworks, bonfires, and the eating of *monkey nuts* (peanuts in the shell). If you're in the country at the end of October and want to find out where the party's going to be, just look for the field or lot where kids are stacking up wood scraps.

November

Belfast Festival at Queens (first week of the month): All-out arts festival hosted by Queen's University featuring ballet, dance, film, opera, jazz, and traditional and classical music. Call ☎ 028-9066-7687 for more information.

December

St. Stephen's Day (December 26): Boys dress up as *Wren boys* (chimney sweeps) and sing carols for charity all over the country.

Chapter 3

Deciding On an Itinerary

In This Chapter

▶ Getting tips for touring Ireland

▶ Determining which itinerary is right for you

▶ Hitting the highlights on a one-week trip

▶ Traveling with family

▶ Planning a trip for golfers

▶ Stepping off the beaten path (on purpose!)

Some people like to travel with absolutely no direction — they just get off the plane and go wherever the wind takes them. Although this approach may sound daring and adventurous, you're probably looking for a little more structure in your tour of Ireland. If you don't want to be locked into a tour group's itinerary, but you'd prefer to have some sort of game plan before crossing the Atlantic, this chapter is for you. I offer suggestions and give you tips for custom-designing your own itinerary. Go anywhere, do whatever you want — it's your trip!

Planning Your Own Itinerary

You can put together your own custom trip in numerous ways, but the two easiest methods for seeing Ireland on your own are the base camp approach and the nomadic approach.

The base camp approach

This approach is the one I recommend. Pick two or three cities and make day-trips out from them. Base yourself in lovely towns like **Cork** or **Killarney** (to explore the South), **Galway** (for the West), or **Dublin** (for, well, Dublin). If you have only one week, you'll have to pick and choose what you see. Planting yourself in Dublin for a couple days, and then staying in a West Coast city like Killarney for a few more is a good idea because many sights are an easy drive from these two points. By staying a couple nights in the same place, you save the time and hassle of switching hotels every day and worrying about check-in times.

Day tours: The *Gilligan's Island* option

You know, a three-hour tour.

City walking tours, bus tours, and tours through museums and castles are excellent ways to discover history and highlights you may otherwise miss.

In general, tours are informative, interesting, and worth the time and expense, but they aren't for everybody. If you're the kind of person who likes to make your own discoveries and do your own homework, you may feel that such a spoon-fed tour is a waste of time. Before you sign on, really get the lowdown on what the tour covers and determine how much time you have to devote to it. Make sure the things you really want to see are covered on the tour and find out if you can leave the group to explore on your own. (Some places require you to stick with the group.) Throughout this book I've listed tours that I can vouch for, but asking questions first — like how long the tour takes, how much it costs, and what it includes — is still smart.

Self-catering is a cost-efficient option that families and groups choosing the base camp approach may want to consider. Self-catering means you rent a home with kitchen facilities for a week or two and head off on your sightseeing excursions from there. You can save money on both accommodations and dining, and some of the cottages and apartments available are just beautiful. (For more information, check out Chapter 8.)

The nomadic approach

The nomadic approach may take more planning and require you to waste time checking in and out of hotels as you move from city to city, but the advantage is that you won't ever see the same thing twice. I've laid out this guidebook to introduce areas in a counterclockwise direction from Dublin to the southern coast, the west, and finally Northern Ireland. If you take the nomadic approach, go in that direction and decide what to see and what to skip based on your interests and the amount of time you have. But don't spread yourself too thin: The longer the distance between each day's destinations, the less time you'll have to stop and really savor the attractions before you run out of daylight.

The most important thing is to have fun. Sit down with this guidebook (and a pint of Guinness, if you like) and pick out some places you really want to see. Be realistic, though. You can spend a full (and tiring) day seeing only a few big sights while driving just the distance between Cork and Waterford. If you're staying in Dingle and the next night in Dublin, you won't have time to see much along the way. The Ring of Kerry, Dingle Peninsula, and the Antrim Coast all deserve a full day. And just one day in either Dublin or Belfast may not be enough to soak up all those cities have to offer.

Dealing with the Daily Tourist Grind

Two things that can really frustrate travelers when it comes to making and fulfilling a custom-made itinerary are

- ✔ Trying to pack too much into one day
- ✔ Burnout

Be realistic about the amount of time you'll spend in the car or bus, burning up precious daylight hours. I suggest getting up and out early to see the sights. And when it's time to move on to your next destination, hit the road late in the day rather than making the trip early and wasting daytime; as an added benefit, you'll have the whole night to rest up before your next round of sightseeing.

You don't always have to act like an army on a campaign, marching, fortifying yourself somewhere, and then attacking. Don't think you always have to go to the hotel first, and then hit the sightseeing trail. Going from Waterford to Cork and you want to see the Blarney Stone? See it on your way to the hotel — you'll save yourself daylight and also assure that you'll get it in (Blarney Castle closes after dark).

You should make an A-list of places you most want to see and a B-list of things to look for only if you have extra time (like my top-ten picks in Chapter 24). Make your A-list items a priority when mapping out your itinerary, and fill in the gaps with secondary sights. (And remember, some places that look small and quick on a map — like the Ring of Kerry — can surprise you and take all day.) Just don't try to cram too much into one day. If you're constantly rushing from one place to the next, you'll enjoy none of them. Relax and enjoy yourself — you're on vacation. See the helpful worksheets printed on yellow paper at the back of this book. The "Going 'My' Way" worksheets will help you efficiently plan your trip.

Saving money: Some tips

If you do plan your trip on your own, turn to the following sections of the book for money-saving advice:

- ✔ Chapter 4 for tips on how to get the best deals on airfares and other money-saving tips
- ✔ Chapter 5 if you're over 50 and you want tips on cost-cutting deals for mature travelers
- ✔ Chapter 7 for the best deals on wheels

Finding the Itinerary That's Right for You

A whole country's worth of attractions to choose from — where do you start? I've given you a hand by putting together three tours that cover the best of what Ireland has to offer. Depending on your interests, you can choose the highlight trip, the family itinerary, or a nine-day golf tour that covers much of the country.

You can find details on all the individual attractions listed in the various destination chapters. See the index for easy reference.

Hitting the highlights: Ireland in one week

If you have only one week, you'll have to make some sacrifices, but I've mapped out a thorough one-week see-the-highlights tour. Follow my itinerary, and you won't go home dissatisfied. Tired maybe, but not dissatisfied.

Day 1: Dublin

Fly into **Dublin** (most flights arrive in the morning). Head to your hotel or B&B if you have it booked in advance, or go straight to the **Dublin Tourism Centre** and have people there find you accommodations in the city. (The Tourism Centre is a good place to start if you arrive with any questions or want to scope out some free literature.) After you're settled, get over to **Trinity College** and take the historical walking tour. Grab a quick lunch at a *chipper* (a fish-and-chips restaurant) and catch the bus or walk out to the **Guinness Brewery.** On your way back, stop and see **St. Patrick's Cathedral, St. Stephen's Green,** and the shopping area of **Grafton Street** and **Nassau Street.** Have a nice sit-down dinner before heading to **Duke's Bar** for the **Literary Pub Crawl** or to **Oliver St. John Gogarty's** for the **Musical Pub Crawl.**

Day 2: Dublin to Waterford

Walk off your traditional Irish breakfast by visiting some of Dublin's landmarks like the **Ha'Penny Bridge** and the **General Post Office** building. Then pick up your rental car and head south. Skip the less-than-stunning southeast coastline and head toward **Waterford.** Stop in **Kilkenny** on the way to stretch your legs and take a picture. By the time you get to Waterford you'll have time for dinner, a walk along the water, and maybe a pint or two.

Day 3: Waterford to Cork

Walk along the river Suir and climb **Reginald's Tower** early, then head to the **Waterford Crystal Factory** before noon. After the tour, pick up a

$100 crystal paperweight in the factory store (or don't), have lunch back in town, and head southwest to Cork. You'll have enough time to visit **Blarney Castle** before checking into your hotel. Go out for dinner and have a pub-crawl afterward on **Oliver Plunkett Street.**

Day 4: Cork to Killarney

Do a little souvenir shopping around **Cork,** maybe ring the bells in **St. Anne's Shandon Church,** and then make a beeline for **Killarney National Park.** You'll see the **Lakes of Killarney,** the **Torc Waterfall,** and **Muckross House,** and end up in **Kenmare,** where you can have a late lunch. Keep your camera handy as you wind along the park's famous mountainous drive (and watch out for sheep in the road). By the time you get back to **Killarney,** where you'll stay the night, you'll be ready for a good meal and a slow stout by the fire. I recommend the restaurant **Teo's** and a raucous good time in **Laurels,** the self-proclaimed "Singing Pub."

Day 5: Killarney to Galway City

Get on the road early because lunch and a visit to **Limerick's Hunt Museum** and **King John's Castle** are your only stops on the way to the majestic **Cliffs of Moher** — a long drive from Killarney, but worth it. The cliffs are one of those sights to which the postcards just can't do justice. Don't stand near the edge and don't wear a hat — the wind gods have been known to take sacrifices. From the cliffs, take the scenic route up to the oft-sung-about **Galway Bay,** snap a picture of the **Aran Islands** off in the distance, and stop on the way to **Galway** to see the **Poulnabrone Dolmen** and **Aillwee Cave** in **The Burren.** You'll get into Galway City early enough for dinner.

How do I find a place when there's no #&@*$! address!?

Welcome to one of the facts of life you'll discover as you plan your trip around Ireland: Outside of the major cities, American-style street names and addresses simply aren't used. If you leaf through this book, you'll often see the address of a B&B listed with just the town name after it. This is just the way it works. In fact, if you were to write a letter to the place, you'd address it the very same way, with just its name and the town.

I know what you're thinking: "How am I supposed to find any of these places?!" Fear not: It's not as hard as it seems. Often these places are right on the town's main thoroughfare (such as R236 or the Dublin-Waterford road), and in these cases, if you drive into the town, you can't miss them. You can find many exceptions to this generalization — for instance, in some cases, a place is on a small side street, and that little street doesn't necessarily have a name. In such cases, I list more-specific directions.

Day 6: Galway City to Dublin

Galway is a great town, compact enough for walking around and shopping — but you're flying back out of Dublin tomorrow morning, and you have a 180-mile drive ahead of you, so don't stay too long. Even though the midlands can be a bit of a yawn, your adventure doesn't have to end. If you still have the stamina, drive north of the city first to see the ancient burial site of **Newgrange** and the **Hill of Tara,** the old seat of the Irish kings, and then head back to Dublin. When you get there, you may be tempted to get a good night's sleep for your early flight the next morning. Nonsense. Tradition requires a pub-crawl through trendy **Temple Bar.** You can sleep on the plane.

Bringing the kids: A one-week itinerary for families

Ireland is a family-friendly place, so with a little planning, there's no reason you can't have a great family vacation here. In this itinerary, I've pulled together some of the most kid-friendly sights, hotels, and restaurants to help you map out a trip that the whole family can enjoy.

Day 1: Dublin

Fly into **Dublin** (most flights arrive in the morning), and head to your hotel or B&B if you have it booked in advance. Your best option for a hotel is **Jury's Christchurch Inn,** which has family-friendly rates and is within walking distance to most sites and restaurants. Kids will love **Dvblinia,** a hands-on museum on the history of the city, connected to **Christ Church Cathedral.** For lunch, head to **Eddie Rockets,** a fun, diner-style place. On your way back to the city center, stop and see **St. Patrick's Cathedral.** A fun dinner pick is **Gallagher's Boxty House,** which has traditional Irish food and group-style dining tables.

Day 2: Dublin to Waterford

The little ones won't be so restless in the car if you take a good walk around Dublin visiting (and photographing) some of the city's landmarks like the **Ha'Penny Bridge** and the **General Post Office** building before you hit the road. Because it's easier to get there by car, on your way out of town stop at **Phoenix Park and Zoo** to take in the animals and maybe have a picnic in the park. As you make your way to **Waterford,** play some good car games, like "Count the Sheep!" Get your bearings in Waterford with a short walk before dinner. The novelty of eating on a boat at the **Galley Cruising Restaurant** should keep the kids from getting bored.

Day 3: Waterford to Cork

Take the time to see **Reginald's Tower** before you leave Waterford; it's a fun climb. Then head to the **Waterford Crystal Factory.** Depending on the age of your kids, you may want to skip this. Young kids may actually like the noise and all the interesting sites, but older kids may be bored. Next stop: **Cork.** You'll have plenty of time to visit **Blarney Castle** on the way, which the young ones will love — not just for the precarious climb to the top of the ruins but also for the trail-heavy grounds. In Cork, **Ristoranti Rossini** is a safe dining bet with traditional Italian fare, and **Jury's Hotel** is a great place for the family to stay.

Day 4: Cork to Killarney

Cork doesn't have much by way of kid-friendly attractions, but about 15 minutes away is the town of **Cobh,** home to the **Fota Wildlife Park.** The park has some great exotic animals like ostriches and kangaroos. Also in Cobh is the **Queenstown Story,** which gives an interesting history of the area. You should also head out to **Killarney National Park** for lakes, waterfalls, and plenty of scenery to keep young tourists occupied while driving through the park. In the town of Killarney, **Allegro Restaurant** has some great pizza — a staple of many a family meal. A good place to stay is **Murphys Guesthouse,** which has a kid-friendly food menu and a baby-sitting service if you have little ones. (*Note:* The Irish call a day-care facility a *creche.*)

Day 5: Killarney to Galway City

Get on the road early because you have a long jump to the **Cliffs of Moher.** Have lunch in **Limerick** at **Nestor's** with its quasi-American menu and visit **King John's Castle** before you make the long-but-worth-it drive out to the majestic cliffs. Keep a close eye on the kids while at the cliffs because strong winds can make the cliff edge very dangerous, and there are no barriers. On the way to Galway, stop and see the **Poulnabrone Dolmen** and **Aillwee Cave** in Burren. You'll get into Galway City early enough for dinner at **Maxwell McNamaras,** a nice family restaurant with a extensive kids' menu. Your best bet for a hotel is the **Galway Great Southern Hotel** — children will love the heated pool and you'll love the special kids' rates.

Day 6: Galway City to Dublin

You have to hit the road early to get back to Dublin, but try to take a walk around Galway before you go and make a fun stop in the resort and amusement park town of **Salthill.** It's a long drive through the midlands from there but, with any luck, the rugrats will be too tired to still be fighting in the backseat. If you still have the stamina after you reach Dublin, drive a little north of the city to see the ancient burial sites of **Newgrange** and the **Hill of Tara** — which the kids can explore à la Indiana Jones. By the time you get back to Dublin, the whole family will be tuckered out.

Hitting the links: The nine-day, all-golf Ireland tour

Although you can't walk too far in any direction in Ireland without stumbling upon a golf course, and almost every hotel and B&B boasts proximity to three or four courses, why play at lesser courses when I can direct you to the very best? See Chapter 1 for more information about golfing in Ireland.

First hole: St. Margaret's

One of the hosts of the Irish Open, St. Margaret's is a new, challenging, and exciting course of the highest standard, with an infamously difficult finishing hole. Located in Stephubble, St. Margaret's, County Dublin (☎ 01-864-0400; E-mail: Stmarggc@indigo.ie). Par: 73. Fees: €50 ($47.50) for 18 holes in the summer, €31.25 ($29.70) in the winter.

Second hole: Portmarnock

This course was the home of the first Irish Open in 1889 and was renovated and reopened in the early 1990s. It's a natural golf course, incorporating the rugged landscape of the region rather than being predesigned. Located 25 minutes from Dublin city center, Portmarnock, County Dublin (☎ 01-846-2968; E-mail: secretary@portmarnockgolfclub.ie). Par: 72. Fees: €81.25 ($77.20) midweek, €100 ($106) weekends.

Third hole: Mount Juliet

This Jack Nicklaus "Signature" course was host of the Irish Open from 1993 to 1995. The lakes and waterfalls make a picturesque backdrop to this course, called the "Augusta of Europe" and voted the best inland course in Ireland. Located on the N9 Waterford-Dublin Road, Thomastown, County Kilkenny (☎ 056-73-000). Par: 72. Fees: €87.50 ($83.10) midweek, €93.75 ($89.05) weekends.

Fourth hole: Old Head Golf Links

A new course located on a stunning outcrop of land and surrounded by the Atlantic, the Old Head Links was a cooperative project, built by the top golfers of the country. It can be challenging and is very expensive. Located in Kinsale, County Cork (☎ 021-477-8444; Internet: www.oldheadgolflinks.com). Par: 72. Fees: €250 ($237.50).

Fifth hole: Killarney Golf and Fishing Club

Home of the 1991 and 1992 Irish Open Championship, this course is nestled among the beautiful lakes of Killarney and below the majestic MacGillycuddy's Reeks Mountains. Located at Mahony's Point, Killarney, County Kerry (☎ 064-33-899; Internet: www.killarney-golf.com). Par: 72. Fees: €70 ($66.50).

Emerald green on the silver screen

If you're a diehard movie buff, you can plan your itinerary around locations from some of your favorite films. Here are several areas and the movies that were filmed there:

Dublin: *Michael Collins, The General, Angela's Ashes, Into the West, In the Name of the Father* (Kilmainham jail), *Educating Rita* (Trinity College), *An Awfully Big Adventure* (Olympia Theatre)

County Wicklow: *Zardoz*

County Wexford: *Saving Private Ryan*

Counties Kildare and Meath: *Braveheart*

Cahir, County Tipperary: *Excalibur* (Cahir Castle)

Cork City: *Angela's Ashes*

Dingle: *Far and Away*

County Galway: *Lion in Winter*

Aran Islands: *Man of Aran*

Limerick: *Angela's Ashes*

Cong, County Mayo: *The Quiet Man*

Donegal: *Dancing at Lughnasa*

Belfast: *The Boxer*

Sixth hole: Ballybunion

A seaside club with two fine 18-hole courses, the old course is the more challenging of the two; the newer Cashen course was fashioned by the legendary Robert Trent Jones. Located on Sandhill Road, Ballybunion, County Kerry (☎ **068-27-146;** Internet: www.ballybunion golfclub.ie). Par: 71. Fees: €75 ($71.25) Cashen course, €110 ($104.50) old course.

Seventh hole: Lahinch Golf Club

Now you're golfing in Ireland! High elevations provide amazing views of sea and valley, and local goats are known to cross the fairway. The club has two 18-hole courses; one is a championship course. Located in Lahinch, County Clare (☎ **065-81003;** E-mail: lgc@iol.ie). Par: 72. Fees: €31.25 ($29.70) midweek, €37.50 ($35.60) weekends.

Getting off the beaten path

Between these itineraries and my top-ten list in The Part of Tens, I cover the most worthwhile destinations for you to see in Ireland, but much has still gone unmentioned. Ireland has a thousand small towns with friendly pubs, and maybe a castle that bears your last name, or a church honoring your favorite saint.

How do you find those places, the ones that are ready to fill you with warm memories and are story fodder for when you get back home? You get off the beaten path. You stay in a small town you like instead of worrying about getting to the next landmark by sundown. You talk to the locals (that's how I found some great stuff that made it into this guide).

Believe me, the lasting memories you have of Ireland can be those from the out-of-the-way village you stumbled upon and the gregarious locals you met, as much as they may be of the Cliffs of Moher and the Blarney Stone.

Eighth hole: County Sligo Golf Club

This difficult course challenges top players, but dabblers have fun playing it, too. The course is set between striking Atlantic beaches and the hill of Benbulben. Located in Rosses Point, County Sligo (☎ 071-77-186; E-mail: cosligo@iol.ie). Par: 71. Fees: €33.75 ($32.05) midweek, €43.75 ($41.55) weekends.

Ninth hole: Royal Portrush

Three excellent 18-hole courses all offer amazing seaside views of the northern Antrim Coast. Located on Dunluce Road, Portrush, County Antrim (☎ 028-7082-2311). Par: 72. Fees: £55 ($81.50) midweek, £65 ($96.35) weekends.

Here's one more course, to round out your golf trip with a little star-gazing: The **Waterville Golf Links,** Newrath, Waterville, County Kerry (☎ 066-74-102). Waterville is scenic, overlooking the Atlantic, but more importantly, it's where Bob Hope and Sean Connery play when they're in Ireland. Par: 71. Fees: €62.50 ($59.35).

Chapter 4

Planning Your Budget

. . . .

In This Chapter

▶ Controlling your total trip costs

▶ Understanding the pricing shorthand in this book

▶ Figuring out a skeleton budget

▶ Discovering how to save big bucks

. . . .

As far as destinations go, Ireland is neither the cheapest nor the most expensive place you can choose. Although this guide gives you lots of money-saving insider tips and offers accommodation and dining selections that won't tap your wallet like a keg of Guinness on St. Patrick's Day, you should have a realistic view of what your vacation will cost you.

Can you do Ireland on $5 a day? Maybe in 1965, but not now. How about $30 a day? Sure, if you don't mind hostel bunk beds and convenience-store dinners. Being realistic, you can bet on a figure more like $50 to $100 per person per day — and that doesn't include a rental car and airfare. When the credit card statement greets you a month after you've returned home, you'll know it was worth every penny; but knowing what you're getting into before you leave is best, so read on.

Getting a Handle on Your Total Trip Costs

So how much is this trip going to cost? It depends how smart a traveler you are. One week in Ireland can cost you thousands of dollars if you let it. You have this guide in your hand, and that's a huge step in the right money-saving direction, but — and this is a big but — keeping to a tight budget does not mean you have to sacrifice a memorable vacation.

Finding out what things cost

To cut out the hassle of closely reading to find out the exact prices of hotels and restaurants, I've denoted the relative cost of things with dollar signs. The actual prices are listed, too, but the dollar signs will allow you to get an idea of a place's price with just a quick glance.

The "Dining" price ranges refer to the average cost of a main course. The "Accommodations" prices are for two people, called *double* in this book.

Dining

$	€8/£5.10/$7.60 or less
$$	€8–€13/£5.10–£8.30/$7.60–$12.35
$$$	€13–€19/£8.30–£12.15/$12.35–$18.05
$$$$	€19/£12.15/$18.05 or more

Accommodations

$ ·	€50/£32/$47.50 or less
$$	€50–€100/£32–£64/$47.50–$95
$$$	€100–€200/£64–£128/$95–$190
$$$$	€200/£128/$190 or more

Sketching a skeleton budget

I list specific money-saving tips later in this chapter, but just to give you an idea, you can try to create a skeleton budget based on the level of luxury you expect and the number of days you'll be visiting Ireland. Look over the sections of this guide that cover the cities and regions you want to see to get an idea of how much a hotel or dinner will cost you. Do you want only the best rooms in the best hotels in the best locations? That will obviously cost you more. Do you plan to play golf every day? Factor in greens fees and the price of renting clubs (assuming you're not lugging your own along). Horseback riding and fishing also mean added costs.

Generally speaking, your costs will be in these ranges:

- ✔ **Airfare:** Airfare to and from Ireland will vary depending on where you're flying from, the time of year, and the totally arbitrary whims of the airline gods. As a vague example, airfare from New York to Ireland and back can run you about $700 — but don't hold me to that! See Chapter 6 for tips on getting the best deals.

- ✔ **Ground transportation:** Transportation costs vary depending on whether you're busing it or renting a car. Driving — the transportation choice for most tourists — costs around $50 a day, plus an additional $15 in gas.

- ✔ **Lodging:** A double room runs about $80; those on the low end go for about $50 and those on the high end about $130 to $170.

- ✔ **Meals:** A good per-person allowance for lunch is $10, and for dinner between $15 and $30. Breakfast is included with most accommodations, so you don't have to figure that in your daily costs.

- ✔ **Attractions**: Even if you see two or three attractions each day, a fair amount to budget for sights is $15 per day.

- ✔ **Shopping:** Are you planning to buy clothes, jewelry, Waterford Crystal, and antiques, or just a few postcards, a snow globe, and a couple other inexpensive souvenirs? A modest piece of Waterford Crystal can set you back $80; a nice Guinness sweatshirt about $50. So gauge your impulse-buying tendencies and factor that in as well.

This budget is a skeleton one. Make sure you have access to emergency money, too.

Outlining a low-end, one-week tour budget

Use the one-week tour budget in Table 4-1 to estimate your per-person costs. When figuring for a second person, deduct the cost of the rental car and gas from the total, and if you're traveling with a child and planning to share a hotel room, you may be able to lower the hotel figure as well by about $10 or $15 (an average rate for a third guest in a room). Keep in mind, though, that many places in Ireland charge by the head for accommodations.

Table 4-1	One-Week Tour Budget
Expense	*Cost*
Airfare (round trip New York to Dublin)	$700
Rental car	$350
Two tanks of gas	$60
Seven nights in hotels ($40 per person average)	$280
Seven lunches (at $10 each average)	$70
Seven dinners (at $22 each average)	$154
Sightseeing admissions ($15 per day)	$105
Souvenirs and miscellaneous ($10 per day)	$70
TOTAL FOR ONE WEEK	**$1,789**

Saving Money: Some Tips

Worried you can't afford your trip? Well, you can rent *Far and Away,* read *Angela's Ashes,* listen to a Chieftains CD, and just pretend you're in Ireland; but what fun is that?

If necessary, you can find lots of corners to cut that will make your vacation quite a bargain. It just takes a little traveling know-how.

For example, stay at smaller lodges and guesthouses and avoid big hotels. And, even if you simply stick to the many free attractions scattered around the country, you'll still see a lot. You can find plenty of ways, some little and some big, to cut down on costs. I scatter various money-saving tips throughout this book, but here's a list of 20 general ones all in one place:

- ✔ **Go in the off-season.** Traveling between November and April will save you a lot on your airfare and the cost of accommodations. Christmas week is the exception — it's the main time of year many Irish in other countries come home to visit, and the airlines cash in. (See Chapter 6 for more information on airfares.)

- ✔ **Travel on off days of the week.** Airfares vary depending on the day of the week. If you can travel on a Tuesday, Wednesday, or Thursday, you may find cheaper flights. Also remember that staying over a Saturday night can occasionally cut your airfare by more than half.

- ✔ **Reserve your flight well in advance by taking advantage of advance-purchase excursion (APEX) fares.** You can also book your ticket through a *consolidator* (also known as a *bucket shop,* for reasons no one in the whole world can explain), which is basically a wholesaler who buys airline tickets in bulk and resells them at a discount. (See Chapter 6 for more information on booking your flight.)

- ✔ **Try a package deal or group deal.** A single phone call to a package tour operator can cover your flight, accommodations, transportation within Ireland, and sightseeing. Packages may not only save time but money as well. Even if you don't want to go with a complete package, you can book directly through some hotels for room/car deals (where they throw in the rental car for free) or other special packages. (See Chapter 6 for more on package deals.)

Whether for packages or for admission to individual attractions, group rates are a fantastic way to save money, and you don't necessarily have to travel with a busload of other people to get them. Sometimes a group is as few as three people, so always ask. And sometimes you and the folks behind you can be a makeshift group to get the discounted price.

- ✔ **Always ask about discounts.** Membership in AAA, frequent-flier plans, trade unions, AARP, the military, or other groups may qualify you for discounted rates on plane tickets, hotel rooms, and car rentals (these apply mainly to U.S. companies). Some car-rental companies give discounts to employees of companies that have corporate accounts. With valid identification, students, teachers, youths, and seniors can be entitled to discounts. Many attractions have discounted family prices. Ask about everything — you could be pleasantly surprised.

✔ **Book your rental car at weekly rates when possible.** Doing so will save you money for sure over the steeper daily rates.

✔ **Walk.** You can easily walk all cities in Ireland and Northern Ireland, even Dublin and Belfast. So save the bus and cab fare (or worse, the rental-car fees) and hoof it to save a few extra pounds or euro.

✔ **Never make a phone call from a hotel.** The marked-up fees hotels charge are scandalous. Walk to the nearest coin or card phone for calls in and out of the country.

✔ **Skimp on souvenirs.** As a general rule, souvenirs (and I'm talking especially about those created for the tourist market) are poorly made and often kitschy. Take pictures, keep a journal, and let your memories suffice. Also, wait to develop your film until you get back home — it'll be cheaper.

✔ **Use American Express to exchange money.** AmEx offers the best rate, and will exchange American Express Travelers Cheques for free. (Do this instead of using the checks as cash at a hotel or restaurant.) American Express charges a small commission to exchange currency, but it still beats the competition, which invariably charges a percentage. (See Chapter 9.)

✔ **Pick up those free, coupon-packed visitor pamphlets and magazines.** Detailed maps, feature articles, dining and shopping directories, and discount and freebie coupons give these pocket-sized giveaways a good wallop. Especially popular and reliable are *Visitor, Discover Ireland, Ireland,* and *Southeast Holiday Guidebook.*

✔ **Skip the fantabulous views.** Rooms with great views are the most expensive rooms in any hotel, and because you probably won't be hanging out in your room all day, why pay the price?

✔ **Get out of town.** In many places, hotels just outside the popular tourist areas may be a great bargain that will only require you to do a little more driving — and they may even offer free parking. The rooms may not be as fancy, but they're just as comfortable and a whole lot cheaper.

✔ **Ask if your kids can stay in your room with you.** Although many accommodations in Ireland charge by the head, some may allow your little ones to stay for free. Even if you have to pay $10 or $15 for a rollaway bed, in the long run you'll save hundreds by not booking two rooms.

✔ **Share a bathroom.** Rooms without a bathroom are cheaper. Sharing a bathroom is a small sacrifice when it comes down to saving money. And it's not going to detract from your trip. Group hostel rooms are even cheaper. (See Chapter 8.)

✔ **Check out self-catering accommodations.** By renting an apartment or house (called *self-catering accommodations* in this guide) for a week or more, you can save money overall on accommodations (especially if you're traveling with a group) and on food, because you'll be able to prepare your own meals in the kitchen. (See Chapter 8.)

✔ **Take advantage of free breakfasts.** Most accommodations include a free Irish breakfast, so don't oversleep. If you have a big breakfast and then wait to have a late lunch or early dinner, you'll save the cost of a meal a day. If the meal is buffet-style, stash away a piece of fruit for an afternoon snack.

✔ **Have the same meal for less money.** If you have a late lunch at a nice restaurant and have a small dinner later, your wallet and stomach will thank you. Lunch menus often offer the same food as on the dinner menu, but the prices are much less expensive — for the same food.

✔ **Look before you tip.** Many restaurants add a service fee (gratuity) onto the bill. Always check, or you may pay a double tip by mistake.

Setting Priorities: Three Corners You Should Not Cut

Now that you know how to save a lot of money on your vacation, here's how I think you should spend it. These are the three most important tactics you can take to ensure you have a great trip:

✔ **Don't skip sightseeing.** The sights are what you came for. If €4 seems like a lot for the Blarney Castle and Stone, remember that this is something you'll wish you had done when you're back home and everyone keeps asking you, "Did you see this? Did you do that?"

✔ **Don't trade money for time.** Maximizing time is essential, so don't wait hours for a cheaper bus when the more expensive one is leaving now. For example, if flying from England costs a little more than coming by ferry, you need to weigh that against the fact that the ferry can take all afternoon and the plane takes an hour. Saving a few bucks just may not be worth it when you're losing a few hours.

✔ **Invest in good shoes.** Whether you like to walk or not, you'll be doing a good bit of it after you're there. So don't bring a pair of cheap sneaks or straight-from-the-box dress shoes and just figure you'll brave the blisters. Go for comfortable and sturdy. And watch out for sandals — they may seem comfy at first, but after ten hours you'll have strap sores that kill!

Chapter 5

Tips for Travelers with Special Needs

●　●

In This Chapter

▶ Sightseeing with your family

▶ Globe-trotting with disabled or senior travelers

▶ Checking out the scene for gay and lesbian travelers

▶ Finding vegetarian restaurants and meals

●　●

*A*lthough every traveler has different needs, some special cases are common enough that special travel services around the world have been set up just for them. In this chapter, I run through some services, give some tips, and note some challenges of travel in Ireland.

Family Planning: Tips on Traveling with Kids

Ah, the Family Vacation. A rite of passage for many households, but one that holds the lurking possibility of becoming a National Lampoon movie. Fear not, adventurous parents: Taking the family to Ireland can be as pleasant a trip as your honeymoon. But you have to lay the groundwork.

The first thing you may notice while traveling in Ireland with children in tow is that you're not alone. Plenty of people make Ireland a family vacation destination each year. Ireland is a kid-friendly place, because it has to be — you know what they say about Irish Catholics and big families.

Throughout this book, I point out the places where kids welcome and will enjoy themselves most. I'll let you know which restaurants are kid-friendly, and point you to the attractions that keep them *ooh*ing and *ahh*ing all day. (Moms and dads: It's okay if you like this stuff, too.)

Hints and special services for families

Before liftoff, take care of a few preliminaries that help ensure a peaceful trip. First, even if your children are old enough to pack for themselves, check what they've packed anyway. If they've never been to Ireland, they can't know the clothes necessary for the weather (see the section on climate in Chapter 2). Also, make sure they don't overdo the packing — you know they can guilt you into lugging their bags for them. Think of it as lower-back self-preservation.

Bring a few toys for younger children, but nothing that you can't replace upon return if they're lost or left behind in a hotel room. Puzzles and car games are great for when the scenery from the back window isn't sufficiently engaging. These, as well as a deck of cards, also work well when children are waiting for the food to come at a restaurant.

Keep in mind that most attractions offer reduced fares for children and occasionally so does public transportation. And most have family group prices (usually for two adults and two or three children), even for attractions that don't seem to be family-oriented. Be sure to ask. (See more money-saving tips in Chapter 4.)

When you book your flight, let the ticket agent know the age of your children. Some airlines offer child-companion fares and have a special kids' menu upon request. Flight attendants are usually happy to warm up baby food and milk if you ask.

Car-rental companies provide necessary car seats, and all vehicles have rear seatbelts. The law requires that children are buckled in the front and back seats.

If your kids will be bunking in a room with you along the way, you may be able to add an extra cot for a child at a small additional cost. Check with the concierge or manager at your hotel, guesthouse, or B&B.

Parents who want to see the sights alone or have a night on the town will be in search of a *creche* (pronounced cresh). This is the Irish term for day care. (And you thought it was some kind of arts and crafts project.) Some hotels offer a creche (for an extra fee). Also, most hotels, guesthouses, and some B&Bs have a baby-sitter list at their fingertips.

Publications for family travelers

For more-specific information and advice on traveling with families, contact **Travel With Your Children (TWCH)** (☎ 212-206-0688) for an information packet. Online, check out Family Travel Times (`www.family traveltimes.com`). This online newsletter requires a subscription for most of its articles ($49 for two years), but there are some articles available for free as well.

A few books geared specifically toward traveling with little ones are also available. Most concentrate on the United States, but two, *Family Travel* (Lanier Publishing International) and *How to Take Great Trips with Your Kids* (The Harvard Common Press), are full of good general advice that applies to traveling anywhere. Another reliable tome with a worldwide focus is *Adventuring with Children* (Foghorn Press).

A World of Possibility: Travel Advice for Savvy Seniors

The worldwide travel market has never been more open to senior citizens. With fantastic discounts available for seniors on almost every aspect of travel, you can hardly find a reason not to pack up and get out there.

Discovering how to get travel discounts

When booking your flight and rental car, remember to ask about senior discounts. In addition, some hotel chains and rental-car companies offer discounts for being a member of **AARP.** Call AARP (☎ **800-424-3410**) for information on Ireland in particular.

Seniors will find many discounts after they actually get to Ireland as well, typically 10% at attractions and theaters, unless otherwise posted.

Publications for senior travelers

Tourism Ireland (☎ **800-223-6470** in the United States; Internet: `www.tourismireland.com`) publishes a list of reduced-rate hotel packages, and also puts out a smaller version of its *Discover Ireland* magazine called *Golden Holidays,* which lists premier accommodations across Ireland that offer special, inclusive price breaks for seniors. You can get this list at any Irish Tourist Board office.

American tour operators that specialize in senior travel programs include **CIE Tours** (☎ **800-CIE-TOUR**), **SAGA Tours** (☎ **800-343-0273**), **Grand Circle Travel** (☎ **800-221-2610**), and **Road Scholar Tours** (☎ **800- 621-2151**). **Elder Hostel** (☎ **877-426-8056**; Internet: `www.elderhostel.org`) has two- and three-week comprehensive educational programs for anyone over 55 and will send you a free catalog of its tours.

Simple Suggestions for Travelers with Disabilities

These days, sensitivity to persons with disabilities extends to most of the world's best-loved travel destinations. So, generally speaking, a physical impairment shouldn't stop you from traipsing the globe. Specifically, getting around Ireland and having a great time won't be too difficult.

Ireland has accessibility regulations for public areas, though they're not as comprehensive as in the United States. Most sidewalks have ramps, and many accommodations are wheelchair accessible. Getting around in cities and towns won't be hard, but Ireland is an old country, and many of its more popular attractions prove it. Not every museum has closed captions for video presentations, and not every castle has an entrance ramp. Calling ahead for attractions (and for B&Bs, many of which aren't disability-friendly) is always a good idea, but you can feel fairly confident that most restaurants and newer hotels are entirely accessible.

Tips and services for travelers with disabilities

Wheelchairs for travelers in Ireland are available from the **Irish Wheelchair Association** (☎ **01-833-8241**) at the cost of €25 ($23.75) a week. It has offices in Dublin, Kilkenny, Cork, Limerick, and Galway.

Ireland tours and vacation planning geared specifically toward the disabled are available through **Grimes Travel** (☎ **800-937-9767;** Internet: www.grimestravel.com). You can also point your Internet browser to www.access-able.com if you're looking for a travel agent who plans trips for travelers with disabilities. Hands down, it's the best source for disabled travelers. This user-friendly site also provides relay and voice numbers for hotels, airlines, and car-rental companies, as well as links to accessible accommodations, attractions, transportation, and tours; local medical resources and equipment repairers; and much more.

Directions Unlimited (☎ **800-533-5343**) and **The Guided Tour, Inc.** (☎ **215-782-1370**) both conduct annual trips to Ireland for mentally challenged travelers.

Publications for travelers with disabilities

For further information, the Access Department of the **National Rehabilitation Board,** 24/25 Clyde Rd., Dublin 4 (☎ **01-68-4181;** Fax: 01-60-9935), has free, comprehensive guides for accommodations, restaurants, attractions, and even pubs with wheelchair accessibility in the Republic. In the North, the **Disability Action's** information center (☎ **028-9032-2504**) offers advice over the phone.

The **American Foundation for the Blind** (☎ **800-232-5463**) offers travel advice for the seeing-impaired, including information on bringing a Seeing Eye dog into Ireland. And you can obtain a copy of its publication *Air Transportation of Handicapped Persons* by writing to Free Advisory Circular No. AC12032, Distribution Unit, U.S. Department of Transportation, Publications Division, M-4332, Washington, DC 20590.

Making a Shoestring Budget Work: Help for Students

Having been a starving college student myself once, I thoroughly understand your situation. Congratulations on not shying away from what I think is a rite of passage — traveling when you're young!

The biggest mistake potential travelers make is assuming that globetrotting is too expensive. Obviously, for some young people this is true, but luckily for you I'm not the only person to respect the plight of fiscally challenged students. An entire market out there is devoted to making travel accessible to you.

Council Travel, under the **Council on International Educational Exchange (CIEE),** is a great source for cheap flights, traveler's insurance, and international student and youth identification cards that get you discounts at many attractions in Ireland. You don't need to bring photos of yourself; they take them at the office. And you don't even have to be a student to use CIEE — it has the same fares available for anyone 25 years and younger, as well as for teachers, as long as you have an ID card to prove it. Call ☎ **800-2-COUNCIL** or access www. ciee.org for information, flight bookings, and the nearest location to you. The Canadian version of CIEE is **Travel CUTS** (☎ **416-979-2406**).

While you're in Ireland, you can look up Council Travel's partner organization, called **usit NOW,** with offices open year-round in Dublin (☎ **01-602-1600**), Cork (☎ **021-27-0900**), Galway (☎ **091-56-5244**), Limerick

(☎ 061-41-5064), Waterford (☎ 051-87-2601), and Belfast (☎ 028-9032-4073). If you lose your ticket or need to change your departure date, these offices can and will happily help you. The CIEE toll-free number for Traveler's Assistance is ☎ 877-370-ISIC. Outside the United States, you can call ☎ 715-342-4104 collect.

The Web site www.collegetravelers.com is another great online resource for young travelers.

A travel-save stamp from usit NOW gives members a 50% discount on Irish Rail and Irish Ferries, as well as discounts on Bus Eireann in the South and Ulsterbus in the North. Other discounts include restaurants, accommodations, and theater. Pop into one of the offices previously mentioned for the free stamp.

Getting an international student, teacher, or youth ID is worth the money. Even if you don't see a sign advertising student discounts, always ask. In some cases the savings cover more than half of the ordinary admission.

Recommendations for Gay and Lesbian Travelers

Although not necessarily the San Francisco of Europe, Ireland is a place where gays and lesbians feel welcomed. This attitude is mainly because of how tolerant the people are in general, rather than because Ireland is exceptionally progressive when it comes to homosexuality. Actually, homosexuality was illegal in Ireland until 1993 (and in Northern Ireland until 1982)! If that attitude seems dated, just remember: Divorce was also against the law until the early 1990s and abortion until 2001.

Today, Dublin has a pretty thriving gay scene. From bars to hotels to magazines, the city offers a niche for the homosexual market. Dublin is where you can find the most gay-friendly places and where the gay nightlife is most active.

As for the rest of the country, again, it's not a place renowned for pro-gressively fostering the homosexual life. Smaller towns and villages won't have a gay club — you can count on that. But then again, you're probably not going to Ireland for the happening nightlife anyway.

Tips and travel services for gay and lesbian travelers

The International Gay & Lesbian Travel Association (IGLTA) (☎ 800-448-8550 or 954-776-2626; Fax: 954-776-3303; Internet: www.iglta.org)

links up travelers with the appropriate gay-friendly service organization or tour specialist. With around 1,200 members, IGLTA offers quarterly newsletters, marketing mailings, and a membership directory that's updated quarterly. Membership often includes gay or lesbian businesses but is also open to individuals for $150 yearly, plus a $100 initial fee for new members. Members are informed of gay and gay-friendly hoteliers, tour operators, and airline and cruise-line representatives. Contact the IGLTA for a list of its member agencies, which are tied into IGLTA's information resources.

Travel agencies geared to both gay men and lesbians include **Family Abroad** (☎ **800-999-5500** or 212-459-1800) and **Yellowbrick Road** (☎ **800-476-5466**). **Above and Beyond Tours** (☎ **800-397-2681**) is primarily geared toward gay men.

The following organizations (all located in Dublin) offer advice and progressive locations:

- ✔ **Gay Switchboard** (☎ **01-872-1055**): Open Sunday through Friday 8 to 10 p.m., Saturday 3:30 to 6:00 p.m.

- ✔ **LEA:** A lesbian organization located at 5 Capel St., Dublin 1. Access the organization's Web site at http://indigo.ie/~leanow, or call them at ☎ **01-872-0460.**

- ✔ **Outhouse** (6 South William St., Dublin 2. ☎ **01-670-6377**; Internet: http://indigo.ie/~outhouse): A good lesbian and gay community resource center in the city. It also has a cafe.

Publications for gay and lesbian travelers

Some good gay guidebooks include *Odysseus* and *Spartacus International Gay Guide* (both focused more on gay men) and *Frommer's Gay and Lesbian Guide to Europe* (published by Wiley). You can get them from most gay and lesbian bookstores and often in the large chain stores as well. Or you can order them from **Giovanni's Room** (☎ **215-923-2960**), or **A Different Light Bookstore** (☎ **800-343-4002** or 212-989-4850). Both lesbians and gay men may want to pick up a copy of *Gay Travel A to Z.*

Out and About, 8 W. 19th St. #401, New York, NY 10011 (☎ **800-929-2268** or 212-645-6922), offers guidebooks and a monthly newsletter (for $49 per year) packed with good information on the global gay and lesbian scene. **Our World,** 1104 North Nova Rd., Suite 251, Daytona Beach, FL 32117 (☎ **904-441-5367**), is a slicker monthly magazine (costing $35 per year) promoting travel bargains and opportunities.

For more information while you're in Ireland, the *Gay Community Newspaper* is a free monthly publication mostly found in Dublin and geared toward both gays and lesbians. The stylish glossy magazine

In Dublin has a section devoted to gay community news and events. It is published twice a month and is available throughout the country.

Finding gay/lesbian B&Bs

In Cork, **Roman House**, 3 St. John's Terrace, Upper John St., Cork City (☎ 021-50-3606), caters to lesbians and gay men and is centrally located in the city. Double rooms run €45 ($42.75).

Dublin has several good gay- and/or lesbian-friendly lodgings. **Horse & Carriage Guest Hotel,** 15 Aungier St., Dublin 2 (☎ 01-478-3537; Fax: 01-478-4010), caters to lesbians and gay men and is located five minutes from Grafton Street and Saint Stephen's Green. Doubles range from €50 to €112.50 ($47.50 to $106.85). **Inn on the Liffey,** 21 Upper Ormond Quay, Dublin 7 (☎ 01-677-0828 or 01-872-4172; Fax: 872-4165), caters to lesbians and gay men. A double costs €56.25 ($53.45) midweek and €68.75 ($65.30) on the weekends.

In Galway, **The Centurion,** 20 Lower Abbeygate St. (☎ 091-561-957), is located in the heart of Galway and caters to gay men. Rooms go for €43.75 ($41.55) per double.

Hunting Down Vegetarian Meals

Any place that loves blood pudding and bacon as much as Ireland does is enough to frighten a vegetarian, but you won't go hungry on your trip, I promise. I include some good vegetarian restaurants in this book (yes, Ireland has some!), and you can rest assured that most restaurants in general have at least a couple of veggie selections.

A traditional Irish breakfast is a pretty meaty event, but you can still partake by asking your host to hold the meat and lavish you with eggs, beans, toast, fried tomatoes, potatoes, and homemade breads and goodies. You can count on a selection of cereals and fruit, too.

Foods in stores carry labels marked by a green leaf icon and the phrase *suitable for vegetarians.* And something that may really shock you is the amount of vegetarian fast food! McDonald's and Burger King both have veggie burgers, and so do many chippers. **Abrakebabra,** the country's own kebab chain, has falafel and other vegetarian options. Strict vegetarians may want to pass on chips — they're fried in the same oil as everything else.

An excellent online resource for finding vegetarian restaurants and whole-food stores in Ireland is www.happycow.net/europe/index.html.

Chapter 6

Getting to Ireland

● ●

In This Chapter

▶ Using a travel agent

▶ Finding a package tour or traveling with a group tour

▶ Booking your flight through a consolidator or over the Internet

▶ Connecting through the U.K. or taking a ferry to Ireland

● ●

Sightseeing, souvenir shopping, and stuffing yourself silly are the easy parts of traveling. Making all the plans to get you there is a little tougher. This chapter outlines the advantages and disadvantages of bargain airfares, travel agents, and package tours.

If you're traveling with children, let your travel agent know their ages when you're booking your flight. Some airlines offer child-companion fares and have a special kids' menu upon request.

Travel Agent: Friend or Foe?

A good travel agent is like a good mechanic or a good plumber: hard to find, but invaluable when you have the right one. The best travel agents can tell you how much time you should budget for each destination, find a cheap flight that doesn't require you to change planes three times on your way to Ireland, get you a hotel room with a view for the same price as a lesser room, and arrange for a competitively priced rental car. Travel agents work on commission. The good news is that you don't pay the commission — the airlines, hotels, and tour companies do. The bad news is that unscrupulous travel agents may try to persuade you to book the vacations that land them the most money in commissions.

In the past few years, many airlines and resorts have limited or eliminated travel agent commissions. The immediate result has been that travel agents don't bother booking these services unless the customer specifically requests them. As other airlines and accommodations follow suit, some travel agents will have to start charging customers for their services.

Here are a few hints for tracking down the travel agent of your dreams:

- ✔ **Ask friends.** Your best bet, of course, is a personal referral. Not only is this agent already a relatively proven commodity, but he's extra-likely to treat you well, knowing that he may lose two customers — not just one — if your vacation gets screwed up.

- ✔ **Go with what you know.** If you're pleased with the service you get from the agency that books business travel at your workplace, ask if it books personal travel, too. Because business travel tends to be booked in volume, the agency may be able to get you a discount.

- ✔ **Go to the travel agent source.** If you can't get a good personal or business referral, contact the **American Society of Travel Agents (ASTA)** (Internet: www.astanet.com), the world's largest association of travel professionals, which can refer you to one of its local member agents. ASTA has its own consumer affairs department to handle complaints and help travelers mediate disputes with ASTA member agencies — which doesn't guarantee anything but does offer you some protection.

The Ins and Outs of Package Tours

Package tours are a way to buy your airfare, accommodations, and other elements of your trip (such as car rentals and airport transfers) at the same time — kind of like one-stop vacation shopping.

For popular destinations like Ireland, packages can be a smart way to go because they save you money. Packages are sold in bulk to tour operators, who resell them to the public. Package tours are kind of like purchasing your vacation at a buy-in-bulk store, except that the tour operator buys the 1,000-count box of garbage bags and resells them ten at a time at a cost that undercuts what you'd pay at your average neighborhood supermarket.

Telling the deals from the duds

When you start delving into packages, you'll find that you have plenty to choose from; in fact, the choices may even overwhelm you. Here are a few tips to help you figure out which package is right for you.

- ✔ **Read this book.** Do a little homework; read up on Ireland. Decide what cities, towns, and attractions you want to visit, and pick some accommodations that you think you may like. Compare the *rack rates* (the published hotel room prices) that I list to the discounted rates being offered by the packagers to see what kinds of deals they're offering; verify whether you're actually being offered a savings. Don't just compare packagers to one another; compare the prices that packagers offer on similar trips. The amount you save depends on the trip; most packagers can offer bigger savings on some trips than others.

✔ **Read the fine print.** When you compare packages, make sure you know exactly what's included in the price you're being quoted, and what's not. Some packagers include extra discounts on restaurants and activities, while others don't even include airfare.

✔ **Know what you're getting yourself into — and if you can get yourself out of it.** Before you commit to a package, make sure you know how much flexibility you have. Some packagers require iron-clad commitments, while others charge minimal fees for changes or cancellations. Ask a lot of questions: What's the cancellation policy? What if I need to reschedule?

✔ **Understand the limitations.** Packages do have some limitations, such as a small selection of hotels or a fixed itinerary. Some packages offer a better class of hotels than others. Some offer flights on scheduled airlines, while others book charters. In some packages, your choices of travel days may be limited.

Picking a peck of pickled packagers

The best place to start looking for packagers is the travel section of your local Sunday newspaper. Also check the ads in the back of national travel magazines like *Travel + Leisure, National Geographic Traveler, Travel Holiday,* and *Condé Nast Traveler.* Then call a few package-tour companies and ask them to send you their brochures.

For one-stop shopping on the Web, go to www.vacationpackager.com, an incredibly extensive Internet search engine where you can link up with hundreds of different package tour operators and custom design your very own package.

The following operators offer the best package tours in the business, with the most options and comprehensive tours. Among them, I believe Moore and CIE to be the best.

✔ **CIE Tours International (☎ 800-CIE-TOUR;** Internet: www.cie tours.com): CIE does tours of Ireland and the U.K., with 14 Irish-only escorted tours and many more that combine Ireland with Britain or Scotland. Its Web site has a helpful tour index, and each package link connects you to price range, description, itinerary, discounts for seniors or early booking, and so on. It has all varieties of tours: rail and bus, escorted, self-drive, B&Bs, and more.

✔ **Grimes Travel (☎ 800-937-9767** or 914-375-3068; Fax: 914-375-3901; Internet: www.grimestravel.com): Grimes organizes airlines, cars, hotels, and all the rest, and offers very-well-priced specials. It mostly handles Ireland but also has links to other destinations.

✔ **Brendan Tours** (☎ **800-421-8446;** Internet: www.brendantours. com): Based out of Dublin, Brendan Tours offers packages all over the world but is most proud of its Irish tours. It has three categories: Escorted, Self-Drive, and Rent an Irish Home.

✔ **Brian Moore International Tours** (☎ **800-982-2299**): Brian Moore Tours has about a dozen escorted tours in different geographic areas, as well as self-drive tours and independent customized travel. It's based out of Boston and specializes in Scotland and Ireland.

✔ **Sceptre Tours** (☎ **800-221-0924;** Internet: www.sceptretours. com): Sceptre custom-tailors its inclusive Irish tours for different interests, and has a specific one for golfers. It requires you to specify lengths of stay and other information to find the tour that is right for you. It also finds weekly specials.

Buying packages through the airlines

Another good resource is the airlines themselves, which often package their flights together with accommodations. The newest of the tours offered by **Aer Lingus "Discover Ireland" Vacations** (☎ **800-223-6537;** Internet: www.aerlingus.ie) is the "Go-As-You-Please" package, which allows you to pick and choose your destinations.

Be sure to give the airline your frequent-flier account number. Most airline packages reward you with miles not only based on the flight, but on all the dollars you're spending — which can really add up.

When escorted-tour brochures say *double occupancy,* they almost always mean a room with twin beds rather than a queen- or king-size bed. If you're committed to cuddling with your honey under the covers, be sure you're familiar with your operator's policy before you commit to a tour.

Touring by Bus: Escorted Tours

Some people love escorted tours. They free travelers from spending a great deal of time behind the wheel; they take care of all the details; and they tell you what to expect at each attraction. You know your costs up front, and you can get to the maximum number of sights in the minimum amount of time.

There are plenty of reasons to take an escorted tour. If your mobility is limited, if you like the ease and security of an escorted tour, or if you're just the sociable type who likes to travel in a group, an escorted tour may be for you.

Asking the escorts: Important questions to keep in mind

If you do choose an escorted tour, ask a few simple questions before you buy:

- ✔ **What's the cancellation policy?** Do you have to put down a deposit? Can they cancel the trip if they don't get enough people? When do you pay? Do you get a refund if you cancel? If they cancel?

- ✔ **How jam-packed is the schedule?** Do they try to fit 25 hours into a 24-hour day, or is there ample time for relaxing, shopping, or hitting the pubs? Will you have to get up at 7 a.m. every day to catch the bus?

- ✔ **How big is the group?** The smaller the group, the more flexible the tour and the less time you spend waiting for people to get on and off the bus. Tour operators may not know the exact size of the group until everybody has made their reservations, but they should be able to give you a rough estimate. Some companies have a minimum group size and cancel the tour if they don't book enough people.

- ✔ **What's included?** Don't assume anything. You may have to pay to get yourself to and from the airport. Or a box lunch may be included in an excursion, but drinks may cost extra. Can you opt out of certain activities, or does the bus leave once a day, with no exceptions? Are all your meals planned in advance? Can they accommodate special diets?

If you choose an escorted tour, think strongly about purchasing travel insurance, especially if the tour operator asks to you pay up front. But don't buy insurance from the tour operator — that's the equivalent of putting all your eggs in one basket. Buy travel insurance through an independent agency. (See Chapter 10 for recommended agencies and other insurance tips.)

Hopping on the magic bus

If you do decide to join an escorted tour, you have lots to choose from. Most of them are priced all-inclusively, which means you pay one price and don't have to worry about paying your hotel bill or tipping your bus driver. Always remember to check whether your airfare is included in the price — some tour operators include it with their quoted prices, and some don't.

For details on the first three companies listed in this section, see "Picking a peck of pickled packagers," earlier in this chapter.

- ✔ **CIE Tours International** (☎ 800-CIE-TOUR; Internet: www.cie tours.com).

- ✔ **Brian Moore International Tours** (☎ 800-982-2299).

- ✔ **Sceptre Tours** (☎ 800-221-0924; Internet: www.sceptretours.com).

- ✔ **Globus** (☎ 800-221-0090; Internet: www.globusandcosmos.com). A first-class worldwide tour company, Globus has four or five tours of Ireland. The lengths of trips run from 8 to 14 days. You have to book these tours through a travel agent, and because the tours all visit different sites, you should be specific with your agent about what you want to see. Price ranges from $950 to $1,400.

- ✔ **Cosmos** (☎ 800-221-0090; Internet: www.globusandcosmos.com). The budget arm of Globus offers downscale versions of the Globus trips (though there isn't so great a price difference), with a tour guide and motorcoach on hand at all times.

The Independent Traveler: Making Your Own Arrangements

Okay, so you're a John Wayne type. You want to get out in front of that wagon train, whip your hat in the air, and hit the trail. In modern terms, that attitude means foregoing both package tours and escorted tours and traveling with total independence. The first step is booking your flight, so in this section I give you a short course in flying to Ireland.

Knowing who flies where

In addition to Aer Lingus (which is Gaelic for — guess what? — *airline*), a few U.S. airlines fly to Shannon and Dublin airports and many more fly to England, where you can catch a connecting flight to Ireland (see "Finding Other Ways to Get There," later in this chapter). Calling more than one airline to compare prices is a good idea.

Here's a list of the major airlines that fly to Ireland from the United States:

- ✔ **Aer Lingus** (☎ 800-223-6537; Internet: www.aerlingus.ie): Out of Boston to Shannon, Dublin, and Belfast; out of Chicago to Shannon and Dublin; and out of New York to Shannon, Dublin, and Belfast.

✔ **Delta Air Lines** (☎ **800-241-4141;** Internet: www.delta.com): Out of Atlanta to Shannon and Dublin; out of New York to Shannon and Dublin.

✔ **Continental** (☎ **800-231-0856;** Internet: www.continental.com): Out of Newark, New Jersey, to Shannon and Dublin.

✔ **American Airlines** (☎ **800-433-7300;** Internet: www.aa.com): Out of New York to Shannon.

Picking an arrival airport

Your options for international airports in the Republic of Ireland are **Dublin Airport** (☎ **01-844-4900**), located 9 miles outside Dublin on the East Coast of Ireland (via the N1), and **Shannon Airport** (☎ **061-47-1444**), located 15 miles west of Limerick, on the West Coast (via the N18).

If you plan to stay in Northern Ireland, **Belfast** also has an international airport, located 19 miles west of the city (☎ **028-9448-4848**).

In general, they're all perfectly fine airports, and no option outweighs the other in terms of niceness or proximity to a city. For more pointers on planning your itinerary, which is the main factor in deciding which airport to choose, see Chapter 3.

Getting the best airfare

Airfares represent capitalism in its purest form. Passengers sitting right next to each other on an airplane rarely pay the same fare; they pay what the market bears on the day they book their flight.

Passengers who can book tickets far in advance, who don't mind staying over Saturday night, and who are willing to travel on a Tuesday, Wednesday, or Thursday pay the lowest fares, usually a fraction of the full fare — what's known in industry lingo as an *APEX* (advance-purchase excursion) fare.

The general guideline about APEX fares is this: As the ticket gets cheaper, the restrictions get tighter. If you luck into a sale fare at the height of the high season, don't be surprised if the schedule isn't changeable. Period.

So when you're quoted a fare, make sure you know exactly what the restrictions are before you commit. And if the restrictions are tight, don't buy until you're sure the schedule you've booked works for you. Otherwise, if your boss doesn't approve your vacation schedule, or your kid comes down with the flu at exactly the wrong moment, you may be stuck with some expensive scrap paper you used to call an airline ticket.

The airlines also periodically hold sales in which they lower the prices on their most popular routes. These fares have advance-purchase requirements and date-of-travel restrictions, but you can't beat the price. So keep your eyes peeled for a sale as you plan your vacation, and pounce if you get wind of one. But don't expect to see a sale around the peak vacation months of July and August, and forget Christmas altogether.

Booking through bucket shops

Consolidators (also known as *bucket shops,* for reasons no one can figure out) buy tickets directly from the airlines and resell them at lower prices. There's nothing shady about the reliable ones — basically, they get discounts for buying in bulk and pass some of the savings on to you. But be careful and make sure you know what you're getting before you give anybody your credit card number; if a fare sounds too good to be true, it probably is.

My favorite consolidators are **Cheap Tickets** (☎ **800-377-1000;** Internet: www.cheaptickets.com) and **1-800-FLY-4-LESS.** I've gotten great deals on a number of occasions from both of these reliable companies. **Council Travel** (☎ **800-226-8624;** Fax: 617-528-2091; Internet: www.ciee.org) is relatively easy to get through to and has also quoted me very competitive fares. Part of the Council on International Educational Exchange (CIEE), it has especially good deals for travelers under age 26.

Reserving your tickets online

Another way to find the cheapest fare is by using the Internet. The number of virtual travel agents on the Internet has increased exponentially in recent years. There are too many companies now to mention them all, but here a few of the better-respected ones:

- ✔ **Travelocity** (www.travelocity.com) includes maps, flights, rooms, cars, packages, a currency converter, weather forecasts, and destination guides featuring updated information on some 260 destinations worldwide.

- ✔ **Microsoft Expedia** (www.expedia.com) has maps, flights, rooms, cars, and packages.

- ✔ **Orbitz** (www.orbitz.com) is a popular site launched by United, Delta, Northwest, American, and Continental airlines. (Stay tuned: At press time, travel-agency associations were waging an antitrust battle against this site.) It has an excellent quick fare finder, but prices are hit or miss.

✔ **American Express** (http://travel.americanexpress.com/ travel) may be the most comprehensive Internet airline information source and reservations service to date. Some of the site's features include links to virtually every airline in the world; Internet-only airfare deals posted on one easy-to-scan page; and, in my opinion, the best fare-finder on the Web. You can call **American Express** (☎ 800-253-9822 or 650-494-1557) before or after you make your reservation if you have any questions or concerns about what you see on-screen.

Getting through security

In the wake of the terrorist attacks of September 11, 2001, the airline industry began implementing sweeping security measures in airports. Expect a lengthy check-in process and extensive delays. Although regulations vary from airline to airline, you can expedite the process by taking the following steps:

✔ **Arrive early.** Arrive at the airport at least two hours before your scheduled flight.

✔ **Be sure to carry plenty of documentation.** A government-issued photo ID (federal, state, or local) is now required. You may need to show this at various checkpoints. With an E-ticket, you may be required to have with you printed confirmation of your purchase, and perhaps even the credit card with which you bought your ticket. This varies from airline to airline, so call ahead to make sure you have the proper documentation. And be sure that your ID is up-to-date. An expired driver's license, for example, may keep you from boarding the plane altogether.

✔ **Know what you can carry on — and what you can't.** Travelers in the United States are now limited to one carry-on bag, plus one personal bag (such as a purse or a briefcase). The Transportation Security Administration (TSA) also has issued a list of newly restricted carry-on items; you can find it on the Internet at www. tsa.gov, or check with your airline.

✔ **Prepare to be searched.** Expect spot-checks. Electronic items, such as a laptop or cellphone, should be readied for additional screening. Limit the metal items you wear on your person.

Finding Other Ways to Get There

If you're driving from the American West or Midwest, just start heading east on any major freeway, start picking up speed when you hit Ohio, and when you see the ocean, pull back on the steering wheel *hard* and hope for liftoff.

But seriously, you have a couple other ways of getting to Ireland besides flying direct, which I discuss in the following sections.

Connecting through Britain

Instead of flying directly into Ireland, you can fly into England and pick up a short connecting flight from there. Many more airlines fly from the United States to England than from the United States to Ireland, so you may be able to find a lower fare.

The major airlines that fly from the United States and Canada to England are

✔ **Air Canada** (☎ **800-776-3000,** from Canada only; Internet: www. aircanada.ca)

✔ **American Airlines** (☎ **800-223-7776;** Internet: www.aa.com)

✔ **British Airways** (☎ **800-247-9297;** Internet: www.british airways.com)

✔ **Continental Airlines** (☎ **800-231-0856;** Internet: www. continental.com)

✔ **Delta Airlines** (☎ **800-241-4141;** Internet: www.delta.com)

✔ **Northwest Airlines** (☎ **800-447-4747;** Internet: www.nwa.com)

✔ **United Airlines** (☎ **800-241-6522;** Internet: www.united.com)

✔ **Virgin Atlantic** (☎ **800-862-8621;** Internet: www.virgin-atlantic.com)

Major airlines that fly between England and Ireland are

✔ **Aer Lingus** (☎ **800-223-6537;** Internet: www.aerlingus.com), from Heathrow and Stanstead

✔ **British Midland** (☎ **800-788-0555;** Internet: www.flybmi.com), from Heathrow

Taking ferry service between England and Ireland

Ferries are not the fastest or cheapest way to come to Ireland, but they're still popular because they're a more interesting and relaxing way to travel than by air — getting there becomes part of the adventure. Ferry service to Ireland leaves from the U.K. and France and brings you within striking distance of Cork, Dublin, or Belfast. After you arrive, public transportation is readily available from the ferry terminals to Belfast, Dublin, and Cork City.

The following companies all offer ferry service to the Emerald Isle:

- ✔ **Irish Ferries:** Sails from Holyhead (Wales) to Dublin or Pembroke (Wales) to Rosslare. For advance reservations in the United States and Canada, contact the **Scots-American Travel Advisors** (☎ 772-563-2856; Fax: 772-563-2087; Internet: www.scotsamerican.com).

- ✔ **Stena Sealink:** Sails from Holyhead (Wales) to Dun Laoghaire, Fishguard (Wales) to Rosslare, or Stranraer (Scotland) to Belfast. For advance reservations in the United States and Canada, contact the **Britrail Travel International** (☎ 800-677-8585). HighSpeed Sea Service (HSS) is also available on all three routes.

- ✔ **Swansea Cork Ferries:** Sails from Swansea (Wales) to Cork. For advance reservations, contact the Swansea offices in Cork (☎ 21-27-6000; Fax: 21-27-5814).

- ✔ **SeaCat Scotland:** Sails from Stranraer (Scotland) to Belfast. For advance reservations, contact SeaCat in Belfast (☎ 01208-81-2508).

Part II
Ironing Out the Details

The 5th Wave   By Rich Tennant

"This afternoon I want everyone to go on line and find all you can about Native American culture, history of the old west, and discount airfares to Ireland for the two weeks I'll be on vacation."

In this part . . .

After you have an idea about which parts of Ireland you want to concentrate on, when you want to visit, and how you're going to get there, it's time to take care of the details. For example, you need to figure out how you're going to get around after you arrive, where you're going to stay, what's your best option for carrying money, and so on.

This part gives you all the information you need to plan a successful trip. In Chapter 6, I discuss your options for getting yourself to the Emerald Isle — from travel agents to package tours. In Chapter 7, I give you the pros and cons of all your options for getting around Ireland after you arrive. You also need to figure out where to rest your tired head (and feet) after long days of sightseeing. You can find information on all your options, from hostels to luxury hotels, in Chapter 8. In Chapter 9, I explain the ins and outs of money in the Republic and Northern Ireland, including where to get the best exchange rates. And, in Chapter 10, I cover loose ends that you may want to know about before you go — including how to get a passport, what you should pack, and options for keeping in touch with the folks back home after you're in Ireland.

And rest assured — I show you how to get the most for your money every step of the way.

Chapter 7

Getting Around Ireland

In This Chapter

▶ Renting a car in Ireland

▶ Getting to know Ireland's road signs and driving rules

▶ Traveling through Ireland by bus and train

*E*enie, meeny, miney, mo. After you get to Ireland you have three choices when it comes to getting around: cars, buses, and trains. For most trips, I recommend renting a car — it's the best way to see the country — but your length of stay and destination choices could make buses or trains preferable. In this chapter, I help you make an informed decision.

Seeing Ireland by Car

I think the best way to see Ireland is by car. No timetables, plenty of leg room, and control over the music — what more could you want? Besides, I can guarantee you'll want to pull over to take in the scenery and snap a few thousand pictures. If this sounds like your cuppa' tea, read on. In the following sections, I focus on how exactly to get those wheels of freedom.

Booking a rental car

In the off-season (between October and March) you should have little difficulty getting a car on short (or no) notice. Booking anything during the summer, however, is a different story. To stay on the safe side, booking anytime from a few weeks to a month in advance is a good idea. Because prices are bound to increase based on demand, the earlier you book your car, the better your chance of getting a deal. Major rental-car companies operating in Ireland include Alamo, Argus, Avis, Budget, Hertz, Murrays Europcar/AutoEurope, and National. The toll-free numbers and Web sites for these companies are listed in the appendix.

Under 25? You can rent a car in Ireland

Unlike the States, Ireland is a place where most people under the age of 25 (but over 21) can rent a car without a problem. Some places will charge an underage-driver fee, so be sure to ask before you make a reservation. Members of Hostelling International not only get discounts on car rentals, they're directed to companies that rent to underage drivers. Here's the scoop on your prospects:

✔ **Alamo:** Must be at least 21; $7.60 a day extra, up to age 25

✔ **Argus:** Must be at least 23; no extra fee

✔ **Avis:** Must be at least 23; no extra fee

✔ **Budget:** Must be at least 23; no extra fee

✔ **Hertz:** Must be at least 21; $17 a day extra, up to age 25

✔ **Murrays Europcar:** Must be at least 21; $15 a day extra, up to age 23

✔ **National:** Must be at least 23; no extra fee

If you fly into Dublin and plan to spend some time there, wait to get a car until you're just about to head out to the countryside. With the public transportation in the city you won't need a car — and with the lack of parking you won't want one. So if you wait to rent, you'll avoid paying for a car you probably won't use. However, if you're planning to leave town straightaway, or if you fly into Shannon airport, getting the car upon arrival is a good idea.

Cars are due back at the same time you picked them up — if, for example, you get the car at 9 a.m., it's due back at 9 a.m. If you return the car late, you usually have to pay for an extra day.

A few companies allow you to drop off cars in places other than where you picked them up, and of course there are other pickup locations than the airports, like Cork, Killarney, and Belfast. Ask about your options and if there are drop-off fees.

If you think you may end up changing your plans, booking your rental car for a shorter amount of time and then extending it from the road with a simple phone call is better. If you do the opposite — booking the car for a week but bringing it back after only four days, for example — you'll still get your credit card refund, but not anytime soon. I found this out the hard way.

Considering your rental options

There are three levels of rental cars: economy (small), compact (medium), and intermediate (large). You may think you want a larger vehicle, but keep in mind that most roads are nail-bitingly narrow, and while winding down a street lined with cars and oncoming traffic you'll appreciate driving a mini-mobile. So, try to get the smallest car you think you'll be comfortable in. Another thought: Smaller is cheaper.

Always expect a stick shift. Unlike the States, where it's standard for rental cars to have an automatic transmission, the standard in Ireland is a manual transmission. You can get an automatic — but it will cost you. Prices vary widely, so if you're sure you want an automatic, shop around for the best deal.

Because the driver's side is on the right-hand side of cars in Ireland, the stick shift is controlled by your left hand, not your right. Sounds wacky and hard to do, but you should get the hang of it in no time.

Air conditioning and unlimited mileage are standard, but a radio isn't necessarily. To be on the safe side, ask if the car has one. The charge isn't any higher for one with, and you probably don't want to rely on your co-riders' musical ability for entertainment between sightseeing stops.

Paying for a rental car

Some companies require a deposit when you make your reservation, generally on a credit card. If you book by phone they may ask for it then; otherwise your credit card will be run through at the rental desk. Don't be shocked if they charge you a gas deposit on your card, too. Just be sure to fill the tank before drop-off and the deposit will be taken off (good thing, because the deposit is always way higher than the actual cost of the gas). And always ask about discounts when you book. Besides obvious big-time groups like AARP and AAA, many companies, both large and small, have corporate accounts with rental companies, and employees can take advantage of this to get a discounted rate. Often you need some sort of proof of affiliation like a business card or pay stub.

Funny, there aren't any road signs

One of the biggest complaints that tourists have about traveling around Ireland is the lack of road signs. The reason for this is somewhat surprising: They get stolen! Pub owners and, yes, tourists, steal signs as decoration and souvenirs, especially if they have a family name or ancestral town name on them. You know the kind: white, arrow-shaped signs that you've undoubtedly seen in Irish bars in the United States. And you thought they were reproductions. . . .

When planning your car trips, you can check out the handy mileage chart I've provided on the tear-out card in the front of this book.

Boots, bonnets, and other brouhaha: An Irish driving glossary

To save you confusion about the odd words and phrases the Irish have for car-related things, here's a list of the most commonly used (and most commonly confused):

✔ **Roundabout:** Circles (or rotaries if you're from New England). These are common, especially entering and leaving cities. Make sure you go left and yield to the right!

✔ **Boot:** Trunk

✔ **Bonnet:** Hood

✔ **Gear stick:** Stick shift

✔ **Footpath:** Sidewalk

✔ **Motorways:** Highways

✔ **Petrol:** Gasoline

Gas, called *petrol* in Ireland, is very costly. You'll notice that the signs at petrol stations advertise prices that seem comparable to home, but those are the prices per liter, not gallon. So in essence you're paying more than four times what you would in the States. This as another good reason to get a smaller car: better gas mileage.

Figuring out the rules of the road

For some people, just the idea of driving in a foreign country is overwhelming. Different cars, different roads, and different laws don't make for a welcome invitation. Don't let that deter you, though — driving a car around Ireland is a great experience, one that shouldn't be missed just because you think it's going to be difficult.

Here are some important traffic rules and laws that will help you get around safely and legally.

✔ **The general speed limit is 60 mph (96 km/h) unless otherwise posted.** Standard 60 mph signs are indicated only by a black circle with a slash mark through it. When the speed limit is other than 60 mph, there'll be a sign with a red circle and the limit written inside in black. You'll see this often when entering small towns where you should reduce speed to 30 mph. On motorways (highways), the speed limit is generally 70 mph.

✔ **A sign that is a red circle with a red X through the middle means no stopping or parking during posted hours.**

✔ **A flashing yellow light means yield to pedestrian traffic but proceed with caution if it's clear.**

✔ **Yield to traffic coming from your right.**

✔ **Seat belts must be worn by drivers and front-seat passengers.** If your car has back seat belts, they must be worn as well.

✔ **Drinking and driving is a serious offense and is dealt with harshly.** Do not drink and drive under any circumstances.

Jane, get me off this crazy thing! There's an arcane law in Northern Ireland that prohibits a driver from going around a roundabout more than three times. So, no getting yourself dizzy just for kicks when you're up North.

If you have any further questions about traffic laws, you can call the **National Safety Council** in Dublin at ☎ **01-496-3422.**

Getting the scoop on driver's licenses and insurance

To drive a car in Ireland, all you need is a valid U.S. driver's license.

Your personal auto insurance doesn't extend to rental cars in Ireland. You must get a Collision Damage Waiver (CDW), which is included in the price of the rental. If you have one, use a Diner's Club Card to pay for the rental (which pays for the CDW at no cost to you). American Express and Visa no longer cover CDW in Ireland, and MasterCard's coverage is only accepted by some companies.

If you plan on taking the car into Northern Ireland, be sure to inform the rental company and ask if additional insurance is required.

Driving on the wrong side of the road

To get an idea of what driving in Ireland is like, simply imagine driving in the U.S., and then turn that image upside down. The steering wheel is on the right-hand side and the gearshift is on the left (the position of the gas, clutch, and brake are the same). This causes most people an initial fright. Thankfully, it's a temporary feeling and soon you'll comfortably drive from town to town (not my guarantee — just my experience!).

In highway traffic, you merge to the right while slower traffic stays on the left. Roundabouts are tricky and you'll probably pop a few curbs while making sharp lefts, but don't get discouraged. Driving in Ireland just takes practice, practice, practice.

Understanding parking rules and regulations

A couple points on parking. First, there's no law, as in the United States, that prohibits you from parking a car facing into traffic. You will often see cars on one side of the road parked in both directions, which makes it tough to tell if you're going the wrong way on a one-way street.

In larger towns, there are some, but not many, parking garages. Street parking is fine, but don't think that parking is free just because there are no meters. In Ireland, you have to buy *parking disks,* which indicate how long you've been in the spot. You can buy disks at machines marked "P," which you may mistake for small phone boxes. Purchase a ticket and stick it to your window. Residential neighborhoods and some towns also require disks but have no parking-disk machines. In those cases, local corner shops usually sell them.

Doing the Bus Thing

Despite their not-so-great reputation, buses are a pretty great way to see Ireland. First, Irish buses are downright posh — they're coaches, really. They make many more stops than the trains, you get a great view of the countryside from the huge windows, they're comfortable, and the cost is soooo much cheaper. On the other hand, you're not free to stop whenever you want, you're stuck with the same people for hours at a time, and not all buses have toilets.

Getting to know the major bus companies

Bus Eireann is the country's principal public coach line, and it has a vast network of routes that webs through all the major towns of Ireland and into Northern Ireland. However, it's pretty much a tool of transportation rather than tourism — it doesn't always pass near all the tourist sights along the way. But after you get to a major town, local transportation can usually get you where you want to go.

Information, prices, times, and routes can be found at **Bus Eireann** on Store Street, Dublin 1 (☎ **01-836-6111;** Internet: www.buseireann.ie/site/home). The number in Limerick is ☎ **061-31-3333.** You must purchase tickets at the station before you board.

Irish Bus Routes

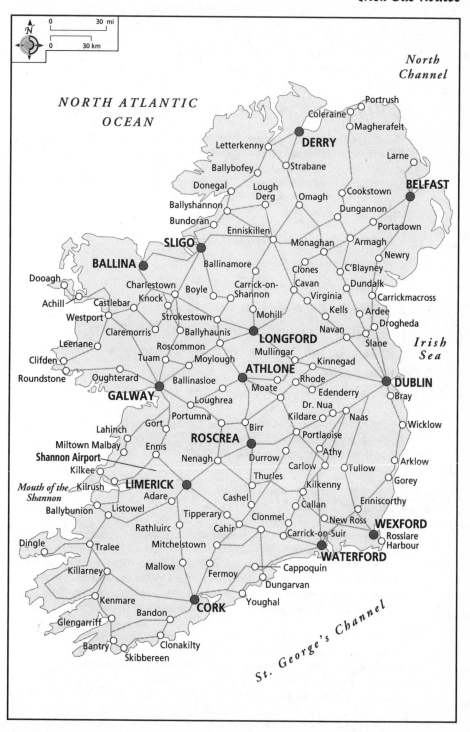

In Northern Ireland, **Ulsterbus** is the area's bus service and it does have routes that pass sights of interest to tourists. The two stations in Belfast are at Europa Bus Station on Glengall Street, and Oxford Street Bus Station. Call ☎ **028-9033-7004** for more information, or call the timetable hot line at ☎ **028-9033-3000.** You can also find information online at www.ulsterbus.co.uk.

Enlisting bus packages and tours

Bus Eireann also has guided sightseeing tours that cover a number of favorite tourist sights and may even pick you up at your hotel (if you're staying at one of its designated pickup points). Routes become more limited in the off-season, so calling ahead to find out which tours will be offered on the dates you're going to be there is best. The major day-trips out of Dublin are

- ✔ Glendalough and Wicklow (for information, see Chapter 13)
- ✔ Newgrange and Boyne Valley (see Chapter 12)
- ✔ Kilkenny City (see Chapter 14)
- ✔ Jerpoint Abbey and Nore Valley Drive (see Chapter 14)
- ✔ Ballykissangel and Wicklow Mountains (see Chapter 13)
- ✔ Russborough House and Powerscourt Garden (see Chapter 13)
- ✔ Waterford (see Chapter 14)
- ✔ The Mountains of Mourne (see Chapter 23)

There are also seasonal trips out to Cork, Galway, Sligo, and Donegal, and a tour of Bunratty Castle, the Cliffs of Moher, and the Burren. For more information call ☎ **1850-36-6222.**

Riding the Rails

Ireland has an excellent rail system that connects the major cities of the Republic and Northern Ireland. The advantages of train travel are that it's fast and very comfortable. On the downside, trains are more expensive and travel to fewer destinations than the buses. So train travel is a comfortable way to get from one part of the country to another, but service isn't comprehensive enough to allow you to see all the sights.

Trains between major cities run three to five times daily and are reliable. Year-round, you should have no problem buying tickets a half-hour before departure, but during the high season calling the day before to confirm availability is advisable. For information about destinations, times, and fares call **Iarnro'd E'ireann** (Irish Rail) at ☎ **01-836-6222** (Internet: www.irishrail.ie). In Northern Ireland, **NI Railways** information is ☎ **028-9066-8258** (Internet: www.nirailways.co.uk).

Irish Rail Routes

Finding train packages and tours

There are packages for train travel that connect to bus tours of more-popular destinations like the Burren, Connemara, and the Ring of Kerry and include hotel accommodations. **Railtours Ireland,** at 58 Lower Gardiner St., Dublin 1 (☎ 01-856-0045), is one private tour operator. Other bus-rail packages are listed in the following section.

Iarnro'd E'ireann (Irish Rail) has Rail Breaks packages that include accommodations as well as family-oriented "InterCity KID +" tickets that go to places like Bunratty Castle or the lakes of Killarney and specialize in commentary and special destinations. Contact the **Travel Centre** at 35 Lower Abbey St., Dublin 1 (☎ 01-836-6222), for more information.

Combining bus and rail packages

The following bus and rail deals are available through **CIE Tours International** (☎ 800-243-7687). For a flat price, you'll get a pass allowing you unlimited use of trains and buses.

- ✔ **Irish Explorer:** Five-day rail only (includes Intercity, DART, and Suburban Rail), $100 adult, $50 under 12. Eight-day combined rail and bus (includes Intercity, DART, and Suburban Rail; Bus Eireann Expressway; Provincial Bus; and city buses in Cork, Limerick, Galway, and Waterford), $150 adult, $75 under 12.

- ✔ **Irish Rover:** Five-day all-Ireland rail only (includes Intercity, DART, Suburban Rail, and Northern Ireland Railways), $124 adult, $62 under 12.

- ✔ **Emerald Card:** Eight-day combined rail and bus (covers Intercity, DART, Suburban Rail, Northern Ireland Railways, Bus Eireann Expressway, Provincial Bus, Ulsterbus Provincial Services, and city buses in Belfast, Cork, Limerick, Galway, and Waterford), $174 adult, $87 under 12. Fifteen-day costs $300 adult, $150 under 12.

Getting Out to the Islands

The only way you can get out to those celebrated islands off the coast of Ireland — the **Arans, Skelligs, Rathlin,** and so on — is by ferry. You can take your car on some, but not all. The famed Aran Islands, for instance, are vehicle-free, and want to stay that way. Check out the chapters for each area you want to visit for more information (Chapter 18 for the Arans, Chapter 16 for the Skelligs, and Chapter 22 for Rathlin). Bad weather can severely limit ferry travel, so always call ahead.

Chapter 8

Booking Your Accommodations

In This Chapter

▶ Figuring out what your accommodations will cost you

▶ Getting the scoop on hotels

▶ Exploring your options: B&Bs, guesthouses, hostels, and self-catering

● ●

So where do you want to stay — castle or cottage? Although Ireland has more than 3,000 castles and more cottages than you can shake a stick at, you'll probably be staying in a hotel or guesthouse.

Hotels in Ireland are rated by the tourist board and range from one to five stars for quality. They're comparable in variety to those you'll find back home. The other option is a guesthouse, which is essentially a bed-and-breakfast (B&B), though sometimes a bit larger. I've included more hotels than B&Bs in this guide because hotels are more often right on the tourist trail, but B&Bs are peppered throughout the country and easy to find.

You have other options as well, from self-catering to hostels, and the following sections tell you more about each, help you find the type of accommodation that's best for you, and fill you in on how to make your reservations before you leave home. If you choose to color outside the lines and stay someplace not in this book, chances are you probably won't be disappointed. Why? Because the Irish really are masters at the art of hospitality. Accommodating people in a friendly and warm way is something they all seem to take quite seriously.

Figuring Out the Costs

You can expect a wide range of prices for accommodations. To make it easy for you to quickly gauge whether one of these options is afford-able to you, I've listed the cost of a *double room* — what it will cost for two people to stay in one room together. The range typically indicates the price for the room during the off-season (the lower price) to the high-season (the highest cost). However, this also refers to the differences in cost of a room with a sea view, extra-large beds, and so on. If you're traveling alone, count on paying more than half the price we've listed for a double. Some hotels charge the same amount for a double room regardless of whether it's being rented to a solo traveler or a couple.

Almost every place I've listed in the book includes a full Irish breakfast.

Use the following scale for quick reference:

$	€50/£32/$47.50 or less
$$	€50–€100/£32–£64/$47.50–$95
$$$	€100–€200/£64–£128/$95–$190
$$$$	€200/£128/$190 or more

Dublin Central Reservations has a fantastic (and free!) **Accommodation Booking Service** (☎ **01-820-0394;** Fax: 01-822-0493; Internet: www.dublinreservations.com) for Ireland and Northern Ireland. It will search out and reserve all levels of accommodations, from five-star hotels to B&Bs, hostels, and self-catering houses. **Res Ireland** is good, too (☎ **800-668-6866** in the U.S.; E-mail: reservations@gulliver.ie).

Lodging in Luxury

The hotel experience in Ireland has a few minor differences from what you'd expect back home. For example, bellhops aren't as common. And smaller hotels sometimes lock up the doors late at night, so you're faced with the situation of having to ring or knock to be let in after hours. (But don't worry; they're used to it.)

Even among hotels, the range of accommodations is wide — from castles on down to small, family-run lodges. Hotels are used to catering to tourists and have a deserved reputation of helpfulness and friendliness. You can expect the furnishings to be comfortable, and you can assume many of the larger and chain hotels will have fitness equipment, room service, and in-house pubs and restaurants.

The following chains have top-quality hotels in major cities throughout the country. I've listed them here starting with the most posh:

- ✔ **Great Southern:** ☎ **01-214-4800;** Fax: 01-214-4805; Internet: www.gshotel.com (Parknasilla, Killarney, Galway, Rosslare, Cork Airport, Dublin Airport, Shannon Airport, Derry)

- ✔ **Tower:** ☎ **071-44-000;** Fax: 071-46-888; Internet: www.towerhotelgroup.ie (Dublin, Waterford, Killarney, Sligo)

Phoning overseas

Before you can book your room, you need to know how to call Ireland. To call Ireland from anywhere in the world, dial the international access code (011 from the United States), then the country code (Ireland is 353; Northern Ireland is 44), then the city code (for example, Dublin is 1), and then the number. Remember, Ireland is five hours ahead of Eastern standard time, so if you're trying to call a business, call between 9:00 and 5:00 *their* time.

For example, if you wanted to call Guinness Customer Service in Dublin to make sure they'll have enough Guinness waiting for you, you would dial 011 (the international access code) + 353 (the country code) +1 (the city code) + 454-3911 (the number).

Note: When calling long-distance within Ireland, you dial a zero before the city code. I've included the zero in the telephone numbers throughout this guide, but you should drop it if you're calling Ireland from the United States.

> ✔ **Jury's:** ☎ 01-660-5000; Fax: 01-660-5540; Internet: www.jurys.com (Dublin, Waterford, Cork, Galway, Limerick, Belfast)
>
> ✔ **Ryan Hotels:** ☎ 01-878-7966; Internet: www.ryan-hotels.com (Dublin, Killarney, Limerick, Galway)
>
> ✔ **Travelodge:** ☎ 800-70-9709; Internet: www.travelodge.co.uk (Dublin, Waterford, Cork)

 Weekends are often the cheapest time to stay at hotels in major cities. These hotels thrive on business travelers, who go home on the weekends. Hotels are eager to keep the house full, so some offer great deals to tourists like yourself. If it means saving a few euro, it's worth asking.

Staying in Casual Comfort: Bed-and-Breakfasts and Guesthouses

B&Bs are a great alternative to hotels. Unlike in a big hotel, you'll get to know the owners of the B&B, because they'll probably be the same folks who check you in, serve your breakfast, and lug your bags upstairs. You may go away from the experience feeling you've made a new friend.

A big advantage of choosing a B&B over a hotel is the price. The cost of a double room averages between €45 ($42.75) and €65 ($61.75). You won't get some of the amenities of a hotel (pool, gym, room service), but most people don't take advantage of those anyway.

Keep in mind that many B&Bs don't accept credit cards, so have enough cash on hand when it's time to check out.

Most B&Bs have between four and ten rooms only, so the better ones fill up quickly during the high-season. You should book at least a week in advance of your trip — even sooner if possible.

Some B&B rooms are not *en suite,* meaning they don't have a private bathroom. So if you're completely against sharing facilities with the folks down the hall, make sure you ask for a room with its own bathroom. It may cost you a little bit more, but for some people, it's worth it.

The Family Homes of Ireland, the largest guide to B&Bs, can be found on the Web at www.familyhomes.ie, or by phone at ☎ **091-55-2000. Town and Country Homes Association** (☎ **072- 51-377**) has information on B&Bs in the Republic. Northern Ireland B&Bs are covered by **Town and Seaside House Association** (☎ **028-7082-3823**; Fax: 028-7082-2741).

Enjoying Self-Catering Cottages

Self-catering cottages are the Irish equivalent of that condo you rented for a week at the beach last year. They're a place for you to drop your bags, settle in, and do things family style, cooking your own meals and making your own beds. If you're making the trip with children, this may be a perfect option, both in terms of convenience and cost.

With self-catering, you pay one price, generally for the week. (Some rent for two to three days.) Compared to the amount of money you would pay for hotels and B&Bs on a nightly basis, it's usually a bargain. Food costs decrease when you're buying your own and cooking it, too.

The drawback is location. Although some self-catering cottages and apartments are in *great* locations, the trouble is that they don't move: Rent one and you're in one place, all week; to see the sights around the country you've got to drive to them, and then drive "home." Of course, this is fine if you intend to spend all your time in one area. But making day-trips to sights in far-flung parts of the country may be tough.

The variety of self-catering options is as diverse as types of hotels. You can stay in actual thatched-roof cottages or completely modernized units. All of these accommodations are registered with the tourism authorities and are rated from one star to four (four being the best).

As with any place to stay, all you have to do is call the tourist board in the area you want to visit, and the staff there will help you with bookings. To get you started, though, here are some organizations that deal solely with self-catering cottages:

✔ **Self-Catering Ireland** (☎ **053-33-999;** Fax: 053-33-808; Internet: www.selfcatering-ireland.com) is the most comprehensive reservation service, offering three- and four-star self-catering apartments throughout Ireland and Northern Ireland.

✔ **Rent an Irish Cottage,** 85 O'Connell St., Limerick (☎ **061-41-1109**), organizes self-catering in traditional whitewashed cottages. In Northern Ireland, contact **Rural Cottage Holidays** (☎ **01232-23-1221;** Fax: 01232-24-0960).

✔ **Irish Farmhouse Holidays** (☎ **01-825-0240**) has lists of rural farmhouses in the Republic that take paying guests.

✔ **Home from Home Holidays,** 26/27 Rossa St. Clonkilty, West Cork (☎ **023-33-110;** Fax: 023-33-131), also offers a good selection.

Exploring Hostel Options

Hostels have a reputation for being the accommodation of choice for the micro-budgeted, and if you've got the image in your head of hostels full of young, tireless travelers who don't mind going long stretches without showers or food, you're partly right — though only partly. Today, hostels serve all kinds of independent travelers who cherish flexibility.

Hostels located across Ireland vary in quality and services. Some offer community kitchens, and the majority sleep people dorm-style, with anywhere from four to dozens of people per room (though a few have private rooms with bathrooms). Many hostels have separate dorm rooms for women and men, but some do have mixed dorms. Families can even stay in hostels, renting a room with four bunks.

Hostels provide a blanket and pillow, and some beds have sheets, but to be safe bring your own sleep-sack — two twin sheets sewn together.

Many people wonder how safe their luggage will be in hostels, because your personal belongings will most likely be sitting at the foot of the bed. It's not a major problem, but it is something to consider. Many hostels provide security lockers, but if not, take some precautions: Make your luggage as difficult to get into as possible by, for instance, stacking bags on top of each other, with the most valuable at the bottom. Also, bring your wallet, passport, purse, and other important personal belongings to bed with you for safekeeping.

As for bathrooms, think of high-school gym restrooms — cold tiles, a row of small sinks and toilet, and shower stalls. You may not love it, but it will get the job done.

I can't vouch for every hostel in Ireland, but if there's one undeniable fact, it's that they're cheap. You can get a warm bed for as little as €8 ($7.60) and never pay more than €28 ($26.60). And, you'll meet people from all over the world doing the same thing as you. Sure, you'll run into your share of hostels that don't exactly disinfect the toilet daily, but on the whole, Irish hostels are the cleanest I've seen anywhere.

Some hostels take reservations, but only a day ahead. Others are first come, first sleep. If you're planning to do the hostel tour of Ireland, you'll really benefit from joining **Hostelling International (☎ 202-783-6161)** before you leave the United States. In fact, some places only accept card-carrying members. Fees are $25 a year; $10 if you're under 18; and $15 if you're over 54. With the card, you'll get discounts at places affiliated with the group and even save on car rentals.

A good hostelling resource is www.hostels.com. This site offers everything a hostel seeker may need: a worldwide hostel database, Q&A about staying in hostels, postings from readers, and maps. The section on finding a hostel in Ireland (Internet: www.hostels.com/ie.html) digs deep.

Discover Ireland Holiday Breaks magazine (available at tourist offices) lists accredited hostels across the country. For more information, contact **An Óige Irish Youth Hostel Association (☎ 01-830-4555;** Fax: 01-830-5808; Internet: www.irelandyha.org) and the **Youth Hostel Association of Northern Ireland (☎ 028-9032-4733;** Fax: 028-9043-9699).

Considering Other Accommodation Options

Here are a few other options for accommodations in Ireland.

✔ **University housing:** Check with local tourist boards or directly with universities to find out if they have unused dorm space in campus housing to rent. Cities with large universities include Dublin, Galway, Cork, and Limerick. Don't count on this being available, though. Currently, housing for students is in high demand all over the country, so it's usually only available during the summer and Christmas holidays.

✔ **Castles and manors:** A company called **Elegant Ireland (☎ 01-475-1665)** rents castles and country houses that are furnished to the nines with antiques and period furniture.

✔ **Camping and caravans:** This option is popular with Irish vacationers. For information, contact **Irish Caravan and Camping,** P.O. Box 4443, Dublin 2, Ireland (no phone; Fax: 098-28-237; E-mail: info@camping-ireland.ie).

Chapter 9

Money Matters

● ●

In This Chapter

▶ Spending and exchanging money in Ireland

▶ Finding ATMs: The traveler's best friend

▶ Figuring out your credit card and traveler's check options

▶ Dealing with a lost wallet

● ●

*M*oney, money, money makes the world go 'round. The rise of the mighty ATM has made money matters a cinch for modern travelers, but you still need to keep a few things in mind. In this chapter, I sort out the euro and the pound and set you up with information about other currency matters in Ireland — what to bring, how to get more, and what to do if you lose your money.

Cash in Hand: Making Sense of the Irish Currency

As of 2002, the currency in the Republic of Ireland is the euro. With denominations and an exchange rate similar to the U.S. dollar, the euro won't be very confusing for American travelers. In Northern Ireland, the currency is the British pound (often called *sterling*).

Understanding the exchange rates

Generally speaking, things are more expensive in Ireland than in the States. On average, I found that things cost about 50% more in Ireland. This disparity isn't true of all items, but it gives you a general idea of how far your new cash and coins can go.

The exchange rate fluctuates daily (by small amounts), but the average rates are similar to those listed in Tables 9-1 and 9-2.

Prices in this guide may reflect a conversion from the price in Irish *punts* (the old currency) and therefore may be a little off the actual price charged. At the time of writing the euro was just recently introduced to Ireland and many establishments were still charging their old rates and converting them to euro for payment. As time passes, every establishment will change their menus, rates, and admission fees to list prices in euro, and in doing so will most likely adjust prices at the same time.

Table 9-1	Republic of Ireland Exchange Rates
Home Currency	*Euro*
$1 U.S.	€1.06 (€1 = 95¢ U.S.)
$1 Canadian	€0.68 (€1 = $1.46 Canadian)
£1 British	€1.56 (€1 = £0.64)
$1 Australian	€0.59 (€1 = $1.69 Australian)
$1 New Zealand	€0.51 (€1 = $1.96 New Zealand)

Table 9-2	Northern Ireland Exchange Rates
Home Currency	*British Pound*
$1 U.S.	£0.68 (£1 = $1.48 U.S.)
$1 Canadian	£0.44 (£1 = $2.28 Canadian)
$1 Australian	£0.38 (£1 = $2.63 Australian)
$1 New Zealand	£0.33 (£1 = $3.06 New Zealand)

A great Internet resource for current currency exchange information is www.oanda.com/convert/classic.

Finding a place to exchange money

You can exchange money anywhere you see the Bureau de Change sign, but generally, you'll get the best rates at banks. The following numbers are for the major banks in Ireland, so call if you have any questions or need to find the nearest location while you're there.

- **Allied Irish Bank** (☎ **800-24-2000,** or 800-AIB-1234 from the United States)
- **Bank of Ireland** (☎ **01-670-0600**)

✔ **National Irish Bank** (☎ 800-60-0600)

✔ **Ulster Bank** (☎ 01-677-7623), a Northern Ireland bank with branches throughout the Republic as well

Accessing ATMs, Just Like at Home

As long as your ATM card is hooked to one of the major networks, you can use your ATM card in Ireland. The machines work just like at home, but they're called *service tills* in Ireland. Most ATMs can give cash advances for major credit cards as well, but you need a personal identification number (PIN). If you don't know your PIN, contact your bank before you leave home and have it mailed to you.

Before you leave, be sure to check the daily withdrawal limit with your bank. Also, if your card covers both your checking and savings accounts, be sure to stow any cash you may need in checking, because that's the only account some overseas ATMs can access (and many won't allow you the option of switching money between the two).

ATMs are linked to networks that most likely include your bank at home. **Cirrus** (☎ 800-424-7787; Internet: www.mastercard.com/atm) and **Plus** (☎ 800-843-7587; Internet: www.visa.com/atms) are the two most popular networks; check the back of your ATM card to see which network your bank belongs to. You can call the toll-free numbers to locate ATMs at your destination.

If you lose your ATM card (or if it's stolen), immediately contact your bank at home and report it. This long-distance call will be expensive, but it's cheaper than it will be if your card (and, in a worst-case scenario, your PIN) falls in the wrong hands. Don't expect the bank to send you an emergency replacement card, though. Some banks take up to a month to replace them.

Using Credit Cards on the Road

Credit cards are invaluable when traveling. They're a safe way to carry money, provide a convenient record of all your expenses, and allow you to take cash advances at any bank or most ATMs, as discussed earlier in this chapter. However, you should know that you'll start paying hefty interest on the cash advance the moment you receive it. Usually the exchange rate you get when you use a credit card is much more favorable than if you exchange cash or traveler's checks at a bank.

Visa, MasterCard, American Express, and Diners Club are all widely used in Ireland, but Discover is not accepted.

If you lose your credit cards (or if they're stolen), every minute counts. Call your credit card companies immediately and have the cards deactivated. Most Irish merchants are careful about checking the signatures on receipts against the cards, but a smart thief can quickly master the fine art of forging your signature. By getting to your credit card company before any illegal purchases are made, you save the hassle of getting those purchases exempted and help the *garda* (the Irish police) find the thief.

Almost every credit card company has an emergency toll-free number that you can call to report a loss or theft. The company may be able to wire you a cash advance from your credit card immediately, and in many places it can deliver an emergency credit card in a day or two.

The issuing bank's toll-free number is usually on the back of the credit card — but that doesn't help you much if the card was stolen, so be sure to write it down somewhere and keep it separate from your credit card.

The phone numbers to report stolen credit cards while in Ireland are

- ✔ **Visa** (☎ 800-55-8002)
- ✔ **MasterCard** (☎ 800-55-7378)
- ✔ **American Express** (☎ 800-62-6000)
- ✔ **Diners Club** (☎ 702-797-5532; members can call collect)

Odds are that if your wallet is gone, the police won't be able to recover it for you. However, after you cancel your credit cards, informing the authorities is still important. Your credit card company or insurer may require you to give a police report number.

If you're an American Express card member, bring a single blank personal check with you on your trip and keep it in a safe place away from your card. If your card is lost or stolen, you can use that check to draw a cash advance against your account. Just bring it, unsigned, into an AmEx office and they can cash it on the spot. The only American Express offices in Ireland are in Dublin (41 Nassau St.; ☎ 01-617-5597) and Galway (c/o International Hotel, East Avenue Road; ☎ 64-35722).

Considering Traveler's Checks: Old-Fashioned or Useful?

Traveler's checks, while providing a measure of security for people away from home (you can get them replaced if they're stolen) are something of an anachronism from the days before ATMs made cash accessible at any time. So what's the plus side of traveler's checks? Many banks impose a fee every time you use an ATM in a different city or bank, which can add up if you withdraw money every day. Traveler's checks eliminate that problem, but they can be a bit of a hassle, because you need to show identification every time you want to cash a check.

Don't use traveler's checks to pay for a meal or a room. The exchange rate is worse than at a bank or exchange bureau. If you're carrying American Express checks, try to cash them at an American Express office to avoid commission costs and get a good rate.

You can get traveler's checks at almost any bank. Here are some of the big guns in the field:

✔ **American Express** Traveler's Cheques are available over the phone by calling ☎ **800-221-7282;** by using this number, AmEx gold and platinum cardholders are exempt from service fees, which range from 1% to 4%. Members of AAA can obtain checks without a fee at most AAA offices.

✔ **Visa** offers traveler's checks at Citibank locations across the United States and at several other banks. You can get Visa checks at most banks. Call ☎ **800-732-1322** for information.

✔ **MasterCard** also offers traveler's checks. Call ☎ **800-223-9920** for a location near you.

If you opt to carry traveler's checks, be sure to keep a record of their serial numbers in a location separate from the checks themselves so you can get a refund if your checks are lost or stolen. Call **American Express** toll free (☎ **800-62-6000** in the Republic, ☎ **0800-521-313** in Northern Ireland) to have the lost checks replaced. The company needs to know exactly which checks were unused. The best way to keep track of this is by creating a list of the check numbers and crossing them off as you use them. If your **Visa** checks are lost or stolen, call ☎ **44-207-937-8091.** You can call the **MasterCard** number listed earlier collect in an emergency.

If you're traveling as a couple, note that dual checks are available that allow either person to sign for them.

Dealing with Stolen Cash and Credit Cards

Don't panic. If you don't have any money or traveler's checks and you've reported all your credit cards and bank cards stolen, you may be in bad shape, but (hopefully!) you still have your return plane ticket, and you still have a couple of ways left to get emergency cash. (Look at it this way: You're sure to stay within your budget.)

First, contact your bank (some larger ones accept collect calls). You may be able to have cash from your checking account wired via money-gram and sent to a travel agent or perhaps to your hotel in Ireland. Fees will apply, but at least you won't starve.

The other option is to have someone back home wire you money through a **Western Union money transfer.** You can do this at more than 400 locations throughout Ireland. Completing the transaction and getting your money takes only minutes. Call the toll-free number (☎ 800-39-5395) for the nearest location and information.

Chapter 10

Tying Up the Loose Ends: Last-Minute Details and Other Things to Keep in Mind

● ●

In This Chapter

▶ Getting a passport or a visa

▶ Dealing with Customs

▶ Insuring yourself

▶ Falling ill in a foreign land

▶ Keeping in touch with the home front

▶ Packing your bags

▶ Making your flight more comfortable

● ●

Deciding to go on a trip is easy; the tough part is preparing for it. In this chapter, I go through some things you need to do before boarding the plane, from getting your passport to packing and figuring out how you can keep in touch with the people back home (assuming you want to, of course).

Papers, Please!: Getting Your Passport

Who needs a passport? You, that's who! A valid passport is the only legal form of identification that every nation recognizes.

Getting an Irish passport

Were your parents or grandparents born in Ireland? If so, you may be eligible for an Irish passport. Why would you want one? Shorter immigration lines for one thing. Having an Irish passport also allows you to work legally anywhere in the European Union (EU). Contact the Irish embassy in your home country for full details about how to get a passport. The Irish embassy in the United States is at 2234 Massachusetts Ave. NW, Washington, DC 20008 (☎ **202-462-3939**; Fax: 202-232-5993).

For U.S. citizens

Getting a passport is easy, but completing the process takes some time. If you're applying for a first-time passport, you can do it in person at one of 13 passport offices throughout the United States; at many federal, state, or probate courts; or at a major post office (call the number listed later in this section to find the ones that accept applications). You need to bring a completed (but not signed) application, which you can get at the post office, and proof of citizenship — a certified birth certificate. It's wise to bring along your driver's license or other identifying documents as well. You'll also need two identical 2 x 2 photos taken within the last six months. You can get these taken at just about any corner photo shop. You cannot use the strip photos from photo vending machines.

When you get your passport photos taken, have them make up some extras. You'll need them to apply for an International Driving Permit and for getting things like student or teacher IDs. Take the extras with you on your trip. If you lose your passport, you can use one as a replacement photo.

For people age 16 and over, a passport is valid for ten years and costs $60 ($45 plus a $15 handling fee); for those age 15 and under, the passport is valid for five years and costs $40.

If you're over 15 and have a valid passport issued less than 12 years ago, you can renew it by mail. Get a renewal application at the places described earlier in this chapter, or at the State Department Web site, http://travel.state.gov. By mail, you bypass the $15 handling fee, and it costs just $45.

Apply for your passport at least two months before your trip — preferably earlier. The processing takes four weeks on average but can run longer in busy periods (especially spring). It helps speed things along if you write on the application a departure date within the next

three weeks. To expedite your passport — in which case you'll get it in
five business days — visit an agency directly (or go through the court
or post office and have them overnight it), and pay an additional $35 fee.

At certain times of the year, travelers literally flood the agencies with
applications. Passport agencies are busiest during January and are
generally jumping constantly from then until fall. To get your passport
quickly (and that's a relative word), the best time to apply is between
September and December.

For more information, and to find your regional passport office,
consult the State Department Web site at http://travel.state.gov
or call the **National Passport Information Center** (☎ **900-225-7778;**
35¢ a minute for automated service; $1.05 a minute to speak with an
operator).

For non-U.S. citizens

Procedures for getting a passport vary from country to country. Here
are some information resources for the English-speaking world:

- ✔ **For British citizens:** You can get applications at British post
  offices. You'll need proof of citizenship (such as a birth certificate)
  and two identical photographs. See the application for specific
  instructions. You can also find more information online at www.
  ukpa.gov.uk.

- ✔ **For Canadian citizens:** To find the nearest passport location call
  ☎ **819-994-3500** within Canada. In addition to the application, you
  must have a birth or citizenship certificate and two matching
  photos.

- ✔ **For Australian citizens:** Contact the Department of Foreign Affairs
  and Trade at ☎ **131-232** within the country or go to www.dfat.
  gov.au/passports for information.

- ✔ **For New Zealand citizens:** Contact the Department of Internal
  Affairs, Documents of National Identity, Passport Division toll-free
  at ☎ **0800-22-5050** within the country or online at www.pass
  ports.govt.nz. In addition to the application, you must have a
  birth or citizenship certificate and two matching photos.

Keeping your passport safe

Finding yourself without your vital documents in a foreign country can
be dangerous and scary, so don't leave it to chance. If they're lost or
stolen, being able to prove who you are is important. Before you go on
your trip, photocopy your passport (and your driver's license, Social
Security card, and any other pertinent information, too). Make a few

copies, and pass them on to friends and family, keeping one set for your luggage, stored separately from the originals.

When you're on the road, always keep your passport with you. Never let it out of your sight. In the event that you do lose your passport while you're in the Republic of Ireland, the first thing you need to do is contact your country's embassy or consulate. People there need to know that someone else may be posing as you, and they can help you get a replacement passport. (You cannot return home without a passport, so getting another one is a top priority.) Bring any identification you have, plus the photocopy of your passport. In the Irish Republic, embassy locations are as follows:

✔ **United States:** 42 Elgin Rd., Ballsbridge, Dublin 4 (☎ **01-668-8777**).

✔ **Canada:** 65/68 St. Stephen's Green, Dublin 2 (☎ **01-478-1988**).

✔ **New Zealand:** The New Zealand Consulate is no longer in operation, so for emergencies contact the High Commission New Zealand House, The Haymarket, London SW1Y42Q UK (☎ **171-930-8422**).

✔ **Australia:** Fitzwilton House, Wilton Terrace, Dublin 2 (☎ **01-676-1517**).

✔ **United Kingdom:** 29 Merrion Rd., Dublin 4 (☎ **01-205-3700**).

The United States is the only one of these countries with a diplomatic presence in Northern Ireland (at 14 Queen St., Belfast, BT1 SEQ; ☎ **028-9032-8239**). Embassies for other countries are all located in London.

And no, you don't need a visa

When people hear the word *visa,* they think it's a formal document they must get before entering a foreign country. For some countries, it is, but not Ireland. There, the word reverts to its less intimidating incarnation: a stamp in your passport, which is a country's okay for you to stay within its borders for a certain amount of time. In Ireland, that means 90 days. If you want to stay longer than that, you have to submit an alien's registration form after you arrive. For more information, contact the **Embassy of Ireland,** 2234 Massachusetts Ave. NW, Washington, DC 20008 (☎ **202-462-3939**). You can also find more information on the Irish embassy's Web site at www.irelandemb.org.

Getting more information on passports

For more information on passports, contact the **Irish Embassy,** 2234 Massachusetts Ave. NW, Washington DC, 20008 (☎ **202-462-3939**; Fax: 202-232-5993). For most questions, the embassy will direct you to Irish consulates in New York (☎ **212-319-2555**), Boston (☎ **617-267-9330**),

San Francisco (☎ 415-392-4214), or Chicago (☎ 312-337-1868). The Irish Embassy in Canada is at 130 Albert St., Suite 1105, Ottawa, Ontario, K1P 5G4 (☎ 613-233-6281).

Well, I Do Declare: Understanding the Customs of Customs

If you come to Ireland bearing gifts, you may not necessarily be that well received. You're limited on what and how much you can bring into the country. These guidelines are strict and can result in a mess if you try to get around them.

What you can't bring in

You cannot bring any of the following: firearms, ammunition, or explosives; narcotics; poultry, plants and their immediate byproducts; domestic animals; and snakes (St. Pat worked so hard to get them all out). Also, you can bring in no more than 200 cigarettes, one liter of liquor, and two liters of wine.

If you're flying out of or back to the United States, information about what goods you can bring in and out is available on the U.S. State Department's Web site at http://travel.state.gov.

Customs channels: Red, green, or blue?

After you arrive in Ireland and gather your luggage, you'll have to confront one last obstacle. Ireland and Northern Ireland have three Customs channels: red, blue, and green.

- **Red:** To make a declaration if you're bringing in more goods than the rules allow
- **Blue:** If you're traveling from another country in the European Union, and you have nothing to declare
- **Green:** If you're traveling from anywhere outside the European Union, and you have nothing to declare

So, if you're not entering Ireland through Britain, you should go through the green channel. Under most circumstances, you won't be asked any questions or have to open your suitcases.

When you go back home, you'll be given a simple Customs form to fill out that you'll present to immigration officials when you arrive stateside. Provided you follow Customs guidelines, you should have no hassles.

Buying Travel and Medical Insurance

The differences between travel assistance and travel insurance are often blurred, but in general the former offers on-the-spot assistance and 24-hour hot lines (mostly oriented toward medical problems), while the latter reimburses you for travel problems (medical, travel, or otherwise) after you have filed the paperwork. The three different kinds of travel coverage are trip-cancellation, lost-luggage, and medical insurance. Trip-cancellation insurance is sensible for many travelers, but most people can do without the other two types. Your homeowner's insurance should cover stolen luggage. If you're carrying anything really valuable, you should keep it in your carry-on luggage rather than checking it. Rule number one: Check your existing policies before you buy any additional coverage.

The cost of travel insurance varies widely, depending on the cost and length of your trip, your age and overall health, and the type of trip you're taking. Insurance for extreme sports or adventure travel, for example, will cost more than coverage for a cruise. Some insurers provide packages for specialty vacations, such as skiing or backpacking. More-dangerous activities may be excluded from basic policies.

And keep in mind that in the aftermath of the terrorist attacks of September 11, 2001, a number of airlines, cruise lines, and tour operators are no longer covered by insurers. The bottom line: Always, always check the fine print before you sign on; more and more policies have built-in exclusions and restrictions that may leave you out in the cold if something does go awry.

For information, contact one of the following popular insurers:

- ✔ **Access America** (☎ 800-284-8300); Internet: www.access america.com)

- ✔ **Travel Guard International** (☎ 800-826-1300; Internet: www. travelguard.com)

- ✔ **Travel Insured International** (☎ 800-243-3174; Internet: www. travelinsured.com)

- ✔ **Travelex Insurance Services** (☎ 800-228-9792; Internet: www. travelex-insurance.com)

Trip-cancellation insurance

There are three major types of trip-cancellation insurance (TCI): one, in the event that you prepay a cruise or tour that gets cancelled, and you can't get your money back; a second when you or someone in your family gets sick or dies, and you can't travel; and a third, when bad weather makes travel impossible. Some insurers provide coverage for events like jury duty, natural disasters close to home, even the loss of a job. A few have added provisions for cancellations due to terrorist activities. Always check the fine print before signing on, and don't buy trip-cancellation insurance from the tour operator that may be responsible for the cancellation; buy it only from a reputable travel-insurance agency. And don't overbuy. You won't be reimbursed for more than the cost of your trip.

Medical insurance

Most health-insurance policies cover you if you get sick away from home — but check, particularly if you're insured by an HMO. With the exception of certain HMOs and Medicare/Medicaid, your medical insurance should cover medical treatment — even hospital care — overseas. However, most out-of-country hospitals make you pay your bills up front, and send you a refund after you've returned home and filed the necessary paperwork. Members of **Blue Cross/Blue Shield** can now use their cards at select hospitals in most major cities worldwide (☎ **800-810-BLUE** or www.bluecares.com for a list of hospitals).

Some credit cards (American Express and certain gold and platinum Visas and MasterCards, for example) offer automatic flight insurance against death or dismemberment in case of an airplane crash if you charged the cost of your ticket.

If you require additional insurance, try one of the following companies:

- ✔ **MEDEX International,** 9515 Deereco Rd., Timonium, MD 21093-5375 (☎ 888-MEDEX-00 or 410-453-6300; Fax: 410-453-6301; Internet: www.medexassist.com).

- ✔ **Travel Assistance International** (☎ **800-821-2828;** Internet: www.travelassistance.com), 9200 Keystone Crossing, Suite 300, Indianapolis, IN 46240 (for general information on services, call the company's Worldwide Assistance Services, Inc., at ☎ **800-777-8710**).

The cost of travel medical insurance varies widely. Check your existing policies before you buy additional coverage. Also, check to see if your medical insurance covers you for emergency medical evacuation: If you have to buy a one-way same-day ticket home and forfeit your non-refundable roundtrip ticket, you may be out big bucks.

Dealing with Getting Sick Away from Home

Finding a doctor you can trust when you're in an unfamiliar place can be hard. If you suffer from a chronic illness, consult your doctor before your departure. For conditions like epilepsy, diabetes, or heart problems, contact **Medic Alert** (☎ **800-825-3785;** Internet: www.medic alert.org) to get an identification tag that will immediately alert doctors to your condition and give them access to your records through Medic Alert's 24-hour hot line. Membership is $35, plus a $15 annual fee.

Pack prescription medications in your carry-on luggage. Carry written prescriptions in generic form rather than under a brand name and carry all prescription medications in their original labeled vials. Also bring along copies of your prescriptions in case you lose your pills or run out.

The **International Association for Medical Assistance to Travelers (IAMAT)** (☎ **716-754-4883;** Internet: www.sentex.net/~iamat) offers tips on travel and health concerns in the countries you're visiting. The **United States Centers for Disease Control and Prevention** (☎ **404-332-4559;** Internet: www.cdc.gov/travel) provides up-to-date information on necessary vaccines and health hazards by region or country.

When you're abroad, any local consulate can provide a list of area doctors. If you do get sick, you may want to ask the concierge at your hotel to recommend a local doctor — even his or her own. Doing so will probably yield a better recommendation than any toll-free number can. You can also try the emergency room at the local hospital. Many emergency rooms have walk-in clinics for emergency cases that are not life threatening.

Communicating with the Folks Back Home

You've just landed in Ireland. So much to do, so much to see. Yet what's the first thing you want to do? Phone home to make sure your plants will be watered and the dog walked twice a day. That's fine. Calling America from Ireland is pretty easy, after you know the basics.

Using the phones

You can find two types of pay phones in Ireland: coin phones and card phones. Both kinds of phones are spread throughout the country, and you may even see them side by side.

If you use a coin phone, read the directions before you start feeding in coins. Some phones require putting the coins in before you dial; others have you put in the coins after the other party answers.

Coin phones in the Republic and Northern Ireland cost 40 eurocents, and the amount of time you get depends on how far you're calling. Have change in hand — the phone gives an extremely short warning before disconnecting.

Got no calling card? Got no change? Got no problem. The Irish have phone cards that work the same as those in the United States, like a debit card, and you can get one in any shop or post office. They come in varying denominations. What's different about the Irish version is that it's used in its own phone booth, designated by the sign *Cardphone*. When you enter the booth, slide the card in the slot like you would a credit card. There's a screen on the phone that says how many units the card has left. The units decrease while you're on the phone, so you know how much time is left before you're hung up on. No more "Time'supI'lltalktoyoulatergoodb—."

Avoid making calls from your hotel room. You may have to foot surcharges, pay astronomical fees, and incur charges even just to get your calling-card company on the line.

Numbers beginning with 800 within Ireland are called *Freephone numbers* and are toll free, but calling a toll-free number in the United States from Ireland is not free. In fact, doing so costs the same as a regular overseas call.

Making calls before or after Irish business hours (8 a.m. to 6 p.m.) is much cheaper. This is sometimes tough to finesse when calling home because of the time difference, but it will save you some bucks if you can swing it. (Ireland is five time zones ahead of the U.S. East Coast, so when it's noon in New York it's 5 p.m. in Ireland, and when it's noon in Los Angeles, it's 8 p.m. in Ireland.)

Making calls from and within Ireland

Here you go: One-stop shopping for all your telephone needs.

- ✔ **To make international calls to places outside the United Kingdom:** You first dial 00 and then the country code (United States and Canada 1, Australia 61, New Zealand 64). Next you dial the area code and number. For example, if you wanted to call the Irish Embassy in Washington, D.C., you would dial 00-1-202-462-3939.

- ✔ **To call Northern Ireland from the Republic:** Dial 08 and then the area code (called *city code* in Ireland) and number.

✔ **To call the Republic from Northern Ireland:** Dial 00-353 and then the area code and number.

✔ **To call the U.K.:** From the Republic, dial 00-44 and then the area code and number. When calling the U.K. from Northern Ireland, just dial the area code and number.

✔ **For directory assistance from the Republic:** Dial ☎ **1190** if you need a number in the Republic and Northern Ireland, ☎ **1197** if you need a number in Great Britain, and ☎ **1198** for a number in all other countries.

✔ **For directory assistance from Northern Ireland:** Dial ☎ **192** if you want numbers in the U.K. and Republic, and dial ☎ **153** for numbers to all other countries.

✔ **Operator assistance:** If you need operator assistance in making a call, dial ☎ **114** if you need to make an international call and ☎ **10** if you want to call a number in Ireland or Britain.

Throughout this guide, phone numbers are preceded by their city codes (Dublin numbers are preceded by the city code 01, for example), but you can drop the city codes if you call within the same city.

Using your U.S. calling card

AT&T, MCI, and Sprint calling cards all operate worldwide, so using any of them in Ireland is no problem. Each has a local access number, which saves you the cost of dialing directly to the United States. When you want to use your card, just call ☎ **800-55-0000** for **AT&T,** ☎ **800-55-5381** for **MCI,** and ☎ **800-55-2001** for **Sprint.** The operator will then explain how to make the call.

If you have a calling card with a company other than one of the three I named, contact the company before you go on the trip to see if it has a local access number in Ireland. After you've arrived, it's too late; directory assistance deals only with AT&T, MCI, and Sprint. Whatever card you have, call the company before you go on your trip to see if it has a discount plan for calling overseas.

Using Internet Cafes

If you're going global, go all the way! By using one of Ireland's many Internet cafes you can send quick e-mail postcards to your friends and retrieve your most pressing (or entertaining) incoming messages as you travel. You can find cybercafes sprinkled throughout the country; I've listed some of them in the "Fast Facts" sections at the end of each area chapter. Most cafes are part of the **Irish Internet Cafe Association.** You can get addresses and phone numbers of cafes from that group's Web site at www.iica.net.

If your Internet provider isn't accessible through a Web site, set up a free Web-based e-mail account through one of the many free services available before you go on your trip. Two popular free e-mail services are Hotmail (www.hotmail.com) and Yahoo! Mail (www.yahoo.com). Give your new address to friends before you go and you can send and receive messages from any cybercafe in the world.

America Online (AOL) is available at many Internet cafes, and if you already have an AOL account, you just have to sign on as a guest or through www.aol.com.

The cost of Internet cafes is generally €5 to €7 ($4.75 to $6.65) an hour, but if you just need to pop in for a quick fix, most cafes allow you to pay by the quarter-hour.

Sending and Receiving Snail Mail in the Republic and Northern Ireland

You do know you'll be hard-pressed to get someone to pick you up at the airport if you don't send home any postcards, right? Post offices in the Republic are called *An Post* (www.letterpost.ie for general information) and are easy to spot: Look for a bright green storefront with the name across it. Ireland's main postal branch, the **General Post Office (GPO),** on O'Connell Street, Dublin 1 (☎ **01-872-6666**), is in the heart of Dublin and is the hub of all mail activity. Its hours are 8 a.m. to 8 p.m., Monday through Saturday; 10 a.m. to 6 p.m., Sunday. Major branches, found in the bigger towns and cities, are open 9 a.m. to 6 p.m., Monday through Saturday. Minor branches, which are in every small town, are open 9 a.m. to 1 p.m. and 2:15 to 5:30 p.m., Monday through Friday, and 9 a.m. to 1 p.m., Saturday. Irish post offices sell phone cards and lottery tickets, and you can even change money at main branches.

It costs you the same to send a postcard to the United States as it does to send a pretty hefty letter (€0.57/65¢), and it usually takes mail about a week to get to the States. If you plan to mail packages, you can save money by sending them economy, or surface, mail. This idea comes in handy when mailing things to yourself. (See "Packing It Up" later in this chapter.)

Sending mail from Northern Ireland is just as easy, though a couple of things make it different. Up north, they're called Post Offices, like in the States. They're also identifiable by color, but here the offices and post boxes are bright red. The general hours are the same as An Post, too. The cost to send a letter outside Europe is 67p Sterling ($1).

If you need mail sent to you while on your trip in Ireland, no problem. Just have the sender address the mail with your name, care of the General Post Office, Restante Office, and the town name (for instance, Joe Smith, c/o General Post Office, Restante Office, Galway, Ireland). Your mail will be held there for you to pick up. Larger post office branches (all those I list in the "Fast Facts" sections of this book) provide this service, but smaller post offices won't.

American Express cardholders can also have mail sent to them at the AmEx office in Dublin (see the AmEx listing in the appendix).

Packing It Up

Know what's much more important than what you bring on your trip? What you leave at home. So many hapless travelers make the easily avoidable mistake of simply bringing too much with them. Believe me: You'll not only not need your bathtub headrest or fur-lined, self-warming slippers, you'll forget all about them.

Keep in mind that there won't be anyone to carry his or her load and take care of yours, too. So fill up those bags and lug them around while you're still at home. If getting your luggage from the door to the driveway is any struggle, you can be sure you'll never make it through the airport, let alone down a crowded street.

Deciding what to bring and what to leave at home

The biggest mistakes you can make when packing are bringing too much clothing and bringing the wrong kind. First, forget about anything that wrinkles easily. Unless you'll be staying in upscale hotels, you'll be hard-pressed to find an iron. Whites are also a no-no for travel in general and Ireland in particular: With so much rain, a white outfit wouldn't make it to the curb before becoming a piece of abstract art, with mud as the medium.

For the most part, Ireland is a casual country, and even if it weren't, what you'll be doing as a tourist pretty much requires warm, loose-fitting clothes. You'll spend a lot of time outside or in drafty castles and abbeys, and you'll want to be comfortable.

Layering is the best way to ensure your comfort no matter what the temperature. The clothes you bring depend on what time of year you'll be visiting, but even if you go in summer, don't bother with shorts and tank tops — the weather is never really warm enough for that. Another reminder: From September to April Ireland is cold enough for sweaters and jackets. (See Chapter 2 for more information on the seasons.)

It does rain a good deal in Ireland, but a raincoat isn't really necessary. A compact umbrella is light and small and will do just fine for the light, yet almost constant, drizzle that's characteristic of the country.

One exception to the Irish casual dress code is Dublin. As in most European capitals, people there dress stylishly to just go down the street. Bring one nice outfit if you plan to spend time there.

Remember: You don't need 14 outfits for a 2-week trip. Nearly every town has a laundry service — for a few pounds you can get your clothes washed and dried, and you'll be lugging around so much less.

Ireland unplugged: Leaving that electric nosehair trimmer at home

My personal recommendation is don't bother bringing anything that must be plugged in or recharged. But if you can't live without that electric nosehair trimmer, and you don't mind the extra space (and weight) they will take up in your luggage, you can purchase adapters that will allow your plug to fit into Ireland's outlets (which are shaped differently from those in the U.S.) and converters that will switch the voltage for you.

In the States the current is 110 volts. In Ireland it's 220 to 240 volts. So if you plug in your hair dryer, it may light up like a Roman candle or blow a fuse. You can buy a voltage transformer, but they're expensive; you'll have to decide if it's worth the cost for a short stay. If you bring electronic items (such as an alarm clock or personal cassette or CD player), it's best to bring battery-powered models, and pack some extra batteries.

Some travel appliances like shavers and irons have a nice feature called *dual voltage* that will adapt to the change, but unless your appliance gives a voltage range (such as 110v to 220v), don't chance it. Most laptop computers have this feature, but always check with the manufacturer as a precaution. Plug adapters are not hard to find; your local hardware store or even the airport should have what you need. For more information, check out www.walkabouttravelgear.com or call the **Franzus Corporation** (☎ **203-723-6664**) for its pamphlet on foreign electricity.

If you plan on bringing a video camera (something I don't encourage — better to look at and remember the country than devote all your attention to the camera), bring enough battery packs but also enough videotape. VHS cassette tapes in Ireland look identical to the ones from home, but they won't work in your camera.

Making Your Plane Ride More Comfortable

Whoever said, "Getting there is half the fun" definitely wasn't referring to international air travel. Plane rides, especially bad ones, can be extremely uncomfortable. Cramped legs, infamously bad cuisine, and a movie you can barely see can put a big damper on the first leg of your trip. But again, your airplane experience comes down to packing. Bringing just a few essential items in your carry-on bag can make the trip great. These things may not make you feel like you're in first class, but they can at least take your mind off the man snoring in your ear.

- ✔ **Water:** Pressurized cabins are notorious for leaving you dehydrated, so bring a large bottle of water to drink throughout the trip. Alcohol can be free-flowing on flights, but beware: The added dehydration will not only knock you for a loop, it will add to jet lag.

- ✔ **Diversions:** The in-flight magazine will soon wear thin, and you can't guarantee the movie will be one you haven't seen already (or that you'll be able to see the screen), so plenty of diversions are a must. A novel, favorite magazine, and crossword puzzles are all good time-passers.

- ✔ **Snacks:** It could take eons for the dinner cart to make it to your row, and even then you may hate the meal, so be prepared! There's nothing worse than starving your way through a long flight. Pack some snacks that are filling but not too salty, like dried fruit or bagels.

These days, airlines are willing to accommodate passenger food restrictions. So if you're a vegetarian, are restricting your salt or fat intake, keep kosher or hallal, or have some other special dietary regime, call the airline two days before you leave and request a special meal. You'd be surprised at how many options they have.

My luggage is where!?!?

There is, of course, a slim chance that your luggage will be lost or delayed. You can prepare yourself for this, though. Simply pack your carry-on bag with a light change of clothes and necessary toiletries. This way, even if you're high and dry for a day or so, you won't frighten the natives.

Part III
Dublin and the East Coast

"OK-we got one cherry lager with bitters and a pineapple slice, and one honey malt ale with cinnamon and an orange twist. You want these in steins or parfait glasses?"

In this part . . .

Sometimes people fly into Dublin airport and immediately whisk themselves off to the western part of the
country in a "see ya, wouldn't wanna be ya" sort of way.
These people are missing out. Dublin and the counties
that surround it — Wickow, Kildare, Meath, and Louth —
are all spectacular places.

Dublin City, with its big-time hotels, restaurants, clubs,
and museums, is a place whose imprint will last in your
memory. In fact, there's so much to do and see in Dublin
that I devote all of Chapter 11 to it. Dublin also makes a
great base camp for exploring the region's many attractions. Just north of the city are Meath and Louth, which
contain Ireland's most magnificent ancient ruins (which I
tell you about in Chapter 12), while to the south there are
Wicklow and Kildare, two counties that contain some of
the very best of Irish outdoors (covered in Chapter 13).
Prepare to be amazed.

And don't forget the southeastern counties of Ireland —
Wexford, Waterford, Kilkenny, and Tipperary — which I
cover in Chapter 14. You'll find a little bit of everything
here: a few castles, beautiful sunny countryside bordered
by the sea, the famous Rock of Cashel, and the even more
famous Waterford Crystal Factory.

Chapter 11

Dublin

● ●

In This Chapter

▶ Arriving in Dublin and getting around after you're there

▶ Getting your bearings in the city's major neighborhoods

▶ Deciding where to stay and where to eat

▶ Finding out more about Dublin's best sites, landmarks, museums, and cathedrals

▶ Shopping for distinctly Irish items

▶ Finding all the top pubs

● ●

Consider a place that combines history, architecture, and rich culture; couples cosmopolitan flair with old-time tradition; and unites the diversity of an entire country. Sounds like a great place to visit, huh? Well, that's just what you're doing, because Dublin provides all this and more.

Once barely passable as a European capital, Dublin is on the fast track these days, quickly becoming a hub of computer software development and booming with the roar of Ireland's "Celtic Tiger" economy. And with such prominence comes the key components to any major city: money, young people, and flair. Dublin is now a hip, young place with excellent international cuisine, five-star hotels, and posh nightclubs.

Fear not: The city retains its original charm and history in the middle of all this modernizing. Along its cobbled streets you'll find buildings that date back to a time before America was a twinkle in England's eye, and the booming economy has allowed Dublin to drop money into restoring public buildings and historical exhibits. There's never been a better time to visit the city.

Getting to Dublin

Dublin is one of Ireland's two international gateways, so if you're flying to the country, there's a good chance it's where you'll be touching down.

County Dublin and the East Coast

By plane

Dublin International Airport (☎ **01-844-1111**; Internet: www.iol.ie/~dkane) is 7 miles north of the city, about a 25-minute drive from the city center (**An Lar** in Gaelic). Aer Lingus, Continental, Delta, and American fly directly into Dublin from the States. British Midlands, Aer Lingus, and Ryanair have regular flights from England.

All the major car-rental companies listed in Chapter 4 have desks in the Arrivals Hall of the terminal. Taxis are available outside the terminal's main entrance — just look for the signs. The fare to downtown Dublin is about €17 to €23 ($16.15 to $21.85), depending on traffic. There are two buses that will take you to downtown Dublin (near O'Connell Street). The number 41 Dublin bus only takes passengers with little or no luggage and the fare is €1.45 ($1.35). You'll need change to pay the fare; the drivers don't carry any. The other option, the AirLink cargo bus (the number 747 or 748), is a cheap way to get to the city from the airport; it costs €4.50 ($4.30) per person, and the buses have room for luggage. You'll be dropped near a taxi rank, and you can take a cab from there to your hotel — much cheaper than taking one from the airport. The buses generally run from 7 a.m. to 11 p.m. daily. Lastly, many of the larger hotels offer airport pickup service to guests.

By ferry

Passenger and car transportation from Britain's town of Holyhead are run by two companies. **Irish Ferries** (☎ 01-855-2222; Internet: www. irishferries.ie) arrive at Dublin Ferryport (on the Eastern tip of the North Docks). **Stena Sealink Line** ferries (☎ 01-204-7777) arrive at the Ferryport in Dun Laoghaire, a southern suburb of Dublin. Public transportation into the city is available from both ports.

By train

Irish Rail (Iarnro'd E'irrann) InterCity service (☎ 01-850-36-6222; Internet: www.irishrail.ie) links Dublin to the major towns of Ireland and to Belfast. Trains arrive at one of three stations: Connolly Station on Amiens Street (serving trains from the North, including Northern Ireland); Heuston Station on Kingsbridge, off St. John's Road (serving trains from the South and West); and Pearse Station on Westland Row, Tara Street (serving trains from the Southeast). The **DART** (Dublin Area Rapid Transit) is a commuter train that connects the city to the coastal towns north (as far as Howth) and south (as far as Greystones); call the same number previously given in this paragraph for more information.

By bus

The city's bus terminal is on Store Street (☎ 1850-36-6222; Internet: www.buseireann.ie), three blocks east of O'Connell Street, north of the river behind the Trading House building. The bus system, **Bus Eireann,** connects Dublin to most cities and towns all over the country.

However you arrive in Dublin, it helps to know that major roads (N1, N2, N3 from the north; N4, N7 from the west; N11 from the south) all lead directly into the center of the city. The M50 Westlink (€1.30 toll) is Dublin's beltway, linking all the major routes (for example N1, N2) out of town.

Orienting Yourself in Dublin

One of the first things you'll notice when you start making your way around Dublin is that the addresses all have a number after their address, such as: General Post Office, O'Connell Street, Dublin 1. These numbers are postal codes, similar to American zip codes. Most of central Dublin is located within postal codes 1, 2, and 8. Odd numbers are north of the River Liffey, and even numbers are south of it.

A few words on street names: They have a tendency to change when you least expect it. One minute you're on Aungiers Street, the next you're on South Great George's Street. Did you make a turn without knowing it? No, that's just how the streets go in Irish cities, so pay careful attention as you explore.

Here's how the different neighborhoods break down:

- **O'Connell Street (north side):** Although this area once thrived as a fashionable and historical part of the city, it's now something of an aging starlet, largely ignored. Between stately buildings like the **General Post Office** and **Gresham Hotel** are fast-food joints, movie theaters, and amusements. O'Connell Street's center median is dotted with impressive statues of noted Irishmen. Just north of the street are the serene **Garden of Remembrance** and the **Dublin Writers Museum,** and only a few blocks away is the famous **Abbey Theatre.** The newest and tallest landmark in the city is the **Millennium Spike**, located in the middle of O'Connell Street itself. This area stands out for its shopping, with Henry and Mary streets providing the city's largest selection of stores.

- **Trinity College Area (south side):** Just across O'Connell Bridge on the south side of the River Liffey stands Trinity College. This sprawling and well-kept campus sits in the heart of the city and is surrounded by classy bookstores and shops.

- **Temple Bar (south side):** Tucked into a spot between Trinity and Dublin Castle is the ever-fashionable Temple Bar. Here you'll find funky shops and hip bars along cobbled alleys. This is the cultural and entertainment hub of the city. There's no shortage of lively pubs, late-night bars, unique shops, and interesting people.

- **Old City–Historical Area (south side):** For a taste of history, step into this area of narrow streets and ancient buildings. Some date as far back as Viking and Medieval times. Some highlights are

Dublin Castle, Christ Church Cathedral, St. Patrick's Cathedral, and the old city walls. A bit further on, you'll find the **Guinness Storehouse.**

✔ **St. Stephen's Green and Grafton Street (south side):** This area begins at the bottom of the pedestrian Grafton Street and finishes up in St. Stephen's Green. This pretty part of town has plenty of upscale shops and cafes, and it's always teeming with people. The green is an enclosed park, and nice weather brings out plenty of Dubliners.

✔ **Merrion and Fitzwilliam Squares (south side):** These two square parks are surrounded by fashionable townhomes, some the best examples of Georgian architecture, and each with a distinctive, brightly-colored door. Some were once the homes of Dublin's most famous citizens, but today many of them house professional offices. Some big names from Dublin's past are said to have lived here on Merion Square: the poet W. B. Yeats, Irish nationalist leader Daniel O'Connell, and writer Oscar Wilde.

You can find interactive maps of Dublin online at `www.visitdublin.com/maps.htm` or order one online at `www.visitdublin.com/books.htm`.

For general visitor information, go to the **Dublin Tourism Centre** on Suffolk Street (☎ **1850-23-0330** from inside the country, ☎ 066-979-2083 from outside the Republic; open year-round). It also provides reservation services. The trendy Temple Bar district has its own information Web site at `www.temple-bar.ie`. For telephone directory assistance, dial ☎ **1190.** A good online source of Dublin information is `www.visit.ie/countries/ie/dublin/index.html`.

Getting Around Dublin

The best way to get around Dublin and really see it is to lace up a good pair of walking shoes and start hoofing. Dublin is entirely accessible by foot, and walking will save you many hassles. Driving a car in the city is like going to war, and it often takes longer to get from point A to point B via mass transit than it does to walk.

Just remember before stepping into the street that the cars are going in a different direction! Coming from a driving-on-the-right country, your tendency will be to look to the left first when stepping onto the street, but the cars will really be coming from the right.

The **DART** connects the city to the suburbs and coastal towns north (as far as Howth) and south (as far as Greystones). Call ☎ **1850-36-6222** (`www.irishrail.ie`) for information. There are only three stops in Dublin: Connolly Station, Pearse Street Station, and Tara Street Station (the closest to the city center, next to the River Liffey just east of the O'Connell Street Bridge). The DART runs from 6:00 a.m. to 11:45 p.m. Monday through Saturday and 9:00 a.m. to 11:45 p.m. on Sundays. Trains run every 5 to 15 minutes, depending on the time of day. (See the Cheat Sheet in the front of this book for a DART map.)

Dublin Bus, 59 Upper O'Connell St., Dublin 1 (☎ 01-872-0000), operates bus service throughout Dublin city and county, with fares under €2. Try to have small change — the newer buses don't give change back. Double-decker buses are still in use, along with a fleet of small, short-distance buses called City Imps. Buses run from 6:00 a.m. to 11:30 p.m. (Sunday service begins at 10 a.m.) and there's a late-night route Thursday through Sunday until 3 a.m. Discounted one-day to four-day passes are available with some restrictions. Call or visit `www.dublin bus.ie` for more details.

To get a taxi in Dublin, go to a taxi rank, where cabs line up along the street. You can hail a cab, but it's not common and the cab may not stop. There are taxi ranks at large hotels, train stations, the bus station, the O'Connell Street median near the General Post Office, opposite St. Stephen's Green shopping center, and near Trinity College in front of the Bank of Ireland. Getting a taxi during the day is usually not a problem, but you can end up waiting up to an hour for one on weekend late nights. As a rule, only get in a cab that's marked (with a rooftop sign or lettering on the doors); unmarked cars may not be sanctioned by the city and therefore have no fixed prices. **Blue Cabs** (☎ 01-676-1111) operates a 24-hour service.

Unlike cab etiquette in the States, it's protocol for passengers to sit up front with the driver rather than in the back seat, chauffeur-style. And hold on to your hats: Dublin cabbies are notorious for their crazy — yet strangely capable — driving.

If you can avoid renting a car while staying in Dublin, do it. If you do drive into the city, blue-and-white signs marked "P" direct you to car parks, and blue computerized signs list the number of spaces available in each. Street parking is on a disk system. You can buy disks from black-box vending machines in the city and from newsstands in outer neighborhoods. The *garda* (police) will clamp your car if you're parked illegally. Dublin's only large 24-hour car park is Usher's Quay on the south of the River Liffey near O'Connell Street.

Where to Stay in Dublin

Dublin is home to what seems like a zillion hotels, ranging from luxurious to simple. I've picked out some of the best, and cover all the bases that'll help you find the kind of place that says "you."

In general, if you're at all concerned about the quality of a hotel you choose, just find out how many stars it's been given by the Irish

Tourist Board. This system ranks hotels from one to five stars. Of course, more stars usually means more euros. The **Dublin Tourism Centre** on Suffolk Street will help you find accommodation based on price, location, and other factors. You can reserve a room (from within Ireland) by whipping out your credit card and calling ☎ **1800-66-8668** or e-mailing reservations@dublintourism.ie.

Dublin Central Reservation (☎ **01-820-0394**; Fax: 01-822-0493; E-mail: bookings@dublin reservations.com; Internet: www.dublin reservations.com) also has a free booking service that will book you into anything from a five-star hotel to a hostel.

The **Self-Catering Accommodation Association** for weekly rentals can be reached at ☎ **01-668-6641**.

Unlike the rest of the country, Dublin hotels don't significantly lower prices during the off-season (October through April). However, city hotels often offer great weekend packages, so be sure to ask about those.

Most accommodations have parking available. The price for parking isn't generally included in the rate, but if it's in a garage, often the price is discounted for guests.

The Clarence

$$$$ Temple Bar, Dublin 2

This high-class, five-star hotel has everything: location, elegance, a modern look, and superior service. You may not want to leave your enormous bed, where you can bliss out to the CDs on the room's stereo (no doubt better than your own). It's even touched by fame: The hotel is partly owned by Bono and the Edge of the Irish rock band U2 (who bought it because they loved the bar). Its decor is simple and chic, and it lies in the heart of the popular Temple Bar area. It also boasts the classy Octagon bar and the raved-about Tea Room restaurant. One of Dublin's poshest night clubs, The Kitchen, is in the basement. Looking for some lavish pampering? This is the place.

6–8 Wellington Quay, Temple Bar, Dublin 2. ☎ *01-407-0800. Fax: 01-407-0820. Internet: www.theclarence.ie. DART: Tara Street Station. Bus: 51, 51B, 68, 68A, 69X, 78A, 79, 90, 210. Valet parking. Rates: €285 –€620 ($270.75–$589) double. Breakfast not included. AE, DC, MC, V.*

College House B&B

$ Dublin 9

The quaint and quiet Victorian residence of Lord Boyce Molloy, across the street from St. Patrick's College, stands out from the many B&Bs in the area. The rooms are comfortable and the location is convenient to the city, airport, and ferries.

Dublin Accommodations and Dining

ACCOMMODATIONS ■
The Clarence **14**
College House B&B **2**
Hotel Isaacs **5**
Hotel St. George **3**
Jury's Christchurch Inn **16**
The Morrison **6**
North Star **4**
Phoenix Park House **1**
Shelbourne **28**
Temple Bar Hotel **9**
Trinity Arch **12**

Church ✝
DART Station ⬭
Information ⓘ
Post Office ✉

DINING ◆
Apache Pizza **13**
Bad Ass Cafe **11**
Beshoff's **8**
Bewley's Oriental Cafe **23**
Botticelli's **10**
Cafe Fresh **22**
Captain America's
    Cookhouse and
    Rock'n' Roll Museum **26**
The Chicago Pizza Pie
    Factory **24**
Eastern Tandoori **21**
Elephant & Castle **10**
Fitzer's **27**
Foggy Dew **12**
Gallagher's Boxty House **9**
Halo **6**
Juice **17**
Leo Burdocks **16**
Oliver Goldsmith's **9**
Oliver St. John Gogarty **11**
Panem **7**
Planet Hollywood **25**
Poco Loco **15**
Stag's Head **18**
Thunder Road Cafe **8**
Tosca **20**
Trocadero **19**
The Unicorn **29**

McKee Barracks
St. Brendan's Hospital
St. Lawrence Hospital
Prussia St.
Aughrim St.
Manor St.
Granggegorman Upper
Kirwan
North Circular Rd.
Oxmantown Rd.
Brunswick St. North
North King St.
Hospital
PHOENIX PARK
Infirmary Rd.
Cricket Ground
Main Rd.
Arbour Hill
Collins Barracks
Blackhall Place
Queen St.
Smithfield St.
Department of Defence
Montpelier Hill
King's Bridge
Benburb St.
Victoria's Bridge
Bow St.
Conyngham Rd.
Parkgate St.
Wolfe Tone Quay
Ellis Quay
Arran Quay
River Liffey
Victoria Quay
Queen's Bridge
Usher's Quay
Heuston Station
St. John's Rd.
West Hospital
Steven's Ln.
Guinness Brewery
Island St.
Bonham St.
Bridgefoot St.
Cook St.
Military Rd.
St. Patrick's Hospital
Thomas St. West
Cornmarket
St. James's St.
Rainsford St.
THE LIBERTIES
Robert St.
Bellevue
Earl St. S.
Meath St.
St. Patrick's Hospital
Bond St.
Pimlico
Ardee St.
St. Kevin's Hospital
Marrowbone Ln.
Grand Canal Bank
Cork St.
South Circular Rd.
Brown St.
Barn St.
Grand Canal
Dolphin's
Hospital

Phoenix Park
✈ **Area of detail**
Liffey
Dublin Bay
DUBLIN

50 Upper Drumcondra Rd., Dublin 9. ☎ *01-836-7070. Bus: 3, 11, 16, 41. Rates: €18.75–€37.50 double ($17.80–$35.60). No credit cards.*

Hotel Isaacs

$$$ O'Connell Street Area, Dublin 1

This moderately priced hotel is right across the street from the Bus Eireann station, close to Dublin's main shopping area and a mere five-minute walk from the city center. Hotel Isaacs is a restored wine warehouse; much of the original brickwork is still visible, giving it a lot of character. Rooms are furnished with a modern and tasteful flair. There's an Italian restaurant, Il Vignardo, downstairs.

Store Street, Dublin 1. ☎ *01-855-0067. Fax: 01-836-5390. Internet:* www.isaacs. ie. *DART: Connolly Street Station. Bus: 90. Rates: €130–€160 ($123.50–$152) double. AE, MC, V.*

Hotel St. George

$$ O'Connell Street Area, Dublin 1

Situated within a row of classic Georgian townhomes, the Hotel St. George stands out for its great location at the top of O'Connell Street on the north side of the city. From here, you're close to the Abbey and Gate theaters, the Writers Museum, the James Joyce Centre, and shopping galore. Rooms are reasonable, too.

7 Parnell Square, Dublin 1. ☎ *01-874-5611. Fax: 01-874-5582. Internet:* indigo.ie/ ~hotels/george.htm. *DART: Connolly Street Station. Bus: 1. Rates: €50– €56.25 ($47.50–$53.45) double. MC, V.*

Jurys Christchurch Inn

$$ Old City (near Temple Bar), Dublin 2

You can't beat Jurys for value if you're traveling as a family: This hotel group is one of the few in Ireland that won't charge extra if more than two people share a room. The rooms here are large and modern, and the hotel offers baby-sitting services. There's live traditional music in the bar on weekend nights. Christchurch Inn is situated conveniently at the top of Dame Street, in the heart of the city.

Christ Church Place, Dublin 8. ☎ *800-843-3311, toll-free from the United States; 01-454-0000. Fax: 01-454-0012. Internet:* www.jurys.com. *DART: Tara Street Station. Bus: 21A, 50, 50A, 78, 78A, 78B. Rates: €87.50 ($83.10) for up to three adults or two adults and two children. AE, DC, MC, V.*

The Morrison
$$$$ North Liffey, Dublin 1

This hotel is Dublin's newest bid for the top-notch hotel of the city, in league with the Clarence and the Shelbourne. The building itself blends an old Georgian townhouse with a modern façade, which speaks to the hotel's combination of old-fashioned guest pampering with modern amenities. Inside, you're met with the visually pleasing mix of high ceilings and stone floors with Irish carpets, with modern art along the walls. The elegant rooms are all decorated with a smart black and white design and come equipped with a state-of-the-art sound system, VCR, modem line, bar, and safe. The service is, in a word, flawless.

Ormond Quay, Dublin 1 (in front of the Millennium Bridge). ☎ *01-887-24000. Fax: 01-878-3185. Internet:* www.morrisonhotel.ie. *DART: Connolly Station. Rates: €270–€445 ($256.50–$422.75) double. AE, DC, MC, V.*

North Star
$$$ O'Connell Street Area, Dublin 1

This family-owned hotel is just a stone's throw from the Connolly rail and DART station on the north side of the River Liffey. It underwent major renovations last year, boosting the number of rooms to more than 130 and transforming it into a plush three-star hotel. The restaurant is grand and the pub is comfortable. Mentioned in Joyce's *Ulysses,* the hotel is a good starting point for sightseeing.

Amien Street, Dublin 1. ☎ *01-836-3136. Fax: 01-836-3561. Internet:* www.regency hotels.com. *DART: Connolly Street Station. Bus: 90. Rates: €150–€200 ($142.50–$190) double. AE, MC, V.*

Phoenix Park House
$ Phoenix Park Area, Dublin 8

This family-run guesthouse is a perfect choice for people entering town from Heuston Station. It's next to the beautiful and serene Phoenix Park and is within walking distance of the Guinness Brewery and National Museum. The city center is very accessible by bus, and besides, it's pretty cheap.

38–39 Parkgate, Dublin 8. ☎ *01-677-2870. Fax: 01-679-9769. Internet:* www.dublin guesthouse.com. *DART: Heuston Street Station. Bus: 25, 26, 51, 66, 67, 68, 69. Rates: Starting at €37 ($35.15) double. AE, MC, V.*

Shelbourne
$$$$ St. Steven's Green, Dublin 2

Since it was opened in 1824, this luxurious hotel has seen its share of history. It was one of the first buildings in Dublin to have electric lights.

Room 112 is the Constitution Room, where Michael Collins and others drafted the constitution of the Irish Free State in 1922. JFK and Jackie stayed during a visit in 1957. If staying here is too much of a splurge, you can have a cup of tea in the Lord Mayor's Lounge and gaze at the grand chandelier in the lobby. No two rooms are the same in this historical tribute to old-world tradition. If you do decide to spend the dough here, get a room overlooking St. Stephen's Green, not one with a bland view from the back of the hotel.

27 St. Stephen's Green, Dublin 2. ☎ *800-848-8415, from the United States; 01-676-6471. Fax: 01-661-6006. Internet:* www.shelbourne.ie. *DART: Tara Street Station. Bus: 32X, 39X, 41X, 66X, 67X. Rates: €315–€340 ($299.25–$323) double. Breakfast not included. AE, DC, MC, V.*

Temple Bar Hotel
$$$ Temple Bar, Dublin 2

As the saying goes: "Location, location, location." This hotel has that, and a lot more. Starting with the courteous staff that's eager to help, and carrying on to the immaculate and comfortable rooms, this is what a hotel should be. They do all they can to make you feel welcome, from the bottled water in your room to the towel warmers in the bathroom. The Terrace Restaurant has good food and it's a pleasure to relax in its atrium-like dining room.

Fleet Street, Temple Bar, Dublin 2. ☎ *01-677-3333. Fax: 01-677-3088. Internet:* www.towerhotelgroup.ie/templebar. *DART: Tara Street Station. Bus to Fleet Street: 51, 51B, 68, 68A, 69X, 78A, 79, 90, 210. Rates: €155–€185 ($147.25–$175.75) double. AE, DC, MC, V.*

Trinity Arch
$$$ Temple Bar, Dublin 2

Nestled in an 18th-century building, this relatively small hotel is on the edge of Temple Bar and smack-dab between Trinity College and Dublin Castle. The elegant Oliver Goldsmith's Bar, downstairs, serves fabulous nibble food at low prices. This is a fine place to stay, especially for its location, right on Dame Street. The price of a room includes use of the nearby Riverside Gym.

46 Dame St., Dublin 2. ☎ *01-679-4455. Fax: 01-679-4511. Internet:* www.trinity archhotel.com. *DART: Tara Street Station. Bus: 51, 51B, 68, 68A, 69X, 78A, 79, 90, 210. Rates: €106.25–€137.50 ($100.95–$130.60) double. AE, DC, MC, V.*

Where to Dine in Dublin

Dublin is chock-full of great places to eat. It may come as a surprise, but Ireland's capital is not the place to find traditional Celtic food. Just

Temple Bar

ACCOMMODATIONS ■
The Clarence **1**
Temple Bar Hotel **19**
Trinity Arch **9**

DINING ◆
Apache Pizza **8**
Bad Ass Cafe **11**
Botticelli's **12**
Elephant & Castle **14**
Gallagher's Boxty
House **14**
Polo Loco **4**

ATTRACTIONS ●
Bank of Ireland **21**
Dublin Castle **5**
Dublin's Viking Adventure
& Feast **2**
Ha'Penny Bridge **13**

NIGHTLIFE ☾
Auld Dubliner **16**
Foggy Dew **10**
Irish Film Centre **7**
The Kitchen **1**
The Left Bank Bar **17**
O'Brien's **8**
Oliver St. John Gogarty **18**
Olympia Theatre **6**

The Palace **20**
Turk's Head Chop House **3**
Temple Bar **15**

Information *i*
Parking P

the opposite is true; Dublin is home to a wide variety of international foods and venues ranging from casual to formal. Looking for Indian or Mediterranean? You've got it. Or is it French haute cuisine, Tex-Mex, or Creole that's tempting your taste buds? No problem. Finding a place to eat in Dublin is easier than finding a politician in Washington.

If you're dining with children, the best chain restaurant for kids is **Eddie Rockets.** This chain of diner-style restaurants features burgers and super-good shakes at family-friendly prices. The service is good and the breakfasts are yummy. Locations include 77 Dame St., 33 Upper Baggot St., 52 Upper O'Connell St., 17 Anne St., and 19 Wexford St.

You don't usually need reservations to dine out in Dublin. If you plan on dining somewhere rather posh in the middle of the summer, it's a good idea to phone a couple days in advance. Off season, it's really not a problem. I suggest going to the place you want to eat during the day and make your reservation. If they happen to be booked that night (which is rare) you can book for the next night.

For more dining options in Dublin, the city's tourist office has recently added a decent guide to dining in the city, broken down by cuisine types. If you max out the excellent options in this section, check out www.visitdublin.com/pubsrestaurants.htm.

Pub grub

Hungry, but don't feel like leaving the bar for some good food? Fear not. You'd be surprised at the quality of meals available at some pubs. The following pubs have great grub:

- ✔ **Oliver St. John Gogarty,** 58 Fleet St., Temple Bar, Dublin 2 (☎ 01-671-1822)

- ✔ **Oliver Goldsmith's,** Trinity Arch Hotel, 46 Dame St., Dublin 2 (☎ 01-679-4074)

- ✔ **Foggy Dew,** 1 Upper Fownes St., Temple Bar, Dublin 2 (☎ 01-677-9328)

- ✔ **Stag's Head,** 1 Dame Ct., Dublin 2 (☎ 01-679-3701)

Dublin's top restaurants

Of course, *top* doesn't mean just fancy places. I've also included a few great little cheap-eats places where you can pick up fast (but good!) food. Being hungry is the easy part. Choosing a place to eat is what's hard. I've done the legwork and found the prime spots so you don't have to waste time, money, or good taste.

Apache Pizza
$ Temple Bar, Dublin 2   PIZZA

Located in the heart of the city, Apache is a perfect stop for some quick chow or a post-bar bite. You can get pizza by the pie or slice, or try a famous Totem Roll — pizza ingredients stuffed into a hoagie bun and baked. There's a fabulous jukebox to sort through while waiting for your order.

58 Dame St., at Eustace Street, Temple Bar, Dublin 2. ☎ *01-677-8888. DART: Tara Street Station. Bus to Fleet Street: 46, 46A, 46B, 63, 150. Main courses: €2.25–€5 ($2.15–$4.75). Open: Mon–Thurs 11:30 a.m.–11:00 p.m., Fri–Sat 11 a.m.–3 a.m.*

Bad Ass Cafe
$–$$ Temple Bar, Dublin 2   PIZZA-AMERICAN

No, you don't have to be tough to come here (the name actually refers to a donkey), but you do have to be hungry! It's an open place, with tons of windows looking out to the teeming streets of Temple Bar. The Bad Ass is an institution, serving up some of the city's best pizza. Plenty of other quasi-American dishes round out the menu, and for the health conscious, the salads are good and fresh. Cleverness abounds in the menu, from the tasty "Confucius say 'noodles'," to the "tsunami salad" ("A tidal wave of Asian vegetables."). It's a place kids will enjoy — not only is it lively (and sometimes noisy), but they'll also get food that will remind them of home. For the parents, there's a great wine list, too.

9–11 Crown Alley, Temple Bar, Dublin 2. ☎ *01-671-2596. Internet:* www.badass cafe.com. *DART: Tara Street Station. Bus to Fleet Street: 46, 46A, 46B, 63, 150. Main courses: €4.45–€8.80 ($4.20–$8.35). AE, MC, V. Open: Mon–Sun 11:30 a.m. to midnight.*

Beshoff's
$ Trinity Area, Dublin 2   FISH AND CHIPS

Although opened the same year as Leo Burdocks (see later in this section), Beshoff's doesn't claim to be the original fish and chips shop — it claims to be the best! And it may well be. The fish, and there's quite a variety, is as fresh as can be, and the chips are crisp and done just right. Unlike its counterpart, Beshoff's has seating, so you can dine in if you want to.

14 Westmoreland St., Dublin 2. ☎ *01-842-4400. DART: Tara Street Station. Bus: 7A, 8, 15A, 15B, 15C, 46, 55, 62, 63, 83, 84. Main courses: €2.50–€6.25 ($2.35–$5.95). Open: Mon–Thurs 11:30 a.m.–11:00 p.m., Fri–Sat 11 a.m.–3 a.m.*

Botticelli's

$$$$ Temple Bar, Dublin 2   ITALIAN

This is food for people who know and love their Italian cuisine. Run by Italians, it's a place oft-frequented by Dubs, making it a hot spot that's nearly impossible to get into on weekends. But the gnocchi or tiramisu alone make it worth the wait you're likely to encounter. The Wellington Quay entrance by the River Liffey well represents the crisp, clean decor, while the Temple Bar entrance makes the place look like an upscale take-out joint. Don't be fooled, though; nothing about Botticelli's is like a pizza place (though they do have great pizza!).

3 Temple Bar Rd., Temple Bar, Dublin 2. ☎ 01-672-7289. DART: Tara Street Station. Bus to Fleet Street: 46, 46A, 46B, 63, 150. Main courses: €26.25–€36.25 ($24.95–$34.45). AE, DC, MC, V. Open: Daily 5 p.m. to midnight.

Café Fresh

$–$$ Trinity Area, Dublin 2   VEGETARIAN

This new and welcome addition on the Dublin healthy eating scene provides a tasty variety of entrees, salads, gourmet sandwiches, soups, and homemade desserts and cakes. They serve mostly vegetarian and vegan dishes and will accommodate other dietary restrictions as well. Housed in a refurbished 18th-century mansion, Café Fresh is a nice place to hang out. The friendly staff won't make you feel hurried, but if you are in a hurry, meals to go come with a 10% discount. The menu changes often but, as the name makes clear, everything is fresh. Don't miss their delicious smoothies, and for those who love guilt-free coffee, Fresh serves up fair-trade beans.

Unit 25 I Powerscourt Townhouse Centre, top floor, Dublin 2. ☎ 01-671-9669. DART: Tara Street Station. Bus to Fleet Street: 10, 16, 22, 46, 46A. Main courses: €5.50–€12 ($5.20–$11.40). MC, V. Open: Mon–Sat 10 a.m.–6 p.m. and Thurs until 8 p.m.

Eastern Tandoori

$$$–$$$$ Trinity Area, Dublin 2   INDIAN

Indian tandoori cuisine enjoys a huge following in Dublin, and this place well represents the best of it. Offering a menu that's sure to please everyone, Eastern Tandoori features a variety of foods that even the pickiest of eaters can choose from and enjoy. Everything inside is authentic, from the food to the comfortable surroundings. It's such a popular restaurant that the owners have branched out across the city and into the South. I recommend the barbecued beef.

34–36 S. William St., Dublin 2. ☎ 01-428-0506. DART: Tara Street Station. Bus to Fleet Street: 10, 16, 22, 46, 46A. Main courses: €16.25–€23 ($15.45–$21.85). AE, DC, MC, V. Open: Mon–Sat noon to 2 p.m. and 6:00–11:30 p.m., Sun 6:00–11:30 p.m.

Elephant & Castle

$$–$$$ Temple Bar, Dublin 2   AMERICAN

What you may notice first about this place is that it's always bustling. So if you won't take my word for how good the place is, take everyone else's. This wide-open restaurant offers interesting twists on American favorites, turning old standbys into sumptuous meals. Hamburgers and nachos will never be the same! And brunches are hugely popular, partly for the great omelets and *huevos rancheros* (fried eggs with a Creole sauce) and partly for the relaxed atmosphere and reasonable prices. Parents, take note: Kids love this place.

18 Temple Bar St., Temple Bar, Dublin 2. ☎ *01-679-3121. DART: Tara Street Station. Bus to Fleet Street: 46, 46A, 46B, 63, 150. Main courses: €6.90–€17.50 ($6.55–$16.60). AE, DC, MC, V. Open: Mon–Thurs 8:00 a.m.–11:30 p.m., Fri 8:00 a.m. to midnight, Sat 10:30 a.m. to midnight, Sun noon to 11:30 p.m.*

Fitzer's

$$–$$$ St. Stephen's Green Area, Dublin 2   CAFE

Owned by the Fitzpatricks of Dublin, a family that began as fruit and vegetable merchants in the city, Fitzer's cafes are a testament to how fresh, quality produce can enhance a meal. From creative and filling salads to innovative pasta dishes, Fitzer's incorporates a worldwide theme in its menu while staying true to the basics of an upscale cafe. The selection is varied without becoming complicated, and the atmosphere is classy without being unapproachable. The staff is smart and friendly, too. You'd never guess, but Fitzer's is a chain. There are four locations in the city, each with different menus and prices. The one located on Dawson Street, just blocks from Grafton Street, is the one I recommend. Just for the record, though, the other locations are in RDS Ballsbridge, Dublin 4 (☎ 01-667-1301); National Gallery, 42 Fownes St., Temple Bar, Dublin 2 (☎ 01-679-0440); and Merrion Square, Dublin 2 (☎ 01-661-4496).

51 Dawson St., Dublin 2. ☎ *01-677-1155. DART: Tara Street Station. Bus: 10, 11A, 11B, 13, 20B. Main courses: €9.95–€17.45 ($9.45–$16.55). AE, DC, MC, V. Open: Mon–Sat noon to 4 p.m. and 5:30–11:30 p.m., Sun 11 a.m.–11 p.m.*

Gallagher's Boxty House

$$ Temple Bar, Dublin 2   IRISH

This is the place to get traditional Irish food, featuring (obviously) *boxty,* a potato pancake filled with various meats or cabbage. Gallagher's also offers a menu full of Irish foods that are sure to stick to your ribs, like smoked Irish salmon, Leitrim corn chowder and, for the brave, the Clonakilty (meat) puddings. The decor instantly reminds you of what you imagined an Irish place to be like: plenty of hardwood, music, and friendly service. One aspect that adds to its hominess: You may be seated at long wooden tables with other diners, family-style. And because most of the patrons are travelers like yourself, you'll have lots to chat about.

20 Temple Bar Rd., Temple Bar, Dublin 2. ☎ *01-677-2762. Internet:* www.boxty house.ie. *DART: Tara Street Station. Bus to Fleet Street: 46, 46A, 46B, 63, 150. Main courses: €5–€11.35 ($4.75–$10.80). AE, MC, V. Open: Mon–Sun noon to 11:30 p.m.*

Halo

$$$$ North Liffey, Dublin 1   FUSION

This is Dublin's latest upscale dining hotspot. Want to indulge yourself in the very best? Leave the fanny pack in the hotel room and shimmy into this beautiful wood and crème-colored cathedral of a restaurant, complete with a beautiful staircase. Keep your cool while warming up to some fiery coconut-chili-cucumber-prawn soup, or try the mushroom dumplings in ginger sauce or the savory peppered rare yellow-fin tuna. If you want something distinctively local, go for the Loin of Wicklow lamb. This is a good place to wear that nice outfit you packed.

Ormond Quay, Dublin 1 (in the Hotel Morrison in front of the Millennium Bridge). ☎ *01-887-2400. DART: Connolly Station. Main courses: €25–€29.50 ($23.75–$28). AE, DC, MC, V. Open: 12:30–2:30 p.m. and 7–11 p.m.*

Juice

$$–$$$ Old City, Dublin 2   CALIFORNIA CUISINE

Juice is a little slice of California in the heart of Ireland. Whether you're simply looking to veg out or want excellent, filling food in cool, stark surroundings, Juice is the place for you. Its high ceilings and funky decor add ambience to the vast menu, which spans all kinds of ethnic foods. Items like tofu miso soup and falafels in a tangy sauce are great, but they're second to the heaping, spicy bean burger, which is a challenge to finish. If fresh-pressed juices are too tame for you, there's a pretty good wine list that includes a delicious organic wine available by the glass or bottle. Although you're not likely to run into too many fellow travelers, you'll probably be waited on by an American eager to find out where you're from.

South St. George's Street, Dublin 2. ☎ *01-475-7856. DART: Tara Street Station. Bus: 50, 50A, 54, 56, 77. Main courses: €7.50–€15 ($7.10–$14.25). DC, MC, V. Service Charge of 10% added. Open: Mon–Wed, Sun 9 a.m.–11 p.m., Thurs–Sat 9 a.m.–4 a.m.*

Leo Burdocks

$ Near Temple Bar, Dublin 8   FISH AND CHIPS

Burdocks, which calls itself the original fish and chips shop, is a Dublin landmark. The smell of frying fish wafts up the street to Christ Church, where you're likely to be when tempted to the "chipper." Don't be surprised if the line (or queue) snakes out the door — but don't pass it up, either!

2 Werburgh St., Dublin 8. ☎ *01-454-0306. Internet:* www.leoburdock.com. *Across from Christ Church Cathedral. DART: Tara Street Station. Bus: 50A, 78, 78A. Main courses: €3–€6.25 ($2.85–$5.95). No credit cards. Open: Mon–Fri 12:30 p.m. to midnight, Sat 2–11 p.m., Sun 4 p.m. to midnight.*

Panem

$ North Liffey 1   CAFE

This popular cafe is a great stop for a little lunchtime nosh of soup or pasta of the day, or perhaps just a superior cup of coffee while you write out a few postcards. The baked goods — focaccia, brioches, cakes, biscuits — are the big draw for Dublin locals. And the coffee and hot chocolate are as savory and delicious as you'll find in this tea town.

Ha'penny Bridge House, 21 Ormond Quay Lower, Dublin 1. ☎ *01-872-8510. DART: Connolly Station. Main courses: €2.25–€5.25 ($2.15–$5). No credit cards. Open: Mon–Fri, 8:00 a.m.–5:30 p.m, Sat 9 a.m.–5 p.m.*

Poco Loco

$–$$ Dublin 2   TEX-MEX

If you're looking for some filling, authentic-tasting Tex-Mex food, this is the place — and all at a cheap price. Some things belie the fact that you're not in a cantina in Austin, like the absence of jalapenós, and refried beans that lack the saltiness you're used to. But when it comes to burritos and enchiladas smothered in cheese, tacos stuffed with spicy beef, and fab nachos, Poco Loco is on the mark. It's small and dim, with painted wooden tables, and you may hear Elvis crooning in the background. Best of all, it has a full liquor license.

32 Parliament St., Dublin 2. ☎ *01-679-1950. DART: Tara Street Station. Bus to Fleet Street: 46, 46A, 46B, 63, 150. Main courses: €4.95–€10.95 ($4.70–$10.40). AE, DC, MC, V. Open: Mon–Thurs 5–11 p.m., Fri and Sat 5 p.m.–2 a.m., Sun 5:00–10:30 p.m.*

Tosca

$$$–$$$$ Trinity Area, Dublin 2   ITALIAN

If you've just spent a long day traipsing in and out of shops on Grafton Street, you're ready for a hearty meal in one of the city's best Italian restaurants. Delicious pasta dishes are the cornerstone of this lively place, owned by Norman Hewson, brother of U2's Bono. The fettuccine alfredo is marvelous, especially with chicken. Check out the bargain early-bird specials. And don't pass up the gourmet sandwiches — the focaccia bread is delicious.

20 Suffolk St., Dublin 2. ☎ *01-679-6744. DART: Tara Street Station. Bus: 5, 7A, 8, 15A, 15B, 15C, 46, 55, 62, 63, 83, 84. Main courses: €14.40–€22.80 ($13.70–$21.65). AE, DC, MC, V. Open: Sun–Wed 12:30–2:30 p.m. and 5:30–11:00 p.m., Thurs–Sat noon to 2:30 p.m. and 5:30 p.m.–1:00 a.m.*

A lovely spot for tea

If there's one thing you just have to do in Dublin, it's partake in the age-old practice of relaxing with a cuppa' at **Bewley's Oriental Cafe.** You'll see Bewley's signs at little mom-and-pop cafes all over Ireland to show they serve the finest tea and coffee, but the Bewley's branch you want to visit is at 78–79 Grafton St., Dublin 2 (☎ **01-677-6761;** Internet: www.bewleys.com). It's open Monday through Wednesday 7:30 a.m. to 1:00 a.m., Thursday through Saturday 8 a.m. to 2 a.m., Sunday 9:30 a.m. to 10:00 p.m.

Trocadero

$$–$$$$ **Trinity College Area** **INTERNATIONAL**

Step one foot in this sunken, red-walled restaurant and you'll get the feeling you're among important people — and it could be true. Trocadero is the place Dublin's literati, actors, and "in" people go for a meal and a bottle of wine while tucking themselves into an oversized half-moon booth. The food is delicious and quite reasonably priced given the chichi atmosphere. It's the kind of place where you feel somewhat lucky to have gotten a table, and dinner here offers a real taste of Dublin. Word has it the Troc comes to life around 1 a.m., when upper-echelon Dubliners settle in. But fear not: You're fine as long as you're out before the theaters let out. I got a table one Monday night only by promising to vacate by a certain time!

3 St. Andrew St., Dublin 2. ☎ 01-677-5545. DART: Tara Street Station. Bus to Fleet Street: 16A, 19A, 22A, 55, 83. Main courses: €9.35–€19.70 ($8.90–$18.70). AE, DC, MC, V. Open: Mon–Sat 6:00 p.m.–12:15 a.m., Sun 6:00–11:15 p.m.

The Unicorn

$$$–$$$$ **Merrion Square Area, Dublin 2** **ITALIAN**

This trendy new addition to the Dublin dining scene fuses old Irish ingredients into fresh and zesty Italian dishes. The prices are on the pamper-yourself side, the service is among the best in the city, and the food is unmatched. Highlights include freshly caught Dublin prawn salad; a full antipasto bar; savory *polpette* with polenta (Italian meatballs in arrabbita sauce with chargrilled polenta); penne with duck breast and truffle oil; and the unforgettable *Scaloppa Di Vitello porcini* (scalloped veal with mushrooms) with risotto cake.

12B St. Merrion Court, Merrion Road, Dublin 2 (next door to the Shelbourne Hotel on an alley off Merrion Road). ☎ 01-676-2182. DART: Tara Street Station. Bus: 32X, 39X, 41X, 66X, 67X. Main courses: €18–€23.50 ($17.10–$22.30). AE, DC, MC, V. Open: Daily 6:30–11:15 p.m.

Exploring Dublin

What's your pleasure? Do you want to spend the day in museums? Duck in and out of historical pubs? Relax in a park? Hunt out exemplary architecture? Dublin's got it all. There's so much to see and do here, you'll have to take a few minutes to set your sightseeing priorities — it's easy to get sidetracked!

Saving yourself some time and money

Here's a time-saving tip: **The Guinness Storehouse, Kilmainham Gaol,** the **Modern Art Museum, Phoenix Park,** and **Dublin Zoo** are all in the same general vicinity — west of the city center. Walking to the park is a good idea, but you can hit these other sites on the way and make it worth the time, or take a bus to the **Guinness Storehouse** and walk a little farther to the **Gaol.**

And, you don't need to bankrupt yourself sightseeing. The following attractions in Dublin are free: **Phoenix Park, St. Steven's Green,** the **Glasnevin Cemetery tours, St. Ann's Church,** the **National Museum,** the **National Gallery,** the **Irish Museum of Modern Art,** and the **National Botanic Gardens.** You can also get combined tickets to some attractions, which could save a few euro (see reviews for further information).

Also, the Dublin Tourism Centre on Suffolk Street sells a **SuperSaver Card** that gives discounts for the **Viking Adventure, Malahide Castle, Fry Model Railway, Dublin Writers Museum, Newbridge House,** and **James Joyce Museum.** It's worth purchasing if you visit at least three of them.

Seeing the top sights

St. Stephen's Green and Newman House
Dublin 2

This beautiful park in the heart of the city provides a welcome rest from the bustle of Dublin. One step through Fusilier's Arch — the entrance at the top of Grafton Street — and you may feel like you've magically left the city and entered an enchanted forest. The park is fully enclosed by trees and is full of shrub-lined walkways, vibrant flowerbeds, and a lake and garden. During summer months, you can enjoy lunchtime concerts with the rest of the city's population. Newman House, on the south side of the green, was once home to the Catholic University of Ireland. You can tour the house to see examples of Georgian furniture and interior design.

Dublin Attractions

Abbey Theatre **25**	Four Courts **8**
Bank of Ireland **23**	Garden of Remembrance **28**
Christ Church Cathedral **12**	General Post Office **26**
Dublin Castle **14**	Guinness Hop Store **5**
Dublin Tourism Centre **22**	Ha'Penny Bridge **24**
Dublin Writers Museum **30**	Irish Museum of Modern Art **3**
Dublin's Viking Adventure & Feast **9**	James Joyce Statue **27**
Dublinia **11**	Kilmainham Gaol **2**

Merrion Square **16**
Molly Malone Statue **20**
National Gallery **17**
National Museum (Collins Barracks) **4**
National Museum (Kildare Street) **18**
National Wax Museum **29**
Old Jameson Distillery **6**
Phoenix Park and Zoological Gardens **1**

St. Ann's Anglican Church **19**
St. Audoen's Church **10**
St. Michan's Church **7**
St. Patrick's Cathedral **13**
St. Stephen's Green and Newman House **15**
The Millenium Spike **26**
Trinity College and the Book of Kells **21**

St. Stephen's Green takes up the block at the top of Grafton Street; Newman House is located at 85–86 St. Stephen's Green, between Harcourt Street and Earlsfort Terrace, Dublin 2. ☎ 01-706-7422. Take Grafton Street away from Trinity College. DART: Tara Street Station. Bus: 10, 11, 13, 14, 14A, 15A, 15B. Admission: Green: Free; Newman House: €4 adults, €3 students and seniors. Green Open: Daylight hours. Newman House Open: June–Sept Tues–Fri noon to 5 p.m., Sat 2–5 p.m., Sun 11 a.m.–2 p.m. Only open to groups Oct–May. Suggested visit: About 1 hour.

Trinity College and the Book of Kells
Dublin 2

This college, founded in 1591 by Elizabeth I, remains today an impressive and refined example of old-world academia. The campus sits in the middle of the busy city, but within its gates everything is composed and quiet. Buildings dating back to antiquity add to the austere atmosphere, and during nice weather, students are splayed on the well-kept greens for picnics or studying. You may even imagine the days when former students Samuel Beckett, Oliver Goldsmith, or Edmund Burke rushed across the cobbled walks to class.

Most people visit Trinity for one reason: to see the Book of Kells. And no wonder! This ancient manuscript, painstakingly crafted by monks around A.D. 800, detail the four gospels of the Bible. Written in Latin in ornate script, the book is one of the oldest in the world and includes vividly colored drawings that are not to be missed (though you'll only be able to see one page on any given visit — they flip to the next page once a day). Included in the tour is admission to the Long Room, a vast hall of 200,000 of the college's oldest books. You can also see Ireland's oldest surviving harp and marble busts of famous historical persons.

Main entrance on College Street at the eastern end of Dame Street, Dublin 2. ☎ 01-677-2941. Walk two blocks south of the River Liffey from O'Connell Street Bridge; entrance will be on your left. Walk through the front entrance arch and follow signs to the Old Library and Treasury. DART: Tara Street Station. Bus: 15, 15A, 15B, 83, 155. Admission: College grounds: Free; Old Library and Book of Kells: €4.40 ($4.20) adults, €3.75 ($3.55) students and under 17, free under 12. Open: June–Sept Mon–Sat 9:30 a.m.–5:00 p.m., Sun 9:30 a.m.–4:30 p.m.; Oct.–May Mon–Sat 9:30 a.m.–5:00 p.m., Sun noon to 4:30 p.m. Closed for ten days during Christmas holiday. Suggested visit: 2½ hours.

Trinity's not-so-noble origins

Trinity College was founded in the 1500s as a Protestant institution as part of an English scheme called *The Ascendancy,* the migration of English Protestants to Ireland to establish a ruling class. Up until 1970, Catholics who wanted to enroll at Trinity had to give up their religion and subsequently face excommunication from the Catholic Church. Today, 70% of the students are Catholic.

Kilmainham Gaol
Dublin 8

The place where rebels were jailed and many awaited the firing squad, Kilmainham Gaol (pronounced *jail*) is one of the most startling testaments to what Irish freedom fighters endured. Exploring this extremely well-put-together museum, you'll learn about the jail's history, what kind of criminals were held here (much more than just dissidents against England), and how prisoners were treated during the jail's 130-year history. You'll shudder at the dank cells of such famous patriots as Charles Stewart Parnell, Joseph Plunkett, and James Connolly. A short movie about the jail is shown in the chapel where Plunkett was allowed to marry Grace Gifford just hours before being shot for his part in the 1916 Rising. You can stand in the very spot where many rebels were shot by firing squads — including Connolly, who was so badly injured he couldn't stand up by himself and had to be strapped into a chair to be shot. Kilmainham was used as the set for the 1993 Daniel Day Lewis film *In the Name of the Father.*

Inchicore Road, Kilmainham, Dublin 8. ☎ *01-453-5984. Bus: 51, 51A, 79. Admission: €3.75 ($3.55) adult, €2.50 ($2.35) seniors, €1.50 ($1.40) student and child. Open: Apr–Sept daily 9:30 a.m.–4:45 p.m., Oct–March Mon–Fri 9:30 a.m.–4:00 p.m., Sun 10:00 a.m.–4:45 p.m. Suggested visit: 2 hours.*

Merrion Square
Dublin 2

This square, one of the most elegant sections of Dublin, is surrounded by some of the best examples of Georgian architecture you'll run across. The row homes retain their original splendor, and many still have the original doors, knockers, and wrought-iron balconies. You'll see plaques that note the former homes of poet W. B. Yeats (Number 82), playwright Oscar Wilde (Number 1), and Catholic liberator Daniel O'Connell (Number 58). Today there is a statue of Wilde reclining on a large rock in the Square, across from his home, now part of the American College. The square served as a soup kitchen in the 1840s, during the Great Famine.

Merrion Square takes up the block directly behind the National Gallery. Take Nassau Street on the south side of Trinity College and continue east for a few blocks until it becomes Merrion Square North. DART: Pearse Street Station and head south on Westland Row and Merrion Street Lower. Bus: 5, 7A, 8 Admission: Free. Open: Daylight hours. Suggested visit: 20 minutes.

Dublinia
Dublin 8

This interactive museum covers Dublin history from the invasion of the Anglo-Normans in 1170 to the mid-16th century. You'll find lots of interesting information about medieval Dublin's religion, trade, and development. An audiovisual tour through a life-sized display depicts milestones in the city's history, such as the Black Plague. Also, a scale model of Dublin circa 1500 shows what the city looked like at the tail end of the Middle Ages. An added plus to this attraction is St. Michael's Tower, located in the building that houses the Dublinia Museum. It's one of the highest, most central points open to the public in this low-rise city. From the top you'll get an astounding view of Dublin, and kids will love it! You have to take the tour to get up into it.

High Street (linked to Christ Church), Dublin 8. ☎ *01-679-4611. Internet: www.dublinia.ie. Bus: 50, 78A. Admission: €5.75 ($5.45) adults, €4.50 ($4.25) children, students, and seniors, €15 ($14.25) family of 2 adults and 2 children; free for children under 5. Open: April–Sept daily 10 a.m.–5 p.m., Oct–March Mon–Sat 11 a.m.–4 p.m., Sun 10:00 a.m.–4:30 p.m. Suggested visit: 1½ hours.*

Dublin Castle
Dublin 2

This impressive building — which looks less like a castle than any other in the country — was once the seat of English government. Now the castle is purely Irish, home to official state functions like the president's inauguration. Check out the Drawing Room, which features a breathtaking Waterford Crystal chandelier, and the Throne Room, which is believed to hold an original seat of William of Orange. St. Patrick's Hall holds the banners of the knights of St. Patrick and historical ceiling paintings. Note the statue of Justice in the courtyard. See how she faces away from the city? Cynical Dubliners will tell you that was intentional.

Cork Hill, off Dame Street, Dublin 2. ☎ *01-677-7129. Bus: 50, 50A, 54, 56A, 77, 77A, 77B. Admission: €3 ($2.85) adult, €2 ($1.90) students and seniors, €1.25 ($1.20) under 16. Guided tours are obligatory. Open: Mon–Fri 10:00 a.m.–12:15 p.m. and 2–5 p.m., Sat and Sun 2–5 p.m. Closed for state functions. Suggested visit: 45 minutes.*

Dublin's Viking Adventure & Feast
Dublin 8

Dublin was actually founded over a thousand years back by Viking invaders, and this attraction gives you a chance to witness their history — live! Interactive and interesting, the Viking Adventure takes you on a journey through time. You'll get to walk the streets of Viking Dublin, talk to its inhabitants, and watch them work. Take a simulated ride on a Viking ship and look over the exhibit of artifacts. On Wednesday through Monday you can participate in a huge Viking feast.

Essex Street West, Temple Bar, Dublin 8. ☎ *01-679-6040. DART: Tara Street Station. Bus: 51, 51A, 51B, 79, 90 Admission: €6 ($5.70) adults, €4.50 ($4.25) age 12–18, €3.75 ($3.55) age 3–11, €16.25 ($15.45) family of 2 adults and 4 children. Viking Feast: €43.75 ($41.55) per person. Open: March–Oct Tues–Sat 10 a.m.–1 p.m. and 2:00–4:30 p.m. Suggested visit: 1½ hours (longer if you participate in the feast).*

A record-setting debate

Is Guinness the beer associated with *The Guinness Book of World Records*? Yes. The story is that in 1951, Sir Hugh Beaver, then managing director of the brewery, missed a bird while hunting and got into a stout-fuelled debate over which bird was fastest. Beaver decided that the company should create a book to settle such barroom arguments.

By the way, the fastest bird is the peregrine falcon. It can go 168 miles an hour.

Guinness Storehouse
Dublin 8

For many years, the Guinness "tour" was simply a one-floor collection of advertisements and history placards with a "bar" where you could only have your complimentary pint. But in 2001 the new Storehouse opened and the tour travels through an old converted warehouse where, until the 1980s, "the Black stuff" fermented and was stored (hence storehouse). The six-floor museum, gallery, and tour takes you through a 100-foot pint glass–shaped atrium (which would hold 14.3 million pints of stout if it were an actual glass), a hands-on display of the ingredients, walk-in copper vats, indoor waterfall, an avant-garde art gallery, an audio-visual display of classic Guinness commercials and advertisements, and the 130-foot high Gravity Bar. The Gravity Bar, located on the roof of the building and looking like a *Jetsons*-themed watering hole, has circular glass walls providing a 360-degree view over the city. If the view isn't intoxicating, the stout will be. Guinness also publishes a free Dublin Pub Trail map with 31 "must-try" pubs for your own pub crawl. Pick one up at the museum or the Suffolk Street tourist office.

St. James's Gate, Dublin 8. ☎ *01-408-4800. Internet:* www.guinness-storehouse.com. *DART: Tara Street Station. Bus: 51B, 78A, 123. Admission: €12 ($11.40) adults, €8 ($7.60) students over 18, €5.30 ($5) seniors and students under 18, €2.50 ($2.35) children 6–12, €26 (24.70) family of 2 adults and 4 children, free for children under 6. Price includes a free pint of stout or a soda. Open: Oct–March Mon–Sat 9:30 a.m.–5:00 p.m., Sun 10:30 a.m.–5:00 p.m.; April–Sep 9:30 a.m.–7:00 p.m. daily. Suggested visit: 2 hours (longer if you hang out at the bar).*

Taking in some Dublin landmarks

Abbey Theatre
Dublin 1

This modern-looking theater was cofounded by poet and playwright W. B. Yeats in 1898. It's survived riots stemming from outrage to J. M. Synge's

The Playboy of the Western World, and has showcased the work of some of Ireland's most famous literary voices. Rebuilt in 1966, its lobby walls are lined with portraits of noted people associated with the theater.

Lower Abbey Street, Dublin 1. ☎ 01-878-7222. Suggested visit: 15 minutes.

The Bank of Ireland
Dublin 2

Once the Parliament House, the Bank of Ireland is a striking 18th-century building. Visit the Irish House of Lords, where Parliament sat before being joined with England's in London. This beautiful chamber features wood-work in Irish oak, period tapestries, and an awesome Irish crystal chandelier dating back to 1765. One thing you'll notice right away: There aren't any windows in the Bank of Ireland! This isn't for security reasons; rather, when it was built, England levied a hefty property tax that increased drastically as the number of windows did. To save money, the building was constructed with a single atrium for light and no windows. Have you heard of the phrase *daylight robbery?* You guessed it — it comes from the government's charging for daylight!

2 College Green, Dublin 2. ☎ 01-677-7155. Cost: €1.90 ($1.80) adult, €1.25 ($1.20) seniors and students. Open: Mon–Wed and Fri 10 a.m.–4 p.m., Thurs 10 a.m.–5 p.m. Suggested visit: 15 minutes.

James Joyce Statue
Dublin 1

This statue pays homage to the wiry, bespectacled man whose inspired words have become the essence of Dublin in the "auld times."

Halfway up O'Connell Street, just at the top of Earl Street North, only blocks away from the James Joyce Cultural Centre, 35 North Great George's Street (☎ 01-878-8547), which all true Joyce fans need to visit. Suggested visit: A few seconds, unless you decide to recite a sentence or two from Finnegan's Wake, which could take a month.

The Ha'Penny Bridge
Dublin 1 and 2

This famous footbridge — the only pedestrians-only bridge across the River Liffey — has connected the north side of the river directly to Temple Bar since 1816. Its name comes from the half-penny toll that it once cost to cross the bridge. You can't miss it — it's baby blue, arches high over the River Liffey, and at night it's brightly festooned with lights. The midway point offers a great photo moment, but take care with the wind — you could lose your hat in a flash!

Over the River Liffey between O'Connell and Grattan bridges, across from Liffey Street Lower on the north side. Suggested visit: 5 minutes.

The Millennium Spike
Dublin 1

Dublin's newest landmark (due to be completed early 2003) has been heavily criticized by locals. Whether this large metal spire in the middle of O'Connell Street is an architectural nightmare or artistic enhancement is your call. The benefit of having a landmark taller than the surrounding buildings is that, as a tourist, you can use it to orient yourself on the north side of the Liffey, or at least to find the General Post Office.

O'Connell Street, Dublin 1 (in front of the main post office). Suggested visit: 15 minutes.

Molly Malone Statue
Dublin 1

Sing along now: "In Dublin's fair city, where the girls are so pretty, there once was a girl named sweet Molly Malone. . . ." Inspired by the traditional song "Cockles and Mussels," this statue is a tribute to the fictional Molly Malone, who represents all the women who hawked their wares on Dublin's busy streets in the past. Affectionately known as "The Tart with the Cart," Molly welcomes shoppers at the head of Grafton Street.

Located on the corner of Nassau and Grafton streets. Suggested visit: About 30 seconds, unless you take time to sing the whole song.

Four Courts
Dublin 8

If you have some time, go in and watch imposing barristers with powdered wigs try court cases with perfect, bookish English. You'll be amazed at the difference from home — this is no *People's Court!* You can also get information about the building's history in the entrance. If you're just taking in the sights, tip your head up to the copper-covered dome that rises above a six-column portico, where you'll find statues of Moses, Justice, and Mercy. This regal building sits on the edge of the River Liffey; you can get a great view of it from the Ha'Penny Bridge.

Inns Quay, west of the O'Donovan Rossa Bridge and facing the River Liffey from the north side. Suggested visit: 1 hour or less.

General Post Office
Dublin 1

Probably the single most striking symbol of the Easter Rising of 1916, the General Post Office (GPO) still bears the scars of that violent battle between Irish patriots and the English (look for bullet holes in the pillars). During the rising, members of the Irish Volunteers and Irish Citizen Army captured the GPO and stayed for a week, barely holding their enemies at bay. From its steps, Patrick Pearse read the Proclamation of the

Irish Republic. British persistence forced the rebels out, and 14 leaders were later shot. Inside this cavernous building — still kicking as Ireland's main post office — stands a statue of ancient Irish hero Cuchulainn, which was dedicated to those who died for their part in the rebellion.

North of the River Liffey, halfway up the left-hand side of O'Connell Street. Suggested visit: 30 minutes.

Garden of Remembrance
Dublin 1

This peaceful and orderly garden is dedicated to the men and women who died in the pursuit of Irish freedom. It's hard not to be touched by the serenity of the spot, with its bright flowers and still reflecting pool. There's a telling statue representing the sad myth of the Children of Lir, who were turned into swans by their selfish and cruel stepmother. A symbolic mosaic at the bottom of the pool depicts broken weapons, standing for peace. Eamon de Valera, veteran freedom fighter, opened the garden on the 50th anniversary of the Easter Rising. The location is significant, too; it was where several leaders of the rising were held overnight before being taken to Kilmainham Gaol — and their deaths.

The north end of Parnell Square at the top of O'Connell Street. Open: Nov–Feb daily 11 a.m.–4 p.m.; March, April, Oct 11 a.m.–7 p.m.; May–Sept 9:30 a.m.–8:00 p.m. Suggested visit: 15 minutes.

St. Audoen's Church
Dublin 8

There are actually two churches of the same name off of Cook Street, but you're looking for the smaller and older of the two. Although the building itself, the only medieval church in the city still standing, will likely be closed, there is a stone gate behind it that is the landmark. The arch and wall are the only surviving parts of the old city gates and date back to 1240. Inside the church are the three oldest bells in Ireland, dating back to 1423.

The gate is on Cook Street near Christ Church Cathedral and on the north side of the old St. Audoen's Church. Suggested visit: 15 minutes

Finding other fun stuff to do

So, you've loaded up on java, worn out the soles of your walking shoes, and seen all the best sights that I listed in this chapter, huh? Get ready for some more fun stuff.

Museums and galleries

The following attractions should round out the Dublin experience for culture buffs.

✔ **National Museum (Collins Barracks and Kildare Street branches):**
These two museums, which between them house Ireland's finest
collection of historical artifacts, are set in two separate parts of
the city but are both worth the trip. Highlights from the Kildare
Street location include the **National Treasury,** which contains the
Ardagh Chalice, the intricately detailed Tara Brooch, and the
Cross of Cong dating back to 1123. **"The Road to Independence"**
exhibit deals with the turbulent time in Irish history between 1916
and 1921. **Collins Barracks** is the oldest military barracks in
Europe and features pieces of the economic, social, political, and
military history of Ireland, including a pocketbook carried by
Wolfe Tone, gauntlets worn by King William in the Battle of the
Boyne, and pieces saved from the wreckage of the *Lusitania.*

Behind Collins Barracks lies the small Arbor Hill Cemetery, bordered by a prison. In the graveyard, you'll find a simple granite
memorial to 14 leaders of the Easter Rising (against the British)
who are buried there.

Location: Collins Barracks, Benburb Street, Dublin 7; Kildare Street
branch at Kildare and Merrion streets, Dublin 2. ☎ **01-677-7444**
(for both). DART to Collins Barracks: Connolly Station. Bus to
Collins Barracks: 25, 25A, 66, 67, 90. DART to Kildare Street: Pearse
Street. Bus to Kildare Street: 7, 7A, 8, 10, 11, 13. Admission: Free.
Open: Tuesday through Saturday 10 a.m. to 5 p.m., Sunday 2 to 5
p.m. Guided tours available. Suggested visit: 2 hours.

✔ **Dublin Writers Museum:** Ireland's love affair with literature and
its illustrious legacy is represented in this gorgeous museum, set
in an 18th-century mansion. Through books, letters, portraits, and
personal items, it explores the lives of Dublin's literary luminaries
from the past 300 years — writers like Jonathan Swift, George
Bernard Shaw, W. B. Yeats, James Joyce, and Samuel Beckett.
Poetry and prose readings and lectures are hosted here. Of
course, there's a bookstore as well. The on-site restaurant,
Chapter One, is excellent.

Location: 18 Parnell Square North, Dublin 1. ☎ **01-872-2077.**
DART: Connolly Station. Bus: 10, 11, 11A, 11B, 13, 16, 16A, 19, 19A,
22, 22A, 36. Admission: €4 ($3.80) adult, €3.50 ($3.30) under 18,
€2 ($1.90) under 12. Open: June to August, Monday through
Saturday 10 a.m. to 6 p.m., Sunday 11 a.m. to 5 p.m.; September to
May, Monday through Saturday 10 a.m. to 5 p.m., Sunday 11 a.m.
to 5 p.m. Suggested visit: 45 minutes.

✔ **The National Gallery:** You may not expect Ireland to be home to a
stellar collection of art, but this gallery should change your mind.
The Gallery has an extensive Irish collection and art from the
major European schools. Some of the most respected pieces are
The Taking of Christ by Caravaggio, *Castle of Bentheim* by Ruisdael,
and *For the Road* by Jack Yeats (poet W. B. Yeats's brother). In
2002, the Millennium Wing opened, an expansive area that
includes the best archive of Yeats paintings in the world. Kids

will want to spend hours in the interactive gallery — an ingenious set of computers that make discovering any aspect of art easy and fun. It'll wow parents, too.

Location: Merrion Square West, Dublin 2. ☎ **01-661-5113.** DART: Pearse Street Station and head south on Westland Row and Merrion Street Lower. Bus: 5, 7A, 8. Admission: Free, although special exhibits may have a cost. Open: Monday through Wednesday, Friday, and Saturday 10:00 a.m. to 5:30 p.m., Thursday 10:00 a.m. to 8:30 p.m., Sunday 2 to 5 p.m. Guided tours available. Suggested visit: 1 hour.

✔ **Old Jameson Distillery:** This small but popular museum is housed in part of Jameson's now-unused Bow Street distillery. It traces the history of Irish whiskey distilling from sixth-century monasteries to the present. Finish off the tour with a sample of the goods at the Ball o' Malt Bar.

Location: Bow Street, Dublin 7. ☎ **01-872-5566.** DART: Connolly Street. Bus: 67, 67A, 68, 69, 79, 90. Admission: €4.40 ($4.20) adults, €3.75 ($3.55) students and seniors, €1.90 ($1.80) children. Open: Daily 9:30 a.m. to 6:00 p.m. Suggested visit: 45 minutes.

✔ **Irish Museum of Modern Art:** Grandly sitting at the end of a tree-lined lane, this is one of Ireland's most magnificent 17th-century buildings, built in 1680 as a hospital for injured soldiers. The building is so impressive that when it was finished, many lobbied to use it as the campus for Trinity College. Even if you couldn't care less about modern art (and the collection's not exactly extensive), you'll probably enjoy just looking at the building and grounds. The Baroque chapel of wood carvings and stained glass is a sight in itself. Exhibits change often but invariably include Irish and international art.

Location: Military Road, Kilmainham, Dublin 8. ☎ **01-612-9900.** Bus: 79, 90. Admission: Free. Open: Tuesday through Saturday 10:00 a.m. to 5:30 p.m., Sunday noon to 5:30 p.m. Suggested visit: 1 hour.

✔ **National Wax Museum:** From the very start, with the wax man reading the *Irish Times* in the lobby, you'll be second-guessing your own wits in this place. Heroes from Irish antiquity to present day are represented. The replica of DaVinci's *Last Supper* is magnificent, and kids will love the Children's World of Fairytale and Fantasy and the Hall of Megastars. If your kids (or you!) are even slightly skittish, though, steer away from the Chamber of Horrors — it's amazingly realistic!

Location: Granby Row, Parnell Square, Dublin 1. ☎ **01-872-6340.** DART: Connolly Station. Bus: 11, 13, 16, 22, 22A. Admission: €4.40 ($4.20) adults, €3.15 ($3) students, €2.50 ($2.35) children. Open: Monday through Saturday 10:00 a.m. to 5:30 p.m., Sunday noon to 5:30 p.m. Suggested visit: 1 hour.

A park and zoo experience

If you need a break from museum-hopping, here's a great back-to-nature option:

✔ **Phoenix Park and Zoological Gardens:** This is Europe's largest enclosed city park — five times the size of London's Hyde Park! You can drive through it, but if the weather's nice don't pass up the chance to walk, because Phoenix Park is more than just a green spot for picnic lunches: Enclosed within it are the homes of Ireland's president and the U.S. ambassador. The **Zoological Gardens** is the world's third-oldest zoo and is home to many animals, including the world's most famous lion — the one that roars before every MGM movie. Other sights include the **Papal Cross,** where Pope John Paul II said Mass to a million Irish in 1979, and **Ashton Castle,** a 17th-century tower house that's now the visitor center. Originally a deer park, the area is still home to many deer, so be watchful when driving.

Location: Park Gate, Conyngham Road; Phoenix Park Visitor Centre, Dublin 8. Visitor Centre ☎ **01-677-0095**, Zoological Park ☎ **01-677-1425**. To the Park: Bus 37, 38, or 39 to Ashtown Cross Gate. To the Zoo: Bus 10, 25, 26. Admission: Free to park; to zoo €7.50 ($7.10) adults, €5.25 ($5) students, €4 ($3.80) under 17. The park is open 9:30 a.m. to 5:30 p.m. daily from late March to May and the month of October; 9:30 a.m. to 6:30 p.m. daily from June to September; and 9:30 a.m. to 4:30 p.m. Saturday and Sunday from November to mid-March. The zoo is open Monday through Saturday 9:30 a.m. to 6:00 p.m., Sunday 10:30 a.m. to 6:00 p.m. Closes at sunset in winter. Suggested visit: 2½ hours.

Cathedrals and churches

I list the big one (St. Patrick's) here, along with a few other religious spots for those looking for some spiritual succor (or just a chance to gape at some amazing architecture):

✔ **Christ Church Cathedral:** This church is the mother of the Church of Ireland in Dublin and the city's oldest building, first founded in 1038 as a simple wooden church. In 1169 the church was rebuilt by Strongbow, the Anglo-Norman conqueror of Dublin, for Laurence O'Toole, archbishop of Dublin. O'Toole was later canonized as the patron saint of the city. Neither lived to see the completed cathedral, but the remains of Strongbow and the heart of St. Laurence are kept here. There are original medieval tiles in the chapels and a basement crypt contains the mummies of a cat and rat found in an organ pipe in the 1860s.

Location: Christ Church Place, Dublin 8. ☎ **01-677-8099.** DART: Tara Street Station. Bus: 50, 50A, 78, 78A. Admission: €1.25 ($1.20). Open: Daily 10 a.m. to 5 p.m. Suggested visit: 45 minutes.

✔ **St. Patrick's Cathedral:** This church, the national cathedral of the Church of Ireland, is as symbolic and historic as it is impressive and beautiful. Because members of the Church of Ireland live in the Republic as well as Northern Ireland, the cathedral is an important bridge between two groups that are desperately trying to meet on a religious middle ground. The famous satirist Jonathan Swift was a dean of St. Pat's, and now enjoys his final resting place here. Legend says that the well inside the cathedral is where St. Patrick baptized converts in the fifth century. Services are given nearly every day. The choir section is amazing to behold, as is the great Willis organ, Ireland's largest.

Location: Patrick's Close, Dublin 8. ☎ 01-475-4817. DART: Tara Street Station. Bus: 50, 54A, 56A. Admission: €2.50 ($2.35) adults, €1.90 ($1.80) students, services free. Open: April through October, Monday through Friday 10 a.m. to 6 p.m., Saturday 9 a.m. to 5 p.m., Sunday 10:00 a.m. to 4:30 p.m.; November through March, Monday through Saturday 9 a.m. to 4 p.m., Sunday 10:00 a.m. to 4:30 p.m. Suggested visit: 45 minutes.

✔ **St. Michan's Church:** Unless you plan to make your next vacation a tour of the ancient pyramids, this may be your best chance to see actual mummies. It's hard to believe, but something in the dry air here preserves bodies, and the vaults contain the remains of such people as Henry and John Sheares, leaders of the Rebellion of 1798. The church also proudly displays an organ believed to have been played by Handel. Don't miss the detailed wood carvings of instruments above the choir area.

Location: Church Street, Dublin 7. ☎ 01-872-4154. DART: Tara Street Station. Bus: 34, 70, 80. Admission: €1.90 ($1.80) adult, €1.25 ($1.20) seniors and students, €0.75 (70¢) under 12. Open: Monday through Friday 10 a.m. to 5 p.m., Saturday 10:00 a.m. to 12:30 p.m. Suggested visit: 1 hour.

✔ **St. Ann's Anglican Church:** In this church, the writer of the creepy novel *Dracula,* Irishman Bram Stoker, married Florence Balcombe, witty playwright and Oscar Wilde's first love. Wolfe Tone, the famous rebel, was also married here. Gorgeous stained-glass windows are found throughout.

Location: Dawson Street, Dublin 2. ☎ 01-676-7727. DART: Tara Street Station. Bus: 10, 11A, 11B, 13, 20B. Admission: Free. Open: Monday through Friday 10 a.m. to 4 p.m. Suggested visit: 30 minutes.

Attractions a little out of town

If you'd like to get out of the city for bit, here are a few options just outside Dublin:

✔ **Malahide Castle:** This castle was witness to the longevity of one of Ireland's great and wealthy families, the Talbots, who resided here from 1185 to 1973. The architecture of the house is varied, and period furniture adorns the rooms. There's a large collection of Irish portrait paintings, many from the National Gallery. The Great Hall chronicles the Talbots, with portraits of family members. One tragic legend details the morning of the Battle of the Boyne in 1690, when 14 members of the family shared a last meal; by nighttime they had all been killed. The grounds are spectacular and probably haven't changed much in the past 800 years. Kids will have a great time at the Fry Model Railway Museum (see the next listing) located on the castle grounds.

Location: Malahide. ☎ **01-846-2516.** Irish Rail: Malahide Station from Connolly Station. Bus: 42. Admission: €3.75 ($3.55) adults, €3.15 ($3) under 18, €2 ($1.90) under 12; combined tickets available with Fry Model Railway Museum (see next listing). Open: April through October, Monday through Saturday, 10 a.m. to 5 p.m., Sunday 11 a.m. to 6 p.m.; November through March, Monday through Friday 10 a.m. to 5 p.m., Sunday 2 to 5 p.m. Suggested visit: 1½ hours.

✔ **Fry Model Railway Museum:** Located on the grounds of Malahide Castle, the Fry Model Railway Museum will entertain kids of all ages. The unique collection of handmade trains spans the history of this mode of transportation in Ireland, from the early days of train travel to present day. The collection is the intricate work of Cyril Fry, a railway engineer from the 1920s and 1930s, and his attention to detail and craftsmanship is evident in each piece.

Location: Malahide. ☎ **01-846-3779.** Irish Rail: Malahide Station from Connolly Station. Bus: 42. Admission: €3.50 ($3.30) adults, €2.50 ($2.35) under 18, €2 ($1.90) under 12; combined tickets available for castle and museum. Open: April through September, Monday through Friday 10 a.m. to 6 p.m., Saturday 10 a.m. to 5 p.m., Sunday 2 to 6 p.m.; October through March, Saturday and Sunday 2 to 5 p.m. Closed Fridays in April and May. Suggested visit: 1 hour.

✔ **Newbridge House and Park:** Walking around Dublin you've seen plenty of examples of Georgian exteriors, but here's your chance to see a fine Georgian interior. This manor perfectly exhibits the refined quality of the Georgian style, and each room is open to the public. Antique and original furniture fill the rooms, and the house looks almost exactly as it did 150 years ago. On the grounds is a traditional farm representative of the time period. It even has animals living on it — kids will love this part!

Location: Donabate. ☎ **01-843-6534.** Irish Rail: Donabate Station from Connolly Station. Bus: 33B. Admission: €3.50 ($3.30) adults, €3 ($2.85) under 18, €2 ($1.90) under 12. Open: April through September, Tuesday through Saturday 10 a.m. to 5 p.m., Sunday 11 a.m. to 6 p.m. Closed 1 to 2 p.m. Suggested visit: 1½ hours.

✔ **National Botanic Gardens:** This is a must for anyone who has a green thumb (or wishes he or she had one). Some of the features of the gardens are an arboretum, a rock garden, and rare Victorian *carpet bedding* — a style of ground cover with spots of colorful flowers interspersed. It's dense and impressive-looking. The glass houses (Irish-speak for *greenhouses*) contain a large palm house, an alpine house, and a complex for ferns, tropical water plants, and succulents.

Location: Glasnevin, Dublin 9. ☎ 01-837-7596. Bus: 13, 19, 134. Admission: Free. Open: Summer, Monday through Saturday 9 a.m. to 6 p.m., Sunday 11 a.m. to 6 p.m.; Winter, Monday through Saturday 10:00 a.m. to 4:30 p.m., Sunday 11:00 a.m. to 4:30 p.m. Suggested visit: 45 minutes.

✔ **Joyce Tower and Museum:** This tower was made famous in the first scene of *Ulysses,* when Joyce has his main character, Stephen Dedalus, stay here with the character Buck Mulligan. Located on a rocky beach in the quaint town of Sandycove, the tower was built with 11 others in 1804 as protection against a possible invasion by Napoleon. Joyce actually did stay in the tower with his friend Oliver St. John Gogarty (the real model for the fictional Mulligan) at the start of the century, and now the place is officially known as Joyce Tower. It houses such Joycean effects as letters, a walking stick, and a cigar case.

Location: Sandycove. ☎ 01-280-9265. DART: Sandycove Station. Bus: 8. Admission: €3.50 ($3.30) adults, €2.50 ($2.35) under 18, €2 ($1.90) under 12. Open: April through October, Monday through Saturday 10 a.m. to 5 p.m., Sunday 2 to 6 p.m. Suggested visit: 1 hour.

Green on green: Dublin's top golfing spots

Just because you're visiting a major city doesn't mean you can't get a few rounds in. Here are my top picks near Dublin:

✔ **St. Margaret's:** One of the hosts of the Irish Open, this is a new, challenging, and exciting course of the highest standard, with an infamously difficult finishing hole.

Location: Stephubble, St. Margaret's, County Dublin. ☎ 01-864-0400. E-mail: Stmarggc@indigo.ie. Par: 73. Fees: €50 ($47.50) for 18 holes in the summer, €31.25 ($29.70) in the winter.

✔ **Portmarnock:** This area was home of the first Irish Open in 1889 and was renovated and reopened in the early 1990s. It's a natural golf course, incorporating the rugged landscape of the region rather than being purpose-built.

Location: Portmarnock, County Dublin. ☎ 01-846-2968. E-mail: secretary@portmarnockgolfclub.ie. Par: 72. Fees: €81.25 ($77.20) midweek, €100 ($95) weekends.

✔ **Royal Dublin:** Situated on man-made North Bull Island in Dublin Bay, only 4 miles from the center of Dublin, this is a championship course that has offered exciting play among great scenery for over 100 years.

Location: North Bull Island, Doillymount, Dublin 3. ☎ **01-833-6346** or 01-833-1236. E-mail: royaldublin@clubi.ie. Par: 72. Fees: €82.50 ($78.35) mid-week, €100 ($95) weekends.

Seeing Dublin by Guided Tour

Unless you're traveling with someone who knows the city, taking a tour may be worthwhile. The tours I've listed here are entertaining and fun.

If you want something more independent, there are lots of self-guided tours you can take in Dublin as well. The **Rock 'n' Roll Trail** focuses on contemporary Irish music like U2, Sinead O'Connor, and Chris de Burgh. The **Georgian Trail** covers five 18th-century squares, surrounded by period homes. The **Old City Trail** concentrates on the medieval area of Dublin. And the **Cultural Trail** covers the city's impressive architecture. Maps are available at the **Dublin Tourism Board** on Suffolk Street. You can also get the information online at www.visitdublin.com/tours trails.htm. Give yourself an afternoon for each tour.

Jameson's Literary Pub Crawl

Literature was never so much fun! This is a fabulous idea, done exceptionally well. Two Irish actors combine talent and comedy for 2½ hours of pure entertainment. They'll take you to pubs of literary fame and interesting stops along the way, the whole time superbly acting out tidbits from famous Irish lit. If you pay attention, there's even a chance to win some prizes at the end. I highly recommend this one — it's so good I did it twice!

Tours generally run every evening during the summer (April—Oct) and in the winter (Nov—March) Thur–Sun starting at 7:30 p.m. as well as Sun at noon year-round. Tickets can be purchased a half-hour in advance at The Duke (Duke Street, off Grafton), where the tour begins. Information: ☎ *01-670-5602. Be sure to call, because times sometimes change seasonally. E-mail:* info@dublin pubcrawl.com. *Internet:* www.dublinpubcrawl.com. *Price: €10 ($9.50) adults, €8 ($7.60) students. Suggested visit: About 3 hours.*

Traditional Irish Music Pub Crawl

Learn the story of Irish music while listening to a professional musician perform some of the songs that made the Celts famous. You don't have to know the music beforehand, but you'll probably want to learn some when it's over. You'll be taken to four musical watering holes in the city. A fun evening!

Tours run nightly during the summer and Fri and Sat nights in the winter (no tours in Dec or Jan), leaving from the Oliver St. John Gogarty Pub in Temple Bar (corner of Fleet and Anglesea streets) at 7:30 p.m. Arrive early. Information: ☎ *01-478-0193. Internet:* www.musicalpubcrawl.com. *Price: €7.50 ($7.10) adults, €6.25 ($5.95) students and seniors.*

Attractions around County Dublin

Fry Model Railway Museum **3**	Newbridge House and Park **1**
Glasnevin Cemetery **6**	Portmarnock Golf Course **4**
Joyce Tower and Museum **7**	Royal Dublin Golf Course **5**
Malahide Castle **3**	St. Margaret's Golf Course **2**
National Botanic Gardens **6**	

Historical Walking Tours

This is a great way to get an interesting and historical perspective of the city. It's called the "Seminar on the Street" and explains the main features of Irish history. The tour is led by history grad students from Trinity and covers Old Parliament House, Dublin Castle, City Hall, Christ Church, and Temple Bar, with entertaining commentary and insight along the way. During the summer, new "special tours" include The Birth of the Irish State (Monday and Friday), Architecture and Society (Tuesday and Thursday), and Sex and the City (Wednesday, Saturday, and Sunday).

Tours run daily at 11 a.m. and 3 p.m. from May to Sept with the special tour at noon. From April to Oct tours run Fri, Sat, and Sun at noon. Leaves from the front gate of Trinity College on College Street, Dublin. Information: ☎ 01-878-0227. E-mail: tours@historicalinsights.ie. *Price: €10 ($9.50) adults, €8 ($7.60) students, seniors, and children.*

Glasnevin Cemetery Walking Tours

Here lie such famous figures as Michael Collins, Charles Stewart Parnell, and Brendan Behan, and you can make it your final stop, too! This is a fine resting place after a day of sightseeing, and you'll learn tons more about Irish history. The grounds feature beautiful sculpture and hand-carved faces of high kings and queens of Ireland. The guide, Shane MacThomas, really knows his stuff.

Tours meet at the main entrance of the cemetery at 2:30 p.m. on Wed and Fri. Information: ☎ 01-830-1133. Internet: www.glasnevin-cemetery.ie. *Take Bus 19. 19A, 13, 40, 40A. Price: Free.*

Hop on–Hop off Bus Tours

I definitely recommend this tour, which is perfect if you want some tour-like guidance but also want the freedom to take as much time as you want checking out the sights. Pretty much every attraction the city has to offer is at one of the bus stops, and there's commentary throughout. The tour takes 1 hour and 15 minutes if you just ride the bus straight through, but you can, as the name says, hop on and hop off, stretching the tour out to a whole day. Some attractions offer discounts for people taking this tour.

All tours leave from Dublin Bus, 59 Upper O'Connell Street, Dublin 1. ☎ 01-872-0000. Internet: www.dublinbus.ie. *Runs every 30 minutes weekdays and every 15 minutes weekends. Credit cards accepted. Price: €7.50 ($7.10) adults, €3.75 ($3.55) child.*

Viking Splash Tours

The newest kid on the tour block opened in 2000 to instant popularity; in fact, one out of three patrons was a Dubliner. Two things make this 75-minute tour a stand out from the competition: First, you're riding around in a WWII amphibious vehicle (called a *duck*) that at one point leaves the normal tourist trail to sail along the Grand Canal. Second, the Viking theme doesn't just color the history trivia along the tour; all riders are given Viking helmets and encouraged to roar at the rival tour groups. Kids, I promise, will not be bored.

All tours leave from Bull Alley beside the gardens of St. Patrick's Cathedral, around the corner from the tour's new ticket office and gift store at 64–65 Patrick St., Dublin 8. ☎ 01-453-9185. Internet: www.vikingsplashtours.com. Runs every half hour on the half hour between 10 a.m. and 5 p.m. every day in the summer and skips Tuesday during the off-season. Price: €13.50 ($12.80) adult, €7.50 ($7.10) child, €45 ($42.75) family.

Dublin Bus Coastal Bus Tours

The two best tours that cover the outlying areas of Dublin are run by Dublin Bus. The "Coast and Castle Tour" travels north and covers the fishing villages of Dublin Bay, the coastline, and Malahide Castle. It leaves at 10 a.m. daily. The "South Coast Tour" covers the port towns of Dun Laoghaire, and Dalkey, Killiney Bay, and the Wicklow Mountains. It leaves at 11 a.m. and 2 p.m. daily.

Tours depart from 59 Upper O'Connell St., Dublin 1. ☎ 01-872-0000. Price: €15 ($14.25) adult, €7.50 ($7.10) under 14.

Suggested One-, Two-, and Three-Day Sightseeing Itineraries

If you just have **one day,** start off with breakfast at Bewley's on Grafton Street. Next, do some shopping on Grafton Street, the main shopping area in the city, and take in the Molly Malone statue at the end of the street, across from Trinity. Walk around Trinity's campus and see the Book of Kells.

From there, walk over the O'Connell Street Bridge, up to the historic Grand Post Office, back over the Ha'Penny Bridge, and then across Dame Street to grab traditional fish and chips at Leo Burdocks — the most famous chipper in the city.

Next, visit Dublin Castle (across the street from the chipper). Go back across Dame for Christ Church Cathedral and then down the road to St. Patrick's Cathedral.

You've worked up an appetite for traditional Irish fare, so it's dinner at Boxty House in Temple Bar and then a pub crawl for Irish music and dancing for as long as you can stay out.

If you have **two days,** follow the previous itinerary for day one. On your second day, have breakfast at your hotel. Put on your comfy walking shoes and make a morning stop at a local shop for some fruit, cheese, bread, and a couple beers for an Irish picnic later in the day.

Head out to South Circular Road and make your first stop the Modern Art Museum, and then go across the street to the infamous Kilmainham Gaol.

Your next stop is Phoenix Park and the Dublin Zoo. Take a breather in the park for your picnic. On your way back toward the city, take the Guinness tour and visit the Hop Store.

Back in the city, treat yourself to a nice dinner at the upscale chain Fitzer's — the one on the lovely Merrion Square. In the evening, do the Literary Pub Crawl that starts at Duke's off Grafton Street.

If you have **three days,** follow the previous itineraries for days one and two. On your third day, after breakfast, make your way to the north side of the River Liffey and pop into the famous Abbey Theatre and the Garden of Remembrance at the top of O'Connell Street. Next head to Parnell Square to see the Dublin Writers Museum and the Wax Museum.

Hop over the Ha'Penny Bridge to Temple Bar and have an authentic pub lunch at one of the pubs, and then head back across the River Liffey to take in the old Jameson Distillery and Collins Barracks.

Have dinner in Temple Bar at the Elephant & Castle. Finally, cross over the Ha'Penny again for upscale cocktails at Zanzibar and Pravda.

Shopping in Dublin

Dublin is the shopping mecca of Ireland. Within the city limits you can easily find all those items that have made Ireland famous, like Donegal tweed, Waterford Crystal, Belleek china, and Claddagh rings.

Locating the best shopping areas

There are two main shopping areas in Dublin. The first, on the North side of the River Liffey, is the **Henry Street–Mary Street area,** at the corner of O'Connell at the GPO. You can find what you need along this gauntlet of department stores and smaller shops, even down to the week's groceries. **Moore Street,** just off the main shopping drag, offers a daily open-air market where you'll find plenty of the freshest (and cheapest) fruits and vegetables in the city. You'll hear the perfected lilt of the vendors hawking their wares — a Dublin attraction in its own right.

Dublin Shopping

Anthony Antiques **10**
Antique Trade Services **2**
Books Upstairs **16**
Brown Thomas **7**
Butler Antiques **23**
Carrolls of Dublin **19**
Cathach Books **9**
Celtic Note Music Shop **12**
Claddagh Records **17**
DESIGNyard Retail Gallery **20**
Dublin Woolen Mills **22**
Dunnes Stores **3**
Fred Hanna Bookstore **14**
Greene's Bookstore **11**
Guinness Storehouse **1**
House of Ireland **13**
The Irish Historical Picture
    Company **21**
John Farrington **6**
Kevin & Howlin **15**
Powerscourt Townhouse
    Shopping Centre **5**
Rainbow Crafts **4**
Temple Bar Outdoor
    Food Market **18**
Walton's **25**
Waterstone's Bookstore **24**
Weir and Sons **8**

To Airport ↗

Mountjoy Square

0 1/4 mi
0 0.25 km
N

Phibsborough

Dominick St.

Dorset St.

Parnell Square East

Parnell Square West

Ballybough Rd.

Portland Row

Constitution Hill

Bolton St.

Capel St.

Green St.

Arran St. E

Summerhill

O'Connell St.

Parnell St.

Lwr. Gardiner St.

Upr. Gardiner St.

Sean Mac Dermott St.

Railway St.

Amiens St.

CONNOLLY

Central Bus Station

Inner Dock

George's Dock

25

Church St.

Mary's Lane

Mary St.

Henry St.

Earl St. N.

Talbot St.

Beresford Place

Customs House

Custom House Quay

24

Liffey St.

Millennium Bridge

O'Connell Bridge

Lwr. Abbey St.

Eden Quay

Butt Bridge

L i f f e y

Gratton Bridge

Abbey St.

Ha'penny Bridge

23

Burgh Quay

City Quay

TARA ST.

Talbot Memorial Bridge

Hanover St.

Four Courts

Richmond Bridge

Ormond Quay Upr.

21 22

Ormond Quay Lwr.

R i v e r

Wellington Quay

Aston Quay

Inns Quay

Merchants Qy.

Wood Qy.

Essex Qy.

Essex St. E.

Temple Bar

Fleet St.

Anglesea St.

Temple Ln.

Townsend St.

Pearse St.

DART

Whitworth Bridge

Lord Edward

(i) 20 19 18

Dame St.

17

16

Westmoreland

College Green

College St.

Trinity College

Westland Row

PEARSE ST.

High St.

Dublin Castle

Ship St.

Exchequer St.

Suffolk St.

(i)

15 14 13

Nassau St.

College Green

Fenian St.

Francis St.

The Coombe

St. Patrick's Park

Golden Ln.

Great Georges St.

William St.

King St.

Aungier St.

York St.

West

6

5

4

3

7 Duke St.

8

9

Anne St.

Dawson St.

10

12

11

Kildare St.

Leinster House

Leinster St. North

Merrion Square

Pembroke St.

2

Bride St.

Wood

Kevin St.

North

St. Stephen's Green

South

Merrion Row

Lwr. Baggot St.

Lad Lane

New Row

New St. Patrick St.

Lower Kevin St.

Cuffe St.

Camden St.

Camden Row

Richmond St.

Harcourt S.

Hatch St.

Lower Leeson St.

Fitz-william Square

Blackpitts

Clanbrassil St.

Lombard St.

Herbesbury St.

Long Lane

Adelaide Rd.

Circular Rd.

Fitzwilliam St.

Church ✝
DART Station ⬭
Information (i)
Post Office ✉

For the more image-conscious, there's **Grafton Street** on the south side of the River Liffey. Here you'll find trendy boutiques and big-name fashions on a perpetually busy pedestrian street. Things tend to cost more here than on the north side — you pay for being in a chic area. Check out the **Guinness clothing store** or Ireland's chichi department store, **Brown Thomas.** Having a cup of tea and people-watching from Bewley's Cafe is a fun way to spend time here — it's like getting your own personal fashion show!

Of course, there are other places to shop aside from these two main areas. If you're looking for funky secondhand fashions, go directly to **Temple Bar,** where you'll also find eclectic jewelry and art, modern home furnishings, and every kind of music there is.

If your idea of shopping consists mostly of pampering yourself, the **Powerscourt Townhouse Shopping Centre,** 59 S. William St., Dublin 2 (☎ 01-679-4144), is for you. This restored Georgian townhouse is home to **The Crafts Council of Ireland.** There are daily piano concerts and shops ranging from clothes boutiques to antique shops.

Finding Ireland's best wares

Known the world over for its handmade products and fine craftsmanship, Ireland offers many unique shopping opportunities. Dublin, as Ireland's commercial center, is a one-stop source for the best shopping in Ireland.

Antiques

There are two main areas of concentration for antique dealers: **Francis Street** (between Thomas Street West and the Coombe) and **Dawson-Molesworth streets** (between St. Stephen's Green and Trinity College). The following places are some of your best bets for quality and value:

- ✔ **The Irish Historical Picture Company,** 5 Lower Ormond Quay, Dublin 1 (☎ 01-872-0144; E-mail: info@irishhistoricalpics.ie), is a vast treasure trove of photographs documenting the life of Ireland since the invention of the camera in every region and theme you can imagine.

- ✔ **Butler Antiques,** 14 Bachelor's Walk, Dublin 1, along the north quays (☎ 01-873-0296), offers a great variety and some good bargains.

- ✔ **Anthony Antiques,** 7 Molesworth St., Dublin 2 (☎ 01-677-7222), specializes in late 19th-century furniture and brass.

- ✔ **Antique Trade Services,** 17 Marks Alley W., Dublin 8, off Francis Street (☎ 01-454-1143), is the place for keen bargain hunters.

Books

Like any section of a city that surrounds a college campus, there are loads of good bookstores near Trinity College. You'll find works of Irish writers that may be hard to find at home.

- ✔ **Waterstone's,** Jervis Centre, Mary Street, Dublin 1 (☎ 01-679-1415), is pretty much the Barnes & Noble of the Emerald Isle.

- ✔ **Fred Hanna,** 29 Nassau St., Dublin 2 (☎ 01-677-1255), is a family-run business with an excellent selection and some secondhand books.

- ✔ **Greene's,** 16 Clare St., Dublin 2 (☎ 01-676-2554), was mentioned in Joyce's *Ulysses* and boasts a huge Irish literature section.

- ✔ **Books Upstairs,** 36 College Green and Dame Street, across from the Trinity College front entrance, Dublin 2 (☎ 01-679-6687), has bargains and a great selection in the arts and humanities.

- ✔ **Cathach Books,** 10 Duke St., off Grafton Street, Dublin 2 (☎ 01-671-8676), has one of Dublin's most thorough stocks of Irish literature.

Clothes

You don't have to go all the way to the Aran Islands or Donegal for authentic Irish knitwear. At these stores, you can find the real McCoy!

- ✔ **Dublin Woolen Mills,** 41 Lower Ormond Quay, Dublin 1, on the north end of the Ha'Penny Bridge (☎ 01-677-5014), has everything from traditional sweaters to kilts, shawls, and scarves.

- ✔ **Kevin & Howlin,** 31 Nassau St., Dublin 2 (☎ 01-677-0257), sells authentic handwoven tweed jackets and hats for men and women.

- ✔ **House of Ireland,** 37 Nassau St., at the corner of Dawson Street, Dublin 2 (☎ 01-677-7949), is a premier shop that sells everything authentically Irish — for a price. You can buy Waterford Crystal, china, jewelry crafted with traditional symbols, woolens, housewares, and more.

Crafts and jewelry

A surge of demand for jewelry and crafts with a Celtic flair is occurring, so if you're looking for the perfect set of wedding bands engraved with the Claddagh symbol or a pendant with the Tara harp, you're sure to find it. The following stores are a great place to start your hunt for all jewelry and crafts Irish:

- ✔ **DESIGNyard Retail Gallery,** 12 E. Essex St., Dublin 2, along Temple Bar's main thoroughfare (☎ 01-677-8453), stocks exquisite and generally affordable contemporary Irish-designed jewelry, textiles, glass, and earthenware.

✔ **Brown Thomas,** 92 Grafton St., Dublin 2 (☎ **01-605-6666**), stocks Irish fashion and giftware.

✔ **Rainbow Crafts,** Westbury Hotel Mall, off Grafton, Dublin 2 (☎ **01-677-7632**), is a great place for European-designed toys and games, and handmade Irish dolls.

✔ **Weir and Sons,** 96 Grafton St., at Wicklow Street, Dublin 2 (☎ **01-677-9678**), sells fine jewelry, Waterford Crystal, silver, leather, and watches in elegant showcases.

✔ **House of Ireland,** Corner of Dawson and Nassau streets, Dublin 2 (☎ **01- 677-7949**), stocks Aran sweaters, Irish tweed, and Celtic jewelry.

✔ **John Farrington,** 32 Drury St., Dublin 2 (☎ **01-679-1899**), is a good bet for vintage jewelry, from Georgian silver earrings to Victorian lockets.

Food

If you've fallen in love with that fabulous and fresh Irish food, take some home:

✔ **Temple Bar Outdoor Food Market,** Meetinghouse Square in Temple Bar, with entrances on East Essex and Eustace streets, Dublin 2 (☎ **01-677-2255**), has Irish gourmet and organic food including delicacies like Chez Emily's chocolates, Llewellyn Apple farm's cider and Noirin Kearney's breads — the kind of goods you won't find in Marks & Spensers. It's open year-round on Saturdays.

✔ **Dunnes Stores,** St. Stephen's Green Shopping Centre, Dublin 2 (☎ **01-478-0188**), stock sausages and vacuum-packed smoked salmon at better prices than you'll find at the airport.

Music and musical instruments

If you're hoping to master the sounds of the traditional session you heard at the pub last night, first you need the instruments. Start with an Irish tin whistle or bodhrán (*bow*-rahn) drum. If you're not that adventurous, just buy a CD!

✔ **Celtic Note Music Shop,** 12 Nassau St., Dublin 2 (☎ **01-670-4157**), is a great place to find any type of Irish music, from traditional to contemporary.

✔ **Claddagh Records,** 2 Cecilia St., Temple Bar, Dublin (☎ **01-677-0262**), specializes in folk and traditional Irish music.

✔ **Walton's,** 2–5 North Frederick St., Dublin 1 (☎ **01-874-7805**), and 69–70 South Great Georges St., Dublin 2 (☎ **01-475-0661**), stocks harps, whistles, pipes, bodhráns, and cassettes and books to help you learn to play them.

Souvenirs

You just can't go home empty-handed! Even if it's just a little shot glass or paper model of an Irish cottage, it wouldn't be a vacation without these goofy reminders. Here are two great places to find the souvenirs you're seeking:

- ✔ **Carrolls of Dublin,** 4 Merchants Arch, Dublin 2 (☎ 01-671-0047), is the hands-down winner for Irish and Guinness souvenirs, from T-shirts to authentic pint glasses and anything else you can imagine, all at better prices than the many specialty shops.

- ✔ **Guinness Storehouse,** St. James's Gate, Dublin 8 (☎ 01-408-4800; Internet: www.guinness-storehouse.com), stocks all things Guinness, from posters and slippers to clocks and candles.

Hitting the Pubs and Enjoying Dublin's Nightlife

Pubs play an integral part in Irish culture, and nowhere is this better represented than in Dublin. Whether you're looking for a warm and smoky traditional enclave where older patrons know each other by name or you're in search of a sleek, neo-Celtic bar that proudly represents the cosmopolitan edge of the city, Dublin has it all.

James Joyce put it best in *Ulysses,* in this thought that flitted through the head of his character Leopold Bloom: "Good puzzle would be cross Dublin without passing a pub." Rather than make you search out the best among Dublin's 1,000 pubs, I've taken on the pleasant task of finding some of the finest.

Pulling a pint: Pub life

Mulligan's

This is an authentic old Dublin pub and favorite watering hole for the journalists of the nearby *Irish Times* newspaper. JFK drank here as a young European correspondent for the Hearst newspapers in 1945 and again when he visited as president. It's also mentioned in *Ulysses.*

8 Poolbeg St. (off south quays near O'Connell Bridge), Dublin 2. ☎ 01-677-5582. Bus: 5, 7, 7A, 7X, 8.

Dublin Nightlife

Church ✝
DART Station ⬭
Information ⓘ
Post Office ✉

McKee Barracks
Dublin Zoo
Garda HQ
Dublin Zoo
PHOENIX PARK
Cricket Ground
Main Rd
Infirmary Rd
North Circular Rd
Oxmantown Rd
Aughrim St
Prussia St
Manor St
Kirwan
Grangegorman Upper
St. Brendan's Hospital
St. Lawrence Hospital
Hospital
Brunswick St. North
North King St.
Arbour Hill
Department of Defence
Montpelier Hill
Collins Barracks
Blackhall Place
Queen St.
Smithfield St.
Bow St.
Parkgate St.
King's Bridge
Benburb St.
Victoria's Bridge
Ellis Quay
Arran Quay
Liffey
Wolfe Tone Quay
Victoria Quay
Queen's Bridge
Usher's Quay
Heuston Station
St. John's Rd.
West Hospital
Island St.
Bonham St.
Bridgefoot St.
Cook St.
St. Patrick's Hospital
Military Rd.
Steven's Ln.
Guinness Brewery
Thomas St. West
Cornmarket
THE LIBERTIES
St. James's St.
Rainsford St.
Meath St.
St. Patrick's Hospital
Basin St. Upper
Bond St.
Robert St.
Bellevue
Earl St. S.
Pimlico
St. Kevin's Hospital
Marrowbone Ln.
Cork St.
Ardee St.
Grand Canal Bank
South Circular Rd.
Brown St.
Grand Canal
Barn St.
Dolphin's
Hospital
Phoenix Park
Liffey
DUBLIN
Area of detail
Dublin Bay

Abbey Theatre **4**
Auld Dubliner **16**
The Ambassador Movie
Theatre **2**
The Brazen Head **10**
The Bridge **32**
The Da Club **28**
The Duke **29**
The Foggy Dew **20**
Gate Theatre **1**
Ha'penny Ha Ha **15**
Harcourt Hotel **26**
Irish Film Centre **14**
Judge Roy Beans **30**
The Kitchen **12**
Lannigans **6**
The Left Bank Bar **19**
The Long Hall **23**
Mulligan's **34**
Murphy's Laughter Lounge **7**
O'Brien's **21**
O'Donoghues **27**
O'Neill's **31**
Oliver St. John Gogarty **18**
Olympia Theatre **13**
The Palace **33**
The Plough **5**
Pravda **8**
Scholar's **25**
The Stag's Head **22**
Temple Bar **17**
Turk's Head Chop House **11**
Virgin Cinema **3**
Whelan's Pub **24**
Zanzibar **9**

The Brazen Head

The Brazen Head claims to be the oldest pub in Dublin. That may or may not be true, but certainly many a pint has been pulled here since its opening in 1198! The unusual name comes from a story about a bold woman who was so curious during one of the country's many rebellions that she stuck her head out of the window — only to have it chopped off! There's live music every night.

20 Lower Bridge St., Dublin 8. ☎ *01-679-5186. Bus: 78A, 79, 90.*

Oliver St. John Gogarty

This popular pub is named for a friend of James Joyce who became the model for Buck Mulligan, a flip character in *Ulysses*. Check out the great lunch buffet.

58 Fleet St., Temple Bar, Dublin 2. ☎ *01-671-1822. Internet:* www.oliver gogartys.com. *Bus: 46, 46A, 46B, 63, 150.*

The Plough

Appropriately across from the Abbey Theatre, this pub was named for Sean O'Casey's *The Plough and the Stars*. The play opens in a pub and dramatizes the Easter Rising of 1916. Drop in for a pint after checking out the theater.

28 Lower Abbey St., Dublin 1. ☎ *01-874-0971. Bus: 29A, 31, 31A, 31B, 32, 32A, 37, 38, 42A, 42B, 51A, 70, 70X, 130.*

The Duke

One of Michael Collins's secret meeting places during the independence movement, The Duke is now decorated in a classic Georgian style. The pub features cozy fires, a maze of rooms, and portraits of Irish literary figures.

9 Duke St. (off Grafton Street), Dublin 2. ☎ *01-679-9553. Bus: 10, 11A, 11B, 13, 20B.*

A Temple Bar pub crawl

Some of the city's best pubs are all located within a stumble of each other in Temple Bar, making the area perfect for a pub crawl. The narrow, cobbled streets between Trinity College and Christ Church Cathedral are nice paths between some fun and classic pubs. Here are some great pubs to include in your crawl: **Auld Dubliner,** 24–25 Temple Bar (☎ 01-677-0527); **Oliver St. John Gogarty,** 57–58 Fleet St. (☎ 01-671-1822); **Temple Bar,** 47 Temple Bar (☎ 01-672-5287); **Foggy Dew,** 1 Upper Fownes St. (☎ 01-677-9328); and for late night, **The Left Bank Bar,** Anglesea Street (☎ 01-671-1822), or **O'Brien's,** 40 Dame St. (☎ 01-677-8816).

The Stag's Head

It's hard to stand out as an exceptional pub in a city that houses nearly 1,000, but The Stag's Head is a landmark. Its Victorian decor includes a massive mahogany bar and stained glass that'll wow you. The food's great — often called the best pub grub in town.

1 Dame Court, Dublin 2. ☎ 01-679-3701. Bus: 21A, 50, 50A, 78, 78A, 78B. Look for the mosaic stag head inlaid into the sidewalk on Dame Street, pointing the way.

O'Neill's

This is a labyrinth of a pub, with many cozy corners and rooms to settle into. Once a hangout of Samuel Beckett's, O'Neill's is now a favorite of students and professors alike, who ramble over from nearby Trinity College. At night it's bound to turn into a noisy, smoky college bar, though, so be warned.

2 Suffolk St. (across from the Dublin Tourism Office), Dublin 2. ☎ 01-679-3614. Bus: 5, 7A, 8, 15A, 15B, 15C, 46, 55, 62, 63, 83, 84.

The Long Hall

Rumored to have the longest bar in the city, The Long Hall is a gorgeous specimen of a pub. There's a vast array of antique clocks, and plenty of cozy compartments (or *snugs*) to get lost in. It backs up to Dublin Castle, so stop in on your way!

51 S. Great George's St., Dublin 2. ☎ 01-475-1590. Bus: 50, 50A, 54, 56, 77.

Scholar's

The spacious bar at Scholar's, a restored all-boy's National School, has a giant screen that offers a perfect view from any seat of the latest football (read: soccer), rugby, hurling, or Gaelic football matches.

Donovan's Lane, off Clanbrassil Street, below St. Patrick's Cathedral, Dublin 8. ☎ 01-453-2000.

Sipping a cocktail: Hip bars

Zanzibar

From the beauty and style of the people inside, you'd think patrons of chic Zanzibar were trying to look as gorgeous as the fabulous decor. It's the hottest of Dublin's hot spots.

35 Lower Ormond Quay, Dublin 1 (facing the River Liffey). ☎ 01-878-7212.

Pravda

The head of the cool department, Pravda is where the fashion-conscious assemble. The decor is grand and Soviet-esque, and there are plenty of couches. Lines reach the Ha'Penny Bridge on weekends.

35 Liffey St. Lower, Dublin 1 (north side of the Ha'Penny Bridge). ☎ *01-874-0076.*

Pulling an all-nighter: Late-night bars

Still up for some partying after last call (at the shocking hour of 11:30 p.m.!)? I personally recommend the following extended-hours pubs:

- ✔ **The Bridge,** 10 Westmoreland St. (directly below O'Connell Street Bridge), Dublin 2. ☎ **01-670-8133.**

- ✔ **The Foggy Dew,** 1 Upper Fownes St., Temple Bar, Dublin 2. ☎ **01-677-9328.**

- ✔ **Judge Roy Beans,** 45 Nassau St. (across from Trinity College), Dublin 2. ☎ **01-679-7539.**

- ✔ **O'Brien's,** 40 Dame St., Dublin 2. ☎ **01-677-8816.**

- ✔ **Turk's Head Chop House,** Parliament Street, Temple Bar, Dublin 2. ☎ **01-679-9701.**

- ✔ **Whelan's Pub,** 25 Wexford St., Dublin 2. ☎ **01-478-0766.**

Tapping your feet: Traditional music venues

Want to hear real Irish music? I suggest the **Traditional Irish Music Pub Crawl** (listed under "Seeing Dublin by Guided Tour," earlier in this chapter), but here are a few pubs where you can listen to the traditional sounds.

- ✔ **O'Donoghues,** 15 Merrion Row, Dublin 2 (☎ **01-676-2807**), is a popular singing pub with traditional Irish music every night. No cover.

- ✔ **Temple Bar,** 47 Temple Bar, Temple Bar, Dublin 2 (☎ **01-672-5287**), is a place to hear often unrehearsed, impromptu, and exceptional traditional sessions. No cover.

- ✔ **Harcourt Hotel,** 60 Harcourt St., Dublin 2 (☎ **01-478-3677**), has traditional music Monday through Wednesday and Saturdays. Occasional cover.

- ✔ **Whelan's Pub,** 25 Wexford St., Dublin 2 (☎ **01-478-0766**), has a cozy, wooden interior with an excellent and eclectic mix of live music. Nice atmosphere. There's a cover charge when there's a band playing; it ranges from €8 to €25 ($7.60 to $23.75).

✔ **Lannigans,** O'Connell Bridge, Dublin 1, in the Clifton Court Hotel (☎ 01-874-3535), is a candlelit pub with real turf fires and music sessions every night. No cover.

There are, literally, hundreds of pubs in Dublin but if you've sipped your way through many of these top options and want more, the Dublin tourist office has created a decent guide at www.visitdublin.com/pubsrestaurants.htm.

Striking a pose: Club life

As in most European capitals, clubbing is taken seriously in Dublin and the hot spots are frequented by local fashionistas. Therefore, dress is pretty important, especially at the trendiest, most popular clubs — don't be surprised it you're turned away because of jeans or sneakers. Often there are cover charges (usually between €5 and €25), and you could need to show an ID. Clubs usually open just when buses stop running (about 11:30 p.m.), so expect to take a cab back to your hotel.

The Kitchen

Frequented by the terminally stylish, The Kitchen is an intimate if cavernous club and one of the coolest places to be seen, if you don't get lost. It boasts the best DJs and modern music. Located under the Clarence Hotel, it can be found at the end of the long line.

East Essex Street, Temple Bar, Dublin 2. ☎ *01-677-6635.*

The Da Club

This small club, located upstairs from a classy bar and restaurant, is known for its diverse nightly offerings: You may find live music, comedy, or a hot new DJ on the bill. Small means small, though — there's only one toilet.

2–5 Johnsons Place, Dublin 2. ☎ *01-670-3137.*

The Palace

A dance-a-holic's dream! Even wallflowers will be lured to the dance floor when the DJ spins favorites from the '70s and '80s. There's a large round bar in the center and intriguing music memorabilia on the walls. The crowd is often younger than in most clubs in the city.

21 Fleet St., Dublin 2. ☎ *01-677-9290.*

Yes, Virginia, there is other nightlife in Dublin

If pubs aren't your thing, you'll still find some mighty fine nightlife in Dublin. From Dublin's legendary theaters to cutting-edge cinema and gut-busting humor, you'll never lack for entertainment. Here are a few things you can do.

See a theatrical show

Dubs have long held theater in high reverence, and today the city's theaters often play host to quality plays that later find their way to the United States and England. Check out what's on at Ireland's most famous playhouse, the **Abbey Theatre,** Lower Abbey St., Dublin 1 (☎ 01-878-7222), where some of the biggest names in Irish drama (like Sean O'Casey and John Millington Synge) first flaunted their work. W. B. Yeats was one of the theater's founders. Or try the **Gate,** 1 Cavendish Row, Dublin 1 (☎ 01- 874-7483), which features classic Irish theater and is the place where Orson Welles got his professional start. If you're in the mood for some lighthearted fare, try the **Olympia Theatre,** 72 Dame St., Dublin 2 (☎ 01-478-2183), where you'll see big-name bands on European tour. Call the theaters or check the *Irish Times* newspaper for details about shows.

Go to the movies

Or, as the Irish say, "the cinema." There are lots of places to catch a flick in Dublin, and all types of filmgoers can find a theater that suits them. **The Ambassador,** Parnell St., Dublin 1 (☎ 01-872-7000), plays only one film at a time, in an old-fashioned theater complete with a balcony and red curtain that opens to a huge screen. **Virgin Cinema,** midway down Parnell Street, Dublin 1 (☎ 01-872-8444), is a streamlined and very modern multiplex, with nine screens and a full-service bar. The **Irish Film Centre (IFC),** 6 Eustace St., Temple Bar, Dublin 2 (☎ 01-679-3477), shows up-and-coming Irish independent cinema, European exclusives, and classics. A place for true film buffs, the IFC is as hip as it gets. There's a cafe, a lively bar, and a book-video shop on the premises (but the videos won't play in your VCR at home — they're formatted for European models).

Have a laugh

Everybody needs a good laugh, and one of the funnier choices includes **Murphy's Laughter Lounge,** Eden Quay, just off O'Connell on the north side of the River Liffey (☎ 01-874-4611), for stand-up. On Tuesday nights, hilarious improv that feeds off of the audience can be found at the **Ha'penny Ha Ha,** upstairs at the Ha'Penny Bridge Inn, 42 Wellington Quay in Temple Bar (☎ 01-677-0616). Prices vary.

Fast Facts: Dublin

Area Code

The area code for Dublin city and county is **01**. Only dial the area code if you're calling Dublin from outside the city. If you're calling from outside the country, you can drop the 0.

Currency Exchange

Currency exchange is indicated by the sign "Bureau de Change." You can exchange money at travel agencies, hotels, and some post offices, but the best rates are to be found at banks. If you have American Express Travelers Cheques you can exchange them without paying any commission at the AmEx office, 41 Nassau St., Dublin 2 (☎ 01-679-9000). A second AmEx exchange is located inside the Dublin Tourism Centre at St. Andrew's Church on Suffolk Street (☎ 01-679-9000).

Dentists

You can get emergency dental care at the Dental Hospital, Lincoln Place, Dublin 2 (☎ 01-612-7200).

Doctors

See "Hospitals."

Embassies and Consulates

United States, 42 Elgin Rd., Ballsbridge, Dublin 4 (☎ 01-668-8777); Canada, 65 St. Stephen's Green, Dublin 2 (☎ 01-478-1988); United Kingdom, 29 Merrion Rd., Dublin 4 (☎ 01-205-3700); Australia, Fitzwilton House, Wilton Terrace, Dublin 2 (☎ 01-676-1517).

Emergencies

Dial ☎ **999** for police, fire, or ambulance.

Hospitals

The two most prominent hospitals in Dublin are St. Vincent's Hospital, Elm Park, Dublin 4 (☎ 01-269-4533), on the south side of the city, and Beaumont Hospital, Beaumont Road, Dublin 9 (☎ 01-837-7755), on the north side.

Internet

The following Internet cafes have World Wide Web access and printing capabilities: Global Internet Cafe, 8 Lower O'Connell St., Dublin 1 (☎ 01-878-0295); Cyberia Internet Cafe, Temple Lane South, Temple Bar, Dublin 2 (☎ 01- 679-7607; Internet: www. cyberia.ie).

Pharmacies

O'Connell's Pharmacies at 55 Lower O'Connell St., Dublin 1 (☎ 01-873-0427), and 21 Grafton St., Dublin 2 (☎ 01-679-0467), have extended hours.

Police

Dial ☎ **999** in case of emergencies. The Dublin Garda (Police) headquarters is at Harcourt Square, Dublin 2 (☎ 01-475-5555).

Post Office

The General Post Office (GPO) is located on O'Connell Street, Dublin 1 (☎ 01-872-6666). Its hours are Monday through Saturday 8 a.m. to 8 p.m., Sunday 10 a.m.to 6 p.m. Branch offices, called An Post and noted with green storefront awnings, are generally open Monday through Saturday from 9 a.m. to 6 p.m.

Chapter 12

Easy Trips North of Dublin: Counties Meath and Louth

. . . .

In This Chapter

▶ Finding the best of the Celtic high crosses

▶ Exploring the Cooley Peninsula

▶ Trying out water sports in the Irish Sea

▶ Running through tombs like Indiana Jones

▶ Visiting the ancient capital of Ireland

. . . .

Collectively, Counties Meath and Louth are typically known as "the ancient land of the Celts." They're the country's hot spots for visiting prehistoric sites, such as ancient burial mounds and places where the old Irish High Kings held court. You can easily take day-trips from Dublin to both counties, which you may well think of as one destination because they're so complementary. But I've also listed a few good hotels in case you want to set up camp for a while.

What's Where?: Meath and Louth's Major Attractions

County Meath has a few of the biggest ancient religious and political attractions in Ireland — the ancient tombs of **Newgrange** and **Knowth** and the **Hill of Tara.** The heart of the area is the River Boyne, home of the famous battle of the same name and one of the region's most fought-over by the country's many invaders. All those invaders, from the Normans to the English, left their mark on the area. Other influences, from the ancient High Kings to Christianity, are evident, too. Ruins, religious sites, and exalted meeting places are just some of the evidence of how the area has been molded over the centuries. The history-rich towns of **Kells, Slane,** and **Trim** (with minor attractions like Slane Castle and Trim Castle) are the best towns for a stopover. Some of County Meath's highlights include

- ✔ **Newgrange and Knowth:** Ancient burial mounds where you can get a feel for really old history.
- ✔ **The Hill of Tara:** And no, this attraction has nothing whatsoever to do with *Gone with the Wind* — it's the ancient seat of Irish kings.

What **County Louth** lacks in big tourist attractions, it makes up for in history and the charm of small towns like **Dundalk** and **Drogheda.** These towns are the stomping grounds of legends such as Cuchulainn, Queen Maeve, and the great warrior Finn MacCool. My favorite part of Louth is the far northern area of the beautiful **Cooley Mountains** and **Peninsula** and the town of **Carlingford.** Although the rest of the county is not as picturesque as these areas, if you happen to be coming from Northern Ireland and have time to make the short Cooley drive, I guarantee you can have a few picture-worthy moments. So, be sure to catch

- ✔ **Dundalk and Drogheda:** Stop by for a pint in one of these charming little towns.
- ✔ **The Cooley Peninsula:** A gorgeous drive with great views of the Irish Sea and Carlingford Lough.

Touring Meath and Louth

Most visitors to Louth and Meath arrive by car, often on a day-trip from Dublin. Take the N2 north toward Slane and the N3 toward Navan and Kells. You can get to most major towns and attractions from these routes — just follow the signs. If you're heading directly to Louth from Dublin, take the N1 north toward Drogheda, Dundalk, and Newry. Most major towns and attractions are along that route. To get to the Cooley Peninsula from Dundalk, take the R173, which loops to the town of Newry.

Irish Rail (☎ 01-836-6222) has stops in the County Louth towns of Drogheda and Dundalk from Dublin.

Bus Eireann (☎ 01-836-6111) has year-round routes to Navan, Kells, Slane, Drogheda, Dundalk, Carlingford, and other smaller towns throughout the area. It also runs a year-round day tour of Newgrange and the Boyne Valley that begins in Dublin. The tour covers all the major sights, including the Hill of Tara. The tour runs May to September, Saturday and Sunday; October through April, Thursday and Saturday. It leaves Central Bus Station in Dublin at 10:00 a.m. and returns at 5:45 p.m. Information: ☎ 01-836-6111. Price: €21.25 ($20.20) adult, €11.25 ($10.70) children.

Counties Meath and Louth

ACCOMMODATIONS	ATTRACTIONS	SHOPPING
Ballymascanlon House Hotel **3**	Causey Farm **9**	Carlingford Adventure Centre **1**
Boyne Valley Hotel & Country Club **7**	Cooley Peninsula **2**	Mary McDonald Craft Studio **6**
Conyngham Arms **6**	Hill of Tara **8**	
The Old Rectory **4**	Knowth **7**	NIGHTLIFE
Station House Hotel **8**	Monasterboice **5**	McManus' **3**
DINING	Newgrange Farm **6**	O'Hare's **1**
Carrick House **10**	Newgrange **7**	Railway Bar **10**
The Gables **4**	Old Mellifont Abbey **7**	
Jordan's **1**		

Where to stay in Meath and Louth

Ballymascanlon House Hotel
$$$ **Dundalk, Louth**

Here you can stay in an authentic Victorian mansion for a moderate price. The house retains an old-world ambience, and rooms are in a traditional style, with antiques and Victorian touches. This hotel is a great place for golfers — complete with an 18-hole course on the grounds — and recent renovations have made way for a leisure center with a pool, Jacuzzi, tennis courts, and more. The hotel also features a restaurant that serves local meats, seafood, veggies from the garden, and a bar that generally plays Irish music on the weekends.

Dundalk, Louth. ☎ *042-937-1124. Fax: 042-937-1598. Internet:* www.global golf.com/ballymascanlon. *By car: N1 from Dublin. Rates:* €102–€145 *($96.90–$137.75) double. AE, DC, MC, V.*

Boyne Valley Hotel & Country Club
$$$ Drogheda, Louth

Though it's in Louth, this hotel is a great starting point for touring the sites of Newgrange, Knowth, and Mellifont Abbey (all located in nearby Meath). Beautiful gardens and woodlands surround the elegant house and make for a pleasant stroll or a great view from the large atrium. All rooms are spacious and have been smartly refurbished. Amenities include a pool. And the fish dishes served in the restaurant are as fresh as it gets; they're prepared from the catch of the Boyne River.

Drogheda. ☎ *041-983-7737. Fax: 041-983-9188. Internet:* www.boyne-valley-hotel.ie. *By car: N1 from Dublin. Rates:* €125–€150 *($118.75–$142.50) double. AE, DC, MC, V.*

Conyngham Arms
$$–$$$ Slane, Meath

Located near Newgrange and Knowth, the Arms is a good base from which to explore the Boyne Valley. The service at this family-run hotel is personable and friendly, and the four-poster beds are a nice touch. You'll think you're staying in a B&B rather than a hotel.

Slane, Meath. ☎ *800-44-UTELL, from the United States, or 041-982-4155. Fax: 041-982-4205. Internet:* www.destination-ireland.com/conyngham. *By car: N2 from Dublin. Rates:* €75–€106.30 *($71.25–$101) double. AE, DC, MC, V.*

The Old Rectory
$$ Ardee, Louth

You won't find a better deal for your euro than this lovely traditional B&B, which is the picture of Irish hospitality. Hostess Janie Jennings will likely welcome you in with a hot tea and homemade scones with gooseberry jam made from berries grown in her garden. Her son Paul loves to chat up the guests, and the rooms are comfortable, with large beds and bathrooms. Don't sleep in; the yummy breakfasts go above and beyond continental fare with hot cereals, fresh fruit, and special concoctions from the kitchen.

Kells Road, Ardee, Louth. ☎ *041-685-3320. Internet:* www.ardeeoldrectory.com. *By car: On the N2 or take the R173 from Dundalk. Rates:* €64 ($60.80) double.

Station House Hotel
$$ Kilmessan, Meath

Located near the Hill of Tara, this unique hotel was once a railway junction building and uses the old ticket office, luggage room, platforms, engine sheds, and signal box for various hotel functions. The rooms are comfortably furnished, the price is right, and the theme is interesting.

Kilmessan, Meath. ☎ *046-25-239. Fax: 046-25-588. Internet:* www.thestation househotel.com. *By car: N3 from Dublin to Dunshaughlin, turn left at end of village and follow signposts for Kilmessan. Rates:* €57 ($54.15) double. AE, DC, MC, V.

Where to dine in Meath and Louth

Carrick House
$–$$$ Kells, Meath   IRISH

The food is good, and the price is even better at this family restaurant and lounge. The service is not the swiftest, but they make up for that with generous portions and comfortable seating. The restaurant also has a nice policy of using local, hormone-free beef. The menu features plenty of variety, so everyone will be happy.

Kells (on the main road), Meath. ☎ *046-40-100. By car: Take the N3 from Dublin to Kells. Main courses:* €6.90–€13.15 ($6.55–$12.50). MC, V. Open: 12:30–10:00 p.m. daily.

The Gables
$$$–$$$$ Ardee, Louth   FRENCH

This fine, classically French restaurant goes out of its way to spoil you. From the service to the wine, everything is top-notch. It's high-class eating minus all the fuss. Specialties include snails in garlic butter, local prawns, venison, and, yes, pigeon. I must tell you: Pigeon is gamy and doesn't taste at all like chicken. I recommend The Gables for New Yorkers in particular.

Dundalk Road, Ardee, Louth. ☎ *041-685-3789. By car: On the N2 or take the R173 from Dundalk. Main courses:* €14.40–€27.50 ($13.70–$26.10). MC, DC, V. *Open: March–Sept daily 12:30–5:00 p.m. and 7–11 p.m. Off-season Sun lunch. Closed in Jan.*

Jordan's
$$$$ Carlingford, Louth   IRISH

Located in a renovated stone warehouse, this Irish restaurant overlooking Carlingford's harbor has excellent dishes made from locally and organically grown ingredients. The interior is classic — ornate wall fixtures, white tablecloths, and fresh flowers — the service top-notch, and the atmosphere casual. You can't go wrong ordering one of its award-winning fish dishes.

Newry Street, Carlingford, Louth. ☎ *042-937-3827. By car: N2 from Dublin. Main courses: €18.15–€30 ($17.25–$28.50). MC, V. Open: Daily 12:30–11:00 p.m.*

Enjoying the area's top attractions

Bru' na Boinne Visitor Centre (Newgrange and Knowth)
Donore, County Meath

This visitor center has combined two of the best sites in Meath into a historic and archeological stop well worth your time (allow about four hours to see everything). In addition to Newgrange Tumulus and Knowth, the center itself contains many interpretive displays about the rich history of the Boyne Valley as well as viewing areas of the Neolithic (New Stone Age) sites. Unlike in the past, you can no longer get direct access to Newgrange and Knowth. You must purchase tickets at the Visitor Centre and take its minibus shuttle to the sites.

More fun than informative, Newgrange Tumulus is a huge, impressively intact round mound — 200,000 tons of earth and stone covering a magnificent and well-preserved 5,000-year-old burial chamber. You enter through a low arch and make your way Indiana Jones–style down the long and narrow stone passage to the central burial chamber. Knowth is an even older and larger tomb, used from the Bronze Age through the Norman periods of Irish history. You can see two burial chambers filled with tomb art and 18 smaller satellite tombs with passages. If you have to choose between Newgrange and Knowth, I recommend Knowth — there's more to see inside, even though Newgrange is prettier from the outside.

Over the entrance stone of Newgrange is a roof box opening that allows light to slowly creep into the burial chamber during the winter solstice, filling the room for about 15 minutes. A sign of the new year or a clue to finding the lost ark? I don't know, because tours during the solstice are booked up years in advance.

Off N51, Donore, east of Slane, County Meath. ☎ *041-988-0300. By car: L21 off N1 from Drogheda or N2 from Slane. By bus: Bus Eireann (☎ 01-836-6111) takes a day tour of Newgrange and the Boyne Valley from Dublin. Admission: Centre and*

Newgrange: €3.75 ($3.55) adults, €2.50 ($2.35) seniors, €2 ($1.90) students and children, €10 ($9.50) family; Centre and Knowth: €2.50 ($2.35) adults, €2 ($1.90) seniors, €1.25 ($1.20) students and children, €6.25 ($5.95) family. Centre, Newgrange and Knowth: €6.25 ($5.95) adults, €4.50 ($4.25) seniors, €3 ($2.85) students and children, €16 ($15.20) family. Open: June to mid-Sept daily 9 a.m.–7 p.m., May and mid-Sept to the end of Sept daily 9:00 a.m.–6:30 p.m.; March, April, and Oct daily 9:30 a.m.–5:30 p.m.; Nov–Feb daily 9:30 a.m.–5:00 p.m. Restricted access for people with disabilities. Suggested visit: 4 hours.

Hill of Tara
South of Navan, County Meath

This Stone Age meeting house was once the seat of the High Kings and capital of Celtic Ireland. A large, round structure raised from the earth, it looks like something out of *The X Files,* and the atmosphere is just a bit creepy. The audiovisual presentation is interesting, but walking about this early Christian religious and political site is a close encounter of its own kind.

South of Navan off the main Dublin road (N3), County Meath. ☎ *046-25-903 May–Oct or* ☎ *041-24-488 Nov–April. By car: From Dublin, take the N3 toward Navan and look for signs beginning about 9 miles before reaching the town. Near the village of Kilmessan. Admission: €2 ($1.90) adults and seniors, €1 (95¢) students and children. Open: Mid-June to mid-Sept daily 9:30 a.m.–6:30 p.m., May to mid-June and mid-Sept to Oct daily 10 a.m.–5 p.m. Visitor center closed Nov–April, but you can still walk up the Hill. Restricted access for people with disabilities. Suggested visit: 45 minutes.*

Newgrange Farm
Slane, County Meath

This is your average working Irish farm turned tourist attraction, where the darn-friendly Redhouse family gives a tour of its farm, livestock, garden, and 17th-century buildings. You can hold a baby chick, watch a threshing machine in action, see a horse get a new pair of shoes, pet a donkey, and more. This attraction is definitely one for the kids, but adults can enjoy themselves as well, and maybe learn a few pointers for the herb garden at home.

Off N51, Slane, County Meath. ☎ *041-982-4119. By car: N2 from Dublin or N51 from Navan or Drogheda. Admission: €3.50 ($3.30) per person, €11.25 ($10.70) family. Open: April–Aug Mon–Sat 9:30 a.m.–5:30 p.m. Suggested visit: 1½ hours.*

Old Mellifont Abbey
Tullyallen, County Louth

Founded by St. Malachy in 1142, Mellifont was the first Cistercian monastery in Ireland. This historic house of worship was suppressed by

Henry VIII, then became a pigsty (literally), and later was the headquarters for William III during the Battle of the Boyne. The site is a peaceful and tranquil place. The unique *octagonal lavabo* (a washing trough for religious ceremonies) remains intact, along with several of the abbey's arches, all set along the River Mattock. The visitor center contains examples of masonry from the Middle Ages.

Tullyallen, Drogheda, County Louth. ☎ *041-982-6459 summer,* ☎ *041-988-0300 winter. By car: N1 from Dublin. Cost: €2 ($1.90) adults, €1.25 ($1.20) seniors, €1 (95¢) students and children. Open: May to mid-June and mid-Sept to mid-Oct daily 10 a.m.– 5 p.m., mid-June to mid-Sept daily 9:30 a.m.–6:30 p.m. Suggested visit: 1 hour.*

Monasterboice
Collon, County Louth

Throughout Meath and Louth you'll see more Celtic high crosses than you can shake a stick at. These imposing crosses, which began being erected in the eighth century, were status symbols for churches and monasteries. Beginning in the tenth century, they were decorated with biblical scenes. It's thought that the crosses were used as teaching tools to help the illiterate better understand the Bible. Two such remarkable ninth-century decorated High Crosses are the highlights of the sixth-century Monasterboice monastery, which was founded by St. Buithe, a follower of St. Patrick. Muiredach's Cross, one of the best examples of the popular Celtic crosses, depicts the Last Judgment and Old Testament scenes. The other cross (sometimes called the West cross) is one of the largest in Ireland. The rest of the area is rather unassuming, with its standard graveyard, round tower, and church ruins, but the crosses in particular make Monasterboice one of the most important religious sites in Ireland.

Off the main Dublin road (N1) near Collon, County Louth. By car: N1 from Dublin. Cost: Free. Open: Daylight hours. Suggested visit: 30 minutes.

Causey Farm
Kells, County Meath

Want to get your hands dirty in some old-fashioned Irish fun? The recently-opened Causey Farm gives you the opportunity to make your own brown bread and scones, cut up some turf in a bog, learn some set dancing and Gaelic, see a sheepdog demonstration, and have a traditional dinner. You'll spend the day learning, dancing, singing, and eating like a local in this ancient bogland, about 45 minutes out of town.

Fordstown, Navan, County Meath. ☎ *046-34-135 or 087-918-1180. Internet: www. causeyexperience.com. Located 4½ miles from Kells off the Kells-Athboy Road. Transportation will pick you up at Nassau Street (beside Trinity College) in Dublin at an arranged time and drop you off at 10 p.m. Cost: €45 ($42.75) per person including transportation, all your activities, entertainment, and dinner. Open: Fridays and Saturdays from May to Sept. Suggested visit: All day.*

Cooley Peninsula, Louth
Outside Dundalk, County Louth

This peninsula offers a great scenic drive with impressive views of the Irish Sea and Carlingford Lough. At one point, the road actually passes through the mountainside. The peninsula is the mythic home of legendary heroes, namely Cuchulainn and Finn MacCool. Dotted along the drive are *dolmen* (Neolithic tombs), forests, mountains, rivers, and quaint fishing villages. The largest village, Carlingford, is a good place to stop for a stretch and to see the ruins of King John's Castle or to visit the Holy Trinity Heritage Centre. Carlingford Lough, across which lies Northern Ireland, is a natural fjord from the Ice Age. Drive the route in a few hours or hike along Tain Trail out of Carlingford in an afternoon.

By car: R173 loops around the Peninsula, off N1 outside Dundalk. Suggested visit: 3 hours.

Shopping and other fun stuff to do

✔ **Mary McDonnell Craft Studio** (Slane, County Meath): Mary personally designs fine cushions, quilts, and wall hangings inspired by the legends and folklore of the Boyne Valley. Other treasures include ceramics, candles, leatherwork, and jewelry.

Location: 4 Newgrange Mall, Slane, Meath. (No phone.) By car: N2 from Dublin or N51 from Navan or Drogheda. Mary's shop is open most days in summer, but hours are very irregular. Because there's no phone, you'll just have to try your luck if you're in the area.

✔ **Carlingford Adventure Centre** (Carlingford, County Louth): Great outdoor fun — like windsurfing, kayaking, and sailing on Carlingford Lough or trekking and rock climbing in the Cooley Mountains — is what the Adventure Centre is all about. The center is fun for the whole family and the best way to experience the area's natural beauty.

Prices and schedules for activities vary. Location: Thosel Street, Carlingford, Louth. ☎ **042-937-3100.** By car: R173 from Dundalk, on the Cooley Peninsula. Open: Year-round.

Perusing Pub Life

McManus'

This family-run establishment is like three pubs in one. The Music Bar often hosts spontaneous traditional music sessions that keep your feet tapping. On cold days, make your way to the back Kitchen Bar, an intimate room with brick interior and a warm cast-iron stove. The Secret

Beer Garden's outdoor seating area has coal and turf fires burning year-round, as well as the occasional barbecue.

17 Seatown, Dundalk. Louth. ☎ *042-933-1632.*

O'Hare's

As part-grocery, part-pub, O'Hare's is a dying breed of places that combine a local watering hole with a neighborhood convenience store. But this popular place brings in the tourists for an even more unique attraction: the leprechaun in a glass case. (Judge its authenticity for yourself.) The pub also features traditional music on Wednesdays. The pub grub is good, but the house specialty — oysters — is a must-try. Simply scrumptious.

Carlingford, Louth (coming from Dundalk, take the first left off the main road and stay to the right until you see the beer garden; it may be easier to park on the main road and walk to the pub). ☎ *042-937-3106.*

Railway Bar

This charming pub is so full of warmth and character that the place often fills up quickly, but fear not: It has a conservatory that opens to a large walled garden out back to handle the overflow.

Kells, Meath. ☎ *046-40-215.*

Fast Facts: Counties Meath and Louth

Area Codes

042 and **046** for Meath, **042** and **041** for Louth.

Emergencies/Hospitals

Dial ☎ **999** for all emergencies. Louth County Hospital is on Dublin Road in Dundalk (☎ 042-933-4701).

Genealogical Resources

In Meath, contact the Meath Heritage Centre, Mill Street, Trim (☎ 046-36-633, Fax: 046-37-502). In Louth, contact MC Research Service, Seabank, Castlebellingham, Dundalk (☎ 042-937-2046; Fax: 042-937-2046).

Information

For visitor information in Meath, go to one of the tourist offices: Trim (☎ 046-37-111; open year-round), Navan (☎ 046-37-426; closed Oct–April), and Kells (☎ 046-49-336; closed Jan). E-mail: info@meathtourism.ie. For telephone directory assistance, dial ☎ 1190. For visitor information in Louth, go to the tourist office at Jocelyn Street, Dundalk (☎ 042-933-5484; Internet: www.louthholidays.com), open year-round. They can also provide reservation services. For telephone directory assistance, dial ☎ 1190.

Post Office

Clanbrassil Street, Dundalk, Louth (☎ 042-933-4444).

Chapter 13

Easy Trips South of Dublin: Counties Wicklow and Kildare

. . . .

In This Chapter

▶ Viewing homes and gardens no magazine could capture

▶ Exploring the Wicklow Mountains and the scenic Wicklow Way

▶ Enjoying high-class dining and accommodations you won't soon forget

▶ Making a pilgrimage to the home of Irish racing

▶ Discovering the history of the area at a pub

. . . .

*I*mmediately south of bustling Dublin, you find the beginnings of all that Irish green you've heard about your whole life. While County Wicklow's people trim all that lush greenery into beautiful gardens, County Kildare's citizens tend to feed theirs to the horses — the county is home to dozens upon dozens of horse farms, as well as racetracks.

What's Where?: Wicklow and Kildare and Their Major Attractions

County Wicklow is affectionately known as "The Garden of Ireland," and it's easy to see why. The county begins just barely out of Dublin's limits, but immediately the cityscape gives way to rural roads and stunning scenery. Wicklow makes for a great day-trip when staying in Dublin, but the area offers plenty of charming places to stay if you'd like to extend your visit.

Wicklow's eastern coast is studded with resort areas and harbor towns, where you can have a fine seafood dinner and stay in a family-run guesthouse to experience Ireland's famed hospitality. But it's County Wicklow's inland that will amaze you. To really get a feel for the area, you should take a walk on a stretch of the **Wicklow Way,** a signposted walking path that follows forest trails, sheep paths, and county roads from just outside Dublin all the way to Clonegal. Nestled among the hills are quaint, not-to-be-missed villages, plus some great attractions like the following:

✔ **Powerscourt House, Gardens, and Waterfall:** This sweeping estate has some of the finest gardens in all of Europe, as well as a beautifully preserved mansion and Ireland's highest waterfall.

✔ **Wicklow Mountains National Park:** Nearly 50,000 acres of nature.

✔ **Glendalough Round Tower and Monastery:** St. Kevin built this monastery in the sixth century, and the remains today give a little peek into how the Irish saved civilization.

✔ **The National Sea Life:** An aquarium and museum explain life in the ocean and bring you face to face with its wonders.

When you drive into **County Kildare,** you drive into horse country. Horse racing is an integral part of Irish culture, and Ireland is known and respected worldwide for its horse breeding. Much of that reputation stems from the work done with horses in County Kildare, where for years breeders have raised and raced some of the finest thoroughbreds the world has to offer.

If you're less than enthusiastic about horses, first, some advice: Don't admit it in these parts! Second, the area offers plenty of other interesting things for you to see. Horse- and non-horse-related attractions include

✔ **Irish National Stud and Japanese Gardens:** Visitors to this state-run stud farm can walk around the grounds and see the prize-winning horses being groomed and exercised, or visit the Horse Museum or the striking Japanese Gardens — one of the finest outside of Asia — which boast bonsai, bamboos, and cherry trees.

✔ **The Curragh:** Ireland's best-known racetrack is often referred to as the Churchill Downs of Ireland.

✔ **Celbridge Abbey Grounds:** Sitting along the River Liffey, these grounds were planted by the daughter of the Lord Mayor of Dublin in 1697 for Jonathan Swift.

✔ **Castletown House:** This impressive, stately, 18th-century house is a standout in Irish architecture.

✔ **Steam Museum:** This collection houses locomotive engines dating all the way back to 1797.

County Wicklow

Wicklow is green, green, green, and you can easily hit the highlights in a day or stick around to really get the flavor of the place. Many Dubliners go on vacation in Wicklow, especially in the area around the River Dargle. But that's not what makes the spot so well known. What's really given it immortality is its use in drinking songs. After all, can you think of another town name that rhymes so easily with the word *gargle?*

Counties Wicklow and Kildare

ACCOMMODATIONS
Annagh Lodge Guesthouse **5**
Curragh Lodge Hotel **7**
Druids Glen Marriott Hotel **14**
Glendalough Hotel **18**
Glenview Hotel **13**
Hillview House **4**
Hunter's Hotel **17**
Royal Hotel **10**
Slievemore **15**
The Sycamores B&B **4**
Tinakilly House **17**

DINING
Coopers **13**
Harbour View **4**
The Hungry Monk **13**
Mitchells of Laragh **18**
Red House Inn **5**
The Roundwood Inn **9**

ATTRACTIONS
Avondale House and
 Forest Park **19**
Castletown House **1**
Celbridge Abbey Grounds **2**
The Curragh **5**
Glendalough Round Tower
 and Monastery **18**
Irish National Stud and
 Japanese Gardens **6**
Killruddery House and
 Garden **11**
Meeting of the Waters **19**
The Millennium Forest **22**
Mt. Usher Gardens **16**
National Sea Life **10**
Powerscourt House
 and Gardens **12**
Russborough House **8**
Steam Museum **3**
Sugar Loaf Mountain **12**
Tullamore Dew **24**
Wicklow Mountains
 National Park **18**

SHOPPING
A La Campagne **17**
Avoca Handweavers **21**
Fisher's of
 Newtownmountkennedy **13**
Glendalough Woolen Mills **18**
Noritake Arklow
 Pottery Ltd. **23**

NIGHTLIFE
Cartoon Inn **19**
The Manor Inn **4**
The Meetings **20**
Old Court Inn **17**
Philip Healy's **17**
Silken Thomas **7**

Getting to and around Wicklow

If you're arriving by car, take the N11 (which becomes M11 periodically) south from Dublin toward Arklow. You can turn off along this route to reach most major towns and attractions. The **Dublin (Connolly Station)–Rosslare Harbour train line** (☎ **01-703-1843**) has stations in Bray, Greystones, Wicklow, Rathdrum, and Arklow. Dublin Area Rapid Transit (DART) extends as far as Greystones. **Dublin Bus** (☎ **01-872-000**) runs from City Centre to Dun Laoghaire and the Bray DART station. **Bus Eireann** (☎ **01-836-6111**) travels year-round between Bray, Wicklow, Arklow, Rathdrum, and Avoca.

Stena Sealink (☎ **01-204-7777**) travels from Holyhead, Wales, to Dun Laoghaire six to eight times a day. You can catch the DART or bus or rent a car at the port town.

Where to stay in Wicklow

Druids Glen Marriott Hotel
$$$–$$$$ Newtownmountkennedy

This new hotel, beautifully situated between the Irish Sea and the Wicklow mountains, has the distinction of being the first Marriott Hotel in Ireland, in case you're a fan of the chain. Built to five-star specifications, it's the best place to stay in the area in terms of service and accommodation. The rooms are larger than most, and the hotel has every amenity you can think of, plus a few you probably wouldn't, like a whirlpool, solarium, and steamroom in the pool area, and its own Enterprise Rent-a-Car desk. If you're a golfer you'll appreciate the location — on the 400-acre Druid's Glen Golf Resort.

Newtownmountkennedy. ☎ *01-287-0800. Fax: 01-287-0801. Internet:* www.marriot thotels.com. *By car: From Dublin, take the N11 national route toward Wexford. Turn off toward Newtownmountkennedy and follow the signs to Druids Glen. Rates:* €190–€310 ($180.50–$294.50) double. AE, MC, V.

Hunter's Hotel
$$$ Rathnew

This family-run hotel is one of Ireland's oldest coaching inns, offering views of breathtaking gardens and nearby mountains. Rooms are huge, with quality furniture and attractive art. Irish dishes, like Wicklow lamb, and fresh vegetables from the hotel's gardens are served in the restaurant. Blazing fires and antique furniture add to its charm.

Newrath Bridge, Rathnew. ☎ *0404-40-106. Fax: 0404-40-338. Internet:* www. hunters.ie. *By car: N11 from Dublin and take a left in Ashford village by the* *bridge and opposite Ashford House pub. Hunter's is 1½ miles (2km) from Ashford. Rates: €131.25–€150 ($124.70–$142.50) double. AE, DC, MC, V.*

Tinakilly House
$$$–$$$$ **Rathnew**

This small country-house hotel brings together everything you've heard about the grandeur and friendliness of Ireland. Staying here may strain your budget, but when your every whim is being catered to and you're lost in the surroundings, you'll be happy you splurged! The hotel is an impressive Victorian home, with rooms that have four-poster beds and overlook gardens that are tended with precision. The menu changes daily, but if you see it, try the turbot with shrimp ravioli and black sesame and soy dressing.

Off the Dublin-Wexford Road, on R750, Rathnew, Wicklow. ☎ **0404-69-274** *or 800-525-4800 from the U.S. Fax: 0404-67-806. Internet:* www.tinakilly.ie. *To get there, take the R750 off the main Dublin-Wexford Road. Rates: €162.50–€225 ($154.35–$213.75) double. AE, DC, MC, V.*

Glenview Hotel
$$$ **Delgany**

This bright, relaxing hotel is easy to reach — off the N11 and just a half-hour from Dublin. Glenview was recently refurbished, and all the bed-rooms are tasteful and have amenities like pants presses and satellite TVs. Its best draw is the Woodlands Restaurant, which overlooks the glen in the hotel's name.

Glen O' The Downs, Delgany. ☎ **01-287-3399.** *Fax: 01-287-511. E-mail:* glenview@iol.ie. *By car: 25 minutes south of Dublin off the N11. Rates: €145–€187.50 ($137.75–$178.10) double. AE, DC, MC, V.*

Royal Hotel and Leisure Centre
$$$ **Bray**

This hotel has it all: luxury for a bearable cost, a prime location in a great town, and tons of extras to tempt you to skip sightseeing. The Royal sits on the picturesque main street of Bray and isn't dubbed a "leisure centre" for nothing. After relaxing in the indoor pool or whirlpool, you can stroll into the hotel's top-grade pub for a meal from the *carvery* (buffet). Rooms are large enough to fit whole families, and the Royal provides child care, too.

Main Street, Bray. ☎ **01-286-2935.** *Fax: 01-286-7373. Internet:* www.regencyhotels.com. *By car: Take N11 to Bray. DART: Bray is 30 minutes from Dublin. Rates: €122.50 ($116.35) double. AE, DC, MC, V.*

Glendalough Hotel
$$–$$$ Glendalough

Any shortcomings to this hotel are made up for by the surrounding vistas. On the whole, it's a charming place. The food served in the impressive dining room is excellent and fresh, and the Glendalough Tavern has some of the best pub food you'll find in a hotel. The rooms are pretty bland and are a letdown compared to the rest of the place, but why would you spend lots of time in your room when there's so much to see?

On the 755, Glendalough. ☎ *0404-45-135. Fax: 0404-45-142. By car: Take the R755 off the N11. Rates: €75–€125 ($71.25–$118.75) double. AE, DC, MC, V. Closed Jan.*

Slievemore
$ Greystones

You won't get a better view of Greystones's spectacular beachfront than from Slievemore, an impeccable, white-washed B&B run by a pleasant couple. Rooms are small but cute and very clean. Bathrooms are in the hall. Step out of the door and take a walk on the beach before having a traditional breakfast in the atrium. This place is a great representation of the quaintness of the town.

The Harbour, Greystones. ☎ *01-287-4724. By car: Follow signs south out of Bray to Greystones village. Rates: €50 ($47.50) double. No credit cards.*

Where to dine in Wicklow

Mitchells of Laragh
$$$$ Glendalough IRISH

Set in a garden among the Wicklow Mountains, this schoolhouse-cum-restaurant is renowned for its Irish fare and mercurial gourmet menu. Inside, the country-style decor and fireplaces are lovely, but ask for a table outside in the summer. Among their specialties, the local rack of Wicklow lamb is a must try, as is the homemade ice cream. Yum!

Laragh, Glendalough. ☎ *0404-45-302. By car: From N11/M11 turn right at Kimacanogue to Glendalough. Main courses: €20.65–€24.40 ($19.60–$23.20). AE, DC, M, V. Open: 9 a.m.–9 p.m. daily, April–Sept; Wed–Sun 9 a.m.–9 p.m., Oct–March.*

The Roundwood Inn
$$–$$$$ Bray SEAFOOD/IRISH/ECLECTIC

Forget about fish and chips! The Roundwood Inn takes the preparation of seafood to new levels, with careful creations and European flair. Nothing's oversauced or tries too hard to be continental; the food is a perfect mix of Irish heartiness and worldly sophistication. The Roundwood also serves pub food that's a step above the norm all day. Try the lobster salad.

Main Street, Roundwood, Bray. ☎ 01-281-8107. Reservations recommended. By car: Out of Bray take R755 to Roundwood. Main courses: €11.85–€21.25 ($11.25–$20.20). AE, DC, MC, V. Open: Wed–Sat 7:30–10:00 p.m., Sun 1–10 p.m. Not wheelchair accessible.

The Hungry Monk

$$$–$$$$ Greystones   IRISH/ECLECTIC

The Hungry Monk, a small, candlelit restaurant on the main street, boasts a menu that's as varied as it is good. The roast rack of Aughrim lamb is delicious, and the starters are tempting enough to order as a meal. Portions are generous, so come hungry. This is a good place to enjoy a romantic meal. It's best to leave the kids with a sitter.

Church Road, Greystones. ☎ 01-287-5759. By car: Follow signs south out of Bray to Greystones village. Main courses: €13.15–€21.25 ($12.50–$20.20). M, V. Open: Tues–Sat 7–11 p.m., Sun 12:30–8:00 p.m. Not wheelchair accessible.

Coopers

$$–$$$ Greystones   SEAFOOD/IRISH/ECLECTIC

Possibly Greystones's greatest claim to fame, Coopers is a restaurant everyone seems to know about — and for good reason. Because of its proximity to the ocean (waves practically hit the place), it's no surprise the fish dishes are delicious, but the quality extends throughout the menu. Try the duck and chicken pâté with cumberland sauce for starters, then the baked salmon on a bed of aubergines. On weekends it's crowded, so call ahead.

The Harbour, Greystones. ☎ 01-287-3914. Reservations recommended. By car: Follow signs south out of Bray to Greystones village. Main courses: €10.65–€13.75 ($10.10–$13.05). AE, M, V. Open: Mon–Sat 5:30–11:30 p.m., Sun 12:30–4:00 p.m. and 5:30–10:00 p.m.

Exploring Wicklow

Gardens and greenery are the big draws here, but Wicklow also has its share of historic houses and monastic sites. In this section, I run through the best of them.

The top attractions

Here are a few of my favorite hot spots in Wicklow.

Powerscourt House, Gardens, and Waterfall
Enniskerry

This sweeping estate has some of the finest gardens in all of Europe, maintained with meticulous care. They cover 100 acres at the base of a Palladian mansion built in the 1730s by the first Viscount Powerscourt, Richard Wingfield. The house was gutted by a fire in 1974 but was recently rebuilt and is now once again open to the public. The sweeping grounds feature Japanese gardens, a beautiful mosaic of pebbles gathered from the beach in Bray, and classically styled statues throughout. An incredible stairway leads to the circular Triton Lake. A crafts center, children's play area, and restaurant on the premises round out the amenities. Also part of the estate is Ireland's highest waterfall.

Off the main Dublin-Wicklow Road (N11), Enniskerry. ☎ *01-204-6000. By car: Take the N11 out of Dublin (it becomes the new motorway M11) and follow signs for the garden. By bus: 44 from Dublin to Enniskerry and Alpine Coach (☎ 01-286-2547), which runs daily buses from Dublin to the gardens. Admission: Garden only: €4.40 ($4.20) adults, €4 ($3.80) students and seniors, €2.50 ($2.35) children under 16; House only: €2 ($1.90) adults, €1.50 ($1.40) students and seniors, €1.25 ($1.20) children under 16; House and Garden: €6.25 ($5.95) adults, €5.50 ($5.20) students and seniors, €3.75 ($3.55) children under 16. Open: Garden March–Oct 9:30 a.m.–5:30 p.m., Nov–Feb 9:30 a.m. to dusk. Waterfall March–Oct 9:30 a.m.–7:00 p.m., Nov–Feb 10:30 a.m. to dusk. Closed for the two weeks prior to Christmas. Suggested visit: 2 hours.*

Wicklow Mountains National Park
Glendalough

This area, covering nearly 50,000 acres, includes large mountain bogs and protects such wildlife as the rare peregrine falcon. The park centers around the beautiful Glendalough, and the Glendalough Wood Nature Reserve serves as the information and education facility for the park. In May the park hosts a two-day walking festival.

Glendalough. ☎ *0404-45-425; winter number* ☎ *0404-45-338. By car: N11 to R755 from Dublin; R752 to R755 from Wicklow. The Information Point is located by Upper Lake, R756 off R755. Admission: Free. Information Point Open: May–Aug daily 10 a.m.–6 p.m., April and Sept Sat and Sun 10 a.m.–6 p.m. Suggested visit: 1 to 3 hours.*

Glendalough Round Tower and Monastery
Glendalough

Despite being sacked, pillaged, and destroyed by fire, this monastery has persevered. St. Kevin built this fortified Irish monastic community in the sixth century, but Vikings invaded it in the ninth century, a fire swept through the second version at the end of the 14th century, and most of what now stands is a restoration from the 1800s. Just beyond the visitor center and through the double-arched stone entryway is St. Kevin's Church, and the chimney-looking building — the Round Tower at Glendalough — was once a bell tower where monks could keep a lookout for potential intruders. One of the first things to attract your attention is the position of the door — 10 feet off the ground! The most accepted explanation for this is that the monks put it there for safety. They would climb to the door on a ladder and then pull up the ladder in case of a threat below.

Glendalough. ☎ 0404-45-325. By car: N11 to R755 from Dublin, R752 to R755 from Wicklow. Admission: €2.50 ($2.35) adults, €2 ($1.90) seniors, €1.25 ($1.20) children and students. Open: Mid-Oct to mid-March daily 9:30 a.m.–5:00 p.m., mid-March to May and Sept to mid-Oct daily 9:30 a.m.–6:00 p.m., June–Aug daily 9:00 a.m.–6:30 p.m. Suggested visit: 1½ hours.

The National Sea Life
Bray

Much more than an aquarium, this interactive museum breaks boundaries to explain life in the ocean and bring you face to face with its wonders. Two hundred tanks house nearly 700 species of aquatic life! Kids have a ball here, following an adventure trail with clues and puzzles or even picking up real ocean dwellers. The Explore Think Tank is an interactive display, with touch-screens and CD-ROM games. You can come and go all day, taking advantage of the feeding demonstrations and talks.

Bray, Strand Road (on the boardwalk). ☎ 01-286-6939. By car: N11 to Bray. DART: The center is a ten-minute walk from the Bray Station. Admission: €7 ($6.65) adults, €6 ($5.70) senior, €5 ($4.75) students, €4.50 ($4.25) children. Open: Oct–March Mon–Fri noon to 4 p.m., March–Sept daily 11 a.m.–6 p.m. Suggested visit: 2 hours.

Other fun stuff to see and do

What? The historic houses and gardens that I mentioned previously aren't enough of a feast for you? Okay, then. Here's some dessert:

✔ **Walk the Wicklow Way:** This 76-mile trail extends from Dublin City to County Carlow. You may not have the time (or energy!) to walk the entire thing, but do drop into parts of it — you won't be disappointed. Beginning at Marlay Park on the outskirts of Dublin, the trail climbs into the Dublin Mountains and then dips into glens in the high Wicklow Mountains, along the way passing places of historical note, farms, and traditional stone walls that separate land ownership. Those stone walls that separate fields in Ireland began out of a practical necessity to clear the earth of all the rocks in order to make the land suitable for crops and grazing.

To get there: A daily bus runs from Dublin and Waterford to Bunclody near the County Carlow end of the trail and local buses run from Dublin to Marlay Park (Bus Eireann, Dublin-Waterford Express). Before you go, be sure to pick up a map at a County Wicklow tourism office, through e-mail at eastwest@ eircom.net, or via the Web at http://homepage.eircom.net/~eastwest.

✔ **Killruddery House and Garden:** Since 1618, this house has been in the family of the Earls of Meath, but the draw of the place is really the gardens. Kilruddery is one of the earliest gardens in Ireland that still survives; it exhibits the 17th-century French style. The garden contains an outdoor theater, foreign trees and shrubs, and a pond with fountains.

Location: Off the main Dublin-Wicklow Road (N11), Killruddery. ☎ 01-286-2777. By car: Take N11 south from Bray. Admission: €5.65 ($5.35) adults, €3.75 ($3.55) seniors and students. Garden only: €3.75 ($3.55) adult, €2.50 ($2.35) seniors and students. Open: Mid-February to June and September, daily 1 to 5 p.m. Garden open April through September. Suggested visit: 1½ hours.

✔ **The Millennium Forest:** Although not a stunning attraction in and of itself, the idea behind this new project makes it a marvel. The goal is for every household in the country to have a tree planted in its name. This is the largest project ever undertaken to restore native Irish woodlands. The trees planted in the People's Millennium Forests come from acorns and other seeds gathered from as close to the forest locations as possible. This forest is the best of the 16 planted around the country in the last couple years; it contains 130,000 ash, alder, hazel, birch, and oak trees planted on 90 acres on behalf of the families in Wicklow and Dublin. If you know a family in Dublin, you can actually locate their tree.

Location: Shelton Abbey. ☎ 045-201-1111. E-mail: info@ millenniumforests.com. By car: From Dublin, take the N11 south and take a right to Shelton just before Arklow. Admission: Free. Open: Dawn to dusk. Suggested visit: 1 hour.

✔ **Russborough House:** This house, built in the mid-1700s in the Palladian style, is home to the world-famous Beit Collection of paintings, which includes pieces by Gainsborough, Rubens, and Vernet. Inside, you can see a fine selection of furniture, tapestries, porcelain, and silver. Stop by the restaurant, shop, children's playground, and lakeside picnic area.

Location: Off N81, Blessington. ☎ 045-86-5239. By car: From Dublin, take the N7 to Naas and pick up the R410. The house is located where the R410 meets the N81. Admission: Main rooms €5 ($4.75) adults, €3.75 ($3.55) seniors and students, €2.50 ($2.35) children under 12. Additional €3.50 ($3.30) for bedroom tour, which includes silver and porcelain displays. Open: June through August daily 10:30 a.m. to 5:30 p.m., September Monday through Saturday 10:30 a.m. to 2:30 p.m., Sunday 10:30 a.m. to 5:30 p.m. Suggested visit: 1 hour.

✔ **Mt. Usher Gardens:** More than 5,000 species of plants from all over the world are spread throughout these gardens, located along the River Vartry. Starting from a humble potato patch in 1860, these 20 acres have blossomed into an ocean of flowers, meadows, and waterfalls and are a playground for birds and wildlife. A particularly nice area is where the suspension bridge spans a little waterfall — quite a romantic spot!

Location: Off the main Dublin-Wicklow road (N11), Ashford.
☎ **0404-40-116.** By car: N11 from Dublin or Rosslare. Admission: €4.50 ($4.25) adults, €3.50 ($3.30) students. Open: Mid-March to October daily 10:30 a.m. to 6:00 p.m. Suggested visit: 1½ hours.

✔ **Avondale House and Forest Park:** Built in 1779 and set in a lush valley, this house was the birthplace of one of Ireland's great leaders, Charles Stewart Parnell (1846–1891), and is now a museum dedicated to his life and memory. Avondale is also the center of Irish forestry, and its plantations have served as a model for the country. The forest park has long, well-marked walks and a picnic area.

Location: Rathdrum. ☎ **0404-46-111.** By car: Take N11 to R752 to Rathdrum crossroads and follow signs to the house. Admission: House €3.75 ($3.55) adults, €3.25 ($3.10) students and seniors, €2 ($1.90) children under 16; Parking fee: €2.50 ($2.35); Park: Free admission. Open: Mid-March to October daily 10 a.m. to 5 p.m. Suggested visit:1½ hours.

✔ **Best View in Wicklow:** You can enjoy a really spectacular view from the top of **Sugar Loaf Mountain.** The climb is pretty easy, and you can get to the top in under an hour. You'll be happy you did — on a clear day you can see all the way to Wales!

Location: Near Kilmacanogue. Take R755 off N11.

✔ **Best Spot for a Picnic:** Just beyond Avondale House is the famed **Meeting of the Waters,** where the Avonmore and Avonbeg rivers come together. This spot is so beautiful it inspired Thomas Moore to write: "There is not in the wide world a valley so sweet / as the vale in whose bosum the bright waters meet."

Location: 3 miles south of Rathdrum heading toward Arklow on the R752 (which becomes the R755 as you leave Rathdrum).

Organized tours

Because Wicklow is so close to Dublin, a number of operators offer bus tours, and others take advantage of the area's beauty to offer such interesting options as horse tours and boat tours.

Wild Coach Tours

Go off the beaten track in a little 29-seater Mercedes coach to see the most amazing spots in the Wicklow Mountains, accompanied by excellent and entertaining guides who fill you in on local legends and folklore. The day-long tour includes Dun Laoghaire Harbour, Sandycove, Killiney Bay, Avoca

Handweavers, Glendalough, Laragh, and the mountains. The half-day tours are called the "The Wild Castle Tour" and "The Wild Powerscourt Tour."

When and where: The full-day tour and the half-day castle tour pick up at three Dublin city hotels and the Dublin Tourism Office daily between 8:50 a.m. and 9:40 a.m. and return at 5:30 p.m. and 1:30 p.m., respectively, to Dublin City Centre. The half-day Powerscourt tour picks up at 1:30 p.m. and returns by 6:30 p.m. Information: Call Aran Tours ☎ 01-280-1899. Internet: www.wildcoachtours.com. *Price: €28 ($26.60) for full day, €20 ($19) for half day. Advanced reservations recommended.*

Bus Eireann Bus Tour

Bus Eireann offers three-day tours of the area from Dublin. The **Glendalough & Wicklow Panorama Tour** (€17.50 to €21.25/$16.60 to $20.20 adult, €8.75 to €11.25/$8.30 to $10.70 child, depending on the season) runs year-round, covering the south coast of Dublin, Killiney Bay, Wicklow, Avoca Handweavers, Roundwood, and Glendalough. The **Wicklow Mountains, Glenroe,** and **Ballykissangel Tour** and the **Russborough House & Powerscourt Gardens Tour** (€21.25/$20.20 adult, €11.25/$10.70 child) each run one day a week June through September.

When and where: All tours leave from the main station, on Store Street behind the Customs building. Information: Bus Eireann. ☎ 01-836-6111. Call for schedule information.

Blessington Lake Cruises

The MV *Blessington* offers hour-long cruises of the beautiful lakes serenely set in the foothills of the Wicklow Mountains, with history, geography, and folklore supplied as you go.

When and where: Take Bus Eireann 005, 132, or 391 to Blessington. Cruises are only in the summer. Call for more details, including prices, which vary. Information: Blessington Lake Cruises, Adventure Centre pier, Blessington. ☎ 045-86-5092.

Brennanstown Riding School Horseback Tours

Brennanstown Riding School offers horseback riding around the trails of Sugarloaf Mountain.

When and where: Take the DART to the end stop at Bray. Information: Brennanstown Riding School, Holybrook, Kilmacanogue, Bray. ☎ 01-286-3778. Price: €18.75 ($17.80) an hour for groups.

Shopping in Wicklow

Wicklow is known for pottery and knitwear. The **County Tourism Office in Wicklow** (☎ 0404-66-057) puts out a publication called the "Pottery Trail," with a full list of pottery, crafts, and knitwear locations throughout the county. I list some of the county's top spots here.

A La Campagne

This little shop offers unique items, including gifts, kitchenware, pottery, and glass; plenty of artsy objects, like candles and holders; and also Irish country pottery. The owner, Stephen Falvin, is often on hand to help pick out a gift or advise on choices.

Main Street, Wicklow. ☎ *0404-61-388.*

Avoca Handweavers

Here, in the oldest handweaving mill in Ireland (dating to 1723), you can find Avoca clothing, knitwear, and a wide range of fine Irish crafts.

Avoca Village. ☎ *0402-35-105. Outlet store: Kilmacanogue, near Bray.* ☎ *01- 286-7466.*

Fisher's of Newtownmountkennedy

Located in a converted schoolhouse, this shop has tons of men's and women's sporting clothes and accessories, as well as cool items like hip flasks and pool cues.

On R765, off N11, Newtownmountkennedy. Look for a big pink building before getting into town. No phone.

Glendalough Woolen Mills

In this old farmhouse, you can find quality wool and also learn how wool goes from sheep to sweater. The jewelry workshop features St. Kevin's medals, Claddagh symbols, and Connemara marble.

Laragh, on the R755. No phone.

Noritake Arklow Pottery Ltd.

Any serious shopper for pottery will find something here, in Ireland's largest pottery factory. Home of Noritake's Celt Craft and Misty Isle lines, this factory puts out everything from earthenware to porcelain in modern and traditional designs plus plenty of teapots, tableware, and gifts. The factory offers free tours from mid-June through the third week of July and during the last two weeks of August.

South Quay, Arklow. ☎ *0402-32-401.*

Wicklow Vale Pottery

This showroom has a complete range of Avoca Blue hand-painted ceramics and Wicklow Vale Ceramics, and you can arrange a tour of the factory. Their "olde worlde" coffee shop is good for a cup and some homemade pastry.

Tinnahask in Arklow, left on South Quay. ☎ *0402-39-442.*

Hitting the pubs

Philip Healy's

This pub is a place where locals meet for a leisurely drink and chat. The high ceilings make it feel open and airy, but the pub has plenty of nooks to settle into if you're looking for some quiet conversation. Healy's is an unpretentious place that serves food but unfortunately doesn't have music. So nip in and have a pint before heading out to tour the Wicklow Mountains.

Main Street, Wicklow. ☎ *0404-67-380.*

Old Court Inn

You can't miss this pub — it's bright yellow and sits at the center of town. Inside, it's quiet, cozy, and warm. If you visit during chillier times, expect fireplaces to be blazing. Even in the summer, you'll want to hunker down in an overstuffed booth. This is the place to relax after you've trekked through the outdoors all day.

Main Street, Wicklow (near the courthouse). ☎ *0404-67-680.*

The Meetings

Sunken down in the beautiful Vale of Avoca, The Meetings has everything you want in a pub. You can get good food all day and hear music at night — and, when the weather's warm, sit outside on the patio and take in the view. It's clearly geared to tourists, but that's not necessarily a bad thing. After all, how many pubs provide a Bureau de Change and a craft shop?

Vale of Avoca. ☎ *0402-35-226.*

Cartoon Inn

You may be more interested in the cartoons than your drink in this themed pub, whose interior walls are covered with artwork by famous cartoonists. The Cartoon Festival (no, I'm not kidding) is held here in early summer. Food is served during lunchtime.

28 Main Street, Rathdrum. ☎ *0404-46-774.*

Fast Facts: County Wicklow

Area Codes

County Wicklow's area codes (or city codes) are **01, 0404, 0402,** and **045.**

Emergencies

Dial ☎ **999** for all emergencies. The main hospital is in Wicklow (☎ 0404-67-108).

Information

For visitor information, go to the tourist office at Rialto House, Fitzwilliam Square, Wicklow

(☎ 0404- 69-117), open year-round. They can also provide reservation services. For telephone directory assistance, dial ☎ 1190.

County Kildare

Welcome to horse country! You can visit Kildare for a quick afternoon with the ponies or settle down for a night or two at one of the hotels I list, and spend a little time at a historic house or the Steam Museum.

Getting to and around Kildare

By car, take the N7 from Dublin or Limerick to get to Kildare. **Irish Rail** (☎ **01-836-6222**) has daily service to Kildare town, and **Bus Eireann** (☎ **01-836-6111**) services Kildare, Straffan, Celbridge, Newbridge, and other towns throughout the area.

Where to stay in Kildare

Annagh Lodge Guesthouse
$$–$$$ **Newbridge**

The newly built Annagh Lodge has pluses you don't generally find in a country guesthouse. With sauna and in-house movies, you may be surprised at the level of pampering. Bedrooms are luxurious, too. This is a good place if you're interested in outdoor activities — eight golf courses and fishing are all within a close drive.

Naas Road, Newbridge. ☎ *045-43-3518. Fax: 045-433-538. Internet:* www.annagh lodge.ie. *By car: N7 from Dublin to Newbridge. Rates: €75–€112.50 ($71.25–$106.85) double. MC, V.*

Hillview House
$$ **Naas**

This lovely guesthouse is situated just far enough from Kildare town to give the feel of country isolation but close enough to be a starting point for touring the best attractions in the area. You'll feel at home and catered to by the Allen family, who runs the house. Having a meal in one of their tearooms is a treat, and the food, served all day, is delicious.

Prosperous, Naas. ☎ *045-86-8252. Fax: 045-892-305. E-mail:* hillview@tinet.ie. *By car: Prosperous is a village on R403 (between N4 and N7) near Naas. From Naas, take the R403 northwest for a few miles. Rates: €62.50–€87.50 ($59.35–$83.10) double. MC, V.*

Curragh Lodge Hotel
$$–$$$ Kildare Town

This hotel is ideal mainly for its location. Just off the N7 and right in Kildare town, the Curragh Lodge Hotel is close to the Irish National Stud and Japanese Gardens. It has clean rooms, serves food, and has a pub, all for a moderate price.

Dublin Road, Kildare. ☎ *045-52-2144. By car: N7 from Dublin to Kildare. Rates: €87.50–€112.50 ($83.10–$106.85) double. AE, DC, MC, V.*

The Sycamores B&B
$ Naas

This is the kind of place you'd love to call home. Noreen Malone's comfortable house is a welcome departure from the sometimes impersonal nature of hotels. The exquisitely manicured lawn hints at the clean and nicely decorated rooms and dining area. The town of Naas is just a five-minute walk away, and the price of this lovely stay-over can't be beat.

Sallins Road, Naas. ☎ *045-89-7598. By car: N7 from Dublin to Naas. Rates: €42.50–€46.25 ($40.35–$43.95) double. No credit cards.*

Where to dine in Kildare

Red House Inn
$$$–$$$$ Newbridge IRISH/MEDITERRANEAN

Set in a country house, this award-winning restaurant blends modern and traditional fare in a unique way. From Irish to Mediterranean food, the Red House Inn is good for a quiet and delicious meal.

Newbridge. ☎ *045-43-1657. Reservations recommended. By car: N7 between Naas and Kildare. Main courses: €15.65–€33.70 ($14.85–$32). AE, DC, MC, V. Open: Tues–Sat 7–10 p.m. Sun, three sittings: 12:30 p.m., 1:00 p.m., and 2:30 p.m.*

Harbour View
$$$–$$$$ Naas IRISH

The food here is what you expect in Ireland: home-cooked, wholesome, delicious, and served in hearty portions. The menu has something for everyone. Don't let the nondescript exterior fool you; one foot in the door and you know you're in for a meal that will keep you going all day long.

Limerick Road, Naas. ☎ *045-87-9145. By car: N7 from Dublin to Naas. Main courses: €11.85–€20 ($11.25–$19). AE, DC, MC, V. Open: Daily 7:30–10:00 a.m. and noon to 9:30 p.m.*

Exploring Kildare: The top attractions

Irish National Stud and Japanese Gardens
Tully

One of the foremost breeding grounds in the country, the National Stud is consistently ranked as one of Ireland's top-20 tourist attractions. Visitors can see the horses being groomed and exercised. Also check out the Horse Museum, with exhibits on racing, hunting, and show jumping, plus the skeleton of the famed Arkle, the renowned king of hunt racing.

On the same grounds are the striking Japanese Gardens, which boast bonsai, bamboos, and cherry trees. The gardens portray the journey of the life of man, starting with birth and going to eternity, which is represented by a Zen rock garden. In all, the grounds make for a nice way to spend a day.

Kildare. ☎ *045-52-1617. By car: Take N7 from Dublin or Naas. By train: Daily service into Kildare Railway Station. Admission: €6.25 ($5.95) adults, €3.75 ($3.55) seniors and students, €2.50 ($2.35) under 12. Open: Mid-Feb–mid-Nov daily 9:30 a.m.–6:00 p.m. Suggested visit: 3 hours.*

The Curragh
Newbridge

This racetrack, the country's best known, is often referred to as the Churchill Downs of Ireland. Races run sporadically from March to October, but you can be sure to catch a race here at least one Saturday a month. In late June, the Curragh is host to the famous Irish Derby.

Dublin-Limerick Road (N7), Newbridge. ☎ *045-44-1205. Internet:* www.curragh.ie. *By car: Take N7 from Dublin or Naas. By train: Daily service into Curragh. Admission: €10–€15 ($9.50–$14.25) for most races, €43.75 ($41.55) for the Derby. Special "Racing by Rail" package for €15 ($14.25) (purchase at Heuston Station in Dublin) includes coach bus to the race track. Call ahead for upcoming dates. Suggested visit: 2 hours.*

Celbridge Abbey Grounds
Celbridge

These grounds were planted by the daughter of the Lord Mayor of Dublin in 1697 for Jonathan Swift. They rest along the River Liffey and feature Rockbridge, the oldest remaining stone bridge over the river. The grounds also boast a model railway, picnic area, and donkey rides, which are a hit with kids. The abbey itself is a private residence, so don't expect a tour.

Right on the main road (403) in Celbridge. ☎ *01-627-5508 or 01-628-8161. By car: From Dublin take the N4 west, picking up the R403 several miles out of the city. By train: Daily service into Hazelhatch Station. By bus: 67 and 67A from Dublin. Admission: €3.50 ($3.30) adults, €2 ($1.90) seniors and children. Open: Daily 10 a.m.–6 p.m. Suggested visit: 1 hour.*

Castletown House

Celbridge

This impressive, stately house was built in the early part of the 18th century for William Connolly, then the Speaker of the Irish House of Commons. Its grandeur is staggering, and it remains a standout in Irish architecture. The mansion was built in the Palladian style, a Renaissance mode meant to copy the classicism of ancient Rome. The interior is decorated with Georgian furnishings, and the main hall and staircase are covered with intricate plasterwork. Run by the state and open to the public, the house is worth the drive — about 10 miles northeast of Naas.

R403, off the main Dublin-Galway Road, Celbridge. ☎ *01-628-8252. By car: From Dublin take the N4 west, picking up the R403 several miles out of the city. Located on the R403 just before you reach the village of Celbridge. By bus: 67 and 67A from Dublin. Admission: €3.50 ($3.30) adults, €2.50 ($2.35) seniors and students, €1.25 ($1.20) children. Open: April–Sept Mon–Fri 10 a.m.–6 p.m., Sat and Sun 1–6 p.m.; Oct Mon–Fri 10 a.m.–5 p.m., Sat and Sun 1–5 p.m; Nov Sun 1–5 p.m. Suggested visit: 1½ hours.*

Steam Museum

Straffan

Anyone with an interest in locomotion will enjoy this museum. This restored church contains a cache of 18th-century locomotive engines that includes Richard Trevithick's Third Model of 1797, the oldest surviving self-propelled machine in existence. It also contains engines from the industrial age. You can find plenty of steam-locomotion literature in the shop.

Off the Dublin-Limerick Road (N7), Lodge Park, Straffan, near Celbridge. ☎ *01-627-3155 summer,* ☎ *01-628-8412 winter. By car: Take the N7 from Dublin or Naas. By train: Daily service into Kildare Railway Station. Admission: €6 ($5.70) adults, €5 ($4.75) seniors, students, and children. Open: April, May, and Sept Sun 2:30–5:30 p.m., June–Aug Tues–Sun 2–6 p.m. Suggested visit: 2 hours.*

More fun things to see and do

Here are some options for the whiskey-lovers and duffers in your group:

✔ After a long hiatus from the public, **Tullamore Dew,** the popular Tullamore Whiskey distillery, is back in the tourist business and it was well worth the refurbishments, and worth the short jaunt from Kildare (it's located just outside County Kildare). The new Tullamore Dew Heritage Centre presents films and interactive displays about the history of the place and a display of the equipment used. Perhaps the most interesting part of the tour is the Irish Mist Liqueur section, home to a community of 70,000 live bees collecting nectar for the popular potent potable. Lest you think this is an adult-only tour, the kids will love the part where you dress in period costume and the huge aquarium displaying local species of fish and fauna. Adults get a complimentary glass of Tullamore Dew Whiskey or Irish Mist at the end of the tour.

Location: Tullamore, County Offlay. ☎ **0506-25-015.** Internet: www.tullamore-dew.org. By car: Take the N7 from Monastereva. Follow signs into Tullamore. The distillary is clearly sign-posted in Tullamore. Admission: €4.45 ($4.20) adults, €3.50 ($3.30) seniors, students, and children, €11.45 ($10.85) family. Open: May through September Monday through Saturday 9 a.m. to 6 p.m., Sunday noon to 5 p.m.; October through April Monday through Saturday 10 a.m. to 5 p.m., Sunday noon to 5 p.m. Suggested visit: 2 hours.

✔ The 18-hole championship **Kildare Country Club (K-Club)** was designed by Arnold Palmer himself. Location: 17 miles west of Dublin in Straffan. ☎ **01-601-7300.** Internet: www.kclub.ie. Par: 72. Fees: €162.50 ($154.35) for 18 holes in the summer, €93.40 ($88.75) in the winter.

Shopping in Kildare

Unless you're in the market for horse saddles or grooming equipment, Kildare's not a shopping extravaganza. But you can buy souvenirs and Irish handcrafts at a few places in town. Here are a couple of the best.

Kildare Woolen Mills

Like many other woolen mills in the country, this one offers traditional Irish clothing — sweaters and tweeds, as well as local crafts and gifts. It has a convenient location right in town.

6 Academy St., Kildare. ☎ *045-52-0190.*

Irish Pewter Mill

In addition to its full selection of original pewter jewelry, this 1,000-year-old mill specializes in crafts like tableware.

On the N9, Timolin, Moone. ☎ *0507-24-164.*

Hitting the pubs

The Manor Inn

This warm and inviting pub is a surprisingly great place to discover the area's history. Pictures and mementos throughout reflect local color and Kildare pride. There's enough information to keep your interest while you wait for some delicious pub grub to come your way. Kids love the children's menu.

On N7, where the N7 meets the N9, 25 Main St. South, Naas. ☎ **045-89-7471.** *By car: N7 from Dublin to Naas.*

Silken Thomas

Silken Thomas is the quintessential roadside pub — it's not one of Kildare's hottest spots for nothing, and the second you see this place you'll understand why. You can hear music six nights a week and fortify yourself with some of Silken Thomas's reputably good food until 8 p.m. Stop in for a nicely pulled pint and end up staying all evening.

The Square, Kildare. ☎ **045-52-1695.** *By car: N7 from Dublin to Kildare.*

Fast Facts: County Kildare

Area Codes
Kildare's area codes (or city codes) are **01, 045, 053,** and **0507.**

Emergencies/Police
Dial ☎ **999** for all emergencies.

Genealogical Resources
Contact the Kildare History and Family Research Centre, Riverbank, Main Street, Newbridge (☎ 045-43-3602; Fax: 045-43-1611; E-mail: capinfo@iol.ie; Internet: www.kildare.ie/genealogy).

Information
The tourist office in Kildare (☎ 045-52-2696) is open mid-May to September. For telephone directory assistance, dial ☎ 1190.

Internet
The Cyberx Internet Cafe (☎ 01-629-1747) in Maynooth has Internet access and printing capabilities.

Chapter 14

The Southeast: Counties Wexford, Waterford, Tipperary, and Kilkenny

● ●

In This Chapter

▶ Traversing the Irish National Heritage Park and the Hook Peninsula

▶ Touring the Waterford Crystal Factory

▶ Visiting Ireland's version of The Rock (the Rock of Cashel, that is)

▶ Reliving history at one of Ireland's top medieval castles

▶ Exploring the Dunmore Caves

▶ Playing at a former Irish Open golf course

● ●

*I*reland's Southeastern counties — Wexford, Waterford, Tipperary (which it's a long way to . . .), and Kilkenny — are often referred to as "the sunny Southeast" because they generally enjoy more sunshine than the rest of the country. They also provide a varied touring experience, whether you're looking to shop at the world-famous Waterford Crystal Factory, visit the huge and impressive Rock of Cashel, or play a few rounds of golf at a championship course.

What's Where?: The Southeast Counties and Their Major Attractions

Located on the southeastern tip of the country, **County Wexford** makes a nice stop on your tour, especially if nature calls (so to speak). The area's dotted with bird sanctuaries, beaches, and pretty countryside. It's bordered by the Wicklow Hills on the north and the Blackstairs Mountains on the west, and the rest is bound by the Irish Sea. The county is also the home to the Kennedys. Yes, *the* Kennedys: The family of the first Irish-Catholic U.S. president hailed from the town of New Ross.

The Southeast

ACCOMMODATIONS
Clone House B&B **28**
Cullintra House B&B **16**
Ferrycarrig **25**
Inistioge **17**
Kelly's Resort Hotel **23**
Riverside Park **27**
Samuels Heritage B&B **20**

DINING
Angela's Wholefood Restaurant **13**
Ballyrafter House **11**
Chez Hanz **7**
The Galley Cruising Restaurant **18**
The Lobster Pot **22**
Neptune **19**
The Tannery **12**

ATTRACTIONS
Brú Ború National Culture Centre **7**
Cahir Castle **8**
Curracloe Nature Trail **26**
Dunmore Cave **4**
Enniscorthy Castle and Wexford
County Museum **27**
Holy Trinity Church **6**
Hook Peninsula **21**
Irish National Heritage Park **25**
Jerpoint Abbey **15**
Johnstown Castle Gardens **24**
Lismore Castle **11**
Mitchelstown Cave **8**
National 1798 Visitor Centre **27**
Rock of Cashel and Museum **7**

SHOPPING
Farney Castle **2**
Hanley's Woolen Mill Shop **1**
Nicholas Mosse **5**
Tipperary Crystal Designs **14**
Tipperary Music **10**
Upper Court Manor **3**

NIGHTLIFE
Antique **27**
Ronald Regan Pub **9**

Some highlights include

- ✔ **The Irish National Heritage Park:** The park traces the region's history from its earliest Stone Age settlements through the Celtic, Viking, and Norman periods.

- ✔ **Johnstown Castle Gardens:** The gardens, lawns, lakes, and ornamental towers of this fairy-tale castle are worth exploring, as is the agricultural museum that's on the grounds.

- ✔ **The Hook Peninsula:** A lovely coastal pathway, an ancient abbey, and a few castles, forts, and lighthouses make this small foot of land well worth visiting.

County Waterford doesn't have an excess of attractions, but the things it does have are well worth a visit, such as the following:

- ✔ **Waterford Crystal Factory:** The place they make the world-famous crystal offers a tour that shows you every step of the crystal-making process. Afterward, you can visit the factory shop.

- ✔ **Reginald's Tower:** This tower, in the heart of Waterford Town, is the only Viking building continuously used since that age.

- ✔ **Lismore Castle:** This 12th-century castle isn't open to the public, but the gorgeous garden and 8,000-acre estate grounds are.

Tipperary is one of the largest counties in Ireland, and it has one of the country's biggest attractions: the Rock of Cashel. This, along with some great places to shop, makes it a nice place to wander through. It's not exactly a bustling area, though, so I don't recommend setting up camp here. Just roll on in and see the sights, such as the following:

- ✔ **Rock of Cashel:** The limestone Rock of Cashel and the medieval towers and monuments built on and around it are among the country's most awesome archeological sites.

- ✔ **Mitchelstown Cave:** You can explore about a half-mile of caverns on this tour, while tour guides explain their formation.

- ✔ **Cahir Castle:** This castle, one of Ireland's largest and best preserved, is the one that was used as the set for John Boorman's film *Excalibur.*

In the past, **County Kilkenny** often made it onto visitor itineraries only because it's one of the counties people would drive through on their way out of Dublin. These days, though, Kilkenny county and town are fighting to become a destination to reckon with by putting money into restoring some historic sights in the area, such as the following:

- ✔ **Kilkenny Castle:** This 12th-century medieval castle sits among beautiful sculptured gardens.

- ✔ **Dunmore Cave:** These large, well-lit chambers and passageways are natural formations of limestone dating back millions of years.

- ✔ **Jerpoint Abbey:** One of the best-preserved monastic ruins in Ireland.

County Wexford

County Wexford was the heartbeat of the 1798 rebellion, when Irish rebels took a brave stand against the strong arm of the Brits, and it was at Vinegar Hill, near Enniscorthy, where 20,000 rebels were massacred by English cannons, effectively ending the rebellion. **Wexford Town** is a fairly attractive harbor town, but not the best town for a lengthy stay. The river's edge is kind of industrial-looking and driving around town, along one-way streets the width of a supermodel's waist, can be frustrating. There's so much to see in the county, though, you shouldn't pass it up.

Getting to and around County Wexford

If you're driving from Dublin, take the N11 (which becomes M11 periodically) south to Enniscorthy and Wexford; from Wexford take the N25 west to New Ross. Most attractions are along this route. A fast and cost-effective shortcut across Waterford Harbour between Passage East, County Waterford, and Ballyhack, County Wexford, is provided by **Passenger East Car Ferry** (☎ 051-38-2480). It runs Sunday through Friday year-round, and will save you a lot of time driving around. Cost per vehicle: €7.50 ($7.10) round-trip, €5 ($4.75) one-way.

The Dublin (Connolly Station)-Rosslare Harbour line of **Irish Rail** (☎ 01-836-6222) has stations in Rosslare, Wexford, and Enniscorthy. **Bus Eireann** (☎ 01-836-6111) travels year-round to Wexford, Enniscorthy, Rosslare, New Ross, and other towns throughout the area.

You may arrive in Ireland via Wexford. **Stena Sealink Line** (☎ 01-204-7777) has passenger and car ferries from Fishguard, Wales, to Rosslare Harbour Ferryport. **Irish Ferries** (☎ 01-855-2222) has service from Pembroke, Wales, to Rosslare. Irish Ferries also makes trips between Rosslare and the French towns of Le Havre, Cherbourg, and Roscoff. Call for more details.

Walking is the best way to get around County Wexford's towns. Even the largest town, Wexford, is easily walkable.

Where to stay in County Wexford

Kelly's Resort Hotel
$$$ Rosslare

Situated along a 5-mile stretch of sandy beach, this family-run hotel is truly a resort accommodation. You'll be spoiled by the two pools, indoor and outdoor tennis courts, and crazy golf and croquet grounds — though you won't exactly feel like you're in the Emerald Isle as you sip cocktails on the beach. It's not far from the ferry port, and in the spring Kelly's hosts special activities like wine tastings.

Rosslare. ☎ *053-32-114. Fax: 053-32-222. Internet:* www.kellys.ie. *By car: Take N25 from Wexford. Rates: €122.50–€165 ($116.40–$156.75) double. AE, MC, V.*

Ferrycarrig
$$$–$$$$ Wexford

This has one of the best locations of all Ireland's hotels, perched over the River Slaney estuary. The rooms and facilities (including a health club, pool, and two waterside restaurants) are unbeatable, and the staff is friendly and warm. There's not a bad view in the house. Ferrycarrig also has the cool Dry Dock Bar, where you'll be tempted to sit and relax the entire time.

Ferrycarrig Bridge, Wexford. ☎ *053-20-999. Fax: 053-20-982. Internet:* www.griffingroup.ie. *By car: Take N11 from Wexford toward Enniscorthy. Rates: €125–€375 ($118.75–$356.25) double. AE, DC, MC, V.*

Riverside Park
$$$ Enniscorthy

The county's newest hotel, Riverside Park, is situated on the banks of the River Slaney. It's difficult to miss coming in or out of town, given its beautiful brick-and-glass seawall and round tower. From the moment you walk in and see the amazing foyer 'til you check out your spacious room (almost all have a fantastic view), you'll know you've made the right choice. You're pretty much guaranteed to thoroughly enjoy your stay, especially if you wander into the unique Mill House pub — what a great hotel bar!

The Promenade, Enniscorthy. ☎ *054-37-800. Fax: 054-37-900. Internet:* www.riversideparkhotel.com. *By car: On the N11 just outside Enniscorthy. Rates: €154 ($146.30) double. AE, DC, MC, V.*

Wexford Town

ATTRACTIONS ●
The Bullring **2**
John Barry Monument **4**
Selskar Abbey **1**

SHOPPING ▲
Faller's Sweater Shop **3**
Hynes Jewelers **3**
Westgate Design **3**
Wexford Silver **3**

NIGHTLIFE ☾
Macken's The Cape
 of Good Hope **2**
Crown Bar **5**

| Church ✝ |
| Information ⓘ |

Clone House B&B
$$ Enniscorthy

This 300-year-old farmhouse set in the picturesque countryside is a quiet getaway spot, and it's almost a surprise to realize it's also close to golf, beaches, and area attractions. The best things about this place are the comfy beds and the Breens, the lovely couple who run the house. They're wonderfully knowledgeable about the area and are eager to help you decide where to go and what to see.

Ferns, Enniscorthy. ☎ *054-66-113. By car: Off the N11 between Enniscorthy and Gorey. Rates: €62.50 ($59.40) double. No credit cards.*

Where to dine in County Wexford

The Galley Cruising Restaurant
$$$$ **New Ross** IRISH

You can enjoy your meal while nestled into the heated salon of a river-boat cruising along the picturesque Barrow and Nore rivers. It's a wonderful experience. The menu of mainly Irish fare is limited and not cheap, but it's worth the price — everything is fresh and well-prepared. There's a bar on board as well. Give yourself three hours for the tour, Gilligan, and don't be late!

New Ross Quay, New Ross. ☎ 051-42-1723. By car: West on N25 from Wexford. Main courses: €25–€30 ($23.75–$28.50). Cost of cruise: €12.50 ($11.90). No credit cards. Leaves at 6 p.m. and 7 p.m. daily. Reservations required.

The Lobster Pot
$$$$ **Carne** SEAFOOD

You couldn't pick a better location for a seafood restaurant than this, the southeastern tip of Ireland, between the Irish Sea and Lady's Island Lake. You can be sure the catch of the day was actually caught that day, and has only traveled a stone's throw to get to your plate. Gastronomic delights and rural hospitality have garnered The Lobster Pot awards for its menu and excellent pub. What should you order? I had some tasty fish, but people were raving about — what else? — the lobster.

Carnsore Point, Carne. ☎ 053-31-110. By car: From Rosslare Harbour or Wexford take the N11 toward Kilmore and follow signs to Carne or Lady's Island. Main courses: €18.75–€22.50 ($17.80–$21.40). AE, DC, MC, V. Open: June–Sept daily noon to 10 p.m., Oct–Dec and Feb–May Tues–Sun noon to 10 p.m. Closed Jan. Reservations required.

Neptune
$$$ **Ballyhack** SEAFOOD

This is as fine a bistro as you'll find in Ireland, attractively decorated with an ever-changing lineup of contemporary Irish art on display. Located in the shadow of Ballyhack Castle, it's growing more and more popular with the tourists. Expect gourmet meals at moderate prices. I recommend the poached hake in lobster sauce.

Ballyhack. ☎ 051-38-9284. By car: Take the R733 west from Wexford or south from New Ross. Main courses: €13.15–€18.75 ($12.45–$17.80). AE, DC, MC, V. Open: Mid-March to mid-Nov Tues–Sat 6–10 p.m. and Mon in July and Aug.

Exploring County Wexford: The top attractions

Irish National Heritage Park
Ferrycarrig

This informative and attention-grabbing place traces the region's history from its earliest Stone Age settlements through the Celtic, Viking, and Norman periods. Visitors receive maps that take them through to 14 historical sites. Re-creations of castles, boats, homes, and dolmen; guides in period dress; and audiovisual presentations bring the dynamic history of Ireland to life. Everything is hands-on, so it's a great place for the kids. Set on a wooded 35-acre site overlooking the Slaney River, the heritage park also has a Celtic-themed restaurant and craft shop on the grounds.

Off the Dublin-Wexford road (N11), Ferrycarrig. ☎ *053-20-733. By car: A few miles west of Wexford off the N11 at Ferrycarrig. Admission: €6.25 ($5.95) adults, €5.50 ($5.25) seniors, €5 ($4.75) students, €2.50 ($2.40) children ages 4–12, €14.50 ($13.80) family. Open: April–Oct daily 9:30 a.m.–6:30 p.m. Suggested visit: About 2 hours.*

Johnstown Castle Gardens
Wexford Town

Only the entrance to this fairy-tale castle is open, but the gardens, lawns, lakes, and ornamental towers are worth exploring. There is an agricultural museum with displays on the potato and everything you ever wanted to know about the Great Famine (but were afraid to ask). The museum also houses a collection of antique farm tools and large-scale replicas of blacksmith and cooper's workshops.

Bridgetown Road, off Wexford-Rosslare Road (N25), Wexford Town. ☎ *053-42-888. By car: A couple miles east of Wexford off the R733. Castle Grounds admission (only charged May–Oct): €3.75 ($3.55) per car or €2 ($1.90) per adult pedestrian, €1 (95¢) student and child pedestrian. Museum admission: €3.50 ($3.35) adults, €2 ($1.90) students and children, €10 ($9.50) family. Gardens Open: Daily 9 a.m.–5 p.m. Museum Open: Mon–Fri 9 a.m.–5 p.m.; Sat and Sun 2–5 p.m. Closed weekends Nov–March. Suggested visit: 2 hours.*

Hook Peninsula

There is so much to see on this small clubbed foot of land (in southwest County Wexford) that it's worth spending the afternoon driving and walking the lovely Slí Charman (Wexford's Coastal Pathway) to the end and back, provided you have the time and it's the peak season (a few places close for the winter). Highlights include the richly ornamented **Tintern Abbey** (which Wordsworth fans will be familiar with), near Saltmills, with its maze of ancient paths, walled gardens, fortified bridge, and church ruin (€2/$1.90 adults, €1.25/$1.19 seniors, €0.75/71¢ children and students); **Ballyhack Castle** (☎ 051-38-9468) with displays on the Crusades (€1.25/$1.19 adult, €0.75/71¢ children and students); **Slade Castle** (☎ 051-38-9454), an amazing fortress ruin near the **Hook Head Lighthouse,** one of the oldest lighthouses in Europe (lighthouse admission €4.50/$4.28 adults, €3.50/$3.33 children and seniors); and **Duncannon Fort** (☎ 051-38-9454), built to fend off attacks from the Spanish Armada.

By car: Tintern Abbey, Ballyhack, and Duncannon are off R733. To get to Hook Head, go south toward Fethard on R734 from New Ross. Park in Fethard and walk the coastal path to Slade Castle, the Lighthouse, and even on to Duncannon. Suggested visit: Varies, depending on the distance you go, but give it a couple of hours.

The National 1798 Visitor Centre
Enniscorthy

The story of the United Irishman's first rebellion against the British is told in multimedia pomp here at this small but fun museum on the struggle for Irish independence. You'll find out about the harsh conditions inflicted on the Irish under English rule and Sir William of Orange and the heroic rebellion that first tried to bring occupation to an end. The museum is a bit cheesy, with plastic historic figures and an oversized chess game, but the kids will enjoy it and the adults will learn something. The center is located on the banks of the scenic River Slaney and makes a nice spot for a picnic lunch as well.

Mill Park Road, Enniscorthy. ☎ 054-37-596. Fax: 054-37-198. Internet: www.1798 centre.com. By car: On the N30 and N11 next to Vinegar Hill. Admission: €6 ($5.70) adults, €3.50 ($3.35) student and child. Open: Mon–Sat 9:30 a.m.–5:00 p.m., Sun 11 a.m.–5 p.m. Suggested visit: 1 hour.

Top landmarks in Wexford Town

The Bullring
Wexford Town

This was the location of the first declaration of independence for the Irish Republic, during the Rebellion of 1798 (commemorated by the Pikeman statue). The area's name comes from the bloody sport of bull-baiting that took place here in the 17th century.

Off Quay Street, Wexford Town.

Selskar Abbey
Wexford Town

This is said to be one the oldest houses of worship in Wexford and was probably built during the Crusades. It's noted for being where King Henry

II spent 40 days of penance for his part in the death of Thomas à Becket, the martyred Archbishop of Canterbury.

Abbey Street, Wexford Town.

John Barry Monument
Wexford Town

"Who's John Barry?" you ask. No less than the father of the American Navy! He bravely went to the colonies and signed up for the Revolutionary War to fight against the British. He was captain of the famous ship *Lexington,* and was appointed by George Washington as com-mander-in-chief of the brand-spanking-new U.S. Navy.

Crescent Quay, Wexford Town.

Other fun stuff to do

Whether you'd like to hit the beach or explore a castle, here are a couple more options for your stay in Wexford:

✔ **Curracloe Nature Trail:** Free and informative maps are available on this excellent nature trail through the seashore dunes. Located 8 miles north of Wexford, this public and sheltered sandy beach is fun for the whole family. To get to the beach: Take the R742 5 miles out of Wexford Town.

Information: Wexford County Council. ☎ 053-42-211. Suggested visit: 1 hour.

✔ **Enniscorthy Castle and Wexford County Museum:** Witness the town's turbulent history and find out about the castle's traditional place in the town over the centuries. The castle is well preserved, and the museum contains historical, religious, industrial, and agricultural artifacts from the 19th and 20th centuries. There's a really complete display dealing with the 1798 uprising — an exceptionally big piece of history in these parts, given the town's participation.

Location: Castle Hill, Enniscorthy. ☎ 054-35-926. By car: North of Wexford off the N11 or east of New Ross off the N30. Admission: €3.75 ($3.55) adults, €2.50 ($2.40) students and seniors, €0.75 (70¢) children, €9.25 ($8.80) family. Open April to September, 10 a.m. to 6 p.m.; October to November and February to March 2:00 to 5:30 p.m. Closed December and January. Suggested visit: 45 minutes.

Organized tours

If you'd like a more in-depth look at Wexford (County or Town), here are a couple of good touring options.

> ✔ **Walking Tours of Wexford:** You can see the sights of Wexford town on this tour, lasting one and a half to two hours, "depending on how interested everyone is." Book ahead — the number of tours and time of departure depend on how many people are involved.
>
> When and where: Generally given daily between 11:30 a.m. and 2:30 p.m. year-round. Meets at the Westgate Heritage Tower, William Street, Wexford. ☎ **053-46-508.** Price: €3.75 ($3.55) adults, €1.25 ($1.20) for children.
>
> ✔ **Galley Cruising:** Travel the calm and brackish waters of the River Barrow for a relaxing tour of the countryside. When and where: June through August, leaves at 3 p.m. daily from New Ross Quay, 15 miles from Waterford on N25. ☎ **051-42-1723.** Price: €6.25 ($5.95). Optional tea and snack, additional €7.50 ($7.15). No credit cards.

Shopping in County Wexford

Faller's Sweater Shop

Far from the Aran Islands, this shop nonetheless specializes in authentic Aran knitwear — sweaters mostly, but also accessories like scarves and hats.

29B N. Main St., Wexford Town. ☎ *053-24-659.*

Hynes Jewelers

This shop carries leading brands of watches and gifts but specializes in Celtic jewelry and claddagh rings.

17 North Main St., Wexford Town. ☎ *053-22-736.*

Westgate Design

A large selection of Irish giftware, from wool clothing to pottery, is the highlight of this little shop.

22 North Main St., Wexford Town. ☎ *053-23-787.*

Wexford Silver

A family of silver- and goldsmiths run this shop, which sells finely crafted pieces, perfect for gifts or keepsakes.

115 N. Main St., Wexford Town. ☎ *053-21-933.*

Pub life in County Wexford

Macken's The Cape of Good Hope

As you venture into Wexford's famous Bullring area, you're sure to do a double take when you see Macken's: The awning over the entrance advertises a bar, undertaker, and grocery. And it's no joke — you can have a pint, pick up a loaf of bread, and make funeral arrangements in one convenient stop! Irish rebels made Macken's a popular meeting place over the centuries, and mementos from their struggles line the walls. Definitely a place like none other.

The Bullring, Wexford Town. ☎ **053-22-949.**

Crown Bar

The oldest pub in Wexford Town, the Crown was formerly a stagecoach inn and is full of antique memorabilia. Dueling pistols and other weapons from the revolutionary days of yore may be the main draw for many who pop in, but the locals go there for the excellent drink and town gossip.

Monck Street, Wexford Town. ☎ **053-21-133.**

Antique

The black-and-white exterior makes this traditional pub easy to recognize. Inside, it's a dark and cozy public house full of revolutionary antiques. Check out the famous weapons of the Pikeman of the 1798 uprising. The balcony is a nice spot for sitting outside when the weather's nice.

14 Slaney St., Enniscorthy. ☎ **054-33-428.**

Fast Facts: County Wexford

Area Code(s)

County Wexford's area codes (or city codes) are **051, 053, 054,** and **055.**

Emergencies/Hospital

Dial ☎ **999** for all emergencies. Wexford General Hospital is on New Town Road, Wexford (☎ 053-42-233).

Genealogical Resources

Contact the County Wexford Heritage Research Centre, Yola Farmstead Folk Park,

Tagoat (☎ 053-32-610; Fax: 053-32-612; E-mail: wexgen@iol.ie; Internet: http://homepage.eircom.net/~yola wexford).

Information

For visitor information, go to the tourist office at Crescent Quay, Wexford (☎ 053-23-111, open year-round). It can also provide reservation services. Seasonal offices (open June through September) are in Enniscorthy at the Town Centre (☎ 054-34-699) and Rosslare

Harbour Terminal Building (☎ 053-33-232). Another great source is the Web site www.wexfordtourism.com. For telephone directory assistance, dial ☎ 1190.

Post Office

The main post office is on Anna Street, Wexford (☎ 053-22-587).

County Waterford and Waterford City

The name Waterford certainly sounds appropriate for a place on the shores of two rivers, but the name actually comes from the Danish for "weather haven," which is funny: I don't know what the Viking invaders who named it were used to in terms of weather, but Waterford sure gets plenty of rain!

Speaking of invaders, Waterford is the only city in Ireland that was spared Oliver Cromwell's brutal and bloody 1649 attack, though not through lack of effort. He attempted to invade Waterford from two routes, through Hook Head and Crooke Village — neither of which are direct or easy ways to enter Waterford. Both tries failed, and from that we get the expression about doing something "by hook or by crook" — when you resort to unconventional and extreme tactics to get something done.

County Waterford isn't exactly chock-full of a zillion things to see and do, but the things it has — such as **Waterford City** itself and the famous **Waterford Crystal Factory** — are amazing in their own right and more than worth the stop. The main part of Waterford City runs along the River Suir and has a wonderful medieval feel to it, with narrow alleyways and the remains of its city wall. The major attraction downtown is the richly historic **Reginald's Tower** (Waterford Crystal is a few miles out of town), there are several nice restaurants and hotels, and although the city has become cosmopolitan thanks to modern shopping and commerce, it's still very much part of the "auld worlde."

Getting to and around Waterford City

If you're driving, take the N25 from Cork or Wexford or N7 to N9 from Dublin to get to Waterford City. Lismore is on the N72 off the N25. A fast and cost-effective route across Waterford Harbour, between Passage East, County Waterford (10 miles east of Waterford), and Ballyhack, County Wexford (20 miles west of Wexford), is provided by **Passenger East Car Ferry** (☎ 051-38-2480). It runs year-round, Sunday through Friday. The cost per vehicle is €7.50 ($7.15) round-trip, €5 ($4.75) one-way.

Waterford City

ACCOMMODATIONS ■
The Bridge **1**
Jury's **2**
Tower **9**

DINING ◆
Jade Palace **10**
The Wine Vault **5**

ATTRACTIONS ●
Reginald's Tower **8**
Waterford Crystal **12**

SHOPPING ▲
Heritage Irish Crystal **6**
Joseph Knox Ltd. **4**
Kelly's Limited **6**
Waterford City Design Centre **6**

NIGHTLIFE ◖
The Munster **7**
The Olde Stand **11**
T&H Doolans **3**

Information ⓘ

Irish Rail (☎ 051-87-401) services Waterford at Plunkett Station, located next to the Ignatius Rice Bridge. **Bus Eireann** (☎ 01-87-9000) travels year-round to Waterford, Lismore, and other major towns in County Waterford. In Waterford City, buses arrive at Plunkett Station, next to the Ignatius Rice Bridge. Bus Eireann also has a tour bus out of Dublin covering the River Barrow and the Waterford Crystal Factory. It leaves Dublin's main bus terminal at 9:30 a.m. and returns at 9 p.m. on Wednesdays, June through October. The cost is €31.30 ($29.75) adults, €21.25 ($20.20) child. The cost includes lunch and a boat tour of the River Barrow.

Waterford is an easily walkable city. Stroll up the Quays toward Reginald's Tower, take a right, and you'll be in the heart of town. You'll need a car to get out to the Waterford Crystal Factory, though, unless you take a taxi (available in the city and mostly found at Plunkett

Station on the Quay; call **Parnell Cabs** at ☎ **051-87-7710** if you need one to pick you up). If you're parking your car here, you'll need parking disks, which you can buy at local shops near the block you're parking on or at the tourist office. Hotels in the city center generally have their own parking areas.

Where to stay in Waterford

Tower
$$$ Waterford City

Here is a three-star hotel that leaves nothing for want. Facing Reginald's Tower and situated next to the river, the Tower is in the heart of the city and is the flagship branch of the Tower Hotel Group. The rooms are large and have wide windows that open to the lovely breezes that come off the water. The finest rooms face the river and allow you to watch the water traffic slowly tug by. The indoor pool and gym are nice amenities and the huge Adelphi Riverside Lounge is a nice spot for a nightcap.

The Mall, Waterford City. ☎ *800-448-8355 from the United States; 051-87-5801. Fax: 051-87-0129. To get there: It's across the street from Reginald's Tower, near The Quay. Rates: €118.60–€131.25 ($112.65–$107.05) double. AE, DC, MC, V.*

The Bridge
$$–$$$ Waterford City

This three-star hotel overlooking the River Suir is one of the oldest in Waterford, but it has been refurbished to provide every modern comfort. The Bridge is what an old Irish hotel should be: It's run like a tight ship by the Treacy family but has a friendly, jovial atmosphere. Three in-house restaurants can serve up just about anything you want.

1 The Quay, Waterford City. ☎ *051-87-7222. Fax: 051-87-7229. Internet:* www. bridgehotel.com. *To get there: Take The Quay to the foot of the Ignatius Rice Bridge. Rates: €82.50–€112.50 ($78.40–$106.90) double. AE, DC, MC, V.*

Jury's
$$$ Waterford City

There's a great view of Waterford and the River Suir from this hotel on a mountain. The spacious rooms are decorated Victorian style. If you can't fully relax there, try the indoor heated pool, the sauna, or the steam room. The Jury's hotel chain always delivers, and this branch in Waterford is no exception.

Ferrybank (across the river bank from city center), Waterford. ☎ *051-83-2111. Fax: 051-83-2863. Internet:* www.jurys.com. *To get there: Take Rice Bridge, from The Quay, across the River Suir. Rates: €118.75–€131.25 ($101.55–$124.70) double. AE, DC, MC, V.*

Samuels Heritage B&B

$ Ballymacode

This beautiful family home is set on 30 acres of farm and garden land overlooking the River Suir. The rooms are all nonsmoking and en suite; televisions are available upon request. It's within close proximity to beaches and four 18-hole golf courses. A nice touch is having your breakfast outdoors if the weather's nice.

Dunmore Road, Ballymacode, Waterford. ☎ *051-87-5094. By car: Take Cork Road from city center 3 miles to Dunmore, beyond the Regional Hospital and Orpens Pub, on the left. Rates: €45 ($42.75) double. No credit cards.*

Where to dine in Waterford

Turn that smile upside down with some blaa! More upscale restaurants may not serve this local specialty, but Waterford locals enjoy their *blaa* (meat, onion, tomato, and lettuce on a roll). Sounds a little blah, but it'll perk you up! The best blaa I had was at Munster's (see the "Pub life in Waterford City" section, later in this chapter).

In addition to the places I list later in the chapter, you can also combine your dinner with a river cruise aboard the **Galley Cruising Restaurant.** Although you catch the boat on the River Barrow in New Ross, County Wexford (see "Other fun stuff to do" in the Wexford section), the trip takes you down to the River Suir and through County Waterford.

The Wine Vault

$$$–$$$$ Waterford City SEAFOOD

Not just a place for excellent oysters, mussels, and fresh prawns, the Vault has historical appeal and is a must-stop for wine enthusiasts. This cavernous yet cozy stone-walled casual restaurant is the former home of Waterford mayor and wine merchant James Rice. Currently, the wine list runs to as many as 250 selections. The Vault's wine shop has an excellent range and you can buy souvenir glasses with the Vault's logo (Bacchus, the Greek god of wine). Try a white wine with the house specialty, panache of seafood in a tarragon and lobster bisque sauce.

Lower High Street, Waterford City. ☎ *051-85-3444. E-mail:* bacchus@tinet.ie. *Main courses: €15–€25 ($14.25–$23.75). AE, V. Open: Mon–Sat 12:30–2:30 p.m., 5:30–10:30 p.m.*

Jade Palace

$$–$$$$ Waterford City CHINESE

Chinese food? In Ireland? Yes. Authentic, mouth-watering, you'll-eat-too-much Cantonese and Szechuan in downtown Waterford. This is the kind of place where you tell the manager what you think you'd like and let him decide for you. Your choice of silverware or chopsticks. The steamed fish with ginger is excellent.

3 The Mall, Waterford, next to Reginald's Tower in city center. ☎ 051-85-5611. Main courses: €11.25–€21.25 ($10.70–$20.20). Service charge of 10% added. AE, MC, V. Open: Mon–Fri. 12:30–2:30 p.m., Sun 1–3 p.m., daily 5:30 p.m. to midnight.

Ballyrafter House
$$$$ Lismore   SEAFOOD

You know you can expect good seafood from a restaurant if the local fishermen recommend it, and Ballyrafter House is no exception. It has a great view of the riverside Lismore Castle, and it's the little touches, like fresh-cut flowers from the garden or the pub's many photographs of smiling fishermen and their big catches, that make this place so memorable. The smoked Blackwater Salmon is delicious and is one of the most popular dishes.

Right on the N72, Lismore. ☎ 058-54-002. By car: From Waterford or Cork take the N25 to the N72 at Dungarvan. Main courses: €22–€26 ($20.90–$24.70); €30 ($28.50) for five course prix-fixe menu. AE, DC, MC, V. Open: March–Dec daily 1:00–2:30 p.m. and 7:30–9:30 p.m.

The Tannery
$$$$ Dungarvin   SEAFOOD

This old leather tannery has been converted into a stylish, contemporary restaurant. The kitchen is wide open so patrons can watch chef Paul Flynn in action. The interior is minimalist — white dishes on unadorned light-wood tables. The roasted red pepper soup with basil aoili is an excellent starter. Follow it with the delicious crispy cod cakes. Desserts are too tantalizing to pass up.

10 Quay St., Dungarvan. ☎ 058-45-420. By car: From Waterford or Cork, take the N25. Main courses: €25–€27.50 ($23.75–$26.15) for five courses. No credit cards. Open: Tues–Thur 12:30–2:30 p.m., 6:30–10:00 p.m.; Fri and Sat 12:30–2:30 p.m., 6:30–10:30 p.m.

Exploring County Waterford: The top attractions

Waterford Crystal Factory
Kilbarry

What makes crystal shine brighter than regular glass? It's the lead, of course! Seems odd, but the addition of a lead oxite called red litharge gives crystal that characteristic gleam. That's the first thing you'll learn in the surprisingly interesting tour of the Waterford Crystal Factory. You'll be shown every step of the meticulous process that goes into making the world-renowned Waterford Crystal, from the blowing to the cutting to the detail decorating. And talk about a stressful job: The Waterford Crystal Factory has a six-step screening process for every piece that's made. Only perfect pieces of crystal make it out of the factory, which means 45% are destroyed for minor flaws. The glass blowers and craftsmen only get paid for perfect pieces. Sometimes on the Waterford Crystal tour you get to see one-of-a-kind pieces in production, like the Millennium Ball that fell in Times Square at midnight in 2000, or the Super Bowl's Vince Lombardi Trophy, which I saw them working on. After the tour, you can stop in the Waterford Crystal Gallery to stock up.

Kilbarry (five minutes out of Waterford). ☎ *051-37-3311. By car: From Waterford, take the main road to Cork (N25); the factory is 5 miles outside town on the right. Admission: €2.50 ($2.40) for tour. Open: April–Oct tours daily 8:30 a.m.–4:00 p.m., showroom daily 8:30 a.m.–6:00 p.m.; Nov–March tours Mon–Fri 9:00 a.m.–3:15 p.m., showroom Mon–Fri 8:30 a.m.–6:00 p.m. Suggested visit: 2 hours.*

Reginald's Tower
Waterford City

Recently refurbished, this small but significant landmark in the heart of Waterford City is worth the three-story climb to the top. The tower, which is the only Viking building continuously used since that age, has seen a lot of history and worn many hats. The ground and first floors were built around the beginning of the 13th century, and the top floors were built as many as 300 years later. Besides being the main tower for the old city walls, the building was the wedding chapel for Norman chief Strongbow, as well as a place for minting money, an ammunition dump, and a police station. If these walls could talk. . . .

The Quay, Waterford City. ☎ *051-30-4220. Admission: €2 ($1.90) adult, €1.25 ($1.20) child. Open: April and May Mon–Fri 10 a.m.–1 p.m. and 2–6 p.m., Sat 10 a.m.–1 p.m.; June–Oct Mon–Fri 10 a.m.–8 p.m., Sat 10 a.m.–1 p.m. and 2–6 p.m. Suggested visit: 30 minutes.*

Lismore Castle
Lismore

This castle was originally built in the 12th century and was owned by Sir Walter Raleigh in the 16th century. Raleigh never actually lived in his castle, which is a shame for him; it rests on a beautiful spot high above the River Blackwater and the view is incredible. The castle itself isn't open to the public, but the gorgeous 8,000-acre estate and garden are, and there's plenty to see.

Lismore. ☎ *058-54-424. By car: From Waterford or Cork take the N25 to the N75 in Dungarvan. Admission: €3.75 ($3.55) per person. Open: April–Sept daily 1:45– 4:45 p.m. Suggested visit: 1½ hours.*

Joining an organized tour

If you'd like some guidance during your visit to Waterford, check out these organized tours.

✔ **Waterford Tourist Services Walking Tours:** Lasting an hour, this tour covers four national monuments, including Reginald's Tower and the Wine Vault Restaurant (see "Where to dine in Waterford City").

Where and when: Leaves from the Granville Hotel (Meagher Quay), March to October daily at noon and 2 p.m. Information: ☎ **051-87- 3711** or 051-85-1043. Price: €3.75 ($3.55) adults, free for children.

✔ **Galley Cruising:** Travel the calm and brackish waters of the River Suir estuary and have a relaxing tour of the countryside.

Where and when: June to August daily 3 p.m., Waterford Harbour, next to the Custom House Parade. Information: ☎ **051-42-1723.** Price: €6.25 ($5.95). The optional tea and snack is an additional €7.50 ($7.15). No credit cards.

Shopping in Waterford City

Heritage Irish Crystal

The other authentic, hand-blown crystal makers in town; excellent quality but not as big or famous as its counterpart — Waterford Crystal.

67–68 The Quay, Waterford City. ☎ *051-84-1787.*

Joseph Knox Ltd.

Established in the 18th century, this gift shop stocks Celtic jewelry, English and Irish china and crystal, porcelain, and linen.

3–4 Barronstrand St., Waterford City. ☎ *051-87-2723.*

Kelly's Limited

At 150 years old, it's one of the oldest businesses in town, selling crafts, linens, Waterford Crystal, and Belleek pottery.

75 The Quay, Waterford City. ☎ *051-87-3557.*

Waterford City Design Centre

Everything you could be looking for is under one roof: gifts, designer Irish clothing, handcrafted ceramics, jewelry, candles, linen, lace, glass, and more.

44 The Quay, Waterford City. ☎ *051-85-6666.*

Waterford Crystal Gallery

This is the most famous showroom of crystal in the world. It's two floors of only the best.

Kilbarry (five minutes out of Waterford). ☎ *051-873-311. By car: Take the main Cork Road (N25). Open: Mon–Fri 8:30 a.m.–6:00 p.m. Plus Nov–March, Sat 8:30 a.m.– 6:00 p.m.*

Pub life in Waterford City

T&H Doolans

The oldest tavern in Waterford, Doolans has long been considered the best establishment in the area. This black-and-white 18th-century pub opens onto a pedestrian street in the center of town and has excellent traditional music sessions every night, warm fires, delicious pub grub, warm welcomes, and a cheerful crowd. Oh, and the stout is perfect as well. What's the T&H stand for? That's for you to find out.

31 George's St., Waterford City. ☎ *051-87-2764.*

The Munster

The Munster (also known as Fitzgerald's) is superbly decorated with Waterford Crystal, antique mirrors, and wood walls taken from the old Waterford toll bridge. There are many sections to this old-world bar and restaurant, and it's a good place to get to know the locals when you find you've been seeing the same ol' tourist faces over and over. Traditional music kicks up on weekends mostly.

Bailey's New Street, Waterford City. ☎ *051-87-4656.*

The Olde Stand

This Victorian Pub — or rather, pubs (there are two downstairs and one upstairs) — is a fine place for a pint or a meal. There's a restaurant upstairs, but you can have a casual meal downstairs as well. Everyone raves about the steak and the fresh seafood dishes. I liked the well-pulled Guinness and the chatty bartender who enjoyed my company as much as I did his.

45 Michael St., Waterford City. ☎ *051-87-9488.*

Fast Facts: County Waterford

Area Code(s)

County Waterford's area codes (or city codes) are **051, 052,** and **058.**

Emergencies/Police

Dial ☎ **999** for all emergencies. Regional Hospital, Cork Road, Waterford (☎ 051-87-3321). Late-night Pharmacy: Mulligans, Dunmore Road, Waterford (☎ 051-84-3700), is open until 9 p.m. Monday through Saturday and 6 p.m. on Sundays.

Genealogical Resources

Contact the Waterford Heritage Survey, Jenkins Lane (St. Patrick's Church), Waterford (☎ 051-87-6123 or 051-87-3711; Fax 051-85-0645; E-mail: mnoc@iol.ie).

Information

For visitor information go to the tourist office at 21 The Quay (☎ 051-87-5788), open year-round. It can also provide reservation services. For telephone directory assistance, dial ☎ 1190.

Internet

Voyager Internet Cafe, Parnell Court, Parnell Street (☎ 051-84-3843), has Internet access and printing capabilities.

Post Office

The main post office is on Parade Quay, Waterford City (☎ 051-74-444).

County Tipperary

Even though it's one of the largest counties in Ireland, Tipperary isn't exactly a bustling area, so I don't recommend setting up camp here (and for that reason haven't provided any lodging choices). Tipperary does have one of the country's largest attractions, though: the **Rock of Cashel.** This, and some great places to shop, makes it a nice place to wander through.

While you're moseying around and hitting the pubs, you're likely to hear the song "It's a Long Way to Tipperary," a happy yet plaintive tune about an Irishman in England missing his home. The song was actually composed by Englishman Jack Judge — a man who'd never been to Ireland in his life! He chose the town's name for his song simply because it made the basis of a good rhyme. But the song is perhaps best known by Americans as the tune the cast of *The Mary Tyler Moore Show* sang as they left the station for the last time.

Getting to and around County Tipperary

If you're coming by car, take the N8 from Cork or Dublin (via N7) to Cashel and Cahir. Take the N24 from Limerick or Waterford to Tipperary and Cahir. **Irish Rail** (☎ 01-836-6222) services Tipperary,

Cahir, and Carrick-on-Suir, and **Bus Eireann** (☎ 01-836-6111) travels year-round to Tipperary, Cahir, Cashel, and Carrick-on-Suir, as well as other major towns in County Tipperary.

Where to dine in County Tipperary

Chez Hanz
$$$$ Cashel   FRENCH

This is French cuisine at its finest, as evidenced by the number of patrons who flock to this converted Baptist chapel. From the black-and-white uniformed waitstaff to the artistic dishes, everything is professional and to the nines. The portions are surprisingly large, the famous Cashel blue cheese finds its way into many dishes, and the fresh desserts are to die for. Don't be afraid to try something you've never had before, like the mussel gratin — everything is simply top-notch.

Rockside, Cashel. ☎ *062-61-177. To get there: Just look for the giant rock. The restaurant is located below it. Main courses: €27.50–€31.25 ($26.15–$26.70). MC, V. Open: Tues–Sat 6:30–10:00 p.m. Closed Jan. Reservations required.*

Angela's Wholefood Restaurant
$ Clonmel   INTERNATIONAL

Angela's Wholefood Restaurant offers scrumptious, substantial fare at remarkable value. The blackboard menu may include custom-made breakfast omelets, spicy Moroccan lamb stew, savory tomato-and-spinach flan Provençal, homemade soups and sandwiches made to order, and an array of delicious salads. The food is vibrant, fresh, and appreciated by the bustling patrons who line up with trays in hand, from barristers (in garb) to baby-sitters.

Clonmel. ☎ *052-26-899. To get there: 14 Abbey St. in Clonmel. Breakfast menu €2.50–€5 ($2.40–$4.75); lunch menu €2–€6.90 ($1.90–$6.55). No service charge. No credit cards. Mon–Fri 9:00 a.m.–5:30 p.m., Sat noon to 5 p.m.*

Exploring County Tipperary: The top attractions

Rock of Cashel and Museum
Cashel

Sure, it's big, but even so, you may be wondering, "What's so important about Cashel?" Here goes: Legend places St. Patrick in Cashel for his famous explanation of the Holy Trinity. He is said to have shown pagans a shamrock, pointing out that the three leaves represent the Father, Son, and Holy Ghost. In the 11th century, Ireland's most important High King, Brian Ború, was crowned King of Ireland here (which explains the presence of the Brú Ború National Culture Centre nearby — see the next listing).

Today, the limestone Rock of Cashel is one of the country's most awesome archeological sites. The Round Tower is perhaps the oldest and most remarkably well preserved building of its kind. Irish Romanesque–style Cormacs Chapel, located on a dramatic outcrop, is ornate with carved beasts and human figures. The unique St. Patrick's Cross (a replica — the original is in the museum) has the carved figure of St. Patrick on one side and Jesus on the other. The roofless cathedral is the largest building on the Rock and was never restored after being set fire (along with the villagers hiding inside) by Oliver Cromwell's men. The museum, housed in the beautifully restored Hall of Vicars, the old choir residence, has great views for photos and contains stone carvings and silver religious artifacts.

Cashel. ☎ 062-61-437. By car: Take N8 from Dublin or N74 east from Tipperary. Admission: €3.75 ($3.55) adults, €2.50 ($2.40) seniors, €1.50 ($1.45) children, €9.50 ($9.05) family. Open: Mid-March to mid-June daily 9:30 a.m.–5:30 p.m.; mid-June to mid-Sept daily 9:00 a.m.–7:30 p.m.; mid-Sept to mid-March daily 9:30 a.m.–4:30 p.m. Suggested visit: 1 hour.

Brú Ború National Culture Centre
Cashel

Located next to the Rock of Cashel, the Culture Centre has advanced family-research facilities but is more popular for the music, theater, and craft exhibits it hosts. The resident group of entertainers has represented Ireland all over the world and was even on *Good Morning America.* Brú Ború means "Palace of King Brian Boru."

Rock of Cashel. ☎ 062-61-122. By car: Take N8 from Dublin or N74 east from Tipperary. Admission: Free. Evening performance: €10 ($9.50) or €31.30 ($29.75) for dinner and show. Open: Mon–Fri 9 a.m.–5 p.m. Folk theater performances 9 p.m. (dinner at 7 p.m.), June–Sept Tues–Sat. Suggested visit: Varies, depending on event.

Mitchelstown Cave
Cahir

You can explore three massive caverns full of cool stalactites and sta-lagmites with biblical names like the Tower of Babel and the Shroud of Turin. Tour guides explain the formation of the caves and describe fea-tures and wall markings as they take you through nearly a half-mile of caverns. *Note:* The caves can get quite chilly, so wear your new Aran sweater.

Burncourt, Cahir. ☎ 052-67-246. By car: Go west of Tipperary off the N7. Admission: €3.75 ($3.55) adults, €3.25 ($3.10) seniors, €1.25 ($1.20) children. Open: Daily 10 a.m.–6 p.m. Suggested visit: Up to 2 hours.

Cahir Castle
Cahir

The castle, one of Ireland's largest and best preserved, sits on an island in the middle of the River Suir. The walls and towers are in near-pristine condition and the interior is fully restored. The audiovisual presentation is interesting as well, covering the history of the castle. Attention movie buffs: The castle was used as the set for John Boorman's film *Excalibur.*

Cahir. ☎ 052-41-011. By car: Off the N8 from Cashel or Cork or N24 from Tipperary. Admission: €2.50 ($2.40) adults, €2 ($1.90) seniors, €1.25 ($1.20) students and children. Open: Mid-March to mid-June and mid-Sept to mid-Oct daily 9:30 a.m.–5:30 p.m.; mid-June to mid-Sept daily 9:00 a.m.–7:30 p.m.; mid-Oct to mid-March daily 9:30 a.m.–4:30 p.m. Suggested visit: 1 hour.

Holy Trinity Church and Medieval Walls
Fethard

Sitting along the River Clashawley, the small town of Fethard (population: under 1,000) claims the most complete circuit of medieval town walls in Ireland. Enter the walled inner city at the cast-iron gateway on Abbey Street, which opens into the pretty churchyard of Holy Trinity. The heather-strewn views of the valley are best from the heights of one of the towers, and the church itself is a fine example of the castle-like construction of medieval churches.

Fethard. No telephone. By car: Take the small road connecting Cashel and Windgap east from Cashel or go north off the N24 to Fethard town. Admission: Free. Open: No official hours, but the Abbey Street gate of the town wall is often locked. During normal business hours you can get a key from Whytes grocery store just a few doors down on Main Street. And if the church is closed and you want to enter, you can get a key from Dr. Stoke's office at the eastern end of Main Street. Suggested visit: 2 hours.

Joining an organized tour

Cashel Heritage Tram Tour provides tours of Cashel's historic sites as well as entry to the Cashel Heritage Centre and Bolton Library. The train leaves from the Heritage Centre (see earlier in this chapter), and you can hop on and off where you please. It operates June through September, Tuesday through Saturday, noon to 6 p.m. Information: ☎ 062-62-511. Price: €3.75 ($3.55) adults, €2 ($1.90), for students.

Shopping in County Tipperary

Farney Castle

Uniquely located inside a medieval castle, this knitwear and porcelain shop has Jacob sweaters (from the un-dyed colored fleece of the rare Jacob sheep), jackets, and fine porcelain figurines and ornaments.

Near Thurles and Holycross, on the R503 from the N8. No phone.

Hanley's Woolen Mill Shop

Located next to the weaving factory in Ballyartella, Hanley's has a fantastic collection of tweed, knitwear, pottery, glassware, and gift items. The Mill Shop provides weaving demonstrations and complimentary tea and coffee.

Ballyartella, Neagh (take the R495 to Dromineer and turn right toward Ballycommon). No phone.

Tipperary Crystal Designs

A band of rebel craftsmen left Waterford Crystal in 1988 and set up this enterprise, where they produce the same top-quality stuff they did under their former label. These folks are so good they're the only Irish crystal producer to supply the prestigious Tiffany & Co. They give free tours Monday through Friday from April to September.

Carrick-on-Suir. ☎ 051-64-1188. By car: Take the N24 from Waterford, located next to Dovehill Castle. Showroom hours: Winter, Mon–Fri 9:00 a.m.–5:15 p.m., Sat 9:30 a.m.–4:45 p.m., Sun 11:00 a.m.–4:45 p.m.; summer, Mon–Sat 9 a.m.–6 p.m., Sun 11:00 a.m.–5:30 p.m.

Tipperary Music

Watch *bodhráns* (traditional Irish drums) being made and wander through the showroom full of other traditional instruments, plus Irish music books, CDs, and crafts.

Main Street, Clogheen. ☎ 052-65-307. By car: Take the R668 from Lismore or Cahir or the R665 from Mitchelstown or Clonmel.

Pub life in County Tipperary

Ronald Reagan Pub

Pints are pulled with a special "trickle-down" tap method that seems to have staved off the inflationary cost of beer at this pub that is, in fact, named after the former president himself. In 1984, Ronnie visited Ballyporeen, hometown of his great-grandfather, and the pub/gift shop/shrine has photos of the historic visit on the walls, as well as mementos for sale. More hype than hops, but an interesting stop.

Main Street, The Square, Ballyporeen. ☎ *052-67-133.*

Fast Facts: County Tipperary

Area Code(s)

County Tipperary's area codes (or city codes) are **051, 052, 062,** and **067.**

Emergencies/Police

Dial ☎ **999** for all emergencies.

Genealogy Resources

Contact the Brú Ború Heritage Centre, Rock of Cashel (☎ 062-61-122; Fax: 062-62-700), or the Tipperary Heritage Unit, The

Bridewell, Michael Street, Tipperary (☎ 062-52-757; E-mail: thu@iol.ie).

Information

For visitor information, go to the seasonal tourist offices at Town Hall, Main Street, Cashel (☎ 062-61-333), open April through September; or James Street, Tipperary (☎ 062-51-457), open May through September. For telephone directory assistance, dial ☎ 1190.

County Kilkenny

Often tourists stop in Kilkenny only because they have to drive through it to get to Dublin. They may stop to see **Kilkenny Castle** or have a pint at the **Marble City Bar,** but often they then just drive on. That could soon change — recently Kilkenny county and town have made an effort to restore some of the historic sights in the area in hopes of becoming a more popular destination. I've listed only the top attractions and most interesting things to see in the time you have, but I've also included a couple of great accommodations and some shopping areas if you choose to extend your stay in County Kilkenny. You won't be disappointed if you do. Kilkenny is fast becoming the preferred route from Dublin, chosen over the nature-oriented route of Wexford or the crystal capital of Waterford.

Getting to County Kilkenny

By car, take the N7 to N9 to N10 south from Dublin or the N9 north from Waterford to Kilkenny City. **Irish Rail** (☎ 01-836-6222) services Kilkenny Town and Thomastown. **Bus Eireann** (☎ 01-836-6111) travels year-round to Kilkenny Town and other towns in County Kilkenny and also has a tour bus out of Dublin covering Kilkenny Town, Jerpoint Abbey, and the Nore Valley. It leaves Dublin's main bus terminal at 9:30 a.m. and returns at 7 p.m. on Wednesdays, June through October.

Kilkenny Town

To Freshford

Green's Bridge

To Castlecomer, Dublin

Troy's Gate

Green St.

Troy's Ln.

Church Ln.

Vicar St.

River Nore

Greensbridge St.

Castlecomer Rd.

Ballybought St.

Grange Rd.

Church Ln.

Irishtown

Coach Rd.

1

Wolfe Tone St.

John's Green

Barrack St.

Castlecomer New Rd.

Thomas St.

Dean St.

Abbey St.

Parliament St.

2

New Building Ln.

John's Quay

Michael St.

John St. Upper

Dublin Rd.

10

To Carlow

Black Mill St.

Evan's Ln.

P

3

James's St.

4

Chapel Ln.

John St. Lower

Maudlin St.

John St. Lower

9

James's Green

Collier's Ln.

Poyntz's Ln.

St. Kieran St.

St. John's Bridge

Dominic St.

P

Guard Ln.

High St.

River Nore

Kickham St.

Garden Row

William St.

P

Rose Inn St.

Canal Walk

Parnell St.

Friary St.

ⓘ

Stephen's St.

Penney's

Father Ln.

5

The Parade

P

Gaol Rd.

Upper Walkin's St.

Lower New St.

Patrick St.

6 **8**

7

Castle Rd.

Gaol St.

Ormonde Rd.

Jacob St.

Fr. Hayden's Rd.

Archers St.

Old Callan Rd.

College Rd.

Patrick St.

Coote's Ln.

Upper New St.

Nuncio Rd.

To Bennettsbridge, Thomastown, Rosslare

Information **ⓘ**

Parking **P**

P To Callan, Cork

To Waterford

NORTHERN IRELAND

Dublin

REPUBLIC ★ OF IRELAND

Kilkenny Town

ACCOMMODATIONS ■	**SHOPPING ▲**
Butler House **5**	Kilkenny Design Centre
DINING ◆	and Crescent Workshops **7**
Lacken House **10**	**NIGHTLIFE ☾**
Rinuccini **6**	Kyteler's **3**
ATTRACTIONS ●	Langton's **9**
Kilkenny Castle **8**	Marble City Bar **4**
St. Canice's Cathedral **1**	Smithwick's Brewery **2**

Where to stay in County Kilkenny

Butler House
$$$ **Kilkenny Town**

This wonderful house was once part of Kilkenny Castle, and the castle gardens out back are proof. The three-story, ivy-covered house overlooks the town's main street, and each of the 14 rooms is decorated individually, tastefully, and comfortably. You couldn't ask for a better location — just stepping out of the front door puts you in the perfect place to start off exploring the city. If you decide to stay in (and I could hardly blame you), you can ask for a VCR and movie from the collection at the front desk.

16 St. Patrick St., Kilkenny Town. ☎ *056-65-707. Fax: 056-65-626. Internet:* www.butler.ie. *By car: Take the N7 to N9 to N10 from Dublin to Kilkenny. Rates: €111.25–€123.75 ($105.70–$117.55) double. AE, DC, MC, V.*

Cullintra House B&B
$$ **Inistioge**

A finely built farmhouse among trees and farmland, this place seems a million miles from everything even though it's just 5 or 6 miles from Jerpoint Abbey and close to Kilkenny. Relax by the fireplace in the living room or take a stroll down to the River Nore. There's a conservatory where you can watch local foxes milling around out back, and nature trails lead from the house. Your host, Mrs. Cantlon, goes the extra distance to make you feel at home.

The Rower, Inistioge. ☎ *051-42-3614. By car: Take R700 south from Kilkenny or north from New Ross. Rates: €50–€62.50 ($47.50–$59.40) double. No credit cards.*

Where to dine in County Kilkenny

Lacken House
$$$$ **Kilkenny Town**   **IRISH/INTERNATIONAL**

In this handsome but unassuming house, the McSweeneys (husband Eugene is the chef, wife Breda is the wine expert) serve the best in Irish and international cuisine and will advise you on exactly which wine goes best with your meal. Try the lamb or the outstanding vegetable soup with nettle pesto.

Dublin Road, Kilkenny (just outside of town). ☎ *056-61-085. By car: Take the N7 to N9 to N10 from Dublin to Kilkenny. Main courses: €28.75 ($27.30) prix-fixe dinner. AE, DC, MC, V. Open: Tues–Sat 7:00–10:30 p.m.*

Rinuccini

$$$ Kilkenny Town ITALIAN

You surely didn't expect to come to Ireland for Italian food, but there's so much of it (and it's so good) that it's hard to pass it by. Rinuccini is a great example. This quaint restaurant is run by an Italian who specializes in homemade pasta dishes, but it also serves veal, seafood, and steaks. It's just across from Kilkenny Castle.

Number 1, The Parade, Kilkenny Town (opposite Kilkenny Castle). ☎ *056-61-575. By car: Take the N7 to N9 to N10 from Dublin to Kilkenny. Main courses: €12.50–€18.75 ($11.90–$17.80). AE, DC, MC, V. Open: Daily 12:30–2:30 p.m. and 6:00–11:30 p.m.*

Exploring County Kilkenny: The top attractions

Kilkenny Castle

Kilkenny Town

This 12th-century medieval castle, the principal attraction in Kilkenny, sits among beautiful sculptured gardens and a formal rose garden on the shore of the River Nore. Guided tours take you through restored rooms, including the 150-foot Long Gallery (which boasts masterpieces by the likes of Dutch master Van Dyck), a library, drawing room, and bedrooms. The castle's Butler Gallery houses modern art exhibits and the National Furniture Collection is like no other in the world. There is also a large outdoor children's play area.

The Parade, Kilkenny. ☎ *056-21-450. By car: Take the N9 north from Waterford or take the N7 to N9 to N10 out of Dublin. Admission: €3.75 ($3.55) adults, €2.50 ($2.40) seniors, €1.50 ($1.45) students and children. Open: April–May daily 10:30 a.m.–5:00 p.m., Oct–March Tues–Sat 10:30 a.m.–5:00 p.m., June–Sept daily 10 a.m.–7 p.m. Suggested visit: 1½ hours.*

Dunmore Cave

Ballyfoyle

These large, well-lit chambers and passageways are natural formations of limestone dating back millions of years. Viking coins and other artifacts are on display. It was here in A.D. 928 that the Vikings discovered and slaughtered more than 1,000 Irish villagers. The skeletal remains of 40 people who were probably hiding from the raids have been found. You can walk the catwalks through the chambers and make the deep descent down.

Off Castlecomer Road (N78), Ballyfoyle (not Dunmore Village, as the name may imply). ☎ *056-67-726. By car: 7 miles north of Kilkenny on the N78 (the Kilkenny-Castlecomer Road). Admission: €2.50 ($2.40) adults, €2 ($1.90) seniors, €1.25 ($1.20) students and children. Open: March–June Tues–Sat 10 a.m.–4 p.m., Sun 2–4 p.m.; July–Sept daily 10 a.m.–6 p.m. Inaccessible for wheelchairs. Suggested visit: About 1 hour.*

Jerpoint Abbey
Thomastown

This Cistercian abbey is considered one of the best-preserved monastic ruins in the country. It houses Celtic crosses and unique stone carvings of knights and dragons. There's a ton to see as you tiptoe through the graveyard and 15th-century cloister grounds. The small visitor center provides information about the history of the carvings and abbey.

Off the Waterford Road (N9), Thomastown. ☎ *056-24-623. By car: It's off the N9. Admission: €2.50 ($2.40) adults, €2 ($1.90) seniors, €1.25 ($1.20) children. Open: April–May daily 10:30 a.m.–5:00 p.m.; Oct–March Tues–Sat 10:30 a.m.–5:00 p.m., Sun 11 a.m.–5 p.m.; June–Sept daily 10 a.m.–7 p.m. Suggested visit: 45 minutes.*

More fun stuff to do

Here are a few great ways to work off the huge Irish breakfast you probably had:

- **Enjoy Kilkenny's best view.** Climb the Round Tower of **St. Canice's Cathedral** for the best view of the city and beyond. There's a small charge and you have to climb all the way to the top, so you'll sweat for this photo op, but I think it's worth it.

  Location: Off St. Canice's Place. Suggested visit: 20 minutes.

- **Golf Kilkenny's top course.** Mount Juliet was host of the Irish Open from 1993 to 1995. The lakes and waterfalls make a picturesque backdrop to this course, called the "Augusta of Europe" and voted the best inland course in Ireland.

  Location: On the N9 Waterford-Dublin Road, Thomastown, County Kilkenny. ☎ **056-73-000.** Par: 72. Fees: €87.50 ($83.15) mid-week, €93.40 ($88.75) weekends.

- **Join a walking tour.** On one of Tynan's Walking Tours, local historian Pat Tynan will take you through the old streets of Kilkenny, mapping out the medieval history of the town.

  Location: Tours depart from the Tourist Office, Shee Alms House, Rose Inn Street, Kilkenny. ☎ **056-65-929.** Price: €3.75 ($3.55) adults, €2.50 ($2.40) seniors and students, €1.25 ($1.20) children. Daily March to October; Tuesday through Saturday November to February. Suggested visit: 1 hour.

Shopping in County Kilkenny

The tourism office puts out a publication called the *Craft Trail Map*, which includes the pottery of Nicholas Mosse, later in the chapter, plus more shops throughout Kilkenny.

Kilkenny Design Centre and Crescent Workshops

Located in the courtyards of Kilkenny Castle, these workshops stock the best in clothing, ceramics, and linens, as well as local gifts.

Castle Yard, Kilkenny. ☎ *056-22-118.*

Nicholas Mosse

Expert craftsman Mosse uses the River Nore to produce the electricity to fire his pots, and each piece is hand-thrown. The earthenware clay pottery, sold as individual pieces or in sets, is designed and detailed for elegance and makes a nice addition to any kitchen. The customer service is outstanding and the shop also stocks linens, baskets, and home accessories.

Bennettsbridge. ☎ *056-27-105. By car: R700 south from Kilkenny.*

Upper Court Manor

This shop is home to the country's largest collection of antique furniture, and housed in one of Ireland's finest 18th-century mansions. It will ship large items to your home.

Freshford. ☎ *056-32-174. By car: R693 north from Kilkenny.*

Pub life in County Kilkenny

Kilkenny is home to one of Ireland's own brews: **Smithwick's,** a thick red ale. The brewery, on Parliament Street (☎ **056-21-014**) churns out this tasty brew as well as an American favorite, Budweiser (which is an import here!). You can't get a tour of the brewery, but they do have an audiovisual display and tasting session, Monday through Friday at 3 p.m., June through August.

Kyteler's

The best feature of this haunting old coaching inn is the outdoor courtyard, where you can enjoy your pint and the weather (the former more predictably good, the latter iffy). The place is named for Dame Alice Kyteler, a woman who, along with her maid, was accused of witchcraft after the mysterious deaths of Alice's four husbands. Alice escaped punishment; the maid burned at the stake. There's an effigy of a witch in the window frame.

27 St. Kieran's St., Kilkenny. ☎ *056-21-064.*

Langton's

This place is a four-time winner of the National Pub of the Year award. You'll find comfortable seating inside the recently renovated interior and a garden enclosed by old city walls outside. Good conversation and friendly faces fill the many small pub sections, each individually decorated. There's toe-tapping, hand-clapping music and dancing four nights a week, as well as a popular Tuesday disco night.

69 John St., Kilkenny. ☎ *056-65-133.*

Marble City Bar

The oldest and most famous pub in Kilkenny gets its name from the local limestone but gets its reputation from great service and a friendly atmosphere. Of course, you'll spend most of your time inside one of Marble City's four floors of *snugs* (small partitioned areas) and bars, but the outside Edwardian facade of brass and carved wood lit by gas lamps is an attraction in itself.

66 High St., Kilkenny. ☎ *056-62-091.*

Fast Facts: County Kilkenny

Area Code(s)

County Kilkenny's area codes (or city codes) are **056** and **051**.

Emergencies/Police

Dial ☎ **999** for all emergencies.

Genealogy Resources

Contact the Kilkenny Archaeological Society, 16 Parliament St., Rothe House (☎ 056-22-893; Fax: 056-51-108).

Information

For visitor information go to Shee Alms House, Rose Inn Street, Kilkenny

(☎ 056-51-500). Open year-round. It can also provide reservation services. For telephone directory assistance, dial ☎ 1190.

Internet

Compustore, Unit 12, Market Cross Shopping Centre, High Street, Kilkenny (☎ 056-71-210), has Internet access plus printing capabilities.

Post Office

The Kilkenny District Post Office is at 73 High St., Kilkenny (☎ 056-21-813).

Part IV
The South

"Let me ask you a question. Are you planning to kiss the Blarney Stone, or ask for its hand in marriage?"

In this part . . .

Counties Cork and Kerry make up what may be Ireland's most visited region — and that's not just by chance. When you spend some time here, you, too, will see why visitors flock to it year after year.

I start with Cork City, a bustling, cosmopolitan city with a small-town feel. This is a great place to set up camp for exploring the south's many historical attractions and natural wonders. If shopping for great Irish products strikes your fancy even a little bit, you could build up a big head of shopping steam in these parts. And don't forget West County Cork — home of Kinsale, Ireland's mecca for gourmet food lovers. If all this isn't enough to get you excited, have I mentioned that County Cork is home to the Blarney Stone as well? For details, turn to Chapter 15.

County Kerry has long been Ireland's hottest tourist spot, in part due to the charming, picturesque town of Killarney. The county is also well known for the Ring of Kerry, a 110-mile route lined with endless scenic views of the mountains and sea, and dotted with charming Irish towns and villages. Add to this the amazing Killarney National Park, a few museums, an amazing re-creation of a medieval town, and a chance to swim with the world's friendliest dolphin. What more could you ask from a vacation destination? All this and more are covered in Chapter 16.

Chapter 15

County Cork

In This Chapter

▶ Kissing the Blarney Stone

▶ Touring Cork City by day, pub-crawling by night

▶ Visiting Cobh — just like the *Titanic* and *Lusitania* did

▶ Eating your way through Ireland's cuisine capital at Kinsale

▶ Getting to the garden isle of Garinish

County Cork occupies the eastern half of Southern Ireland and has the country's second-largest city (Cork City), one of its most beautiful golf courses (at the Old Head of Kinsale), a host of historical sights, and, bar-none, the most famous rock on the island: the Blarney Stone. Pucker up!

Many travelers breeze into Cork City, look around, stop at Blarney Castle on the way out for a quick kiss, and then head right for Killarney, but to that I say: *big mistake*. The stretch of coast from the lovely seaside town of Kinsale to the tip of Bantry Bay is just too beautiful to pass up. My advice: Stick around a while. And because East Cork is a good strategic starting point from which to explore the entire Southern Coast of Ireland, I've given you plenty of great options for accommodations.

What's Where?: County Cork's Major Attractions

Cork City has the cosmopolitan atmosphere you would expect from the second-largest city in the Republic, yet unlike Dublin, Cork hasn't lost any of its small-town friendliness. This dichotomy mixes architecture of auld and a history of political activism with contemporary shopping and dining. You'll also find attractions like the following:

✔ **St. Finbarre's Cathedral:** Before Cork existed as a city, the area was a monastic settlement established by St. Finbarre in 606. This cathedral stands on the site of his original monastery and university.

> ✔ **Old English Market:** This pretty, old-world stone-floored market has been in use for over 200 years.

Outside the city, in **East County Cork,** lie some of the really big attractions you come to this area for, especially the following:

> ✔ **Blarney Castle and the Blarney Stone:** Legend says kissing the rock is better for your public-speaking skills than a night course at your local community college.
>
> ✔ **Fota Wildlife Park:** Lions and tigers and bears (and cheetahs, ostriches, and giraffes), oh my! Fota is a little bit of the wild world, where you can check out the animals with no bars between you.
>
> ✔ **Jameson Heritage Centre:** Jameson's Midleton Distillery is the largest distillery in Ireland, producing many different whiskies. You can tour the place and then sample some of the product yourself.
>
> ✔ **Cobh, The Queenstown Story:** This fascinating exhibit tells the story of Cobh and details the part it played in Irish emigration and the stories of the *Titanic* and the *Lusitania*.

The lovely seaside town of **Kinsale** is known as the Gourmet Capital of Ireland, and I've included some of the best dining you'll find among the town's narrow, winding streets, which are dominated by **Charles Fort,** Ireland's largest fortification.

West County Cork is the epitome of the quaint Ireland you see on post-cards and television commercials. It's full of small fishing villages, joyful pubs, and marvelously interesting history. With everything from fortified towers to inspiring gardens, you won't be in want of things to do and see, like the following:

> ✔ **Mizen Head:** At the very tippy-tip of this point you'll get priceless views of the wild Atlantic waves and the jagged rocks.
>
> ✔ **Bantry House and Gardens:** More than 250 years old, Bantry House contains a unique collection of tapestries, furniture, and art from around the world, and its exquisite Italian gardens overlook Bantry Bay.
>
> ✔ **Garinish Island:** Take the ferry over from Glengariff and what do you find? An uninhabited 37-acre island that was bare rock before someone brought in hundreds of tons of topsoil and planted an exotic Italian garden.

Cork City and East County Cork

County Cork has always been associated with the sea. In 1669, Quaker leader William Penn, founder of the state of Pennsylvania, sailed to America from Cork Harbor. It was also the last port of call for the first

County Cork

ACCOMMODATIONS ■

Ashbourne House **14**
Ballylickey Manor **4**
Innishannon House **8**
Lotamore **15**

DINING ◆

Aherne's **18**
Blair's Cove **2**
Mary Anne's **6**

ATTRACTIONS ●

Blarney Castle **9**
Bantry House and Gardens **5**
Cobh, The Queenstown Story **11**
Fota Wildlife Park **13**
Garinish Island **3**
Jameson Heritage Centre **16**
Mizen Head **1**
Royal Gunpowder Mills **10**
Scott's Square **12**
Youghal's Medieval Walls **18**

SHOPPING ▲

Blarney Woolen Mills **9**
The Craft Shop **5**
Stephen Pearce Pottery **17**
Youghal Pottery &
  Craft Centre **18**

NIGHTLIFE ☾

DeBarra's **7**

steamship to cross the Atlantic westward, *The Sirius,* in 1838. Appropriately, Cork's coat of arms contains the inscription *Statio Bene Fide Carinis* — "safe harbor for ships." The nearby village of **Cobh,** in addition to being the jumping-off point for most of the Irish who emigrated to America, was also the last port of call ever for the most famous ship to ever *not* cross the Atlantic, the *Titanic.* Cork City is the home of Beamish beer and the birthplace of antiwar activist and labor organizer Mary Harris, better known as Mother Jones.

Getting to Cork City

To get to **Cork City** by car, take the N25 west from Waterford; the N20 south from Limerick; or the N22 east from Kilkenny. The towns of East Cork are located off the N25. If you're coming to Cork City from the east, you can save lots of time by taking the **Cork Harbour Crossing Car Ferry** (☎ 021-81-1223) between Cobh on the east side of the bay and Ringaskiddy (10 miles south of Cork) on the west side. The scenic trip only takes about five minutes and runs year-round, 7:15 a.m. to 12:30 a.m. daily. The cost is €4.50 ($4.25) round-trip or €3 ($2.85) one-way.

Irish Rail (☎ 021-50-4888) services Cork City, Fota, and Cobh regularly, and **Bus Eireann** (☎ 021-50-8188) services Cork City, Cobh, Youghal, and other cities throughout County Cork daily. The main bus depot is located at the **Travel Centre,** Parnell Place, Cork.

You can travel right to Cork from Britain and France as well. **Swansea Cork Ferries** (☎ 021-27-1166) sails to Cork from Swansea, Wales. **Brittany Ferries,** 42 Grand Parade, Cork (☎ 021-27-7801), sails from Roscoff and LeHavre, France.

Getting around Cork City

Cork City can be confusing to find your way around, specifically because the River Lee forks and creates two sets of *quays* (wharfs or piers). Although roads are not as narrow as in most towns, the one-way streets can be frustrating when you're carried across a bridge you don't mean to cross or you see where you want to go but can't quite seem to get there.

Most of the smaller roads and alleys are open exclusively to pedestrian traffic. If you're in Cork City to see the sights and do some shopping, just park when you get downtown and see the city by foot. (Parking in Cork City runs on a paper disk system. Disks can be purchased at small shops on each block. There's also a multistory parking garage in Cork City at Lavitt's Quay.) Most of the attractions and shopping lie on the island between the two tributaries. **St. Patrick's Street** is the city's hub for shopping, and **Oliver Plunkett Street** is the main place for a Cork City pub-crawl. If you end up needing a taxi in town, call **Taxi Co-op** (☎ 021-27-2222).

Cork City

ACCOMMODATIONS ■
Isaac's **6**
Jury's Hotel **22**
Jury's Inn **8**

DINING ◆
Arbutus Lodge **1**
Café Paradisio **23**
Gingerbread House Cafe **14**
Isaacs **7**
Ristoranti Rossini **16**

ATTRACTIONS ●
City Hall **9**
National Monument **19**
Old English Market **18**
St. Ann Shandon Church **2**
St. Finbarre's Cathedral **21**

SHOPPING ▲
Cork Butter Exchange **4**
The Living Tradition **5**
Merchants Quay
Shopping Centre **10**
Mercier Bookshop **15**
Prince's Street Market **17**

NIGHTLIFE ☾
An Spailpin **20**
Chimes **3**
Henchy's **13**
Le Chateau **12**
The Long Valley **11**

Church
Footbridge
Information

It's best to have a car for getting to and from attractions and towns in East Cork. Car-rental companies include **Great Island Car Rentals,** MacCurtain Street, Cork (☎ 021-50-3536), and Rushbrooke, Cobh (☎ 021-81-1609). **Bus Eireann** (☎ 021-50-8118) also operates local service around Cork City to neighboring towns like Blarney, Cobh, and Fota. Most buses leave from the Parnell Place Bus Station. If you need a taxi in the outlying towns, call **Castle Cabs** (☎ 021-38-2222) in Blarney and **Harbour Cabs** (☎ 021-81-4444) in Cobh.

Where to stay in Cork City and East County Cork

Isaac's
$–$$ Cork City

Rustic charm, a literary theme, a great location, and a courtyard garden featuring a beautiful waterfall are the highlights of this comfortable hotel. The rooms are uniquely (some oddly) decorated, but all are comfortable. This oasis of a hotel also has 2- and 3-bedroom apartments that are a better deal if you're traveling with couples.

48 MacCurtain St., Cork City. ☎ *021-450-0011. Fax: 021-450-6355. Internet:* www. isaacs.ie/hotelc. *To get there: Above the north channel, take a right off of St. Patrick's Hill. Rates: €45–€55 ($42.75–$52.50) double. AE, MC, V.*

Jury's Inn
$$ Cork City

The service is par for the course and rooms are comfortable, but there's nothing exceptional about Jury's Inn — except the low price. A flat rate for up to three adults or two adults and two children makes this a good deal for traveling families. Even though the high-rise inn faces the north tributary of the River Lee, the view's not tremendous, and there are no extra amenities like its out-of-town sister hotel — Jury's Hotel (see the next review) — although there's a decent casual restaurant and it's only a block away from the Cork City bus station.

Anderson's Quay, Cork City. ☎ *021-27-6444. Fax: 021-27-6144. Internet:* www. jurys.com. *To get there: Between the Custom House and bus station at the mouth of the north channel. Rates: €58.75–€71.25 ($55.81–$67.95) up to three adults or family of four. AE, DC, MC, V.*

Jury's Hotel
$$$ Cork City

As at all the jewels in the Jury's Hotel crown, the service here is professional and efficient and the rooms are modern and cookie-cutter standard. The major feature that makes this one stand out is the enclosed grounds, featuring a walking path, pool, and outdoor sunbathing. The amenities are what you're paying for when you compare the price to the downtown Jury's Inn (mentioned in the previous entry) to this one, located about three minutes outside the city.

Western Road, Cork City. ☎ *021-27-6622. Fax: 021-27-4477. Internet:* www.jurys. com. *To get there: Take Lancaster Quay from city center, which becomes Western Road. Rates:* €137.50 ($130.65) double. AE, DC, MC, V.

Ashbourne House
$$–$$$ Glounthaune

This ideal country house was once called Harmony Lodge, a fitting name for a peaceful retreat that's right on the tourist route. Cork City is only ten minutes away and the Fota Wildlife Park (see "Exploring East County Cork," later in this chapter) is just five minutes from here. Golfers will appreciate the proximity to four 18-hole courses. Every inch of this place is flawless, from four-poster beds to the tiny fireplace-warmed bar to the large and relaxing Oakroom lounge. Look out any window and see the award-winning gardens and verdant grounds. All this harmony overlooks the River Lee and is attended to by a small but competent staff.

Glounthaune, Cork. ☎ *021-35-3319. Fax: 021-35-4338. By car: From Cork, take the N25 east for ten minutes and look for signs for Glounthaune on the left. Rates:* €80–€107.50 ($76–$102.10) double. No credit cards.

Lotamore
$$ Tivoli

This 20-room Georgian-manor-turned-guesthouse functions like a four-star hotel and is beautifully furnished with antiques. It's only ten minutes from the center of Cork City — just far enough to be a quiet respite from the beaten path yet in easy reach to Cobh, Fota Island, Blarney, and several golf courses. You can't beat the price for the pampering you'll receive. If you get sick, worry not — the manor is run by two doctors. The estate overlooks the River Lee and castle ruins.

Tivoli, Cork. ☎ *021-82-2344. Fax: 021-82-2219. E-mail:* lotamore@iol.ie. *By car: East off the main road to Waterford (N25). Rates:* €62.50–€63.75 ($59.40–$60.55) double. AE, MC, V.

Where to dine in Cork City and East County Cork

Before I take you into some of Cork's best restaurants, I feel it's my duty to introduce you to the local specialties — because if you're a picky eater, there's a lot of Cork cuisine you may not like. Food in East County Cork can be a little tricky — and perhaps a little disgusting. Cork people love their local dishes, but you may not. You should know these handy translations: *crubeens* are pig's feet, *Drisheens* are local blood sausage, and *tripe* is animal stomach. Does that sound good? If not, I've listed some nice Italian restaurants for you.

Café Paradiso

$$–$$$ Cork City   VEGETARIAN

Before you even sit down, you'll feel the vibe. This bright and electric restaurant is filled with books and toys and a certain . . . energy. Then there's the food, a vegetarian's nirvana with an eclectic and fresh menu with offerings such as roasted tomato soup with basil pesto; mushroom fritters fried in ginger butter; gingered sweet potato spring rolls with sesame cabbage; panfried couscous; feta and almond cake with arribiata sauce; and for dessert try the rich fudge cake with orange sauce. Is your mouth watering yet? You can even purchase *The Café Paradiso Cookbook* and try out the recipes at home.

16 Lancaster Quay, Cork City. ☎ *021-27-7937. To get there: Just beyond Wood Street down the south channel of the river, across the street from Jury's Hotel. Main courses: €8.50–€16.50 ($8.10–$15.70). MC, V. Open: Tues–Sat 12:30–3:00 p.m., 6–10 p.m. Closed Sun, Mon.*

Gingerbread House Cafe

$–$$$ Cork City   CAFE

Good food, bread that's baked in-house, and probably the best slow-roasted coffee you'll find in Ireland are yours for the taking in this little cafe. The modern, open dining area looks out onto a pedestrian square in the heart of town. In an effort to break out of its breakfast and lunch, coffeehouse-crowd niche, the Gingerbread has created an impressive full menu that extends through dinnertime and has one of the best wine selections in Cork City.

Paul Street Plaza, Cork City. ☎ *021-27-6411. To get there: One block north of Patrick Street. Main courses: €6.25–€15 ($5.95–$14.25). AE, MC, V. Open: Mon–Wed 8:30 a.m.– 9:30 p.m., Thurs–Sat 8:30 a.m.–10:30 p.m.*

Isaacs

$$–$$$ Cork City   INTERNATIONAL-PIZZA

An informal and trendy restaurant that doesn't act like it, Isaacs is an amalgam of contemporary and traditional — much like Cork City itself. Located in a converted Victorian warehouse with a vaulted ceiling, Isaacs has red brick walls adorned with local art pieces. But this place isn't all atmosphere; the international cuisine is reliably delicious, too. I recommend the specialty pizzas.

48 MacCurtain St., Cork City. ☎ *021-50-3805. To get there: Above the north channel, take a right off of St. Patrick's Hill. Main courses: €6.90–€17.50 ($6.55–$16.65). AE, MC, V. Open: Mon–Sat 10:00 a.m.–10:30 p.m., Sun 6:30–9:30 p.m.*

Ristoranti Rossini
$$–$$$ Cork City   ITALIAN

Quintessentially Italian, down to the elegant blue plates and matching blue candles dripping over chianti bottles, this charming and authentic restaurant is located down one of the side streets off Oliver Plunkett Street. The pasta is homemade by the chef, and you can't go wrong with the speciality *Italia de la Casa* — pasta and seafood with the chef's own sauce creation. If you don't have a pleasant meal here, you just don't like Italian food, period.

34 Princes St., Cork City. ☎ *021-27-5818. To get there: Between Oliver Plunkett Street and South Mall. Main courses: €6.50–€13.75 ($6.20–$13.05). MC, V. Open: Mon–Sat noon to 3 p.m. and 6:00 p.m.–12:30 a.m., Sun 5 p.m. to midnight.*

Arbutus Lodge
$$$$ Montenotte   IRISH-FRENCH-INTERNATIONAL

You'll find the best in local dishes here, up a hill just outside Cork City — tripe, crubeens, and ham with cabbage, as well as French and international cuisine. The meals are gourmet, the decor relaxing, the service friendly, and the wine list extensive, so don't be afraid to ask your server for recommendations. The lobster, straight from the tank, is exceptional and tender, and not so big that the meat gets tough.

St. Luke's Hill, Montenotte, Cork. ☎ *021-50-1237. To get there: North on St. Patrick's Hill from the north channel. Main courses: €18.75–€24 ($17.80–$22.80). AE, DC, MC, V. Open: Mon–Sat 1:00–2:30 p.m., 7:00–9:30 p.m.*

Aherne's
$$$ Youghal   SEAFOOD

This port town restaurant has a reputation for serving the freshest and tastiest seafood in this part of the country. Don't expect a lot of fanciness and formality with your dishes: The chef is more concerned about taste than presentation. New Englanders may never order cod back home again after having it at Aherne's. The seafood chowder is unmatched as well. If you're really hungry, go for the award-winning six fish, four shellfish platter.

163 N. Main St., Youghal. ☎ *024-92-424. To get there: Take the main road to Waterford (N25), and then turn off onto Main Street. Main courses: €14–€23.75 ($13.30–$22.55). AE, DC, MC, V. Open: Tue–Sun 11 a.m.–8 p.m.; Mon in July and Aug.*

Exploring East County Cork

The really big attractions in East County Cork are outside Cork City. I detail a few of the finest in the following sections.

The top attractions and monuments

Blarney Castle
Blarney

You've just got to see this place, one of the greatest tourist attractions in Ireland. The seat of the Munster province, Blarney is one of the most for-tified castles in Ireland — its walls are 18 feet thick in some parts. But the highlight of your self-guided romp through this 17th-century castle, is of course, the Blarney Stone, located at the top of the castle (after a fair amount of climbing up narrow, twisted stairways). The world's most famous rock allegedly imparts eloquence, or "the gift of gab," to those daring enough to contort upside down from the parapet walk and kiss it. It's a real feat to lean back into nothing and tip your head to kiss that smooth rock — it may even be a little frightening to people afraid of heights (or germs!). It's customary to tip the guy who holds your legs, and you may want to give it over *before* he holds you over the faraway courtyard.

Don't leave Blarney without seeing the enchanted castle grounds. You'll go through odd foliage, ancient trees, and mystic stones along this walk, and even wander through a witch's kitchen and leprechaun-sized tunnel!

Wondering just where the old "gift of gab" lore stems from? Well, we've all heard some blarney in our lives, but the person who did it best (and first) was the charismatic Lord of Blarney, Cormac McDermot McCarthy. When Queen Elizabeth was asking all Irish lords to effectively sign over their land to the crown, McCarthy was determined not to. For every demand the Queen made, he responded with eloquent letters that claimed undy-ing loyalty and dripped with flattery, although he had no intention of giving in to her demands. After receiving yet another crafty letter, the Queen, exasperated, explained that it was "all blarney" and that the Lord never meant what he said or did what he promised. So, today, anyone who uses a lot of eloquence and empty phrases and playfully deceives or exag-gerates is said to be talking "blarney."

Off the N20, Blarney. ☎ *021-38-5252. By car: Off the N20 north of Cork City, head-ing toward Limerick. By bus: You can catch a Bus Eireann round trip to the castle from Cork. Admission: €3.75 ($3.55) adults, €2.50 ($2.40) children. Open: June–Aug Mon–Sat 9 a.m.–7 p.m., Sun 9:30 a.m.–5:30 p.m.; May and Sept Mon–Sat 9:00 a.m.–6:30 p.m., Sun 9:30 a.m.–5:30 p.m.; Oct–April Mon–Sat 9 a.m. to dusk, Sun 9:30 a.m. to dusk. Not accessible by wheelchair. Suggested visit: 2 hours.*

Cobh, The Queenstown Story
Cobh

Cobh Harbour was the main point of departure for thousands of starving Irish on their way to the United States during the Great Famine. Annie Moore, along with her two brothers, left Cobh for America and became a footnote in the history books: She was the first immigrant ever to be processed at Ellis Island. At this top attraction, you'll learn all about Cobh's part in the emigration, as well as the town's history. Elsewhere in this guide I tend to ignore all the sleep-inducing attractions that focus on small-town history, but the presentation Cobh puts on is fascinating and shown with several dramatic exhibitions throughout the restored Victorian Railway Station and Customs Hall. The most interesting exhibits detail the experiences of an Australian-bound convict ship and the ill-fated tragedies of both the *Titanic* and the *Lusitania* — both of which made Cobh their last port of call.

In case you skip this attraction, here are a few tidbits: The word *Cobh* means "cove," in Gaelic, which makes sense, because the town's obviously a little cove for Cork's harbor. But in the mid-1800s, the town was renamed Queenstown after a visit from Queen Victoria. Later, when the novelty of having a queen drop by wore off (or after she'd been dead long enough), the town's original name was restored.

Cobh Railway Station, Cobh. ☎ *021-81-3591. To get there: Off the N25, east of Cork City and west from Youghal. Admission: €4.50 ($4.30) adults, €2.50 ($2.40) children, €12.50 ($11.90) family of two adults and three children. Open: Daily 10 a.m.–6 p.m. Suggested visit: 1 hour.*

Fota Wildlife Park
Carrigtwohill

Here you'll find a bit of the African savanna in Ireland, and more. View 70 species of exotic wildlife without any cages between you and the animals (except for the cheetahs — Fota is the world's largest breeder of this endangered species). See ostriches, zebras, giraffes, monkeys, and kangaroos. There's a train tour that takes you around the park. Also check out the arboretum and the snack and gift shops. This is a perfect place for the kids.

Carrigtwohill, Cork Harbour. ☎ *021-81-2678. To get there: 10 miles from Cork City toward Cobh off the N25. Admission: €4.75 ($4.50) adults, €4.25 ($4.05) students, €3 ($2.85) children and seniors, €18.75 ($17.80) family. Open: April–Oct Mon–Sat 10 a.m.–5 p.m., Sun 11 a.m.–5 p.m. Suggested visit: 1½ hours.*

Jameson Heritage Centre
Midleton

Journey through the history of Irish whiskey! You'll see a great audiovisual presentation and parts of the restored 18th-century distillery, including the largest Pot Still in the world, able to hold an intoxicating 30,000 gallons! Midleton Distillery is the largest in Ireland, producing many different whiskies, including Jameson and Tullamore Dew. At the end of the tour you get to sample some of the smoothest whiskey ever made. The souvenir shop will sell you anything from a shot glass to a bottle of the Water of Life.

Distillery Road, off Main Street, Midleton. ☎ *01-872-5566 (Dublin number). To get there: Off the N25, east of Cork City and west from Youghal. Admission: €4.50 ($4.30) adults, €2 ($1.90) children. Open: March–Oct daily 10 a.m.–6 p.m.; Nov–Feb Mon–Fri 10 a.m.–6 p.m. with tours departing at noon and 3 p.m. Suggested visit: 2 hours.*

Youghal's Medieval Walls
Youghal

This lovely little port town is worth a stop to get out and stretch your legs and see what Dublin might look like if it hadn't become the capital of the country. Like Dublin, Youghal (pronounced *yawl*) was settled by the Vikings and later fortified by the Normans, who built a wall around the city, half of which still stands. As you make your way from the main Water Gate along the old wall, you'll see several towers (originally built close enough to allow guards to shout to one another) and the main arched gate, called Cromwell's Arch because it's believed Oliver Cromwell ended his bloody English campaign here. Don't miss the restored Clock Gate (formerly Trinity Gate) at the southern entrance to the town, once the execution site and prison and at interesting incorporation of modern municipal building and medieval town wall.

Also, be sure to visit St. Mary's Collegiate Church, inside the walls where you will notice coffin-shaped indentations in the nave. Coffins were stood up in the wall so that bodies carrying the plague would, as required by law, fall outside the city wall into a pit of limestone. Next to the church is Myrtle Grove house, believed to have been occupied by a famous former mayor of Youghal, Sir Walter Raleigh. Look for the weathervane depicting the famous story of Raleigh throwing down his cloak for Queen Elizabeth.

Youghal. You can purchase a guide to the wall, Youghal: Historic Walled Port, at the visitor center by the Water Gate between Strand and Gratten streets in front of Youghal harbor. To get there: On the N25 east of Middleton. Suggested visit: 2 hours.

The top Cork landmarks

City Hall
Cork City

Lit up every night in spectacular glory and reflected off the river, this is where JFK gave a speech during his historic visit to Ireland in 1963.

On Albert Quay, between Anglesea Street and the South City Link Road, Cork City.

St. Ann Shandon Church

Until 1986, when they were repaired, each of the four clock faces on the tower of St. Ann Shandon, on Church Street, gave a different time, earning it the nickname "The Four-Face Liar." Today, you can stop in anytime

Monday through Saturday 10 a.m. to 5 p.m., climb the bell tower, and see the city's best view. And, there's an added attraction: You get to ring the bells yourself!

Church Street, Cork City.

National Monument
Cork City

A unique and grand memorial to the Irish patriots who lost their lives in the struggle for independence between 1798 and 1867.

At the river end of Grand Parade, Cork City.

Old English Market
Cork City

This pretty, old-world, stone-floored market was originally the Root Market (from 1788 to 1862). The area was destroyed by fire in 1980. The market you see today contains the original cast-iron fountain, columns, and railings. Meats, fish, vegetables, fruit, and some Irish delicacies (like tripe and Drisheens) are sold at numerous stands throughout the market.

Between Grand Parade and Princes Street.

Royal Gunpowder Mills
Ballinollig

Between 1794 and 1903, these mills — the largest of their type in Europe — manufactured and supplied gunpowder to European armies. So important were they that when Napoleon threatened the United Kingdom (which then included Ireland), the British government sent an envoy to control and protect the mills. Today the site, set along the pretty banks of the River Lee, is an excellent attraction, with guided tours through the canal- and tree-lined complex ending at a functioning water-powered mill wheel.

Right off the N22 in Ballinollig (look for the signs). ☎ *021-87-4430. To get there: Only five minutes west of Cork on N22 toward Killarney. There is a Bus Eireann from Cork that runs round-trip. Admission: €3.75 ($3.55) adults, €3.50 ($3.35) students and seniors, €2.25 ($2.15) children, €10 ($9.50) family. Open: March–Oct daily 10 a.m.– 6 p.m. Suggested visit: 1 hour.*

St. Finbarre's Cathedral
Cork City

This cathedral was built on the site of the monastery and university that served the settlement St. Finbarre established here in 606 — long before Cork City existed. Interesting highlights of the *cruciform* (cross-shaped) cathedral include the one-of-a-kind underground church organ, zodiac symbols on the stained glass, and gilded ceilings. You'll get more out of your visit to this French Gothic-styled Protestant cathedral if you take the short but informative tour, rather than see it alone.

Dean Street, Cork City. ☎ *021-32-2993. To get there: Take Bishops Street from Sullivan Quay. Admission: Free, €1.25 ($1.20) for the tour. Open: Mon–Fri 10 a.m.– 1 p.m. and 3:00–5:30 p.m. Suggested visit: 30 minutes.*

Scott's Square
Cobh

An impressive and sobering memorial stands in honor of the 1,195 people who died aboard the *Lusitania* when it was hit by a German torpedo off the Irish coast in 1915. The sinking prompted America's entry into World War I.

Cobh Harbour, on the square right by the water. The little road that takes you onto the Island from the N25 ends at the village.

Joining an organized tour

These tours will give you a more in-depth look at Cork, both the county and the city.

- ✔ **Bus Eireann Heritage Tour:** Visits Blarney, Cobh, and Midleton. Sundays in July and August. Leaves from Cork Bus Station at 10 a.m. and returns at 10 p.m.

  Information: ☎ **021-50-8188.** Price: €17.50 ($16.60) adult, €12.50 ($11.90) child.

- ✔ **Bus Eireann Open-Top City Tour:** This tour leaves from Cork Bus Station regularly between June and September. The tour lasts three hours and visits all the major city sites.

  Information: ☎ **021-50-8188.** Price: €7.50 ($7.15) adult, €3.75 ($3.55) child.

Shopping in Cork City and East County Cork

Cork is a diverse city for shopping. From the highbrow stores on Patrick's Street to the eclectic mix of small retail shops along Oliver Plunkett Street, you'll find everything from designer clothing and linen to gourmet cheese and homemade crafts. Patrick Street is the location of Cork's only mall, the **Merchants Quay Shopping Centre,** home to 40 shops and the upscale department stores Roches and Marks & Spencer.

There are two main markets in Cork as well. The **Cork Butter Exchange** (John Redmond Street) is a cobblestone rotunda housing many craft workshops and summertime music sessions. The **Prince's Street Market** is a grand old indoor market with gourmet delights of all kinds, but with an emphasis on fish.

Here are a few of my favorite shops in the area.

Blarney Woolen Mills

This is the original in a string of famous stores. In addition to the wares (cashmere sweaters, tweeds, hats, and signature wool sweaters), this one has several craft demonstrations you can watch — including handweaving, of course.

Near Blarney Castle, off the N20, Blarney. ☎ *021-38-5280.*

The Living Tradition

One of the best traditional music shops in Ireland, this store offers a large variety of *bodhráns* (Irish drums), tin whistles, and sheet music.

40 McCurtain St., Cork City. ☎ *021-50-2040.*

Mercier Bookshop

Mercier sells a wide selection of titles, from Irish history to cult fiction. It also stocks the complete collection of the Cork-based Mercier Press, Ireland's oldest independent publishing house.

18 Academy St., Cork City. ☎ *021-27-5040.*

Stephen Pearce Pottery

Come here for unique handmade earthenware, handblown Simon Pearce glass, linen, and jewelry.

On the R629. Shanagarry. ☎ *021-64-6807.*

Youghal Pottery & Craft Centre

This store has one of the single largest selections of pottery styles under one roof, specializing in the colorful and unique smoke-fired Raku pottery. It stocks knitwear, crafts, and gifts as well.

Foxhole. Take the N25 east from Cork. Foxhole is just a little beyond Youghal — you don't even realize you've left Youghal — and the pottery center is the biggest thing going on there; there are signs for it on the N25. ☎ *024-91-222.*

Pub life in County Cork

An Spailpin

Low ceilings, plenty of brickwork, and traditional music six nights a week make An Spailpin (that's "The Loft" in Gaelic) one of the best pubs in town. It's also one of the oldest pubs in Cork, and the old-time furnishings help prove it. An Spailpin is located opposite the Beamish Brewery, which should give you a good idea what you should order.

28 S. Main St., Cork City. ☎ *021-27-7949.*

Chimes

This is a popular working-class pub and the best place to watch a football or hurling match on the telly. I suggest you drink the local beers — smooth Murphy's or sharp Beamish. Foot-stomping accordion music usually plays on weekends.

27 Church St., Cork City. ☎ *021-30-4136.*

Henchy's

Perhaps the highlight of this stylish pub is the legitimate *snug* (a separate room where women were once relegated to drink), which has its own entrance. The mahogany bar and stained glass are staples of a traditional pub, but the frequent poetry readings Henchy's hosts set it apart.

40 Saint Luke's St., Cork City. ☎ *021-50-7833.*

Le Chateau

Centrally located in the heart of Cork and built more than 200 years ago, this labyrinthine Victorian-decorated pub with an inexplicably French name is one of the oldest and most-favored places in town. City memorabilia is featured prominently throughout the many sections and snugs. And the Irish coffee is legendary.

93 Patrick St., Cork City. ☎ *021-27-0370.*

The Long Valley

This quixotic watering hole is popular with college students and locals, but things never get out of hand under the watchful, motherly eye of Mrs. Moynihan. She may even let you peek at the list of celebs who have visited The Long Valley through the years. Always fun, and always good music playing.

10 Wintrop St., at the corner of Oliver Plunkett (across from the General Post Office), Cork City. ☎ *021-272-144.*

Fast Facts: Cork City and East County Cork

Area Code(s)

Cork City and East County Cork's area codes (or city codes) are **021, 022,** and **024.**

Emergencies-Police

Dial ☎ **999** for all emergencies. Cork Regional Hospital is on Wilton Road (☎ 021-54-6400).

Genealogy Resources

Mallow Heritage Centre, 27–28 Bank Place, Mallow. ☎ 022-21-778. Fax: 022-20-276.

Information

For visitor information go to Aras Fáilte, Tourist House, Grand Parade (near Oliver Plunkett Street), Cork (☎ 021-27-3251). Open year-round. It can also provide reservation services. For telephone directory assistance, dial ☎ 1190.

Internet

FutureKids Internet Centre, South Douglas Road (☎ 021-89-3800), has Internet access and printing capabilities.

Post Office

The General Post Office in Cork is on Oliver Plunkett Street (☎ 021-27-2000).

Kinsale and West County Cork

If you've ever seen quaint postcards or television commercials of Ireland, **West Cork** will look familiar to you. It's full of the small fishing villages and joyful pubs that probably come to mind when you think of the Emerald Isle. But it has more than just scenery to offer — in County Cork you can see fortified towers, stroll through inspiring gardens, or explore a former earl's estate.

You can also feast on some of the finest cuisine available in Ireland at the port city of **Kinsale,** which is known as the Gourmet Capital of Ireland. In this section, I include information on some of the country's best dining, located among the ancient buildings rising throughout the town's narrow, winding streets.

Getting to Kinsale and West County Cork

To get to Kinsale by car, take the R600 south from Cork or the R605 south from Inishannon. The N71 links Cork to most of the major towns in West County Cork. **Bus Eireann** (☎ **021-50-8188**) travels year-round to Kinsale, Bantry, and other major towns in West County Cork. Bus Eireann also has a special day-trip bus to Kinsale from Cork from April to mid-September.

Where to stay in Kinsale and West County Cork

Actons Hotel
$$–$$$ **Kinsale**

Three stories high and contemporarily furnished with big beds, Actons Hotel has exceptional amenities, like an indoor heated pool, gym, sauna, steam room, outdoor tub, jacuzzi, children's pool, and solarium. Pay the extra €20 ($21.20) for a sea view overlooking Kinsale's beautiful harbor and yachting marina — it's worth it. An outdoor breakfast is another nice feature, and you can take your lunch or dinner at the hotel's excellent Captain's Table restaurant, which is also quite good. On Sundays lunch is served to an excellent soundtrack of jazz.

Pier Road, Kinsale. ☎ *021-477-2135. Fax: 021-477-2231. Internet:* www.actons hotelkinsale.com. *To get there: Take the N71 to R605 if coming from West Cork (Clonakilty) direction and R600 from Cork City direction. Rates: €78.75–€136 ($74.80–$129.20) double. AE, DC, MC, V.*

Blue Haven
$$$ **Kinsale**

There's nothing fishy about this award-winning hotel, located on the site of Kinsale's old fish market. The townhouse-style interior, rooms decorated with local crafts, and a super-friendly staff combine to make Blue Haven the quintessential small-town accommodation. It was recently expanded and refurbished and is centrally located in the heart of town. See the next section for a review of Blue Haven's restaurant.

3–4 Pearse St., Kinsale. ☎ *021-77-2209. Fax: 021-77-4268. Internet:* www.blue havenkinsale.com. *To get there: Pearse Street becomes Long Quay at the harbour. Rates: €100–€187.50 ($95–$178.15) double. AE, DC, MC, V. Closed Jan.*

Scilly House
$$$ **Kinsale**

A lovely mix of Irish and American styles, Scilly House is decorated with antique pine, folk art, and American quilts. The hotel's restaurant serves Californian cuisine and the lovely library and wine bar has a grand piano and hearty fire. The rooms are spacious, uniquely decorated, and all non-smoking. The bedroom suites, dining rooms, and three patios all overlook the sea, Charles Fort, and the house's professional gardens. Ask your host to tell you the hotel's haunting tale of the White Lady.

Scilly, Kinsale. ☎ *021-77-2413. Fax: 021-77-4629. To get there: From Kinsale, take Scilly Road (R600) toward the Charles Fort. After you cross the bay, Scilly House is on the right. Rates: €125–€130 ($118.75–$123.50) double. AE, MC, V. Closed Nov–March.*

Kinsale

ACCOMMODATIONS ■
Actons Hotel **8**
Blue Haven **1**
Scilly House **11**

DINING ◆
Blue Haven **1**
Man Friday **10**
Max's Wine Bar **5**

ATTRACTIONS ●
Charles Fort **12**

SHOPPING ▲
Boland's Irish Craft Shop **2**
Granny's Bottom Drawer **6**

NIGHTLIFE ☾
Kieran's Folk House **4**
Lord Kingsale **7**
The 1601 **3**
Spaniard Inn **9**

Castle
Church
Information
Parking
Post Office

NORTHERN IRELAND
REPUBLIC OF IRELAND
Dublin
Kinsale

SUMMERCOVE

Kinsale Harbour

Castle Park

Marina

Harbour Master

Scilly Rd.

River Rd.

High Rd.

Scilly Walk

Eastern Rd.

Featherbed Lane

Barrack Hill

Quay

Long Quay

Denis Quay

Pier Rd.

Lower O'Connell St.

The Green

St. John's Hill
Compass Hill

The Mall

Outdoor Education Centre

Winter's Hill

Compass Hill Walk

Town Park

The New Rd.

The Glen

Place Newman's Mall

Market Square

Market Quay

Pearse St.

Emmet St.

Guardwell

Main St.

Higher O'Connell St.

The Ramparts

Ramparts Ln.

Convent School

Gate

Blind Gate

Desmond Castle

St. John's Church

Friars St.

Church St.

St. Multose Church

Rose Abbey

Butchers Row

The Rock Friars Gate

Cork St.

Ballylickey Manor

$$$$ **Ballylickey**

One of the few great accommodations overlooking Bantry Bay, this 17th-century manor house is flanked by modern cottages, an outdoor heated pool, and a private fishing area. Standard and luxury rooms are available, but all guests will enjoy the pretty grounds and views.

Ballylickey, Bantry Bay. ☎ *027-50071. Fax: 027-50-124. Internet:* www.bally lickeymanorhouse.com. *To get there: From Bantry Town go 3 miles north on the N71 toward Glengarriff. Ballylickey Manor is on the left, facing the water. Rates: €200–€309 ($190–$293.55) double. AE, DC, MC, V. Closed Nov–March.*

Innishannon House

$$–$$$ **Innishannon**

Innishannon House boasts of being "the most romantic hotel in Ireland." Although the romance pretty much depends on you, the top-shelf wine cellar, fine dining, woodland walks, river's-edge locale, rose garden, and rooms with Irish country house decor will undoubtedly help things along. There's boating and private salmon and trout fishing available.

On the N71 in Innishannon, west of Cork and east of Clonakilty. ☎ *800-44-UTELL in the United States, or 021-77-5121. Fax: 021-77-5609. Internet:* www.iol.ie/ hotels. *To get there: Take the N71 west from Cork and east from Clonakilty. Rates: €93.75–€185 ($89.05–$175.75) double. AE, DC, MC, V. Closed Jan–mid-March.*

Where to dine in Kinsale and West County Cork

Blue Haven

$–$$$$ **Kinsale   ECLECTIC**

Look for the ornate blue-and-gold clock above the entrance to this multi-award-winning restaurant. When you enter, you'll notice the maritime theme and skylit dining area. The atmosphere is not the least bit stuffy and the menu has a large range, making this a good place to bring the whole family. There's everything from seafood pancakes, pasta, and lamb stew to farmyard duck and local venison. The house specialty is oak-chip-roasted salmon. Next door is Blue Haven's wine and cheese shop, so you can take some of your favorites home.

3 Pearse St., Kinsale. ☎ *021-77-2209. To get there: Pearse becomes Long Quay by the harbour. Main courses: €5.50–€22.50 ($5.25–$21.40). AE, DC, MC, V. Open: Daily 7:45–10:30 a.m., 12:30–3:00 p.m., and 7:00–10:30 p.m. Closed two weeks in mid-Jan.*

Man Friday

$$–$$$$ **Kinsale   SEAFOOD**

Like most of Kinsale's top restaurant picks, the specialty here is seafood, caught locally and served up fresh. The wood-and-stone decor give the place a warm and cozy feel. The portions are huge, the sole is perfectly grilled to the bone, and the desserts are piled high.

On the Scilly Road, Kinsale. ☎ 021-77-2260. To get there: On the Scilly Road. Main courses: €11.25–€18.75 ($10.70–$17.80). AE, MC, V. Open: Daily 7:00–10:30 p.m., Sun 12:30–3:00 p.m.

Max's Wine Bar

$$–$$$ **Kinsale   CONTEMPORARY IRISH**

Located in the heart of Kinsale, this small and unassuming restaurant is one of the best gourmet dining experiences you'll have in the area — the *Irish Independent* newspaper put it best when it wrote, "No visit to Kinsale is complete without a visit to Max's." The scallops poached in vermouth and cream are heavenly, and the rack of lamb with red wine and rosemary sauce is unforgettable.

Main Street, Kinsale. ☎ 021-77-2443. To get there: One block from harbour. Main courses: €8.15–€15.65 ($7.70–$14.85). MC, V. Open: Daily 12:30–3:30 p.m. and 6:30–10:30 p.m. Closed Nov–Feb.

Blair's Cove

$$$$ **Darrus   SEAFOOD**

For starters, let's talk about the starters — a host of delicious options, arranged buffet-style for you to pick and choose among. Then come the main-course options, mostly fish and meat, all grilled to perfection. And finally, the piano becomes a dessert tray, with a vast array of to-die-for sweet delectables. Go for the complete package, because you'll probably only get to eat here once in your life (twice if you're lucky). The Cove is on the water and has an open terrace for summer dining. During the off-season, you can have a romantic meal in a candlelit stone barn.

Barley Road, Durrus. ☎ 027-61-127. To get there: 1 mile from Durrus on the road to Barleycove. Main courses: €27.50–€35 ($26.15–$33.25). AE, DC, MC, V. Open: March–June and Sept–Oct Tues–Sat 7:00–9:30 p.m., July–Aug Mon–Sat 7:00–9:30 p.m.

Mary Anne's

$$$–$$$$ **Skibbereen   SEAFOOD**

Although located in a traditional 150-year-old pub, Mary Anne's doesn't just serve up the old standards of pub grub. A shared treasure of the locals and visitors in the pleasant small town of Castletownshed, this is known as *the* place to go for top-notch seafood. Popular dishes include filleted sole with Mornay sauce glaze, scallops meunière, and deep-fried prawn (large shrimp). Also delicious and popular are the local West Cork cheeses.

Castletownshed, Skibbereen. ☎ 028-36-146. To get there: N71 to Skibbereen and then 5 miles south on the Castletownshed Road (R596). Main courses: €15–€24.40 ($14.25–$23.15). MC, V. Open: Tues–Sun 12:30–2:00 p.m. and 6–10 p.m. Closed Tues during winter.

Exploring Kinsale and West County Cork: The top sights

In this section, I list the big attractions in West County Cork, but if you've a mind to skip the forts, gardens, and the like for a good game of golf, the **Old Head Golf Links** beckon (☎ 021-477-8444; Internet: www.oldhead golflinks.com). This brand-new, challenging course is located on a stunning outcrop of land surrounded by the Atlantic Ocean, just south of Kinsale. Par is 72 and greens fees are €250 ($237.50) for 18 holes.

Bantry House and Gardens
Bantry

This mostly Georgian house was built in 1750 for the earls of Bantry. Every room contains a unique collection of tapestries, furniture, and art from around the world, all carefully collected by the Earl of Bantry. The stately home and exquisite Italian gardens overlook Bantry Bay. The highlights include the Rose Room, Dining Room, and Rose Garden. If you fall in love with this pleasant brigadoon (and have deep pockets), you can stay overnight in the expensive (up to €120 per night) B&B. (Call for more information.)

On the N71, Bantry. ☎ 027-50-047. By car: On N71 between Glengarriff and Skibbereen. By bus: Eireann Bus from Cork, €11 ($10.45) round-trip. Admission: €7.50 ($7.15) adults, €5.50 ($5.25) seniors, €5 ($4.75) students, free under 12. Open: March–Oct daily 9 a.m.–6 p.m. Suggested visit: 2 hours.

Charles Fort
Kinsale

Ireland's largest fortification is impossible to miss when you're in Kinsale, because it guards the city. The nicest way to get there is along a neat coastal path. The classically star-shaped fort was in continual use from 1677 until it was destroyed in 1922 during the Irish Civil War.

Kinsale. ☎ 021-77-2263. To get there: Scilly Road or coastal walk from Kinsale. Admission: €3.50 ($3.35) adults, €2.50 ($2.40) seniors, €1.25 ($1.20) students and children, €6.25 ($5.95) family. Open: Mid-April to mid-June Mon–Sat 9 a.m.–5 p.m., Sun 9:30 a.m.–5:30 p.m.; mid-June to mid-Sept Mon–Sun 9 a.m.–6 p.m.; mid-Sept to Oct Mon–Sat 9 a.m.–5 p.m. Restricted access for the disabled due to uneven terrain. Suggested visit: About 1 hour.

Garinish Island

This little island is an amazing sight — an Italian garden of rare trees and shrubs set along walkways and pools, and all propped out in the sea on an uninhabited 37-acre island. Before the owner brought over hundreds of tons of topsoil to grow the exotic plants, the island was bare rock. Half the fun is the short journey getting there on one of the small ferries that service the island.

Ilnacullin (Garinish Island). ☎ *027-63-040. To get there: The Blue Pool Ferry leaves from the harbor in Glengarriff every half-hour or so and takes 15 minutes to reach the island. Ferry prices are €6.25 ($5.95) adults, €5 ($4.75) students and seniors, €2 ($1.90) children. Admission: €3.50 ($3.35) adults, €2.50 ($2.40) seniors, €1.25 ($1.20) children and students, €7.50 ($7.15) family. Open: June–Sept daily 10 a.m.– 6 p.m.; mid-March to May and Oct daily 10:30 a.m.–5:00 p.m.; Nov to mid-March Sat and Sun 11 a.m.–5 p.m. Suggested visit: 1½ hours, including ferry trip.*

Mizen Head

The Visitor Centre and the Fog Signal Station on the very tippy-tip of this point are exciting additions to an already popular spot, where you'll get priceless views of the wild Atlantic waves and the jagged rocks of Ireland's southwestern-most point. Take your pictures, and then walk the station grounds, including the keeper's house, observation area, and engine room. Then traverse the famous suspension bridge and climb to the top of Mizen Head. Set down as far as you can go on the Bantry Peninsula, Mizen Head seems a little out of the way, but this exhilarating experience is worth a detour.

Mizen Head. ☎ *028-35-115 or 028-35-591. To get there: From Skibbereen, the drive is about an hour. Take the N71 to the R592 in Ballydehop to the R591 in Toomore and follow the signs for Mizen Head. (You don't really know you're on the R591. You begin seeing signs for Mizen back in Skibbereen and you're basically just following the signs to get there.) Admission: €3.50 ($3.35) adults, €2.25 ($2.15) students and seniors, €1.75 ($1.65) under 12, free for under 5, €9 ($8.55) family of two adults and three children. Open: June–Sept daily 10 a.m.–6 p.m.; mid-March to May and Oct daily 10:30 a.m.–5:00 p.m.; Nov to mid-March Sat and Sun 11 a.m.–5 p.m. Suggested visit: 30 minutes.*

Joining an organized tour

Need a break from driving? Here are a couple of good guided tour options.

> ✔ **Bus Eireann Day Tour:** This tour visits Bantry, Glangarriff, Kenmare and more. It leaves at 11 a.m. from Cork Bus Station on Fridays only, June through August, and it returns at 8:15 p.m.
>
> Information: ☎ 021-50-8188. Price: €17.50 ($16.35) adult, €12.50 ($11.90) child.

✔ *Harbour Queen* **Boat Tour:** Leaving from Glengarriff, the *Harbour Queen* makes trips to Garish Island and hosts seal-watching cruises to Seal Island from March to October.

Call for prices and times of departure. Information: ☎ **027-63-116.**

Shopping

Boland's Irish Craft Shop

From the pretty to the pretty unusual, Boland's has a variety of items — Aran vests, Kinsale smocks, ceramic sheep, and miniature paintings.

Pearse Street, Kinsale. ☎ *021-77-2161.*

The Craft Shop

The Craft Shop offers the best of everything: pottery by Nicholas Mosse and Stephen Pearse, glass by Jerpoint Glass Studio, silver jewelry by Linda Uhleman, plus candles, leatherwork, book binding, baskets, and more.

Glengarriff Road, Bantry. ☎ *027-50-003.*

Granny's Bottom Drawer

Come here for traditional linen and lace: pillowcases, placemats, table-cloths, and more, all handwoven with delicate care.

53 Main St., Kinsale. ☎ *021-77-4839.*

Pub life in Kinsale and West County Cork

Kieran's Folk House

Who doesn't come to Kieran's? This place is popular with both locals and visitors (a rare combination in itself) as well as with the angling and diving crowds. Small but vivacious, it really kicks up on the weekends, when live music is featured. If you're hungry, the Bacchus Brasserie serves up some delicious dishes (although it's only open April to October).

Guardwell, Kinsale. ☎ *021-77-2382.*

Lord Kingsale

A classic black-and-white exterior pub, Lord Kingsale is a romantic little spot, with small snug areas, music on weekends, and even poetry readings.

Delicious home-cooked food is served all day long and a comfortable, lived-in atmosphere draws a pleasant, subdued crowd.

4 Main St., Kinsale. ☎ *021-77-237.*

The 1601

The front bar is essentially a memorial to the town's most famous battle, and the back bar doubles as an art gallery. The pub-grub menu is always changing, but the locals assure me that it never falls short of "superb." Modern and traditional music plays on Mondays and Tuesdays. The Irish lost the Battle of 1601, but this great bar reminds us who won the war.

Pearse Street, Kinsale. ☎ *021-77-2529.*

Spaniard Inn

The best part of the Spaniard is a whole lot of outdoor seating that over-looks the harbor. Inside are cozy turf and log fires and traditional, jazz, folk, and blues music. This fisherman-theme pub is built over the ruins of a castle and named in honor of Don Juan del Aquila, commander of the Spanish fleet and ally to the Irish during the Battle of Kinsale in 1601.

Scilly Road, Kinsale. ☎ *021-77-2436.*

DeBarra's

From top to bottom and inside and out, everything about this lovely tra-ditional pub is authentic. The musicians hail from the local Irish-speak-ing area (called a *Gaeltacht*) and you'll see hand-painted signs and old-fashioned whiskey jars. People come from far and wide to enjoy the ambience of one of County Cork's finest pubs.

Main Street, Clonakilty. ☎ *023-33-381.*

Fast Facts: Kinsale and West County Cork

Area Code(s)

Kinsale and West County Cork's area codes (or city codes) are **021, 027**, and **028**.

Emergencies-Police

Dial ☎ **999** for all emergencies.

Information

For visitor information go to the tourist office at Town Hall, Skibbereen (☎ 028-21-788), open year-round. It can also provide reser-vation services. A seasonal tourist office in Kinsale, on Pier Road (☎ 021-77-2234), is open March through October. For telephone directory assistance, dial ☎ 1190.

Chapter 16

County Kerry

· ·

In This Chapter

▶ Visiting lovely Killarney Town

▶ Exploring Killarney National Park by car, cart, bike, or waterbus

▶ Visiting the home of an Irish chieftain

▶ Taking Ireland's most famous scenic drive: the Ring of Kerry

▶ Meeting Ireland's most famous (and friendliest) dolphin

· ·

*C*ounty Kerry, located at the bottom of Ireland, is home to some of the country's most spectacular scenery, including the famous Ring of Kerry. It also has Ireland's two highest mountains, Carrantuohill and Mount Brandon, as well as some great golf courses, pubs, and charming towns.

What's Where?: County Kerry's Major Attractions

One glance at the picturesque, whimsical **Killarney** and you'll know why it's probably Ireland's most visited town. Charming streets lined with pubs, restaurants, hotels, and shops give way to outlying areas of breathtaking scenery and Killarney's most popular attractions:

✔ **Killarney National Park:** The drive around the three lakes and towering mountains that make up the park is one of the best time investments you can make in Ireland.

✔ **Muckross House and Gardens:** This stirring Victorian mansion is one of Ireland's finest stately manors, and provides a venue for traditional craftsmen.

✔ **Ross Castle:** Built in the 1400s, this castle is the perfect example of the home of an Irish chieftain during the Middle Ages, when the chieftain kings ruled the area.

The drive around the **Ring of Kerry** is one of the most gratifying you'll make during your trip around Ireland. The 110-mile route is along the Iveragh Peninsula, providing endless and beautiful views of the sea, mountains, and quaint towns. Most people make the drive counter-clockwise, beginning in Killarney or Killorglin and going around to the picturesque town of **Kenmare,** where you can enjoy fine hotels, restaurants, shopping, and pubs. Other attractions in the area include

- ✔ **The Skellig Experience:** Ten miles off the coast of the Iveragh Peninsula lie the Skellig Islands, **Skellig Michael** and **Little Skellig,** two impossibly steep and rocky little points on which a community of Irish monks built a monastery in the sixth or seventh century. A sea cruise from the center circles the rocks, but you can also visit Skellig Michael via ferry from Ballyskellig.

- ✔ **Kenmare Heritage Centre and Heritage Trail:** The town of Kenmare has an interesting story to tell, and the Heritage Centre tells it, from a display on lacemaking to the effects of the Great Famine.

- ✔ **Derrynane House National Historic Park:** This beautiful home was where the Great Liberator, Daniel O'Connell, lived for most of his life.

- ✔ **Kerry Bog Village Museum:** C'mon, don't tell me you've never wanted to visit a bog. In addition to displays on peat bog, there are thatched-roof cottages, a blacksmith's forge and house, a stable, and a dairy house.

Northwest of Killarney and the Ring, **Tralee** is the capital town of County Kerry, and a pleasant place to stay overnight. It's the home of the **Rose of Tralee Festival,** and you'll also find plenty of culture, as well as, of course, a pub or two. From here you can set off on a tour of the **Dingle Peninsula,** just north of the Ring of Kerry, which offers historic sights and stunning mountain and seacoast scenery. The town of **Dingle** is a vibrant fishing port full of shops, pubs, seafood restaurants, and an astounding natural beauty. Some Dingle Peninsula highlights include

- ✔ **Kerry the Kingdom:** Ever wanted to know what life was like in Kerry in the 15th century? Here's your chance. Kerry the Kingdom includes a very realistic re-creation of a medieval street as well as a museum.

- ✔ **The Aqua Dome:** It isn't particularly Irish, but it's fun. Under a big dome there's a main pool, kiddie pool, and sky-high waterslides, as well as a sauna dome, a steam room, a cool pool, and a sunbed.

- ✔ **Fungi the Dolphin:** Fungi the Dolphin has lived in the waters around Dingle since 1984. Today, you can ride a fishing boat out for a visit or even put on a wet suit and take a dip with him.

County Kerry

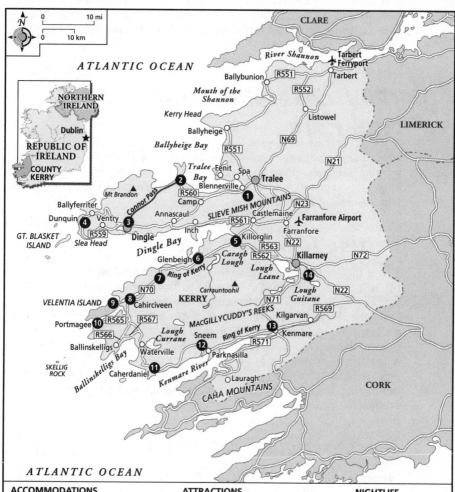

ACCOMMODATIONS
Alpine House **3**
Captain's House **3**
Carhoomeengar Farmhouse **13**
Connor*s **3**
Oakley House **1**
Pax House **3**
Scarriff Inn **11**
Towers Hotel **6**

DINING
Beginish Restaurant **3**
The Blue Bull **12**
Doyles Seafood Bar **3**
The Forge Restaurant **3**
Waterside Restaurant
  & Coffee Bar **3**

ATTRACTIONS
Blasket Centre **4**
Conor Pass **3**
Derrynane House National
  Historic Park **11**
Fungi the Dolphin boat docks **3**
Kerry Bog Village Museum **6**
Killarney National Park **14**
The Skellig Experience **9**
Skellig Islands boat docks **10**

SHOPPING
Brian de Staic **3**
Irish Crafts and Gifts **3**
Pat's Craft Shop **7**

NIGHTLIFE
Bianconi **5**
Caitin Baiters **8**
Dick Mack's **3**
The Dingle Pub **3**
Natterjack **2**
O'Flaherty's **3**
The Point Bar **8**

✔ **Blasket Centre:** For years, there was an isolated, Irish-speaking community on the Blasket Islands, off the coast of the Dingle Peninsula. The islands were abandoned in the 1950s, but at this cultural center you can find out all about the islands and the former inhabitants.

Killarney Town and Killarney National Park

One glance at picturesque, whimsical Killarney Town and you'll know why it's a popular place to visit. And if the town itself isn't enough to keep you occupied, it makes a great base for seeing the amazing mountain scenery of the region.

Getting to Killarney

To get to Killarney by car, take the N21 southwest from Limerick or the N22 northwest from Cork. To get to Tralee from Killarney take the N22 north. To continue on to Dingle, take the N86 from Tralee. The tip of the Dingle Peninsula can be driven via the R559, beginning and ending in Dingle. **Irish Rail** (☎ **064-31-067** or 066-26-555) services Killarney from Dublin, Limerick, Cork, and Galway. Trains arrive daily at the Killarney Railway Station, Railway Road, off East Avenue Road. **Bus Eireann** (☎ **064-34-777**) operates daily scheduled trips from all over Ireland to Killarney. The bus depot is across from the train station.

Getting around Killarney

This compact town is entirely walkable. There's a "Tourist Trail" that takes you past all the best sights and attractions in the town. Just follow the signs, or get a pamphlet about the trail at the tourist office (see "Fast Facts: Killarney," later in this chapter, for the address). If you have a rental car with you, I recommend just parking it at your hotel until you're ready for a day-trip to Killarney National Park. Most accommodations offer free parking for guests, but there's also street parking. During the day you'll need to display a parking disc in your car; discs are available at shops and hotels. There's no bus service within the town, but you can get a taxi if you need one at the taxi rank on College Square, between 8 a.m. and midnight. Otherwise, call **O'Callaghan's Cab & Chauffeur Service** (☎ **064-37-555**) or **Dero's Taxi Service** (☎ **064-31-251**).

Where to stay in Killarney

Killarney Park Hotel
$$$$ Killarney

Every inch of this luxurious hotel says, "Pamper me." This place is for people who want comfort, class, and a taste of old-world refinement. Kids are also welcome and a few family rooms are available. The lobby alone has many plush areas to relax (whether in front of a fire or not), including an ornate and fully stocked library where you can plan out your day over a cuppa' tea. The Garden Bar maintains traditional style, with wood everywhere and strategically placed fireplaces and snugs. You'll be amazed at the breakfast, served in a vaulted dining room complete with life-sized portraits and plush, high-backed chairs. This hotel definitely is worth a splurge.

Kenmare Place, Killarney. ☎ *064-35-555. Fax: 064-35-266. Internet:* www.killar-neyparkhotel.ie. *To get there: Located between the railway station and the Cineplex. Rates: €220–€335 ($209–$318.25) double. AE, DC, MC, V.*

Great Southern Hotel
$$$ Killarney

With its manor-house style, the Great Southern doesn't look like part of a chain, but after you experience the amenities and service they lavish on you, it becomes obvious they know the routine. Everything looks polished, the rooms overlook gorgeous grounds, and the breakfast is a diner's dream. The hotel has a leisure center with pool and Jacuzzi, a baby-sitting service, and a cocktail bar with a conservatory. You'll feel completely isolated from the world, but the hotel's just a short walk to the center of town.

Railway Road, off East Avenue Road, Killarney. ☎ *800-44-UTELL, from the United States or 064-31-262. Fax: 064-31-642. Internet:* www.gsh.ie. *To get there: Located between the railway station and the Tourist Office. Rates: €120–€188 ($114–$178.60) double. AE, DC, MC, V.*

Arbutus Hotel
$$–$$$ Killarney

This hotel in the center of town is decorated with traditional Irish luster. Plush, high-backed chairs are arranged around an old-time turf fire in the lobby, and the rooms are large and decorated with fine taste. Buckley's pub has an oak-paneled bar, and local opinion has it that the bartenders there pull the best pint of Guinness in town. Good traditional music fills the air nightly. The Arbutus is a family-run hotel (three generations of the Buckley family), and the entire staff is friendly and willing to help with anything.

College Street, Killarney. ☎ *064-31-037. Fax: 064-34-033. Internet:* www.arbutus killarney.com. *To get there: From Main Street, turn onto Plunkett Street (it only goes one way). Plunkett becomes College, and the hotel is at the roundabout where College meets Lewis Road. Rates: €82.50–€137.50 ($78.40–$130.65) double. AE, DC, MC, V.*

McSweeney Arm

$$–$$$ Killarney

If you're not the extravagant type, and a simple place to lay your head is fine, then this is the place for you. The location is mainly what you pay for — it's perfect, right in the center of town. Don't get me wrong, though: It's also homey and nice and the family that runs it covers all the bases. One of the highlights is the great food in the restaurant, beginning with the hearty breakfasts and on to savory dinners.

College Street, Killarney. ☎ *064-31-211. Fax: 064-34-553. To get there: Located at the roundabout in the town center. Rates: €75–€125 ($71.25–$118.75) double. AE, DC, MC, V. Closed Jan and Feb.*

Murphys Guesthouse

$$ Killarney

This is one of those ideal places that you'll remember long after going home. A great and, therefore, popular pub downstairs makes it the perfect place to have a guesthouse — at the end of the night, after a few pints and music, you just go upstairs to your bed! The friendly owners will ensure you enjoy yourself. All rooms are newly refurbished but still retain that old-world ambience. And parents, take note: They have a baby-sitting service and children's menu.

18 College St., Killarney. ☎ *064-31-294. Fax: 064-34-507. Internet:* www.murphys bar.com. *To get there: Go through the roundabout and down College Street. Rates: €50–€59.40 double. ($47.50–$66.25). AE, DC, MC, V.*

Carhoomeengar Farmhouse

$ Kenmare

A gem of a farmhouse B&B, John and Maureen Harris have restored this pretty white, yellow-trimmed home into a warm and welcoming respite after touring the Ring of Kerry. The rooms are nice enough (small, but cute and homey in a grandmotherly sort of way) and the house is full of lovely antiques. A golf course is nearby on which you can practice your swing. The delicious menu boasts organic farm produce and the grounds include some rare breeds of poultry, but the main draw is an excellent price for what you get: a little bit of home.

Carhoomeengar East, Kenmare. ☎ *064-41-987. To get there: Located 4 miles from Kenmare on the N71. Rates: €25.50–€26.50 ($24.25–$25.20) double. No credit cards.*

Killarney

NORTHERN IRELAND
REPUBLIC OF IRELAND
Dublin ★
Killarney ●

N

Railway Station
Bus Station
17
18
Park Rd.
Fair Hill
16 15
14
Lewis Rd.
College St.
13
East Ave.
Countess Rd.
Woodlawn Rd.
Mill Rd.
Loreto Rd.
Killarney Bypass
St. Anne's Rd.
Muckross Rd.
Plunkett St.
12
8 8
10 11
High St.
Rock Rd.
Tralee Rd.
9
Main St.
4 3
5 2
i
Ross Rd.
6
Shopping Arcade
Innisfallen Mall
7
New St.
1
St. Margaret's Rd.
New Rd.
Bishop's Path
Cathedral Place
Port Rd.
Deenagh River
Lower Lake

ACCOMMODATIONS ■
Arbutus Hotel **14**
Great Southern Hotel **17**
Killarney Park Hotel **1**
McSweeney Arms **16**
Murphys Guesthouse **13**

DINING ◆
Allegro Restaurant **8**
Foley's Seafood & Steak Restaurant **10**
Gaby's Seafood Restaurant **11**
Killarney Manor **18**
Teo's **6**

SHOPPING ▲
Blarney Woolen Mills **2**
Brian de Staic **9**
De Courcy Dodd **4**
Killarney Bookshop **4**
The Sweater Company **7**

NIGHTLIFE ☾
Buckley's **15**
Courtneys **12**
Laurels **3**
O'Connors **8**
Scoundrels **5**

i Information
⊠ Post Office

Where to dine in Killarney

There are some who say that because Killarney tourists are pretty much hungry captives in the town, restaurants don't try very hard to make food palatable. I disagree; there are loads of really good places to get delicious and varied food. Here are my top picks.

Gaby's Seafood Restaurant
$$$$ Killarney SEAFOOD

Make this stop for the finest seafood in Killarney. It's well known for its lobster dishes, but the Kerry shellfish platter takes the cake. The rustic brickwork and wooden floors make for pleasurable surroundings. And enjoying dinner in the raised dining area is a welcome break from sitting amid the chaos of some restaurants. The excellent food, which includes tons more than vittles from the sea, is complimented by the diverse wine list from Gaby's cellar. Altogether, you're practically guaranteed a great meal — and you may not even mind what it'll cost you.

27 High St., Killarney. ☎ 064-32-519. To get there: Follow Main Street until it becomes High Street. Main courses: €18.75–€23.75 ($17.80–$22.55). MC, V. Open: Tues–Sat 12:30–2:30 p.m., Mon–Sat 6–10 p.m.

Foley's Seafood & Steak Restaurant
$$–$$$ Killarney SEAFOOD-IRISH

The elegant black and white exterior of Foley's is an adequate indicator of what to expect inside. It's primarily a seafood restaurant, but it's the land-lubber's food that will surprise you. The menu changes all the time, but it's not everywhere you can count on such meat entrees as duck or pheasant. Whatever you choose, you'll be blessed with homemade brown bread. Even vegetarians will enjoy a fabulous meal at Foley's.

23 High St., Killarney. ☎ 064-31-217. Main courses: €11.25–€18.15 ($10.70–$17.20). MC, V. Open: 12:30–2:30 p.m. and 6–10 p.m.

Allegro Restaurant
$$ Killarney PIZZA-IRISH

Like its sister take-out version down the street, Allegro makes a mean pizza! But here you can get much more, from salads to traditional Irish eats. Prices are unbeatable, especially for the good food and huge portions. Fresh ingredients and homemade dough make for incredible pizza. The single-serve pizzas can feed two, even if you're extra-hungry. The house wine is surprisingly good, and sinking into an oversized booth is rewarding after a day of seeing sights.

9 High St., Killarney. ☎ 064-32-816. Main courses: €6.25–€11.50 ($5.95–$10.95). MC, V. Open: 5:00–10:30 p.m.

Teo's
$-$$ Killarney   ECLECTIC

A restaurant to satisfy any taste, whether it be for Greek, Italian, or French cuisine, or even a tangy Szechuan stir-fry. Teo's covers it all, with plenty of vegetarian food, too. Italian dishes make up the bulk of the menu, but there are plenty of other Southern European influences throughout that give the food zest — and if you don't want anything very exotic, you can always count on standard (and tasty) spaghetti and lasagna. Teo's is also a good place for a light meal before dinner hours.

13 New St., Killarney. ☎ *064-36-344. Main courses: €6.25–€11.25 ($5.95–$10.70). MC, V. Open: noon to 10:30 p.m.*

Killarney Manor
$$$$ Killarney   IRISH

Here's your big chance to have dinner in an authentic vintage manor, in the most authentic way — just like it was in the 19th century. Of course, there's electricity and you'll arrive by car, but nearly everything else is the same. You become part of the act in this entertaining (and appetizing) feast, as guests of "Lord and Lady Killarney" in their stately home. You'll start with a welcome drink in the imposing Gallery Room and then move into the Great Hall for a five-course meal. All the while, the captivating sounds and poetry of the auld days are played for you. The rousing after-dinner entertainment is characteristic of a great Irish house — you'll really feel like an honored guest when the players sing and dance for you. It's fun! It's exciting! It's dinner! Older kids will love it.

Note: At press time, Killarney Manor was nonoperational due to a fire, and I didn't have details concerning when it will re-open, so it's essential that you call before planning on having dinner here.

Loreto Road, Killarney (about 2 miles out from town). ☎ *064-31-551. Open nightly April–Oct. Dinner is served from 7:45 to 10:00 p.m. The cost is €35 ($33.25). AE, DC, MC, V. Reservations are a good idea in the summer.*

Exploring Killarney and Killarney National Park: The Top Attractions

Killarney Town is a "wander around, do some shopping, and have a pint" kind of place, but the outskirts are another matter entirely, providing some of the most amazing things to see in all Ireland, including the beautiful Killarney National Park and the famed Lakes of Killarney. The drive around the lakes is one of the best time investments you can make in Ireland, so setting aside a day to focus on it by itself is best. In autumn, you'll pass mountains covered with beautiful purple heather — the subject of many an Irish song. A curve in the road may open up to a deep and far-reaching valley dotted with brooks and goats. You'll want to spend more time outside of the car than in it.

If you get a yen to do the golf thing while you're in the midst of all this green, visit the **Killarney Golf and Fishing Club.** Home of the 1991 and 1992 Irish Open Championship, this course is nestled among the beautiful Lakes of Killarney and below the majestic Macgillycuddy's Reeks mountains. It's on Mahony's Point, Killarney (☎ **064-33-899;** Internet: www.killarney-golf.com). Par is 72, and the greens fees are €70 ($66.50).

Killarney National Park
Just outside Killarney

Three thrilling lakes surrounded by towering mountains comprise this state-owned park. A well-defined (but occasionally dippy and curvy) road winds throughout the park, making for an incredible drive. There are plenty of places to park and take pictures, or even do a little climbing. Be careful not to drive too fast or you'll pass the parking areas before you know it (not to mention flatten a few sheep, who have a tendency to wander into the road). Without stopping, the drive takes just over an hour, but undoubtedly you'll stretch it out for longer — there's just so much to see and do within the park's limits.

Just inside the park, about a mile in on the left, is parking for **Torc Waterfall.** Only a few steps into the forest and you see the bottom of it, but don't be fooled and think that's it. The waterfall trail is easy to walk and will take you to the top of the mountain and the head of the falls. From here (about an hour's climb), you'll get the most exhilarating view of the lakes.

Continuing on, you'll pass **Ladies View,** which is marked by a pretty large parking area. Definitely stop for the view: It's extraordinary. How did it get its name? In the 1800s, Queen Victoria of England made a momentous trip to Killarney and took her entourage through what is now the National Park. Along the way, the Queen's ladies in waiting were so overcome with marvel at the landscape from this particular spot, they stopped for a Kodak moment (sans the camera). From that moment on, the spot's been known as "Ladies View."

About midpoint in the park is **Moll's Gap,** where the mountains are highest. Here you can stop for a bite to eat (there's a cafe-bakery, but it's also a good spot for a picnic if you've brought some grub with you) or some shopping before heading down. The park drive dumps you in the town of Kenmare (see "Tralee and the Dingle Peninsula," later in this chapter). You don't have to go back through the park to return to Killarney; there's a route that bypasses the mountains.

Killarney National Park

ATTRACTIONS

The Head of the Gap of Dunloe **2**
Kate Kearney's Cottage **1**
Ladies View **3**
Muckross Friary **5**
Muckross House & Gardens **6**
Muckross Traditional Farms **6**
Ross Castle **4**
Torc Waterfall **7**

Cliff ⊔⊔⊔⊔⊔
Hiking Trails - - - - -
Bicycle Route ■ ■ ■ ■
Alternate Bicycle Route ● ● ●

Information ⓘ
Parking Ⓟ

Killarney. ☎ **064-31-440**. *To get there: Take Kenmare Road (N71) out of town. Signs indicate the park (and guide throughout it). Admission: Free. Open: Daylight hours. Suggested visit: Anywhere from 1 hour to all day, depending on your interests.*

Muckross House, Gardens, and Traditional Farm
Killarney National Park

This Victorian mansion is within the National Park and is one of Ireland's finest stately manors. The decor of the home, down to tiny furnishing details, silently explains the lifestyle of the gentry of the mid-19th century. The basement portrays the harsher environment of the life of the domestic servants. Also on site, you can watch traditional craftsmen weaving, bookbinding, and making pottery. There are landscaped grounds, known for their rhododendrons and azaleas; a traditional farm that preserves the way things were run before modern conveniences; and the Mucros Garden Restaurant. Restricted accessibility for the disabled.

Killarney National Park, Killarney. ☎ *064-31-440. Internet:* www.muckross-house.ie. *To get there: Take Kenmare Road (N71) out of town. Admission: For either Muckross House or Farm €4.75 ($4.50) adults, €3.50 ($3.35) seniors, €2 ($1.90) children and students, €11.25 ($10.70) family. Combined ticket €7 ($6.65) adults, €5 ($4.75) seniors, €3.50 ($3.35) children and students, €17.50 ($16.65) family. House Open: Mid-March to June, Sept and Oct daily 9 a.m.–6 p.m.; July and Aug daily 9 a.m.–7 p.m.; Nov to mid-March daily 9:00 a.m.–5:30 p.m.; Farm Open: June–Sept daily 10 a.m.–7 p.m.; May daily 1–6 p.m.; mid-March to April and Oct Sat and Sun 2–6 p.m. Suggested visit: 2 to 3 hours.*

Ross Castle
Killarney

This castle stronghold was probably built in the 1400s by a member of the O'Donoghue Ross clan. Today it serves as a perfect example of the home of an Irish chieftain during the Middle Ages, when the chieftain kings ruled the area. The castle itself looks a lot like a huge tower and is surrounded by a wall with four smaller towers at each corner — clearly, fortification was a priority. Inside is an admirable collection of furniture from the 16th and 17th centuries. This was the last place in the province of Munster to surrender to Cromwell in 1652. The castle sits on a peninsula that projects onto Lough Leane, and you can rent boats from here to explore the lake, Killarney's largest.

Ross Road, Killarney. ☎ *064-35-851. To get there: Head south from town, on Ross Road. Admission: €3.50 ($3.35) adults, €2 ($1.90) seniors, €1.25 ($1.20) children and students, €7.50 ($7.15) family. Open: April daily 11 a.m.–6 p.m.; May and Sept daily 10 a.m.–6 p.m.; June–Aug daily 9:00 a.m.–6:30 p.m.; Oct Tues–Sun 10 a.m.–5 p.m. Suggested visit: 1½ hours.*

Joining an organized tour

If you want the information of a guided tour but could do without the guide, try the **Killarney Tourist Trail,** which takes you through the town's most interesting parts, keeping you on track through a series of signposts. The tour begins at the Killarney of the Welcomes tourist office on Beech Road (for information, call ☎ **064-36-622**), and takes about two hours if you walk at a leisurely pace.

If you're looking to go off the beaten trail on your own, pick up **Simple Pocket Maps for Walkers and Cyclists in Killarney** at the Killarney of the Welcomes office or the Killarney Tourist office at Town Hall (see "Fast Facts: Killarney" later in this chapter). These are concise color maps that will guide you into some of the area's hidden and delightful scenery. If you want to cover any of these routes by bike, you can rent a mountain bike, tandem bike, touring cycle, or kid's bike by the day or week from **O'Neill Cycle Store Rent-A-Bike**, 6 Plunkett St., Killarney (☎ **064-31-970**). This is a popular option, so call ahead to be sure they'll have a bike for you.

If you'd prefer a little more organization to your tour, here are some options:

- ✔ **Killarney Highlights Bus Tour:** This bus tour takes you to the main sights around Killarney. You'll see the lakes, Ross Castle, Muckross House and Gardens, and Torc Waterfall, and then head up to the Gap of Dunloe.

    Where and when: May to September daily at 12:30 p.m. The tour takes about three hours and departs from Dero's Tours office at 22 Main St., Killarney. Information: ☎ **064-31-251.** Price: €11.25 ($10.70) per person.

- ✔ **Gap of Dunloe and Lakes of Killarney Horse Cart Tour:** This is the real way to see the spectacular Kerry mountains — up close and personal! You can't take cars through the Gap of Dunloe, so you'll get a bus to famous local beauty Kate Kearney's Cottage, once her inn but now home to craft and coffee shops. From there you'll take a horse or a pony cart for the 7 miles through the famous Gap. You'll get lunch at Lord Brandons Cottage and then hop on a boat for a tour of the Lakes of Killarney. You'll stop at Ross Castle before taking a boat back to town. It takes a full day and really is an adventure.

    Where and when: Runs year-round at varying times. Information: Castlelough Tours Ltd., 7 High St. ☎ **064-32-496.** E-mail: `loch@ tinet.ie`. Price: €16.25 ($15.45) per person for bus and boat (plus a small fee for lunch).

- ✔ **Jaunting Car Tour:** These horsedrawn buggies are as much a part of Killarney as the lakes and mountains. The drivers will take you through the town or as far as the Gap of Dunloe. They'll go into the Killarney National Park as far as Muckross House and Torc Waterfall, too. The drivers are characters, and pretty persuasive — even if you had no intention of taking one, you could find yourself bouncing in the back of a buggy with a blanket snug around your legs.

    Where and when: There's no phone number or central place to find a jaunting car, but you can find them all over town — or rather, they'll find you. Price: It's not like the carts have meters, so check with the tourist office or your hotel; they'll tell you what price to expect for where you're going. To be on the safe side, have the driver quote a price before heading out. The going rate ranges from €4 ($3.80) to €8 ($7.60) per person.

✔ **The Pride of the Lakes Waterbus Tour:** This tour takes you around Lough Leane, Killarney's largest lake, in a luxurious passenger cruiser.

Where and when: Tours leave from the pier at Ross Castle, from April to October, and last about an hour. Information: Destination Killarney, East Avenue Road, Killarney. ☎ **064-32638.** E-mail: destinationkillarney@eircom.net. Price: €6.25 ($5.95) per person.

Shopping in Killarney

Killarney provides plenty of places for buying Irish treasures. You'll find the best shopping right in town, but there are some exceptions, like handweavers smack dab in the middle of the mountains. Some of the best, for value and selection, are listed in this section.

Avoca Handweavers

This vast shop has a huge selection of sweaters and tweeds for men and women. You'll also find unique pottery and crafts, as well as plenty of souvenirs.

Molls Gap (midway through the Killarney National Park). ☎ *064-34-720.*

Blarney Woolen Mills

Here you'll find quality Irish items, from real Aran knit sweaters to linen and tweed. You can even watch sweaters being handframed and knit.

10 Main St., Killarney. ☎ *064-34-843.*

Brian de Staic

This handcrafted jewelry ranks among the most respected in Ireland. Goldsmith de Staic is renowned for his work, which captures the best of Celtic design.

18 High St., Killarney. ☎ *066-33-822.*

de Courcy Dodd

You'll find fine antiques of all kinds for serious collectors and people just dabbling at de Courcy Dodd.

68 New St., Killarney. ☎ *064-31-351.*

Killarney Bookshop

A comprehensive collection of both Irish and worldwide authors. You can have the shop's mail-order catalog sent to your home.

32 Main St., Killarney. ☎ *064-34-108.*

The Sweater Company

If you're in the market for just sweaters and handknits, this is the place for you. From cardigans to pullovers, you'll get the finest Irish knitwear here.

3 New St., Killarney. ☎ *064-35-406.*

Pub-crawling in Killarney

Killarney has been welcoming tourists for years now, and the town has perfected the art of making strangers feel welcome. Music, too, plays a huge part of the Killarney pub scene. So settle in and enjoy!

If you've been touring around Ireland for a while, you've probably heard people referring to *yer man* (as in, "I was talking to *yer man* the other day . . ."), and by now you're wondering who this incredibly popular guy is. Well, he's the fella Americans might call *this guy* (for example, "I was talking to this guy the other day . . ."). You may also hear yer man's feminine counterpart, *yer won.*

Buckley's

Locals say this pub pulls the best pint of Guinness in town, and I agree — try for yourself. The interior is oak paneled and turf fires burn, making it cozy and welcoming. As the story goes, Publican Tim Buckley had spent some time in New York, and in the 1920s returned to Ireland, deeply missing his hometown. So, he created the bar to combine all the great things he missed about Ireland while in the States. Maybe that's why it exudes Irish comfort. Pub grub is served all day, and music plays every night in the summer.

College Street, Killarney. ☎ *064-31-037.*

Laurels

This pub offers more than meets the eye. If you stick around until the music begins, you'll understand why Con O'Leary's place has been dubbed "The Singing Pub." It really comes to life after the music starts. When the back room opens up, the pub doubles in size. Soon it seems like everyone's raising their pints to one another. Music is scheduled from April to October. A rousing good time!

Main Street, Killarney. ☎ *064-31-149.*

O'Connors

Wood from floor to ceiling adds to the decor of this old-style pub. Stools and tables low to the floor and wonderful stained glass throughout add to the ambience. A friendly place, where locals meet and tourists drop in, the pub has been run by the O'Connor family for three generations. Good soup and sandwiches are served all day.

7 High St., Killarney. ☎ *064-31-115.*

Courtneys

This tiny place, with its blazing turf fires, sawdust on the floor, and light emanating from the candles on low-rising tables, is a true Irish pub with nothing pretentious about it. Everyone knows each other (and so will you, by the end of the evening), and there's always a pickup game of chess being played in a corner. Things are a bit low-key here; you're more likely to hear Celtic or jazz background music than stirring rebel ballads.

24 Plunkett St. (below Courtneys restaurant), Killarney. ☎ *064-32-688.*

Going clubbing in Killarney

If you prefer club hopping to pub-crawling, fear not! Here's a cool place to dance the night away.

Scoundrels

The focus of this club is dance, dance, dance. Most of the place is taken up by a huge dance floor in the center, and the rest of the club resembles an overcarpeted 1970s venue, though it's so dark inside that the dated decor hardly matters. With the jumpy music the DJs spin, you'll be dancing too much to care!

New Street (below Eviston House Hotel), Killarney. ☎ *064-31-640.*

Finding live music

Most pubs in town have traditional music nightly during the spring and summer. Another customary form of Irish entertainment is the cabaret, a variety show featuring folk music and sing a-longs. "An Evening In Killarney" is one cabaret hosted by Great Southern Hotel, Railway Road, off East Avenue Road, Killarney (☎ **064-33-911**), July and August on Monday, Wednesday, and Friday at 8:45 p.m.

Fast Facts: Killarney

Area Code

Most numbers have the area code **064.**

Currency Exchange

In addition to the standard Bureau de Change, travel agencies, and hotels, you can change money at the American Express office on Kenmare Place (open from March through October).

Emergencies

Dial ☎ **999** for all emergencies.

Genealogical Resources

Contact the Killarney Genealogical Centre, Cathedral Walk, Killarney (☎ 064-35-946).

Information

For visitor information go to Killarney of the Welcomes, on Beech Road (☎ 064-36-622), or the Killarney Tourist Office, in the Town Hall, Church Place, off Main Street (☎ 064-31-633). Both are open year-round and provide many brochures. A great resource is the free publication *Where: Killarney,* which includes useful information like maps, events, and entertainment. It's available at most hotels and guesthouses in town.

Post Office

The Killarney Post Office (☎ 064-31-051) is on New Street.

Kenmare and the Ring of Kerry

The drive around the Ring of Kerry, a 110-mile route along the Iveragh Peninsula, is one of the most scenic and gratifying you'll make during your trip around Ireland, varying from town to town and providing endless and beautiful views of the sea, mountains, and quaint villages. (See the Cheat Sheet at the front of this book for a map of the Ring of Kerry.)

The standard route begins in **Killorglin,** known as the gateway to the Ring. Next comes **Glenbeigh,** a town partially surrounded by a ring of mountains. At **Rossbeigh** you'll first catch sight of the Atlantic, and then comes the town of **Cahirsiveen,** where you're likely to stop for a bite to eat. **Portmagee** is a pretty fishing harbor where you cross the bridge to **Valentia Island. Ballinskelligs** is a *Gaeltacht,* or Irish-speaking area, that has an Irish college where children can attend summer classes to learn the language.

Waterville, the next town on the Ring, is known as a fishing resort, but there are plenty of other sporting attractions to divert you from the drive. In **Caherdaniel** you can see the home of Daniel "The Liberator" O'Connell, and nearby **Castlecove** is loaded with sandy beaches. The lovely village of **Sneem,** one of my favorite little towns, has mountain and river scenery and is a haven of peace and quiet. **Parknasilla** benefits from the Gulf Stream, and has a (comparably) warm climate and even subtropical plants. Finally, the Ring of Kerry ends in the picturesque town of **Kenmare,** where you'll enjoy fine hotels, restaurants, shopping, and pubs.

The Ring is traditionally driven counterclockwise, beginning in Killarney or Killorglin and going around to Kenmare. During the peak tourist seasons, you'll encounter a good number of other drivers along this route. So, if you want to avoid the crowds, begin in Kenmare and go clockwise — that way, you'll be going against the traffic.

Getting to and around Killarney and the Ring

By car, take the N70 south from Tralee, or the N71 southwest from Killarney. A car is the best way to get to the Ring of Kerry, and the best way to see it all. **Bus Eireann** (☎ **064-34-777**) has limited service from Killarney to Cahersiveen, Waterville, Kenmare, and a few other towns on the Ring of Kerry.

Where to stay in Kenmare and along the Ring

Stretching about 110 miles, the Ring of Kerry is short enough to drive in a single day, but there are lots of things to see and do throughout the peninsula, and the coastline is dotted with places to stay overnight.

Foley's Shamrock

$–$$ Kenmare

This B&B has everything: location, food, drink, and comfort, all for a reasonable price. Set in the heart of Kenmare, Foley's is the kind of place Ireland is known for. It's small, so Ms. Foley can care for you personally, and it's within walking distance to golf, horseback riding, and fishing. The restaurant serves Irish and international food (but there are some really great places to eat in town). The downstairs pub is a place that makes you feel secure and snug the second you walk inside.

Henry Street, Kenmare. ☎ *064-42-162. Internet:* www.foleyskenmare.com. *To get there: Where the N70 and N71 meet. Rates: €40–€80 ($38–$76) double. MC, V.*

Wander Inn

$$ Kenmare

This charming B&B may have a silly name, but the O'Sheas, the couple in charge, take their job seriously. You'll feel very welcome and comfortable here, and each room is decorated uniquely with antiques. Rooms all have a TV and phone. If a pint is what you're after, there are two (count 'em, two) pubs in the B&B to choose from, both with traditional music every night. You can get a picnic lunch for the road, and the owners will even organize guided tours of the area.

2 Henry St., Kenmare. ☎ *064-41-038. Fax: 064-41-318. To get there: Located where the N70 and N71 meet, in the center of town. Rates: €50–€62.50 ($47.50–$59.40) double. MC, V.*

Towers Hotel
$$–$$$ Glenbeigh

This elegant hotel is a great place to spend the night after the first leg of your drive around the Ring. Sandy beaches and towering mountains are just a short walk away, and fishing and golfing are nearby. The hotel's classy restaurant creates superb seafood dishes, and the traditional pub draws locals, so even if you just go in for a bite, you'll get to see a real slice of this part of Kerry.

Glenbeigh. ☎ *066-976-8212. Fax: 066-976-8260. To get there: Right off the N70, between Killarney and Cahirsiveen. Rates: €95–€117.50 ($90.25–$111.65) double. AE, DC, MC, V. Closed Nov–March.*

Scarriff Inn
$$ Caherdaniel

You'll get a fantastic view of Derrynane Harbor from this family-run inn, located on the Ring of Kerry and offering a perfect place to rest your weary head after a long day of sightseeing. There's a seafood restaurant that offers full meals or just nibblers, and even a bar. If you decide to stay for a while, you can explore the countryside from here. Whether it's fishing, diving, or plain relaxation you're looking for, this is a fine spot to set up camp.

Caherdaniel. ☎ *066-947-5132. Fax: 066-947-5425. To get there: On the N70. Rates: €50–€58 ($47.50–$55.10) double. MC, V. Closed Nov to mid-March.*

Where to dine in Kenmare and along the Ring

One thing you'll notice about Kenmare is the number of restaurants in this small town. It's chock full o' them! I don't want you to have to eat through them all until you find a great place, though, so I've taken the burden upon myself. I don't want to think about the number of hours I had to spend on the Stairmaster to work it all off. . . .

The rest of the Ring is a bit more spotty in terms of places to eat, so I've picked out one of the best.

d'Arcy's
$$–$$$$ **Kenmare** **IRISH**

Get ready for real gourmet Irish food, prepared with fresh ingredients by a talented chef. This is the kind of food that's changing stereotypes about Ireland's culinary capabilities — it's not just meat and potatoes anymore. Choose from baked sea trout in puffed pastry with smoked salmon, or loin of Kerry lamb with eggplant, tomato, and garlic. The kitchen accommodates vegetarians, too. The dining room has a big, open fireplace that creates a welcome, cozy climate.

Main Street, Kenmare. ☎ *064-41-589. To get there: In the center of town. Main courses: €11.85–€21.25 ($11.25–$20.20). MC, V. Open: March–Oct daily 6–10 p.m.; Nov–Feb Wed–Sat 7:00–9:30 p.m. Closed Mon Sept–June.*

Purple Heather
$–$$$ **Kenmare** **HAUTE PUB**

Here's a switch: hearty, delicious pub grub with a haute-cuisine edge. Perfect for a light meal or snack and guaranteed not to be ordinary. Tasty seafood salads, vegetarian omelets, soups, and platters piled high with farmhouse cheese are just some of the offerings. It's situated in the heart of town, too.

Henry Street, Kenmare. ☎ *064-41-016. To get there: In the center of town. Main courses: €4.50–€12.50 ($4.30–$11.90). No credit cards. Open: Mon–Sat 11 a.m.– 7 p.m.*

Virginia's Restaurant and Wine Bar
$$ **Kenmare** **IRISH**

Chef and owner Virginia Harrington specializes in traditional and modern Irish food at good prices. Seafood dishes are a staple of the menu, which uses only fresh local produce. Meals are succulent and imaginative, like the house special: supreme of chicken stuffed with farmhouse cheese.

36 Henry St., Kenmare. ☎ *064-41-021. To get there: In the center of town. Main courses: €10–€16.25 ($9.50–$15.45). MC, V. Open: Mon–Sat 5:00–9:30 p.m., Sun 12:30–9:30 p.m.*

The Blue Bull
$$–$$$ **Sneem** **SEAFOOD-IRISH**

This quaint roadside restaurant is known throughout County Kerry for its fresh seafood. There are also steaks and hearty soups, and specials include traditional Irish dishes. Check out the bar inside, where good pub grub is served all day long. Stick around after dinner for some Irish music in the pub.

South Square, Sneem. ☎ *064-45-382. To get there: On the Ring of Kerry, 15 miles west of Kenmare. Main courses: €11.85–€18.75 ($11.25–$17.80). AE, DC, MC, V Open: April–Oct 6–10 p.m.*

Exploring Kenmare and the Ring: The Top Attractions

In this section, I take you to a forbidding island where Irish monks helped save civilization, to a historic home and a cultural center, and then dump you in a bog. If you want to add a little golf to round out the experience, visit **Waterville Golf Links,** Newrath, Waterville (☎ **066-74-102**), the course to the stars. It's scenic, overlooking the Atlantic, but more importantly, it's where Bob Hope and Sean Connery play when they're in Ireland. It's a par-71 course, and greens fees are €62.50 ($59.40).

The Skellig Experience
Valentia Island

At this heritage center, located close to the Ring of Kerry, you'll learn all about the two Skellig Islands off the coast of the Ring, which were once the home of monks. The Skellig Experience, located on the beautiful Valentia Island, explains the life and work of early Christian monks on Skellig Michael and how the lighthouses of the islands guided seafarers. You'll also learn about the sea birds and sea life in and around the Skellig Rocks, and there's a stone theater (where you'll watch a video about the islands) and a place to get a light lunch.

Skellig Heritage Centre, Valentia Island. ☎ *066-76-306. To get there: Only 7 miles from the Ring of Kerry (N70). Take the R565 to Portmagee and Valentia Island. The Heritage Centre is just across the bridge from Portmagee as soon as you cross over onto Valentia Island. Admission: €3.75 ($3.55) adults, €3.25 ($3.10) seniors and students, €2 ($1.90) children under 12. Open: April–June and Sept daily 10 a.m.–7 p.m.; July–Aug daily 9:30 a.m.–7:00 p.m. Suggested visit: 2 hours.*

Sailing to the Skelligs
Portmagee

You can take a boat out to the larger of the Skellig Islands, Skellig Michael. It is definitely worth the 45-minute trip to see the island. My favorite thing to do is to climb to the monastic ruins (dating back to the 12th century) at the top of Skellig Michael. You can have a picnic near there as well. Bird-lovers will enjoy seeing all the nesting seabirds on the islands, especially gannets and puffins (in the summer).

The trip takes about 45 minutes and costs €25 ($23.75) per person. Ferries run April–Sept daily, leaving between 10 a.m. and 11 a.m. (weather permitting, so call the evening before to make sure). For a ferry from Portmagee to Ballyskellig (on Skellig Michael), call Joe Roddy (☎ 066-9474-268).

Derrynane House National Historic Park
Caherdaniel

This beautiful home was where the Great Liberator, Daniel O'Connell, lived for most of his life. The lawyer and politician fought for the repeal of anti-Catholic laws, and the home is now a museum that displays many personal pieces from his life and career and includes a 25-minute video. The house sits on gorgeous grounds along the coast.

Right off the Ring, in Caherdaniel. ☎ 066-9475-113. To get there: From Killarney, take the Ring of Kerry (N70) to Caherdaniel. You will see a sign 1 mile north of the village for parking. Admission: €2.50 ($2.40) adults, €2 ($1.90) seniors, €1.25 ($1.20) students and children, €6.25 ($5.95) family. Open: Oct–April Tues–Sun 1–5 p.m.; May–Sept Mon–Sat 9 a.m.–6 p.m., Sun 11 a.m.–7 p.m. Suggested visit: About 1 hour.

Kerry Bog Village Museum
Glenbeigh

This is a slice of life in Kerry in the 1800s, featuring thatched-roof cottages, a blacksmith's forge and house, a stable, and a dairy house. You'll also see the homes of the craftspeople of the area, including a laborer, a turf-cutter, a thatcher, and a tradesman. Of course, plenty of freshly cut turf is lying about, coming from the bog; it was once a huge part of Irish life, used as heating fuel. Inside the home are authentic pieces from across County Kerry.

Ring of Kerry Road (N70), Glenbeigh. ☎ 066-976-9184. To get there: From Tralee, take the Ring of Kerry (N70) south to Glenbeigh. Follow signs from the village. Admission: €3.50 ($3.33) adults, €2 ($1.90) students, €1.25 ($1.19) children. Open: March–Nov daily 9 a.m.–6 p.m.

Joining an organized tour

If you'd like to take a break from driving around the Ring, one of these tours will give you a day off:

✔ **Bus Eireann Day Tour:** Bus Eireann makes a day tour of the Ring of Kerry. The buses don't stop very often, so you lose a lot of freedom picking a tour over driving the ring yourself. But if you're not too comfortable driving, a tour beats a white-knuckled trip down narrow, windy roads with sharp drop-offs and no shoulders.

Where and when: From Cork Bus Station, daily between May and September leaves 10 a.m. and returns 10 p.m. Information: ☎ 021-50-8188. Price: €17.50 ($18.55) adult, €12.50 ($11.90) child.

✔ **Seafari Scenic & Wildlife Cruises:** See Kenmare Bay aboard this covered and heated cruising boat, which holds up to 150 people. For two hours you'll get an informed tour of the history, geography, and geology of the area. You may even see some sea otters, gray seals, and herons. There are evening music cruises during the high season, and you can purchase food and drink on board.

Where and when: Leaves from Kenmare Pier, Kenmare. Departs every two hours beginning at sunrise, April to October. Information: ☎ 064-83-171. Price: €12.50 ($11.90) adults, €10 ($9.50) students, €6.25 ($5.95) children.

✔ **The Kerry Way Self-Guided Walking Tour:** This self-guided walk goes throughout the Ring of Kerry and is for seasoned walkers only.

Where and when: Pick up maps at a tourist office in Killarney or Kenmare (see "Fast Facts: Kenmare and the Ring of Kerry" later in this chapter).

Shopping

There are plenty of small craft shops along the Ring of Kerry, but the best shopping is in the town of Kenmare. You'll find a variety of specialty shops and souvenir stores, and plenty of what the town is known for: Kenmare lace.

Cleo

This women's shop has stylish Irish clothes and is noted for colorful tweeds and linen.

2 Shelbourne Rd., Kenmare. ☎ *064-41-410.*

Nostalgia

Nostalgia stocks the finest collection of the famed Kenmare lace, in tablecloths, bed linens, doll clothes, and more.

27 Henry St., Kenmare. ☎ *064-41-389.*

Pat's Craft Shop

Here's a one-stop shop for souvenirs and crafts, with crystal, china, clothes, and more.

Kells Post Office, between Glenbeigh and Cahirsiveen on the Ring. ☎ *066- 9477-601.*

Defending Ireland's turf

You may be one of the last tourists to ever get a whiff of the not-so-wonderful aroma of burning peat. Special conservation areas are now preserving bogs throughout Ireland, and a recent European Union directive has decreed that all turf-cutting be halted by 2008.

Quills Woolen Market

Quills (part of a chain) has a fine selection of Irish crafts, like Aran sweaters, Donegal tweeds, and Waterford Crystal.

The Square, Kenmare. ☎ 064-32-277. Outlet store at North Square, Sneem. ☎ 064-45-277.

Pulling a pint: Pub life along the ring

Bianconi

This will probably be your first stop along the Ring of Kerry. An interesting little pub, Bianconi's offers good Irish lunches — you can even splurge on some smoked salmon or oysters. There's folk music most evenings, and you can count on a friendly welcome from the staff.

Right on the N70 (near where it meets the N72), Killorglin. ☎ 066-61-146.

Caitin Baiters

This thatched-roof pub is as authentic as they get, and inside you'll enjoy hearty food and a well-pulled pint, both at reasonable prices! Some nights (it's hit and miss) there are music sessions.

Kells Bay, Cahirsiveen (from the town's main street, follow the turnoff to Kells Bay; it's on that little road). ☎ 066-947-7614.

The Point Bar

If the weather's good, this is the place to be. Sitting outside on the patio sipping a pint and looking out at the water is simply idyllic. If you're hungry, there are plenty of good, fresh seafood dishes, served 12:30 to 3:00 p.m. and 6:30 to 9:30 p.m.

On the road to Renard Point (off the Ring road) in Cahirsiveen, just a minute or two from the N70). ☎ 066-947-2165.

Fast Facts: Kenmare and the Ring of Kerry

Area Code

Most numbers on the Ring of Kerry have the area code **064**.

Emergencies

Dial ☎ **999** for all emergencies.

Information

For visitor information go to the Kenmare Tourist Office at Market Square

(☎ 064-41-233). For telephone directory assistance, dial ☎ 1190.

Internet

Tanamara Ltd., Mountain Ash, Gortalinney, Kenmare (☎ 064-41-358), offers Internet access.

Tralee and the Dingle Peninsula

You'll begin your exploration of the Dingle Peninsula (just north of the Ring of Kerry) in **Tralee,** the quaint "Gateway to Kerry." This is the capital town of County Kerry, a pleasant place to stay overnight, and the home of the world famous **Rose of Tralee Pageant,** the highlight of the annual Festival of Kerry. The festival lasts for five days at the end of August and includes concerts, street entertainment, and horse races leading up to the beauty-talent contest that names the Rose herself (call the festival office at ☎ **066-712-1322** for more information).

From Tralee you can set off on a driving tour through Castlemaine, Inch, and Annascaul before reaching **Dingle,** the primary town of the peninsula. Don't pass by this gem of a town before taking in all that it has to offer (which invariably means at least a night's stay). The town is small, but chock full of the things that epitomize Ireland: shops, pubs, seafood restaurants, and an astounding natural beauty. All these explain its popularity as a tourist locale. But tradition's been preserved, too: Dingle is one of the few remaining *Gaeltachts,* or Irish-speaking areas.

The drive around the Dingle Peninsula affords some sights you may not expect to see in Ireland. The first weird thing you'll probably notice are palm trees. That's right — palm trees. The Gulf Stream sweeps up to the peninsula and its warm waters provide fertile ground for the trees. Next, you'll notice sandy, clean beaches that lie tucked between jagged coves. At the very tip of the peninsula is Slea Head, where the land rounds out and you'll get spectacular views of the ocean and Blasket Island. It's a sight that's well worth going out of your way to experience.

Tralee

ACCOMMODATIONS ■
The Abbey Gate Hotel **2**
Oakley House **8**

DINING ◆
Val O'Shea's Bar & Bistro **4**

ATTRACTIONS ●
The Aqua Dome **5**
Kerry the Kingdom **6**

NIGHTLIFE ◖
Kirby's Brogue Inn **1**

SHOPPING ▲
The Tralee Gift Shop **3**
Walter Lyons **7**

Information ⓘ

Getting to and around Tralee and the Dingle Peninsula

If you're coming by car from Dublin, follow signs for N7 south to Limerick and then N21 or N69 (Coast Road) to Tralee. To get to Dingle at the head of the Dingle Peninsula, take the R559. Trains to Tralee arrive daily from Dublin, Cork, and Limerick to the railway station on John Joe Sheehy Road (☎ **066-712-3522**). No trains go to Dingle. Buses arrive in Tralee daily from all over Ireland at the Bus Eireann depot on John Joe Sheehy Road. **Bus Eireann** provides service to Dingle daily; the depot is on Upper Main Street (☎ **066-712-3566**).

Where to stay in Tralee and Dingle

In this part of Kerry, you've essentially left the big city (well, you know what I mean) and entered the heartland. You're not going to find much along the lines of huge hotels with room service and leisure centers. But fear not, you'll run across plenty of hospitable and welcoming places to stay. Read on for my favorites.

The Abbey Gate Hotel
$$–$$$ Tralee

The Abbey Gate is a great all-in-one place. The hotel is elegant and rooms are spacious, and everyone's extremely helpful. To sweeten the pot, just downstairs is the quite good Vineyard Restaurant. Using only fresh local produce, it whips up Irish and European meals that everyone will like. And the pub, The Old Market Place, has open fires and a cozy atmosphere — a nice stop after dinner and before climbing up to bed.

Maine Street, Tralee. ☎ *066-712-9888. Fax: 066-712-9821. Internet:* www.abbey gate-hotel.com. *To get there: Located right in the center of town. Rates: €62.50–€122.50 ($59.40–$116.40) double. AE, DC, MC, V.*

Oakley House
$ Ballymullen

If you don't mind being just barely outside of town, this gorgeous guest-house is for you. It's a grand restored period house with tons of charac-ter and charm. Tralee is less than a ten-minute walk away, and the house is close to beaches, golf, and horseback riding. There's a guest lounge with tea- and coffeemaking facilities and television. Here, rooms are much like those in a home, rather than in a hotel. It makes for a great atmos-phere, but don't expect tons of amenities. The couple who run the house are certain to make you feel welcome.

Ballymullen, south of Tralee along the N70. ☎ *066-712-1727. Fax: 066-712-1727. To get there: Right on the N70. Rates: €45–€50 ($42.75–$47.50) double. MC, V.*

Alpine House
$–$$ Dingle Town

This is a guesthouse that people rave about. The sizable rooms offer all the best pluses, like tea- and coffeemaking facilities, hair dryers, direct-dial phones, and central heating (sure beats huddling next to a radiator on chilly days!). Plus, you have use of a roomy guest lounge and can enjoy the hospitality of the O'Shea family. The heart of Dingle Town is only a two-minute walk away. There's a wide choice for breakfast, too.

Mail Road, Dingle Town. ☎ *066-915-1250. Fax: 066-915-1966. To get there: Off the main road (N86). Rates: €42.50–€62.50 ($40.40–$59.40) double. MC, V.*

Captain's House
$$ Dingle Town

When you step over the footbridge and enter the yard of the Captain's House, you'll think you've entered a new world. Hospitality reigns at this family-run B&B. Even breakfast is delightful, featuring homemade bread and preserves in a room overlooking the flawless and award-winning gardens. The rooms are pleasant and the rest of the house is interestingly decorated with the spoils of the now-retired Captain's voyages.

The Mall, Dingle. ☎ *066-915-1531. Fax: 066-915-1079. Internet:* http://home page.tinet.ie/~captigh. *To get there: Located right in the center of town Rates: €57.50–€62.50 ($54.65–$59.40) double. AE, DC, MC, V. Closed Jan–mid-March.*

Connors
$–$$ Dingle Town

For the price and location, Connors is a great place to stay in Dingle. It's been refurbished, and rooms have TV, clock radio, hair dryer, and tea- and coffeemaking facilities. None of the rooms are exactly enormous, but they're all comfortable and homey. At breakfast, you can even ask for a packed lunch to take with you on the road. Main Street is only a hop away, and pubs and restaurants are next door.

Dykegate Street, Dingle. ☎ *066-915-1598. Fax: 066-915-2376. To get there: Just up from the harbor. Rates: €45–€62.50 ($42.75–$59.40) double. AE, MC, V.*

Pax House
$$ Dingle Town

The first thing that you'll notice about this place is the view — it's spectacular. Overlooking the water, with mountains looming in the distance, Pax House will tempt you to just lounge around on its comfortable balcony all day. Inside, everything's meticulously decorated, and rooms are gorgeous. A gourmet breakfast will welcome you in the morning.

Upper John Street, Dingle. ☎ *066-915-1518. Fax: 066-915-2461. Internet:* www.pax-house.com. *To get there: In the center of town. Rates: €56.25–€100 ($53.45–$95) double. MC, V. Closed Nov–Feb.*

Where to dine in Tralee and Dingle

Visiting a place right on the water pretty much promises you'll find plenty of good seafood, and the restaurants on the Dingle Peninsula won't fail you. From elegant to simple, the dishes in these parts are delicious.

Val O'Shea's Bar & Bistro
$–$$ Tralee   IRISH

Looking for some hearty, real Irish food? Look no further. Don't expect bland pub food; the chefs focus on creating traditional Irish meals at a high standard, and they offer vegetarian dishes, too. Expect soups and salads that will fill you up, and fresh seafood dinners that will surprise you. Despite the full bar and a fairly extensive wine list, it's not exactly a chichi place — you'll be comfortable with the whole family, and you won't drop too large a chunk of change in the process.

6 Bridge St., Tralee. ☎ *066-712-1559. To get there: In the center of town. Main courses: €5.50–€12.50 ($5.25–$11.90). MC, V. Open: Daily 12:30–2:30 p.m. and 6:30–10:00 p.m.*

Beginish Restaurant
$$$ Dingle Town   SEAFOOD

Seafood is in order when you come to this classy restaurant. That's the easy choice; if it's not too busy, you can pick between the cozy old dining room with the huge fireplace or the serene conservatory looking out on the gardens. Then you have to decide among such imaginative dishes as scalloped wild salmon with tarragon sauce or a seafood medley of mussels, prawns, scallops, and monkfish in a liqueur broth.

Green Street, Dingle Town. ☎ *066-9151-588. To get there: In the town center. Main courses: €12.50–€21.25 ($11.90–$20.20). AE, DC, MC, V. Open: Tues–Sun 12:30–2:15 p.m., 6–10 p.m. Closed mid-Nov to mid-March.*

The Forge Restaurant
$$–$$$$ Dingle Town   IRISH

This popular restaurant is a family haven. The prices are reasonable, and there's a special menu for kids. The menu covers seafood, steaks, and vegetarian dishes, and all meals are made with fresh local produce. The Forge is family-run and popular with tourists and locals alike. The Fentons also own and run Fenton's Restaurant on Green Street, which offers great food but doesn't really cater to the whole family.

Holyground Road, Dingle. ☎ *066-915-1209. To get there: Just up from the Main Street. Main courses: €10.65–€20.95 ($10.10–$19.90). AE, DC, MC, V. Open: Daily 12:30–2:30 p.m. and 6:00–10:30 p.m. Closed mid-Nov to mid-March.*

Doyles Seafood Bar
$$$–$$$$ Dingle Town   SEAFOOD

If you're looking for lobster, look no further. Here, when you have the specialty of the house, you pick it out of a tank in the bar. And you won't be disappointed! The rest of the menu depends on the fresh seafood caught daily by local fishermen. So although you can't always depend on a certain dish, you can be sure whatever you get will be fresh. The dining room is cozy, with plenty of brick and stone, and you may feel like you're eating in someone's wide-open kitchen.

John Street, Dingle. ☎ *066-915-1174. To get there: In the center of town. Main courses: €14–€22.50 ($13.30–$21.40). AE, DC, MC, V. Open: Mon–Sat 6:30–10:00 p.m. Closed mid-Nov to mid-March.*

Waterside Restaurant & Coffee Bar
$$–$$$ **Dingle Town**   **CAFE-IRISH**

The Waterside combines a place to have a refreshing light lunch or coffee with a perfect summertime dinner restaurant. At lunch, you can slip in while walking around the marina for a cup of joe and a pastry or a delicious Dingle seafood salad sandwich. Then, come back for a relaxing dinner in the conservatory. If the weather's nice, you can even eat alfresco on the patio. Young and daring chef John Dillon is a master with innovative Irish dishes, and fresh local produce underscores the entrees.

Quay Street, Dingle Marina. ☎ *066-9151-458. To get there: At the marina. Main courses: €11.25–€16.90 ($10.70–$16.05). MC, V. Open: Cafe: Easter–Sept 10 a.m.–6 p.m. Restaurant: June–Aug 7 a.m.–10 p.m. Closed Oct–Easter.*

Exploring Tralee and Dingle Peninsula: The Top Attractions

In this section, I'll take you down a medieval street, to a domed pool, and out into the ocean to swim with a dolphin. If your idea of fun leans more toward duffing, there are a couple good choices in the area. On Sandhill Road you'll find **Ballybunion** (☎ 068-27-146; E-mail: bbgolfc@iol.ie), a seaside club with two fine 18-hole, par-71 courses. The Old Course is the more challenging of the two, and the newer course was fashioned by the legendary Robert Trent Jones. Greens fees are €110 ($104.50). The par-71 **Tralee,** located at West Barrow, Ardfert, in Tralee (☎ 066-713-6379), is the original European Arnold Palmer–designed course. This up-and-coming course is staged before an amazing backdrop, boxed in by river, the sea, and the crumbling castles of Ardfert. Greens fees are €56.25 ($53.45).

Kerry the Kingdom
Tralee

This is your chance to really witness life in the Middle Ages — on a busy market day in 1450, to be exact. When you enter the gates, you'll walk down a street re-created to look, smell, and sound just like it did centuries ago. The museum comes next, allowing you to look closely at many of the elements the market day highlighted. There are artifacts, scale models, and video presentations to fully explain what life was like in Kerry in the 15th century. The rest of the county's history doesn't go unnoticed, either. Kerry's progression through time, starting 7,000 years ago, unfolds before you. This place is loaded with interactive displays and interesting presentations.

Ashe Memorial Hall, Denny Street, Tralee. ☎ *066-712-7777. To get there: Located in the same building as the Tourist Office. Admission: €5.25 ($5) adults, €3.50 ($3.35) children, €16.25 ($15.45) family. Open: Mid-March–July and Sept–Oct daily 10 a.m.–6 p.m., Aug daily 10 a.m.–7 p.m., Nov–Dec daily noon to 7 p.m. Suggested visit: 1½ to 2 hours.*

The Aqua Dome
Tralee

Fun for the whole family! Kids can splash around in the kiddie pools, fly down the sky-high slides, or really get berserk in the raging rapids — all under one roof. Meanwhile, adults can relax in the sauna dome, which has two saunas, a steam room, a cool pool, and a sunbed. The main pool is for the whole family, and next door is an over-16-only "health suite" (which is really just a spot with hot tubs and a relaxing place to read the paper). There's plenty to do in the Aqua Dome, whether you're looking to chill out or get rid of some pent-up energy. There's also a restaurant and shop inside, and at night the dome is amazingly lit up.

Dingle Road, Tralee. ☎ *066-712-8899, 24-hour information line; 066-29-150. To get there: Next to the steam railway heading out of town. Admission: April–Aug €9 ($8.55) adults, €8 ($7.60) children; Sept–March €8 ($7.60) adults, €7 ($6.65) children. Open: June–Aug daily 10 a.m.–10 p.m., Sept–May, phone for details. Suggested visit: As long as you want!*

Fungi the Dolphin
Dingle

Dingle's most famous resident, Fungi the Dolphin, is friendlier and more accessible than those at larger water parks. The water around Dingle is tinged with the Gulf Stream, so Fungi's arrival in 1984 wasn't a huge surprise. But when the super-friendly mammal stayed long enough to be named by local fishermen, people knew he'd made a home. Today, the colorful fishing boats bobbing at the Dingle Pier are waiting to ferry you out to see the gregarious dolphin, who will jump up and greet you. One warning: Don't lean over too far. You don't want to explain that you got a black eye from a dolphin! The trip takes about an hour. **The Fungi the Dolphin Tour** also arranges actual encounters with Fungi. You can rent everything you need (wet suit, mask, snorkel, and fins) for €17.50

($18.55), plus another €12.50 ($11.90) for the boat ride. The morning swim with Fungi is from 8 to 10 a.m. He's not in captivity, so theoretically he could take off for greener waters at any time, but he's lived here since 1984, so odds are good that he's in Dingle to stay.

The Pier, Dingle. ☎ 066-9151-967. To get there: At the waterfront. Cost: €7.50 ($7.15) adults, €3.75 ($3.55) children. Buy tickets at a kiosk at the pier. Open: Daily 10 a.m.–5 p.m.

Blasket Centre
Dunquin

This heritage center celebrates the Blasket Islands, a group of islands headed by the Great Blasket. On it, a number of Irish people lived in isolation from the world, speaking Gaelic and penning some of the greatest Irish-language literature. In the 1950s, the island was abandoned when isolation and loneliness drove the inhabitants out. At the very tip of the Dingle Peninsula stands the Blasket Centre, where you can learn all about the islands and the former inhabitants. Through displays, exhibits, and a video presentation you'll come to understand the phenomenon of the people who lived there and enriched Irish literature; there's also a bookshop specializing in Irish literature.

Dunquin, Tralee, County Kerry. ☎ 066-915-6025. To get there: At the tip of the Dingle Peninsula on the R559. Admission: €3.50 ($3.35) adults, €2 ($1.90) seniors, €1.25 ($1.20) children and students, €7.50 ($7.15) family. Open: Easter–June daily 10 a.m.–6 p.m.; July and Aug daily 10 a.m.–7 p.m.; Sept and Oct daily 10 a.m.–6 p.m. Suggested visit: 1 hour.

Conor Pass
Outside Dingle Town

Don't miss the spectacular view from Conor Pass, outside Dingle Town. A twisty, white-knuckle drive up to this spot will reward you with an astonishing view. When you reach the top, you're at the dead center of the peninsula, and between lush mountains you'll see Brandon Bay and Dingle Bay on either side. If it's a bit foggy when you get up there, don't rush off — the fog comes and goes. The drive down the other side of the mountain is equally scary, and if you're squeamish, don't look left — there's nothing there!

To get there: Take Saint's Road out of Dingle Town.

Joining an organized tour

In addition to the organized tours in this section, you can take self-guided tours in Tralee. Check out the **Walk Information Centre,**

40 Ashe St., Tralee (☎ **066-712-8733**), for details on self-guided walks, maps, and books on the Tralee and Kerry area. It's open Monday through Saturday from 8:30 a.m. to 6:00 p.m.

- ✔ **Bus Eireann Tour:** This tour runs a day tour of Killarney, Inch Strand, Dingle, and Tralee.

  Where and when: From Cork Bus Station. Leaves daily at 10:00 a.m. and returns at 9:30 p.m., July and August only. Information: ☎ **021-50-8188.** Cost: €17.50 ($16.65) adults, €12.50 ($11.90) children.

- ✔ **Sciuird Tours Bus and Walking Tour:** If you're interested in archeology, this tour is for you. It lasts two to three hours and is run by an expert who'll show you four or five monuments from the Stone Age to the Middle Ages. You'll take a short bus trip and do some easy walking.

  Where and when: Tours begin at the Tourist Office at the head of the Pier of Dingle. Information: Holy Ground, Dingle. Price: €8 ($7.60) per person. May to September, daily 10:30 a.m. and 2:00 p.m.

Shopping

You'll find the most shopping in the heart of Dingle and Tralee towns. However, there are some great pottery shops along roadsides throughout the Dingle Peninsula; just drop in when you come across them.

Brian de Staic

This shop offers unique, handcrafted jewelry made by the artist in his studio-workshop in Dingle. Pieces highlight Celtic art, and you can watch jewelry being made in the studio.

Studio Shop, The Wood, Dingle. ☎ *066-915-1298. Outlet store on Green Street, Dingle.*

Irish Crafts and Gifts

From souvenir gifts to keepsakes for yourself, from Waterford Crystal to sweaters to books, this is a one-stop shop.

Green Street, Dingle. ☎ *066-915-1433.*

The Tralee Gift Shop

Here's where you can get all those kitschy gifts you promised to bring home, like ceramic cottages and locally made crafts.

Russell Street, Tralee. ☎ *066-712-4233.*

Walter Lyons

This is the largest antique and secondhand store in Ireland; it doubles as a flea market. The owners welcome browsers, too.

JJ Sheehy Road, Tralee. ☎ *066-712-2603.*

Pulling a pint: Pub life in Tralee and Dingle

Local color is a staple of the pub scene in this part of County Kerry. The small but bustling little town of Tralee has pubs galore to suit tourist tastes. In Dingle, tradition reigns, so you may hear locals chatting to each other in their mother tongue, Gaelic.

Dick Mack's

Undoubtedly one of Ireland's quaintest pubs, Dick Mack's retains an aura of times gone by — years ago, pubs often doubled as bars and groceries; this one doubled as bar and cobbler, and one side of the place still holds the leather-working tools of the late owner. There's a great little snug at the end of the bar side, and an authentic back room that once served as the kitchen. Apparently, when Tom Cruise and Nicole Kidman stayed in Dingle while filming *Far and Away,* they fell in love with the place. Many other stars have stopped in for a pint, leaving their mark on the street out front. See for yourself!

Green Street, Dingle Town. ☎ *066-915-1960.*

The Dingle Pub

Facing the harbor and easily distinguished by the green-and-white shamrock outside, this place is just what it sounds like: the pub that represents Dingle. The inside of the pub is much like Dingle itself: It seems as if nothing's changed in generations, and you can relax in the laid-back atmosphere. Stop in for a pint and a talk with the locals.

Main Street, Dingle Town, at the harbor. ☎ *066-915-1370.*

Kirby's Brogue Inn

This bright-yellow alehouse has dubbed itself "your landmark in Tralee." Given the great atmosphere and food, it probably will be. Its quaint exterior gives way to a wonderful old pub inside, where you'll hear traditional sessions and jazz in the summers, and where you can nosh on glorified pub grub all day — steaks and seafood barside are quite a treat.

Rock Street, Tralee. ☎ *066-712-3221.*

Natterjack

This pub hearkens back to days of old, and it's a perfect place to stop in for a bite and a refreshing pint after the drive to the north end of the peninsula. This old-fashioned place concentrates more on good music and food than the latest trend in decor. There's a children's menu, and a beer garden in summertime.

The West End, Castlegregory. ☎ *066-713-9491.*

O'Flaherty's

You can count on the music in O'Flaherty's to be good — the owner frequently performs. Check out the posters and clippings that line the walls to get a real feel for Dingle Town. Everything about this place screams "authentic," and the locals who frequent it don't bother speaking English for the tourists' sake. It's big and open, and because of the stone-flagged floor, it doesn't exactly get cozy until it gets full. Stop in for a real taste of Ireland.

Bridge Street, Dingle Town. ☎ *066-915-1983.*

Fast Facts: Tralee and Dingle Peninsula

Area Code

The main area code for Tralee and Dingle is **066**.

Emergencies-Hospital

Dial ☎ **999** for all emergencies. In Tralee, the Tralee General Hospital is on Killarney Road (N22) (☎ 066-7126-222). In Dingle, the Dingle District Hospital is on Upper Main Street (☎ 066-9151-455).

Information

For visitor information go to the tourist office at Ashe Memorial Hall, Denny Street, Tralee (☎ 066-712-1288), which is open year-round. For visitor attraction information, call ☎ 066-712-7777. The office can also provide reservation services. For telephone directory assistance, dial ☎ 1190.

Internet

Computronics Cyber Suite, 33 Ash St., Tralee (☎ 066-712-9794), and DingleWeb, Lower Main Street, Dingle (☎ 066-52-477), both have Internet access and printing capabilities.

Part V
The West and Northwest

The 5th Wave By Rich Tennant

We've been through the thin and the thick of it
So lost that we're thoroughly sick of it
     Our errors so far
     Leave us in Erin go braugh
It's Limerick, the town that we're looking for.

In this part . . .

*I*n this region, you'll find that legendary Irish hospitality just about everywhere you go. You'll also find the lush countryside that inspired some of the most famous Irish ballads and rebel songs like "Galway Bay," "It's a Long, Long Way from Clare to Here," and "Sean South of Garryowen."

I start this section with Counties Limerick and Clare, in Chapter 17. The dilapidated Limerick City that author Frank McCourt describes in *Angela's Ashes* is largely a thing of the past. Today, the city sucessfully strikes that difficult balance of mixing old and new, with enough historic sights, fantastic restaurants, and elegant hotels to satisfy discriminating travelers. County Clare is also well worth a visit. This is where you'll find Bunratty Castle as well as the stunning Cliffs of Moher.

You could say that County Galway is a mini version of the country — a wonderful combination of a major city, quaint small towns, and outdoor wonders — but that may really anger a lot of people who think their own county is just as grand, so I'll pretend the subject never came up. But given all the county's assets, I *will* say I think you should make a visit here a priority. Turn to Chapter 18 for more details.

Poetry and film fans alike should be excited about a visit to Counties Mayo and Sligo (covered in Chapter 19). John Ford's classic Irish romance *The Quiet Man* was filmed in beautiful Mayo, and you can hardly swing a fisherman's sweater in Sligo without hitting a tribute to the great W. B. Yeats. This region was once the source of divine inspiration as well — Crough Patrick (in County Mayo) is said to be where St. Patrick fasted and prayed for 40 days.

In the last chapter of this section (Chapter 20), I tell you about County Donegal, Donegal Town (a great place to just walk around), the highest sea cliffs in Europe, a couple of impressive castles, a ring fort, and some of the freshest seafood you can get anywhere.

Chapter 17

Counties Limerick and Clare

- -

In This Chapter

▶ Making a pilgrimage to the literary world of Frank McCourt

▶ Hunting for historical artifacts in the Hunt Museum

▶ Eating in a thatched hut

▶ Visiting the famous Cliffs of Moher

▶ Touring the Burren

▶ Walking through prehistoric Ireland

▶ Learning to do the Riverdance . . . sort of

- -

*F*or years, Counties Limerick and Clare were the first places visitors to Ireland saw, because all international flights used to go to Shannon Airport. Nowadays Dublin Airport has snagged a lot of that business, but whether you fly in directly or visit as part of the typical clockwise swing from Dublin south through Cork and Kerry and then up to Galway, Limerick and Clare have more than enough history, culture, and positively Irish sights to justify your investment of time.

What's Where?: Limerick and Clare's Major Attractions

In recent years, **Limerick City** has risen from near dilapidation to achieving a cosmopolitan flair that may soon make it the Dublin of the West. It can't be denied that Pulitzer Prize–winning author Frank McCourt has finally brought this city to the forefront of tourism, but what you'll be surprised to see is how different the Limerick of today is from the Limerick McCourt remembers from his youth.

Some of the major sights in Limerick City and the surrounding area include

✔ **King John's Castle:** This castle is known as one of the finest examples of a fortified Norman structure in Ireland.

✔ **Hunt Museum:** Even the most reluctant museum-goer will be wowed by the wide-ranging and impressive art collection at the Hunt.

✔ **Lough Gur:** This incredible mass of prehistoric remnants includes burial mounds, a wedge tomb, and a 4,000-year-old stone circle, all explained at the interpretive center.

✔ **Adare Town and Heritage Centre:** Adare is that picturesque town of thatched-roof cottages, narrow streets, and ivy-covered churches that you thought only existed in movies and on postcards. The Heritage Centre explains how the beautiful village evolved.

County Clare often gets lost somewhere between the dazzle of Counties Galway and Kerry, but people who skip this county are missing out on some of Ireland's best attractions. Clare doesn't boast any large cities, but it's dotted with quaint towns and villages that serve nicely as stopovers and starting points for sightseeing. The narrow streets of Ennis, the main town in the county, are lined with places to stay and see. The tiny towns of Ennistimon, Kilkee, and Lahinch have nothing if not character; the pubs, restaurants, and shops are reason enough to drop in and stay awhile. If you've flown into Shannon Airport, you're in the heart of County Clare anyway and all the following sights are a short, attractive drive away:

✔ **Bunratty Castle and Folk Park:** Built in 1425, Bunratty is today one of Ireland's most authentic medieval castles. Bunratty Folk Park is a re-creation of an Irish village of the 19th century.

✔ **Knappogue Castle:** This imposing 15th-century castle has been extraordinarily refurbished, and the interior is overflowing with antiques and period furnishings.

✔ **A Medieval Feast:** Both Bunratty and Knappogue castles host medieval-style banquets, full of meat, mead, and music, plus storytelling and more, and speaking of more. . . .

✔ **The Cliffs of Moher** (pronounced *more*): Rising over 700 feet above the crashing Atlantic in places and stretching for miles in both directions, these incredible cliffs offer a view of the Clare coast, the Aran Islands, and, on a clear day, mountains as far away as Kerry and Connemara.

✔ **The Burren:** This vast expanse of limestone, stretching as far as the eye can see, is home to unique plants and animals, massive Neolithic tombs, and a maze of underground caves.

✔ **Aillwee Cave:** Located on the Burren (or rather, beneath it), this cave has ancient stalagmites and stalactites, bridges that span frighteningly deep chasms, and an underground waterfall.

✔ **Craggaunowen Castle and Project:** Ever wonder about life during the Bronze Age? You can see it firsthand here, with actors performing daily tasks in costume, a guide describing life in a ring fort, an Iron Age roadway and cooking site, and a restored castle.

Counties Limerick and Clare

ACCOMMODATIONS

Aran View House Hotel **5**
Berry Lodge **10**
Bunratty Castle Hotel **16**
Carrabawn House **17**
Dunraven Arms **17**
Queens Hotel **12**
Shamrock Inn Hotel **7**
Stella Maris **11**

DINING

Ailwee Cave **1**
Barrtra **8**
Bruach na hAille **5**
The Cloister **12**
Cruises **12**
The Inn Between Restaurant **17**
MacCloskey's **16**
The Mustard Seed **18**

SHOPPING

Antique Loft **13**
Avoca Handweavers **16**
Belleek Shop **12**
Burren Perfumery **2**
The Burren Smokehouse **3**
Craft Showcase Kilkee **11**
Traditional Music Shop **5**

NIGHTLIFE

The Cloister **12**
Durty Nelly's **16**
Galvins **7**
Monk's Pub **1**
O'Brien's **9**
O'Connor's **5**

ATTRACTIONS

Adare Town and Heritage Centre **17**
Ailwee Cave **1**
Bunratty Castle and Folk Park **16**
The Burren and Burren
  Visitor Centre **4**
Cliffs of Moher **6**
Craggaunowen Castle
  and Project **14**
Eamon de Valera statue **12**
Knappogue Castle **15**
Lahinch Sea World **7**
Lough Gur **19**
Poulnabrone Dolmen **2**

Airport ✈
Ferry - - -

10 mi
10 km

✔ **Lahinch Sea World:** At this fascinating Atlantic aquarium you'll come face to face with creatures from the Irish coast, like sharks, lobsters, rays, and Conger eels. There's even a touch pool, where kids can plunge their hands into the water and feel the (less-threatening) underwater life.

County Limerick and Limerick City

County Limerick has never exactly been the tourist hub of the country, but most visitors to Ireland end up there at some point in their travels. Whether you're heading north to Galway, west to Clare, or south to Kerry, Limerick is sure to be a stopover — and a worthwhile one, too. The area is rich with history, culture, and distinctly Irish sights, from lush scenery to city- and townscapes.

In *Angela's Ashes,* author Frank McCourt described **Limerick City** as a place wracked with poverty, unemployment, alcoholism, and rain — lots of rain. "Out in the Atlantic Ocean," he wrote, "great sheets of rain gathered to drift slowly up the River Shannon and settle forever in Limerick. . . . The rain drove us to the church — our refuge, our strength, our only dry place. . . . Limerick gained a reputation for piety, but we knew it was only the rain."

Rain is rain, of course, but you'll be surprised to see how different in all other respects the Limerick of today is from the Limerick McCourt remembers from his youth. In recent years, the city has pulled itself up from near dilapidation to become a bustling place full of great restaurants and hotels, all sharing space with historic sights. A stroll along the River Shannon offers a striking vista of the city, and the imposing sight of King John's Castle is never far from view.

The area west of the River Shannon was once the West Bank or Gaza Strip of Ireland. In 1654, the Parliament of England decreed that "Under penalty of death, no Irish man, woman, or child, is to let himself, herself, itself be found east of the River Shannon." The Irish wouldn't gain their freedom for another 200 years after that.

Getting to and around Limerick

Shannon International Airport (☎ 061-47-1444), located on the N19, off the N18, south of Ennis and 15 miles west of Limerick, has direct flights from the United States, through Continental, American Airlines, Delta, and Aer Lingus. Aer Lingus also has flights from all areas of Ireland. Several airlines have flights from England (see Chapter 6 for more information).

Limerick City

ACCOMMODATIONS ■
Alexandra Guest House **17**
Jury's Inn Limerick **16**
Limerick Ryan **1**

DINING ◆
Jasmine Palace **13**
Mustang Sally's **14**
Nestor's **13**

ATTRACTIONS ●
Hunt Museum **8**
King John's Castle **3**
Old Court House **7**
Treaty Stone **2**
St. Mary's Cathedral **5**

SHOPPING ▲
Arthur's Quay Centre **9**
Decorum **9**
Milk Market **12**
O'Mahony's **15**

NIGHTLIFE ☾
Castle Lane Tavern **4**
The Holy Ground **11**
The Locke **6**
M. J. Finnegans **10**
W. H. South **18**

If you're coming by car, Limerick can be reached by the N20 from Cork, N21 from Tralee, N24 from Tipperary, N7 from Dublin, or N18 from Ennis and Galway. Rental-car company desks are located at Shannon Airport's Arrivals Hall. All the major car-rental companies listed in Chapter 7 are represented there.

Irish Rail (☎ **061-31-5555**) services Limerick from Dublin, Cork, Killarney, and other cities throughout Ireland. Trains arrive at Colbert Station, Parnell Street, Limerick. **Bus Eireann** (☎ **061-31-333**) has daily service to Limerick City and most towns in County Limerick. For 24-hour automated time schedules out of Limerick, call ☎ **061-31-9911**.

Limerick City is best seen on foot. Park near King John's Castle (for free!) and hoof it from sight to sight. (Parking elsewhere in Limerick City requires disks that can be purchased at local shops.) A car is your best way of getting to the major attractions throughout the county, though Limerick has local bus service that covers the city's suburbs, running from Colbert Station on Parnell Street. You can also catch a cab at Colbert Station, or call **Top Cabs** (☎ 061-32-8011).

Where to stay in County Limerick

In and around Limerick City, there are a number of nice places to stay. So whether you prefer to be in the heart of the city or out in the 'burbs, I have a place for you.

Limerick Ryan
$$–$$$$ Limerick City

Set just outside of the city, this classy hotel has a section that has been around since 1780. Additions have increased the number of rooms and transformed the Ryan into a lovely hotel that echoes times past. The architecture is Georgian, and the grounds are carefully groomed. There's the Ardhu Restaurant (taking its name from the original building), the staid Ardhu Bar, and a more laid-back sports bar with a giant television screen to watch football (read: soccer). Breakfast is buffet style and is served until noon for late-risers. (Due to a change in management, the hotel's name will soon change to the Gresham Ardhu.)

Ardhu House, Ennis Road, Limerick. ☎ *061-45-3922. Fax: 061-32-6333. Internet:* www.Gresham-hotels.com. *To get there: Take Ennis Road (N18) from the Sarsfield Bridge in town. Rates: €87.50–€275 ($83.15–$261.25) double. AE, DC, MC, V.*

Jury's Inn Limerick
$$$ Limerick City

Much like a Ramada in the States, this hotel is your standard, comfortable place to stay, and though the rooms are rather nondescript, the place is located in the heart of city. Best of all, though, kids stay free. This is one of the few places in Ireland that charges a flat room rate for up to three adults or two adults and two children, so if there are more than two of you, it's a great value. There's a parking garage (that you pay to use), an informal restaurant, and a pub.

Lower Mallow Street, Limerick. ☎ *061-20-7000. Fax: 061-40-0966. Internet:* www.jurys.com. *To get there: In the city center, just over the Shannon Bridge (N18). Rates: €110–€127.50 ($104.50–$121.15) double. AE, DC, MC, V.*

Alexandra Guest House
$–$$ Limerick City

This elegant Victorian house sits among a row of classy homes just a few minutes' walk from city center, on Limerick's main street. Here, rooms are big and comfortable and there's a guest lounge to relax in and enjoy a cup of tea or coffee. The lovely couple who run the guesthouse are happy to organize day tours, and they have nonsmoking rooms, which is rare. Another nice treat, if you've had you're share of greasy breakfasts, is the healthy meal option you can choose.

O'Connell Avenue, Limerick. ☎ *061-31-8472. Fax: 061-40-0433. To get there: O'Connell Avenue is an extension of O'Connell Street from city center. Rates: €32.50–€56.25 ($30.90–$53.45) double. MC, V.*

Dunraven Arms
$$$ Adare

Other hotels are going to seem like roughing it after you stay in the luxurious Dunraven Arms, built in 1792 and surrounded by the well-preserved thatched cottages of little Adare, often called the prettiest village in all of Ireland. The charm of the village is carried into the hotel, where the Old World lives on. Rooms are exquisite, with beautiful antique furniture and even a dressing room. Modern day does seep into some parts, though: There's a pool, steam room, and gym for guests' use.

Main Street (N21), Adare. ☎ *800-44-UTELL, from United States; 061-39-6633. Fax: 061-39-6541. Internet:* www.dunravenhotel.com. *To get there: From Limerick City, take the N18 southwest on the N21. Rates: €157.50–€196.25 ($149.65–$196.45) double. AE, DC, MC, V.*

Carrabawn House
$$ Adare

Attention to detail and warm hospitality are the cornerstones of this luxurious guesthouse. It's not a thatched-roof cottage, but it is a comfortable, roomy house that you're sure to feel welcome in. It's right on Adare's main road, putting all of County Limerick's attractions practically at the doorstep. Rooms are fully equipped with conveniences: television, phone, hair dryer, and tea and coffee.

Killarney Road (N21), Adare. ☎ *061-39-6067. Fax: 061-39-6925. To get there: From Limerick City, take the N18 southwest on the N21. Rates: €50–€75 ($47.50–$71.25) double. MC, V.*

Where to dine in County Limerick

Nestor's
$$–$$$$ Limerick City   QUASI-AMERICAN

The brass rails and wood paneling found throughout this exceptional restaurant are a good indicator of what to expect: classy atmosphere and a tasteful menu. Whether you choose the traditional restaurant or Cafe

Bar, you'll get friendly service and delicious, varied food. The restaurant features steaks (the house specialty), Tex-Mex, and pizza, while the Cafe serves continental French (don't be fooled by the fancy title; it's standard cafe-Irish luncheon fare). After 8 p.m., you can often enjoy musical accompaniment with your dinner. The quasi-American menu makes this a good place for kids (American ones, at least).

O'Connell Street, Limerick. ☎ 061-31-7334. To get there: In city center. Main courses: €10–€22.50 ($9.50–$21.40). MC, V. Open: Daily noon to 11 p.m.

Jasmine Palace
$$–$$$ Limerick City   CHINESE

You've had Chinese food before — most likely from a white paper container with little metal handles. Now's your chance to see what Chinese food can really be. The Irish have a passion for Asian food, and Jasmine Palace delivers (so to speak). Not only is the food fantastic, but the crisp table linens and silver cutlery holders really add to the ambience. Best of all, it's affordable. (A word to the wise: If you're really starving, get some soup as a starter, because service can be slow.)

O'Connell Mall, O'Connell Street, Limerick. ☎ 061-41-2484. To get there: Between Cecil and Roaches streets in the city center. Main courses: €8.45–€15.65 ($8.20–$14.85). AE, DC, MC, V. Open: Mon–Thurs 5 p.m. to midnight, Fri and Sat 5:00 p.m.–12:30 a.m., Sun 1–3 p.m. and 5 p.m. to midnight.

Mustang Sally's
$$ Limerick City   TEX-MEX

South of the border meets the Emerald Isle at Mustang Sally's, Ireland's award-winning Tex-Mex restaurant. The inside resembles any Mexican cantina worth its salt (the kind that rims margarita glasses, that is), and the food is as authentic. When you've had your share of shepherd's pie and lamb stew at other places, drop in here for a memorable enchilada.

103 O'Connell St., Limerick. ☎ 061-40-0417. To get there: In city center. Main courses: €6.55–€15 ($6.25–$14.25). AE, DC, MC, V. Open: Mon–Fri 5–11 p.m., Sat and Sun 1:00–11:30 p.m.

The Mustard Seed
$$$$ Adare   IRISH

The surroundings are gorgeous enough to distract your attention, but even endless gardens and a beautiful country manor can't take away the impact of the food at The Mustard Seed. Nothing's thrown together here; it all creatively flows. You'll spend a bit more than at many other places mentioned in this book, but you'll get a true gourmet meal in return. Organic vegetables and cheeses are the foundation of the meals, which range from intriguing meatless entrees to savory poultry dishes. The atmosphere is calming and soft arias fill the room.

Echo Lodge, Ballingarry, Adare. ☎ 069-68-508. To get there: From Limerick City, take the N18 southwest to Adare, and then the R519 south for ten minutes. Main courses: €37.50 ($35.65) prix fixe. AE, MC, V. Open: Daily 7–10 p.m. Closed Sun and Mon in winter.

The Inn Between Restaurant
$$–$$$ Adare SEAFOOD-IRISH

Some thatched-roof cottages offer more than backdrop for great pictures — The Inn Between, for instance. The cheery yellow thatched cottage is nestled between a row of others. The bright, homey atmosphere helps contribute to a great meal. If you're good and hungry, try the always satisfying Inn Between burger, served with fries and homemade relish. If you're looking for something a little less hands-on, you can find plenty of more upscale meals, and the Inn's particularly proud of its fish dishes. In the warm months, you can sit out back in a lovely courtyard.

Main Street (N21), Adare. ☎ 061-39-6633. To get there: From Limerick City, take the N18 southwest on the N21; the Inn is in the center of the village. Main courses: €8.45–€14.40 ($8.10–$13.65). AE, DC, MC, V. Open: Daily 10:00 a.m.–10:30 p.m.

Exploring County Limerick: The Top Attractions

This section includes the major sights in and around Limerick City, as well as some big-time city landmarks.

Hunt Museum
Limerick City

Located in Limerick's beautifully refurbished Custom House, this museum's art collection was generously donated by the Hunt family and includes many world-class pieces that occasionally go out on loan to international exhibitions. The range of art is extremely wide, with Picasso and da Vinci sculptures; medieval paintings, jewelry, and crystal; Egyptian, Greek, and Roman pieces; and a great deal of Irish art from as far back as prehistoric times. There's a fabulous shop in the lobby that sells classy souvenirs, and the museum restaurant serves light meals.

The Custom House, Rutland Street, Limerick City. ☎ 061-31-2833. To get there: Next to Arthurs Quay, on the River Shannon. Admission: €3.75 ($3.55) adults, €2 ($1.90) students and children. Open: Tues–Sat 10 a.m.–5 p.m., Sun 2–5 p.m. Suggested visit: 2 hours.

King John's Castle
Limerick City

This sturdy, impressive fortress on the River Shannon's banks was the brainchild of King John, who commissioned it in 1210, and whose name will forever be linked with it in the public mind (even though its real name is Limerick Castle). Clearly a place built to keep people out rather than hold court or host lavish parties, this castle is known as one of the finest examples of a fortified Norman structure in Ireland. Fierce war defenses sit in the courtyard (how often do you get to manhandle a real battering ram?), and you can get a great view of the city from the corner towers. The interior has been completely restored. To get a complete understanding of the castle's function over the centuries, check out the interpretive center. Models, displays, and graphics combine to explain the past, and the show *The Story of Limerick* explains the turbulent history of this city in an interesting way.

Nicholas Street, Limerick. ☎ 061-41-1201. To get there: East of the Thomond Bridge, corner of Nicholas and Castle streets. Admission: €4.50 ($4.30) adults, €2.50 ($2.40) students and children. Open: Daily 9:30 a.m.–5:30 p.m. Suggested visit: 1½ hours.

Lough Gur
Southeast of Limerick City

If you're at all interested in prehistoric times, Lough Gur is for you. There are burial mounds, a wedge tomb, and the highlight: the 4,000-year-old Great Stone Circle. Evidence shows this Stone Age settlement was thickly settled in 3000 B.C., but what's left is now this archeological "park" of sorts. The interpretive center is housed in authentic-looking Stone Age huts right on the location of the original settlement. Inside are models of unearthed tools, weapons, and pottery, plus audiovisual displays. There are regular walking tours of the area, but you're welcome to walk around on your own (and save the cost of entering the interpretive center).

Lough Gur. ☎ 061-36-1511. To get there: 7 miles southeast of Limerick City off the N24 and R513. Museum admission: €2 ($1.90) adults, €1.25 ($1.20) students. Open: Mid-May–Sept daily 10 a.m.–6 p.m. Suggested visit: 45 minutes.

Adare Town and Heritage Centre
Adare

Thatched-roof cottages, narrow streets, ivy-covered churches — the Ireland you dreamed about but figured was an exaggeration of the movies, right? Think again. The picturesque town of Adare is just that, and more. Just a short drive outside of Limerick City, Adare takes great pride in being one of the prettiest villages in the country, if not *the* prettiest. The town history, like its past owners and how it came to be such a quaint and clean place (a concerted effort was put into its renovation), is all explained at the Adare Heritage Centre. In this attractive building, you can walk through a display of the town history, plus see a model of how Adare looked in the Middle Ages. A 20-minute video also presents the town as it is today — which is interesting, but I suggest you spend the time seeing the real thing instead. Stop into the craft and knitwear shops, and pop into the cafe for some fresh-baked bread. Books are available if you want to learn more about the area.

Main Street, Adare. ☎ *061-39-6666. To get there: From Limerick City, take the N18 southwest on the N21; to the middle of the village. Admission: €2.50 ($2.40) adults, €1.25 ($1.20) seniors, students, and children. Open: May–June, Sept and Oct daily 9 a.m.–6 p.m.; July–Aug daily 9 a.m.–7 p.m. Suggested visit: 1½ hours.*

Top Limerick City landmarks

Treaty Stone

This noble slab of limestone is reportedly where the Treaty of Limerick was signed in 1691, ending the bloody Siege of Limerick led by William of Orange. Catholic King James II was defeated, so this stone also marks the sad end of his reign.

Across the Thomand Bridge, facing King John's Castle across the Shannon.

St. Mary's Cathedral

Built in 1172, this is the oldest building in Limerick City. Inside are many beautiful carvings in black oak. Mass is said daily.

Bridge Street, one block south of King John's Castle on Nicholas Street.

Old Court House

One of the most salacious trials in Ireland's history, the famous Colleen Ba'n trial occurred more than a century ago, but it could be in any of today's newspapers. The case involved the body of a young woman found on the banks of the Shannon. Turns out she was a servant girl, and her murderer was a wealthy landowner. The high-profile case was tried in Limerick's Old Court House, and people came from far and wide to follow it. A public hanging followed, in the center of the city. But the sad fate of Colleen Ba'n resonated among people across the country, and a play was written about the case. An opera followed suit, but presumably because Limerick didn't make for a sexy enough set, it was renamed *The Lilly of Killarney*.

Bridge Street, one block south of King John's Castle, across from St. Mary's Cathedral.

Joining an organized tour

Historical Walking Tours

Join experienced tour guides for an informative and interesting 90-minute tour, either of King's Island (really just a jut of land over the Shannon) or St. Mary's Parish (including Merchant's Quay, St. Mary's Cathedral, King John's Castle, the Treaty Stone, and much more).

Where and when: Leave from St. Mary's Action Centre, 44 Nicholas St., Limerick, daily at 11:00 a.m. and 2:30 p.m. Information: ☎ 061-31-8106. Price: €5 ($4.75) per person, €9.50 ($9) family.

Self-Guided Walking Tours

The Tourist Office has two interesting self-guided walking trail maps. The English Town Walk covers the southern part of town and the Viking and Norman influence there. The New Town Walk covers the development of Limerick since the mid-18th century.

Information: Tourist Office, Arthur's Quay, Limerick. ☎ 061-31-7522. Price: One booklet covers both tours and costs €2 ($1.90).

Gray Line Bus Tour

Gray Line runs a full-day comprehensive tour covering the areas around Limerick, the Cliffs of Moher, the Burren, Bunratty Castle, and Galway Bay.

Where and when: Leaves Arthur's Quay, Limerick at 10 a.m. daily from May until Oct. Information: ☎ 061-41-3088. Price: €33.75 ($32.05).

Bus Eireann Bus Tour

A city "Open Top Tour" with commentary that includes the city's medieval and Georgian history, rivers, bridges, and King John's Castle.

Where and when: Leaves daily from Limerick Tourist Office, Arthur's Quay, June–Aug. Information: ☎ 061-31-3333. Price: €6.25 ($5.95) adults, €5 ($4.75) seniors and students, €3.50 ($3.35) for children, €15 ($14.25) for a family of two adults and four children.

Angela's Ashes Bus Tour

The tour covers the sites from Frank McCourt's Pulitzer Prize–winning book, like South's Pub, St. Joseph's Church, and Leamy's School.

Where and when: Tour leaves twice a day Mon–Sat June–Aug. Information: Tourist office, ☎ 061-31-7522. Price: Call for current prices.

Shopping

Limerick, like nearly all of Ireland's major cities, is a hub of shopping for the surrounding region. The main city thoroughfares, O'Connell Street and William Street, are lined with small shops and department stores. You won't find a load of places that sell souvenirs, though. The shopping here is vast and varied, but it mainly suits the needs of the people who live here.

There are two major shopping areas in Limerick City — one new and one old. The **Milk Market** (corner of Wickham and Ellen streets) is a restored medieval marketplace. Bordered by the original city walls, this quaint area offers country produce on Saturdays and local arts and crafts on Fridays. Stalls and open-fronted shops make up the market, where you can find quality secondhand clothes and books, too. The city's real shopping gets done at **The Arthur's Quay Centre,** a modern mall in the heart of town. Inside this open, multistoried mall are 30 stores and places to eat, plus little cafes and child-care facilities.

Here are a couple other, more specific picks.

O'Mahony's

O'Mahony's has a great selection of books, maps, and stationery so you can catch up on your Joyce or write friends back home in style.

120 O'Connell St., Limerick City. ☎ *061-41-8155.*

Decorum

Decorum has a small but high-quality selection of glassware, pottery, mirrors, rugs, candles, and potpourri.

Arthur's Quay Centre, Limerick City. ☎ *061-41-975.*

Pub-crawling in Limerick

Castle Lane Tavern

This beautiful tavern's decor (a medieval re-creation, in sort of a Disney way) is so detailed and authentic-looking you may be tempted to summon the barmaid with a hearty "beer wench!" but I don't recommend it. I do suggest you grab a drink and maybe some soup or a sandwich and settle into one of the comfortable sunken benches or stools. The tavern is right next to King John's Castle and just down a cobbled alleyway. The whole area gives the pleasant feeling of being in a time warp.

Nicholas Street (next to St. John's Castle), Limerick City. ☎ *061-31-8044.*

The Holy Ground

Welcome to the world's only bar in a graveyard! That's right, a corner of the Holy Ground backs up to an old graveyard and a section of it actually sits in it. It was once the home of the graveyard's *sexton* (or keeper) but was later transformed into a pub (and later still, it was featured on the television program, *Ripley's Believe It or Not*). It's a thrill to go in, have a pint, and be able to say you drank in a graveyard, but that's about the only draw. It's pretty cramped (a few notches above cozy), and although regulars are used to tourists eagerly filing in, they're not always ready to open up to a chat. Go on in; it's a rare opportunity to (legally) be part of something so macabre and weird.

1 Church St., south off of John's Square, Limerick City. ☎ *061-41-2583.*

The Locke

Dating back to 1724, The Locke is one of Limerick City's oldest and best pubs, and it's got a great location, too, right on the bank of the river, amid some of the city's oldest landmarks — the Old Custom House (now the Hunt Museum) and the Old Court House. When weather permits, there's seating across the street on the quay. Inside, you can warm up at the open fires and listen to traditional music every Tuesday and Sunday night. Hot, home-cooked food is served until 6 p.m.

3 George's Quay, Limerick City. ☎ *061-41-3773.*

W. H. South

Made famous by Frank McCourt's *Angela's Ashes,* this pub still basks in the glory bestowed by the Pulitzer Prize–winning author. The walls bear witness to newspaper accounts of the local uproar that occurred when the book was published (many Limerick natives objected to the negative light it shone on their city). Of course, there are also those who consider McCourt the local boy who made good. Star element aside, South's is a gorgeous pub, all wood and snugs, and always buzzing with people. During the day, hot and delicious lunches are served; and the soup is consistently good.

The Crescent, O'Connell Street, Limerick City. ☎ *061-31-8850.*

M. J. Finnegans

Beautifully stylized to echo an old-world appeal, this pub combines elegance with homey comforts. Inside you'll be surrounded by brickwork, wood, stone, and almost distracting vintage decor. If you're hungry, you're in luck; the food is especially good and above the usual pub-grub standards, and steaks and seafood are a specialty. There's seating outside for nice weather, so you can enjoy your pint next to a blossoming rose garden. If you've tackled James Joyce's *Finnegans Wake* and recognize the name, you're right on — the tavern is a kind of homage to the opus. Finnegans is just outside of Annacotty on the main Dublin Road.

Dublin Road, Annacotty (take the N7 south from the city). ☎ *061-33-7338.*

Fast Facts: County Limerick

Area Code(s)

County Limerick's area codes (or city codes) are **061, 063, 068,** and **069.**

Emergencies-Hospital

Dial ☎ **999** for all emergencies. St. John's Hospital is on St. John's Square, Limerick (☎ 061-41-5822).

Genealogy Resources

Contact the Limerick Regional Archives, The Granary, Michael Street (☎ 061-41-0777; Fax: 061-41-5125).

Information

For visitor information, go to the tourist office at Arthur's Quay, Limerick

(☎ 061-31-7522), or Shannon Airport (☎ 061-47-1664). Both are open year-round. They can also provide reservation services. For telephone directory assistance, dial ☎ 1190.

Internet

Websters Internet Cafe, 44 Thomas St., Limerick (☎ 061-31-2066), has Internet access and printing capabilities.

Post Office

The General Post Office is on Post Office Lane, off Lower Cecil Street, Limerick (☎ 061-31-4636).

County Clare

Sadly, visitors to Ireland are often so drawn by the giant tourist magnets known as Counties Galway and Kerry that they ignore County Clare completely. Well, listen up: I'm going to change that, because I don't want you to miss out on Clare's attractions, which I think are among Ireland's best. Think about it — where else can you poke around in completely restored and furnished castles from the Middle Ages **(Bunratty** and **Knappogue),** see prehistoric villages and 19th-century towns come to life **(Craggaunowen Castle** and **Bunratty Folk Park),** travel across a unique natural phenomenon **(the Burren),** and stand on the precipice of cliffs that will take your breath away **(the Cliffs of Moher)?** And that's just for starters. The county is dotted with quaint towns and villages that serve nicely either as stopovers or starting points for sightseeing.

Getting to and around County Clare

Shannon International Airport (☎ **061-47-1444**), located on the N19, off the N18, south from County Clare's main town of Ennis and 15 miles west of Limerick, has direct flights from the United States through

Continental, American, Delta, and Aer Lingus. Aer Lingus also has flights from all areas of Ireland, and several airlines have flights from England. See Chapter 6 for more information.

If you're coming by car, take the N18 north from Limerick or south from Galway to Ennis. There are rental-car company desks at Shannon Airport's Arrivals Hall representing all the major car-rental companies listed in Chapter 7. The **Shannon Ferry Ltd.** runs a car ferry connecting Tarbert, County Kerry, with Killimer, County Clare, bypassing Limerick. It runs year-round between 7:30 a.m. and 9:00 p.m. (until 7 p.m. October through March) and costs €8.75 ($9.30) one way, €12.50 ($11.90) round-trip.

Irish Rail (☎ 065-40-444) services Ennis at the Ennis Rail Station on Station Road. All routes run through Limerick. **Bus Eireann** (☎ 065-682-4177) travels year-round to Ennis, Ballyvaughan, Doolin, Kilkee, and most towns in County Clare.

Where to stay in County Clare

Aran View House Hotel
$$–$$$ Doolin

Built in 1736, this gorgeous Georgian house overlooks some of Ireland's most fabulous vistas — you can see the Cliffs of Moher and the Aran Islands while you're being pampered. Rooms are big and tasteful, and the house sits on 100 acres of farmland. The restaurant is comfortable and full of atmosphere, and fish is the house specialty. Horse riding, golf, and fishing are all close, too.

Coast Road, Doolin. ☎ *065-707-4061. Fax: 065-707-4540. To get there: On the road to the Cliffs of Moher, R487 northwest from Lahinch or southwest from Lisdoonvarna. Rates: €75–€137.50 ($71.25–$130.65) double. AE, DC, MC, V. Closed Nov–March.*

Berry Lodge
$$ Annagh

This is a must-stay for any serious gourmet or gourmand. Originally a well-known cooking school, this 17th-century country house near the sea offers surprisingly inexpensive accommodation now as well. The rooms are simple and colorfully decorated but the real draw of the place is the food, grown and caught locally. You'll want to have dinner at the Lodge and even consider taking one of the cooking classes. They offer special weekend rates combining rooms with classes.

Annagh, Miltown Malbay. ☎ *065-708-7022. Fax: 065-708-7011. Internet:* www. berrylodge.com. *To get there: From Kerry take the car ferry from Tarbert to Killimer. Take the N67 into Quilty village; take the third turn right and then take the first right into Berry Lodge. Rates: €60–€70 ($57–$66.50) double. AE, MC, V.*

Bunratty Castle Hotel
$$–$$$ Bunratty

This bright yellow Georgian hotel is in the center of Bunratty village, with the famed Bunratty Castle pub Durty Nelly's just across the street. The hotel is only a few years old and all rooms are tastefully decorated in Irish traditional style. Rooms have every convenience, including air conditioning — pretty rare in Ireland. Everyone is friendly and willing to help, and from here County Clare's best sights are only a short drive. Kathleen's Irish pub is pleasant and serves food, and you're likely to run across plenty of people to chat with.

Bunratty. ☎ *061-70-7034. To get there: Off the N18 between Limerick and Ennis. Rates: €98.75–€188 ($93.80–$178.60) double. AE, DC, MC, V.*

Queens Hotel
$$–$$$ Ennis

Everything about this hotel is perfectly charming. Old-world hospitality reigns, and the style is traditional Irish. From here, in the center of Ennis, all of County Clare's sights are only a stone's throw away. The bedrooms are completely decked out, with TV, video player, and radio. At the famous Cruise's Pub and Restaurant (which adjoins the hotel), you'll find home-cooked Irish food and traditional music nightly.

Abbey Street, Ennis. ☎ *065-682-8963. Fax: 065-682-8628. E-mail:* www.irish courthotel.com. *To get there: In city center. Rates: €70–€150 ($66.50–$142.50) double. AE, DC, MC, V.*

Shamrock Inn Hotel
$$ Lahinch

This little hotel, located in the heart of the pretty seaside resort town of Lahinch, is pleasant and has it all. Rooms are nicely decorated and have a TV, hair dryer, and tea and coffee. The restaurant is popular in town, which is no surprise. It's cozy and relaxing, the menu is varied, and they're happy to cater to your tastes. In the pub, food is served during the day and music lilts at night.

Main Street, Lahinch. ☎ *065-708-1700. Fax: 065-708-1029. To get there: Take the N85 northwest from Ennis. Rates: €75–€100 ($71.25–$95) double. AE, MC, V.*

Stella Maris
$$ Kilkee

This small, family-run guesthouse located in the heart of town perfectly reflects the quaintness of Kilkee. Open peat fires burn inside, or you can sit out on the veranda overlooking the bay. The staff is friendly and welcoming, and they want to make your stay a good one. The bar features traditional music and hearty, home-cooked food.

O'Connell Street, Kilkee. ☎ *065-905-6455. Fax: 065-906-0006. To get there: Take N67 south from Ennistimon or N68 southwest from Ennis. Rates: €50–€70 ($47.50–$66.50) double. AE, MC, V.*

Where to dine in County Clare

MacCloskey's
$$$$ Bunratty IRISH

This restaurant has been called one of the finest in Ireland by visitors and natives alike. Set in the downstairs of a 19th-century mansion, MacCloskey's is intimate and cozy, and great care is taken to ensure you enjoy everything about the meal. The food is Irish in spirit, with traditional and nouveau flair. Mussels in champagne, crab crepes, and duck a l'orange are some house specialties. Finish off with one of the incredible desserts — go on, you're on vacation!

Bunratty Mews House, Bunratty. ☎ *061-36-4082. To get there: Off the N18 north of Limerick. Main courses: €32.50 ($30.90) prix fixe. AE, DC, MC, V. Open: March–Dec Tues–Sat 7:00–9:30 p.m.; July and Aug daily 6:30–9:30 p.m. Reservations required.*

Barrtra
$$–$$$$ Lahinch SEAFOOD

Down a wee farm road and overlooking Liscannor Bay stands this small and homey kitchen of a restaurant rated one of the top 100 in the country. The seafood is some of the freshest lobster, oysters, mussels, and salmon you'll find on the west coast and the wine list is extensive — just the kind of thing called for after an adventure at the nearby Cliffs of Moher. The inventive menu also has some delights by chef Teresa O'Brien, like the gin-and-tonic sorbet.

Lahinch. ☎ *065-708-1280. To get there: 2 miles south of Lahinch off the Lahinch/Miltown Malbay coast road (N67) you'll see the small road to the restaurant. Main courses: €8.50–€19 ($8.10–$18.05). AE, MC, V. Open: March–Dec, Mon–Sat 6–10 p.m. Reservations required.*

The Cloister
$$$–$$$$ Ennis SEAFOOD

Delicious food is served all day at this restaurant, which sits in the shadow of an ancient abbey. The interior is warm and refined, and turf fires burn. The daytime menu features local mussels, fresh fish, and lively sandwiches. The quality of the food becomes obvious when the place fills up at night with people who clearly come time and again. For dinner try the warm farmhouse cheese salad or Ballyvaughan mussels. Meals come with fabulous bread — you'll be tempted to stuff yourself before your meal even comes.

Club Bridge, Abbey Street, Ennis. ☎ 065-682-9521. To get there: It's in the Ennis town center. Main courses: €13.75–€20 ($13.05–$19). AE, MC, V. Open: Daily noon to 10:30 p.m.

Bruach na hAille
$$–$$$ Doolin SEAFOOD

This cottage-like restaurant offers a simple menu, but the food is delicious. Local seafood is the highlight of the fare, and it's prepared in a unique way. Everything's incredibly fresh and from the area. Seafood's not the only thing on the menu, but don't miss the baked seafood au gratin or filet of sole in cider with shellfish cream sauce.

On the coast road, Roadford, Doolin. ☎ 065-707-4120. To get there: Drive through Doolin north along the coast road (R479) 1 mile. Main courses: €11.15–€17.50 ($10.55–$16.65). No credit cards. Open: April–Oct daily 6:00–9:30 p.m.

Cruises
$$–$$$ Ennis IRISH

Stone walls and open fires characterize this homey restaurant and pub, and you're sure to get a hot, hearty meal. Pub grub ranges from club sandwiches and seafood soups to the house special — the thick, meaty Friars Irish Stew. Expect more selection at night, when meals become quite sophisticated, from seafood and steaks to vegetarian offerings. Often, music sessions erupt during dinner, but they aren't so noisy that they'll interrupt your enjoyment of the meal.

Abbey Street, Ennis. ☎ 065-684-1800. To get there: Ennis town center, next to the Queens Hotel. Main courses: €8–€16.90 ($7.60–$16.05). AE, DC, MC, V. Open: Daily 12:30–10:30 p.m.

Exploring County Clare

Here are my top picks for sights to see in County Clare.

The top attractions

Bunratty Castle and Folk Park
Bunratty

This formidable castle, built in 1425 and pillaged many times over, is one of Ireland's biggest attractions. It's one of the most authentic medieval castles in the country, and great care has been taken to ensure the interior is as it was in the 15th century, with furnishings and tapestries that replicate the era. Great halls and tiny stairways characterize the castle, and the dungeon is so eerie you just may get a serious spook unless you bring someone down there with you. On the castle grounds is the Bunratty Folk Park, a re-creation of a 19th-century Irish village. You can poke your head into farmhouses, a blacksmith's forge, and a watermill, and go down a typical village street that has it all: post office, school, pawn shop, doctor's house, printers, hardware shop, and a real pub, where you can stop in for a bite and a drink. This really is an awesome and complete reproduction — don't miss it.

Bunratty. The short exit ramp off the N18 takes you to the entrance of the castle. ☎ *061-36-1511. To get there: On the N18 north of Limerick. Admission: €6.25 ($5.95) adults, €5.50 ($5.25) seniors and students, €3.50 ($3.35) children. Open: June–Aug daily 9:00 a.m.–7:30 p.m.; Sept–May daily 9:30 a.m.–5:30 p.m. Suggested visit: At least 2 hours.*

The Burren and Burren Visitor Centre
Kilfenora

Don't miss this amazing phenomenon of Ireland — a vast expanse of limestone, as far as you can see, and the home to unique plants and animals. The name Burren comes from the Irish *bhoireann* for "a barren, rocky place," and that's pretty much what it is. Instead of bogs and pastures, you'll find limestone mountains, rocky valleys, underground rivers and fields of stone. Still, man settled here ages ago, a fact proved by the massive neolithic tombs located in the area. The distinct spread of limestone covers a maze of underground caves where water drains from the ground. Plants that otherwise only live in the Arctic and Mediterranean thrive here, thanks to the limestone and the Gulf Stream winds. And 26 species of butterflies have been seen here, including one that's indigenous to the area, the Burren Green. From various spots on the Burren, you can see for miles and get views of Clare and Galway Bay. The Burren Display Centre is a good reference and helps explain this amazing area.

The Burren Display Centre is located in Kilfenora. ☎ *065-7088-030. To get there: Take the R476 southeast from Lisdoonvarna. Admission: €2.75 ($2.60) adult, €2 ($1.90) seniors, €1.25 ($1.20) children. Open: July and Aug daily 9:30 a.m.–7:00 p.m., March–Oct daily 10 a.m.–5 p.m. Suggested visit: 1 hour.*

The Cliffs of Moher
On the Atlantic Coast

"Spectacular" doesn't begin to describe the view from these breathtaking cliffs. At places they rise more than 700 feet above the crashing Atlantic, and stretch for miles in both directions. On the highest cliff is O'Brien's Tower, built in the 1800s as a viewing point for tourists. From the tower you can see the span of the Clare coast, the Aran Islands, and, on a clear day, mountains as far away as Kerry and Connemara. When it's sunny, the cliffs take on a purple hue (hence the "Purple Cliffs of Moher" of story and song), and when the wind and rain blow in, it can be a bit harrowing up there. There's a lovely little shop and tearoom in the visitor center.

You've been invited to the castle for a feast!

History comes alive at night when Bunratty and Knappogue castles stage their medieval banquets, complete with a feast of food and lively entertainment. At Bunratty, the Earl of Thomond hosts the amazingly authentic evening, beginning with a cup of honey mead, heading into a delicious feast, and finishing with period entertainment. The banquet at Knappogue celebrates the women of Celtic Ireland, both historical and mythical — queens, saints, and sinners. The entertainment centers around storytelling, singing, and music, all masterfully done, leaving you haunted and enchanted.

Bunratty's Golden Vale farmhouse also hosts **Traditional Irish Nights,** which are banquets taken down a notch, but no less fun and delicious. Here you won't dine with royalty, but rather with the *Fear an Ti,* or man of the house. You'll be very welcome to have a homey meal (Irish stew) and wine, and listen to traditional music that's likely to get your toes tapping. Irish instruments, like the pipes and bodhrán (drum), accompany singers and dancers for your entertainment. A fun, lively night!

For reservations to either Bunratty or Knappogue, call **Shannon Medieval Castle Banquets** at ☎ 061-360-788.

Be extremely careful when walking along the cliffs! There are no rails separating you from the rocks far below, and sometimes wind gusts can push you around, so take extreme care when approaching the edges. Watch kids carefully, too. They may be tempted to climb down to some lower cliff shelves, but it's not at all a good idea.

Off the R478 on the Atlantic coast. ☎ *065-708-1565. To get there: R487 northwest from Lahinch or southwest from Lisdoonvarna. O'Brien's Tower Admission: €1.25 ($1.20) adult, €1 (95¢) children. Parking: €1.25 ($1.20). Open: May–June daily 9:00 a.m.–6:30 p.m.; July–Aug daily 9 a.m.–9 p.m.; Sept–April daily 9:30 a.m.–6:00 p.m. O'Brien's Tower opens a half-hour later and closes a half-hour earlier than regular times. Suggested visit: 45 minutes.*

Knappogue Castle
Quinn

This imposing 15th-century castle has seen its share of history. Built by the McNamaras, it was the pride of the tribe, which dominated the area for 1,000 years. But the stronghold had its troubles, too. In the 1700s, Cromwell's troops occupied the castle for ten years, and during the War of Independence (in the 1920s) revolutionary forces camped within its walls. The castle has been extraordinarily refurbished, and the interior is overflowing with antiques and period furnishings.

Just off the Ennis-Killmury roads, Quinn. ☎ *061-36-8103. To get there: Off the R469 southeast from Ennis. Admission: €3 ($2.85) adult, €2 ($1.90) children. Open: May–Oct daily 9:30 a.m.–5:30 p.m. Suggested visit: 1 hour.*

Aillwee Cave
The Burren

You'll get a better understanding of the effects of the Burren on the land when you climb into the depths of Aillwee Cave. Your guide will take you down into this vast cave, where you'll see ancient stalagmites and stalactites, cross bridges that span frighteningly deep chasms, and get wet from the crashing underground waterfall. And you'll be taken into the eerie hibernation chamber of the extinct brown bear. When you're back above ground, you can shop in the many craft shops selling minerals, fossils, and handmade gifts. There's a dairy where you can watch cheese being made and a tearoom where light snacks are served. You can also have a drink on the terrace and enjoy the view.

The Burren, Ballyvaughan. ☎ *065-707-7036. To get there: Off the R480 south of Ballyvaughan. Admission: €6 ($5.70) adult, €4.50 ($4.30) students, €3.25 ($3.10) children. Open: July and Aug daily 10:00 a.m.–6:30 p.m.; mid-March to Nov daily 10:00 a.m.–5:30 p.m. Suggested visit: 2 hours.*

Craggaunowen Castle and Project
Quinn

Ever wonder about life during prehistoric times? You can see it firsthand here, where the life and times of man during the Bronze Age comes alive. Yabba-dabba-doo! You'll see actors performing daily tasks in costume, a guide describing life in a ring fort, and an Iron Age roadway and cooking site. Probably the most interesting site is the *crannóg,* a man-made home made from mud and reeds, sitting right in the middle of a lake (a type of construction that helped protect against enemy pillage). The project surrounds Craggaunowen Castle, the restored home to an impressive furniture collection from the Hunt Museum in Limerick.

Quinn. ☎ *061-36-7178. To get there: Ten miles east of Ennis off the R469. Admission: €5 ($4.75) adult, €3.25 ($3.10) children. Open: April–Oct 10 a.m.–6 p.m. Suggested visit: 1 hour.*

Lahinch Sea World
Lahinch

This fascinating Atlantic aquarium will entertain all ages. You'll come face to face with creatures from the Irish coast, like sharks, lobsters, rays, and Conger eels. Kids love the touch pool, where they can plunge their hands into the water and feel underwater life. There's a fisherman's cabin, lobster breeding station, and regular feeding sessions. Want a chance to swim like the fishes? Lahinch Sea World also has a huge indoor heated pool, Jacuzzi, sauna, and kiddie pool. The souvenir shop is well stocked, and the cafe serves light meals and snacks.

The Promenade, Lahinch. ☎ 065-708-1900. To get there: West of Ennistimon on the N67. Admission: Aquarium Only €5 ($4.75) adult, €3.75 ($3.55) seniors and students, €3 ($2.85) children, €14 ($13.30) family of two adults and three children. Pool and Aquarium €7.50 ($7.15) adult, €6 ($5.70) seniors and students, €5 ($4.75) children, €21.25 ($20.20) family of two adults and three children. Open: June–Aug daily 9:00 a.m.–9:30 p.m. Suggested visit: 2 hours.

The top landmarks

Poulnabrone Dolmen
The Burren

These structures are ancient burial monuments, dating back 6,000 years. They're a prominent aspect of the Burren, and more people photograph this landmark than almost any other in Ireland. Go on — stand under the humongous stone and pretend you're holding it up. Say "cheese!"

The Burren. To get there: Off R480 south from Ballyvaughan.

Eamon de Valera Statue
Ennis

Eamon de Valera, Irish freedom fighter, president, and prime minister, is honored with a bronze statue in the Ennis town park. De Valera was born in New York; his American citizenship kept him from facing the firing squad after his part in the Easter Rising of 1916.

Ennis. To get there: In the town park off Gort Road (R352).

Other fun things to do

Here's a fine course for any golfers in your group, plus an opportunity to dance off your dinner.

- ✔ **Golfing at the Lahinch Golf Club:** Now you're golfing in Ireland! High elevations provide amazing views of sea and valley and local goats are known to cross the fairway. There are two 18-hole courses here, and one is a championship course.

  Lahinch, County Clare. ☎ 065-708-1003. Par: 72. Fees: €31.25 ($29.70) midweek, €37.50 ($35.65) weekends.

- ✔ **Dancing Irish-style:** Some people spend their whole lives learning those magnificent Irish dance steps. Lucky for you, it only takes a night . . . sort of. Every Wednesday in Ennis between May and October there's Irish dancing, and you're welcome to come and learn a few steps. Who knows? Drop in on enough sessions and you could be the next Michael Flatley!

Fees: €2 ($1.90). For information call Dick O'Connell (☎ 065-20-996). Venue changes periodically.

Joining an organized tour

DolphinWatch Boat Tour

This is a fun and informative two-hour boat trip among a resident group of friendly bottleneck dolphins. The boat is equipped with a hydrophone, so you can listen to dolphins communicate underwater.

Runs daily May–Sept, weather permitting. You must book ahead. Leaves from the port village of Carrigaholt. Information: ☎ 065-905-8156 or 088-258-4711. Price: €12.50 ($11.90) adults, €7.50 ($7.15) children (children under 5 are not permitted).

Fertile Rock Study Tours

Don't let the name fool you, this isn't a boring geology tour. Your guide, Christy Browne, is a renowned scholar of the Burren and hands-down the best guide you'll find to the wonders of Ireland's lunar landscape. The tour (which has a loyal following), covering the history, folklore, animal and plant life, and, yes, the geology of the area, is as funny as it is informative. You'll no doubt have an excellent time.

Fertile Rock Study Tours, Station Road, Lahinch. Be sure to call ahead to make meeting arrangements (if you fly into Shannon airport, Christy will meet you there) and find out the length of the tour. Information: ☎ 065-708-1168. Price: Depends on length and size of tour and can even include an overnight stay in the Burren.

Healy's Bus Tours

This is the best coach tour of the sights of County Clare, covering the Burren, Poulnabrone Dolmen, the Cliffs of Moher, Aillwee Cave, and more for a bargain of a price.

Departs from Salthill Tourist Office (on the main road next to the Atlanta Aquarium) at 9:45 a.m. and Galway Tourist Office (Merchants Road) at 10 a.m. Returns 5 p.m. Runs daily in summer. Call for schedule in off-season. Information: ☎ 091-77-0066 or 088-259-0160. You can purchase tickets on the bus or at the Galway and Salthill tourist offices. Price: €12.50 ($11.90) adults, €10 ($9.50) students, €6.25 ($5.95) children.

O'Neachtain Bus Tours

This tour rivals the Healy tour by covering several extra sights, such as Lisdoonvarna and Leamanah Castle. But this tour takes the same amount of time as the other — and therefore allows you less time at each place. It's a tradeoff.

Departs from Salthill Tourist Office (see previous entry) at 9:55 a.m. and Galway Tourist Office (stop marked "O'Neachtain") at 9:45 a.m. Returns 4:45 p.m. Information: ☎ 091-56-5056. Price: €12.50 ($11.90) adults, €10 ($9.50) students, €6.25 ($5.95) children.

Shopping

Antique Loft

Interesting and unique pieces of all varieties, styles, and periods.

Clarecastle (south of Ennis and north of Limerick on the N18). ☎ 065-41-969.

Avoca Handweavers

This is the newly relocated and bigger shop housing the famous clothing and accessories from the Avoca Mill in County Wicklow.

Bunratty (off the N18 north of Limerick). ☎ 061-36-4029.

Belleek Shop

More than crafts, this is the best store in the area for Waterford Crystal, china, Irish tweed, and cashmere fashions. They have top-notch customer service as well.

36 Abbey St., on the corner of Francis Street in the Ennis city center. ☎ 065-682-9607.

Burren Perfumery

The oldest perfumery in Ireland, Burren Perfumery uses local flora to create unique fragrances.

Carron (take the R480 to the Carron turnoff; shop is located just north of town). ☎ 065-89-102.

The Burren Smokehouse

This gourmet store and visitor center sells the finest smoked Irish Atlantic salmon. They own the neighboring pub, The Roadside Tavern, which serves up freshly smoked salmon, trout, mackerel, and eel.

Lisdoonvarna, on the N67 south of Ballyvaughan and north of Ennistimon. ☎ 065-74-432.

Craft Showcase Kilkee

The store is new but the crafts, from ceramics and sheepskin rugs to Celtic jewelry and basketware, are as authentic and traditional as you'll find.

O'Connell Street, Kilkee (on the main Kilkee-Kilrush Road, on the right from Kilkee city center). ☎ *065-56-880.*

Traditional Music Shop

The best shop in the area for Irish instruments (like an authentic tin whistle), plus a large variety of Irish music on CD and cassette — a little traveling music for the rental car!

Doolin, off the N67 west of Lisdoonvarna. ☎ *065-74-407. Closed mid-Oct through March.*

Pulling a pint: Pub life

The Cloister

This pub sits next to the famed Ennis friary, and in the summer you can sit outside within arm's length of the landmark. Inside, the pub is comfortable and homey, and pub grub is served all day.

Abbey Street, Ennis (in the center of town). ☎ *065-682-9521.*

Durty Nelly's

No trip to Clare is complete without a stop in this world-famous pub. Since 1620, this tavern has been a thirst-quencher for everyone from the guards who once protected Bunratty Castle to the tourists who explore it today. The interior looks like it hasn't changed over the centuries, with sawdust-strewn floors, low lighting from lanterns, and traditional music sessions that commence at any time in any room of the pub. There's seating outside for nice days, and a pretty good restaurant upstairs.

Next to Bunratty Castle, County Clare (take N18 north from Limerick). ☎ *061-36-4861.*

Galvins

You won't be able to sit still in this interesting pub — there's too much to see. Don't worry, they're used to people wandering around with a pint and looking at the pictures that line the walls. When it was built in 1840, stones from the nearby shore were used in the construction. It's a great place to hear music, and musicians passing through the area often drop in to play.

Church Street, Lahinch (in the center of town). ☎ *065-81-045.*

Monk's Pub

A taste of the olde world is retained here, where peat fires burn and rustic furnishings invite you to take a seat. It's right on the water, and good pub grub is served all day. Music fills the air most nights.

Ballyvaughan (take the R476 to the R480 north from Ennis). ☎ *065-707-7059.*

O'Briens

This is the cutest pub in all of Ireland. It is just larger than a walk-in-closet — room enough for one bench, two bar stools, a 4-foot bar and a single Guinness tap (don't worry, the pints are full size). Joe Murray runs the place and keeps things in ship-shape, no *large* task mind you.

Main Street, Miltown Malbay. No phone.

O'Connor's

If the prospect of hearing Irish music plays any part in your choice of pubs, then O'Connor's is for you. This is one of the premier spots in the country for traditional sessions, and fans travel from all over to hear them. The family has run this combination pub and market for more than 150 years. The pub sits amid a row of thatched fisherman cottages and really comes to life at night.

Doolin, off the N67 west of Lisdoonvarna. ☎ *065-707-4168.*

Fast Facts: County Clare

Area Code(s)

County Clare's area codes (or city codes) are **061** and **065**.

Emergencies-Police

Dial ☎ **999** for all emergencies.

Genealogy Resources

Contact the Clare Heritage Centre, Church Street, Corofin (☎ 065-683-7955).

Information

For visitor information, go to the tourist office at Clare Road, Ennis (☎ 065-28-366),

open year-round. They can also provide reservation services. For telephone directory assistance, dial ☎ 1190.

Internet

MacCools Internet Cafe, Brewery Lane, Ennis (☎ 065-682-1988), and Kilrush Internet Cafe, The Monastery, Kilrush (☎ 065-51-061), have Internet access and printing capabilities.

Chapter 18

County Galway and Galway City

In This Chapter

▶ Getting to the Aran Islands

▶ Exploring the vast and amazing Connemara National Park

▶ Shopping for your Aran sweater and everything else on your list

▶ Pub-crawling through Galway

*N*ot making it to every major county in Ireland is no crime, but County Galway's just plain too great to pass up. It's one of the few counties that combines a major city, great small towns, and a healthy dose of scenic outdoors. Given all its assets, Galway should head your to-do list.

What's Where?: Galway's Major Attractions

Galway City serves as the gateway to the rest of the county. This is a major city in Ireland, with a great a variety of places to eat, sleep, drink, and shop. But don't be fooled: Inside that city veneer is the heart of a small town, with all the hospitality and approachability that implies. Amazingly, while keeping apace of fast-moving progress of the day, Galway manages to hold onto the easygoing way of the Irish: It's both a buzzing college town and a star on the European stage of cities.

Anchored by **Eyre Square** (Eyre is pronounced *air*), a pretty park surrounded by hotels and pubs, the city's picturesque streets stretch down to the harbor. It's said that Christopher Columbus made his last European stop here before setting sail on his famous trip for the New World. Although most people don't arrive by galleon these days, tourism is still huge here. Even so, there's nothing tacky about the city. Discriminating shoppers won't be disappointed by the quaint little stores, and pubs and restaurants accommodate city dwellers and visitors alike.

County Galway

ACCOMMODATIONS ■
Alcock and Brown Hotel **3**
Hotel Carraroe Best Western **5**
O'Grady's Sunnybank Guesthouse **3**
Pier House **6**

DINING ◆
Aran Fisherman Restaurant **6**
Mitchell's Restaurant **3**
O'Grady's **3**

ATTRACTIONS ●
Aran Islands **6**
Connemara National Park
   and Visitors Centre **2**
Coole Park **9**
Dunguaire Castle **8**
Kylemore Benedictine Abbey **1**
Salthill **7**
Thoor Ballylee **10**

SHOPPING ▲
Roundstone Music **4**

NIGHTLIFE ☾
E. J. Kings **3**

Galway's not exactly known for its attractions or major historical sites, but the city itself is enough of a draw. Among other things, it supposedly has more stone carvings of mermaids than any other place in Ireland. Mermaids play an integral part in Irish folklore, often representing something that's alluring but dangerous. Galway, a sea town, has apparently taken them to heart. You can see some in the window of St. Nicholas's, in the center of town. According to legend, if you happen to see a real mermaid sitting on a rock, it means bad luck is coming your way. So don't stare out at the rocks too long! Instead, spend your time walking around the city, which you can cover easily in an hour or so — but stay overnight so you can dip into Galway's vibrant pub scene.

Moving out from Galway City, the major attractions include

➤ **The Aran Islands:** On these three isolated islands, old ways flourish even though many, many people visit. The islands are best known for the thick, cabled wool fisherman's sweaters that come from here.

➤ **Thoor Ballylee:** Located south of Galway City, this tower was poet W. B. Yeats's summer home, and where he wrote most of his work. Everything about the place has been restored to look just like it did when the famous poet lived here.

➤ **Kylemore Benedictine Abbey:** Built by an English tycoon for his wife, and today the home of a group of Belgian nuns, this abbey looks like a storybook castle.

➤ **Clifden:** This little town is the unofficial capital of Connemara. Nestled in a valley at the foot of a mountain range, it has a number of great accommodations for visitors.

➤ **Connemara National Park:** Combining the imposing mountains of the Twelve Bens range, boglands that provide peat for the area's fuel, unique flora and fauna, and the famous Connemara ponies, the 5,000-acre park provides a breathtaking day's scenic driving.

Getting To and Around Galway City

Aer Lingus has daily local service from Dublin into Galway Airport, in Carnmore (☎ 091-75-5569).

If you're driving to Galway City, take the N18 from Limerick, the N4 and N6 from Dublin, or the N17 from Sligo. Most attractions in County Galway are located off the N59 from Galway. The rental-car company in downtown Galway is **Budget** (☎ 091-56-6376), on Eyre Square.

Irish Rail (☎ 091-56-144) services Galway daily from Dublin. The Ceannt Station is off Eyre Square. **Bus Eireann** (☎ 091-56-2000) travels year-round to Galway (Ceannt Station) and most towns in County Galway. The private coach service **CityLink** (☎ 091-56-4163) travels between Galway and Dublin for a better price than Bus Eireann. CityLink departs from Galway's Forster Street Coach Park to Dublin Airport and leaves from Dublin to Galway at SuperMacs on O'Connell Street in Dublin.

Galway City is best seen on foot. Many of the pubs and shopping areas are not accessible at all by car. Naturally, a car is best for getting to the major attractions throughout the county. Parking in Galway City requires disks that you can purchase at local shops. Galway also has a local bus service that covers the city's suburbs. Buses run along Eyre Square and go to Connemara, Salthill, and the coast. Call ☎ 091-56-2000 for information. Alternatively, you can pick up a taxi on Eyre Square or by calling **Galway Taxi Co-op** (☎ 091-56-1111).

Galway City

Church ✝
Information ⓘ
Post Office ✉

University College

PUBLIC PARK

Waterside

Wood Quay

Headford Rd.

St. Bridget's Pl.

Prospect Hill

St. Brendan's Ave.

St. Vincents Ave.

Eyre St.

Frances St.

Eglinton St.

KENNEDY PARK

Station Rd.

Eyre Sq.

Nuns Island

River Corrib

Abbeygate St.

Bowling Green

Post Office

Victoria Place

Train Station

Market St.

Shop St.

William St.

Tourist Office

Eglinton Canal Rd.

Eglinton Canal

Gaol Rd.

Presentation Rd.

Newcastle Rd.

University Rd.

Newcastle Rd.

N59

St. Mary's Rd.

St. Helens St.

New Rd.

Mill St.

Nuns Island St.

Lombard St.

High Street

Middle St.

St. Augustine St.

Merchants Rd.

Queen St.

Dock Rd.

Lough Atalia Rd.

Henry St.

Wm. O'Brien Bridge

Raleigh Row

Upper/ Lwr. Dominic St.

Lwr. Dominic St.

William St. W.

Sea Rd.

Munster Ave.

Father Griffin Rd.

Fr. Burke Rd.

Father Griffin Rd.

Faithill

St. Nicholas Rd.

Claddagh Quay

Quay St.

Grattan Rd.

Dock St.

The Long Walk

Commercial Dock

Old Dock

River Corrib

Nimmo's Pier

SOUTH PARK

NORTHERN IRELAND

Galway City

REPUBLIC OF IRELAND

ATTRACTIONS ●
Browne Doorway **3**
John F. Kennedy Plaque **3**
Lynch Memorial Window **13**
Lynch's Castle **11**
Spanish Arch **20**

ACCOMMODATIONS ■
Corrib Haven **1**
Eyre Square **6**
Galway Great Southern Hotel **4**
Imperial Hotel **2**

SHOPPING ▲
Eyre Square Shopping Centre **7**
Galway Saturday Market **14**
Galway Woolen Market **16**
Kennys Bookshop and Art Gallery **16**
Thomas Dillon's **17**
Treasure Chest **10**

DINING ◆
Brannagans **12**
Maxwell McNamaras **8**
McDonagh's Seafood House **19**
The Skeff Bar **5**

NIGHTLIFE ☾
The Kings Head Pub **15**
Monroe's Tavern **21**
The Quays Bar **18**
The Skeff Bar **5**
The Snug **9**

Getting to and around the Aran Islands

The most common way to get to the Arans is by ferry. **Aran Ferries** (☎ 091-56-8903), located at the Galway Tourist Office off Eyre Square, operates ferries that depart from the Galway Docks (Price: €22.50/ $21.40). Ferries also depart from Rosaveal Pier in Connemara (Price: €18.75/$17.80). If you'd rather fly, **Aer Arann** (☎ 091-59-3034) takes off from Connemara Airport, Inverin, near Galway. Interestingly, the ten-minute flight is the shortest scheduled flight in the world (Price: €43.75/$41.55 round-trip).

You can't bring your car to the Arans, and there are no car rentals, so when you've reached the islands you have a couple choices. You can rent a bike at **Rothar Arainn Teo,** Frenchman's Beach, Kilronan (☎ 091-61-132), which is what I recommend. Or you can hire a driver and minibus (Hernon Aran Tours, ☎ 099-61-001 or 099-61-109) or a bumpy horse and cart (Cyril Flaherey, ☎ 099-61-001).

You can also tour the Arans by foot. Walking-tour maps are available at the **tourist office** (☎ 099-61-263). Each route takes a couple of hours.

For more information on the islands check out the Web sites www. aran-islands.com and www.aranislands.net.

Where to Stay in County Galway

Corrib Haven
$–$$ **Galway City**

If, at this point in your traveling, you stay at Corrib Haven, there are two things you'll probably notice straightaway. First, the showers are exceptionally powerful, given the general absence of water pressure throughout Ireland; secondly, the beds are about as comfortable as I like to think they'll be in heaven. This wonderful new guesthouse is located just out of Galway City, on the way to Connemara and the Aran Islands, so it makes a convenient stopover. This is a B&B run with the professionalism of a hotel, and there's even a menu to choose from at breakfast.

107 Upper Newcastle, just outside Galway City. ☎ *and Fax:* ***091-52-4171.*** *To get there: On the N59 just out of Galway City. Rates: €45–€75 ($42.75–$71.25) double. MC, V.*

Eyre Square
$$–$$$ **Galway City**

This newest addition to the Galway hotel scene puts as much care and detail into its 45 rooms as it does its exquisite lobby, so amble in off the street to get an idea of what's in store. The hotel is right in the thick of things, facing Eyre Square, but you may not venture out to nearby pubs and restaurants with the hotel's Red Square Bar staring you down: There you can have a carvery lunch or nice dinner, and then stick around for some drinks and music later. All rooms are comfortably furnished with the standard amenities.

Forster Street, Galway City. ☎ 091-56-9633. Fax: 091-56-9641. To get there: Off the south side of Eyre Square. Rates: €75–€175 ($71.25–$166.25) double. AE, DC, MC, V.

Galway Great Southern Hotel
$$$–$$$$ **Galway City**

A room on one of the higher floors of this incredibly refined hotel will give a view of the entire city and beyond. From the heated rooftop pool you may fool yourself into thinking you can see all the way to England! This hotel, overlooking Eyre Square and amid the city's best offerings, was built in 1845 and is an elegant example of Victorian style. The spacious lobby and sitting rooms are nice just to look at, with high ceilings and detailed furnishings like crystal chandeliers and fireplace marble from the nearby hills of Connemara. Rooms are exquisite, furnished with style and attention, and with lots of amenities. There are special low rates for children and a baby-sitting service is available. If you're looking for fine dining, book a table at the Oyster Room. For a more relaxed meal, stop into O'Flaherty's Pub. The food is excellent and the atmosphere matches it.

15 Eyre Square, Galway City. ☎ 800-44-UTELL, from the United States; 091-56-4041. Fax: 091-56-6704. Internet: www.gsh.ie. To get there: On the south side of the square. Rates: €145–€217.50 ($137.75–$206.65) double. AE, DC, MC, V.

Imperial Hotel
$$–$$$ **Galway City**

The best thing about the Imperial is how inexpensive it is for such an incredible location. It's probably the cheapest place on Eyre Square, Galway City's center point. From here, you're only feet from the bus depot, train station, main shopping streets, restaurants, and pubs. Inside, you'll find quality and subdued elegance. I beg you not to be put off by what seems like the lobby of a second-rate hotel. It's a little cramped and maybe hasn't been redecorated in a few years, but the rooms really make up for that. They're all big and tastefully decorated, and the spacious, modern bathrooms are a treat in a country full of tiny ones. The hotel's pub, called Blakes Bar but locally known as the "Meeting Place," is a nice place for a drink and some local color.

Eyre Square. ☎ *091-56-3033. Fax: 091-56-8410. To get there: On the north side of the square. Rates: €75–€137.50 ($71.25–$130.65) double. AE, DC, MC, V.*

Hotel Carraroe Best Western
$$ Carraroe

This may be one of the quieter areas of the country (west of Galway City), but you (and especially the kids) won't be in want of things to do at this family-run hotel. There's an outdoor swimming pool, game room, play area, and tennis court, and boats leave daily for the Aran Islands from the nearby Rossaveal Harbour. You'll get a taste of tradition in the little village of Carraroe, where Irish music is taken very seriously and Old World values hold sway. If you have questions about touring Connemara, just ask the friendly staff; they're helpful and knowledgeable.

Carraroe, near Rossaveal. ☎ *091-59-5116. Fax: 091-59-5187. To get there: From Galway take the R336 west to the R343 south into Carraroe. Rates: €75–€100 ($71.25–$95) double. AE, MC, V. Closed Oct–April.*

Alcock and Brown Hotel
$–$$ Clifden

Clifden is a quaint village famous for being near the landing spot of Alcock and Brown, who completed the first transatlantic flight in 1919. It's now a perfect liftoff location for touring the spectacular Connemara National Park, which it's situated at the base of. The Alcock and Brown Hotel is a wonderful family-run hotel known for its fantastic restaurant. The inside is modestly and very tastefully furnished, and rooms are spacious. The bar is comfortable and often filled with people relaxing after a day of sightseeing.

Clifden, Connemara. ☎ *095-21-206. Fax: 095-21-842. Internet:* www.alcockand brown-hotel.com. *To get there: Take the N59 northwest from Galway or southwest from Westport. Rates: €48–€62 ($45.60–$58.90) double. AE, DC, MC, V.*

O'Grady's Sunnybank Guesthouse
$$ Clifden

This first-rate guesthouse is sure to surprise you. How often do little family-run B&Bs have heated pools, a sauna, a sunbed, and a tennis court? Having scoured the country, I can categorically say, "Not many." This gorgeous period home even has a fish pond and little waterfall in the landscaped gardens. The inside of the house is just as fantastic. It's only feet from the town center, too. You'll be doing yourself a favor by staying here.

Church Hill, Clifden. ☎ *095-21-437. Fax: 095-21-976. To get there: Take the N59 northwest from Galway or southwest from Westport. Rates: €57.50–€75 ($54.65–$71.25) double. MC, V. Closed Nov–Feb.*

Pier House

$–$$ Lower Kilronan, Inishmore, Aran Islands

Located on a small island, you're pretty much guaranteed a view of the water from anywhere; but from a room in the Pier House, you'll get that and more. Only feet from the harbor, this guesthouse is a lovely place to stay while visiting the Aran Islands. Sandy beaches, pubs, and restaurants are all a short walk away, and the ocean breeze will make its way into your room's open window at night. Rooms are quite nice, and it's obvious that great care goes into ensuring a guest's comfort. Given all this, you can't beat it for the price.

Lower Kilronan, Inishmore, Aran Islands. ☎ *099-61-417. Fax: 099-61-122. Internet:* www.galway.net/pages/pierhouse. *To get there: See "Getting to and around the Aran Islands" earlier in this chapter. Rates: €35–€55 ($33.25–$52.25). MC, V. Closed Nov–Feb.*

Where to Dine in County Galway

Brannagans

$$$ Galway City INTERNATIONAL-ECLECTIC

Versatility is at the heart of this little restaurant, where the menu spans the globe. You're practically guaranteed to find what you're craving, whether it's a steak, pizza, pasta, seafood, or Asian cuisine. The best thing about it is that it's all done surprisingly well. You may think a place with so many offerings overdoes it, not managing to create any one thing that's noteworthy, but that's not the case here. The fajitas are especially good, with plenty of meat and sautéed veggies to cram into warm tortillas. The atmosphere is cozy, with brick and pine and giving you the feeling that you're in someone's spacious kitchen.

36 Upper Abbeygate St., Galway City. ☎ *091-56-5974. To get there: Near Lynch's Castle. Main courses: €12.50–€18.75 ($11.90–$17.80). MC, V. Open: Daily 5:00–10:30 p.m.*

Maxwell McNamaras

$$–$$$ Galway City IRISH-SEAFOOD-PASTA

Serving the good people of Galway since 1016, McNamara's is an institution. Waiting for dinner was never so interesting — with so much history to this comfortable and tasteful place, you're bound to get caught up reading the back of the menu. I'm not sure if it's true that Columbus brought a McNamara burger with him when he set sail for the New World, but it makes for good conversation! (And who knows? Maybe he did. After all, the food is quite good.) You'll find plenty of traditional dishes on the menu, but the Mixed Grill stands out as even more decadent than usual: lamb cutlet, sausage, bacon, burger, black-and-white pudding, tomato, and mushrooms. Irish dishes, seafood, and creative pasta dishes round out the menu, and the children's menu will make even the pickiest eater happy. The drink list is vast, with liqueurs, coffee drinks, draft beer, and an extensive wine list.

Williamsgate Street, Galway City. ☎ *091-56-5727. To get there: Off Eyre Square, on the corner of Williamsgate and Eglinton streets. Main courses: €6.55–€14.05 ($6.25–$13.35). AE, DC, MC, V. Open: Daily 9 a.m.–10 p.m.*

McDonagh's Seafood House
$–$$$ **Galway City** **SEAFOOD**

Fish doesn't get fresher or better than at this popular place. The McDonaghs, who've been at it for four generations, have had plenty of practice in the trade. The day's catch is personally inspected and chosen before it comes in the door. You choose exactly how you'd like your fish cooked, whether it's salmon, trout, or sole. Shrimp and lobsters come the way the sea made them: in the shell. If you're in the market for a light meal but don't want to pass up the chance for this great seafood, there's a fish-and-chips shop in the front of the house for take-out.

22 Quay St., Galway City. ☎ *091-56-5001. To get there: Located beside Jury's Inn, near the Spanish Arch. Main courses: €5.65–€15 ($5.35–$14.25). AE, DC, MC, V. Open: Daily noon to midnight.*

The Skeff Bar
$–$$$ **Galway City** **AMERICAN**

Don't be scared off by the fact that this is a bar — it's also a fantastic, informal restaurant with a separate dining room. And if you're hankering for a little good ol' American fare, this is it. You can get burgers, chicken fingers, pizza, pasta, and vegetarian dishes, all at decent prices. The servings are sure to fill you, but the appetizer list is too enticing to pass up. Of course, there's a full bar, but the wine list is pretty great too, with good choices from South Africa and Chile. If you do opt to sit somewhere in the vast pub area, you'll be in a lively atmosphere with a beautiful dark wooden decor.

Eyre Square, Galway City. ☎ *091-56-3173. To get there: On the west side of the square. Main courses: €6.25–€16.25 ($5.95–$15.45). MC, V. Open: Daily 11:00 a.m.– 10:30 p.m.*

Mitchell's Restaurant
$$–$$$ **Clifden** **IRISH-ECLECTIC**

Hearty, traditional fare is the staple of this restaurant, and thick stews, steaks, and fish dishes stand out. Noteworthy lighter meals — like seafood pastas, quiche, and salads — are served during the day. The decor is warm and rustic, with stone and brick walls, a big open fireplace, and local memorabilia throughout. There's also a children's menu.

Market Street, Clifden, in the center of town. ☎ *095-21-867. To get there: Take the N59 northwest from Galway or southwest from Westport. Main courses: €8.15–€13.70 ($7.70–$13). MC, V. Open: Mid-March–mid-Nov noon to 11 p.m.*

O'Grady's
$$–$$$$ Clifden IRISH

This restaurant has thrived in Clifden for decades, thanks to fine food and cozy surroundings. When you settle into one of the dimly lit nooks and scan the menu, you'll know why visitors and locals alike return to this little converted shop. Here you'll get simple foods done well, which may remind you of a home-cooked meal. But, of course, local lobster and lamb isn't often what you get at home! Desserts here are a wonderful end to a delicious meal.

Lower Market Street, Clifden. ☎ *095-21-450. To get there: Take the N59 northwest from Galway or southwest from Westport. Main courses: €9.35–€25 ($8.85–$23.75). AE, MC, V. Open: Mon–Sat 12:30–2:30 p.m. and 6–10 p.m.*

Aran Fisherman Restaurant
$–$$$ Kilronan, Inishmore, Aran Islands SEAFOOD-IRISH

Having a seafood meal on an island where the main livelihood is fishing is kind of like having a cheese steak in Philly — heavenly. Just a stone's throw from where the seafood comes out of the sea, this restaurant offers shark, lobster, fish, and crab along with meat and vegetarian dishes. Meals come with organic vegetable salads from the island. Sitting on the outside patio completes the meal.

Kilronan, Inishmore, Aran Islands. ☎ *099-61-363. To get there: Three minutes walk west from the harbor, on the only road. Main courses: €6.25–€15.65 ($5.95–$14.85). MC, V. Open: Daily noon to 10 p.m.*

Exploring County Galway

Ever wondered about the intricate patterns in an Aran knit sweater? Or where the verb "to lynch" comes from? Or where the smallest church in the world is? Read on for the answers.

Galway's top attractions

The Aran Islands

If you've held out long enough, now's your chance to buy an authentic, often-copied-but-never-reproduced, hand-knit fisherman's sweater from the Aran Islands. And what a shopping excursion you're in for! The

Inishmore, Aran Islands

Rock Island

North Sound

Brannock
Islands

Onaght

Kilmurvy

Killmurvey
Bay

Dun Aengus
Ring Fort

Oatquarter

Kinereigh

Oghil

NORTHERN
IRELAND

Inishmore

Dublin ★

REPUBLIC
OF IRELAND

Inishmore

Kilronanan

Killeany
Bay

Straw
Island

Black Fort ■ Killeany

Temple Benen ■

Dog's
Head

ATLANTIC OCEAN

Gregory's
Sound

ACCOMMODATIONS ■
Pier House **1**

Lightouse ⚓

Clinewalee
Point

South Sound

DINING ◆
Aran Fisherman Restaurant **2**

Tourist Information ⓘ

Primary Road ═══
(Mostly Paved)

ATTRACTIONS ●
Ionad Arann (Aran Islands Heritage Centre) **3**

Secondary Road ∙∙∙∙∙
(Unpaved)

0   1 mi

0   1 km

Rossaveal • GALWAY • Oranmore
Spiddal • Galway
Inishmore • Galway Bay
Inishmaan • Ballyvaughan • Kinvara
Inisheer
Doolin • Lisdoonvarna
CLARE

islands — Inishmore, Inishmaan, and Inisheer — are famous for being
havens of traditional Irish culture. From the Gaelic language that
islanders speak to their methods of livelihood (mainly fishing and
tourism), this truly is the place to witness a way of life that the fast-paced
world barely touches. People live in stone cottages and get around
in horse-drawn carts, but conditions are a bit more advanced for tourists.
You won't be able to bring your car there, and you'll have to rely on
carts or bikes to get around. But there are a number of fine accommodations, restaurants, and amazing little pubs. The main place to stay is
Kilronan, on Inishmore, where the ferries drop off visitors and where
you'll find the most amenities. There you'll also be in among sandy
beaches and one of the Arans' most notable sites: prehistoric stone forts.
Also, Inishmore has the smallest church in the world, taking up a measly
7 feet by 11 feet. Maybe they thought just a little prayer is better than
nothing?

Located out in the middle of the Atlantic Ocean. To get there: See "Getting to and around the Aran Islands," earlier in this chapter. Suggested visit: Several hours at least.

Connemara National Park and Visitors Centre
Letterfrack

Some of the absolute best scenery in this part of Ireland is contained in this 5,000-acre park. Mountains, bogs, valleys, and forests make up the region, but most people come to catch sight of the famous Connemara ponies that make the park home. Four of the mountains that make up the impressive Twelve Bens range are in the park, including Benbaun, the highest of the 12. It reaches 2,400 feet — pretty high for a country this size. If you keep a careful watch, you'll glimpse some of the park's hidden wonders. There are 4,000-year-old prehistoric structures, flowers that only grow here, and rare plants and animals. For instance, Connemara ponies were once the only purebred horses native to Ireland. As for the ones roaming Connemara National Park today, a fantastic legend says they are the direct descendants of the Arab horses that struggled ashore when the Spanish Armada was wrecked against the coast in 1588.

To make sure you don't miss a thing, the Visitors Centre (on the N59) organizes nature trail walks. Loners can take one of the two marked paths. For the less adventurous, the center also has exhibitions and audiovisual shows.

Letterfrack, County Galway. ☎ 095-41-054 or 095-41-006. To get there: Clifden-Westport Road (N59). Bus Eireann (☎ 091-56-2000) takes a day tour of Connemara from Galway Bus Station between June and Sept. Park admission: €2.50 ($2.40) adults, €2 ($1.90) seniors, €1.25 ($1.20) children and students, €6.25 ($5.95) family. Open: Park open year-round. Visitor Centre open April, May, and Sept daily 10:00 a.m.–5:30 p.m.; June daily 10:00 a.m.–6:30 p.m.; July–Aug daily 9:30 a.m.–6:30 p.m. Suggested visit: Several hours.

Thoor Ballylee (W. B. Yeats's Summer Home)
Gort

One look from the battlements of this stone tower and you'll see what the famous poet W. B. Yeats drew inspiration from, and why. This tower was the poet's summer home and where he wrote most of his work. The view includes Galway's lush fields and forests. There's an audiovisual tour and museum dedicated to Yeats's life and work. Everything about the place has been restored to look just like it did when the poet lived there in the 1920s. Fans can buy his writings in the bookshop, and there are gardens and a picnic area that make for a gorgeous lunch stop when the weather's nice.

Gort, County Galway. ☎ 091-64-1436. To get there: Off Limerick-Galway Road (N18) or the Gort-Loughrea Road. Look for the sign. Admission: €3.75 ($3.55) adults, €3.50

($3.35) seniors and students, €1 (95¢) children. Open: April–Sept daily 10 a.m.–6 p.m. Suggested visit: 1½ hours.

Kylemore Benedictine Abbey
Kylemore

Sitting at the base of the mountains and on the shores of the lake, this abbey looks like a storybook castle — and it is, in a way. An English tycoon ordered the gorgeous Gothic building constructed for his adored wife, but when she died suddenly, he abandoned it. Later, a group of nuns escaping the horrors of World War I in Belgium took up residence and began the lengthy process of restoring the old place. They're still at it, but now they also run a world-renowned girls' boarding school here. You can visit the striking reception rooms, where you'll see a video about the history of the estate; walk along the lake to the restored Gothic church; and visit the magnificent walled Victorian garden. The Abbey is known for its pottery, which you can watch being made (and can purchase in the craft shop). There's also a restaurant on the grounds.

Kylemore, Connemara. ☎ 095-41-145. To get there: On the Clifden-Westport Road (N59), east of Letterfrack. Admission: €2 ($1.90) adults, €1.25 ($1.20) seniors and students, €0.75 (70¢) children. Open: April–Oct daily 9:30 a.m.–6:00 p.m. Suggested visit: About 1 hour.

The top Galway City landmarks

Spanish Arch

During Medieval times, Galway Harbor was outside the thick city walls, leaving it exposed to any trouble. In the late 1500s, Spanish ships often sailed into the harbor with valuable cargos — wine, brandy, and produce. To protect against any trouble from the foreigners, a stone archway was constructed, and the Spanish would pass their goods through without coming into town.

Located between Wolfe Tone Bridge and The Long Walk, at the mouth of the river.

Browne Doorway

Looking pretty odd at the head of Eyre Square, the Browne Doorway is a towering stone archway that's connected to nothing. For more than 75 years it's stood there, and although the park is accessible from any point (there are no walls), you'll be amazed to see how many people take the trouble to walk through the doorway. Dating from 1627, it comes from an old mansion on Lower Abbeygate Street, and it has the coat of arms of the families Browne and Lynch.

Located on the northwest side of the square.

Lynch's Castle (now AIB Bank)

If this isn't your first castle in Ireland you may expect something, well, larger. This 14th-century home of the legendary Lynch family was restored and now houses a bank, though you can still marvel at the coats of arms and stonework on the exterior.

Located on Abbeygate Street Upper between Shop and Market streets.

John F. Kennedy Plaque

In 1963, just months before he was assassinated, JFK spoke in Eyre Square on his historic trip to Ireland — the first time a sitting U.S. president had visited the country. From the park in the center of the square, which is named after him, Kennedy spoke to the people and received the "freedom of the city" (like the key to a city). There's a bronze plaque in the park showing the slain president's profile.

Located in Eyre Square.

Lynch Memorial Window

James Lynch Fitzstephen, unyielding magistrate and mayor of Galway, earned his place in the dictionaries when he condemned and executed his own son (convicted for murder) in 1493 as a demonstration that the law does not bend even under family ties. That's where we get the word *lynch*. The Lynch Memorial Window commemorates this event. It's set into a wall just above an ornate Gothic doorway on Market Street.

Located on Market Street, one block northwest of Eyre Square.

Other fun stuff to do

If you've seen the top sites and still have some time, these attractions are worth a stop, too:

✔ **Salthill:** This fun little resort town is Ireland's closest thing to Coney Island. It makes for a fun day with the family. Walk along the boardwalk, eat fast food, play arcade games, and visit the Leisureland amusement park (☎ 091-52-1455) to ride the Ferris wheel (possibly the only one in the country) and other amusement rides.

Location: To get there, take the R336 west from Galway.

✔ **Coole Park:** Once home to Lady Gregory — writer, friend of many an Irish luminary, and cofounder of Dublin's Abbey Theatre — the park is now home to red deer, red squirrels, and badgers, among others, and boasts beautiful nature trails, a lake, bountiful gardens, and a farmlike atmosphere, though the estate manor is gone. One of the most interesting parts of the park is the "Autograph Tree," which bears the carved initials of such famous people as George Bernard Shaw, Oliver St. John Gogarty, Sean O'Casey, and W. B. Yeats, Lady Gregory's friend and partner in the Abbey. In the restored courtyard there's a visitor center, a place to buy light snacks, and picnic tables. The courtyard is also the starting point for nature walks.

Location: Gort, County Galway. ☎ **091-63-1804.** To get there: North of Gort on the N18. Admission: €2.50 ($2.40) adults, €2 ($1.90) seniors, €1.25 ($1.20) children and students, €6.25 ($5.95) family. Open: Mid-April to mid-June Tuesday to Sunday 10 a.m. to 5 p.m.; mid-June to August daily 9:30 a.m. to 6:30 p.m.; September daily 10 a.m. to 5 p.m. Suggested visit: 1 or 2 hours.

✔ **Dunguaire Castle:** How better to tell the story of a castle's rich history than to show it? Each floor of Dunguaire Castle reflects a different and very colorful time in its history. It's been perfectly restored, and the interior is one of the finest in its class, with furnishings that interestingly mirror the time. According to legend, the castle was built on the site of the Palace of Guaire, sixth-century king of Connaught, and that's where the name comes from. Later it was owned by Oliver St. John Gogarty, poet, surgeon, and satirical model for Buck Mulligan, one the characters of James Joyce's *Ulysses.* Although born in Dublin, Gogarty lived mostly in Connemara.

Location: Kinvarra, County Galway. ☎ **091-637-108.** To get there: From the Gort-Kilcolgan Road (N18), take the N67. Admission: €3.50 ($3.35) adults, €2.50 ($2.40) seniors, €2 ($1.90) children and students. Open: April to September daily 9:30 a.m. to 5:30 p.m. Suggested visit: 1½ hours.

Joining an Organized Tour

O'Neachtain Bus Tours

Connemara and Kylemore Abbey are the highlights of this scenic tour that includes other picture-taking highlights like Connemara ponies, the Quiet Man Cottage in County Mayo (see Chapter 19), turf-cutting bogs, Clifden, and the coast.

Departs Salthill Tourist Office daily at 9:55 a.m. and Galway Tourist Office (O'Neachtain Bus Stop, Kinlay House) daily at 9:45 a.m., both year-round. Returns 4:45 p.m. Information: ☎ 091-56-5056. Price: €12.50 ($11.90) adults, €10 ($9.50) students, €6.25 ($5.95) children.

Bus Eireann Connemara Bus Tour

This day tour of Connemara takes you through Clifden with a stop at Kylemore Abbey, but the focus of the tour is the beautiful mountain scenery. There are also some designated picture-taking stops.

Leaves Salthill at 9:45 a.m. and Galway Railway Station at 10 a.m. Runs Sun–Fri in July and Aug and Sun, Tues, and Thurs in June and Sept. Returns at 5 p.m. Information: ☎ 091-56-3081. Price: €11.25 ($10.70) adults, €9.50 ($9.05) students and seniors, €6.25 ($5.95) for children, €22 ($20.90) for a family of two adults and three children.

Corrib Cruises Cruise Tour

Aboard the *Corrib Queen* (either of them — there are two boats with the same name), you'll tour the unspoiled shoreline of the lovely Lough Corrib, monastic ruins, and the village of Cong. The tour provides the best opportunity to photograph Ashford Castle.

Departs from Oughterard and Cong daily at 11:00 a.m., 2:45 p.m., and 5:00 p.m., May–Sept. Information: ☎ 092-46-029. Price: €7.50 ($7.15) per person.

Shopping

I know what you want: You want one of those thick Aran sweaters that'll make you look like one of the Clancy Brothers. In this section, I tell you where to find them.

Aran sweaters may be one of Ireland's biggest exports today, but they came from humble beginnings. Originally, the almost-waterproof wool sweaters were knit by the women of the islands to ensure fishermen stayed warm (the waterproofing comes from natural oils from the sheep's skin, which remain on the wool). The wives and mothers of the fishermen created a different pattern for each family. Sadly, this was to identify their men, should they drown off the dangerous coast.

Another great Galway item is Claddagh rings — you know, the ones with two hands clasping a heart below a crown. The hands symbolize friendship, the crown symbolizes loyalty, and the heart represents love. According to tradition, the wearer wears his or her ring with the crown pointing toward the fingertips to show he or she is in love or married. If, on the other hand, the heart is pointing toward the finger-tips the wearer is said to be unattached. Traditionally, the ring is worn on one's ring finger and serves as an engagement ring. The name comes from Claddagh, the oldest fishing village in Ireland, located on the west bank of the Corrib Estuary in Galway. In Gaelic, *An Cladach* means "flat, stony shore."

There are a few shopping areas in Galway, but the best is the **Eyre Square Shopping Centre** (☎ **091-56-8302**). It has more than 50 shops and an antique market under one glassed roof, and it's lined by old stone walls. It's also home to the Vidiwall, a giant screen displaying music, tourism information, and animated shows. On Saturdays year-round there's also a traditional **Galway Saturday Market** next to the Collegiate Church of St. Nicholas.

Here are some specific shops to check out in Galway City and around the county.

Galway Woolen Market

The market specializes in Aran hand-knits and other knitwear, linen, lace, sheepskin, and gifts.

21–22 High St., Galway City. ☎ *091-56-2491.*

Kennys Bookshop and Art Gallery

This shop houses an excellent collection of contemporary Irish literature (including secondhand and antiquarian books), art prints, and maps. They locate the difficult-to-find stuff.

High Street, Galway City. ☎ *091-56-2739.*

Roundstone Music

Famous for making a large and high-quality selection of *bodhráns* (Irish drums), this music shop features all kinds of other well-crafted instruments as well. Owner Malachy Kearns is something of a celebrity: He made the drums for the *Riverdance* ensemble and is even featured on an Irish postage stamp.

Roundstone, Connemara. ☎ *095-35-808. Internet:* www.bodhran.com.

Thomas Dillon's

Thomas Dillon's is Galway's original maker of Claddagh rings, creating the famous rings since 1750. Also home of the Claddagh Ring Museum, which has on display the oldest rings in existence. There's no charge for checking out their tiny museum.

1 Quay St., Galway. ☎ *091-56-6365.*

Treasure Chest

The Treasure Chest has just about every local gift item you could want under one roof. Waterford Crystal, Royal Tara china, Belleek china, Claddagh rings, Aran knitwear, Irish linen, souvenirs, and more.

31–33 William St., Galway City. ☎ *091-56-7237.*

Pub-Crawling in Galway City

Galway's not just a thriving city, it's a college town, and with that comes a pretty healthy nightlife. In this section, I list a number of great pubs for your enjoyment.

Monroe's Tavern

Feeling footloose? Monroe's regularly packs the place every Tuesday night (after 9:30 p.m.) for *set dancing* — a precursor to American square dancing. And every night features live music — whirling reels keeping a fast, sweaty pace as onlookers shout on in a frenzy of good *craic* (fun). And the crowd isn't all tour-bus shutterbugs; the tavern is most popular with locals. Set in an old house with low ceilings and timber floors, it may seem large for a pub, but it needs the room so you can get your jig on. During the day you should stop in for a bite: Monroe's actually specializes in organic fare — delicious!

Dominick Street, Galway City. ☎ *091-58-3397.*

The Kings Head Pub

The Middle Ages live on in The Kings Head, if just for the original medieval fireplaces and windows. But it's all or nothing here, and every bit of the place looks the part of a pub from the 1500s. There's history galore associated with this place, and a chat with the barkeep will reveal some of its rich stories. This isn't a cramped, elbow-room pub, either: It's spread over three floors, though you'll probably stay downstairs with the music. There are Sunday brunch-time jazz sessions, too. And you can take your picture sitting on the throne, next to the downstairs fireplace!

15 High St., Galway City. ☎ *091-56-6630.*

The Quays Bar

No trip to Galway is complete without a stop at this lively pub, a city institution since its opening in the 1600s, and today a place known for its live music. The whole thing is set in an old stone mansion: The front of the house has an authentic bar and is small with an old-world feel, and the back — while retaining the same traditional look — is vast, with plenty of room to move around. The pub grub is especially good, as locals will attest to.

Quay Street and Chapel Lane, Galway City. ☎ *091-56-8347.*

Skeff Bar

Every corner of this sprawling pub is distinct and impressive, making it an unquestioned must-see. Some parts look like an upper-crust drawing room, with elegant couches, coffee tables, and Persian rugs, while other parts are distinctly Irish pub, with low stools or tall booths. Fireplaces, intricate ceiling work, and stained glass give the pub a posh feel. Staircases throughout lead to more bars upstairs. The food is American-ish and tasty, and there's music on weekends. Expect this popular pub to fill up almost any night of the week.

Eyre Square, Galway City. ☎ *091-56-3173.*

The Snug

A gigantic, ceiling-high fireplace from the 16th century dominates this traditional pub, and smack inside the hearth are the best seats in the house! This is one of Galway's oldest buildings, and part of the fun is meandering around with a pint and reading all the articles on the walls that describe the place. It may be called The Snug, but it has to have one of the most open interiors in the city. Traditional music sessions are held every weekend, beginning on Thursday night.

William Street, Galway City. ☎ *091-56-2831.*

E. J. Kings

Almost anyone who's been to Clifden is familiar with E. J. Kings, because when you go, you can't forget it. Always humming, Kings has many floors, and in the high season music fills the air. Seafood is the feature of the fantastic pub-food menu, but there's also good traditional fare. When it's cold, a welcoming fire warms the pub, and in nice weather the outdoor patio is the hottest spot. The atmosphere in Kings is relaxed and you're sure to get a warm welcome from the young, chatty staff.

The Square, Clifden. ☎ *095-21-330.*

Fast Facts: County Galway

Area Code(s)

County Galway's area codes (or city codes) are **091** and **099**.

Emergencies-Hospital

Dial ☎ **999** for all emergencies. University College Hospital is on Newcastle Road, Galway (☎ 091-58-0580). Need a late-night pharmacy? Try Matt O'Flaherty Chemist, 39 Eyre Sq., Galway (☎ 091-56-3526).

Genealogy Resources

Contact Shoemakers Tower, Medieval Street, Eyre Square Centre, Galway (☎ 091-56-9649), or Galway Family History Society West, Venture Centre, Liosbaun Estate, Taum (☎ 091-75-6737).

Information

For visitor information and reservation services go to Aras Fa'ilte, Victoria Place, Eyre

Square (☎ 091-56-3081), open year-round. They can also provide reservation services. For telephone directory assistance, dial ☎ 1190.

Internet

The NetAccess Internet Cafe, Olde Malte Arcade, Hight Street (☎ 091-56-9772), has Internet access and printing capabilities.

Post Office

Galway Post Office is on Eglinton Street, Galway City (☎ 091-56-2051).

Chapter 19

Counties Mayo and Sligo

● ●

In This Chapter

▶ Exploring Yeats Country

▶ Touring Stone Age monuments in Ceide Fields

▶ Making the religious pilgrimage to Croagh Patrick

▶ Finding the best crafts

● ●

*N*orth of County Galway, Counties Mayo and Sligo boast some of the most beautiful scenery you can imagine — so beautiful that Mayo became the setting of *The Quiet Man,* a movie with John Wayne and Maureen O'Hara. And it was in Sligo that poet W. B. Yeats found the inspiration for some of his greatest work.

What's Where?: Mayo and Sligo's Major Attractions

Many of **County Mayo's** attractions relate to its proximity to water, with most of the area touching either the Atlantic or calm and striking **Clew Bay.** Beaches, of course, are a big part of life in this region. Mountains tower over the county, providing the best views, while bogs and cliffs add to the stunning, unspoiled scenery. The N5 (and a few smaller roads) take you to the towns of Westport, Castlebar, and Mayo's largest, Ballina. Venturing out for a drive west on the N59 takes you along twisty roads that lead to some of the most isolated and sparsely populated regions in the country. Around the county, the top attractions include

✔ **Westport House and Children's Zoo:** This grand 18th-century limestone house features an extraordinary interior. The zoo houses ostriches, llamas, camels, and more.

✔ **Clare Island:** Sandy beaches and walking trails share space on this island with the ruins of **Clare Castle and Abbey,** huts from the Iron Age, and wildlife that includes seals and dolphins.

✔ **Ceide Fields:** This is the world's most extensive Stone Age monument, dating back 5,000 years.

✔ **Croagh Patrick:** This mountain is said to have been where St. Patrick fasted and prayed for 40 days, finally achieving divine inspiration.

✔ **The Quiet Man Heritage Cottage:** In the movie *The Quiet Man,* American John Wayne comes back to his birthplace in Ireland, falls in love with Maureen O'Hara, and gets into a knock-down, drag-out brawl with her brother, played by Victor McLaglen. Romance! Excitement! And one of the best Irish-American films ever. The Quiet Man Heritage Cottage isn't the real thing, but it's close enough to make you feel like you're there with the Duke in person.

Maybe the best compliment given to **County Sligo** comes from the many Irish writers who have fallen in love with the area over the years. Much of the county is known as Yeats Country, because of the fondness the great poet W. B. Yeats had for the place — his last wish was to be buried here. The relatively small county has tributes to the poet in every corner, but its history goes back much further. You can find a heavy concentration of megalithic sites here, and in the towns of Carrowmore, Carrowkeel, and Knocknarea you can see ancient cemeteries and graves. **Sligo Town** is a walkable little metropolis where you can have a nice meal or find a place to stay. South of Sligo Town, **Strandhill** offers sandy beaches for relaxation. Major sights in County Sligo include

✔ **Sligo Abbey:** This medieval building, constructed in the mid-13th century for Dominican monks, contains tomb sculptures and a superbly carved high altar from the 15th century.

✔ **Sligo County Museum & Art Gallery:** This museum and gallery features memorabilia of the great poet William Butler Yeats (including his Nobel Prize) and paintings by his brother Jack and father John.

✔ **Lissadell House:** Owned by a family that was friendly with W. B. Yeats, this Georgian mansion has an impressive interior and contains a collection of family memorabilia.

Because Mayo and Sligo are typically visited together, usually either en route from Galway north to Donegal or Northern Ireland or as a round-trip visit from Galway City, I discuss them together in this chapter.

Counties Mayo and Sligo

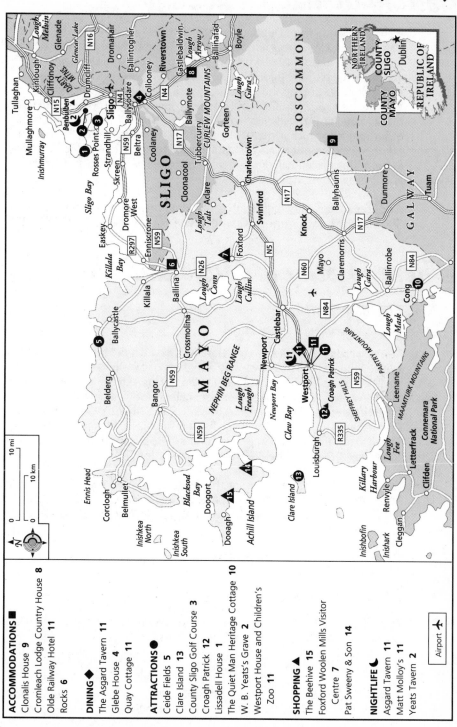

ACCOMMODATIONS ■
Clonalis House **9**
Cromleach Lodge Country House **8**
Olde Railway Hotel **11**
Rocks **6**

DINING ◆
The Asgard Tavern **11**
Glebe House **4**
Quay Cottage **11**

ATTRACTIONS ●
Ceide Fields **5**
Clare Island **13**
County Sligo Golf Course **3**
Croagh Patrick **12**
Lissadell House **1**
The Quiet Man Heritage Cottage **10**
W. B. Yeats's Grave **2**
Westport House and Children's
  Zoo **11**

SHOPPING ▲
The Beehive **15**
Foxford Woolen Mills Visitor
  Centre **7**
Pat Sweeny & Son **14**

NIGHTLIFE ♩
Asgard Tavern **11**
Matt Molloy's **11**
Yeats Tavern **2**

✈ Airport

Getting to Mayo and Sligo

If you're driving from Dublin, take the N4 to Sligo City or the N5 to Castlebar and Westport in County Mayo. From Galway, take the N17 to meet the N5 in County Mayo or straight to Sligo. From Donegal, go south on the N15 to Sligo. **Irish Rail** (☎ 071-69-888) services Sligo at Plunkett Station by the Ignatius Rice Bridge, and also services Westport, Foxford, Ballina, and Castlebar in County Mayo. **Bus Eireann** (☎ 071-60-066) travels year-round to Sligo, Strandhill, Drumcliff, and other major towns in County Sligo, and to Westport, Cong, Ballina, and other towns in County Mayo. In Sligo City, buses arrive at McDiarmada Station. Bus Eireann also has local service between Sligo and Strandhill and Rosses Point in July and August.

Aer Lingus has daily flights into both Sligo Airport (Strandhill, ☎ 071-68-280) and Knock Airport (Charlestown, County Mayo, ☎ 094-67-222).

Where to Stay in Mayo and Sligo

Olde Railway Hotel
$–$$ Westport, County Mayo

You're sure to have a relaxing time at this 18th-century coaching inn, where your comfort is obviously a high priority. Open fires blaze and a glass conservatory overlooks a garden patio. Antique period furniture fills the place, and they also serve excellent food (a new vegetable and herb garden adds fresh additions to the menu). Expect lobster, Connemara lamb, and a vast wine list. This inn is in the heart of Westport. There are standard and superior rooms. The latter are much larger and have king-size beds; they're worth the splurge.

The Mall (in the town center, overlooking the Carrowbeg River), Westport, County Mayo. ☎ 098-25-166. Fax: 098-25-090. Internet: www.anu.ie/railwayhotel. *To get there: In the center of town. Rates: €40–€90 ($38–$85.50) double. AE, DC, MC, V.*

Rocks
$ Ballina, County Mayo

This gorgeous home was designed and built by the owners, and it provides you with a perfect place to settle and explore the Northwest of the country. You have excellent fishing and swimming nearby and you can arrange pony-riding excursions. Kids will love the playground in back and the spacious lawns, and the home has a barbecue for grilling your own catch of the day.

Foxford Road, Ballina, County Mayo. ☎ 098-22-140. To get there: Take Foxford Road from the town center. Rates: €45–€50 ($42.75–$47.50) double. No credit cards.

Sligo Town

N

N15

Sligo Bay

Duck St.

Barrack St.

Holborn Hill

Ash Lane

Ardaghowen

NORTHERN IRELAND

Sligo Town

Dublin ★

REPUBLIC OF IRELAND

Harbour Rd.

Garavogue River

Markievicz Rd.

Lower Quay St.

Union Place

Union St.

Quay St.

Holborn St.

4

Stephen St.

2 The Mall

Wine St.

Lord Edward St.

Adelaide St.

O'Connell St.

3

Bridge St.

Kennedy Parad

Riverside

St. Anne's

Abbeyville

Garavogue River

5 **6**

11

John St.

Grattan St. Castle St.

Abbey St.

Church Hill

Wolfe Tone St.

Charles St.

Harmony Hill

Market St.

Teeling St.

Thomas St.

Chapel St.

7

8

9

Temple St.

High St.

Old Market St.

Burton St.

Cranmore

College Rd.

Connolly St.

10

■ Cranmore Estate

St. Joseph's

Mall Coach Rd.

Pearse Rd.

N4

■ Cleveragh Race Course

Circular Rd.

To Lough Gill ↘

To Dublin ↓

ACCOMMODATIONS ■
Lisadorn **1**
Sligo Park Hotel **10**
Tower Hotel **4**

DINING ◆
The Cottage **8**
Truffles **2**

ATTRACTIONS ●
Sligo Abbey **11**
Sligo County Museum
  & Art Gallery **3**
Yeats Statue **3**

SHOPPING ▲
Cat and Moon **9**
Kate's Kitchen **7**

NIGHTLIFE ☾
Beezie's **5**
Hargadon **6**

Church ✝

Clonalis House
$$ Castlrea, County Roscommon

Just over the County Mayo border is the Victorian Italianate mansion and ancestral home of the O'Conors of Connacht, descendants of Ireland's last High Kings. If you're an O'Connor yourself, you'll find the library and historical heirlooms of particular interest, but everyone else will enjoy the four-poster beds, beautiful estate grounds, and nearby woods. The caretaker, Pyers O'Conor-Nash, will gladly chat about his family's history or the area attractions over whiskey by the fireplace if you'd like. You'll want to have dinner at the manor as well; there are no decent restaurants in the vicinity.

Castlrea. ☎ *907-20-014. Email:* clonalis@iol.ie. *To get there: Take the N60 west from Castlerea or east from Ballyhaunis. Rates: €61–€73 ($57.95–$69.35) double. AE, MC, V. Closed Oct—mid-April.*

Cromleach Lodge Country House
$$$ Castlebaldwin, County Sligo

The western wilds of Ireland and luxury don't normally go together — unless you're staying at the Cromleach Lodge, a modern inn overlooking Lough Arrow. Enjoy the view of the lake and its little islands from the glass-walled sun porch or just enjoy your large, posh, comfortable room. The lauded restaurant has local seafood and an excellent prix-fixe seven-course meal, which may very well be the most memorable meal of your trip.

Castlebaldwin. ☎ *071-65-155. Fax: 071-65-455. Internet:* www.cromleach.com. *To get there: Take the N4 south from Sligo town toward Boyle. Rates: €105–€165 ($99.75–$156.75) double. AE, DC, MC, V.*

Lisadorn
$ Sligo Town, County Sligo

This stately home is at the end of a flower-lined drive; a perfect welcome to Sligo's only three-star guesthouse. The place offers amazing hospitality and comfort for the cost, and all rooms provide the best conveniences. Only five minutes from town and ten minutes from the beautiful Rosses Point, Lisadorn is a great location.

Donegal Road, Sligo Town. ☎ *071-43-417. Fax: 071-46-418. To get there: From the center of town, take the N15 north. Rates: €43.75–€48.75 ($41.55–$46.30) double. MC, V.*

Sligo Park Hotel
$$$ Sligo Town, County Sligo

This is one of those hotels that makes you feel like you're spoiling yourself — especially after you put your travel-weary body back together in the leisure center, featuring a pool, steam room, and workout equipment. The hotel sits on well-groomed gardens with scenic countryside all around. The rooms have large windows overlooking the landscaped gardens. You can't help but feel comfortable here, in Sligo's most modern accommodation.

Pearse Road, Sligo Town. ☎ *071-60-291. Fax: 071-69-556. Internet:* www.lee hotels.ie. *To get there: N4 becomes Pearse in town. Rates: €100–€150 ($95–$142.50) double. AE, DC, MC, V.*

Tower Hotel
$$–$$$ Sligo Town, County Sligo

If you want to stay in the heart of Sligo Town, this place is for you: You can walk out the door and see the town, and the countryside is only a short way off. It's a luxury hotel but small enough to pamper you with personal service. The rooms have lots of amenities, including a pants press and tea and coffee facilities. Off from the lobby is the Links bar, proving the emphasis on golf in these parts.

Quay St., Sligo Town. ☎ *071-44-000. Fax: 071-46-888. Internet:* www.tower hotelsligo.com. *To get there: In the center of town, next to the City Hall. Rates: €87.50–€150 ($83.15–$142.50) double. AE, DC, MC, V.*

Where to Dine in Mayo and Sligo

Quay Cottage
$$–$$$$ Westport, County Mayo   SEAFOOD

This little restaurant overlooks the harbor and is appropriately decked out with nautical treasures. Freshly prepared seafood is the focus of the menu, as well as daily specials and a surprisingly large vegetarian selection. Best of all, the prices are extremely reasonable for such quality food.

The Harbour, Westport, County Mayo. ☎ *098-26-412. To get there: On Westport Harbour at the entrance to Westpor. AE, MC, V. Open: Mon–Sat 6–10 p.m., Sun 1:00–9:30 p.m. Main courses: €9.90–€20.65 ($9.40–$19.60)*

The Asgard Tavern
$$–$$$ Westport, County Mayo   IRISH-STEAKS-SEAFOOD

This nautical-themed restaurant is right on the water and serves award-winning food. Its filling and hearty lunches, such as stews and creamy pasta dishes, are served all day downstairs in the relaxing atmosphere of the pub. Dinner is served upstairs, in the tasteful, candlelit dining room. There, the menu is varied, including creatively-prepared steaks and seafood. The Asgard Tavern pub serves exceptional pub food from noon to 3 p.m. and 6 to 10 p.m. There's also music in the pub most nights.

The Quay, Westport, County Mayo. ☎ *098-25-319. To get there: Drive through Westport, take Coast Road 1 mile. Main courses: €9.25–€17.50 ($8.80–$16.65). AE, DC, MC, V. Open: Sept–June Mon–Sat 6:30–9:30 p.m.; July and Aug daily 6:30–9:30 p.m.*

Glebe House

$$–$$$$ Collooney, County Sligo   IRISH

An elegant Georgian house set amid gardens makes for a classy restaurant. The menu, which changes daily, includes organically grown vegetables from the house gardens. You can always expect a fish dish — the catch of the day — and you can expect beef and chicken meals creatively and tastefully prepared. Fresh herbs underscore the delicious food.

Collooney, County Sligo. ☎ *071-67-787. To get there: From the Collooney-Ballysadare Road, turn left toward Collooney Railway Station. Main courses: €11.85–€21.25 ($11.25–$20.20). AE, MC, V. Open: May–Oct daily 6–9 p.m.; Nov–April Thurs–Sat 6:30–9:30 p.m.*

Truffles

$–$$$ Sligo Town, County Sligo   PIZZA

This little restaurant creates some absolutely delicious pizza, featuring fresh local herbs and vegetables and trademark Irish cheeses. The owner takes a hands-on approach to her work, and you can see her kneading dough or chopping up veggies to prepare her unique fare. The Irish cheese pizza stands out, and the sausage is like none you can have at home.

11 The Mall, Sligo Town. County Sligo. ☎ *071-44-226. To get there: On the north side of the Garavogue River, same street as Stephen Street (Stephen Street turns into The Mall.) Main courses: €7.45–€14.95 ($7.05–$14.20). No credit cards. Open: Tues–Sat 5:00–10:30 p.m., Sun 5–10 p.m.*

The Cottage

$ Sligo Town, County Sligo   VEGETARIAN

Looking for a quick, wholesome vegetarian lunch? Try this little cafe. You don't have to be vegetarian to enjoy the food here, and given the choices, you probably won't miss the lack of beefiness. The fare is tasty and you get plenty of it. The Cottage features chili, pizza, and stuffed baked potatoes. Soups, salads, and melted cheesy sandwiches are also common fare. You can get table service or grab something to take out.

4 Castle St., Sligo Town. ☎ *071-45-319. To get there: Located in the center of town, near the post office. Main courses: €2.50–€6.25 ($2.40–$5.95). No credit cards. Open: Mon–Fri 8:30 a.m.–9:00 p.m., Sat 8:30 a.m.–6:00 p.m.*

Exploring Mayo and Sligo

You may find tearing yourself away from all the gorgeous scenery in Mayo and Sligo hard, but there are several historic and cultural sites that you should see while you're there. I list some of the best in this section.

The top attractions

Westport House & Children's Zoo
Westport, County Mayo

This limestone house, sitting at the head of Clew Bay, is a gorgeous place with an extraordinary interior. Built in the late 18th century, it features a marble staircase and a dining room full of antiques and Waterford Crystal. The children's zoo features ostriches, llamas, camels, and more. You can also enjoy boating, a miniature railroad, and dungeons.

Westport, County Mayo. ☎ 098-25-430. To get there: City center in Westport. Admission: €7.50 ($7.15) adult, €3.75 ($3.55) children. Open: mid-May–June and Sept daily 2–6 p.m.; July and Aug Mon–Sat 10:30 a.m.–6:00 p.m., Sun 2–6 p.m. Suggested visit: 2 hours or more.

Clare Island
Clew Bay, County Mayo

This island is a sanctuary of gorgeous sandy beaches and walking trails. Knockmore Mountain is the heart of the island, and the ruins of Clare Castle and Abbey are nearby. The island is a historian's delight, with huts from the Iron Age and cooking implements from the Bronze Age (the island is the resting place of pirate queen Grace O'Malley as well). There's also a hotel you can stay at if you feel like sticking around (contact the hotel through the *Pirate Queen* ferry number in the following paragraph).

Clew Bay, County Mayo. ☎ 01-872-4154. To get there: The Pirate Queen ferry (☎ 098-26-307) runs daily (weather permitting) and costs €12.50 ($11.90). It leaves from Roonagh Quay, Louisburgh, at 11:00 a.m., 2:25 p.m., and 6:00 p.m., and leaves from Clare Island at 10:00 a.m., 1:15 p.m., and 5:00 p.m. To get to Roonagh Quay: Follow signs from Louisburgh off the R335. Admission: Just ferry cost. Suggested visit: Varies, depending on length of stay.

Ceide Fields
Ballycastle, County Mayo

Here lies the world's most extensive Stone Age monument, with a dwelling area, grazing grounds, and megalithic tombs from 5,000 years ago. Tools and pottery have recently been uncovered. Although a bog now covers most of the fields, portions have been cut out to show where the fields were partitioned by stone walls for growing food and grazing animals. The wild plants and flowers are world renowned, and the fields back up to some of the most captivating cliffs and rock formations in the country. The interpretive center explains the area's past.

Ballycastle, County Mayo. ☎ 096-43-325. To get there: Take the R314 coastal road north from Ballina, 5 miles west of Ballycastle. Admission: €3.50 ($3.35) adult, €2 ($1.90) seniors, €1.25 ($1.20) children and students; €7.50 ($7.15) family. Open: Mid-March–May Tues–Sun 10 a.m.–5 p.m.; June–Sept daily 9:30 a.m.–6:30 p.m.; Oct daily 10 a.m.–5 p.m. Suggested visit: 1 hour.

Croagh Patrick
Murrisk, County Mayo

According to legend, St. Patrick achieved divine inspiration on this mountain after praying and fasting for 40 days — although I don't suggest staying up there that long, no matter how beautiful the view. On the last Sunday of July, devout Irish Catholics climb the 2,500-foot mountain (some barefoot) in memory of their patron saint. This famous mount is more than a religious site, though. Mayo and Clew Bay provide the absolutely gorgeous view from the mountain top. The climb takes about two hours and is tough work, but not impossible. And you can wear your shoes.

Murrisk, County Mayo. To get there: Between Louisburgh and Westport off the R395. Admission: Free. Open: Daylight hours. Suggested visit: Generally a few hours.

Sligo Abbey
Sligo Town, County Sligo

This is the city's only surviving medieval building, constructed in the mid-13th century for Dominican monks. Inside are carvings and tomb sculptures, but the highlight is the superbly carved high altar from the 15th century; the altar is the only one of its kind in a monastic church in Ireland. The abbey was burned down in 1414 by a single lit candle and then was damaged again in the 1641 Rebellion. According to legend, worshippers saved the Abbey's silver bell from thieves by putting it in Lough Gill; it was retrieved later and is back in the Abbey. Legend also says that only those free from sin can hear its toll. I didn't hear it. I don't think anyone has heard it for a long time.

Abbey Street, Sligo Town. ☎ 071-46-406. To get there: One block south from Kennedy Parade in the center of Sligo Town. Admission: €2 ($1.90) adult, €1.25 ($1.20) seniors, €0.75 (70¢) children and students; €5 ($4.75) family. Open: Mid-June–Sept 9:30 a.m.–6:30 p.m. Suggested visit: 45 minutes.

Sligo County Museum & Art Gallery
Sligo Town, County Sligo

The Yeats family legacy is the cornerstone of this museum and gallery, which features memorabilia of the great poet William Butler and paintings by his brother Jack and father John. The special W. B. Yeats section includes his Nobel Prize for Literature (1923) and first editions of his complete works. Also inside is a small collection of objects from Sligo and all over Ireland, from prehistoric times to the Irish war for independence.

Stephen Street, Sligo Town. ☎ 071-42-212. To get there: North side of the Garavogue River. Admission: Free. Museum Open: Tues–Sat 10:30 a.m.–12:30 p.m. and 2:30–4:30 p.m. Gallery Open: Tues, Thurs, and Sat 10 a.m. to noon and 2–5 p.m. Suggested visit: About 1 hour.

Lissadell House
Drumcliffe, County Sligo

W. B. Yeats called Lissadell House "that old Georgian mansion," which just doesn't do the place justice. It's a huge, square stone house full of grandeur. Most notably, Lissadell House is owned by the Gore-Booth family, friends of Yeats. One of the daughters was Countess Markievicz (she married a Polish count), famous for her part in the Easter Rising and her trailblazing in British and Irish politics. Her sister, Eva, was a poet. During the Famine, Sir Robert mortgaged the house to help feed the starving. The interior of the house is impressive and contains a collection of family memorabilia.

Drumcliffe, County Sligo. ☎ 074-63-150. To get there: Off the N15 between Sligo and Donegal. Admission: €3.50 ($3.35) adult, €0.75 (70¢) children. Open: June to mid-Sept Mon–Sat 10:30 a.m.–12:15 p.m., 2–4 p.m. Suggested visit: 2 hours.

The Quiet Man Heritage Cottage
Cong, County Mayo

Have you ever see the movie *The Quiet Man?* It's the one where American John Wayne comes back to his birthplace in Ireland and falls in love with Maureen O'Hara. In the movie, Wayne's character tells a local that he'd been born in the thatched-roof cottage, just like the seven generations of his family before him, and the local makes a wisecrack about Wayne buying the place to turn it into a tourist attraction. Ironically, you can now visit a replica of the original house — and yes, they do charge a small fee to the tourists. Unfortunately, no movie memorabilia remains, so all there is to see is the house.

Circular Road, Cong, County Mayo (☎ 092-46-089). Admission: €3.50 ($3.35) adult, €1.25 ($1.20) children. Suggested visit: 30 minutes.

Other fun things to do

Here are some Yeats-related activities for literary travelers, and a challenging golf course for the duffers in your group:

✔ **Visiting W. B. Yeats's grave:** Yeats died in France but in 1948 his remains were brought to rest in Sligo — the place he always considered home. His grave in the Drumcliff churchyard is near a beautiful Celtic High cross. On the grave itself is an epitaph Yeats wrote: "Cast a cold eye on life, on death. Horseman pass by."

Location: 5 miles north of Sligo on the main Donegal road (N15).

✔ **Reading the Yeats statue:** One of the more interesting statues you'll find in Ireland is a cartoonish likeness of Sligo's famous poet near the banks of the Garavogue River, in town. Scrawled over his entire figure are the words of his own verse.

Location: On Stephen Street, just across Hyde Bridge.

✔ **Taking the Yeats Water Bus Tour:** This boat tour takes you out on Lough Gill, from which you can view W. B. Yeats's Isle of Innisfree, and stops at Parkes Castle and Church Island. As you go, Yeats's poems are recited to coincide with visited areas.

Location: Between Doorley Park in Sligo and Parkes Castle, 7 miles west from Sligo on the Dromahair road (R287). Daily between March and October. The first trip leaves at 12:30 p.m. from the castle and the last leaves from Sligo at 5:30 p.m. The length of the trip is 50 minutes. Information: ☎ **071-64-266** or 087-259-8869. Price: €6.25 ($5.95) adults, €2.50 ($2.40) children, free under 12.

✔ **Golfing at the County Sligo Golf Course:** This course challenges even top players, but dabblers can have fun playing it, too. It's set between striking Atlantic beaches and the hill of Benbulben.

Location: Rosses Point, County Sligo. ☎ **071-77-186.** E-mail: cosligo@iol.ie. Par: 71. Fees: €33.75 ($32.05) midweek, €43.75 ($41.55) weekends.

Shopping in Mayo and Sligo

The Beehive

Shop here for high-quality local crafts and traditional home baking from around Achill Island. Location overlooks the scenic Minaun Cliffs. Open Easter through November.

Keel, Achill Island, County Mayo (follow signs from Louisberg off the R335). ☎ *098-43-018.*

Foxford Woolen Mills Visitor Centre

The locally famous Foxford wool tweeds, rugs, blankets, and much more are all here. The mill, which you can tour, was started by a nun in 1892 and used to help the poor during the Famine.

Foxford, County Mayo (from Westport N5 northeast to N58 north). ☎ *094-56-756.*

Pat Sweeny & Son

This shop, a fascinating example of a local trading store, dates back to 1870. It has "everything from a needle to an anchor" and all the gifts, clothing, fishing gear, food, and petrol in between.

Achill Sound, Achill Island, County Mayo (follow signs from Louisburgh off the R335). ☎ *098-45-211.*

Cat and Moon

This one-of-a-kind store sells Irish handcrafted jewelry, contemporary art, Celtic-inspired home furnishings, and more.

4 Castle St., Sligo Town. ☎ *071-43-686.*

Kate's Kitchen

Stop here for picnic food: meats, cheeses, salads, pâté, homemade baked bread, Irish chocolates, and preserves. The store also has soaps and pot-pourri.

24 Market St., Sligo Town. ☎ *071-43-022.*

Pub Life in Mayo and Sligo

Beezie's

The interior of this pub is beautiful — although from the bland exterior you may not guess it. Stained glass and fireplaces are located through-out, and you can settle in easily. The name pays homage to a woman who would row from her home on Cottage Island to the pub until her death in the 1950s. Mondays and Thursdays live music draws a lively crowd.

45 O'Connell St., Sligo Town. ☎ *071-43-031.*

Hargadon

This is the kind of pub that's so interesting to look at you may not notice the pint in front of you! The superb decor features dark wood walls, stone floors, and lots of colored glass. You have plenty of little snugs to settle into, and you can look at various prints of the city in its early days. The pub used to also be a grocery, and the walls still bear shelves with old goods.

4 O'Connell St., Sligo Town. ☎ *071-70-933.*

Matt Molloy's

If you like traditional Irish music, this pub is worth visiting. It was started by the flutist from the famous band The Chieftains, who are often credited with the revival in Irish folk music. Inside, the pub is traditionally decorated and pretty roomy, and the back room features music nearly every night.

Bridge Street, Westport, County Mayo. ☎ *098-26-655.*

Yeats Tavern

Just a short walk from the grave of poet W. B. Yeats, this pub is a popular watering hole for locals and tourists alike. Inside you can find plenty of Yeats memorabilia. This pub features good pub grub at even better prices, and traditional music during the summer. In winter, they have music on weekends.

Drumcliff Bridge. Five miles out of Sligo Town on the main Donegal road. ☎ *071-63-117.*

Fast Facts: Counties Mayo and Sligo

Area Code(s)

071 and **074** for County Sligo; **092, 094, 096, 097,** and **098** for County Mayo.

Emergencies-Hospital

Dial ☎ **999** for all emergencies. Sligo General Hospital is on Malloway Hill (☎ 071-42-212).

Genealogy Resources

Contact the Sligo Heritage and Genealogy Centre, Temple Street, Sligo (☎ 071-43-728); the Mayo North Family History Research Centre, Castlehill, Ballina (☎ 096-31-809; Fax: 096-31-885); or the South Mayo Family History Research Centre, Main Street, Ballinrobe (☎ 092-41-214; Internet: www. mayoireland.ieroots.html).

Information

Tourist offices are located at Aras Reddan, Temple Street, Sligo (☎ 071-61-201); and James Street, Westport, County Mayo (☎ 098-25-739; Internet: www.visit mayo.com), both open year-round. They can also provide reservation services. For telephone directory assistance, dial ☎ 1190.

Internet

Futurenet Internet Cafe, Pearse House, Pearse Road, Sligo (☎ 071-50-345), has Internet access and printing capabilities.

Post Office

The Sligo General Post Office is on Wine Street (☎ 071-42-646).

Chapter 20

County Donegal

In This Chapter

▶ Touring Glenveagh Castle and its extensive grounds

▶ Staying in a room with a view — of Donegal Bay

▶ Making an excursion to Lough Derg

▶ Exploring an unmatched art collection

*D*onegal isn't a tourist hub of Ireland — not yet, anyway — but its people are proud of their county, and rightfully so. This northern-most corner of the country has plenty to boast about: brilliant coastline scenery, mountains, little seaside villages, museums, and exceptionally fresh seafood. About a third of the county is Irish-speaking. Natives love to think that these perks make Donegal a particularly nice place to visit. (I agree.) The people you meet in the pubs here may not be quite as willing to start up a chat as, say, folks in Kerry, but given the chance, you'll find they're as warm and friendly as anyone in the country.

What's Where?: County Donegal's Major Attractions

The heart of the county, **Donegal Town,** is a pretty tiny hamlet that nevertheless has plenty to offer in terms of places to eat, sleep, and drink — but don't expect to be wowed by attractions. The main draw is the town itself — a delightful, walkable village along the **River Eske.**

On your way to **Donegal Town,** from Sligo on the N15, you ramble into the resort town of **Bundoran.** This town is a popular vacation spot for Irish people from all over the island. In the summertime, the place takes on a carnival-like atmosphere. Farther up the road, right on the water, you hit **Ballyshannon,** one of the oldest towns in Ireland. Keeping along the main road, you get to the town of **Ballybofey,** which is a great start-ing point for touring the far reaches of the county. If you have the time and the inclination, steer your touring-mobile onto the N56 and head to the coast. You can start in Donegal Town and round the coast clock-wise, or head north and focus on the gorgeous **Inishowen Peninsula.** Either way, you'll creep along craggy cliffs that frame the wild ocean.

County Donegal

10 mi

10 km

NORTHERN IRELAND

Dublin ★

REPUBLIC OF IRELAND

COUNTY DONEGAL

DERRY (NORTHERN IRELAND)

TYRONE (NORTHERN IRELAND)

Greencastle

Kinnagoe Bay

Culdaff Bay

Malin

Moville

Lough Foyle

Muff

Limavady

Derry

Cranaugh

A37

A2

A2

A6

A5

5

Clonmany

INISHOWEN PENINSULA

Ballyliffin

Buncrana

Fahan

Pollan Bay

R238

Grianán Of Ailéach (Stone Fort) 9

Lifford

Strabane

A5

N13

N14

Lough Swilly

Carrowkeel

Rathmullan

Inch Island

Rathmelton

Letterkenny 7

Raphoe

N56

N15

Fanad

Carrigart

Millford

GLENVEAGH NATIONAL PARK 8

Rosguill

R247

N56

N56

Horn Head

Dunfanaghy

Creeslough

ARDS FOREST PARK

Mount Errigal

Garrian Lough

Slieve Snacht

N56

DONEGAL

Ballybofey 6 6

Tory Sound

Inishbofin

Bloody Foreland

Bunbeg

Gweedore

Lough Beagh

Derryveagh Mountains

Fintown

N15

Tory Island

Gola Island

Dunglow

Doocharry

Lough Finn

Blue Stack Mountains

Lough Eske

Pettigo

Lough Derg 5

FERMANAGH (NORTHERN IRELAND)

Owey Island

Rosses Bay

Burtonport

R259

R250

Glenties

N56

Mountcharles

DONEGAL

Ballyshannon

N15

Aranmore Island

Gweebarra Bay

Ardara 2

Killybegs

Rossnowlagh 3

N56

3

4

4

Loughros More Bay

Inver Bay

Donegal Bay

Bundoran

Glencolumbkille 1

R263

Glen Bay

Malin Bay

Slieve League

ATLANTIC OCEAN

ACCOMMODATIONS ■
Creevy Pier **4**
Kee's Hotel **6**
Sand House Hotel **3**

DINING ◆
Smuggler's Creek **3**

ATTRACTIONS ●
The Glebe House and Gallery **7**
Glenveagh Castle and National Park **8**
Griana'n Ailigh **9**
Lough Derg **5**
Slieve League **1**

SHOPPING ▲
Donegal Parian China **4**
Kennedy of Ardara **2**

NIGHTLIFE ☽
Corner Bar **6**
McGinley **6**

Some great County Donegal attractions include

✔ **Glenveagh Castle and National Park:** Take a tour through this gorgeous castle, built in 1870 and filled with imposing rooms and incredible furnishings. The castle's gardens are beautiful, and the surrounding **National Park** features lakes, glens, woods, and red deer, and backs up to the **Derryveigh Mountains.**

✔ **Griana'n Ailigh:** This ring fort dates back to 1700 B.C., and looking out from it you can see **Lough Swilly** and **Lough Foyle.** A refurbished old stone church houses an *interpretive center* (similar to a visitor center, with exhibits explaining the site), which also has a restaurant and craft shop.

✔ **Lough Derg:** Legend says that St. Patrick spent a Lenten season fasting on one of this lake's tiny islands. At the interpretive center you can get a real feel for the area's religious and historical import.

✔ **Donegal Castle:** Sitting beside the River Eske, this impressive 15th-century castle is filled with lovely furnishings, including Persian rugs and French tapestries.

✔ **The Glebe House and Gallery:** The late art collector Derek Hill's 1828 mansion is now open for visitors, who can see works by Picasso and Renoir, Jack Yeats, and many other Irish and Italian artists. The decor of the house is an exhibit in itself, with Islamic ceramics, Japanese art, and priceless wallpaper and textiles.

Getting to and around County Donegal

Local flights come into Donegal Airport, Carrickfinn, Kincasslagh (☎ 075-48-232), located 40 miles from Donegal Town. If you come by car, take the N15 north from Sligo or south from Strabane to Donegal Town. **Bus Eireann** (☎ 074-21-309) travels year-round to Donegal, Killybegs, Ballyshannon, and other towns in County Donegal. Bus pickup in Donegal is at the **Abbey Hotel,** on **The Diamond** in the town center.

There's no local bus service, but you can easily walk through and around Donegal Town if you don't have a car.

Where to Stay in County Donegal

All the accommodations I list in this section have surprisingly great restaurants and pub grub on the premises, so you can get a warm bed and a good meal in one swipe!

Abbey Hotel
$$ Donegal Town

This comfortable hotel has tasteful and spacious rooms — some over-looking Donegal Bay, so be sure to ask about them. The hotel is in the heart of town, and beaches, boating, and horseback riding are all nearby. The comfortable, homey Abbey restaurant is a real treat — not only is the food great, but the decor looks just like a traditional Irish kitchen. There's also a modern-looking bar, the Eas Dun, that serves hot pub grub all day.

The Diamond, Donegal Town. ☎ *073-21-014. Fax: 073-23-660. To get there: In the town center. Rates: €87.50–€100 ($83.15–$95) double. AE, DC, MC, V.*

Creevy Pier
$–$$ Ballyshannon

This family home offers a spectacular view of Donegal Bay, and swimming, fishing, and windsurfing happen at the doorstep. Staying here puts you in a great spot for touring the western part of the county. All rooms are comfortable and nice, and the restaurant specializes in international seafood dishes. The Captain's Cabin pub is a draw — sitting in front of the big stone fireplace with a drink is particularly relaxing.

Creevy Pier, Ballyshannon. ☎ *072-51-236. Fax: 072-51-236. To get there: On the N15 south from Donegal Town or north from Sligo. Rates: €48.75–€62.50 ($46.30–$59.40) double. MC, V.*

Kee's Hotel
$$–$$$ Stranorlar

This lovely hotel is a historic coaching inn, situated in a village that's perfect for touring Donegal. More than that, Kee's is a superb hotel. Friendliness abounds, the rooms are big and comfortable, and guests can enjoy a pool, open fireplaces, and a gym. The restaurant serves excellent food, and you can rent bikes from the hotel for seeing the village.

Stranorlar, Ballybofey, right where the N13 meets the N15. ☎ *074-31-018. Fax: 074-31-917. To get there: On the N15 northeast from Donegal Town. Rates: €90–€117.50 ($85.50–$111.65) double. AE, DC, MC, V.*

The Sand House Hotel
$$$ Rossnowlagh

The Britton family recently made a €4 million renovation to this ocean-side fishing lodge-turned-four-star hotel, adding a marine spa, an outdoor hot tub, and a new panoramic elevator with sea views. When you're not sleeping the sleep of the dead in your overstuffed bed, you can take a

Donegal Town

To Lough Eske

Presbyterian
Church

Methodist
Church

Library

Waterloo
Place

Tirconnail St.

Castle St.

Bridge St.

Church of Ireland

BANK WALK

River Eske

River Eske

River Eske

Upper Main St.

Hospital

To Ballybofey,
Letterkenny
& Derry

Quay St.

Pier

Donegal
Bay

Shopping
Centre

To Ballyshannon
& Sligo

NORTHERN
IRELAND

Donegal

Dublin

REPUBLIC
OF IRELAND

ACCOMMODATIONS ■
Abbey Hotel **4**

DINING ◆
Errigal Restaurant **5**

ATTRACTIONS ●
Donegal Castle **1**

SHOPPING ▲
Donegal Craft Village **6**
Magee of Donegal **3**

NIGHTLIFE ☾
McGroarty's Bar **2**

Information *i*
Parking P
Post Office ✉
Public Toilet 🚻
Telephone ℅

walk along the cliffs, play some golf at one of the three nearby courses, or just take in comforts of the hotel itself, like the rooftop garden, warm fires, fresh flowers, and homemade scones and pies. For a little extra, you can get a room with a view of the Atlantic Ocean and Donegal Bay — and it's well worth it.

Stranorlar, Ballybofey, right where the N13 meets the N15. ☎ 072-51-777. Fax: 072-52-100. Internet: www.sandhousehotel.ie. *To get there: On the N15 northeast from Donegal Town. Rates: €140–€180 ($133–$171) double. AE, DC, MC, V.*

Where to Dine in County Donegal

Errigal Restaurant
$–$$ Donegal Town FISH AND CHIPS (AND MORE)

Fish and chips is the house specialty at this local favorite. Errigal is a family-run restaurant and the menu is varied enough to appeal to any taste. It features fish dishes, steaks, chicken curry (an Irish favorite), sandwiches, and burgers. Don't look for a light meal here; you'll leave full and satisfied. And with the cost, you won't go off your budget.

Upper Main Street, Donegal. ☎ 073-21-428. To get there: In the town center. Main courses: €5.65–€9.35 ($5.35–$8.85). No credit cards. Open: Mon–Sat 9 a.m.–3 p.m. and 5:30–11:00 p.m., Sun 3:30–11:00 p.m.

Smuggler's Creek
$$–$$$ Rossnowlagh SEAFOOD

The view itself is enough to make a meal at Smuggler's Creek memorable. From the conservatory dining room sitting atop a cliff, you can look out at Donegal Bay, and if your timing's good, you may catch a fantastic sunset. Inside, the stone building is comfortable and aptly decorated with wooden stools, lobster pots, and porthole windows. Not surprisingly, seafood is a specialty here. What is surprising, considering the low prices, is the gourmet menu. You can nosh on wild salmon hollandaise or the rich Smuggler's sea casserole — scallops, salmon, and prawns in a cream sauce. You can also sample steaks with trademark Irish whiskey sauce and pasta dishes. Even the bar menu is a notch above, with fresh pâté and garlic mussels amid your usual soup and sandwiches.

Rossnowlagh. ☎ 072-52-366. To get there: A quarter mile off the R231, off the main Sligo-Donegal road (N15). Take the little, no-name side road from the R231 to get closer to the water. Signs won't let you miss the turnoff. Main courses: €10–€16.90 ($9.50–$16.05). AE, DC, MC, V. Open: Daily noon to midnight.

Exploring County Donegal: The Top Attractions

Glenveagh Castle and National Park
Churchill

This gorgeous castle was built in 1870 and modeled after the royal Balmoral Castle in Scotland. Tours take you through the imposing rooms, each filled with incredible furnishings. Before it was built, the infamous landowner John George Adair evicted 244 tenants during the harsh winter of 1861 to clear the land for construction. The surrounding National Park is a natural beauty. It backs up to the Derryveigh Mountains and includes the highest mountain in Donegal, Mount Errigal. The huge valley contains lakes, glens, woods, and alpine gardens. A herd of red deer has made the valley its home. Closer to the castle are fantastic gardens, some of the finest in the country. A visitor center has an audiovisual show that explains the park interior.

Churchill, Letterkenny. ☎ 074-37-088. To get there: Northwest from Letterkenny on the main road to Kilmacrennan (N56). Admission: For Park or Castle, €2.50 ($2.40) adult, €2 ($1.90) seniors, €1.25 ($1.20) children and students, €6.25 ($5.95) family. Open: Mid-April–Sept daily 10:00 a.m.–6:30 p.m.; Oct Sat–Thur 10:00 a.m.–6:30 p.m. Suggested visit: 2 to 3 hours.

Griana'n Ailigh
Burt

You'll be amazed by the view from the battlements of this ring fort, which dates back to 1700 B.C. From them, you can perfectly see Lough Swilly and Lough Foyle. A refurbished old stone church houses an interpretive center, which also has a restaurant and craft shop. You can visit the ancient woods next to the fort and a wetland habitat that's home to Hooper swans.

Burt, Inishowen. ☎ 077-68-000. To get there: Off the N13 northeast from Letterkenny or west from Derry. Admission: €2.50 ($2.40) per person, €6.25 ($5.95) family. Open: Summer daily 10 a.m.–6 p.m., winter daily noon to 6 p.m. Suggested visit: 45 minutes.

Lough Derg
Pettigo

I certainly won't ask you to participate in the three-day religious retreat on the island of St. Patrick's Purgatory each summer, but going to the visitor center is a good idea. Legend has it St. Patrick spent a Lenten season fasting on one of the lake's tiny islands, and since then devout Catholics have gone there for penance. Pilgrims must stay awake for three days, eating only one meal a day of dry bread and black tea. Visitors are welcome to visit the island, but I recommend investing the time in the visitor center to get a real feel for the area's religious and historical import.

Pettigo. To get there: From the Sligo-Donegal Road (N15) take R232 to Pettigo, and then R233 for 5 miles. The R233 ends at the water's edge, where you'll find a ferry (more like a rowboat, actually) to get to the island. Admission: Free, but you have to contact the visitor center in Pettigo (☎ 072-61-546) before visiting the island. Open: April–Sept. Suggested visit (at the visitor center): 30 minutes.

Donegal Castle
Donegal Town

Built in the 15th century by the O'Donnell chieftain, this impressive castle sits beside the River Eske. Inside, the lovely furnishings include Persian rugs and French tapestries — 17th-century supplements by the last owner, Sir Basil Brooke. He also added gables and many windows. You can take a half-hour guided tour.

For the "how to annoy insurance adjusters" file: Hugh Roe O'Donnell, descendant of the O'Donnell clan and 16th-century owner of Donegal Castle, burned down his own family home. Why? To ensure the English, who mounted a great campaign to seize Irish land and great homes, never got their hands on it. It was later rebuilt.

Donegal Town. ☎ 073-22-405. To get there: In Donegal City center. Admission: €2.50 ($2.40) adult, €2 ($1.90) seniors, €1.25 ($1.20) children and students, €6.25 ($5.95) family. Open: June–Sept daily 9:30 a.m.–6:30 p.m. Suggested visit: 1 hour.

The Glebe House and Gallery
Churchill

This house was the pride of art collector Derek Hill, and now the mansion allows visitors to see his grand collection. Hill's taste was diverse, and inside the gallery are works by Picasso and Renoir, as well as Jack Yeats and many other Irish and Italian artists. The decor of the house is an exhibit in itself, with Islamic ceramics, Japanese art, and priceless wallpaper and textiles. The 1828 building is set amid gardens and woods.

Churchill, Letterkenny. ☎ 074-37-071. To get there: From Donegal Town take the N15 north to Ballybofey and then the N13 north into Letterkenny. Admission: €2.50 ($2.40) adult, €2 ($1.90) seniors, €1.25 ($1.20) children and students, €6.25 ($5.95) family. Open: Mid-May to Sept Sat–Thurs 11:00 a.m.–6:30 p.m. Suggested visit: 1½ hours.

Slieve League
Southwest County Donegal

The true fearless traveler shouldn't miss this attraction — an amazing view from the highest sea cliffs in Europe. At Carrick, turn off for the viewing point. There, you can decide whether to take the challenge and walk the ridge or just take in the view from the car.

Southwest County Donegal. To get there: From town, follow the main road, N56. Admission: Free. Suggested visit: Including walk, 2 hours.

Shopping in County Donegal

Donegal Craft Village

Come here to see a collection of professionals working their crafts — pottery, jewelry, uilleann pipes (Irish bagpipes), ceramics, batik, and more.

On the Ballyshannon-Sligo Road, Donegal Town. ☎ *073-23-312.*

Donegal Parian China

You can find this distinctive brand of pottery within a huge visitor center that gives you the opportunity to see craftspeople at work.

On the main Bundoran Road (N15), 500 yards from Ballyshannon. ☎ *072-51-826. Open weekdays, plus Sat and Sun from June until Sept.*

Kennedy of Ardara

This Aran sweater shop also features tweed suits, Irish table linen, cashmere sweaters, and lambswool knitwear.

Ardara (take the N56 northwest from Donegal). ☎ *075-41-106.*

Magee of Donegal

This is the largest fashion store in the county and the best source for the famous Donegal tweed.

On The Diamond in Donegal Town center. ☎ *073-22-660.*

Pub Life in County Donegal

McGroarty's Bar

This wonderful stone building houses a warm and cozy pub that's chock full of atmosphere. You won't find anything dreary about this brightly decorated pub, and the food is fantastic and varied. The music ranges from traditional Irish to folksy ballads on weekends, beginning on Thursday. An extra-pleasant aspect is the nonsmoking room — a rare thing in Ireland!

The Diamond, Donegal Town. ☎ *073-21-049.*

McGinley

This pub was recently renovated but great care was taken to retain its traditional decor and atmosphere. The bar is huge, making plenty of places to pull up a stool. But if you'd rather, the lounge is spacious and comfortable. You can hear music four nights a week — traditional, as well as an Irish favorite: American country-and-western. Pub grub is served all day.

Glenfinn Street, Ballybofey. ☎ *074-31-150.*

Corner Bar

If you're hankering for a pint and some conversation, go to the Corner. This is a no-nonsense Irish pub, where you can find plenty of locals engaged in lively chats who are eager to let you in. Friendliness is a staple of this pub, and the brick interior and smiling faces make it warm and comfortable.

Glenfinn Street, Ballybofey. ☎ *074-31-361.*

Fast Facts: County Donegal

Area Code(s)

County Donegal's area codes (or city codes) are **072, 073, 074, 075,** and **077.**

Emergencies-Hospital

Dial ☎ **999** for all emergencies. Donegal District Hospital is on Upper Main Street (☎ 073-21-105).

Genealogy Resources

Contact Donegal Ancestry, Old Meeting House, Back Lane, Ramelton, Letterkenny (☎ 074-51-266; E-mail: donances@ indigo.ie; Internet: http://indigo. ie-~donances). Fee: €15 ($14.25)

Information

For visitor information go to the Donegal Tourist Office, Quay Street, Donegal (☎ 073-21-148; Internet: www.donegal. ie). Open year-round. For telephone directory assistance, dial ☎ 1190.

Post Office

Donegal Post Office, Tirconnail Street (☎ 073-21-001).

Part VI
Northern Ireland

The 5th Wave   By Rich Tennant

In this part . . .

Welcome to the North! Whether you immediately notice much difference or not, you've entered another country — one that's gotten a bit of a bad reputation after years of political violence. But don't be scared away. Northern Ireland has enjoyed a season of peace not seen in decades. If you choose to visit, I think you'll experience enough history, culture, stunning scenery, and warm hospitality to make the trip well worth your time.

I start this section with Derry City, Northern Ireland's second-largest city and one of the best examples of a walled city in Europe. I cover Derry City as well as County Derry and Counties Fermanagh and Tyrone in Chapter 21.

Next I take you to Belfast and the surrounding County Antrim. As Northern Ireland's largest city, Belfast has all the hotels and restaurants you'd expect, along with streets crammed with people pub-crawling and club-hopping into all hours of the night. It also makes a perfect home base for exploring County Antrim's great attractions. I cover all this and more in Chapter 22.

I end the tour of Northern Ireland with Counties Down and Armagh, where St. Patrick first started the spread of Irish Christianity. You can visit his grave here, but there are lots of other things to see, including an impressive 18th-century mansion surrounded by gardens, a unique aquarium, and some spectacular scenery courtesy of the Mountains of Mourne. For details, turn to Chapter 23.

Chapter 21

Counties Derry, Fermanagh, and Tyrone

. . . .

In This Chapter

▶ Exploring inside and outside Derry's impressive walled city

▶ Finding your roots in the Ulster-American Folk Park

▶ Touring underground caves and rivers

▶ Perusing famous Belleek china

. . . .

*A*surefire way to detect when someone has definite opinions about Britain's presence in Northern Ireland is if they have strong feelings about what to call the main city of County Derry. *Nationalists* — people who think Northern Ireland should be part of the Republic — say "Derry," the name of the area before Britain entered the picture in the 17th century. *Loyalists* — people who are loyal to England's crown — say "Londonderry." In general, most people, intending no political overtone, simply call the town "Derry" because it has half the syllables. However, those in the public eye, like newscasters, often take the middle ground and say "Derry-Londonderry" to avoid any problems.

What's Where?: Derry, Fermanagh, and Tyrone's Major Attractions

Northern Ireland's second-largest city after Belfast, **Derry City,** is framed by huge 17th-century city walls that are about 30-feet thick and a mile in circumference. The walls are in such pristine condition that Derry ranks as one of the best examples of a walled city in Europe. There are also plenty of examples of Georgian architecture in Derry, which surrounds a square called the Diamond. Some other highlights include

Counties Derry, Fermanagh, and Tyrone

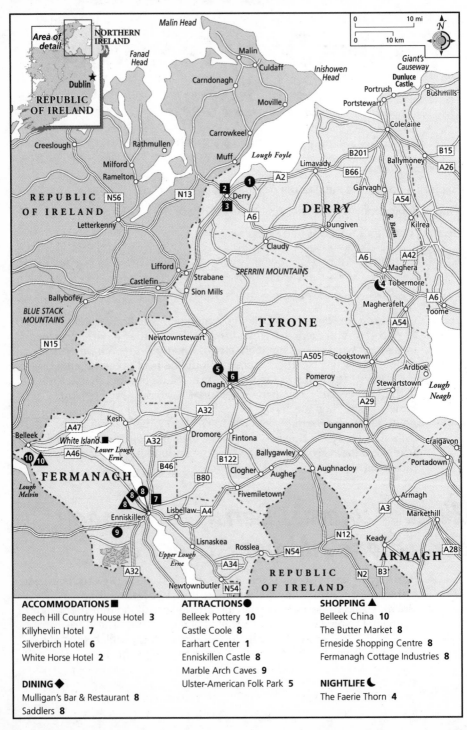

Area of detail

NORTHERN IRELAND

Malin Head

Fanad Head

Malin

Culdaff

Carndonagh

Inishowen Head

Giant's Causeway

Dunluce Castle

Portrush

Bushmills

Portstewart

Moville

Dublin

REPUBLIC OF IRELAND

Carrowkeel

Coleraine

Creeslough

Rathmullen

Muff

Lough Foyle

B201

Ballymoney

B15

Limavady

Milford

A2

B66

A26

Ramelton

Garvagh

REPUBLIC

N56

N13

2

1

Derry

DERRY

A54

OF IRELAND

3

A6

Dungiven

Kilrea

Letterkenny

Claudy

A6

A42

Lifford

SPERRIN MOUNTAINS

Maghera

Castlefin

Strabane

4

Tobermore

Sion Mills

Magherafelt

A6

Ballybofey

Toome

BLUE STACK MOUNTAINS

TYRONE

A54

N15

Newtownstewart

A505

Cookstown

Ardboe

5

Pomeroy

Stewartstown

Lough Neagh

Omagh

6

A29

A32

Dungannon

Kesh

A47

Dromore

Fintona

Craigavon

Belleek

White Island

A46

Lower Lough Erne

A32

Ballygawley

Portadown

10

10

B46

B122

Clogher

FERMANAGH

B80

Augher

Aughnacloy

Lough Melvin

8

8

7

Fivemiletown

Armagh

8

Lisbellaw

A4

A3

Markethill

Enniskillen

9

Lisnaskea

Rosslea

N12

Keady

A28

Upper Lough Erne

N54

ARMAGH

A32

A34

REPUBLIC

N2

B3

Newtownbutler

N54

OF IRELAND

ACCOMMODATIONS ■	ATTRACTIONS ●	SHOPPING ▲
Beech Hill Country House Hotel **3**	Belleek Pottery **10**	Belleek China **10**
Killyhevlin Hotel **7**	Castle Coole **8**	The Butter Market **8**
Silverbirch Hotel **6**	Earhart Center **1**	Erneside Shopping Centre **8**
White Horse Hotel **2**	Enniskillen Castle **8**	Fermanagh Cottage Industries **8**
	Marble Arch Caves **9**	
	Ulster-American Folk Park **5**	**NIGHTLIFE** ☾
DINING ◆		The Faerie Thorn **4**
Mulligan's Bar & Restaurant **8**		
Saddlers **8**		

✔ **St. Columb's Cathedral and Chapter House Museum:** This 1613 Gothic cathedral towers above Derry's city walls.

✔ **Tower Museum:** This museum, housed in a replica 16th-century fort, covers Derry's history from prehistoric times to the present day.

✔ **Earhart Center:** Amelia Earhart landed in Derry in 1932, becoming the first woman to fly solo across the Atlantic, and this center in Ballyarnet will tell you the story.

Further south on the A5 is the town of Omagh, in **County Tyrone,** and past that the quaint **County Fermanagh,** which attracts vacationers for its resortlike qualities. **Lough Erne,** a long, pretty lake, runs the length of County Fermanagh and is dotted with 154 little islands. The highlights of the county include **Enniskillen,** a small town set on an island that connects the upper and lower parts of Lough Erne. Some of the best attractions in Tyrone and Fermanagh are

✔ **Ulster-American Folk Park:** A stop not to be missed! This outdoor folk park traces the roots of Irish emigration to America during the 18th and 19th centuries.

✔ **Marble Arch Caves:** Tour the caves on boats that glide through an underground river while the great cave guides point out rivers, waterfalls, winding passages, and echoing chambers.

✔ **Enniskillen Castle:** The vaults of this 15th-century castle, located in the west end of Enniskillen, hold 15th- and 17th-century models and figurines of old-time castle life.

✔ **Belleek Pottery Factory:** Belleek is Ireland's oldest and most famous pottery, and on these tours you can watch the Belleek craftspeople create the famous fine bone china.

✔ **Castle Coole:** This 18th-century neoclassical-style house is one of the finest of its kind in the country.

Getting to and around Derry, Fermanagh, and Tyrone

The **City of Derry (Eglinton) Airport** (☎ 028-7181-0784) is several miles from the city and serviced by **British Airways Express** (☎ 01496-30-2022). To get to Derry from the airport, take a cab. The fare is around £6 ($9.90) to the city center.

To get to Derry by car from Donegal, take the N15 to Strabane and then take the A5 north. To get to Enniskillen from Sligo, take the N16 (which becomes the A4 in Northern Ireland) east. To get to Omagh from Derry or Strabane, go south on the A5; from Enniskillen go north on the A32.

If you're driving from the Republic into Northern Ireland, make sure you notify your rental-car company; extra insurance may be required.

Northern Ireland Railways (☎ **028-7134-2228**) services Derry year-round, and **Ulsterbus** (☎ **028-7126-2261**) travels year-round to Derry, Omagh, Enniskillen, and other major towns in Counties Derry, Tyrone, and Fermanagh.

Where to Stay in Derry, Fermanagh, and Tyrone

Tower Hotel Derry

$$$ **Derry City, County Derry**

The excellent Tower Irish hotel chain opened the only hotel within the historic city walls in 2002, which means the rooms and amenities are as new as you'll find in the country and the location is the best in the city. The rooms are typical chain-style — nothing fancy, but with plenty of room and comfort. The hotel has a gym and sauna, and the staff is eager to please.

Butcher Street, Derry City, County Derry. ☎ *028-713-71000. Fax: 028-713-71234. Internet:* www.towerhotelgroup.com. *To get there: Just off the Diamond in city center. Rates: £89 ($94.34) double. AE, MC, V.*

The Beech Hill Country House Hotel

$$$ **Derry City, County Derry**

Whether you're strolling the gorgeous grounds of this elegant country house or curling up before the fire with a cup of tea, you'll know this is pampering at its best. Every detail of this hotel exudes style, from the canopy beds to the conservatory dining area. Every room is separately decorated and furnished to the hilt, and the Ardmore Restaurant serves locally caught seafood and homegrown seasonal vegetables. It's just outside of Derry City and within easy driving distance of the region's biggest attractions.

32 Ardmore Rd., Derry City, County Derry. ☎ *028-7134-9279. Fax: 028-7134-5366. Internet:* www.beech-hill.com. *To get there: Take the A6 south out of the city, toward Belfast, and follow signs. Rates: £75–£80 ($123.80–$132) double. AE, MC, V.*

The Trinity Hotel

$$$ **Derry City, County Derry**

This ultra-elegant hotel almost seems out of place in Derry, contrasting with the medieval look of the city. You'll find it simple, yet, despite the reasonable cost, posh. The architecture and materials are modern, but traditional Celtic designs give it a characteristically Irish feel. Although the

Derry City

ACCOMMODATIONS ■
The Trinity Hotel **1**
Tower Hotel Derry **5**

DINING ◆
Schooner's **10**

ATTRACTIONS ●
Bloody Sunday Monument **2**
Derry City Walls **8**
St. Columb's Cathedral and
  Chapter House Museum **7**
Tower Museum **3**

SHOPPING ▲
Richmond Centre **6**
Austins **6**
The Craft Village **4**

NIGHTLIFE ☾
The Metro **9**

rooms aren't the most spacious around, the beds are super-comfortable and the furnishings are simple and sleek. Before you head into Derry City, be sure to check out one of the hotel's three bars, especially the stunning Conservatory Lounge.

22 Strand Rd., Derry City, County Derry. ☎ *028-7127-1271. Fax: 028-7127-1277. To get there: Strand Road is just north of the city center and south of Foyle Bridge. Rates: £80–£100 ($132–$165) double. AE, MC, V.*

The White Horse Hotel
$$ Derry City, County Derry

On the main road to the Giants Causeway in County Antrim (see Chapter 22) and only a few minutes from the airport, this hotel is great for venturing out to see the North. Although the dining and pub life the hotel offers are pretty run-of-the-mill, the rooms are fabulous. They've got canopy beds and porches that lead out to the groomed lawn, and tasteful wallpaper and pine furniture give each room a country feel. There's fishing and golfing nearby.

68 Clooney Rd., Derry City, County Derry (5 miles outside the city). ☎ *028-7186-0606. Fax: 028-7186-0371. To get there: From Derry take the A2 toward Limavady. Rates: £50–£60 ($82.50–$99) double. AE, DC, MC, V.*

The Killyhevlin Hotel
$$$ Killyhevlin, County Fermanagh

Located on the serene and beautiful shore of Lough Erne, The Killyhevlin Hotel provides views of the best this area has to offer, from the lounge and the exceptional restaurant and from your room. Or you can walk just a few steps out of the door and take in the lake up close and personal. Rooms here make you feel immediately welcome, as does the staff. You can get bar snacks all day, and there's a lunchtime buffet.

Dublin Road, Killyhevlin, Enniskillen, County Fermanagh. ☎ *028-6632-3481. Fax: 028-6632-4726. Internet:* www.killyhevlin.com. *To get there: Less than a mile north of Enniskillen, off the A32. Look for the sign. Rates: £80–£95 ($132–$156.75) double. AE, DC, MC, V.*

The Silverbirch Hotel
$$–$$$ Omagh, County Tyrone

This hotel, recently renovated and featuring a beautiful atrium, is by far one of the finest in the mid-Ulster region. Although the hotel has become quite modern, it's fantastically hidden on the outskirts of Gortin Glen National Park, giving it a timeless, rustic feel. The Buttery Grill is known throughout the area for its top-notch cuisine. The friendly and efficient hotel staff may be the highlight of your stay; someone's always on hand to help out.

5 Gortin Rd., Omagh, County Tyrone. ☎ 028-8224-2520. Fax: 028-8224-3360. Internet: www.silverbirchhotel.com. To get there: Just north of Omagh, on the B48. Rates: £35–£82 ($57.75–$135.35) double. AE, DC, MC, V.

Where to Dine in Derry, Fermanagh, and Tyrone

What's the difference between a traditional Irish breakfast and an Ulster Fry? Well, along with your fried egg, sausage, bacon, black pudding, fried tomatoes, and toast you get *soda farls* and *potato cakes*. Soda farls are soft bread, fluffed with soda and buttermilk; potato cakes are made with mashed potatoes, flour, and butter. They're both fried up with the rest of the breakfast and are incredibly good.

But that's only one meal of the day, and you've got two or three still to take care of. Here are some picks that'll make your stomach happy.

Schooner's
$$$–$$$$ Derry City, County Derry   SEAFOOD

Even if the food weren't great, the decor of Schooner's would be enough to make the place popular. (After all, how many restaurants can you name that have a 30-foot schooner incorporated into the furnishings?) But the food *is* great! Seafood dishes like baked filet of trout with hazelnut butter or plaice stuffed with smoked salmon and prawns fill the menu, but non–seafood lovers will love the rest. There's the mushroom stroganoff, for instance, plus various steaks and the Schooner's Specialty, a chicken breast stuffed with broccoli and cheese and wrapped in a puff pastry. The price is right, especially for food of this quality.

59 Victoria Rd., Derry City, County Derry. ☎ 028-7131-1500. To get there: Located on the east bank of the River Foyle. Main courses: £9.95–£13.50 ($16.40–$22.30). AE, MC, V. Open: Daily 8:30 a.m.–10:00 p.m.

Saddlers
$$–$$$ Enniskillen, County Fermanagh   EUROPEAN

Horse lovers will delight at the equestrian atmosphere at Saddlers, where equipment and trappings cover the walls. The food is hearty and varied, from salads to steaks, plus barbecued pork ribs, pizzas, and mixed grills. The restaurant sits above the Horse Show bar, a great place for an after-dinner drink.

66 Belmore St., Enniskillen, County Fermanagh. ☎ 028-6632-6223. To get there: Dublin Road (A4) into town becomes Belmore Street. Main courses: £5.95–£10.95 ($9.80–$18.05). MC, V. Open: Daily noon to 2:30 p.m. and 4:00–10:45 p.m.

Mulligan's Bar & Restaurant
$$$–$$$$ Enniskillen, County Fermanagh
IRISH-INTERNATIONAL

This family-run restaurant serves a wide selection that emphasizes local ingredients. The variety of dishes strikes a balance between local favorites and international cuisine. Everything that reaches the table is homemade, and it shows. For starters, there are savory pâtés and soups, which make way for tasty seafood dishes like local mussels or salmon, or Ulster meat dishes. The atmosphere is inviting and rustic, and there's live music to set the tone for a relaxing meal. Top pick: the Irish stew, which is made with a generous amount of Bushmills whiskey — it may be the best stew you'll ever eat.

33 Darling St., Enniskillen, County Fermanagh. ☎ 028-6632-2059. To get there: Main Street in city center. Main courses: £8–£12 ($13.20–$19.80). MC, V. Open: Daily noon to 3 p.m. and 4–10 p.m.

Exploring Counties Derry, Fermanagh, and Tyrone: The Top Attractions

St. Columb's Cathedral and Chapter House Museum
Derry City, County Derry

This cathedral — named for Saint Columb, founder of Derry — towers above the city walls. There's stained glass inside this Gothic cathedral that depicts the grim tale of one of the city's many sieges, this one involving the Protestants and Jacobites. James I ordered the construction of the cathedral in 1613, and a year later Londoners sent over a bell for the steeple with "Fear God. Honour the King" engraved on it. The Chapter House Museum displays the original keys to the city gates and an audio-visual presentation of the history of Derry City.

London Street, Derry City, County Derry. ☎ 028-7126-7284 or 028-7126-7313. To get there: Inside the city walls south of The Diamond. Admission: £1 ($1.65) per person. Open: March–Oct daily 9 a.m.–1 p.m. and 2–5 p.m.; Nov–Feb daily 9 a.m.–1 p.m. and 2–4 p.m. Suggested visit: 45 minutes.

Tower Museum
Derry City, County Derry

This museum really gets at the heart of Derry, covering its history from prehistoric times to the present day. It's housed in the O'Doherty Tower, a replica of the 16th-century medieval fort that stood in that spot. Upstairs are mementos from the wrecks of the Spanish Armada, and multimedia displays examine the city history, even delving into Northern Ireland's political "Troubles."

Union Hall Place, Derry City, County Derry. ☎ 028-7137-2411. To get there: Inside the city walls, north of The Diamond. Admission: £3.50 ($5.75) per person, £7 ($11.55) family. Open: Oct–June Tues–Sat 10 a.m.–5 p.m.; July–Sept Mon–Sat 10 a.m.– 5 p.m., Sun 9:00 a.m.–5:30 p.m. Suggested visit: 1 hour.

Earhart Center
Ballyarnet, County Derry

Amelia Earhart landed in Derry in 1932, becoming the first woman to fly solo across the Atlantic. To find out more about her historic flight, you can visit the Earhart Center in Ballyarnet.

Ballyarnet, County Derry. ☎ 02871-35-4040. To get there: 3 miles north of Derry City on the A2. Admission: Free. Open: Mon–Thurs 9 a.m.–4 p.m., Fri 9 a.m. to noon. Suggested visit: About an hour.

Marble Arch Caves
Florencecourt, County Fermanagh

Exploring the Marble Arch Caves is a thrill. Visitors tour on boats that glide through an underground river while guides point out waterfalls, winding passages, and echoing chambers. The guides are great, giving detailed information about stalagmites and stalactites and the minerals that coat the walls. The tour includes walking sections, but nothing's dangerous or exhausting.

The Marble Arch Caves are hugely popular, so it's wise to book ahead. Also, it gets pretty chilly "down under," so bring a sweater. If there's been heavy rain, the caves occasionally close for safety reasons, so call if there's been bad weather.

Marlbank Scenic Loop, Florencecourt, County Fermanagh. ☎ 028-6634-8855. To get there: Off the A35, 12 miles south of Enniskillen. When you're in the village of Florencecourt, near the border, there is a loop road that takes you out to the caves, with plenty of signs to point the way. Admission: £5 ($9.05) adults, £3 ($4.95) students and seniors, £2 ($3.30) children. Open: Mid-March to Sept daily 10:00 a.m.– 4:30 p.m. Suggested visit: About 2½ hours.

Enniskillen Castle
Enniskillen, County Fermanagh

This 15th-century castle, once the stronghold of powerful Irish chieftains, sits majestically in the west end of town, overlooking the River Erne. The castle contains a county museum with exhibits on the area's history, wildlife, and landscape, as well as the museum of the Royal Inniskilling Fusiliers. There are also models and figurines depicting old-time castle life.

Castle Barracks, Enniskillen, County Fermanagh. ☎ 028-6632-5000. To get there: West end of town across Castle Bridge from the A4. Admission: £2 ($3.30) adults,

£1.50 ($2.50) seniors and students, £1 ($1.65) children, £5 ($8.25) family of two adults and two children. Open: May, June, and Sept Mon and Sat 2–5 p.m., Tues–Fri 10 a.m.–5 p.m.; July and Aug Sat–Mon 2–5 p.m., Tues–Fri 10 a.m.–5 p.m.; Oct–April Mon 2–5 p.m., Tues–Fri 10 a.m.–5 p.m. Suggested visit: 1½ hours.

Belleek Pottery Tours
Belleek, County Fermanagh

Belleek is Ireland's oldest and most famous pottery works, and on these tours you can watch the highly trained craftspeople create the famous fine bone china and then pick up some of the delicate ivory pottery to take home. There are guided tours, a museum, and a theater that shows a video about china making. The showroom tours (an overview of what the company makes and sells) run only on weekdays and last 30 minutes.

Main Street, Belleek, County Fermanagh. ☎ 028-6865-8501. To get there: Take the A46 northeast from Enniskillen. Admission: Free. Tours £1 ($1.65). Visitor center open: April–June and Sept Mon–Fri 9 a.m.–6 p.m., Sat 10 a.m.–6 p.m., Sun 2–6 p.m.; July and Aug Mon–Fri 9 a.m.–8 p.m., Sat 10 a.m.–6 p.m., Sun 11 a.m.–6 p.m.; Oct Mon–Fri 9:00 a.m.–5:30 p.m., Sat 10:00 a.m.–5:30 p.m., Sun 2–6 p.m.; Nov–March Mon–Fri 9:00 a.m.–5:30 p.m. Tours: Mon–Fri 9:30 a.m.–12:15 p.m. and 2:15–4:15 p.m (Fri last tour at 3:30 p.m.). Suggested visit: 1 hour (including tour).

Castle Coole
Enniskillen, County Fermanagh

This 18th-century neoclassical-style house was completely refurbished by the state, resulting in its becoming one of the finest of its kind in the country. Most of the stone fittings and fixtures are from England and, extraordinarily, almost all the original furniture is in place. The opulent State Bedroom has a bed that was specially made for King George IV to use during his 1821 visit to Ireland. You'll also notice a Chinese-style sitting room and gorgeous woodwork and fireplaces throughout.

Off the Belfast-Enniskillen Road (A4), Enniskillen, County Fermanagh. ☎ 028-6632-2690. To get there: About a mile out of Enniskillen, just off the Belfast-Enniskillen Road (A4). Admission: £2.60 ($4.30) adults, £1.30 ($2.15) children, £6.50 ($10.75) family. Open: April Mon–Fri 1–6 p.m., Sat and Sun 5–9 p.m.; May–Aug Fri–Wed 1–6 p.m.; Sept Mon–Fri 1–6 p.m. Suggested visit: 1 hour.

Ulster-American Folk Park
Castletown, County Tyrone

This immensely interesting folk park traces the roots of Irish emigration to America during the 18th and 19th centuries. It's outdoors, and visitors walk through re-creations of Irish villages and town streets, and of an emigrant ship. The park also exhibits re-creations of the places Irish emigrants went to as well, like an American street and a log cabin. The park sits on land where Thomas Mellon, who founded the Pittsburgh banking dynasty, lived as a boy.

The Ulster-American Folk Park has an excellent lineup of events to appeal to American visitors young and old alike. These include Independence Day celebrations in July, an Appalachian and Bluegrass music festival in September, and a Halloween Festival in October.

Mellon Road, Castletown, Camphill, Omagh, County Tyrone. ☎ 028-8224-3292. To get there: Off the A5, 3 miles north of Omagh. Look for the signs. Admission: £3.50 ($5.75) adults, £1.70 ($2.80) students and children, £10 ($16.50) family. Open: Oct–March Mon–Fri 10:30 a.m.–5:00 p.m.; April–Sept Mon–Sat 11:00 a.m.–6:30 p.m., Sun 11:30 a.m.–7:00 p.m. Suggested visit: 2 hours.

More Fun Things to Do: The Top Derry Landmarks

Check out the following landmarks while touring Derry:

✔ **Derry City Walls:** At 26 feet high and about 30 feet thick, the walls encircling the city are an impressive sight and make Derry one of Europe's only completely walled-in cities. They were built in 1618 and succeeded in keeping Derry safe from many attacks. In fact, the walls have never been breached and are so impenetrable that they earned Derry the nickname "The Maiden City."

✔ **Bloody Sunday Monument:** Outside Butcher's Gate in the old city walls is an area known as the Bogside. This is where the Bloody Sunday massacre occurred in 1972, in which British soldiers shot 13 demonstrators dead. There's a moving monument on Rossville Street that honors them. The event inspired Brit Paul McCartney's song "Give Ireland Back to the Irish," which has become an unofficial anthem of the Irish struggle for independence, as well as the song "Sunday, Bloody Sunday" by U2. Nearby is the "Free Derry Corner," an area of detailed and artistic wall murals. The most famous is the "You Are Now Entering Free Derry" mural.

Joining an Organized Tour

Guinness Essential Walking Tour of Historic Derry

This award-winning walking tour covers the city, pointing out major historical sites. It's run by the North's only member of the Association of Approved Tour Guides of Ireland.

Tours depart from the Tourist Information Centre at 10:30 a.m. and 2:30 p.m. daily between May and Oct. Information: Tourist Information Centre, 44 Foyle St., Derry, County Derry. ☎ 028-7126-7284. Price: £3 ($4.95) adults, children free. Price includes refreshments.

Lough Erne Boat Tour

You can take a boat tour of Upper Lough Erne River aboard the 63-seater *Kestrel*. The trip is fully narrated and covers a good deal of the nature and history of the lake. It includes a half-hour stop at Devenish Island, where you can get off and explore some ruins.

Trips last just under two hours and depart from Round O Jetty, Enniskillen. Tours daily in July and Aug at 10:30 a.m., 2:15 p.m., and 4:15 p.m.; in May and June on Sun 2:30 p.m.; and in Sept on Tues, Sat, and Sun at 2:30 p.m. Information: Erne Tours Ltd., 84 Drumeer Rd., Maguiresbridge. ☎ 028-6632-2882. Price: £3 ($4.95) adults, £1.50 ($2.50) children under 14.

Charabanc Horse-Drawn Carriage Tours

This is the way to see the city! Get a tour of Derry while riding in a horse-drawn charabanc carriage.

Call ☎ 028-7127-1886 to be picked up anywhere in the city center. First tour begins at 10 a.m., and then every hour thereafter until sunset. Runs daily May 1–Oct 1. Information: Contact Martin McGowan, ☎ 028-7127-1886. Price: Varies depending on the phase of the moon (or Martin's whim). Ask when you call.

The Kingfisher Trail Holiday Guide

Anyone interested in cycling around Northern Ireland should pick up this guide, which allows you to custom-pick the route you'd like to make, no matter what level of cycling skill you have. With the guide, you can book accommodations along the trail and choose activities to do along the way. The trail loops around lakes, goes through forests, and winds into villages. Your tour can last anywhere from half a day to eight days. You can also create a multi-activity vacation by adding canoeing, jet-skiing, mountain biking, or archery into your cycling tour.

You can get the guide from the Tourist Information Centre, Wellington Road, Enniskillen, County Fermanagh (☎ 028-6632-0121).

Shopping

In Derry, the best shopping is found in the inner city, in the **Richmond Centre,** a modern mall facing The Diamond and featuring more than 30 shops and boutiques. Enniskillen's large shopping complex, **Erneside Shopping Centre,** is a bi-level modern mall off Wellington Road. And don't forget you can pick up some Belleek china at the factory's showroom. (For details, see "Exploring Counties Derry, Fermanagh, and Tyrone: The Top Attractions," earlier in this chapter.)

Austins

This Victorian-style department store is a city landmark. It specializes in clothes, perfume, china, crystal, and linens. The coffee shop on the third floor has a great view of Derry City.

The Diamond, Derry City, County Derry. ☎ *028-7126-1817.*

The Butter Market

This historic market has studio workshops that make and sell all sorts of local crafts, including ceramic jewelry, screen prints, Celtic-inspired statuary, and leather goods. The cobble courtyard is nice just for browsing.

Enniskillen, County Fermanagh. ☎ *028-6632-4499.*

The Craft Village

Painstakingly restored, this little "village" has loads of craft shops specializing in a variety of handmade Irish products. There's also a restaurant and coffee shop.

City center, Derry City, County Derry. ☎ *028-7126-0329.*

Fermanagh Cottage Industries

Here's where you'll find traditional handmade Irish crafts, like blackthorn *shillelaghs* (walking sticks), Celtic jewelry, and hand-cut glass.

14 East Bridge St., Enniskillen, County Fermanagh. ☎ *028-6632-2260.*

Pulling a Pint: Pub Life

Want to hear traditional Irish music in Derry? Head to **Waterloo Street,** just outside the city walls in front of Butcher and Castle Gates. Some of the best pubs for informal sessions lie along this route, including **Dungloe Bar** (☎ 028-7126-7761), **Bound for Boston** (☎ 028-7126-6351), **Castle Bar** (☎ 028-7126-3118), and **Peadar O'Donnell's** (☎ 028-7137-2318).

The Faerie Thorn

Two gorgeous gardens are the highlight of this traditional pub, which dates back to the 1600s and sits at the feet of the Sperrin Mountains. It used to be a grocery and pawn shop. The gardens have spectacular views of the countryside. Sit with a pint and take it all in. As for the food, you'll be ruined by the steak-and-Guinness pie.

14 Main St., Tobermore, County Derry. ☎ *028-7964-4385.*

The Metro

Plenty of little alcoves and mementos from across the globe make the Metro an interesting stop. The pub sits in the shadow of Derry's old city walls and serves a mean beef Guinness stew.

3–4 Bank Place, Derry City, County Derry. ☎ *028-7126-7401.*

Fast Facts: Counties Derry, Fermanagh, and Tyrone

Area Code

The area code (or city code) for Derry, Fermanagh, and Tyrone is **028**.

Emergencies

Dial ☎ **999** for all emergencies.

Genealogy Resources

Contact The Genealogy Centre, 4–22 Butcher St., Derry, County Derry (☎ 028-7137-3177; Fax: 01504-3-3177), which has a computerized database with records as far back as the early 17th century, or Heritage World, 26 Market Sq., Dungannon, County Tyrone (☎ 01868-72-4187).

Information

For visitor information in Derry, go to the tourist office at 44 Foyle St., Derry (☎ 028-7137-7577), open year-round. It can also provide reservation services. In County Tyrone, contact the Omagh Tourist Information Centre at 1 Market St., Omagh, County Tyrone (☎ 028-8225-0033; Fax: 028-8225-1744; E-mail: tourism@omagh.gov.uk; Internet: www.omagh.gov.uk-tourism.htm). The Fermanagh Tourist Information Centre is located on Wellington Road, Enniskillen (☎ 028-7032-3110). For telephone directory assistance, dial ☎ 192.

Chapter 22

Belfast and County Antrim

● ●

In This Chapter

▶ Getting a room with a view along the coast

▶ Finding the best places to eat or just have a pint

▶ Bringing out your inner adventurer

▶ Taking a *Titanic* (or other) tour of the city

● ●

*W*hat do you think of when you first hear the name Belfast? A fantastic city surrounded by gorgeous and striking scenic drives, charming little towns, and amazing natural sights?

No, you probably think of news stories about sectarian violence. And although it's true that the region has seen its share of "Troubles" for many years, it's also true that things aren't what they were five or ten years ago. Belfast isn't the militarized city it once was, though there is still some tension. The peace accords signed in 1998 prove that there is a real desire for stability in the region, but old wounds take a long time to heal.

Beyond politics and religion, beyond intolerance and nationalism, there's one undeniable fact about Northern Ireland: It's one of the most beautiful areas in the country.

What's Where?: Belfast and County Antrim's Major Attractions

Belfast, Ireland's second-largest city after Dublin, sits at the southern end of County Antrim. It's an architectural delight, with grand Victorian buildings among the stretches of shops. Much like Dublin, the city is having a renaissance of sorts. It's a cosmopolitan place, with pubs and restaurants crammed with people until the wee hours. Highlights include

County Antrim

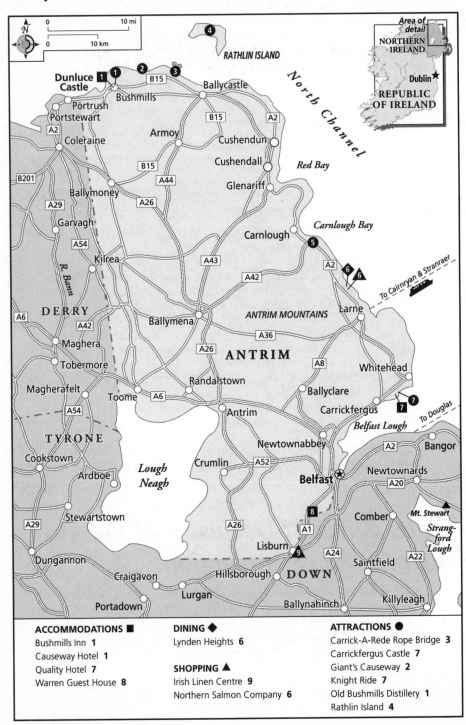

ACCOMMODATIONS ■
Bushmills Inn 1
Causeway Hotel 1
Quality Hotel 7
Warren Guest House 8

DINING ◆
Lynden Heights 6

SHOPPING ▲
Irish Linen Centre 9
Northern Salmon Company 6

ATTRACTIONS ●
Carrick-A-Rede Rope Bridge 3
Carrickfergus Castle 7
Giant's Causeway 2
Knight Ride 7
Old Bushmills Distillery 1
Rathlin Island 4

✔ **The Belfast Zoo:** This zoo has a children's farm, an island of spider monkeys, a Polar Bear Canyon, and much more.

✔ **Ulster Museum:** Northern Ireland's national museum has a collection that ranges from local history to ancient artifacts, plus works of art by Francis Bacon and Henry Moore.

✔ **Bailey's Belfast Pub Tour:** Bailey's Irish Cream hosts a good pub tour that visits six of Ireland's finest pubs.

To travel north out of the city toward the finest attractions around **County Antrim,** I suggest driving along the **Antrim coast** on the A2. The route takes you to **Carrickfergus,** where you can visit **Carrickfergus Castle,** the best example of a Norman fortified castle in Ireland.

Continuing up the A2, a day's drive will take you past gorgeous scenery — both the coastline on the right and the green landscape on the left. Eventually you'll reach the **Causeway Coast,** where sights to see include **Giant's Causeway,** the **Bushmills Distillery,** and for the adventurous, the **Carrick-A-Rede Rope Bridge.**

Getting to Belfast and County Antrim

Belfast International Airport (☎ **028-9448-4848**) is about 19 miles from the city. British Airways, British Midland, and Aer Lingus fly into the airport daily. **Belfast City Airport** (☎ **028-9045-7745**) handles flights within the country. Take the Airbus from Belfast International Airport to get to the city center. The fare is £4.10 ($6.75). From Belfast City Airport, take a cab. The fare is around £4 ($6.60).

Another option if you're coming from Britain or Scotland is the ferry. The **Argyll & Antrim Steam Packet** (☎ **0870-552-3523**) makes the trip between Campbeltown and Ballycastle, County Antrim, in under three hours. Call for bookings. Other ferry services include **SeaCat** (☎ **01208-81-2508**), which travels between Stranraer, Scotland, and Belfast; **P&O European Ferries** (☎ **0990-98-0980**), which travels between Cairnryan, England, and Larne, County Antrim; and **Norse Irish Ferries** (☎ **0151-944-1010**), between Belfast and London (though this trip takes a whopping 11 hours). All ferries can carry vehicles.

If you're coming by car from Dublin take the N1 (which becomes the A1) north to Belfast. To get to the Antrim Coast from Belfast, take the A2, which runs along the entire coast. If you're driving from the Republic into Northern Ireland make sure you notify your rental-car company because extra insurance may be required. Rental cars available in Belfast include **Avis** (☎ **028-9024-0404**), **Budget** (☎ **028-9023-0700**), **Hertz** (☎ **028-9073-2451**), and **National** (☎ **028-9032-5520**).

Northern Ireland Railways (☎ **028-9066-8258**; Internet: www.nirailways.co.uk) services County Antrim extensively. Belfast Central Railway Station is located on East Bridge Street. **Ulsterbus** (☎ **028-9033-7004**) travels year-round to Belfast, Larne, Ballycastle, Bushmills, and other major towns in County Antrim. The main bus stations in Belfast are Europa Bus Centre on Glengall Street and Langanside Bus Centre near the rail station.

Getting Around Belfast and County Antrim

Unlike most towns in Ireland, Belfast is accessible by car. Parking is widely available and meters are used for pay parking. If you're walking Belfast, consider investing in an all-day bus ticket. **Belfast Citybus** (☎ **028-9024-6485**) operates throughout the city. Most buses depart from Donegall Square in the city center. Exact change is required. Multijourney tickets are available at most newsagents.

You can also get around by bike. **Recycle,** 1–5 Albert Square (☎ **028-9031-3113**), rents bikes and provides helmets, locks, and delivery to your accommodation. **Irish Cycle Tours** (☎ **028-9064-2222**) will do you one better by renting you a bike and then taking you on a tour of the city. If you need a cab, you'll find **taxi ranks** at Central Station, both bus stations, and at City Hall. The metered cabs in Northern Ireland are standardized London-style black taxis with yellow disks on the windshield. I recommend you take those rather than a non-meter cab, where your foreign accent may cost you extra.

Where to Stay in Belfast and around County Antrim

Some Belfast hotels have lower rates for the weekends than during midweek. While business people are at home on weekends, you can benefit from cheap rooms at great hotels in the heart of the city.

Ash-Rowan Guest House
$$ Belfast

This beautiful Victorian row home is tucked into a quiet, tree-lined avenue and offers a comfortable, serene place to stay. All four stories are decorated with country-style furniture, antiques, and fresh flowers from the garden in back. You have a choice of eight different breakfasts here, including the traditional (and filling) Ulster fry.

Belfast

ACCOMMODATIONS
Ash-Rowan Guest House **25**
Benedicts of Belfast **22**
Europa Hotel **17**
Madison's Hotel **24**
The McCausland Hotel **7**

DINING
Aero **19**
Benedicts of Belfast **22**
Copperfields Bar & Restaurant **11**
Harveys **20**
Nick's Warehouse **5**
Roscoff **21**

ATTRACTIONS
Belfast Zoo **1**
City Hall **13**
Ulster Museum **26**
W5 **6**

SHOPPING
Craftworks, Bedford House **15**
Irish Linen Stores **12**

NIGHTLIFE
The Beaten Docket **18**
Crown Liquor Saloon **16**
Duke of York **3**
Empire **23**
Front Page **4**
Kelly's Cellars **10**
Kitchen Bar **8**
Madisons **24**
Madden's **2**
The Manhattan Bar **22**
The Morning Star **9**
The Shenanigan Rooms **14**

Church ⛪
Information ⓘ

12 Windsor Ave., Belfast. ☎ *028-9066-1758. Fax: 028-9066-3227. To get there: From city center, follow Bedford Street south past Queen's University and make a right on Windsor. Rates: £60 ($99) double. MC, V.*

Benedicts of Belfast
$$–$$$ Belfast

Only a few years old, Benedicts has been hailed by the *Irish Times* as one of the best recent additions to Belfast. Rooms are big and airy and decorated in minimalist style, but the real attraction is the Gothic-looking bar and restaurant, with intricate woodwork, chandeliers, and stained glass. Also, it's just minutes' walk to Queens University, the Ulster Museum, and a great shopping district.

7–21 Bradbury Place, Shaftsbury Square, Belfast. ☎ *028-9059-1999. Fax: 028-9059-1990. Internet:* www.benedictshotel.co.uk. *To get there: From the Westlink (M1) take Grovesnor Road toward City Hall, go right on Great Victoria Street. Rates: £70 ($115.50) Mon–Thurs, £50 ($82.50) Fri–Sun, double. AE, MC, V.*

Europa Hotel
$$$–$$$$ Belfast

The rooms in this world-class hotel are decked to the nines — huge beds and sofas and beautiful oak furnishings. Despite this, you'll probably spend most of your time in the palatial Gallery Lounge or the cozy, traditional Lobby Bar, which features nightly music sessions. This hotel is a veritable landmark and is just a short walk to the heart of Belfast. President Bill Clinton stayed here on his historic trip to the country.

Great Victoria Street, Belfast. ☎ *028-9032-7000. Fax: 028-9032-7800. Internet:* www.hastingshotel.com. *To get there: From the Westlink (M1) take Grovesnor Road toward City Hall, go right on Great Victoria Street. Rates: £158 ($260.70) Mon–Thurs, £80 ($132) Fri–Sun, double. AE, DC, MC, V. Weekend price doesn't include breakfast.*

Madison's Hotel
$$–$$$ Belfast

This terminally stylish hotel sits on a tree-lined street in Belfast's university district, so plenty of restaurants and shops are right there. This place really epitomizes the hipness of Belfast, where European style meets casual Irish taste. Rooms have all the best amenities, like satellite TV and safe-deposit boxes. The artsy-looking restaurant has been acclaimed by just about every food critic.

59–63 Botanic Ave., Belfast. ☎ *028-9033-0040. Fax: 028-9032-8007. Internet:* www.madisonshotel.com. *To get there: From the Westlink (M1) take Grovesnor Road toward City Hall, go right on Great Victoria Street. From the square, pick up Botanic Avenue. Rates: £75 ($123.75) Mon–Thurs, £60 ($99) Fri–Sun, double. AE, MC, V.*

The McCausland Hotel
$$$ Belfast

This hotel, the newest bid in the one-upmanship of new and trendy Belfast hotels, is probably the best, maintaining the classic feel of an old hotel with the modern bells and whistles of a new one. The rooms are quite large (which is good because the height-of-comfort beds are as well), the television has cable, the towel rack is heated, and you even have a complimentary membership to a local gym. A big treat in the bathrooms is the exclusive use of Neutrogena bath products. The staff is one of the friendliest and best trained I've ever seen and the breakfasts are feasts that will keep you full until dinner. Everything about the place is of the highest quality.

34–38 Victoria St., Belfast. ☎ *028-9022-0215. Fax: 028-9022-0220. Internet:* www.mccauslandhotel.com. *To get there: From the M3 take the Queen's Bridge across the river and make a right onto Victoria. Rates: £140–£180 ($231–$297). AE, DC, MC, V.*

Quality Hotel
$$$–$$$$ Carrickfergus

Outfitted with Mediterranean stylings, this luxury hotel has a lot of the grandeur of its American counterparts. All rooms are deluxe, with king-sized beds and plenty of space, and there are incredible suites with Jacuzzis. Some rooms have views of the water — on a clear day you can see Scotland. Mac's Pub is traditional-looking and cozy, and the Boardwalk Restaurant is sleek and modern — the chef prepares your meal at an island in the center of the dining room. The hotel is only 20 minutes from Belfast.

75 Belfast Rd., Carrickfergus, County Antrim. ☎ *028-9336-4556. Fax: 028-9335-1620. To get there: Downtown, near Carrickfergus Castle. Rates: £120–£170 ($198–$280.50) double. AE, DC, MC, V.*

The Bushmills Inn
$$$–$$$$ Bushmills

The warm glow from a turf fire greets you when you enter this fantastic inn. Then come the grand staircase, cozy oil lamps, and curious antiques that line the halls. The quaint, individually decorated rooms in the Coaching Inn are complimented by the much larger cottage-style rooms in the Mill House on the banks of the River Bush. The round library and the oak-beamed loft will tempt you to skip sightseeing for a day. Don't pass up excellent Irish coffees (made, of course, with premium Bushmills whiskey) by the fire or a superb meal in the dining room. All around, an incredible place.

9 Dunluce Rd. (A2), Bushmills, County Antrim. ☎ *028-2073-2339. Fax: 028-2073-2048. Internet:* www.bushmillsinn.com. *To get there: On the North Antrim Coast.*

Bushmills Inn is located on the A2 (called Main Street in Bushmills) on the banks of the Bush River. Rates: £68–£178 ($102–$267) double. AE, MC, V.

The Causeway Hotel
$$$ Bushmills

Located right next to the famed Giant's Causeway, this hotel's view of the spectacular coast cannot be beaten. The rooms are large, but the furnishings aren't remarkable. That won't matter, though, because you'll be on the tip of the Antrim Coast and spending all your time looking at the amazing scenery! This old, family-run hotel dates back to 1836, and although it's been restored and has modern conveniences, it hasn't lost its feel of the old days.

40 Causeway Rd., Bushmills, County Antrim. ☎ 028-2073-1226. To get there: Off the A2, follow signs to Giant's Causeway. Rates: £65 ($107.25) double. MC, V.

Warren Guesthouse
$$ Dunmurry

Mary Hughes *is* the Warren Guesthouse. She'll pick you up from the airport, take care of your every need and make sure you're well rested and fed before she sees you off. It's like staying at your mother's house without any of the prying or guilt. Located on the River Ferriaghy and containing three spacious luxury rooms (better book ahead) at non-luxury prices, this a great place from which to explore nearby Belfast and the Antrim coast.

10 Thornhill Rd., Dunmurry, Belfast. ☎ 028-9061-1702. Fax: 028-9062-0654. E-mail: mary@warrenguesthouse.freeserve. To get there: From Belfast take the A1 south toward Lisburn to Kingsway. Rates: £50 ($75) double.

Where to Dine in Belfast and around County Antrim

Aero
$$$ Belfast INTERNATIONAL

Stylish, modern decor gives Aero a crisp feel, and its big windows look out over Belfast's busy streets. The menu is difficult to classify — dishes hail from all over the globe and are uniquely and creatively prepared. Excellent starters include chicken spring rolls with black bean and ginger dressing or *crostini* of Italian Coppa ham with moon-dried tomatoes. Don't miss the spinach, brie, and sun-dried tomato *samosas*.

44 Bedford St., Belfast. ☎ 028-9024-4844. To get there: From the Westlink (M1) take Grovesnor Road to Bedford Street. Main courses: £9.25–£11.25 ($15.25–$18.55). AE, MC, V. Open: Daily 5:00–10:30 p.m.

Benedicts of Belfast
$$$–$$$$ Belfast EUROPEAN

Intricate woodwork, brick, and stone give this restaurant an old-world feel. The interior is beautiful, but the food is to die for. Dishes like seared loin of wild boar on white crab mash with tarragon and prawn cream and red pepper oil are for the adventurous eaters, but there are also old standbys (like honey and mustard–marinated pork cutlets) done in a new and creative way. Save room for the mouthwatering white chocolate and caramel cheesecake.

7–21 Bradbury Place, Shaftsbury Square, Belfast. ☎ 028-9059-1999. To get there: From the Westlink (M1) take Grovesnor Road toward City Hall, go right on Great Victoria Street. Main courses: £9.95–£13.50 ($16.40–$22.30). AE, MC, V. Open: Mon–Sat noon to 2:30 p.m. and 5:00–10:30 p.m., Sun noon to 4 p.m. and 5:00–9:30 p.m.

Copperfields Bar & Restaurant
$–$$$ Belfast IRISH

You can't beat the location or the prices at this great restaurant. The food, crafted by chef Arthur Corry, is varied but focuses mainly on traditional Irish dishes — with fantastic flair. Specials change daily and are always creative, and all ingredients are fresh and local. What makes this place so popular, in addition to the food, are the comfy sofas and cozy booths.

9 Fountain St., Belfast. ☎ 028-9024-7367. To get there: From the Westlink (M1) take Divis Street and a right on Fountain Street. Main courses: £4–£10 ($6.60–$16.50). AE, DC, MC, V. Open: Sun–Wed 11:30 a.m.–8:00 p.m., Thurs–Sat 11:30 a.m.–9:00 p.m.

Harveys
$$–$$$ Belfast AMERICAN

Feeling homesick? One foot into Harveys and you'll be transported back to the ol' U.S. of A. American flags adorn the walls and the menu is chock-full of favorites from home. For a break from stews and sausages, you can have burgers, pizza, tacos, and steaks, and the house specialty is the "Frisco Bay," a mixture of shrimp, crab claws, lobster, and mussels in a scampi sauce.

95 Great Victoria St., Belfast. ☎ 028-9023-3433. To get there: From the Westlink (M1) take Grovesnor Road toward City Hall, go right on Great Victoria Street. Main courses: £4.95–£8.50 ($8.15–$14.05). MC, V. Open: Mon–Thurs and Sun 5:00–11:30 p.m., Fri and Sat 5 p.m. to midnight.

Nick's Warehouse
$$–$$$$ Belfast INTERNATIONAL

Set in an old warehouse, this restaurant exudes charm, and despite the size of the place, it is quite intimate. The service is wonderful (I recommend you let them choose something for you if you can't decide). The menu changes frequently, but you won't be disappointed with the options.

35 Hill St., Belfast. ☎ 028-9043-9690. To get there: From the Westlink (M1) take Divis Street and a left on Skipper Street. Main courses: £5.95–£18.50 ($9.80–$30.55). AE, DC, MC, V. Open: Mon–Fri noon to 3 p.m., Tues–Sat 6–9 p.m.

Roscoff
$$$$ Belfast   SEAFOOD

The decor is simple at this sleek restaurant, with frosted glass, black-and-white furnishings, and walls filled with modern art. But the food's not so simple. Much of it is seeped in citrus tastes, reminiscent of the Mediterranean. Try the steamed seafood platter of salmon, mako, monkfish, sole, prawns, and lobster; or the filet of salmon with asparagus and chervil.

7 Lesley House, Shaftsbury Square, Belfast. ☎ 028-9023-0356. To get there: From the Westlink (M1) take Grovesnor Road toward City Hall, go right on Great Victoria Street. Main courses: £29.95 ($49.40) set menu. AE, DC, MC, V. Open: Mon–Fri 12:30–2:15 p.m. and Mon–Sat 6:30–10:15 p.m.

Lynden Heights
$$$–$$$$ Ballygarry   IRISH

Situated on the southern end of the Glens of Antrim, this restaurant probably has the best view of any restaurant on the Northern Coast. The staff is friendly and chatty, and the wine list is as good as it is long. Regional dishes like duck, pheasant, and salmon fill the menu, and everything's enhanced by fresh local produce. This is a wonderful stop for anyone driving the coast road, both for a delicious meal and a chance to see the view at leisure.

97 Drumnagreagh Rd., Ballygally, County Antrim. ☎ 028-2858-3560. To get there: On the Antrim Coast Road, off the A2 on the B148. Main courses: £10–£18 ($16.50–$29.70). AE, MC, V. Open: Wed–Sat 5:00–9:15 p.m. and Sun 12:30–8:00 p.m.

Exploring Belfast and County Antrim

Most of the attractions in this section are around County Antrim rather than in Belfast itself, but Belfast is a great city to walk around and explore, and also makes an ideal base for visiting the rest of the County.

The top attractions

Belfast Zoo
Belfast

This zoo includes a Children's Farm, an island of spider monkeys, an enclosure for primates and other African animals, a Polar Bear Canyon, and pools for penguins and sea lions, to name a few. The zoo houses many endangered animals, and it faces a fantastic view of Belfast Lough. You can have lunch in the Ark Restaurant.

Antrim Road, Belfast. ☎ 028-9077-6277. To get there: Take Donegall Street from the city center north and go right on Antrim Road. Bus: 45, 46, 47, 48, 49, 50, 51. Admission: £4.40 ($7.25) adult, £2.20 ($3.65) child. Open: April–Sept daily 10 a.m.– 5 p.m.; Oct–March 10:00 a.m.–3:30 p.m. Suggested visit: 2 hours.

City Hall
Belfast

Modeled on St. Paul's Cathedral in London, Belfast's City Hall was built in 1888 after Queen Victoria conferred city status on Belfast. The building is made of Portland stone with a central copper dome that rises 173 feet into the sky and is visible for miles. In front, there's a statue of the queen and a memorial to the victims of the *Titanic,* which was built in a Belfast shipyard.

Donegall Square, Belfast. ☎ 028-9032-0202, ext. 2618. Admission: Free tours of the interior available. Tour times: June–Sept Mon–Fri 10:30 a.m., 11:30 a.m., 2:30 p.m.; Sat 2:30 p.m. Oct–May Mon–Sat 2:30 p.m. Otherwise by arrangement. Reservations required. Suggested visit: 45 minutes.

W5: Whowhatwherewhenwhy
Belfast

The newest museum in Belfast is this science and art complex with a name that evokes the fun of the place. Jutting out over the city's waterfront down at the docklands, this flashy steal and neon complex is also home to the Belfast Giants, the city's ice-hockey team. From hands-on lie detectors to moving tennis ball art, the place is a wonder for all ages. Be sure to explore the Tomb of Homunculus Hibericus, the cabinet of wonders made with actual bones!

2 Queen's Quay, Belfast (in the Odyssey Center). ☎ 028-9046-7700. Internet: www. w5online.co.uk. *To get there: Cross Queen Elizabeth Bridge from city center, make the first left, and follow instructions on parking. Admission: £5.50 ($8.25) adult, £3.50 ($5.25) child. Open: Mon–Fri 10 a.m.–6 p.m.; Sat–Sun noon to 6 p.m. Suggested visit: 2 hours.*

Giant's Causeway
Bushmills

It's likely you'll never see another site as strange and awesome as the Giant's Causeway, a 3-mile stretch of roughly 40,000 tightly packed, mostly hexagonal basalt rock columns — some up to 40 feet tall — that jut up from the foot of a cliff and eventually disappear under the sea. The experts will tell you the Causeway was formed by an ancient volcanic eruption, but according to legend, Finn MacCool built the causeway as a path across the sea to a rival giant in Scotland, where there are similar formations. (An aside: In 1842, the writer William Thackeray noted in his *Irish Scetch Book,* "Mon Dieu! And I have traveled a hundred and fifty miles to see that?" Just goes to show, even the eighth wonder of the world can't please everybody!)

44 Causeway Rd., Bushmills, County Antrim. ☎ *028-2073-1855. To get there: Off the A2 along the North Antrim Coast. Bus Eireann (☎ 071-60-066) takes a day tour of Giant's Causeway from Donegal Bus Station for £9 ($13.30) adult, £7 ($10.35) child July and Aug. Admission: Free. Open: Mid-March to May daily 11 a.m.–5 p.m.; June daily 11:00 a.m.–5:30 p.m.; July–Aug daily 10 a.m.–7 p.m.; Sept–Oct Mon–Fri 11 a.m.–5 p.m., Sat–Sun 10:30 a.m.–5:30 p.m. Suggested visit: 45 minutes to 1 hour.*

The Old Bushmills Distillery
Bushmills

A thorough and well-guided tour of the world's oldest distillery awaits you at Bushmills. One highlight: a room that's so heady with whiskey fumes the workers have to get a ride home at the end of the day because they've inhaled so much alcohol! (No fear; a couple minutes won't affect you.) The shop has every Bushmills product you can imagine, from fudge to golf towels, and of course every kind of whiskey they make. The tour ends with a taste test.

Main Street, Bushmills, County Antrim. ☎ *028-2073-1521. To get there: On the A2 along the North Antrim Coast. Admission: £2.50 ($4.15) adults, £2 ($3.30) seniors and students, £1 ($1.65) children. Open: Jan–May and Sept–Dec Mon–Thurs 9 a.m. to noon and 1:30–3:30 p.m., Fri 9 a.m. to noon; June–Aug Mon–Thurs 9 a.m.–4 p.m. Suggested visit: 2½ hours.*

Carrick-A-Rede Rope Bridge
Larrybane

Here's one for the Indiana Jones in all of us! This heart-stopping rope bridge, spanning a chasm 60 feet wide, is not for the fainthearted: It wiggles and shakes underfoot while the sea crashes 80 feet below, and no matter how brave you are, you're in for a scare (though later you can tell yourself it was a thrilling adventure). The bridge is the only access to a sometimes-smelly salmon fishery on the small island at its far end.

Larrybane, County Antrim. ☎ *028-2073-2143. To get there: On the A2 along the North Antrim Coast. Admission: Free. Open: April to mid-Sept during daylight hours. Suggested visit: 30 minutes.*

Carrickfergus Castle
Carrickfergus

During this impressive, well-preserved castle's 800-year history, it grew from a small castle to an unequaled Norman fortress. Historic, life-sized figures make an eerie presence throughout the grounds, and a fascinating audiovisual presentation really brings the castle's exciting history to life. You'll have fun walking along the parapets and looking out to sea. The Castle's keep doubles as a unique period "game room," where you can try on costumes or engage in some oversized medieval games, like chess or "Dragons and Ladders."

Marine Highway, Carrickfergus, County Antrim. ☎ *028-9335-1273. To get there: Take the A2 north of Belfast. Admission: £2.70 ($4.45) adults, £1.35 ($2.25) child and senior citizen, £7.30 ($12.05) family. Combined tickets are available for Carrickfergus Castle and Knight Ride at £4.85 ($8) adults, £2.40 ($3.95) child and senior citizen, £13.50 ($22.30) family. You can purchase the tickets at either venue. Open: April–Oct Mon–Sat 10 a.m.–6 p.m.; April–May Sept–Oct Sun 2–6 p.m.; Jun–Aug Sun 11 a.m.– 8 p.m.; Nov–March Mon–Sat 10 a.m.–4 p.m., Sun 2–4 p.m. Suggested visit: 2 hours.*

Knight Ride
Carrickfergus

This is the fun way to learn! Kids travel throughout the interactive history tour while sitting in a giant helmet that weaves through Carrickfergus's lively past. Sounds, smells, and sights of battles and a 19th-century market highlight this exciting ride. There's even a spooky haunted house in the "Dark Ride." Afterward, a fantastic walk-through exhibit incorporates the information, with a scale model of the town and audiovisual presentations.

Heritage Plaza, Carrickfergus. ☎ *028-9336-6455. To get there: Take the A2 north of Belfast. Admission: £2.70 ($4.45) adults, £1.35 ($2.25) child and senior citizen, £7.30 ($12.05) family. Combined tickets for Carrickfergus Castle and Knight Ride at £4.85 ($8) adults, £2.40 ($3.95) child and senior citizen, £13.50 ($22.30) family. Open: April–Sept Mon–Sat 10 a.m.– 6 p.m., Sun noon to 6 p.m.; Oct–March Mon–Sat 10 a.m.–5 p.m., Sun noon to 5 p.m. Suggested visit: 1½ hours.*

More fun stuff to do in Belfast and around County Antrim

Here are a few more fun things to do with your time in Antrim — including a great place for a round or two of golf:

✔ **Taking Bailey's Belfast Pub Tour:** Belfast has some of Ireland's finest pubs, many authentically Victorian. The famed Bailey's Irish Cream hosts a good pub tour of the city that covers six of the best, most with traditional music. The tour lasts about four hours.

Location: Great Victoria Street, Belfast. Tour departs from the Crown Bar, upstairs from Flannigan's Pub. ☎ **094-9068-3665.** To get there: From Donegall Square go about three blocks east to Victoria Street. Admission: £5 ($8.25) adult. Tours: April through September Tuesday 7 p.m., Saturday 4 p.m.

✔ **Visiting the Ulster Museum:** This is Northern Ireland's national museum, with a diverse collection that ranges from local history to ancient artifacts, including treasures from sunken ships of the Spanish Armada. The fourth floor houses an impressive art gallery with works by greats like Francis Bacon and Henry Moore.

Location: Stranmillis Road, Belfast. ☎ **028-90381-2251.** To get there: From city center, take Great Victoria Street south to University Road, and veer left onto Stranmillis Road. Bus: 69, 70, 71. Admis-zsion: Free. Open: Monday through Friday 10 a.m. to 5 p.m., Saturday 1 to 5 p.m., and Sunday 2 to 5 p.m. Suggested visit: 1 hour.

✔ **Touring the Antrim Coast:** This spectacular drive takes you along sea-splashed cliffs and into small coastal towns with picturesque harbors. Major attractions along the road include the Giant's Causeway and Carrick-A-Rede Rope Bridge (covered earlier in this chapter) plus Dunluce and Kinbane Castle ruins — both of which offer beautiful views of the sea and cliffs.

Location: Start off from Belfast on the A2 north, which stretches as far as Derry. Suggested visit: Anywhere from several hours to two days, depending on how many stops you make.

✔ **Exploring Rathlin Island:** Rathlin's strategic position between Ireland and Scotland has made it the site of many battles over time. Today the tiny, boomerang-shaped island is a peaceful place and the home of thousands of seabirds, including puffins, and only about 100 people. Storytelling, song, and music flourish here, and islanders are always happy to welcome visitors. On the eastern end of the island is Bruce's Cave, where the Scottish King Robert the Bruce hid after being defeated by the English, before returning to his country and winning back his kingdom.

Location: Off the coast of Ballycastle. To get there: Take the ferry from Ballycastle (call ☎ **028-2076-9299** for information). Ferry prices: Round trip £7.60 ($12.55) adults, £5.60 ($9.25) seniors, £3.80 ($6.25) children. Runs daily at 10:30 a.m. and 5:00 p.m. from Ballycastle and at 9 a.m. and 4 p.m. from Rathlin during the spring and summer. During the winter, 10:30 a.m. and 4:00 p.m. from Ballycastle and 9 a.m. and 3 p.m. from Rathlin.

✔ **Golfing at Royal Portrush.** These are three excellent 18-hole courses, all of which offer amazing seaside views of the northern Antrim Coast.

Location: Dunluce Road, Portrush, County Antrim. ☎ **028-7082-2311.** To get there: From Belfast, take the M2 north to Ballymena and then the A26 to Ballymoney. At the roundabout, follow the sign to Portrush (about 10 miles down the road). Par: 72. Fees: £55 ($90.75) midweek, £65 ($107.30) weekends. Open: 6:30 a.m. until sundown.

Joining an Organized Tour

In addition to the tours in this section, see "Taking Bailey's Belfast Pub Tour" in the previous section.

Citybus Bus Tours

A three-hour tour covering all the high points of Belfast. The commentary is very interesting, and this is probably the fastest way to see and hear it all.

Tours operate June–Sept and depart from Castle Place, two blocks north of Donegall Square. Information: City Bus, Donegall Square West Ticket kiosk. ☎ *028-9045-8484. Price: £8 ($13.20) adults, £7 ($11.55) students, £5.50 ($9.07) seniors and children, £18 ($29.70) family.*

Titanic — A (Bus) Tour to Remember

Offered by Citybus, this tour goes out to the Harland and Wolff shipyards, where the *Titanic* was built; stops in the office of the designer, Thomas Andrews; and visits the *Titanic* memorial at City Hall, the *Titanic* exhibition at Cultura's Folk and Transport Museum, and the little town of Comber, home to Mr. Andrews and the statue they erected in his honor. It lasts three and a half hours and the fare includes entry to the transport museum.

See the previous Citybus listing for all information.

The Old Town of Belfast Walking Tour

Local experts lead this 90-minute tour of the original city ramparts and trace the city back to its origins. Guides are extremely knowledgeable.

Runs year-round on Saturdays, departing at 2 p.m. from the Tourist Information Centre on North Street. Information: Tourist Information Centre, ☎ *028-9023-1221.*

Shopping in Belfast and County Antrim

Belfast's City Hall is a perfect landmark for the shopping district, which is just across the street. There you'll find posh (and expensive) British department stores, Irish shops, and some American chains.

Craftworks

A wide range of quality crafts fill this shop, and all products are beautifully displayed. You'll find ceramics, jewelry, hand-painted silk scarves, musical instruments, and more.

Bedford House, 16 Bedford St., Belfast. ☎ *028-9224-4465.*

Halls

This shop was established in 1850, and its years of experience show. Halls specializes in Celtic jewelry, but it also has Donegal tweed rugs, Aran sweaters, and figurines made from compressed peat.

Queen's Arcade, Belfast. ☎ *028-9032-0446.*

Irish Linen Centre

Much more than just a shop, this center gives the history of the famous Ulster linen and conducts handweaving demonstrations — and of course sells plenty of Irish linen, from coats to clothes.

Market Square, Lisburn. ☎ *028-9066-3377.*

Irish Linen Stores

A variety of Irish linen fills this shop, with tea towels the specialty. Most of the linen carries the trademark green shamrock design.

Fountain Centre, College Street, Belfast. ☎ *028-9032-2727.*

Northern Salmon Company

Chemical-free fresh and smoked salmon is yours to take home from this respected company. You can watch the entire process, from salmon harvesting to packaging.

New Road, Glenarm, Ballymena. ☎ *028-2884-1691.*

Enjoying Nightlife in Belfast and County Antrim

Belfast is a bustling city, so you may want to broaden your scope beyond the pubs to include a few clubs. But true to form, I include the best of both in the following sections.

Pulling a pint: Pub life

Though all the exceptional watering holes that follow are located in Belfast, I also want to make a plug for the local pubs I had the pleasure to find in small towns around Antrim. Although none were remarkably decked out or steeped in history, some of my fondest evenings were spent in these anonymous coastal pubs, chatting with the friendly locals. Belfast may have the most atmospheric pubs in the county, but the best ones are what you make them.

Crown Liquor Saloon

Unquestionably the most famous pub in Belfast, the Crown is owned by the state (by the National Trust, to be exact). Inside you'll be taken aback by the wonderful traditional design that includes hand-painted tiles, carved wood, brass fittings, and gas lamps. Truly a perfect Irish watering hole. You've got to try the local Strangford Lough oysters — they're excellent. You may want to find a seat early — the Crown fills up most evenings.

44 Great Victoria Street, Belfast. ☎ *028-9024-9476.*

Kelly's Cellars

Not only is this the oldest continuously used licensed pub in Belfast, but Kelly's was the popular meeting place for the United Irishmen, who organized the 1798 Rebellion. The name is misleading; Kelly's Cellars is a two-storied building with a stone-floored bar downstairs and restaurant upstairs. If you get hungry, try the incredible Black Velvet Steak Pie.

30 Bank St., Belfast. ☎ *028-9032-4835.*

Madisons

One of the city's newest and most stunning bars, Madisons is named for the modern hotel it's housed in. Using an Art Nouveau theme and sporting a striking copper and ceramic bar top, it's a sophisticated and hip gathering place of young professionals and students from the nearby Queens University. There's an over-25 club downstairs that's great for dancing.

59–63 Botanic Ave., Belfast. ☎ *028-9033-0040.*

The Morning Star

You have to go down an alley between High and Ann streets to find this historic pub, but you can't miss its striking green-and-red facade, and anyway, it's worth the hunt. The Star serves up the best pint of Caffrey's (Belfast's hometown brew) in town. That's reason enough to go, but the comfortable interior and unique horseshoe bar are attractions as well.

17–19 Pottingers Entry, Belfast. ☎ *028-9032-3976.*

The Shenanigan Rooms

It's all about ambience here. Pull up a stool and rest a pint on a huge old beer barrel. The more sociable can sit at the long, medieval feasting tables. It's always jumping here, which probably has as much to do with the great atmosphere as it does the incredible pub grub.

21 Howard St., Belfast. ☎ *028-9023-0603.*

Best pubs for traditional music

Some of the best pubs in Belfast to get those toes a-tappin' include **Madden's**, 74 Smithfield (☎ **028-9024-4114**); the **Duke of York**, 11 Commercial Court, off Lower Donegall Street (☎ **028-9024-1062**); the **Empire**, 42 Botanic Avenue (☎ **028-9032-8110**); **Front Page**, 106–110 Donegall Street (☎ **028-9032-4924**); and **Kitchen Bar**, 16 Victoria Square (☎ **028-9032-4901**).

Striking a pose: Club life

The Manhattan Bar

This flashy neon dance club is where all the clubbers go. It's an exciting late-night venue with a carnival atmosphere. *Warning:* The popularity of Manhattan means less-than-friendly doormen.

23 Bradbury Place, Belfast. ☎ *028-9023-3131.*

The Beaten Docket

This modern and popular bar turns into a great nightclub on Friday and Saturday nights and is open into the wee hours of the morning. The best part about the club is that the minimum age is set at 30, which tends to filter out the young'uns. You'll have a blast and wonder where the time went.

48 Great Victoria St. (opposite the Europa hotel), Belfast. ☎ *01232-24-2986.*

Fast Facts: Belfast and County Antrim

Area Code

The area code (or city code) for County Antrim is **028**.

Emergencies-Hospital

Dial ☎ **999** for all emergencies. The Belfast City Hospital is on Lisburn Road (☎ 028-9032-9241).

Genealogy Resources

Contact the Irish Heritage Association, Queens Road, Belfast, BT39DT (☎ 028-9045-5325), or the Ulster Historical Foundation, Balmoral Buildings, 12 College Square East, Belfast BT1 6DD (☎ 01232-33-2288; Fax: 01232-23-9885; E-mail: enquiry@uhf.org.uk; Internet: www.uhf.org.uk).

Information

For visitor information, go to the tourist office at St. Anne's Court, 59 North St. (☎ 028-9023-1221), open year-round. They can also provide reservation services (☎ 0800-40-4050). Belfast has a new tourist Web site as well (www.gotobelfast.com). For telephone directory assistance, dial ☎ 192.

Chapter 23

Counties Down and Armagh

* *

In This Chapter

▶ Finding St. Patrick's grave

▶ Touring the Mourne Mountains

▶ Discovering the history of transportation

* *

South of Belfast, with the Irish Sea on the east, and the border of the Republic just below, Counties Down and Armagh boast several important religious sites. You can visit them either as day-trips from Belfast or en route between Belfast and Dublin.

This is the land of St. Patrick, the patron saint of the country, who planted the first roots of Irish Christianity here in the fifth century. Born in Britain somewhere around A.D. 389 and brought to Ireland as a slave, Patrick spent four years as a shepherd for a Druid. During that time his spirituality flourished, and after escaping slavery, Patrick trained for the priesthood, probably in France. He returned to Ireland as a missionary, sure that God was directing him to spread Christianity in the pagan land, and began the difficult task of converting the Irish and establishing churches.

Over the years, people around the world have gotten to know Patrick as the inspiration for annual drunken revelries every March 17, but believe it or not, St. Patrick's Day is a holy day in Ireland. People attend mass, businesses and schools are closed, and until recently, pubs were closed, too. Some cities and towns in Ireland hold parades on March 17, but doing so is really an American practice, and all the drunkenness such parades inspire is not necessarily held in high regard in the auld country.

What's Where?: Counties Down and Armagh and Their Major Attractions

The little town of Downpatrick, in **County Down,** is filled with fine Georgian architecture and is where you can find the grave of St. Patrick. It's located in a staid graveyard behind a pretty church on a hill.

Counties Down and Armagh

ACCOMMODATIONS ■
Burrendale Hotel **10**
Culloden Hotel **3**
Dufferin Coaching Inn **8**

DINING ◆
El Porto Cafe **13**
The Lobster Pot **7**
The Olde Priory Inn Bar & Restaurant **3**

SHOPPING ▲
Ferguson Linen Centre **12**

ATTRACTIONS ●
Exploris **6**
Mountains of Mourne **11**
Mountains of Mourne Information Centre **10**
Mount Stewart House and Gardens **5**
St. Patrick's Grave **9**
Ulster Folk & Transport Museum **1**

NIGHTLIFE ☾
Grace Neill's Inn **2**
Harry's Bar **12**
Siglu **8**
Tourist Trophy Lounge **4**

But first things first. If you're coming from Belfast, here are some of the attractions you can see along the way:

✔ **Ulster Folk and Transport Museum:** Only about 5 miles from Belfast on the A2, this outdoor museum is devoted to presenting rural life as it was in the 1800s.

✔ **Mount Stewart House and Gardens:** Located in **Newtownards,** about 10 miles east of Belfast, this impressive 18th-century mansion is surrounded by spectacular gardens.

✔ **Exploris:** Underwater tunnels give you a fish-eye view of life in the Irish Sea.

✔ **The Mountains of Mourne:** These enthralling mountains (along the A2 coastal road) contain the highest peaks in Northern Ireland.

Moving farther south and a little west, you reach **County Armagh.** **Armagh City** is one of Ireland's oldest towns — going as far back as St. Patrick. Christianity took hold here and eventually spread out across the country, and two **St. Patrick's Cathedrals** are here — one Catholic and one Protestant. The Protestant one provides the greater draw for visitors: It boasts the remains of Brian Boru, the great High King.

Getting to Counties Down and Armagh

The nearest airports are in Belfast, which is also the destination for ferries from England and Scotland. See Chapter 22 for information.

If you're coming by car from Dublin, take the N1 north to Newry (N1 becomes the A1 in Northern Ireland). From Newry take the A28 to Armagh. To get to the coast, from Newry take the A2 southeast (the A2 runs along the entire coast). If you're driving from Ireland into Northern Ireland make sure you notify your rental-car company because extra insurance may be required.

Northern Ireland Railways (☎ **028-9127-0141**) services Newry, Portadown, Lurgan, Lisburn, and Bangor year-round. **Ulsterbus** (☎ **028-9033-3000**) travels year-round to Newry, Portadown, Armagh City, and other major towns in Counties Armagh and Down.

Where to Stay in Counties Down and Armagh

Culloden Hotel
$$$–$$$$ **Holywood, County Down**

This is the only five-star hotel in Northern Ireland, and it wears that distinction well. Set in a former Gothic mansion on 12 acres of beautiful, secluded gardens and surrounded by the picturesque Holywood Hills, the Culloden will blow you away. Even from the outside, the hotel is gorgeous, and the posh rooms and antique-studded lobby drive the point home. British prime ministers Tony Blair and John Major have stayed here.

Bangor Road, Holywood, County Down. ☎ *028-9042-5223. Fax: 028-9042-6777. Internet:* www.hastingshotels.com. *To get there: On the A2, northeast of Belfast. Rates: £88–£186 ($145.20–$306.90) double. AE, DC, MC, V.*

Burrendale Hotel
$$$ **Newcastle, County Down**

This hotel really has it all. Between the beauty salon, bistro, and bar, there are enough reasons to stay in for the day, but with the Mourne Mountains, a sandy beach on the Irish Sea, and two large parks at the hotel's doorstep, I bet you'll hardly be in your room at all. Locals and visitors alike rave about the Vine Restaurant and the Cottage Kitchen Restaurant. They have varied menus so everybody's happy. Golfers can go crazy: There are 15 courses nearby — including one of the best on the island, Royal County Down.

51 Castlewellan Rd., Newcastle, County Down. ☎ *028-4372-2599. Fax: 028-4372-2328. To get there: Off the A2 toward Downpatrick. Rates: £90–£110 ($148.50–$181.50) double. AE, DC, MC, V.*

Dufferin Coaching Inn
$$$ **Killyleagh, County Down**

Sitting in the shadow of Killyleagh Castle, this charming inn is nestled in the little town of Killyleagh, on the road between Downpatrick and Belfast. It has some of the finest and most comfortable rooms you can find, all decorated in country colors and with beautiful wooden furniture — some rooms even have four-poster beds. The whole place is much larger than it looks from the outside, with a pub, library, guest lounge, and a downstairs dining area that's so cozy you may think you're in someone's warm kitchen. The inn has been operating since 1803, and you won't find an unfriendly face.

31 High St., Killyleagh, County Down. ☎ *028-4482-8229. Fax: 028-4482-8755. E-mail:* dufferin@dial.pipex.com. *To get there: On the A22, south of Belfast. Rates: £65 ($107.30) double. MC, V.*

Where to Dine in Counties Down and Armagh

The Lobster Pot
$$$–$$$$ **Strangford, County Down   SEAFOOD-IRISH-EUROPEAN**

Lobster is, not surprisingly, the house specialty here. Plenty of really great Irish and classically European dishes are served, but the seafood is the highlight of the fare. The house has recently been refurbished, but none of the old-fashioned style has been lost. The decor is comfortable and homey, and the service is quick and quick to please. For when the weather's nice, you can drink your dessert in the lovely beer garden.

9–11 The Square, Strangford, County Down. ☎ *028-4488-1288. To get there: Take the A25 east from Downpatrick. Main courses: £9.95–£15.50 ($16.40–$25.60). AE, MC, V. Open: Mon–Sat 11:30 a.m.–9:30 p.m., Sun 12:30–8:30 p.m.*

The Olde Priory Inn Bar & Restaurant
$$–$$$ Holywood, County Down   IRISH

This is the most popular place to eat and meet in Holywood, and the eclectic decor and super-friendly staff make it a gem. The head chef, well known in these parts, utilizes the best produce of the area and creates a unique and ever-changing daily-specials board. The menu features many kid-friendly meals, but the real draw is the Sunday brunch, which is a four-course feast. There's an in-house baby-sitting service on Sundays as well, so parents can enjoy their meal without the kinder!

13 High St., Holywood, County Down. ☎ *028-9042-8164. To get there: On the A2, northeast of Belfast. Main courses: £5–£10.50 ($8.25–$17.35). AE, DC, MC, V. Open: Daily 11:30 a.m.–10:30 p.m.*

El Porto Cafe
$–$$ Portadown, County Armagh   EUROPEAN

This popular place is really two restaurants in one. Downstairs is a busy European-style cafe, serving mostly sandwiches (such as the house's special hot roast beef on a baguette) and homemade soups. The atmosphere is friendly, and good music is always playing in the background. Upstairs, a classy old-world restaurant offers a gourmet but well-priced menu in comfortable surroundings.

10 Market St., Portadown, County Armagh. ☎ *028-3839-4343. To get there: On the A3 west from Belfast or the A27 north from Newry. Main courses: £3.50–£7.50 ($5.75–$12.40). MC, V. Open: Mon–Sat 9:00 a.m.–5:15 p.m.*

Exploring Counties Down and Armagh

St. Patrick's grave is one of the biggest draws for tourists in the area, but there are plenty of other things to occupy your time. In this section, I run through the best of them.

The top attractions

Here are the top spots in Down and Armagh.

St. Patrick's Grave
Downpatrick, County Down

Sitting atop the Hill of Down is Down Cathedral, a small yet austere church, but what's next to the church makes it famous. The little church-yard reputedly has the remains of Ireland's patron saint, St. Patrick. A rock slab with the word *Patric* across it marks the spot, which sits in the shadow of a tenth-century cross.

Down Cathedral, 33 Cathedral St., Downpatrick, County Down. ☎ 028-4461-4922. To get there: On the A7 south from Belfast. Admission: Free. Open: Daylight hours. Suggested visit: 15 minutes.

Ulster Folk & Transport Museum
Holywood, County Down

Original 19th-century buildings that once stood throughout Northern Ireland now make up this outdoor museum devoted to presenting rural life in the 1800s. You can walk among farmhouses, churches, houses, schools, a bank, and a print shop, just to name a few. You can even see people demonstrating how to thatch a roof and cook over an open fire, and others practicing traditional Ulster crafts like lacemaking, spinning, and printing. Across the road is an exhibit on Irish railways, considered among the finest of its kind in Europe. An exhibit called "Car in Society" shows a fine collection of automobiles. You can also find out about a couple of Belfast-built creations-cum-disasters: the *Titanic* and the DeLorean automobile.

153 Bangor Rd., Holywood, County Down. ☎ 028-9242-8428. To get there: Off the A2, 7 miles east of Belfast. Admission: £3 ($4.95) adults, £2 ($3.30) children. Open: July–Aug Mon–Sat 10:30 a.m.– 6:00 p.m., Sun noon to 5 p.m.; Apr–June and Sept Mon–Fri 9:30 a.m.–5:00 p.m., Sat 10:30 a.m.–6:00 p.m., Sun noon to 6 p.m.; Oct–March Mon–Fri 9:30 a.m.–4:00 p.m., Sat and Sun 12:30–4:30 p.m. Suggested visit: 1½ hours.

Mount Stewart House and Gardens
Newtownards, County Down

Though its interior is just grand, with a fabulous entrance hall and the famous George Stubbs painting *Hambletonian,* this impressive 18th-century mansion almost pales in comparison to the spectacular gardens surrounding it. There's a fabulous Shamrock Garden, which has an Irish harp-shaped topiary and a flowerbed shaped like a red hand (the emblem of Ulster) enclosed in a hedge shaped like a shamrock. Spanish and Italian gardens are in the back, and a colorful sunken garden sits in the east yard.

Newtownards, County Down. ☎ 028-4278-8387. To get there: On the A2 3 miles southeast of Newtownards, along the Ards Peninsula. Admission: House, garden, and temple £3 ($4.95) adults, £1.50 ($2.50) children. Garden and temple £2.70 ($4.45) adults, £1.35 ($2.30) children. Open: House Apr and Oct Sat and Sun 1–6 p.m.;

May–Sept Mon and Wed–Sun 1–6 p.m. Garden Apr–Sept daily 10:30 a.m.–6:00 p.m.; Oct Sat and Sun 10:30 a.m.–6:00 p.m. Suggested visit: 1 hour.

Exploris
Portaferry, County Down

Exploris is Northern Ireland's only public aquarium, giving a fish-eye view of life in the Irish Sea via dark, underwater tunnels of stone with windows giving views of the illuminated green waters. It's the closest you can come to being underwater, short of strapping on a wetsuit. You can get an up-close view and find out about all marine life, from tiny plankton to deadly sharks, and see unique species like camouflage octopi and wolf fish. You may also have an opportunity to feel starfish, sea urchins, and stingrays in the Touch Tank. Exploris is an undersea adventure you won't soon forget.

The Rope Walk, Portaferry, County Down. ☎ 028-4272-8062. To get there: On the A2, on the tip of the Ards Peninsula. Admission: £3.85 ($6.35) adults, £2.70 ($4.45) children, seniors, and students, £12 ($19.80) family of three adults and four children. Open: March–Aug Mon–Fri 10 a.m.–6 p.m., Sat 11 a.m.–6 p.m., Sun 1–6 pm; Sept–Feb Mon–Fri 10 a.m.–5 p.m., Sat 11 a.m.–5 p.m., Sun 1–5 p.m. Suggested visit: 2 hours.

The Mountains of Mourne
County Down

You can drive or take a bus tour on the circular route around these enthralling mountains, but either way you pass 15 striking summits, all rising more than 2,000 feet. Every few miles present different, exciting vistas, and lakes, streams, beaches, and heather-covered valleys fill out the landscape. One of the highlights of the area is the Annalong Cornmill, an old, working mill with a water wheel and an exhibition on water-powered technology.

The Information Centre is located at 10 Central Promenade, Newcastle, County Down. ☎ 028-4372-2222. To get there: Take the coastal road (A2). Bus Eireann gives a day tour of Mountains of Mourne from Dublin for £20 ($33) (including lunch) in July and Aug. Call ☎ 01-836-6111 for information. Suggested visit: Several hours.

More fun stuff to see and do

Ready for more? Here are a couple more ideas to round out your time in Down and Armagh:

 ✔ **Ferguson Linen Centre** is the world's only manufacturer of double damask linen — the store even supplies the White House. You can get a guided tour of the factory or simply pick up some linen sheets, tablecloths, handkerchiefs, or napkins.

 Location: 54 Scarva Rd., Banbridge, County Down, ☎ 028-4062-3491.

✔ You can have all kinds of historical and cultural experiences in Down and Armagh, but if you want to sneak away for a game of golf, I won't tattle on you. The par-71 **Royal County Down** is the top course in the area, attracting the best players in Europe with stunning views and challenging holes.

Location: Newcastle, County Down (☎ **028-4372-3314;** Internet: www.royalcountydown.org). Greens fees £90 ($135) mid-week, £100 ($150) weekends.

Pulling a Pint: Pub Life

In addition to the places that I list in this section, there's another so weird that I just can't leave it out. About a mile from Killyleagh Town, in Delamont Country Park, is **Siglu** (☎ **028-4482-8333**), a clear structure that looks like an igloo. Originally designed as a place for skiers to slide in for a schnapps or a warm drink, it's now a popular spot for merry-makers. From afar, Siglu looks like a glowing dome, and inside it has a center bar and plenty of room to relax with a drink. Check it out; it's an experience you won't forget!

Grace Neill's Inn

Many pubs claim to be the oldest in Ireland, but this one really is. Don't believe me? *The Guinness Book of World Records* says so, and those people know their pubs. The old part of the tavern practically defines what an Irish pub should look like, and even though it's been extended to include a lounge and conservatory, the whole place keeps the old-school style. The pub grub is great, too.

33 High St., Donaghadee, County Down. ☎ *028-9188-2553.*

Harry's Bar

The best thing about Harry's is what it serves: 14 draft beers! You won't be left wanting, that's for sure. The pub is traditionally decorated, and the pub grub is fantastic. Try the boiled ham with Irish whiskey sauce.

7 Dromore St., Banbridge, County Down. ☎ *028-4066-2794.*

Tourist Trophy Lounge

You may think this pub is about you. Actually, the TT is on the route of the famous Tourist Trophy car races of the 1920s. The lounge is full of photos and mementos of those crazy racy days, so there's always entertainment. Downstairs is the traditional North Down House pub, a favorite of locals. The combination makes for a great "pit stop" in this small town just southeast of Belfast, on the A21.

1–3 Railway St., Comber, County Down. ☎ *028-9187-4554.*

Fast Facts: Counties Down and Armagh

Area Code

The area code (or city code) for counties Down and Armagh is **028**.

Emergencies

Dial ☎ **999** for all emergencies.

Information

For visitor information go to the tourist offices at 74 Market St., Downpatrick, County Down (☎ 028-4461-2233), or Town Hall, Newry, County Down (☎ 028-3026-8877). For telephone directory assistance, dial ☎ 192.

Part VII

The Part of Tens

The 5th Wave   By Rich Tennant

"Douglas, I'd like to talk to you about
the souvenirs you brought back from
our trip to Ireland."

In this part . . .

In this part, I give you a couple of fun "extras." You can skip this part completely and still have a great trip, or read on for some bonus information.

In Chapter 24, I tell you about what I consider to be the top ten, absolute-best highlights of my travels through Ireland and Northern Ireland. If you're still undecided about what to see in Ireland after reading the previous chapters, maybe this will help you out.

If you're a serious shopper, check out Chapter 25. There I give you ten shopping tips — from how to find the best bargains to the best ways to get all your treasures home in one piece. I also give you the scoop on the best and most popular Irish products and where to find them.

Chapter 24

The Top Ten Highlights of Ireland and Northern Ireland

In This Chapter

▶ Circling the Ring of Kerry

▶ Planting a kiss on the Blarney Stone

▶ Blowing glass — and some cash — at the Waterford Crystal Factory

▶ Exploring the mountains and lakes of Killarney

These attractions and experiences rank as some of the biggest and best in the Republic and the North (refer to the chapters noted in parentheses for more information).

Driving the Ring of Kerry

The Ring, a southeast peninsula jutting out into the Atlantic Ocean, runs you past stunning coastline, craggy mountains, and colorful fishing villages. (See Chapter 16.)

Standing atop the Majestic Purple Cliffs of Moher

You can look down 760 feet to the crashing waves of the Atlantic, and possibly see the Aran Islands in the distance. (See Chapter 17.)

Bending Over Backward to Kiss the Blarney Stone

You have to lean backward with your head upside down to kiss the smooth stone, but it's worth the effort: At worst, you can say you did it; at best, you walk away with the gift of gab — the legendary reward for your kiss. (See Chapter 15.)

Pub-Crawling in Temple Bar

You'll feel like a Dubliner for sure winding down the cobbled streets of Dublin's trendy Temple Bar neighborhood on an authentic pub-crawl, sipping creamy pints of Guinness and tapping your feet to traditional Irish music. (See Chapter 11.)

Watching Glass Blowers at the Waterford Crystal Factory

Watch as Waterford Crystal pieces are blown before your very eyes. Afterward, you can tour the factory and buy a flawless piece from the gallery/shop. (See Chapter 14.)

Taking a Ferry out to the Stark Aran Islands

Once there, you can tour the islands by horse-pulled cart and have a fresh-fish dinner before leaving with a signature wool fisherman's sweater. (See Chapter 18.)

Driving Around Killarney's Mountains and Lakes

Make your way through the mountains that surround the still and awesome lakes of Killarney, while hunting down waterfalls and slowing to avoid the goats that sleep in the road. (See Chapter 16.)

Walking Out on the Giant's Causeway

This mysterious stretch of pillar-like stones reaches out into the sea and was, legends say, mythical giant Finn MacCool's walkway to Scotland. (See Chapter 22.)

Strolling amid the Stately and Magnificent Powerscourt Gardens

Ponds and statues accent the vast spread of flowers, plants, and shrubs that make these gardens among the finest in Europe. (See Chapter 13.)

Discovering the Ancient Secrets of Newgrange and the Hill of Tara

In County Meath, just north of Dublin, prehistoric tombs and the meeting place of Ireland's High Kings help explain the county's early history. (See Chapter 12.)

Chapter 25

Ten Tips for Shopping Wisely in Ireland

● ●

In This Chapter

▶ Deciding what to purchase

▶ Getting the best prices

▶ Figuring out what to lug home

● ●

Sure, a handful of travelers come back from their trip with nothing more than a few blisters, maybe a tan, and a notebook full of observations and sketches, but most people are a little bit more acquisitive than that. In this chapter, I offer a few tips on buying an Irish sweater (or whatever else you're looking for) without losing your shirt.

Shop Around

Prices vary dramatically from shop to shop and market stall to market stall. They usually go down as you get farther away from touristy places, and you may find the same item for less in a shop on a lower-rent street. Let the store owners know you're comparing prices, and the asking rate may go down on the spot. Also, be sure to check prices for items available at home so you know if you're getting a bargain by buying them abroad.

Peruse Street Markets

This is a fun way to do business, especially if it comes to haggling, which is likely. Irish street vendors are real characters and you'll have an experience that's hard to come by at home. The quality of the merchandise is iffier than in established shops, but you can get great deals on everything from designer knockoffs to identical items from shops that are overstocked.

Finding Ireland's best buys

Shopping on the Emerald Isle means much more than buying cheesy leprechauns and mini thatched-roof cottages as souvenirs, and in fact, Ireland is known for certain products that people travel from around the world to buy. For instance, wool fishermen's sweaters from the Aran Islands have come to signify Ireland like almost nothing else, and people return home wearing them as if they're the Irish flag itself (check the tag before you buy — it will mention the Aran Islands if it's authentic). Here are some items you may want to shop for on your trip.

✔ **China:** Fine bone china is made in Belleek, a tiny town in Northern Ireland, but you can purchase it all over the country. The operation there is reportedly Ireland's oldest pottery, in operation since 1857, and the china is characterized by its ivory color flecked with pink.

✔ **Crystal:** One of Ireland's finest exports, Waterford Crystal, is a perfect example of classic craftsmanship. A whopping 45% of the pieces produced by the factory are thrown out for slight imperfections — the company doesn't sell any seconds. You'll find the best selection of Waterford Crystal at the source: Waterford City, County Waterford.

✔ **Lace:** In the 1860s, Poor Clare nuns in Kenmare began teaching local girls to make lace in hopes of helping the struggling economy. The beautiful needlepoint lace is now famous worldwide. A great place to see examples of (and purchase) the lace is at the courthouse next to the tourist office in Kenmare.

✔ **Linen:** Irish linen is characterized by its delicate weavings and how it gracefully adorns any table. You'll find linen-makers throughout Ireland, but Belfast is known as the linen capital of the world, and it sells some of the finest and best linen selections.

✔ **Pottery:** Irish pottery is a treasure, made daily by local artisans and often bearing Celtic and country designs. County Clare is Ireland's pottery haven, where you'll find unique and traditional styles.

✔ **Tweed:** The best place to find handmade clothing is in the northwest, in County Donegal. (There are loads of hand-weaving shops throughout the rest of the county as well.)

Forget Designer Clothing

Unless you're looking for particularly Irish clothes, you probably won't find any bargains on European designer clothes. Just because you're in Europe doesn't mean you'll get great deals on French or Italian clothes hot off the runway.

Shop Selectively

Don't buy every trinket you see. Go for the items that truly capture the spirit and culture of Ireland and will hold the best memories. Before you buy it, make sure that leprechaun doll or Guinness keychain is something you really want. Also, take into consideration that whatever you buy should be able to fit in your luggage (unless you're planning to mail some things home).

Don't Let Yourself Be Led by the Nose

On most escorted tours, the guide will take or direct you to shops that offer "special prices" to people on your tour. Ninety percent of the time this means the tour guide is getting a kickback for bringing in revenue. Usually, the store passes the burden along to you by jacking up the prices. Although some guides do give honest recommendations, and some of those kickback arrangements don't adversely affect you via markups, knowing when a recommendation is on the level is impossible. Be cynical and comparison shop. If it seems too expensive, it probably is.

Act like an Old Shopping Hand

Scrutinize labels, kick the proverbial tires, and otherwise show that you know what you're doing (even if you don't, really). Shopkeepers who see a savvy customer are less likely to try to pull the wool over your eyes — even when you're trying on sweaters.

Dress Respectably, but Not Too Well

You want merchants to know you're a potential paying customer and not riffraff, but you don't want to give them the idea you're loaded. Especially in markets, prices can go up on the spot if you look willing to pay anything.

Count Your Change and Check Your Receipt

Make sure the receipt is complete and accurate. Don't be rude about it, but make sure you aren't dealing with a rotten shopkeeper who's trying to scam or shortchange you. (Even if there's no malice aforethought, cashiers have been known to make mistakes.) The receipt is important because you'll need it for a VAT refund (see the Appendix for more on this).

Ship Breakables Home

It may cost a bit more, but the longer you lug your purchases around with you, the greater the chances that your Waterford Crystal will end up Waterford shards.

Some antique shops have the resources to ship large items to you back home. If you're in the market for furniture, be sure to ask about shipping before you fall in love with the Victorian dining room table that won't quite fit in your suitcase. Also, you can save yourself time and hassle should something go wrong with a purchase being shipped home if you snap a photo of it before it's wrapped up. This photo makes excellent proof of purchase when it comes to insurance claims.

Evaluate Your Carrying Capacity

If you find that you're running out of room in your luggage, pack fragile items first, and then mail home any unneeded personal stuff (like dirty laundry) rather than entrusting all your purchases to the postal system.

Irish clothing sizes

The United States and Ireland have different systems for measurements (except for men's shirt and suit sizes, which are the same in both countries). Use the following charts only as guides to steer you toward a near fit. As in the United States, clothing size is often much more subjective than it should be, and sizes vary among manufacturers and from store to store.

Women's Coats and Dresses

United States	4	6	8	10	12	14	16	18
Ireland	6	8	10	12	14	16	18	20

Women's Shoes

United States	5	6	7	8	9	10
Ireland	4	5	6	7	8	9

Men's Shoes

United States	7	8	9	10	11	12
Ireland	6	7	8	9	10	11

Appendix

Quick Concierge

Fast Facts

American Express

The only American Express offices in Ireland are in Dublin (41 Nassau St.; ☎ 01-617-5597) and Galway (International Hotel, East Avenue Road; ☎ 64-35722). In an emergency, you can dial collect ☎ 1-44-1-273-571-600 to report lost or stolen traveler's checks.

ATMs

ATMs (called *service tills* in Ireland) are located all over the country. The major networks are Plus and Cirrus.

Business Hours

Banks are open Monday through Wednesday and Friday from 10:00 a.m. to 12:30 p.m. and from 1:30 to 3:00 p.m.; on Thursday from 10:00 a.m. to 12:30 p.m. and from 1:30 to 5:00 p.m. Some banks are beginning to stay open through the lunch hour. Most business offices are open from 9:00 a.m. to 5:00 p.m., Monday through Friday. Most stores and shops are open from 9:00 a.m. to 5:30 p.m. Monday through Wednesday and Friday through Saturday, and from 9 a.m. to 8 p.m. on Thursday. Some stores offer Sunday hours, especially during tourist season.

Credit Cards

Visa, MasterCard, American Express, and Diners Club are widely used in Ireland, but Discover is not accepted.

Currency

The Republic of Ireland uses the new euro, while Northern Ireland uses the British pound. The best source for current currency exchange information is on the Internet, at www.oanda.com/convert/classic. You can exchange money anywhere you see the Bureau de Change sign, but generally, you get the best rates at banks or American Express offices.

Customs

You can't bring firearms, ammunition, explosives, narcotics, poultry, plants and their immediate byproducts, domestic animals, or snakes into Ireland. Also, you may bring in no more than 200 cigarettes, one liter of liquor, and two liters of wine.

If you're flying out of or back to the United States, you can find information about what goods you can bring in and out on the U.S. State Department's Web site at http://travel.state.gov.

Dentists and Doctors

If you need to see a dentist or physician, your best bet is to ask the concierge or host at your hotel or guesthouse for a recommendation. Otherwise, consult the Golden Pages of the Irish telephone book or the Yellow Pages of the Northern Ireland telephone book, or contact your local consulate for a recommendation. Many emergency rooms have walk-in clinics if you can't find a doctor who can help you right away. Expect to pay for treatment up front; you won't be reimbursed by your insurance company until after the fact.

Driving Rules

You must have a valid driver's license from your home country to drive in Ireland. The speed limit is 60 mph (96 km/h) unless otherwise posted. Speed limit signs have a red circle with the limit written inside in black. The Irish drive on the left side of the road.

Drugstores

Drugstores are usually called *chemist shops* or *pharmacies*. Look under "Chemists — Pharmaceutical" in the Golden Pages of the Irish telephone book or "Chemists — Dispensing" in the Yellow Pages of the Northern Ireland telephone book.

Pack prescription medications (in their original-label vials) in your carry-on luggage. Bring along copies of your prescriptions, in generic form rather than under a brand name, in case you lose your pills or run out.

Electricity

The standard electrical current is 220 volts in the Republic of Ireland, 240 volts in Northern Ireland. You need both a transformer and a plug adapter (available at many hardware stores and sometimes airports) for appliances such as hair dryers. Computers and sensitive electronic equipment may require more than the standard over-the-counter voltage converter.

Embassies and Consulates

The American Embassy is at 42 Elgin Rd., Ballsbridge, Dublin 4 (☎ 01-668-8777); the Canadian Embassy resides at 65/68 St. Stephen's Green, Dublin 2 (☎ 01-678-1988); the British Embassy is at 33 Merrion Rd., Dublin 4 (☎ 01-205-3700); and you can find the Australian Embassy at Fitzwilton House, Wilton Terrace, Dublin 2 (☎ 01-676-1517). In addition, there is an American Consulate at 14 Queen St., Belfast BT1 6EQ (☎ 028-9032-8239).

Emergencies

For the Garda (police), fire, or other emergencies, dial ☎ **999**.

Internet Access and Cybercafes

You can find public access terminals in shopping malls, hotels, and hostels, especially in the larger towns and more tourist-centered areas. Additionally, an increasing number of Internet cafes are sprouting up across the island. I list some in the "Fast Facts" section at the end of each chapter. You can also find out the addresses and phone numbers of cafes online from www.iica.net.

Liquor Laws

You must be 18 or older to be served alcoholic beverages in Ireland. Likewise, you can purchase alcoholic beverages by the bottle at liquor stores, pubs displaying *off-license* signs, and at most supermarkets. Ireland has very severe laws and penalties regarding driving while intoxicated, so don't even think about it.

Mail

Post offices in the Republic are called *An Post* and are bright green. In Northern Ireland, they're called *Post Offices* and are red. The Republic's main postal branch is on O'Connell St., Dublin 1 (☎ 01-872-6666). Major branches in the Republic and Northern Ireland are open 9 a.m. to 6 p.m., Monday through Saturday.

If you need mail sent to you while on your trip, have the sender address the mail with your name, care of the General Post Office, Restante Office, and the town name. Your mail will be held there for you to pick up. Only the larger post office branches (those that we list in the "Fast Facts" sections of this book) provide this service.

Police

In Ireland, a law enforcement officer is called a *garda;* in the plural, it's *gardai* (pronounced *gar*-dee) or simply "the Guards." Dial ☎ **999** to reach the *gardai* in an emergency in both the Republic of Ireland and Northern Ireland.

Restrooms

Public restrooms are usually simply called toilets or are marked with international symbols. In the Republic of Ireland, some older toilets carry the Gaelic words *Fir* (Men) and *Mna* (Women). You can find restrooms at shopping complexes and multistory car parks. Some are pay toilets. Free restrooms are available to customers of sightseeing attractions, museums, hotels, restaurants, pubs, shops, theaters, and department stores. Gas stations normally do not have public toilets.

Safety

The Republic of Ireland has enjoyed a traditionally low crime rate, particularly when it comes to violent crime. However, you should take normal precautions to protect yourself and your belongings. Don't carry large amounts of money or important documents like your passport or airline tickets when strolling around. Don't leave cars unlocked or cameras, binoculars, or other expensive equipment unattended. Be alert and aware of your surroundings, and don't wander in lonely areas alone at night. Ask at your hotel about which areas are safe and which are not.

In the north of Ireland, safety is a somewhat greater concern because of the political unrest that has prevailed there for the past 30 years. Before traveling to Northern Ireland, contact the U.S. State Department and the Northern Ireland Tourist Board to obtain the latest safety recommendations. The U.S. Department of State 24-hour hotline (☎ 202-647-5225) provides travel warnings and security recommendations, as well as emergency assistance.

Smoking

Recent legislation makes it illegal to smoke in public areas (such as public offices, schools, and banks), but it's still legal in pubs and many restaurants. Smoking is banned on public transportation and in taxis.

Some B&Bs do not allow smoking; check before making a reservation.

Taxes

Sales tax is called *value-added tax* (VAT) and is often already included in the price quoted to you or shown on price tags. In the Republic, VAT rates vary — for hotels, restaurants, and car rentals, it's 12.5%; for souvenirs and gifts, it's 17.36%. In Northern Ireland, the VAT is 17.5% across the board. You can obtain a VAT refund on products such as souvenirs. The easiest way to make a VAT-free purchase is to arrange for a store to ship the goods directly abroad to your home; such a shipment is not subject to VAT.

If you want to take your goods with you, you must pay the full amount for each item, including all VAT charges. To have the tax refunded to you, get a full receipt that shows the store's name and address, as well as VAT paid. (Customs does not accept cash register tally slips.) When you depart Ireland; go to the Customs office at the airport to have your receipts stamped. Send the stamped receipts to the store where you made the purchase, which will then issue a VAT refund check to you by mail or refund the amount to your credit card.

Telephone

The Irish toll-free number for directory assistance is ☎ 1190. From the United States, the (toll) number to call for directory assistance is ☎ 00353-91-770220.

Coin phones in the Republic and Northern Ireland are available but the amount of time you get to talk depends on how far you're calling. The most efficient way to make calls from public phones is to use a Callcard (in the Republic) or Phonecard (in the North). Both are prepaid cards that you can purchase at phone company offices, post offices, and many retail outlets (such as newsstands).

Throughout this guide, phone numbers are preceded by their city codes (Dublin numbers are preceded by the city code 01, for example), but you can drop the city codes if you call within the same city. Also, if you're calling from outside Ireland, drop the zero that preceeds the city code.

If you think that you'll want to call home regularly while in Ireland, you may want to open an account with Swiftcall (toll-free in Ireland ☎ 0800-794-381; Internet: www. swiftcall.com). Its rates offer you considerable savings, not only from Ireland to the United States but also vice versa. Premiere WORLDLINK (☎ 800-432-6169) offers an array of additional services for overseas travelers — such as toll-free voice-mail boxes, fax, mail, and news services.

Time

Ireland is five time zones ahead of the eastern United States (when it's noon in New York, it's 5 p.m. in Ireland).

Tipping

Most hotels and guesthouses add a service charge to the bill, usually 12.5% to 15%. Always check to see what amount, if any, has been added to your bill. Giving additional cash gratuities is appropriate if you've received exceptional service or if the hotel has charged less than 12.5%. For porters or bellhops, tip €1 ($1.05) per piece of luggage. For taxi drivers, hairdressers, and other providers of service, tip as you would at home, an average of 10 to 15%.

A 10 to 15% tip is appropriate at restaurants, but make sure it hasn't already been added to your check before leaving anything.

Weather Updates

The best site on the Web for Ireland's weather forecasts is http://cnn.com/WEATHER/cities/world.html.

Toll-Free Numbers and Web Sites

Airlines

Air Canada
☎ 800-361-5373
www.aircanada.ca

Aer Lingus
☎ 800-223-6537
www.aerlingus.ie

American Airlines
☎ 800-433-7300
www.americanair.com

British Airways
☎ 800-AIRWAYS
www.britishairways.com

Continental Airlines
☎ 800-231-0856
www.continental.com

Delta Air Lines
☎ 800-241-4141
www.delta.com

Northwest Airlines
☎ 800-225-2525
www.nwa.com

United Airlines
☎ 800-241-6522
www.ual.com

US Airways
☎ 800-428-4322
www.usairways.com

British Midland
☎ 800-788-0555
www.britishmidland.co.uk

Virgin Atlantic
☎ 800-862-8621
www.virgin.com

Car-rental agencies

Alamo
☎ 800-327-9633
www.goalamo.com

Hertz
☎ 800-654-3131
www.hertz.com

Argus
☎ 01-490-9999
www.argus-rentacar.com

Murrays Europcar/AutoEurope
☎ 800-223-5555
www.europcar.ie

Avis
☎ 800-331-1212 in continental United
States; 800-TRY-AVIS in Canada
www.avis.com

National
☎ 800-CAR-RENT
www.nationalcar.com

Budget
☎ 800-527-0700
www.budgetrentacar.com

Where to Get More Information

Contacting Irish tourist boards

In 2002, the Irish Tourist Board and the Northern Ireland Tourist Board consolidated into one entity: **Tourism Ireland.** You can contact its helpful staff at a regional office below or simply go to its Web site at www.tourismireland.com.

In the United States

345 Park Ave, New York, NY 10154; ☎ 800-223-6470 (within the United States), or 212-418-0800; E-mail: .

In Canada

2 Bloor St. W., Suite 1501, Toronto, ON, M4W 3E2; ☎ 800-223-6470; E-mail: info.ca@tourismireland.com.

In the United Kingdom

Britain Visitor Center, 1 Lower Regent St., London SW1Y 4XT; ☎ 0800-039-7000; E-mail: info.uk@tourismireland.com.

In Australia

36 Carrington St., 5th Level, Sydney, NSW 2000; ☎ 02-9299-6177; E-mail: info@tourismireland.com.au.

Surfing the Net

The following sites provide a variety of cultural and visitor information:

- ✔ **D-Tour: A Visitor's Guide to Ireland for People with Disabilities** (http://ireland.iol.ie/infograf/dtour): A site offering various resources for disabled travelers in Ireland, including extensive listings of wheelchair-accessible accommodations

- ✔ **Go Ireland** (www.goireland.com): A well-organized guide to lodging, dining, pubs, getting around, entertainment, sightseeing, and car rentals

- ✔ **Heritage of Ireland** (www.heritageireland.ie): A lovely tour of Ireland's historic attractions

- ✔ **Ireland for Visitors** (http://goireland.about.com): A compendium of Web sites from About.com that includes dozens of categories, from Dining to Package Tours to Travelogues

- ✔ **Tourism Ireland** (www.tourismireland.com): The official and most comprehensive online guide to travel in the Republic of Ireland and Northern Ireland, providing information for most tourism facilities as well as access to an online accommodations booking service

Making Dollars and Sense of It

Expense	Daily cost	x	Number of days	=	Total
Airfare					
Local transportation					
Car rental					
Lodging (with tax)					
Parking					
Breakfast					
Lunch					
Dinner					
Snacks					
Entertainment					
Babysitting					
Attractions					
Gifts & souvenirs					
Tips					
Other					
Grand Total					

Fare Game: Choosing an Airline

When looking for the best airfare, you should cover all your bases — 1) consult a trusted travel agent; 2) contact the airline directly, via the airline's toll-free number and/or Web site; 3) check out one of the travel-planning Web sites, such as www.frommers.com.

Travel Agency_____ Phone_____
    Agent's Name_____ Quoted fare_____

Airline 1_____ Quoted fare_____
    Toll-free number/Internet_____

Airline 2_____ Quoted fare_____
    Toll-free number/Internet_____

Web site 1_____ Quoted fare_____

Web site 2_____ Quoted fare_____

Departure Schedule & Flight Information

Airline_____ Flight #_____ Confirmation #_____

Departs_____ Date _____ Time _____ a.m./p.m.

Arrives_____ Date _____ Time _____ a.m./p.m.

Connecting Flight (if any)

Amount of time between flights_____ hours/mins

Airline_____ Flight #_____ Confirmation #_____

Departs_____ Date _____ Time _____ a.m./p.m.

Arrives_____ Date _____ Time _____ a.m./p.m.

Return Trip Schedule & Flight Information

Airline_____ Flight #_____ Confirmation #_____

Departs_____ Date _____ Time _____ a.m./p.m.

Arrives_____ Date _____ Time _____ a.m./p.m.

Connecting Flight (if any)

Amount of time between flights_____ hours/mins

Airline_____ Flight #_____ Confirmation #_____

Departs_____ Date _____ Time _____ a.m./p.m.

Arrives_____ Date _____ Time _____ a.m./p.m.

Going "My" Way

Day 1

Hotel _____ Tel. _____

Morning _____

_____

Lunch _____ Tel. _____

Afternoon _____

_____

Dinner _____ Tel. _____

Evening _____

_____

Day 2

Hotel _____ Tel. _____

Morning _____

_____

Lunch _____ Tel. _____

Afternoon _____

_____

Dinner _____ Tel. _____

Evening _____

_____

Day 3

Hotel _____ Tel. _____

Morning _____

_____

Lunch _____ Tel. _____

Afternoon _____

_____

Dinner _____ Tel. _____

Evening _____

_____

Going "My" Way

Day 4

Hotel_____ Tel._____

Morning_____

_____

Lunch_____ Tel._____

Afternoon_____

_____

Dinner_____ Tel._____

Evening_____

_____

Day 5

Hotel_____ Tel._____

Morning_____

_____

Lunch_____ Tel._____

Afternoon_____

_____

Dinner_____ Tel._____

Evening_____

_____

Day 6

Hotel_____ Tel._____

Morning_____

_____

Lunch_____ Tel._____

Afternoon_____

_____

Dinner_____ Tel._____

Evening_____

_____

Index

• A •

The Abbey Gate Hotel (Tralee), 293
Abbey Hotel (Donegal Town), 370
Abbey Theatre (Dublin), 14, 122, 145–146, 172
Abrakebabra, 66
accessibility issues, 62
accommodations
  bathroom, sharing, 57–58, 94
  Belfast, 396, 398–399
  booking service, 92
  breakfast, free, 58, 92
  camping or caravan, 96
  castle or manor, 96
  Counties Derry, Fermanagh, and Tyrone, 382–385
  Counties Down and Armagh, 413–414
  Counties Mayo and Sligo, 356–359
  Counties Meath and Louth, 177–179
  County Antrim, 399–400
  County Clare, 320–322
  County Cork, 246–247, 258, 260
  County Donegal, 369–372
  County Galway, 337–340
  County Kildare, 199–200
  County Kilkenny, 233
  County Limerick, 310–311
  County Wexford, 210–211
  County Wicklow, 188–190
  Dublin, 124–130
  gay or lesbian traveler, 66
  guesthouse, 91, 93–94
  hostel, 95–96
  Kenmare and Ring of Kerry, 284–285
  kids, sharing room with, 57, 60
  Killarney Town, 271–273
  luxury chains, 92–93
  parking and, 125
  prices, 54, 57, 91–92
  ratings of, 91, 124–125
  self-catering, 44, 58, 94–95
  Tralee and Dingle Peninsula, 293–294
  university housing, 96
  Waterford City, 220
Actons Hotel (Kinsale), 258
Adare Town and Heritage Centre (County Limerick), 306, 314–315
address, 47, 122
advance-purchase excursion (APEX) fare, 73
Aer Lingus, 70, 72
Aero (Belfast), 400
Aherne's (County Cork), 249
Aillwee Cave (County Clare), 306, 326
airfare, 54, 56, 73–75
airlines
  connecting through Britain, 76
  contact information, 434–435
  to Dublin, 120–121
  international travel, 116
  kids, traveling with, 60
  package tours and, 70
  security, 75
  selecting, 72–73
  Web sites, 74–75, 434–435
airport
  Belfast, 73, 395
  choosing arrival, 73
  Dublin, 120–121
  Shannon, 73, 306, 308, 319–320
Alcock and Brown Hotel (County Galway), 339
Alexandra Guest House (Limerick City), 310–311
Allegro Restaurant (Killarney), 274
All-Ireland Hurling and Football Finals, 42
Alpine House (Dingle Town), 293
American Express, 57, 100, 101
An Spailpin (Cork City), 256
ancestors. See genealogy research
Angela's Wholefood Restaurant (County Tipperary), 227

Annagh Lodge Guesthouse (County Kildare), 199
Antique (County Wexford), 217
Antrim, County, 395
Apache Pizza (Dublin), 133
APEX (advance-purchase excursion) fare, 73
Aqua Dome (County Kerry), 269, 297
Aran Fisherman Restaurant (Aran Islands), 342
Aran fisherman sweater, 348, 428
Aran Islands (County Galway), 335, 337, 342–343, 424
Aran View House Hotel (County Clare), 320
Arbutus Hotel (Killarney), 271, 273
Arbutus Lodge (County Cork), 249
art, 149–150, 194, 369, 374
The Ascendancy, 142
The Asgard Tavern (County Mayo), 359–360
Ashbourne House (County Cork), 247
Ash-Rowan Guest House (Belfast), 396, 398
ATMs (tills), 99, 431
attractions
  accessibility issues, 62
  Belfast and County Antrim, 402–406
  costs, 55, 60
  Counties Derry, Fermanagh, and Tyrone, 386–389
  Counties Down and Armagh, 411–413, 415–418
  Counties Meath and Louth, 180–183
  County Clare, 306, 308, 323–328
  County Cork, 249–254, 262–264
  County Donegal, 367–369, 373–375
  County Galway, 333–335, 342–347
  County Kerry, 267–270
  County Kildare, 201–203
  County Kilkenny, 234–235
  County Limerick, 305–306, 313–315
  County Mayo, 353–354, 361–362, 363
  County Sligo, 354, 362–363
  County Tipperary, 227–229
  County Waterford, 222–224
  County Wexford, 213–216
  County Wicklow, 191–196
  Kenmare and Ring of Kerry, 287–288
  top ten, 423–425
  Tralee and Dingle Peninsula, 296–298
Avondale House and Forest Park (County Wicklow), 195

• B •

Bad Ass Cafe (Dublin), 133
Bailey's Belfast Pub Tour, 395, 405
Ballybunion golf course, 51, 296
Ballylickey Manor (County Cork), 260
Ballymascanlon House Hotel (County Louth), 177–178
Ballyrafter House (County Waterford), 222
Bank of Ireland (Dublin), 146
Bantry House and Gardens (County Cork), 242, 262
Barrtra (County Clare), 322
bars in Dublin, 169–170
Beaver, Hugh (brewery director), 145
Beckett, Samuel (writer), 14
The Beech Hill Country House Hotel (Derry City), 382
beer, 24–25
Beezie's (Sligo Town), 365
Beginish Restaurant (Dingle Town), 295
Behan, Brendan (writer), 14
Belfast, 393, 395
Belfast airports, 73, 395
Belfast City Summer Fest, 40
Belfast Festival at Queens, 42
Belfast Zoo, 402–403
Belleek Pottery Factory (County Fermanagh), 381, 388
Benedicts of Belfast (Belfast), 398, 401
Berry Lodge (County Clare), 320
Beshoff's (Dublin), 133
Bewley's Oriental Cafe (Dublin), 138
Bianconi (Ring of Kerry), 290
Blair's Cove (County Cork), 261
Blarney Castle and Blarney Stone (County Cork), 242, 250, 423–424
Blasket Centre (County Kerry), 270, 298
Bloomsday, 40–41
The Blue Bull (Ring of Kerry), 286–287
Blue Haven (Kinsale), 258, 260
Bono (musician), 125, 137
Book of Kells (Dublin), 142
Botticelli's (Dublin), 134
Boyne Valley Hotel & Country Club (County Louth), 178
Brannagans (Galway City), 340
The Brazen Head (Dublin), 168
Brendan (saint), 14

Brendan Tours, 70

Brian Boru (king), 11, 16, 228

Brian Moore International Tours, 70, 72

The Bridge (Waterford City), 220

Brown Thomas (Dublin), 162, 164

Brú Ború National Culture Centre (County Tipperary), 228

Bruach na hAille (County Clare), 323

Bru'na Boinne Visitor Centre (County Meath), 180–181

bucket shop, 56, 74

Buckley's (Killarney), 281

budget, 53–55, 63–64. *See also* money

Budweiser Irish Derby, 32, 41

Buithe (saint), 182

Bullring (County Wexford), 214

Bunratty Castle and Folk Park (County Clare), 306, 323–324, 325

Bunratty Castle Hotel (County Clare), 321

The Burren (County Clare), 306, 324

Burrendale Hotel (County Down), 414

bus tour, 70–72, 88, 90. *See also* tours

bus travel, 86–88, 121–122, 123–124

The Bushmills Inn (County Antrim), 399–400

business hours, 431

Butler House (County Kilkenny), 233

• **C** •

Café Fresh (Dublin), 134

Café Paradiso (Cork City), 248

Cahir Castle (County Tipperary), 208, 229

Caitin Baiters (Ring of Kerry), 290

calendar of events, 39–42

camping or caravan, 96

Captain's House (Dingle Town), 294

car, renting. *See* rental car

Carhoomeengar Farmhouse (Kenmare), 273

Carlingford (County Louth), 183

Carrabawn House (Adare), 311

Carrick House (County Meath), 179

Carrick-A-Rede Rope Bridge (County Antrim), 404

Carrickfergus Castle (County Antrim), 41, 395, 404–405

Cartoon Inn (County Wicklow), 198

Castle Coole (County Fermanagh), 381, 388

Castle Lane Tavern (Limerick City), 317

Castletown House (County Kildare), 186, 202

Catholicism, 11

Causeway Coast (County Antrim), 395, 406

The Causeway Hotel (County Antrim), 400

Causey Farm (County Meath), 182

Ceide Fields (County Mayo), 354, 361–362

Celbridge Abbey grounds (County Kildare), 186, 201–202

Celtic high crosses, 182

Charles Fort (Kinsale), 262

Chez Hanz (County Tipperary), 227

children. *See* family

Children of Lir, 13, 148

Chimes (Cork City), 256

Christ Church Cathedral (Dublin), 151

Christmas Horse Racing Festival, 32

CIE Tours International, 69, 72, 90

City Hall (Belfast), 403

City Hall (Cork City), 252

Claddagh rings, 348

Clare, County, 306, 308, 319–331

Clare Island (County Mayo), 354, 361

The Clarence (Dublin), 125

Clifden (County Galway), 335

Cliffs of Moher (County Clare), 306, 324–325, 423

climate, 38–39

The Cloister (County Clare), 322–323, 330

Clonalis House (County Roscommon), 358

Clone House B&B (County Wexford), 211

clubs, 171, 282, 410

Cobh (County Cork), 244

Cobh, The Queenstown Story (County Cork), 242, 250–251

College House B&B (Dublin), 125, 128

Collins, Michael (leader), 129–130

comedy venues in Dublin, 172

Connemara National Park (County Galway), 335, 343

Connolly, James (leader), 143

Connors (Dingle Town), 294

Conor Pass (Dingle Town), 298

consolidator, 56, 74

Conyngham Arms (County Meath), 178

Coole Park (County Galway), 346–347

Cooley Mountains and Peninsula (County Louth), 176, 183

Co-operation North Maracycle Event, 30

Coopers (County Wicklow), 191
Copperfields Bar & Restaurant
    (Belfast), 401
Cork City
  accommodations, 246–247
  attractions, 241–242, 252–254
  pubs, 256
  restaurants, 247–249
  shopping, 254–255
  transportation, 244, 246
Cork, County, 241–244
Corner Bar (County Donegal), 376
Cosmos, 72
The Cottage (County Sligo), 360
Council Travel, 63, 74
County Sligo Golf Club, 51
coupons, 57
Courneys (Killarney), 282
Craggaunowen Castle and Project (County
    Clare), 306, 326
craic, 23
creche, 60
credit card, 2, 99–100, 431
Creevy Pier (County Donegal), 370
Croagh Patrick (County Mayo), 354, 362
Cromleach Lodge Country House (County
    Sligo), 358
Crown Bar (County Wexford), 217
Crown Liquor Saloon (Belfast), 409
Cruinniu' na mBad, 31
Cruises (County Clare), 323
Cuchulainn (warrior), 13, 32, 148, 183
cuisine
  Cork City, 247–248
  Dublin, 130, 132, 135
  overview of, 20–21
  Waterford, 221
Cullintra House B&B (County
    Kilkenny), 233
Culloden Hotel (County Down), 413–414
Curracloe Nature Trail (County
    Wexford), 215
The Curragh (County Kildare), 186, 201
Curragh Lodge Hotel (County Kildare), 200
currency, 97, 431. See also money
customs, 107, 431
cybercafes, 112–113, 432
cycling, 30

• D •

The Da Club (Dublin), 171
d'Arcy's (Kenmare), 286
day tours, 44, 88
daylight, hours of, 39
De Valera, Eamon (leader), 148, 327
DeBarra's (County Cork), 265
Derry City, 379, 381, 389
Derrynane House National Historic Park
    (County Kerry), 269, 288
Dick Mack's (Dingle Town), 300
Dingle Peninsula (County Kerry), 269, 291
The Dingle Pub (Dingle Town), 300
Dingle Town (County Kerry), 269, 291
dining. See pubs; restaurants
disability, traveler with, 62–63
discounts
  for child, 60
  Dublin, 139
  finding, 56–57
  for rental car, 83
  for senior traveler, 61
  for student traveler, 64
doctor, finding, 110
Donegal, County, 367–376
Donegal Castle (County Donegal), 369, 374
Downpatrick, 40
Doyles Seafood Bar (Dingle Town), 295–296
dress code, 114–115
drinking and driving, 85
driving rules, 83–86, 123, 124, 284, 432
Drogheda (County Louth), 176
Druids Glen Marriott Hotel (County
    Wicklow), 188
Dublin, 33, 35, 40, 64, 119
Dublin Airport, 73
Dublin Castle, 144
Dublin Film Festival, 40
Dublin International Airport, 120–121
Dublin Tourism Center, 46, 125, 139
Dublin Writers Festival, 41
Dublin Writers Museum, 122, 149
Dublinia, 143–144
Dublin's Viking Adventure & Feast, 144
Dufferin Coaching Inn (County Down), 414
The Duke (Dublin), 168
Dundalk (County Louth), 176
Dunguaire Castle (County Galway), 347

Dunmore Cave (County Kilkenny), 209, 234–235
Dunraven Arms (Adare), 311
Durty Nelly's (County Clare), 330

• *E* •

E. J. Kings (Clifden), 351
Earhart Center (Derry City), 381, 387
Easter Rising, 12, 143, 147–148
Eastern Tandoori (Dublin), 134
Eddie Rockets (Dublin), 132
the Edge (musician), 125
El Porto Cafe (County Armagh), 415
Elder Hostel, 61
electricity, 115–116, 432
Elephant & Castle (Dublin), 135
embassy, 106, 173, 432
emergency, 110, 173, 431, 432
Enniscorthy Castle (County Wexford), 215
Enniskillen Castle (County Fermanagh), 381, 387–388
Errigal Restaurant (Donegal Town), 372
escorted tour, 70–72
euro, 97
Europa Hotel (Belfast), 398
events, 39–42
exchange rate, 97–98
Exploris (County Down), 413, 417
Eyre Square (Galway City), 338

• *F* •

The Faerie Thorn (County Derry), 391
family. *See also* genealogy research
    accommodations for, 128, 178
    one-week itinerary for, 48–49
    restaurants for, 179
    sharing room with kids, 57
    traveling with kids, 59–61
Ferguson Linen Centre (County Down), 417
Fermanagh, County, 381
ferry travel, 76–77, 90, 121, 337
Ferrycarrig (County Wexford), 210
Festival of Kerry, 291
festivals, 39–42
Finn MacCool (hero), 13, 183, 403–404
fishing, 30

Fitzer's (Dublin), 135
Fitzstephen, James Lynch (mayor), 346
Fitzwilliam Square (Dublin), 123
flag, 12
Foggy Dew (Dublin), 132
Foley's Seafood & Steak Restaurant (Killarney), 274
Foley's Shamrock (Kenmare), 284
The Forge Restaurant (Dingle Town), 295
Fota Wildlife Park (County Cork), 242, 251
Four Courts (Dublin), 147
Fry Model Railway Museum (Dublin), 153
Fungi the Dolphin (County Kerry), 269, 297–298

• *G* •

The Gables (County Louth), 179
Gaby's Seafood Restaurant (Killarney), 274
Gaelic, 18–19, 291
Gaelic football, 32, 42
Gaeltachts, 291
Gallagher's Boxty House (Dublin), 21, 135–136
The Galley Cruising Restaurant (County Wexford), 212, 221
Galvins (County Clare), 330
Galway, County, 333–335
Galway Arts Festival, 41
Galway City, 333, 335, 345–346, 350–351
Galway Great Southern Hotel (Galway City), 338
Galway Oyster Festival, 42
Garden of Remembrance (Dublin), 122, 148
gardens
    Counties Down and Armagh, 412, 416–417
    County Cork, 242, 262
    County Kerry, 267, 277–278
    County Wexford, 208, 213
    County Wicklow, 186, 192, 194, 195, 201, 425
    Dublin, 122, 148, 153–154
    Northern Ireland, 416–417, 425
Garinish Island (County Cork), 242, 263
gay or lesbian traveler, 64–66
genealogy research, 15–17, 184, 204, 217
General Post Office (Dublin), 122, 147–148
Giant's Causeway (County Antrim), 403–404, 424

Gingerbread House Cafe (Cork City), 248
Glebe House (County Sligo), 360
Glebe House and Gallery (County Donegal), 369, 374
Glendalough Hotel (County Wicklow), 190
Glendalough Round Tower and Monastery (County Wicklow), 186, 192–193
Glenveagh Castle and National Park (County Donegal), 369, 373
Glenview Hotel (County Wicklow), 189
Globus, 72
Gogarty, Oliver St. John (poet), 347
"Going 'My' Way" worksheet, 45
Golden Pages Dublin Marathon, 30
golf. *See also specific golf courses*
    Dublin, 154–155
    Irish open, 41
    Kildare Country Club, 203
    Kilkenny, 235
    nine-day tour, 50–52
    overview of, 28–29
    Tralee and Dingle Peninsula, 296
Gorrib Haven (Galway City), 337
Grace Neill's Inn (County Down), 418
Grafton Street (Dublin), 123, 162
Great Southern Hotel (Killarney), 271
Gresham Hotel (Dublin), 122
greyhound racing, 32
Griana'n Ailigh (County Donegal), 369, 373
Grimes Travel, 69–70
group rates, 56
guesthouse, 91, 93–94
Guinness beer, 24
The Guinness Book of World Records, 145
Guinness Storehouse (Dublin), 145

● *H* ●

Halloween (Shamhana), 42
Halo (Dublin), 136
Ha'Penny Bridge (Dublin), 146
Harbour View (County Kildare), 200
Hargadon (Sligo Town), 365–366
Harry's Bar (County Down), 418
Harveys (Belfast), 401
Henchy's (Cork City), 256
Henry Street–Mary Street area (Dublin), 159
Hewson, Norman (restaurant owner), 137

high crosses, Celtic, 182
high season, 36, 37
Hill of Tara (County Meath), 176, 181, 425
Hillview House (County Kildare), 199
history, 9, 11–12
The Holy Ground (Limerick City), 318
Holy Trinity Church and Medieval Walls (County Tipperary), 229
Hook Peninsula (County Wexford), 208, 213–214
horse racing, 31–32, 186, 201
horseback riding, 31, 196
hostel, 95–96
Hotel Carraroe Best Western (County Galway), 339
Hotel Isaacs (Dublin), 128
Hotel St. George (Dublin), 128
hotels. *See* accommodations
The Hungry Monk (County Wicklow), 191
Hunt Museum (Limerick City), 306, 313
Hunter's Hotel (County Wicklow), 188–189
hurling, 32, 42

● *I* ●

illness, dealing with, 110
Imperial Hotel (Galway City), 338–339
The Inn Between Restaurant (Adare), 313
Innishannon House (County Cork), 260
insurance, 85, 108–109
International Driving Permit, 104
International Gay & Lesbian Travel Association, 64–65
International Pan-Celtic Festival, 40
Internet access, 112–113, 432
Irish dance, 327–328
Irish Grand National, 32
Irish Museum of Modern Art (Dublin), 150
Irish National Heritage Park (County Wexford), 208, 213
Irish National Stud and Japanese Gardens (County Kildare), 186, 201
Irish Open, 41
Isaac's (Cork City), 246, 248
itinerary
    base camp approach, 43–44
    burnout and, 45
    Dublin, 158–159

family one-week, 48–49
golf nine-day, 50–52
nomadic approach, 44
one-week, 46–48

• **J** •

Jade Palace (County Waterford), 221–222
Jameson Heritage Centre (County Cork), 242, 251–252
Jameson's Literary Pub Crawl (Dublin), 155
Jasmine Palace (Limerick City), 312
Jerpoint Abbey (County Kilkenny), 209, 235
John Barry Monument (County Wexford), 215
Johnstown Castle Gardens (County Wexford), 208, 213
Jordan's (County Louth), 180
Joyce, James (writer), 14, 40–41, 146, 165, 318–319
Joyce Tower and Museum (Dublin), 154
Judge, Jack (songwriter), 226
Juice (Dublin), 136
Jurys Christchurch Inn (Dublin), 128
Jury's Hotel (Cork City), 246–247
Jury's Inn (Cork City), 246
Jury's Inn Limerick (Limerick City), 310
Jury's (Waterford City), 220

• **K** •

Kee's Hotel (County Donegal), 370
Kelly's Cellars (Belfast), 409
Kelly's Resort Hotel (County Wexford), 210
Kenmare (County Kerry), 269, 283, 284–286, 289–290
Kenmare Heritage Centre and Heritage Trail (County Kerry), 269
Kenmare Walking Festival, 30
Kennedy, John F. (president), 205, 252, 346
Kerry, County, 267–270. *See also* Dingle Peninsula; Kenmare; Killarney; Ring of Kerry; Tralee
Kerry Bog Village Museum (County Kerry), 269, 288
Kerry the Kingdom (County Kerry), 269, 296–297
Kerrygold Dublin Horse Show, 32

Kevin (saint), 186, 192
Kieran's Folk House (Kinsale), 264
Kildare, County, 186, 199–203
Kilkenny, County, 208–209, 231, 233–237
Kilkenny Castle, 209, 234
Killarney (County Kerry), 267, 270–275, 280–282, 424
Killarney Golf and Fishing Club, 50, 276
Killarney Manor (Killarney), 275
Killarney National Park (County Kerry), 267, 276–278
Killarney Park Hotel (Killarney), 271
Killruddery House and Garden (County Wicklow), 194
The Killyhevlin Hotel (County Fermanagh), 384
Kilmainham Gaol (Dublin), 143
King John's Castle (Limerick City), 305, 314
The Kings Head Pub (Galway City), 350
Kinsale (County Cork), 242, 257, 258, 260–261, 264–265
Kirby's Brogue Inn (Tralee), 300
The Kitchen (Dublin), 171
Knappogue Castle (County Clare), 306, 325–326
Knight Ride (Carrickfergus), 405
Knowth (County Meath), 176, 180–181
Kylemore Benedictine Abbey (County Galway), 335, 345
Kyteler's (County Kilkenny), 236–237

• **L** •

lace, 428
Lacken House (County Kilkenny), 233
Lahinch Golf Club, 51, 327
Lahinch Sea World (County Clare), 308, 326–327
lake cruise (County Wicklow), 196
Lakes of Killarney (County Kerry), 275–276, 424
Langton's (County Kilkenny), 237
language, 18–20, 291
Laurels (Killarney), 281–282
Le Chateau (Cork City), 256
Leo Burdocks (Dublin), 136–137
Limerick, County, 305–306, 310–315
Limerick City, 305–306, 308, 315, 317–318
Limerick Ryan (Limerick City), 310

liquor laws, 85, 432
Lisadorn (County Sligo), 358
Lismore Castle (County Waterford),
     208, 223–224
Lissadell House (County Sligo), 354, 363
literature, 14–15, 155
The Lobster Pot (County Down), 414–415
The Lobster Pot (County Wexford), 212
The Locke (Limerick City), 318
lodging. *See* accommodations
The Long Hall (Dublin), 169
The Long Valley (Cork City), 256
Lord Kingsale (Kinsale), 264–265
lost or stolen item
  ATM card, 99
  cash, 101–102
  credit card, 100, 101–102
  luggage, 108
  passport, 106
  traveler's check, 101
Lotamore (County Cork), 247
Lough Derg (County Donegal), 369, 373–374
Lough Gur (Limerick City), 306, 314
Louth, County, 176–184
luggage, 108, 114–115, 116, 430
Lughnasa Fair, 41
Lynden Heights (County Antrim), 402

• *M* •

M. J. Finnegans (Annacott), 318–319
MacCloskey's (County Clare), 322
Macken's The Cape of Good Hope (County
     Wexford), 217
Madisons (Belfast), 409
Madison's Hotel (Belfast), 398
Maeve (queen), 13
mail, 113–114, 432
Malahide Castle (Dublin), 152–153
Man Friday (Kinsale), 261
The Manor Inn (County Kildare), 204
maps
  Belfast, 397
  bus routes, 87
  Cork City, 245
  Counties Derry, Fermanagh, and
     Tyrone, 380
  Counties Down and Armagh, 412
  Counties Limerick and Clare, 307
  Counties Mayo and Sligo, 355
  Counties Meath and Louth, 177
  Counties Wicklow and Kildare, 187
  County Antrim, 394
  County Cork, 243
  County Donegal, 368
  County Dublin and East Coast, 120
  County Dublin attractions, 156
  County Galway, 334
  County Kerry, 268
  Derry City, 383
  Donegal Town, 371
  Dublin accommodations, 126–127
  Dublin attractions, 140–141
  Dublin nightlife, 166–167
  Dublin restaurants, 131
  Dublin shopping, 160–161
  Galway City, 336
  Inishmore, Aran Islands, 344
  Ireland, 10
  Kilkenny Town, 232
  Killarney, 272
  Killarney National Park, 277
  Kinsale, 269
  Limerick City, 309
  regions of Ireland, 34
  Sligo Town, 356
  southeastern counties, 206–207
  train routes, 89
  Tralee, 292
  Waterford City, 219
  Wexford Town, 211
Marble Arch Caves (County Fermanagh),
     381, 387
Marble City Bar (County Kilkenny), 237
markets
  Cork City, 242, 253
  Dublin, 159, 164
  Galway City, 349
  shopping in, 427
Mary Anne's (County Cork), 261–262
Matt Molloy's (County Mayo), 366
Max's Wine Bar (Kinsale), 261
Maxwell McNamaras (Galway City),
     340–341
Mayo, County, 353–354, 361–362, 363
The McCausland Hotel (Belfast), 399
McCourt, Frank (author), 305, 308, 318
McCroarty's Bar (Donegal Town), 375

McDonagh's Seafood House (Galway City), 341
McGinley (County Donegal), 376
McManus' (County Louth), 183–184
McSweeney Arms (Killarney), 273
meals. *See* pubs; restaurants
Meath, County, 175–176, 178, 179–184
Medic Alert, 110
medical insurance, 109
medical services, 431
medication, 110
medieval banquets, 325
The Meetings (County Wicklow), 198
mermaids, 334
Merrion Square (Dublin), 123, 138, 143
The Metro (County Derry), 392
Millennium Forest (County Wicklow), 194
Millennium Spike (Dublin), 122, 147
Mitchells of Laragh (County Wicklow), 190
Mitchell's Restaurant (County Galway), 341–342
Mitchelstown Cave (County Tipperary), 208, 228–229
Mizen Head (County Cork), 242, 263
Molloy, Boyce (Lord), 125
Molly Malone Statue (Dublin), 147
Monasterboice (County Louth), 182
money. *See also* currency
exchanging, 57, 98–99
saving, 45, 56–58, 139
Monk's Pub (County Clare), 331
Monroe's Tavern (Galway City), 350
Moore Street (Dublin), 159
The Morning Star (Belfast), 409
The Morrison (Dublin), 129
Mount Juliet golf course, 50, 235
Mount Stewart House and Gardens (County Down), 412, 416–417
Mountains of Mourne (County Down), 413, 417
movie locations, 51, 143, 353
movies in Dublin, 172
Mt. Usher Gardens (County Wicklow), 195
Muckross House and Gardens (County Kerry), 267, 277–278
Mulligan's (Dublin), 165
Mulligan's Bar & Restaurant (County Fermanagh), 386
The Munster (Waterford City), 225

Murphys Guesthouse (Killarney), 273
museums
Belfast, 395, 403, 406
Counties Down and Armagh, 412, 416
County Kerry, 269, 288, 296–297
County Kildare, 186, 202
County Sligo, 354, 363
County Wexford, 214, 215
County Wicklow, 195
Derry City, 386–387
Dublin, 122, 143–144, 149, 150, 153, 154
Limerick City, 306, 313
music
Belfast, 410
Dublin, 155, 164, 170–171
festivals, 40, 42
importance of, 27–28
Killarney, 282
Wexford, 42
Music Festival in Great Irish Houses, 40
Mustang Sally's (Limerick City), 312
The Mustard Seed (Adare), 312–313

• *N* •

names
Gaelic place, 19
origins of, 16
National Botanic Gardens (Dublin), 153–154
National Gallery (Dublin), 149–150
National Monument (Cork City), 253
National Museum (Dublin), 149
National Sea Life (County Wicklow), 186, 193
National 1798 Visitor Centre (County Wexford), 214
National Wax Museum (Dublin), 150
Natterjack (Dingle Peninsula), 301
neighborhoods in Dublin, 122–123
Neptune (County Wexford), 212
Nestor's (Limerick City), 311–312
Newbridge House and Park (Dublin), 153
Newgrange (County Meath), 176, 180–181, 425
Newgrange Farm (County Meath), 181
Newman House (Dublin), 139, 142
Nick's Warehouse (Belfast), 401–402
North Star (Dublin), 129

• *O* •

Oakley House (Dingle Peninsula), 293
O'Briens (County Clare), 331
O'Carolan, Turlough (harper), 13
O'Casey, Sean (writer), 14, 347
O'Connell, Daniel (leader), 143, 269, 283, 288
O'Connell Street neighborhood (Dublin), 122, 128, 129
O'Connor's (County Clare), 331
O'Connors (Killarney), 282
off the beaten path, 51
off-season, 56, 125
O'Flaherty's (Dingle Town), 301
O'Grady's (County Galway), 342
O'Grady's Sunnybank Guesthouse (County Galway), 339
O'Hare's (County Louth), 184
The Old Bushmills Distillery (County Antrim), 404
Old City (Dublin), 122–123, 128, 136
Old Court House (Limerick City), 315
Old Court Inn (County Wicklow), 198
Old English Market (Cork City), 242, 253
Old Head Golf Links, 50
Old Jameson Distillery (Dublin), 150
Old Mellifont Abbey (County Louth), 181–182
The Old Rectory (County Louth), 178–179
The Olde Priory Inn Bar & Restaurant (County Down), 415
Olde Railway Hotel (County Mayo), 356
The Olde Stand (Waterford City), 225
Oliver Goldsmith's (Dublin), 132
Oliver St. John Gogarty (Dublin), 132, 168
O'Neill's (Dublin), 169
one-week itinerary, 46–48
online, booking air tickets, 74–75
Ossian (leader), 13

• *P* •

package tours, 28–29, 56, 68–70
packing, 60, 114–116, 430
The Palace (Dublin), 171
palm trees, 39, 291
Panem (Dublin), 137

parades, 40
parks
  County Clare, 306, 323–324, 325
  County Cork, 242, 251
  County Donegal, 369
  County Galway, 335, 343, 346–347
  County Kerry, 267, 269, 276–278
  County Tyrone, 381, 388–389
  County Wexford, 208, 213
  County Wicklow, 195
  Dublin, 139, 142, 151, 153
Parnell, Charles Stewart (leader), 195
passport, 103–107
Patrick (saint)
  in Cashel, 227–228
  in County Mayo, 354, 362
  grave of (County Down), 416
  life of, 9, 13, 411
  St. Patrick's Day, 411
Pax House (Dingle Town), 294
Pearse, Patrick (leader), 147–148
peat bogs, 290
Penal Laws, 11
Philip Healy's (County Wicklow), 198
Phoenix Park and Zoological Gardens (Dublin), 151
Phoenix Park House (Dublin), 129
phone calls, 57, 93, 110–112, 433–434
Pier House (Aran Islands), 340
"Places to Go, People to See, Things to Do" worksheet, 45
planning trip. *See also* tours
  base camp approach, 43–44
  burnout and, 45
  costs, 53–54, 97
  family, one-week itinerary for, 48–49
  golf, nine-day tour, 50–52
  low-end, one-week budget, 55
  money-saving tips, 45, 56–58, 139
  nomadic approach, 44
  off the beaten path, 51
  one-week itinerary, 46–48
  package tours, 28–29, 56, 68–70
  prioritizing, 58
  seasons, 36–38
  skeleton budget, 54–55
  travel agent, 67–68
The Plough (Dublin), 168
Plunkett, Joseph (leader), 143

Poco Loco (Dublin), 137
The Point Bar (Ring of Kerry), 290
police, 432
Portmarnock golf course, 50, 154
post office, 113–114, 173
poteen, 25
pottery
  Belleek Factory, 381, 388
  County Galway, 345
  County Wicklow, 196, 197
  shopping for, 428
Poulnabrone Dolmen (County Clare), 327
Powerscourt House, Gardens, and Waterfall
    (County Wicklow), 186, 192, 425
Powerscourt Townhouse Shopping Center
    (Dublin), 162
Pravda (Dublin), 170
prescription medication, 110
pubs
  beer, 24–25
  Belfast and County Antrim, 408–410
  Cork City, 256
  Counties Derry, Fermanagh, and Tyrone,
    391–392
  Counties Down and Armagh, 418
  Counties Mayo and Sligo, 365–366
  Counties Meath and Lough, 183–184
  County Clare, 330–331
  County Donegal, 375–376
  County Kildare, 204
  County Kilkenny, 236–237
  County Tipperary, 230–231
  County Wexford, 217
  County Wicklow, 198
  Dublin, 165–169, 424
  food in, 26, 132
  Galway City, 350–351
  history of, 23
  hours and prices, 27
  Kenmare and Ring of Kerry, 290
  Killarney, 281–282
  Kinsale and West County Cork, 264–265
  music in, 28
  rounds, buying, 23
  snugs, 24
  tipping in, 27
  Tralee and Dingle Peninsula, 300–301
  Waterford City, 225
  whiskey, 25–26
Purple Heather (Kenmare), 286

• Q •

Quality Hotel (Carrickfergus), 399
Quay Cottage (County Mayo), 359
The Quays Bar (Galway City), 350
Queens Hotel (County Clare), 321
The Quiet Man Heritage Cottage (County
    Mayo), 354, 363

• R •

rack rate, 2
Railway Bar (County Meath), 184
rain, 38
Rathlin Island (County Antrim), 406
Reagan, Ronald (president), 230–231
Red House Inn (County Kildare), 200
Reginald's Tower (County Waterford),
    208, 218, 223
rental car. See also driving rules
  age and, 82
  booking, 81–82
  contact information, 435
  costs, 54, 57
  driver's license and insurance, 85
  in Dublin, 121, 124
  gas costs, 84
  kids, traveling with, 60
  levels of, 82–83
  paying for, 83
  Web sites, 435
researching family tree. See genealogy
    research
reservations for accommodations, 125
resources. See also Web sites
  disabled traveler, 63
  family travel, 60–61
  gay or lesbian traveler, 65–66
  senior traveler, 60
restaurants
  Belfast and County Antrim, 400–402
  Cork City and East County Cork, 247–249
  Counties Derry, Fermanagh, and Tyrone,
    385–386
  Counties Down and Armagh, 414–415
  Counties Mayo and Sligo, 359–361
  Counties Meath and Louth, 179–180
  County Clare, 322–323
  County Donegal, 372

restaurants *(continued)*
County Galway, 340–342
County Kildare, 200
County Kilkenny, 233–234
County Limerick, 311–313
County Tipperary, 227
County Waterford, 221–222
County Wexford, 212
County Wicklow, 190–191
cuisine, 21, 130, 132, 135, 221, 247–248
dining customs, 22
Dublin, 130–138
Kenmare and Ring of Kerry, 285–287
Killarney, 274–275
Kinsale and West County Cork, 260–262
meal times, 22
menus, reading, 22–23
prices, 21–22, 54, 55
tipping, 58
Tralee and Dingle Peninsula, 294–296
vegetarian, 66
restrooms, 433
Ring of Kerry (County Kerry), 269,
    283–284, 423
Rinuccini (County Kilkenny), 234
Ristoranti Rossini (Cork City), 249
River Boyne, 175
River Liffey, 146
River Shannon, 308
Riverside Park (County Wexford), 210
Rock of Cashel (County Tipperary),
    208, 226, 227–228
Rocks (County Mayo), 356
Ronald Reagan Pub (County Tipperary),
    230–231
Roscoff (Belfast), 402
Rose of Tralee Festival, 41, 269, 291
Ross Castle (County Kerry), 267, 278
roundabout, 84, 85
The Roundwood Inn (County Wicklow),
    190–191
Royal County Down golf course, 418
Royal Dublin golf course, 154–155
Royal Gunpowder Mills (County Cork), 253
Royal Hotel and Leisure Centre (County
    Wicklow), 189
Royal Portrush golf course, 51, 406
running, 30
Russborough House (County Wicklow), 194

• S •

Saddlers (County Fermanagh), 385
safety, 75, 433
sailing, 31
St. Ann Shandon Church (Cork City),
    252–253
St. Ann's Anglican Church (Dublin), 152
St. Audoen's Church (Dublin), 148
St. Canice's Cathedral (County
    Kilkenny), 235
St. Columb's Cathedral and Chapter House
    Museum (Derry City), 381, 386
St. Finbarre's Cathedral (Cork City),
    241, 253–254
St. Margaret's golf course, 50, 154
St. Mary's Cathedral (Limerick City), 315
St. Michan's Church (Dublin), 152
St. Patrick's Cathedral (Dublin), 152
St. Patrick's Day, 40, 411
St. Stephen's Day, 42
St. Stephen's Green (Dublin), 123, 129–130,
    135, 139, 142
Salthill (County Galway), 346
Samuels Heritage B&B (County
    Waterford), 221
The Sand House Hotel (County Donegal),
    370, 372
Scarriff Inn (Ring of Kerry), 285
Sceptre Tours, 70, 72
Scholar's (Dublin), 169
Schooner's (Derry City), 385
Scilly House (Kinsale), 258
Scotch whisky, 25–26
Scott's Square (County Cork), 254
Scoundrels (Killarney), 282
seasons, 36–38
self-catering, 44, 58, 94–95
Selskar Abbey (County Wexford), 214–215
senior traveler, 61
session, 28
Shamrock Inn Hotel (County Clare), 321
Shannon International Airport, 73, 306, 308,
    319–320
Shaw, George Bernard (writer), 14, 347
Shelbourne (Dublin), 129–130
The Shenanigan Rooms (Belfast), 409

shopping
Belfast and County Antrim, 407–408
Cork City and East County Cork, 254–255
costs, 55
Counties Derry, Fermanagh, and Tyrone, 390–391
Counties Mayo and Sligo, 364–365
Counties Meath and Louth, 183
County Clare, 329–330
County Donegal, 375
County Galway, 348–349
County Kildare, 203
County Kilkenny, 236
County Tipperary, 230
County Wexford, 216
County Wicklow, 196–197
Dublin, 159–165
Kenmare and Ring of Kerry, 289–290
Killarney, 280–281
Kinsale and West County Cork, 264
Limerick City, 317
tips for, 427–430
Tralee and Dingle Peninsula, 299–300
Waterford City, 224–225
sickness, dealing with, 110
Silken Thomas (County Kildare), 204
The Silverbirch Hotel (County Tyrone), 384–385
Sinn Fein, 12
The 1601 (Kinsale), 265
The Skeff Bar (Galway City), 341, 350–351
Skellig Experience (County Kerry), 269, 287
Skellig Islands (County Kerry), 287–288
Slieve League (County Donegal), 374–375
Slievemore (County Wicklow), 190
Sligo, County, 354, 362–363
Sligo Abbey (County Sligo), 354, 362
Sligo County Museum & Art Gallery (County Sligo), 354, 363
Sligo Golf Course, 364
Sligo Park Hotel (County Sligo), 358–359
Smithwick's (ale), 236
smoking, 433
Smuggler's Creek (County Donegal), 372
The Snug (Galway City), 351
southeastern counties, 35, 205–209. *See also* Kilkenny, County; Tipperary, County; Waterford, County; Wexford, County

southern counties, 35
souvenirs, 57, 165, 428–429
Spaniard Inn (Kinsale), 265
sports, 28–32
The Stag's Head (Dublin), 132, 169
Station House Hotel (County Meath), 179
Steam Museum (County Kildare), 186, 202
Stella Maris (County Clare), 321–322
stolen item. *See* lost or stolen item
student traveler, 63–64
The Sycamores B&B (County Kildare), 200
Synge, John Millington (writer), 15, 145–146

• T •

The Tannery (County Waterford), 222
Tara Harp, 27
taxes, 433
taxi in Dublin, 121, 124
tea, 138
telephone, 57, 93, 110–112, 433–434
temperature, average monthly, 39
Temple Bar (Dublin)
accommodations, 125, 130
neighborhood, 122
pub crawl, 168, 424
restaurants, 133, 134, 135–136
shopping, 162
Temple Bar Hotel (Dublin), 130
Teo's (Killarney), 275
T&H Doolans (Waterford City), 225
theatres in Dublin, 172
Thoor Ballylee (County Galway), 335, 344–345
tills (ATMs), 99, 431
time zone, 434
Tinakilly House (County Wicklow), 189
Tipperary, County, 208, 226–231
tipping, 27, 58, 434
Tosca (Dublin), 137
tourist information
Dublin Tourism Center, 46, 123, 125, 139
Web sites, 435–436
Tourist Trophy Lounge (County Down), 418
tours. *See also* package tours
Belfast, 395, 405, 407
bus, 70–72, 88, 90
Counties Derry, Fermanagh, and Tyrone, 389–390

tours *(continued)*
  County Clare, 328–329
  County Cork, 254
  County Galway, 347–348
  County Limerick, 316
  County Sligo, 364
  County Tipperary, 229
  County Waterford, 224
  County Wexford, 216
  County Wicklow, 195–196
  day, 44, 88
  disabled traveler, 62
  Dublin, 155, 157–158
  escorted, 70–72
  golf, 28–29
  Kenmare and Ring of Kerry, 288–289
  Killarney, 278–280
  Kinsale and West County Cork, 263–264
  senior traveler, 61
  shopping and, 429
  train, 90
  Tralee and Dingle Peninsula, 298–299
  Tullamore Dew Heritage Centre, 203
  Waterford Crystal Factory, 35
Tower (Waterford City), 220
Tower Hotel (County Sligo), 359
Tower Hotel Derry (Derry City), 382
Tower Museum (Derry City), 381, 386–387
Towers Hotel (Ring of Kerry), 285
Traditional Irish Music Pub Crawl
    (Dublin), 155
train travel, 88–90, 121
Tralee (County Kerry), 269, 291
Tralee golf course, 296
transportation. *See also* airlines
  Belfast and County Antrim, 395–396
  bus, 86–88
  Cork City, 244, 246
  costs, 54
  Counties Derry, Fermanagh, and Tyrone,
    381–382
  Counties Down and Armagh, 413
  Counties Mayo and Sligo, 356
  Counties Meath and Louth, 176
  County Clare, 319–320
  County Donegal, 369
  County Kildare, 199
  County Kilkenny, 231
  County Tipperary, 226–227

County Wexford, 209
County Wicklow, 188
Dublin, 120–122, 123–124
ferry travel, 76–77, 90, 121, 337
Galway City, 335
Killarney Town, 270
Kinsale and West County Cork, 257
Limerick City, 308–310
train, 88–90, 121
Tralee and Dingle Peninsula, 292
Waterford City, 218–220
travel agent, 67–68
travel insurance, 71, 108
traveler's check, 100–101
Trinity Arch (Dublin), 130
Trinity College (Dublin), 142
Trinity College area (Dublin), 122, 133,
    134, 138
The Trinity Hotel (Derry City), 382, 384
trip-cancellation insurance, 108–109
Trocadero (Dublin), 138
Truffles (County Sligo), 360
Tullamore Dew (County Kildare), 203
Tyrone, County, 381

Ulster Folk and Transport Museum (County
    Down), 412, 416
Ulster Harp National Steeplechase, 32
Ulster Museum (Belfast), 395, 406
Ulster-American Folk Park (County Tyrone),
    381, 388–389
The Unicorn (Dublin), 138
U2 (rock band), 125, 137, 389

• V •

Val O'Shea's Bar & Bistro (Tralee), 295
value-added tax (VAT), 433
vegetarian food, 66
video camera, 115–116
Viking Splash Tours (Dublin), 157–158
Virginia's Restaurant and Wine Bar
    (Kenmare), 286
visa, 106

• *W* •

W. H. South (Limerick City), 318
walking
  Belfast, 407
  County Wexford, 216
  County Wicklow, 195
  Dublin, 123, 139, 157
  festivals, 30
  Galway City, 335
  Glasnevin Cemetery tour, 157
  Kilkenny Town, 235
  Killarney, 278–279
  Limerick City, 316
  Ring of Kerry, 289
  saving money by, 57
  shoes for, 58
  trails, 31
  Tralee and Dingle Peninsula, 298–299
  Waterford City, 219–220, 224
  Wicklow Way, 193–194
Wander Inn (Kenmare), 284–285
Warren Guesthouse (County Antrim), 400
Waterford, County, 208, 218–225
Waterford Crystal Factory, 35, 208, 218,
    222–223, 424
Waterside Restaurant & Coffee Bar
    (Dingle Town), 296
Waterville Golf Links, 51, 287
weather, 36–39, 434
Web sites
  accommodation booking services, 92
  airlines, 74–75, 434–435
  American Society of Travel Agents, 68
  car-rental agencies, 435
  currency exchange, 98
  Dublin, 123
  Family Travel Times, 61
  genealogy research, 16–17
  hostel, 96
  medical insurance, 109
  package tours, 69
  student traveler, 64
  Tourism Ireland, 61
  tourist information, 435–436
  travel insurance, 108
  U.S. State Department, 107
  vegetarian food, 66
  weather, 39, 434
western counties, 35
Westport House and Children's Zoo
    (County Mayo), 353, 361
Wexford, County, 205, 209–217
Wexford County Museum, 215
Wexford Opera Festival, 42
W5 (Belfast), 403
whiskey, 25–26
The White Horse Hotel (Derry City), 384
Wicklow, County, 185–198
Wicklow Mountains May Walking
    Festival, 30
Wicklow Mountains National Park, 186, 192
Wicklow Way, 193–194
Wild Coach Tours (County Wicklow),
    195–196
Wilde, Oscar (playwright), 143
The Wine Vault (County Waterford), 221
writers, 14–15

• *Y* •

Yeats, W. B. (writer)
Yeats Tavern (Sligo Town), 366
  Abbey Theatre and, 14, 145
  Coole Park and, 347
  County Sligo and, 354, 363, 364
  grave of, 364
  homes of, 143, 335, 344–345
  poems of, 14
yer man, 281
Youghal's Medieval Walls (County
    Cork), 252

• *Z* •

Zanzibar (Dublin), 169
zoos, 151, 353, 361, 395, 402–403

Notes

Cobb
327-330
Clifden (Alcock & Brown)

FOR DUMMIES

Helping you expand your horizons and realize your potential

PERSONAL FINANCE & BUSINESS

0-7645-2431-3

0-7645-5331-3

0-7645-5307-0

Also available:

Accounting For Dummies
(0-7645-5314-3)

Business Plans Kit For
Dummies
(0-7645-5365-8)

Managing For Dummies
(1-5688-4858-7)

Mutual Funds For
Dummies
(0-7645-5329-1)

QuickBooks All-in-One
Desk Reference For
Dummies
(0-7645-1963-8)

Resumes For Dummies
(0-7645-5471-9)

Small Business Kit For
Dummies
(0-7645-5093-4)

Starting an eBay Business
For Dummies
(0-7645-1547-0)

Taxes For Dummies 2003
(0-7645-5475-1)

HOME, GARDEN, FOOD & WINE

0-7645-5295-3

0-7645-5130-2

0-7645-5250-3

Also available:

Bartending For Dummies
(0-7645-5051-9)

Christmas Cooking For
Dummies
(0-7645-5407-7)

Cookies For Dummies
(0-7645-5390-9)

Diabetes Cookbook For
Dummies
(0-7645-5230-9)

Grilling For Dummies
(0-7645-5076-4)

Home Maintenance For
Dummies
(0-7645-5215-5)

Slow Cookers For
Dummies
(0-7645-5240-6)

Wine For Dummies
(0-7645-5114-0)

FITNESS, SPORTS, HOBBIES & PETS

0-7645-5167-1

0-7645-5146-9

0-7645-5106-X

Also available:

Cats For Dummies
(0-7645-5275-9)

Chess For Dummies
(0-7645-5003-9)

Dog Training For
Dummies
(0-7645-5286-4)

Labrador Retrievers For
Dummies
(0-7645-5281-3)

Martial Arts For Dummies
(0-7645-5358-5)

Piano For Dummies
(0-7645-5105-1)

Pilates For Dummies
(0-7645-5397-6)

Power Yoga For Dummies
(0-7645-5342-9)

Puppies For Dummies
(0-7645-5255-4)

Quilting For Dummies
(0-7645-5118-3)

Rock Guitar For Dummies
(0-7645-5356-9)

Weight Training For
Dummies
(0-7645-5168-X)

Available wherever books are sold.
Go to www.dummies.com or call 1-877-762-2974 to order direct

FOR DUMMIES®

A world of resources to help you grow

TRAVEL

Italy
0-7645-5453-0

Hawaii
0-7645-5438-7

Walt Disney World & Orlando
0-7645-5444-1

Also available:

America's National Parks For Dummies
(0-7645-6204-5)

Caribbean For Dummies
(0-7645-5445-X)

Cruise Vacations For Dummies 2003
(0-7645-5459-X)

Europe For Dummies
(0-7645-5456-5)

Ireland For Dummies
(0-7645-6199-5)

France For Dummies
(0-7645-6292-4)

Las Vegas For Dummies
(0-7645-5448-4)

London For Dummies
(0-7645-5416-6)

Mexico's Beach Resorts For Dummies
(0-7645-6262-2)

Paris For Dummies
(0-7645-5494-8)

RV Vacations For Dummies
(0-7645-5443-3)

EDUCATION & TEST PREPARATION

Spanish
0-7645-5194-9

Algebra
0-7645-5325-9

U.S. History
0-7645-5249-X

Also available:

The ACT For Dummies
(0-7645-5210-4)

Chemistry For Dummies
(0-7645-5430-1)

English Grammar For Dummies
(0-7645-5322-4)

French For Dummies
(0-7645-5193-0)

GMAT For Dummies
(0-7645-5251-1)

Inglés Para Dummies
(0-7645-5427-1)

Italian For Dummies
(0-7645-5196-5)

Research Papers For Dummies
(0-7645-5426-3)

SAT I For Dummies
(0-7645-5472-7)

U.S. History For Dummi
(0-7645-5249-X)

World History For Dummies
(0-7645-5242-2)

HEALTH, SELF-HELP & SPIRITUALITY

Diabetes
0-7645-5154-X

Sex
0-7645-5302-X

Parenting
0-7645-5418-2

Also available:

The Bible For Dummies
(0-7645-5296-1)

Controlling Cholesterol For Dummies
(0-7645-5440-9)

Dating For Dummies
(0-7645-5072-1)

Dieting For Dummies
(0-7645-5126-4)

High Blood Pressure For Dummies
(0-7645-5424-7)

Judaism For Dummies
(0-7645-5299-6)

Menopause For Dumm
(0-7645-5458-1)

Nutrition For Dummies
(0-7645-5180-9)

Potty Training For Dummies
(0-7645-5417-4)

Pregnancy For Dummi
(0-7645-5074-8)

Rekindling Romance F
Dummies
(0-7645-5303-8)

Religion For Dummies
(0-7645-5264-3)
